976.4
DOCUMENT
COLLEGE STATION PUBLIC LIBRARY

Documents of Texas history.

39873003001828

# Documents
## of
# Texas History

# Documents
## of
# Texas History

SECOND EDITION

*edited by*
Ernest Wallace
David M. Vigness
&
George B. Ward

STATE HOUSE PRESS
Austin, Texas
1994

Reference

Copyright © 1963 by The Steck Company
Copyright © 1994  State House Press
Second Edition 1994
All Rights Reserved

*Library of Congress Cataloging-in-Publication Data*

Documents of Texas history / edited by Ernest Wallace, David
M. Vigness & George B. Ward. — 2nd ed.
p.    cm.
Includes index.
ISBN 1-880510-08-1  (alk. paper)
ISBN 1-880510-09-X  (pbk. : alk paper)
ISBN 1-880510-10-3  (ltd. : alk. paper)
1.  Texas—History—Sources.  I.  Wallace, Ernest.  II.  Vigness,
David M., 1922-   .  III.  Ward, George B.

F386.W32  1994
976.4—dc20                                                 94-12996

Printed in the United States of America

*cover design by David Timmons*

STATE HOUSE PRESS
P.O. Box 15247
Austin, Texas  78761

# Introduction

When *Documents of Texas History* was originally published in 1963, the world was a different place. Certainly Texas was a different place. While maintaining important continuities with its past and its traditions, Texas has experienced enormous and sometimes wrenching change in the past three decades. Just months after this book's initial publication, President John F. Kennedy was assassinated in Dallas. If only as a symbolic reference point, this shocking moment in Texas and national history ushered in several decades of upheaval and change that affected the state and the nation: the civil rights movement; assassinations (successful and attempted) of important public figures; the protracted and controversial war in Vietnam (pursued, in part, by a Texas president, Lyndon B. Johnson); the youth movement (including its component parts: student rebellion, the drug culture, the sexual revolution); the women's movement; the environmental movement; the Watergate crisis and subsequent distrust of authority; urban riots and escalating rates of crime and violence; sky-rocketing divorce rates and the crumbling of the traditional family; and the list goes on. Only time and history will sort out the complex impact—for better and for worse—of these changes.

In response to this ongoing cultural and political change, we sometimes seem to have lost faith in our institutions and leaders. We also seem to have lost a sense of compromise, consensus, and balance. Often the voices of debate have come not from a common middle ground of shared values but from alienated fringes, from angry partisans who have driven each other to extremes. Battles have raged between the "religious right" and the "politically correct" left; between preservationists and developers; between blacks and whites; between men and women. Whatever middle ground remains seems shaky and unsure, populated by angry special interest groups. Like the nation itself, Texas has experienced all of this turmoil.

During this thirty-year period, the political pendulum has swung from the tradition-bashing of the 1960s to the conservative backlash of the "silent majority" against "amnesty, acid, and abortion" represented by the elections of Richard Nixon in 1968 and 1972 and continuing with the string of Republican presidents since that time, excepting the Democratic interludes of Jimmy Carter and Bill Clinton. Only perhaps in the moon landing, the Gulf War, and precious few other national events has there been anything like national consensus. And these moments of good feeling have been brief indeed. Shrill anger and character assassination seem to have replaced political debate.

The three decades of national divisiveness and soul-searching that followed the 1963 publication of *Documents of Texas History* have also seen a rise in regional and ethnic pride. With national institutions and authorities challenged and in doubt, people have turned to personal, ethnic, racial, and local sources of identity. Texas has had a long tradition of celebrating its distinctive culture, but this recent surge of regional pride and identification has often gone national in the form of periodic crazes for things Texan. The Dallas Cowboys ("America's Team"), Willie Nelson and urban cowboys, Janis Joplin and George Strait, bluejeans and cowboy hats, LBJ and Barbara Jordan, Tex-Mex food and barbeque, George Bush and Ann Richards, *Dallas* on television and *Lonesome Dove* in the bookstores—all these are only the tip of the Texas iceberg on the national scene.

Virtually all of the nation's significant events and debates have had an important Texas component, or have been strongly reflected in the state's experience. This new edition of *Documents of Texas History* is designed to bring the volume up to date by focusing on the evolving history of Texas since the early 1960s, especially including those crucial, often divisive moments and events that have had national significance or impact. The original 1963 volume, edited by Ernest Wallace and David M. Vigness, included 126 documents which related to important events in Texas history, beginning with Cabeza de Vaca's shipwreck on the Texas coast in 1528 and extending to Hurricane Carla which devastated that same coast in 1961. The documents for the former included portions of Buckingham Smith's 1871 translation of Cabeza de Vaca's famous narrative, and for the latter, a U.S. weather bureau summary of the destructive hurricane. In between these two events—separated by more than four centuries— the book reprinted documents including Travis's famous letter from the Alamo, the Texas Declaration of Independence, Comanche Chief Ten Bears' speech setting forth the case of his people at the Council of Medicine Lodge in 1867, and the 1923 creed of the Ku Klux Klan. Preceding each document was a brief paragraph by the editors which provided background and interpretation of the document and the event which it describes.

The additional documents chosen for this new edition cover a broad range of social, cultural, and political movements which have shaped the history of Texas, and which address important national issues as well. The constraints of space made it necessary to choose representative events and documents which speak to a variety of critical issues. The environmental movement in Texas, for example, could be symbolized by any number of events and documents, such as the establishment of the Padre Island National Seashore or the battle in Austin to control development in the Barton Creek watershed. The documents chosen, however, focus on the federal legislation which established the Big Thicket National Preserve in 1974. The struggle to preserve this unique and diverse East Texas environment was a hard-fought battle. Unlike other Western territories, which transferred their land to the federal government when they became one of the

United States, Texas retained her vast public lands which eventually fell into private hands. Thus the tradition of local and private control naturally made Texas somewhat more reluctant to set aside land for anything other than farming, ranching, development, or oil exploration. The establishment of the Big Thicket preserve therefore symbolized a change in Texas's complex attitude towards the land and its uses.

The documents added to fill out the last three decades in Texas history, like those selected for the first edition of the book, are sources which present history through documents of the moment—living records which do not necessarily tell the entire story, or even a balanced one, but which are starting places for understanding crucial moments in the life of our state and nation. The chosen documents range from speeches and legal cases to topical newspaper reports and book reviews, although it is worth noting that there are many significant historical artifacts of a different nature which would have been just as appropriate. Photographs, paintings, advertisements, folktales, and popular songs, for instance, are, in their own way, every bit as valuable as traditional written documents for understanding a culture and cultural change. An image from the Zapruder film of the Kennedy assassination, for example, or a Mexican-American *corrido* (ballad) about the death of JFK, are powerful, revealing "documents" of that numbing event.

All the documents used in this volume are sources and beginning points for research. Each is preceded by a brief introduction which provides background and context for the subject at hand. Each document (and the event that it describes) stands alone, but together they provide a broad historical overview of Texas history to the present day. The documents, and the introductions which precede them, are not a continuous narrative history. They are representative snapshots of important moments and movements. They are the raw material from which history is made and understood.

I would like to thank my many friends and colleagues in Texas history who helpfully provided lists of potential events and documents for this book, and who subsequently reviewed my choices and introductions. The choices for the years 1963 to 1994 were endless and no two people recommended exactly the same list. I am grateful for their assistance but assume responsibility for the subjects and documents that made it into the book.

George B. Ward
Austin, Texas
June, 1994

# Preface

This is a source book on Texas history. It consists of a series of contemporary documents that provide examples of what seems most worthy of preservation in the Texas heritage. The work is aimed at meeting the need for a convenient and accessible compilation of significant sources that will illustrate, as no secondary writing can, that the obscure, dim past was a fascinating experience, a vivid reality, and its strange personalities real flesh and blood people. The book is directed particularly to students who seek a mature yet easily comprehensive understanding of Texas History, but it is hoped that it may be useful also to those who read for their own cultural enrichment, and perhaps to those who desire a handy reference on some particular subject within its scope. Judiciously used as a supplement to the organized formal textbook, it will enable the reader to see events through the eyes of the people of the time and serve as an introduction to rich stores of contemporaneous writings that provide the material for secondary works.

Source material is essential for learning the right lessons from history. It is the historian's laboratory. The use of sources in the study of history gives the student a sense of reality of the past that never could be obtained through secondary narratives or descriptions. In the utterances of its contemporaries a vanished age returns, the old quarrels are fought out again, the old aspirations and ideals are revealed, and the earnest reader more fully understands. The motives, both sordid and unselfish, that gave impulse to the work of the Spaniards, Frenchmen, and Anglo-Americans, the toil and privations by which the land was won and a new society created, and the pleasures and sorrows experienced in the process, become clear. And, unlike a textbook, sources provide the student with an exercise in analyzing and evaluating evidence, whereas he who fails to go beyond the textbook is apt to acquire a genuinely timid dependence on authority. The history of Texas is marked at every stage by dramatic and exciting decisions and events of far-reaching significance, of which fascinating accounts have been narrated by the men and women who experienced them. Unfortunately, for the majority many of these are unavailable or unknown.

The necessity of keeping this volume in reasonable bounds makes the propriety of many omissions sufficiently evident. The selections, therefore, have been limited to those which most graphically illustrate the Texas past as it has unfolded. Some of the documents are extracts, irrelevant matter being pruned, and those of excessive length have been reduced considerably; but in both instances effort has been made to retain the portions where the sentiments expressed are those of living people, whose words vividly convey their interests, their land, and their society. Some are well known; others are rare; but the majority are not readily accessible to students. Obviously all the foregoing will not entirely satisfy every one, for selection is, after all, largely a matter of individual judgment as to what is of primary importance. Certainly, many other documents would illustrate equally well, but those included in most instances a serious student of the period cannot afford to neglect.

The selections are arranged in chronological order for convenient use separately or in conjunction with a textbook. Such an arrangement possibly makes for as nearly a continuous narrative of Texas history as any. Originals, official copies, and reputable translations of documents generally have been used when available. Special pains have been taken to reproduce the text of each document with scrupulous fidelity, including spelling, punctuation, and capitalization, in order to convey as fully as possible the sense of the past. This may hinder easy and rapid reading, but it is believed that it will make perusal more interesting and fruitful, and hence well worth the additional effort. An omission is indicated by the ellipse (. . .); necessary glosses are enclosed in brackets; and, to avoid distraction as much as possible, the use of "[sic]" is limited to a few cases where it might logically be assumed that an error had occurred in the reproduction of the text. In this connection, the reader is reminded that during the period covered by this work many of the peculiarities of spelling and grammar which would now be errors then had no fixed rules, and that some of the writers had little formal education.

Each document is prefaced by a short introduction, limited to the circumstances of the document itself. As the volume is designed for use either in connection with a narrative textbook or a series of lectures, or for the purpose of a textual examination of a particular document, no attempt has been made to have the introductions, taken together, form a connected story. They are meant, rather, to supply the essential information for orienting the reader.

This volume was conceived by the undersigned and final responsibility for it rested with him. In putting it together, however, he had the able collaboration of his colleague, Professor David M. Vigness. Professor Vigness made many suggestions for its general improvement, translated and edited several of the Spanish sources, and provided a critical reading of the others. Indebtedness to Professor Everett Gillis of the English Staff of Texas Technological College for reading some of the introductions and those who generously granted permission for the reproduction of published material, especially the liberal use of that from *The Southwestern Historical Quarterly*, is gratefully acknowledged. The staffs of the Texas State Library, the University of Texas Library, the Library of Congress, and the Southwest Collection of Texas Technological College rendered valuable aid in locating and reproducing selections. Dr. Odie B. Faulk and Mrs. Martha Webster assisted with the proofreading. Finally, had it not been for the interest of Mr. R. C. Janeway, Librarian, and Dr. R. C. Goodwin, President, of Texas Technological College this book likely would have remained an unpublished manuscript.

Ernest Wallace

Lubbock, Texas
October 22, 1962

# Table of Contents

# Documents of Texas History

## 1. THE FIRST EUROPEANS IN TEXAS

### 1528-1536

Alvar Núñez Cabeza de Vaca and three companions, the first Europeans to penetrate the interior of Texas, were members of the ill-fated Pánfilo de Narváez expedition from Cuba to Florida in 1527. The 242 Spaniards, stranded there, constructed five frail boats in which they attempted to sail along the coast to Mexico. The boats were destroyed by a storm in November, 1528, and all the explorers perished except De Vaca and three others. After nearly six years of servitude to the Indians and two years of wandering across strange lands the four survivors arrived on May 18, 1536, at Culiacán, the northern outpost of New Spain near the Gulf of California. After preparing a report of his adventures at Mexico City, De Vaca left for Spain to seek royal favor and a commission to lead an exploring expedition into the country he had visited. He landed at Lisbon on August 9, 1537, and went directly to the Court of Spain, where he learned that the commission he sought had been granted already to Hernando de Soto. Excerpts from De Vaca's account of the shipwreck and of his return to the Spanish Court follow.

### 1. CABEZA DE VACA SHIPWRECKED ON THE TEXAS COAST

From Buckingham Smith (trans.), *The Narrative of Alvar Nuñez Cabeza de Vaca* (New York, 1871), 61-77.

. . . Thus we continued in company, eating a daily allowance of half a handful of raw maize, until the end of four days, when we lost sight of each other in a storm; . . . Because of winter and its inclemency, the many days we had suffered hunger, and the heavy beating of the waves, the people began next day to despair in such a manner that when the sun sank, all who were in my boat were fallen one on another, so near to death that there were few among them in a state of sensibility. Of the whole number at this time not five men were on their feet; and when the night came, only the master and myself were left, who could work the boat. Two hours after dark he said to me that I must take charge of her as he was in such condition he believed he should die that night. . . .

Near the dawn of day, it seemed to me I heard the tumbling of the sea; for as the coast was low, it roared loudly. Surprised at this, I called to the master, who answered me that he believed we were near the land. . . . Near the shore a wave took us, that knocked the boat out of water the distance of the throw of a crowbar, and from the violence with which she struck, nearly all the people who were in her like dead, were roused to consciousness. Finding themselves near the shore, they began to move on hands and feet, crawling to land into some ravines. There we made fire, parched some of the maize we brought, and found some rain water. From the warmth of the fire the people recovered their facul-

ties, and began somewhat to exert themselves. The day on which we arrived was the sixth of November [1528]. . . .

After the people had eaten, I ordered Lope de Oviedo, who had more strength and was stouter than any of the rest, to go to some trees that were near by, and climbing into one of them to look about and try to gain some knowledge of the country. He did as I bade, and made out that we were on an island. . . .

[He] found some huts, without tenants, they having gone into the woods. He took from these an earthen pot, a little dog, some few mullets, and returned. . . . Three Indians with bows and arrows followed and were calling to him, while he, in the same way, was beckoning them on. Thus he arrived where we were, the natives remaining a little way back, seated on the shore. Half an hour after, they were supported by one hundred other Indian bowmen, who if they were not large, our fears made giants of them. They stopped near us with the first three. It were idle to think that any among us could make defence; for it would have been difficult to find six that could rise from the ground. The Assessor and I went out and called to them, and they came to us. We endeavored the best we could to encourage them and secure their favor. We gave them beads and hawkbells, and each of them gave me an arrow, which is a pledge of friendship. They told us by signs that they would return in the morning and bring us something to eat, as at that time they had nothing.

At sunrise the next day, the time the Indians appointed, they came according to their promise, and brought us a large quantity of fish with certain roots, some a little larger than walnuts, other a trifle smaller, the part got from under the water and with much labor. In the evening they returned and brought us more fish and roots. They sent their women and children to look at us, who went back rich with the hawk-bells and beads given them, and they came afterwards on other days, returning as before. Finding that we had provision, fish, roots, water and other things we asked for, we determined to embark again and pursue our course. Having dug out our boat from the sand in which it was buried, it became necessary that we should strip, and go through great exertion to launch her, we being in such a state that things very much lighter sufficed to make us great labor.

Thus embarked, at the distance of two cross-bow shots in the sea we shipped a wave that entirely wet us. As we were naked, and the cold was very great, the oars loosened in our hands, and the next blow the sea struck us, capsized the boat. The Assessor and two others . . .

1

were drowned under her. As the surf near the shore was very high, a single roll of the sea threw the rest into the waves. . . . The survivors escaped naked as they were born, with the loss of all they had; and although the whole was of little value, at that time it was worth much, as we were then in November, the cold was severe, and our bodies were so emaciated the bones might be counted with little difficulty, having become the perfect figures of death. . . .

At sunset, the Indians thinking that we had not gone, came to seek us and bring us food; . . . [and] seeing no better course, and that any other led to a nearer and more certain death, I disregarded what was said, and besought the Indians to take us to their dwellings. They signified that it would give them delight, and that we should tarry a little that they might do what we asked. . . . Because of the extreme coldness of the weather, lest any one should die or fail by the way, they caused four or five very large fires to be placed at intervals, and at each they warmed us; and when they saw that we had regained some heat and strength, they took us to . . . their habitations, where we found that they had made a house for us with many fires in it. . . .

Captains Andrés Dorantes and Alonzo del Castillo [having come up with all the persons of their boat] . . . were surprised at seeing us in the condition we were, and very much pained at having nothing to give us, as they had brought no other clothes than what they had on.

Thus together again, they related that on the fifth day of that month, their boat had capsized a league and a half from there, and they escaped without losing anything. We all agreed to refit their boat, that those of us might go in her who had vigor sufficient and disposition to do so, and the rest should remain until they became well enough to go, as they best might, along the coast until God our Lord should be pleased to conduct us alike to a land of Christians. Directly as we arranged this, we set ourselves to work. Before we threw the boat out into the water, Tavera, a gentleman of our company, died; and the boat, which we thought to use, came to its end, sinking from the unfitness to float.

As we were in the condition I have mentioned, the greater number of us naked, and the weather boisterous for travel, and to cross rivers and bays by swimming, and we being entirely without provisions or the means of carrying any, we yielded obedience to what necessity required, to pass the winter in the place where we were. We also agreed that four men of the most robust should go on to Pánuco, which we believed to be near, and if, by Divine favor, they should reach there, they could give information of our remaining on that island, and of our sorrows and destitution. These men were excellent swimmers. . . .

The four Christians being gone, after a few days such cold and tempestuous weather succeeded that the Indians could not pull up roots, the cane wears in which they took fish no longer yielded any thing, and the houses being very open, our people began to die. Five Christians, of a mess on the coast, came to such extremity that they ate their dead; the body of the last one only was found unconsumed. . . . This produced great commotion among the Indians, giving rise to so much censure that

had they known it in season to have done so, doubtless they would have destroyed any survivor, and we should have found ourselves in the utmost perplexity. Finally, of eighty men who arrived in the two instances, fifteen only remained alive.

After this, the natives were visited by a disease of the bowels, of which half their number died. They conceived that we had destroyed them, and believing it firmly, they concerted among themselves to dispatch those of us who survived. When they were about to execute their purpose, an Indian who had charge of me, told them not to believe we were the cause of those deaths, since if we had such power we should also have averted the fatality from so many of our people, whom they had seen die without our being able to minister relief; already very few of us remained, and none doing hurt or wrong, and that it would be better to leave us unharmed. . . .

To this island we gave the name Malhado [Misfortune]. The people we found there are large and well formed. . . . The stay they make on the island is from October to the end of February. Their subsistence then is the root I have spoken of, got from under the water in November and December. They have wears of cane and take fish only in this season; afterwards they live on the roots. At the end of February, they go into other parts to seek food; for then the root is beginning to grow and is not good. . . .

There is another custom, which is, when a son or brother dies, at the house where the death takes place, they do not go after food for three months, but sooner famish, their relatives and neighbors providing what they eat. As in the time we were there a great number of the natives died, in most houses there was very great hunger, because of the keeping of this their custom and observance; for although they who sought after food worked hard, yet from the severity of the season they could get but little; in consequence, the Indians who kept me, left the island, and passed over in canoes to the main, into some bays where are many oysters. For three months in the year they eat nothing besides these, and drink very bad water. There is great want of wood; misquitos are in great plenty. The houses are of mats, set up on masses of oyster shells, which they sleep upon, and in skins, should they accidentally possess them. In this way we lived until April [1, 1529], when we went to the sea shore, where we ate blackberries all the month, during which time the Indians did not omit to observe their areitos [mystic dancing and singing] and festivities. . . .

## 2. CABEZA DE VACA AT THE SPANISH COURT

From Buckingham Smith, *Narratives of the Career of Hernando de Soto in the Conquest of Florida as Told by a Knight of Elvas* (New York, 1866), 7-10.

. . . After Don Hernando [de Soto] had obtained the concession, a fidalgo arrived at Court from the Indias, Cabeça de Vaca by name, who had been in Florida with Narvaez; and he stated how he with four others had escaped, taking the way to New Spain; that the

Governor had been lost in the sea, and the rest were all dead. He brought with him a written relation of adventures, which said in some places: Here I have seen this; and the rest which I saw I leave to confer of with His Majesty; generally, however, he described the poverty of the country, and spoke of the hardships he had undergone. Some of his kinsfolk, desirous of going to the Indias, strongly urged him to tell them whether he had seen any rich country in Florida or not; but he told them that he could not do so; because he and another (by name Orantes [Dorantes], who had remained in New Spain with the purpose of returning into Florida) had sworn not to divulge certain things which they had seen, lest some one might beg the government in advance of them, for which he had come to Spain; nevertheless, he gave them to understand that it was the richest country in the world.

Don Hernando de Soto was desirous that Cabeça de Vaca should go with him, and made him favorable proposals; but after they had come upon terms they disagreed, because the Adelantado would not give the money requisite to pay for a ship that the other had bought. Baltasar de Gallegos and Cristóbal de Espindola told Cabeça de Vaca, their kinsman, that as they had made up their minds to go to Florida, in consequence of what he had told them, they besought him to counsel them; to which he replied, that the reason he did not go was because he hoped to receive another government, being reluctant to march under the standard of another; that he had himself come to solicit the conquest of Florida, and though he found it had already been granted to Don Hernando de Soto, yet, on account of his oath, he could not divulge what they desired to know; nevertheless, he would advise them to sell their estates and go, — that in so doing they would act wisely.

As soon as Cabeça de Vaca had an opportunity he spoke with the Emperor; and gave him an account of all that he had gone through with, seen, and could by any means ascertain. . . .

## 2. THE DE SOTO-MOSCOSO EXPEDITION

### 1539-1543

From Buckingham Smith (trans.), *Narratives of the Career of Hernando de Soto in the Conquest of Florida as Told by a Knight of Elvas* (New York, 1866), 5-6, 145-148, 161-164.

On April 20, 1537, before Cabeza de Vaca arrived at the Spanish Court, the King named Hernando de Soto, conquistador from Peru and Nicaragua, governor of Cuba and adelantado (military chief) of Florida. With more than six hundred men, not including sailors, and 223 horses, De Soto sailed from Cuba on May 18, 1539, to explore the country north of the Gulf of Mexico. After marching from western Florida northeastward to North Carolina, and then westward possibly as far as eastern Oklahoma and southern Missouri, he returned to the Mississippi at the mouth of the Arkansas River where he died on May 21, 1542. The explorers, led by De Soto's successor, Luis Moscoso de Alvarado, then attempted to reach the settlements of Mexico by traveling overland. They crossed the Red River, passed through eastern Texas, and traversed the buffalo plains westward probably as far as the headwaters of the Trinity River or the Brazos. With inadequate supplies to carry through the winter, the expedition early in October returned to the Mississippi. In July, 1543, having constructed seven brigantines, the 320 survivors set sail, and on September 10 reached the Spanish settlement at the mouth of the Pánuco River in Mexico.

### 1. WHO DE SOTO WAS

. . . Hernando de Soto was the son of an esquire of Xérez de Badajóz, and went to the Indias of the Ocean Sea, belonging to Castilla, at the time Pedrárias Dávila was the Governor. He had nothing more than blade and buckler: for his courage and good qualities Pedrárias appointed him to be captain of a troop of horse, and he went by his order with Hernando Pizarro to conquer Peru [in 1531]. According to the report of many persons who were there, he distinguished himself over all the captains and principal personages present, not only at the seizure of Atabalípa [Atahualpa], lord of Peru, and in carrying the City of Cuzco, but at all other places wheresoever he went and found resistance. Hence, apart from his share in the treasure of Atabalípa, he got a good amount, . . . which he brought with him to Spain. Of this the Emperor borrowed a part, which was paid . . . in duties on the silks of Granada, and the rest at the Casa de Contratacion.

In Sevilla, Soto employed a superintendent of household, an usher, pages, equerry, chamberlin, footmen, and all the other servants requisite for the establishment of a gentleman. Thence he went to Court, and while there was . . . accompanied by Luis Moscoso de Alvarado, [who] . . . came with him from Peru; and . . . Soto, although by nature not profuse, as it was the first time he was to show himself at Court, spent largely, and went about closely attended by . . . his dependents, and by many others who there came about him. He married Doña Ysabel de Bobadilla, daughter of Pedrárias Dávila, Count of Puñonrostro. The Emperor made him Governor of the Island of Cuba and Adelantado of Florida, with title of Marquis to a certain part of the territory he should conquer. . . .

### 2. DE SOTO'S DEATH AND THE SELECTION OF HIS SUCCESSOR

. . . The Governor, conscious that the hour approached in which he should depart this life, commanded that all the King's officers should be called before him, . . . [and] asked that they be pleased to elect a principal and able person to be governor, one with whom they should all be satisfied, and, being chosen, they would swear before him to obey: that this would greatly satisfy him, abate somewhat the pains he suffered, and moderate the anxiety of leaving them in a country, they knew not where.

Baltasar de Gallegos responded in behalf of all, . . . that . . . whomsoever his Excellency should name to the command, him would they obey. Thereupon the Governor nominated Luys Moscoso de Alvarado to be his Captain-General; when by all those present was he straightway chosen and sworn Governor.

The next day, the twenty-first of May, departed this life the magnanimous, the virtuous, the intrepid Captain, Don Hernando de Soto, . . .

Luys de Moscoso determined to conceal what had happened from the Indians; for Soto had given them to understand that the Christians were immortal; besides, they held him to be vigilant, sagacious, brave; and, although they were at peace, should they know him to be dead, they, being of their nature inconstant, might venture on making an attack; and they were credulous of all that he had told them, who made them believe that some things which went on among them privately, and he had come at without their being able to see how, or by what means, that the figure which appeared in a mirror he showed, told him whatsoever they might be about, or desired to do; whence neither by word nor deed did they dare undertake any thing to his injury.

So soon as the death had taken place, Luys de Moscoso directed the body to be put secretly into a house, where it remained three days; and thence it was taken at night, by his order, to a gate of the town, and buried within. The Indians, who had seen him ill, finding him no longer, suspected the reason; and passing by where he lay, they observed the ground loose, and looking about, talked among themselves. This coming to the knowledge of Luys de Moscoso, he ordered the corpse to be taken up at night, and among the shawls that enshrouded it having cast abundance of sand, it was taken out in a canoe and committed to the middle of the stream [Mississippi]. The Cacique of Guachoya asked of him, saying: "What has been done with my brother and lord, the Governor?" Luys de Moscoso told him that he had ascended into the skies, as he had done on many other occasions; but as he would have to be detained there some time, he had left him in his stead. The Chief, thinking within himself that he was dead, ordered two well-proportioned young men to be brought, saying, that it was the usage of the country, when any lord died, to kill some persons, who should accompany and serve him on the way, on which account they were brought; and he told him to command their heads to be struck off, that they might go accordingly to attend his friend and master. Luys de Moscoso replied to him, that the Governor was not dead, but only gone into the heavens, having taken with him of his soldiers sufficient number for his need, and besought him to let those Indians go, and from that time forward not to follow so evil a practice. . . .

## 3.   WHERE AND WHY MOSCOSO TURNED BACK

. . . The Governor [Luis Moscoso], having been led for two days out of the way, ordered the Indian guide to be put to the torture, when [he] confessed that his master, the Cacique of Mondaco, had ordered him to take them in that manner, we being his enemies, and he, as his vassal, was bound to obey him. He was commanded to be cast to the dogs, and another Indian guided us to Soacatino [possibly in the Upper Cross Timbers of Texas], where we came the following day.

The country was very poor, and the want of maize was greatly felt. The natives being asked if they had any knowledge of other Christians, said they had heard that near there, towards the south, such men were moving about. For twenty days the march was through a very thinly peopled country, where great privation and toil were endured; the little maize there was, the Indians having buried in the scrub, where the Christians, at the close of the day's march, when they were well weary, went trailing, to seek for what they had need of to eat.

Arrived at a province called Guasco [probably on the Brazos River], they found maize, with which they loaded the horses and the Indians; thence they went to another settlement, called Naquiscoça, the inhabitants of which said that they had no knowledge of any other Christians. The Governor ordered them put to torture, when they stated that farther on, in the territories of another chief, called Naçacahoz, the Christians had arrived, and gone back toward the west, whence they came. He reached there in two days, and took some women, among whom was one who said that she had seen Christians, and, having been in their hands, had made her escape from them. The Governor sent a captain with fifteen cavalry to where she said they were seen, to discover if there were any marks of horses, or signs of any Christians having been there; and after traveling three or four leagues, she who was the guide declared that all she had said was false; and so it was deemed of everything else the Indians had told of having seen Christians in Florida [Texas].

As the region thereabout was scarce of maize, and no information could be got of any inhabited country to the west, the Governor went back to Guasco. The residents stated, that ten days' journey from there, toward the sunset was a river called Daycao whither they sometimes went to drive and kill deer, and whence they had seen persons on the other bank, but without knowing what people they were. The Christians took as much maize as they could find, to carry with them; and journeying ten days through a wilderness, they arrived at the river of which the Indians had spoken. Ten horsemen sent in advance by the Governor had crossed; and, following a road leading up from the bank, they came upon an encampment of Indians living in very small huts, who, directly as they saw the Christians, took to flight, leaving what they had, indications only of poverty and misery. So wretched was the country, that what was found everywhere, put together, was not half an alquieire [less than a peck] of maize. Taking two natives, they went back to the river, where the Governor waited; and on coming to question the captives, to ascertain what towns there might be to the west, no Indian was found in the camp who knew their language.

The Governor commanded the captains and principal persons to be called together, that he might determine now by their opinions what was best to do. The majority declared it their judgment to return to the River Grande of Guachoya, because in Anilco and thereabout was much maize; that during the winter they would build brigantines, and the following spring go down the river in them in quest of the sea, where having arrived, they would follow the coast thence along to New Spain, — an enterprise which, although it appeared to be one difficult to accomplish, yet from their experience it offered the only course to be pursued. They could not travel by land, for want of an interpreter; and they considered the country farther on, beyond the River Daycoa, on which they were, to be that which Cabeça de Vaca had said in his narrative should have to be traversed, where the Indians wandered like Arabs, having no settled place of residence, living on prickly pears, the roots of plants, and game; and that if this should be so, and they, entering upon that tract, found no provision for sustenance during the winter, they must inevitably perish, it being already the beginning of October; and if they remained any longer where they were, what with rains and snow, they should neither be able to fall back, nor, in a land so poor as that, to subsist.

The Governor, who longed to be again where he could get his full measure of sleep, rather than govern and go conquering a country so beset for him with hardships, directly returned, getting back from whence he came. . . .

# 3.  THE CORONADO EXPEDITION
## 1540-1541

From George Parker Winship, "The Coronado Expedition, 1540-1542," *Fourteenth Annual Report of the Bureau of Ethnology* (2 pts.; Washington, 1896), I, 491-583.

Cabeza de Vaca's report of his adventures aroused great excitement in Mexico. The most influential of those who decided to investigate the mysterious north country was Viceroy Antonio de Mendoza, who commissioned Governor Francisco Vásquez Coronado of Nueva Galicia for the purpose. Accordingly, Coronado, leaving Compostela in February, 1540, with 370 Spaniards and a large number of Indian allies and relying on the reconnaissance report of Fray Marcos de Niza, proceeded up the Western Corridor to the shabby Indian pueblos near the present Arizona-New Mexico line. While in this area, one of his captains on a side excursion discovered the Grand Canyon of the Colorado River. After spending the winter at the Indian village of Tiguex on the Rio Grande near present Albuquerque, Coronado in the spring of 1541 went in search of the Gran Quivira, reported by the Indians to be somewhere to the east. Guided by a plains Indian known as "The Turk," the Spaniards wandered for many days through western Texas. Upon reaching the eastern escarpment of the Llano Estacado, possibly Palo Duro Canyon, Coronado sent his army back to New Mexico to await his return, and with thirty horsemen headed northward until, finally, in present Kansas, he reached the Gran Quivira — a miserable Indian village of tents. The following extracts, two from the chronicle of Pedro de Castañeda and the third from Coronado's report of October 20, 1541, to the King, illustrate what the Spaniards hoped to find, what they saw, and their opinion of the country they traversed.

## 1. THE NATURE OF GRAN QUIVERA

. . . The Spaniards enjoyed themselves here [Cicuye or Pecos] several days and talked with an Indian slave, a native of the country toward Florida, which is the region Don Fernando de Soto discovered. This fellow said there were large settlements in the farther part of that country. Hernando de Alvarado took him to guide them to the cows; but he told them so many and such great things about the wealth of gold and silver in his country that they did not care about looking for cows, but returned after they had seen some few, to report the rich news to the general. They called the Indian "Turk," because he looked like one. . . . [The general] felt no slight joy at such good news, because the Turk said that in his country there was a river in the level country which was 2 leagues wide, in which there were fishes as big as horses, and large numbers of very big canoes, with more than 20 rowers on a side, and that they carried sails, and that their lords sat on the poop under awnings, and on the prow they had a great golden eagle. He said also that the lord of that country took his afternoon nap under a great tree on which were hung a great number of little gold bells, which put him to sleep as they swung in the air. He said also that everyone had their ordinary dishes made of wrought plate, and the jugs and bowls were of gold. . . . For the present he was believed, on account of the ease with which he told it and because they showed him metal ornaments and he recognized them and said they were not gold, and he knew gold and silver very well and did not care anything about other metals. . . .

## 2. CASTANEDA'S DESCRIPTION OF THE HIGH PLAINS

Now we will speak of the plains. The country is spacious and level, and is more than 400 leagues wide in the part between the two mountain ranges—one, that which Francisco Vasquez Coronado crossed, and the other that which the force under Don Fernando de Soto crossed, near the North sea, entering the country from Florida. No settlements were seen anywhere on these plains.

In traversing 250 leagues, the other mountain range was not seen, nor a hill nor a hillock which was three times as high as a man. Several lakes were found at intervals; they were round as plates; a stone's throw or more across, some fresh and some salt. The grass grows tall near these lakes; away from them it is very short, a span or less. The country is like a bowl, so that when a man sits down, the horizon surrounds him all around at the distance of a musket shot. There are no groves of trees except at the rivers, which flow at the bottom of some ravines where the trees grow so thick that they were not noticed until one was right on the edge of them. They are of dead earth. There are paths down into these, made by the cows when they go to the water, which is essential throughout these plains. As I have related in the first part, people follow the cows, hunting them and tanning the skins to take to the settlements in the winter to sell, since they go there to pass the winter, each company going to those which are nearest, some to the settlements at Cicuye, others toward Quivira, and others to the settlements which are situated in the direction of Florida. These people are called Querechos and Teyas. . . .

Who could believe that 1,000 horses and 500 of our cows and more than 5,000 rams and ewes and more than 1,500 friendly Indians and servants, in traveling over those plains, would leave no more trace where they had passed than if nothing had been there—nothing—so that it was necessary to make piles of bones and cow dung now and then, so that the rear guard could follow the army. The grass never failed to become erect after it had been trodden down, and, although it was short, it was as fresh and straight as before. . . .

Another thing worth noticing is that the bulls traveled without cows in such large numbers that nobody could have counted them, and so far away from the cows that it was more than 40 leagues from where we began to see the bulls to the place where we began to see the cows. The country they traveled over was so level and smooth that if one looked at them the sky could be seen between their legs, so that if some of them were at a distance they looked like smooth-trunked pines whose tops joined, and if there was only one bull it looked as if there were four pines. When one was near them, it was impossible to see the ground on the other side of them. The reason for all this was that the country seemed as round as if a man should imagine himself in a three pint measure, and could see the sky at the edge of it, about a crossbow shot from him, and even if a man only lay down on his back he lost sight of the ground. . . .

Many fellows were lost at this time who went out hunting and did not get back to the army for two or three days, wandering about the country as if they were crazy, in one direction or another, not knowing how to get back where they started from, although this ravine extended in either direction so that they could find it. Every night they took account of who was missing, fired guns and blew trumpets and beat drums and built great fires, but yet some of them went off so far and wandered about so much that all this did not give them any help, although it helped others. The only way was to go back where they had killed an animal and start from there in one direction and another until they struck the ravine or fell in with somebody who could put them on the right road. It is worth noting that the country there is so level that at midday, after one has wandered about in one direction and another in pursuit of game, the only thing to do is to stay near the game quietly until sunset, so as to see where it goes down, and even then they have to be men who are practiced to do it. . . .

## 3. CORONADO'S REPORT TO THE KING

. . . while I was engaged in the conquest and pacification of the natives of this province, some Indians who were natives of other provinces beyond these had told me that in their country there were much larger villages and better houses than those of the natives of this country, and that they had lords who ruled them, who were served with dishes of gold, and other very magnificent things; and although, as I wrote Your Majesty, I did not believe it before I had set eyes on it, because it was the report of Indians and given for the most part by means of signs, yet as the report appeared to me to be very fine and that it was important that it should be investigated for Your Majesty's service, I determined to go and see it with the men I have here. I started from this province on the 23d of last April, for the place where the Indians wanted to guide me. After nine days' march I reached some plains, so vast that I did not find their limit anywhere that I went, although I traveled over them for more than 300 leagues. And I found such a quantity of cows in these, of the kind that I wrote Your Majesty about, which they have in this country, that it is impossible to number them, for while I was journeying through these plains, until I returned to where I first found them, there was not a day that I lost sight of them. And after seventeen days' march I came to a settlement of Indians who are called Querechos, who travel around with these cows, who do not plant, and who eat the raw flesh and drink the blood of the cows they kill, and they tan the skins of the cows, with which all the people of this country dress themselves here. They have little field tents made of the hides of the cows, tanned and greased, very well made, in which they live while they travel around near the cows, moving with these. They have dogs which they load, which carry their tents and poles and belongings. These people have the best figures of any that I have seen in the Indies. They could not give me any account of the country where the guides were taking me. I traveled five days more as the guides wished to lead me, until I reached some plains, with no more landmarks than as if we had been swallowed up in the sea, where they strayed about, because there was not a stone, nor a bit of rising ground, nor a tree, nor a shrub, nor anything to go by. There is much very fine pasture land, with good grass. And while we were lost in these plains, some horsemen who went off to hunt cows fell in with some Indians who also were out hunting, who are enemies of those that I had seen in the last settlement, and of another sort of people who are called Teyas; they have their bodies and faces all painted, are a large people like the others, of a very good build; they eat the raw flesh just like the Querechos, and live and travel around with the cows in the same way as these. I obtained from these an account of the country where the guides were taking me, which was not like what they had told me, because these made out that the houses were not built of stones, with stories, as my guides had described it, but of straw and skins, and a small supply of corn there. This news troubled me greatly, to find myself on these limitless plains, where I was in great need of water, and often had to drink it so poor that it was more mud than water. Here the guides confessed to me that they had not told the truth in regard to the size of the houses, because these were of straw, but that they had done so regarding the large number of inhabitants and the other things about their habits. The Teyas disagreed with this, and on account of this division between some of the Indians and the others, and also because many of the men I had with me had not eaten anything except meat for some days, because we had reached the end of the corn which we carried from this province, and because they made it out more than forty days' journey from where I fell in with the Teyas to the country where the guides were taking me, although I appreciated the trouble and danger there would be in the journey owing to the lack of water and corn, it seemed to me best, in order to see if there was anything there of service to Your Majesty, to go forward with only 30 horsemen until I should be able to see the country, so as to give Your Majesty a true account of what was to be found in it. I sent all the rest of the force I had with me to this province, with Don Tristan de Arellano in command, because it would have been impossible to prevent the loss of many men, if all had gone on, owing to the lack of water and because they also had to kill bulls and cows on which to sustain themselves. And with only the 30 horsemen whom I took for my escort, I traveled forty-two days after I left the force, living all this while solely on the flesh of the bulls and cows which we killed, at the cost of several of our horses which they killed, because, as I wrote Your Majesty, they are very brave and fierce animals; and going many days without water, and cooking the food with cow dung, because there is not any kind of wood in all these plains, away from the gullies and rivers, which are very few.

It was the Lord's pleasure that, after having journeyed across these deserts seventy-seven days, I arrived at the province they call Quivira, to which the guides were conducting me, and where they had described to me houses of stone, with many stories; and not only are they not of stone, but of straw, but the people in them are as barbarous as all those whom I have seen and passed before this; they do not have cloaks, nor cotton of which to make these, but use the skins of the cattle they kill, which they tan, because they are settled among these on a very large river. They eat the raw flesh like the Querechos and Teyas; they are enemies of one another, but are all of the same sort of people, and these at Quivira have the advantage in the houses they build and in planting corn. In this province of which the guides who brought me are natives, they received me peaceably, and although they told me when I set out for it that I could not succeed in seeing it all in two months, there are not more than 25 villages of straw houses there and in all the rest of the country that I saw and learned about, which gave their obedience to Your Majesty and placed themselves under your royal overlordship. The people here are large. I had several Indians measured, and found that they were 10 palms in height; the women are well proportioned and their features are more like Moorish women than Indians. The natives here gave me a piece of copper which a chief Indian wore hung around his neck; I sent it to the viceroy of New Spain, because I have not seen any other metal in these parts except this and some little cop-

per bells which I sent him, and a bit of metal which looks like gold. I do not know where this came from, although I believe that the Indians who gave it to me obtained it from those whom I brought here in my service, because I can not find any other origin for it nor where it came from. The diversity of languages which exists in this country and my not having anyone who understood them, because they speak their own language in each village, has hindered me, because I have been forced to send captains and men in many directions to find out whether there was anything in this country which could be of service to Your Majesty. And although I have searched with all diligence I have not found or heard of anything, unless it be these provinces, which are a very small affair. The province of Quivira is 950 leagues from Mexico. Where I reached it, it is in the fortieth degree. The country itself is the best I have ever seen for producing all the products of Spain, for besides the land itself being very fat and black and being very well watered by the rivulets and springs and rivers, I found prunes like those of Spain [*or* I found everything they have in Spain] and nuts and very good sweet grapes and mulberries. I have treated the natives of this province, and all the others whom I found wherever I went, as well as was possible, agreeably to what Your Majesty had commanded, and they have received no harm in any way from me or from those who went in my company. I remained twenty-five days in this province of Quivira, so as to see and explore the country and also to find out whether there was anything beyond which could be of service to Your Majesty, because the guides who had brought me had given me an account of other provinces beyond this. And what I am sure of is that there is not any gold nor any other metal in all that country, and the other things of which they had told me are nothing but little villages, and in many of these they do not plant anything and do not have any houses except of skins and sticks, and they wander around with the cows; so that the account they gave me was false, because they wanted to persuade me to go there with the whole force, believing that as the way was through such uninhabited deserts, and from the lack of water, they would get us where we and our horses would die of hunger. And the guides confessed this, and said they had done it by advice and orders of the natives of these provinces. At this, after having heard the account of what was beyond, which I have given above, I returned to these provinces to provide for the force I had sent back here and to give Your Majesty an account of what this country amounts to, because I wrote Your Majesty that I would do so when I went there. I have done all that I possibly could to serve Your Majesty and to discover a country where God Our Lord might be served and the royal patrimony of Your Majesty increased, as your loyal servant and vassal. For since I reached the province of Cibola, to which the viceroy of New Spain sent me in the name of Your Majesty, seeing that there were none of the things there of which Friar Marcos had told, I have managed to explore this country for 200 leagues and more around Cibola, and the best place I have found is this river of Tiguex where I am now, and the settlements here. It would not be possible to establish a settlement here, for besides being 400 leagues from the North sea and more than 200 from the South sea, with which it is impossible to have any sort of communication, the country is so cold, as I have written to Your Majesty, that apparently the winter could not possibly be spent here, because there is no wood, nor cloth with which to protect the men, except the skins which the natives wear and some small amount of cotton cloaks. I send the viceroy of New Spain an account of everything I have seen in the countries where I have been, and as Don Garcia Lopez de Cardenas is going to kiss Your Majesty's hands, who has done much and has served Your

Majesty very well on this expedition, and he will give Your Majesty an account of everything here, as one who has seen it himself, I give way to him. And may Our Lord protect the Holy Imperial Catholic person of Your Majesty, with increase of greater kingdoms and powers, as your loyal servants and vassals desire. From this province of Tiguex, October 20, in the year 1541. Your Majesty's humble servant and vassal, who would kiss the royal feet and hands:

FRANCISCO VAZQUEZ CORONADO.

# 4. LA SALLE IN TEXAS

## 1685-1687

From Henri Joutel, *Joutel's Journal of La Salle's Last Voyage* (Chicago, 1896; facsimile of the first English translation, *A Journal of the Last Voyage Perform'd by Monsr. de la Sale, to the Gulph of Mexico, to Find the Mouth of the Missisipi River*, London, 1714), 45-57, 66-78, 96-132.

After founding Quebec in 1608, the French pushed their control westward along the St. Lawrence River and beyond the Great Lakes. Réné-Robert Cavelier, Sieur de la Salle, one of their most aggressive and daring explorers, descended the Mississippi River to its mouth in 1682 and claimed the area drained by it and all its tributaries for Louis XIV. Returning to France, he obtained permission from the King to found a colony at or near the mouth of the Mississippi.

La Salle's colonizing expedition of four vessels and 280 persons sailed from Rochelle, France, on July 24, 1684, and, missing the mouth of the Mississippi, landed on Matagorda Bay, Texas, in February, 1685. After building Fort St. Louis a few miles above Lavaca Bay and exploring toward the west, La Salle attempted to return to the Mississippi River by land. While on this expedition, he was murdered on March 20, 1687, by one of his men. Six faithful survivors, led by Joutel, reached Montreal, Canada, on July 14, 1688. In 1713 Joutel published in Paris an account of the ill-fated expedition, from the translation of which the following excerpts are taken.

### 1. ESTABLISHING FORT ST. LOUIS

. . . When Monsr. de Beaujeu . . . [the naval commander, sailed for France], we fell to Work to make a Fort, of the Wreck of the Ship that had been cast away, and many Pieces of Timber the Sea threw up; and during that Time, several Men deserted, . . .

When our Fort was well advanc'd, Monsr. *de la Sale* resolv'd to clear his Doubts, and to go up the River, where we were, to know whether it was not an Arm of the *Missisipi*, and accordingly order'd fifty Men to attend him, of which Number were Monsr. *Cavelier*, his Brother, and Monsr. *Chedeville*, both Priests, two Recolet Fryars, and several Volunteers, who set out in five Canoes we had, with the necessary Provisions. There remain'd in the Fort about an hundred and thirty Persons, and Monsr. *de la Sale* gave me the Command of it, with Orders not to have any Commerce with the Natives, but to fire at them if they appear'd. . . .

[Upon his return La Salle] told us he had found a good Country, fit to sow and plant all Sorts of Grain,

abounding in Beeves and wild Fowl; that he design'd to erect a Fort farther up the River, and accordingly he left me Orders to square out as much Timber as I could get, the Sea casting up much upon the Shore. . . .

About the Beginning of *April*, we were alarm'd by a Vessel which appear'd at Sea, near enough to discern the Sails, and we supposed they might be *Spaniards*, who had heard of our Coming and were ranging the Coast to find us out. That made us stand upon our Guard, to keep within the Fort, and see that our Arms were fit for Service. We afterwards saw two Men in that Vessel, who instead of coming to uss, went towards the other Point, and by that Means pass'd on, without perceiving us. . . .

Thus we spent the rest of the Month, till the Beginning of *June*. In the mean Time, Monsieur *de la Sale* had begun to make another Settlement, in the Place he before told us of, looking upon it as better, because it was further up the Country. To that Purpose he sent . . . Orders . . . that all the Men should march, except 30 of the ablest to make a good Defence, who were to stay with me in the Fort. The rest being seventy Persons, as well Men and Women as Children, set out with the Sieur *Moranget*; and we being but a small Number remaining, I caused the Fort to be brought into a less Compass, to save posting so many Sentinels. . . .

About the Middle of *July*, the Bark *la Belle* came and anchor'd near us. An Order was brought me from Monsieur *de la Sale*, directing me to put aboard it all the Effects that were in our Fort, to make a Float of the Timber I had caused to be squar'd, if Time would permit, if not to bury it in the Ground. Every Man set his Hand to the Work, . . . but the Weather proving very stormy, and holding very long, I was oblig'd to cause what had been done to be taken in Pieces, and to bury the Timber in the Sand, the best we could, that the Natives might not find it.

We then set out . . . and join'd Monsieur *de la Sale* the next Day, at the Place where he had resolv'd to make his new Settlement. I gave him an Account of all that had happen'd, and was amaz'd to see Things so ill begun and so little advanc'd. As for the Plantation, the Seed and Grain put into the Ground, was either lost through Drought, or eaten by Birds or Beasts. There were several Dead, and among them the Sieur de *Villeperdry*; many sick, and of that Number Monsier *Cavalier* the Priest; no Shelter but a little square Place stak'd in, where the Powder was and some Casks of Brandy; many other Inconveniences there were, which made all Things appear in a miserable Condition.

It was requisite to think of building a large Lodgment, Monsieur *de la Sale* design'd it, but the Difficulty was to get proper Timber for Building. . . . The Trees were cut down and squar'd, . . . but all cost so much Labour, that the ablest Men were quite spent.

Notwithstanding all those Disappointments, enough Timber was carry'd or rather dragg'd, to build the House Monsieur *de la Sale* design'd, . . . but the Timber we brought [that had been buried at the first fort] was a mighty help towards carrying on his Design, and much fitter than that we had hew'd in the Wood, with so much Labour; so that this Timber occasion'd the raising another Structure contiguous to the former. All was cover'd with Planks, and Bullocks Hides over them. The Apartments were divided, and all of them well cover'd. The Stores had a Place apart, and that Dwelling had the name of St. *Lewis* given it, as well as the Neighbouring Bay.

Monsieur *de la Sale* being desirous to take a Progress, to find his fatal *Missisipi* River, and only expecting the Recovery of his Brother Monsieur *Cavalier,* who was to bear him Company, he began to make some Preparations toward it, and in the mean time, took some small Journeys of four or five Leagues about, but could learn nothing further, than that it was a very fine Country, hem'd in on one Side by a small Mountain, which appear'd at about Fifteen or Twenty Leagues distance; beautify'd with very fine Trees, and water'd by many little Rivers, whereof that, on which we had built our Habitation was the least. We call'd it *la Riviere aux Boeufs,* that is the River of Bullocks [Lavaca], by reason of the great Number of them there was about it. These Bullocks are very like ours, there are Thousands of them, but instead of Hair they have a very long curl'd Sort of Wool. . . .

Monsieur *Cavalier* the Priest, being recov'd, Monsieur *de la Sale* prepar'd to set out with all Speed. He was pleas'd to Honour me with the Command, during his Absence, and left me an Inventory of all that was in our Habitation, consisting of Eight Pieces of Cannon, two Hundred Firelocks, as many Cutlaces, an Hundred Barrels of Powder, three Thousand Weight of Ball, about three Hundred Weight of other Lead, some Bars of Iron, twenty Packs of Iron to make Nails, some Iron Work and Tools, as Hatchets and the like.

As for Provisions, all that were left me amounted to twenty Casks of Meal, one Cask and a half of Wine, three Quarters of a Cask of Brandy, and for living Creatures some few Swine, a Cock and a Hen; . . . thirty-four Persons, Men, Women, and Children, and of that Number were three *Recolet* Friars, the Sieur *Hurie,* who was to command in my Absence, one of the Sieurs *Duhaut,* the Sieurs *Thibault* and a Surgeon. . . .

## 2. LA SALLE'S SEARCH FOR THE MISSISSIPPI

Monsieur *de la Sale* had been now long gone, and we began to be in Pain for him, when about the Middle of *March* 1686, hapning to be on the Top of the House, I spied seven or eight Persons coming towards us. I presently ordered eight arm'd Men to follow me, to go meet them; and as soon as we drew near them, we knew Monsieur *de la Sale,* Monsieur *Cavelier,* his brother, Monsieur *Moranget,* his Nephew and five or six Men with them, the rest being gone another Way to find out the Bark *la Belle,* to give Notice of Monsieur *de la Sale's* Arrival.

They were in bad Condition, their Cloaths ragged, Monsieur *Cavelier's* short Cassock hung in Tatters; most of them had not Hats, and their Linen was no better; however the Sight of Monsieur *de la Sale* rejoyc'd us all. The Account he gave us of his Journey reviv'd our Hopes, tho' he had not found the fatal River, and we thought only of making ourselves as merry as we could. . . .

All these Designs being disappointed, he resolved to set out a second Time, and travel by Land, to find out his River. He staid to rest him a while, and to provide for his Departure, and . . . all . . . Things being thus provided, Monsieur *de la Sale* took twenty Men along with him, . . . and they set out towards the latter End of *April* 1686, after having given me the necessary Orders, and we parted without Ceremony, Monsieur *de la Sale* desiring it should be so. . . .

Some Time passed . . . [and] most of our Men seeing Monsieur *de la Sale* did not return, began to mutter. The Sieur *Duhaut,* who perhaps had been the first Fomenter of those Discontents, back'd the Complaints of the disgusted Party, promis'd them great Matters under his Conduct, and offer'd to supply them with such Effects as he had in Possession, endeavouring, as I suppose, by those Means, to gain their Affections, for a mischievous Design, which it is likely he had even then conceiv'd.

It was not long before, I had Intimation of the whole Affair, and I had done Monsieur *de la Sale* a singular Piece of Service, had I then put to Death the Person, who was to be his Murderer; but I rested satisfy'd with giving him a severe Reprimand, and threat'ning to cause him to be secur'd if he persisted, being able to do no other under my present Circumstances. However, I talk'd to all concern'd, and put them in such Hopes of Monsieur *de la Sale's* Return, and that Things would soon change to their Satisfaction, that they were all pacify'd. . . .

Whilst we thus pass'd away the Time the best we could, Monsieur *de la Sale* had penetrated very far up into the Country, inclining towards the Northern Part of *Mexico.* He had travell'd through several Nations, the Inhabitants whereof were, for the most Part, sociable, and had concluded a Sort of Alliance with them, and particularly with the *Cenis* and others whose names I shall mention. He had discover'd charming Countries abounding in all Things that could be wish'd, as well for Sustenance, as for making of easy Settlements, and after he and his Nephew *Moranget* had escap'd two Dangerous Sicknesses, he return'd to our Habitation, with five Horses he had purchas'd and arriv'd at it in *August* 1686. . . .

We were extraordinary glad to see our Commander in Chief return safe, tho' his Journey had not advanc'd his Design. Monsieur *de la Sale* had not found out his River, nor been towards *Illinois* as we had hoped. Only eight Men return'd with him of twenty he carry'd out, . . . [but] after some Time of Rest, he propos'd to undertake a Journey towards the *Illinois*, and to make it the main Business, by the Way, to find the Missisipi; but it was thought proper to let the great Heats pass, before that Enterprise was taken in Hand. . . .

Monsieur *de la Sale* being recover'd of his Indisposition, Preparations were again made for his Journey; but we first kept the *Christmas* Holy-Days. The Midnight Mass was solemnly sung, and on *Twelve-Day*, we cry'd, *The King drinks, (according to the Custom* of France) tho' we had only Water: When that was over we began to think of setting out. Monsieur *de la Sale* gave the Command of the Settlement to the Sieur *Barbier*, directing him what he was to do and observe in his Absence.

There remain'd in that Habitation, the Farmers *Maximus* and *Zenobius*, Recolets, Monsieur *Chedeville*, the Priest, the Marquis *de la Sablonniere*, the Sieur *Barbier*, Commander, his Wife, a Surgeon and others, to the Number of twenty, among whom were seven Women, or Maids, and only the Sieur *Barbier* marry'd; . . . As for Beasts, they amounted to seventy, or seventy five Swine, great and small, which was a good Stock; for Fowl, eighteen or twenty Hens; some Casks of Meal, which was kept for the Sick; Powder, Ball, and eight Pieces of Cannon, without any Bullets.

We set out the 12th of *January*, in the Year 1687, being seventeen in Number, *viz.* Monsieur *de la Sale*, Monsieur *Cavelier*, the Priest, his Brother, Father *Anastasius*, the Recolet, Missieurs *Moranget* and *Cavelier*, Nephews to Monsieur *de la Sale*, the Sieurs *Duhaut*, the Elder, *l'Archeveque*, *Hiens*, *Liotot*, Surgeon, young *Talon*, an *Indian*, and a Footman belonging to Monsieur *de la Sale*, &c. We carried along with us Part of the best Things every Man had, and what was thought would be of Use, wherewith the five Horses were loaded, and we took our Leaves with so much Tenderness and Sorrow, as if we had all presaged, that we should never see each other more. . . .

## 3. THE END OF LA SALLE'S EXPEDITION

The 15th [of March], we held on our Journey with them, and found a pleasanter Country than that we had pass'd thro'; and Monsieur *de la Sale* having in his former Journey hid some Indian Wheat and Beans, two or three Leagues from that Place, and our Provisions beginning to fall short, it was thought fit to go to that Place. Accordingly he order'd the Sieurs *Duhaut*, *Hiens*, *Liotot* the Surgeon, his own *Indian*, and his Footman, whose Name was *Saget*, who were followed by some Natives, to go to the Place he described to them, where they found all rotten and quite spoilt.

The 16, in their Return, they met with two Bullocks, which Monsieur *de la Sale's Indian* kill'd, whereupon they sent back his Footman, to give him Notice of what they had kill'd, that if he would have the Flesh dry'd, he might send Horses for it. The 17th, Monsieur *de la Sale* had the Horses taken up, and order'd the Sieurs *Moranget* and *de Male* and his Footman, to go for that Meat, and send back a Horse Load immediately, till the rest was dry'd.

Monsieur *Moranget*, when he came thither, found they had smoak'd both the Beeves, tho' they were not dry enough; and the said Sieurs *Liotot, Hiens, Duhaut* and the rest had laid aside the Marrow-Bones and others to roast them, and eat the flesh that remain'd on them, as was usual to do. The Sieur *Moranget* found fault with it, he in a Passion seiz'd not only the Flesh that was smoak'd and dry'd, but also the Bones, without giving them any Thing; but on the contrary, threatening they should not eat so much of it, as they had imagin'd, and that he would manage that Flesh after another Manner.

This passionate Behavior, so much out of Season, and contrary to Reason and Custom, touch'd the Surgeon *Liotot, Heins* and *Duhaut* to the Quick, they having other Causes of Complaint against *Moranget*. They withdrew, and resolv'd together upon a bloody Revenge; they agreed upon the Manner of it, and concluded they would murder the Sieur *Moranget*, Monsieur *de la Sale's* Footman and his *Indian*, because he was very faithful to him.

They waited till Night, when those unfortunate Creatures had supp'd and were asleep. *Liotot* the Surgeon was the inhuman Executioner, he took an Ax, began by the Sieur *Moranget*, giving him many Strokes on the Head; the same he did by the Footman and the *Indian*, killing them on the Spot, whilst his Fellow Villains, *viz. Duhaut, Hiens, Teissier* and *Larcheveque* stood upon their Guard, with their Arms, to fire upon such as should make any Resistance. The *Indian* and the Footman never stirr'd, but the Sieur *Moranget* had so much Vigour as to sit up, but without being able to speak one Word, and the Assasins obliged the *Sieur de Marle* to make an End of him, tho' he was not in the Conspiracy.

This Slaughter had yet satisfy'd but one Part of the Revenge of those Murderers. To finish it and secure themselves it was requisite to destroy the Commander in Chief. They consulted about the safest Method to effect it, and resolv'd to go together to Monsieur *de la Sale*, to knock out the Brains of the most resolute immediately, and then it would be easier to overcome the rest. But the River, which was . . . swollen, the Difficulty of passing it made them put it off the 18th and 19th. On the other Hand Monsieur *de la Sale* was very uneasy, on Account of their long Stay. His Impatience made him resolve to go himself to find out his People and to know the Cause of it.

This was not done without many previous Tokens of Concern, and Apprehension. He seem'd to have some Presage of his Misfortune, enquiring of some, whether the Sieur *Liotot, Hiens* and *Duhaut* had not express'd some Discontent; and not hearing any Thing of it, he could not forbear setting out the 20th, with Father *Anastasius* and an *Indian*, leaving me the Command in his Absence, and charging me from Time to Time to go the Rounds about our Camp, to prevent being surpriz'd, and to make a Smoke for him to direct his Way in Case of Need. When he came near the Dwelling of the Murderers, looking out sharp to discover something, he observed Eagles fluttering about a Spot, not far from them, which made him believe they had found some Carrion about the Mansion, and he fired a Shot, which was the Signal of his Death and forwarded it.

The Conspirators hearing the Shot, concluded it was Monsieur *de la Sale*, who was come to seek them. They made ready their Arms and provided to surprise him. *Duhaut* passed the River, with *Larcheveque*. The first of them spying Monsieur *de la Sale* at a Distance, as he was coming towards them, advanc'd and hid himself among the high Weeds, to wait his passing by, so that Monsieur *de la Sale* suspecting nothing, and having not so much as charg'd his Piece again, saw the aforesaid *Larcheveque* at a good Distance from him, and immediately ask'd for his Nephew *Moranget*, to which *Larcheveque* answer'd, That he was along the River. At the same Time the Traitor *Duhaut* fired his Piece and shot Monsr. *de la Sale* thro' the Head, so that he dropp'd down dead on the Spot, without speaking one Word. . . .

When [the assassins] were come to the Camp, . . . I was absent at that Time; he they call'd *Larcheveque*, who, as I have said, was one of the Conspirators, had some Kindness for me, and knowing they design'd to make me away too, if I stood upon my Defence, he parted from them, to give me . . . Assurances of my Life, provided I was quiet and said Nothing, . . .

*Duhaut*, puff'd up with his new gotten Authority, procur'd him by his Villany, as soon as he saw me, cry'd out, Every Man ought to command in his Turn; to which I made no Answer; and then we began to talk of proceeding on our Journey. . . .

We . . . had travell'd . . . till the Sixth of *April*, when the two *French* Men, I have spoken of [deserters from the previous expedition], came both, in the *Indian* Dress, . . . [and] confirm'd what I had been told before, that the Natives had talk'd to them of the great River, which was forty Leagues off, towards the N.E. and that there were People like us, that dwelt on the Banks of it. This confirm'd me in the Opinion, that it was the River so much sought after, and that we must go that Way to return to *Canada* or towards *New England*. . . .

After [the conspirators and some of the others refused to go to Canada with us], . . . we resolv'd not to put off our Departure any longer. Accordingly, we made ready our Horses, . . . and we set forward without *Larcheveque* and *Meunier*, who did not keep their Word with us, but remain'd among those Barbarians, being infatuated with that Course of Libertinism they had run themselves into. Thus there were only seven of us that stuck together to return to *Canada, viz.* Father Anastasius, Messieurs *Cavelier* the Uncle and Nephew, the *Sieur de Marle* [who drowned en route while taking a bath], one Teissier, a young Man born at *Paris*, whose Name was *Bartholomew* and I, with six horses and the three *Indians*, who were to be our Guides; . . .

## 5. THE SPANIARDS FIND LA SALLE'S SETTLEMENT

### April 22, 1689

From "Derrotero de la Jornado que hizo el General Alonzo de León para el descubriemento de la Bahia del Espiritu Santo, y Poblacion de Franceses," in *Documentos para la Historia Eclesiastica y Civil de la Provincia de Texas* (Archivo General de la Nación, Mexico, Vol. XXVII; transcript, Archives, University of Texas Library, Austin).

When word of La Salle's colonizing venture reached Mexico, the aroused Spanish authorities sent out several expeditions by land and by sea to destroy the French settlement. Alonzo de León, governor of the frontier province of Coahuila, located the site in 1689 on his fourth trip into Texas. Setting out with a hundred men in the latter part of March, De León marched eastward across Texas, making contact on April 16 with Indians who reported that Frenchmen had been in the vicinity. Six days later, led by local Indians, he found the remains of Fort St. Louis. He then explored Matagorda Bay, discovered a river he named the San Marcos (the Lavaca), and arrived back in Coahuila on May 13. The following extract from his journal of the expedition describes his finding the fort.

. . . April 16, Saturday 16 of this month, in accordance with the consultation of the previous day, the Governor with the well-equipped sixty soldiers left, after having sung a solemn Mass to Our Lady of Guadalupe; at the same time the force moved out. Having traveled about three leagues with the sixty men, the rearguard discerned an Indian in the brush, and taken to the Governor and examined, although by a poor interpreter, the result was that he declared that his village was near, and that four Frenchmen had been in it. We hastened our pace, our Indian guiding us, having sent word to the force to proceed to the place where the Indian had said. Before our arrival at the village, all the people disappeared. We saw they had gone into some clumps of brush, and with them went eight or ten dogs, loaded with buffalo hides. We sent the same Indian that guided us to call them, and most of them came. It was ascertained that the four Frenchmen were not there, but had passed toward the Texas Indians. In this village we found two Indians, who told us that in two days' journey we would find them. We made presents of some tobacco, knives, and other things to those Indians, so that they would guide us. They did, we took a route to the north, until sundown, and in a brush area found a town of more than 250 persons. Here we were able to learn of the aforementioned French, our French prisoner always serving as interpreter, and they responded that four days before they had passed to the Texas Indians, and that the rest had been settled on the little Sea (that is, the Bay), and that all had died at the hands of the Indians of the coast; that the referred-to French had six houses, and that it had been three months since it had happened; and that previously, an epidemic of small pox had killed the rest. This day the force went toward the East, and it stopped where the Governor settled it, who with the sixty men had gone eight leagues toward the north. . . .

April 21. . . . Thursday, 21st of said month, we left with the force in an easterly direction, and at times east by northeast, and northeast by north. We went through some great plains in which there were not many trees in great distances. We went eight leagues until we reached a creek of good water, and here the guide told us that the settlement of the French had been on the bank of this creek, and near. The land all seemed pleasant, and we saw many buffalo.

22. Thursday, 22 of the said month, notwithstanding the fact that the day dawned raining, we left with the force because we were close to the settlement and at a distance of three leagues down the stream, we found it, and having stopped the force an arquebus shot from it, we went to look, and found all the houses sacked, the boxes all broken, and the bottle cases also, the other furnishings that the settlers had had; more than 200 books (it seemed) in the French language, broken, and the pages thrown in the patios were rotten. We discerned that the aggressors of these dead had taken all that they had outside the houses, and divided it, and that which was of no use to them they destroyed, thus making horrible sack of all that they had had, as the evidence of the act, in having found it in this form, indicated. In the villages through which we passed before arriving at the settlement we found some books that the Indians had in the French language, and in very good condition,

with other trinkets of little value. We took the books and memorized the titles.

The Indians did not only ravage the furnishings, but their arms as well. We found more than a hundred stocks (*cabezas*) of flintlock arquebuses, without hammers nor barrels which they must of taken with them, ascertained by a barrel that was found some distance from the houses. We found three dead bodies strewn in the field, one of which seemed to be a woman by the clothes that still clung to the bones, which we gathered and gave burial to with a Mass sung with the bodies present.

The principal house of this settlement is of ships' timber made in the manner of a boarded fort, and an upper story also of boards with a roof to fend off the rains, and connected with this, without division, another room which must have served as a chapel where they celebrated Mass. The other five houses were of stakes lined with mud on the inside and the roofs were lined with buffalo skin. They were all quite unsuited for any defense. There were near and in the fort and the houses eight pieces of Artillery of Iron, of medium weight of four and six pound shot, and three very old swivel guns, which lacked chambers. Some iron bars were found, bolts that came to twenty *arrobas* weight. Some of the pieces were thrown on the ground and others were in their carriages, although the carriages were broken; there were some ship's guns from off the ships; and as all were in the street it was no accident. In the same way some ship's tackle, much the worse for wear, was found around the main house. We looked for more dead bodies, and could not find them, which caused us to conclude that they had been cast into the arroyo and that the alligators, many in number, had eaten them. The settlement was located in a good place, on a plain good enough for defense from whatever might happen.

On the doorcase of the principal door of the fort was located the year of the settlement, which was 1684. . . .

## 6. SPAIN'S FIRST OCCUPATION OF EAST TEXAS

### 1690

From Lilia M. Casis (trans.), "Letter of Don Damian Manzanet to Don Carlos de Siguenza Relative to the Discovery of the Bay of Espiritu Santo," *The Quarterly* of the Texas State Historical Association, II (1899), 293-309.

Father Damian Massanet (Manzanet), a Franciscan friar of the College of the Holy Cross of Querétaro and assigned to Coahuila as a missionary in 1687, accompanied Captain Alonzo de León on his fourth and fifth journeys into East Texas. The purpose of the last trip, described in the following excerpts from Massanet's letter, included the destruction of the remains of La Salle's fort and the establishment of missionary activity among the East Texas Indians. The first mission in the region, San Francisco de los Tejas, was founded in May, 1690.

. . . When I was in Mexico and had spoken to His Excellency [the Viceroy of New Spain] at different times concerning a second expedition to the bay of Espiritu Santo and a visit to the Tejas His Excellency resolved to call a general meeting in order to decide what

should be done. Taking for granted the information given by Captain Alonso de Leon about a settlement of Frenchmen among the Tejas, and concerning the death of those who had settled on the bay of Espiritu Santo, it was uncertain whether some French vessel might have come afterwards with settlers for the bay; besides, there were other grounds for action in the fact that the Tejas were asking for priests for their country. All these grounds being taken into account in the general meeting, there were various opinions, and finally His Excellency decided that a second expedition should be undertaken to the bay of Espiritu Santo. Previously Captain Alonso de Leon had already made known to His Excellency all that was necessary for that journey in case it should be undertaken. His Excellency ordained that Captain Alonso de Leon should go as commander, taking with him a hundred and ten soldiers—twenty from the presidios of Viscaya, those nearest Coahuila, forty who enlisted in Sombrerete and Zacatecas, the rest from Saltillo and the Nuevo de Leon—one hundred and fifty loads of flour, two hundred cows, four hundred horses, fifty long firelocks, twelve hundred weight of powder, and three hundred weight of shot. They were to inspect the bay of Espiritu Santo and to ascertain whether there were any Frenchmen left of those who used to live there, or whether others had recently arrived; the wooden fort built by the French was to be burnt down, and Captain Alonso de Leon was to communicate with the Governor of the Tejas from the bay of Espiritu Santo as to whether he would be willing to have the ministers of the Holy Gospel enter into his territory, as he had promised Father Fray Damian Manzanet a year previous. If the governor consented, then they should escort the priests, proceeding with every precaution, and should dispatch an order requesting and charging the Very Reverend Father Commissary General to send with Father Fray Damian Manzanet those of the brethren of the Holy College of the Cross who should prove suitable, the said father to decide how many priests would be needed at first. At the same time he was to be provided with all the necessaries for the journey. And I, being present at this general meeting, remarked that I would take along three priests for the Tejas, myself being the fourth, . . . and in the event of the Tejas receiving the faith, then the college should send whatever other priests would be required. This was resolved by the general meeting. . . .

We left Coahuila [Monclova] for the Tejas on the third day of the Easter feast, March 28, '90. When we left, the twenty soldiers from Vizcaya had not yet arrived. The forty from Zacatecas were for the most part tailors, shoemakers, masons, miners—in short, none of them could catch the horses on which they were to ride that day, for when they had once let them go they could manage them no longer. Besides, we had saddles that could not have been worse.

Thus we went on travelling by the route described in the journal which was kept of this expedition. What I noticed was that on our first trip we had found many Indians along the rivers and everywhere else, while this time we went to inspect the bay of Espiritu Santo and returned to the Guadalupe river without having found a single Indian in all the country. Twenty of us reached the fort built by the Frenchmen, the rest remained with the horses by the Guadalupe river. We saw no trace of Frenchmen having been there during our absence, all being as we had left it the year before, except that certainly there were signs that the Indians had dwelt there. I myself set fire to the fort, and as there was a high wind—the wood, by the way, was from the sloop brought by the Frenchmen, which had sunk on entering the bay—in half an hour the fort was in ashes. This was at the hour of noon; afterwards we went down to the coast of the bay, all along the banks of the arroyo by which the Frenchmen passed in and out of the bay with their barges and canoes. And after we had arrived, some of the soldiers of Reyno de Leon said that they

wished to bathe, in order to be able to tell that they had bathed in the sea, this being esteemed so remarkable a thing that they carried away flasks of seawater which later, in their own country of Monterey, it was held a great favor to try and to taste, because it was seawater. . . .

We returned to the main body of the army, . . . [and on April 29] we left for the country of the Tejas, and . . . [on May 9 reached the Colorado River where Indians were encountered who] said that further along there were other Indians, and with them two Frenchmen. Leon . . . sent for them and they came. The one was named Pedro Muñi [Pierre Meunier], a Creole, from the city of Paris, the other, Pedro Talo [Pierre Talon], a Creole, from New France; these had firelocks, a sack of powder, and shot, more than twenty reales of the lowest value, in silver, Spanish money, and eighty gold eight-dollar doubloons, French money. . . . One of the two Frenchmen mentioned, P. Muñi, must have been about twenty years old; the other, Pedro Talo, eleven or twelve. . . .

There came also to that spot an Indian who was thoroughly acquainted with the road into the country of the Tejas, and he showed us the way until we met with the governor of the Tejas [on May 18], together with fourteen or fifteen of his Indians, and the Indian whom we had sent to him with our message. . . . As soon as the governor saw me he came forward to embrace me; we sat down to talk by signs—this being the most usual mode of communication in those regions; and he produced a small sack of powdered tobacco, of the kind which they grow, and another small sack of *pinole*, white, and of very good quality. . . .

Three days later, on Monday, May 22, 1690, we entered the village [situated northwest of the present town of Weches in Houston County]. It was raining heavily on our arrival. That year it had, up to that time, rained but little, and already the corn was suffering from the drought, but every day of the eleven that we spent in the village it rained very hard. . . .

We came to the governor's house, where we found a number of Indians—men, women, and children. Kneeling, we concluded the Litany, and we blessed the house. Soon the governor and the other Indians came up to kiss my robe, and the former bade us enter, in order to look at his house. The house is built of stakes thatched over with grass, it is about twenty *varas* high, is round, and has no windows, daylight entering through the door only; this door is like a room-door such as we have here. In the middle of the house is the fire, which is never extinguished by day or by night, and over the door on the inner side there is a little superstructure of rafters very prettily arranged. Ranged around one-half of the house, inside, are ten beds, which consist of a rug made of reeds, laid on four forked sticks. Over the rug they spread buffalo skins, on which they sleep. At the head and foot of the bed is attached another carpet forming a sort of arch, which, lined with a very brilliantly colored piece of reed matting, makes what bears some resemblance to a very pretty alcove. In the other half of the house, where there are no beds, there are some shelves about two *varas* high, and on them are ranged large round baskets made of reeds (in which they keep their

Reference

corn, nuts, acorns, beans, etc.), a row of very large earthen pots like our water jars, these pots being used only to make the *atole* when there is a large crowd on the occasion of some ceremony, and six wooden mortars for pounding the corn in rainy weather (for, when it is fair, they grind it in the courtyard). . . .

Using the Frenchman as an interpreter I told the governor with many kind expressions that his house was very fine, and that I heartily appreciated his desire to have the priests in his household, but that since we had to build a house for the celebration of masses, it might be well to build likewise a dwelling for the priests, because they must needs live near the church. Thereupon the governor said that we should build the house in the most suitable place, that he would show us the village, and that I might choose the spot. We agreed to visit the village on the following day in order to look for a favorable location for the church and the priests' dwelling; accordingly next day we went with the governor, who took us to the place the French had selected for their settlement, pleasantly and favorably situated on the riverbanks. We did not locate the convent there because it was so far out of the way of the Indians. Just at that spot they showed us two dead bodies of Frenchmen who had shot each other with carbines. All this day we were unable to find a place which suited me.

The next morning [May 26] I went out with Captain Alonso de Leon a little way, and found a delightful spot close to the brook, fine woods, with plum trees like those in Spain. And soon afterwards, on the same day, they began to fell trees and cart the wood, and within three days we had a roomy dwelling and a church wherein to say mass with all propriety. We set in front of the church a very high cross of carved wood. . . .

When the church and the dwelling intended for the priests had been finished [on May 31] they carried into these buildings all that was to be left for the priests, and on the morning of the first of June, the octave of the feast of Corpus Christi, we consecrated the church and celebrated mass, after which the Te Deum Laudamus was sung in thanksgiving, the soldiers firing a royal salute. The church and village were dedicated to our Holy Father St. Francis. . . .

If the Tejas asked for priests and desired baptism, the priests were to remain there. And if the Tejas proved quite friendly and no danger was to be expected at their hands, no large garrison was to be left behind; if, on the other hand, they proved troublesome, as many soldiers should remain as seemed needful, according to the advice and with the consent of Father Fray Damian Manzanet. It was at no time necessary for the safety of the priests to leave soldiers among the Tejas, for from the very first they welcomed us with so much affection and good will, that they could hardly do enough to please us. Yet, in the face of all this, Captain Alonso de Leon made arrangements to leave fifty men, under the command of Captain Nicolas Prietto, an incapable and undeserving old man. . . .

However, in the end, it was arranged that the three soldiers recommended by me should remain there. They were willing to do so, and were quite content. . . .

On the 2nd of June we took our departure, and the priests walked with us a little way out of the village. Then we took leave of one another with many tears of joy and gladness, for these men did not sorrow at being left behind, nay, rather, they gave thanks to God for having merited such a grace as to be called to save the souls of the heathen. . . .

## 7. THE SPANISH REOCCUPATION OF TEXAS: THE RAMON EXPEDITION

### April-July, 1716

From Rev. Gabriel Tous, T. O. R. (trans.), "Ramón Expedition: Espinosa's Diary of 1716," *Mid-America*, XII, New Series I (April, 1930), 339-361. By permission of the publisher, the Institute of Jesuit History.

Their first occupation of eastern Texas having failed, the Spaniards made no further effort to reclaim the country until a new French threat appeared. In 1713, Governor Antoine de la Mothe Cadillac of French Louisiana commissioned Louis Juchereau de St. Denis, an enterprising Frenchman with considerable experience in dealing with the Indians, to establish trade across Texas with the Spanish settlements of northern Mexico. When St. Denis appeared, unannounced, at San Juan Bautista on the Rio Grande on July 18, 1714, the startled Spanish officials sent him under arrest to Mexico City. Alarmed over the westward movement of the French and St. Denis' proposal, the Viceroy of Mexico ordered the reoccupation of Texas. For that purpose, an expedition, commanded by Domingo Ramón and guided by St. Denis, set out from the Rio Grande on April 27, 1716. The following selection describes the expedition and the founding of the East Texas missions.

In the name of the Most Holy Trinity. The diary of the expedition from the Rio Grande del Norte to the Province of Texas, undertaken by order of His Excellency, the Duke of Linares, Viceroy of this New Spain, in concurrence with the two Colleges of the Propaganda Fide of Santa Cruz of Querétaro and Our Lady of Guadalupe of Zacatecas, compiled and written by Rev. Father Fray Isidro Felis de Espinosa. Domingo Ramón was captain of the twenty-five soldiers and carried along also twenty-two other men with eight married women to attend to the beasts of burden.

We registered from the College of Querétaro Rev. Father Fray Isidro Felis de Espinosa, President, the Rev. Father Fray Francisco Hidalgo, the Apostolic Preachers; Rev. Fathers Fray Benito Sanchez, Fray Gabriel de Vergara and Fray Manuel Castellanos. The Rev. Father Fray Antonio Margil de Jesus of the College of Zacatecas became seriously ill at the Mission of San Juan Bautista on the Rio Grande. The Apostolic Preacher

Rev. Father Fray Pedro de Santa Maria y Mendoza, the lay-brother Fray Francisco Xavier Cubillos and Fray Domingo de Vrioste with the habit of Donado remained with him. Don Luis de San Dionisio, (Louis of St. Denis), a Frenchman, was captain of the convoy, and two others of the same nationality enrolled with him.

### A. D. 1716

April 25—Saturday. Feast of St. Mark the Evangelist. Mass was sung at the Mission of San Bernardo; rogation prayers proper to the day recited, and a procession formed. These were offered for the success of our journey. At the conclusion of the ceremonies all accompanied the priest who went to administer the Viaticum to our Rev. Father Margil. In the afternoon the Fathers Fray Francisco Hidalgo, Fray Benito Sanchez, Fray Gabriel Vergara and Fray Manuel Castellanos crossed to the other side of the Rio Grande. Commenting on the Gospel of the day *Designavit Dominus* (the Lord hath chosen) all gave thanks to His Divine Majesty for having chosen us for so glorious an enterprise, . . .

June 23—Tuesday. While some went to repair the pass of the river and to make a bridge over a muddy stream, we said five Masses. Soon afterwards all crossed the river, which we named San Juan Bautista [Trinity], because this was the eve of his feast. Then we walked about half a league through a thin forest of oaks in the direction of east-northeast. We crossed the muddy stream by means of the bridge and the expedition stopped at its margin. . . .

June 25—Thursday. The soldiers went with some Indians to take the goats across the river. The son of our captain and a Teja Indian arrived, bringing us news of Don Luis, and how he was engaged in assembling the Asinai Indians, who were still unaware of our arrival. In order to give him sufficient time [for his task] we did not travel this day.

June 26—Friday. After three Masses were celebrated we went on towards the northeast through a forest of scattered pines, walnut trees, common oaks, evergreen oaks, and grapevines with grapes larger than those already mentioned. We . . . stopped early so as to give the Indians time to approach. Four leagues were travelled.

June 27—Saturday. . . . News was brought of the approach of Don Luis with the Indians, and we got ready to receive them. About eight o'clock in the morning thirty-four Indians arrived, five of them being leaders. They came in file behind Don Luis, and were received in the following manner: We arranged the soldiers in two files placing our Captain in the center with the Religious, and in this order we went to greet and embrace them, our hearts overflowing with joy. In order to enter befittingly, the Indians left their horses behind, their bows and arrows and the firearms that some brought they left in the hands of other Indians who ministered to them as servants. There was a general salute on our part, and in the meantime we went to the place prepared for the reception, which was a hut of boughs of trees, carpeted with blankets; the pack-saddles serving as stools. There, all seated according to rank, a page of the Tejas drew out a pipe full of tobacco which they cultivate on their lands. The pipe was very much ornamented by white feathers—a sign of peace among

them. He lighted the pipe and made each of us take a puff of smoke. We returned the compliment with the same ceremony and served chocolate to them. The function terminated with a very serious discourse by an Indian chief, in which he gave us to understand the pleasure with which all desired to receive us in their midst, as Don Luis de San Dionisio, (Louis of St. Denis) who understands and speaks much of their language, made known to us. This day was most pleasing to us, holding out, as it did, such great prospects of attaining our end and achieving the purpose so much desired. That night the Indians gave a salute and feasted on an ox which the chief served them at their pleasure.

June 28—Sunday. We went on, accompanied by many of the Indians, towards the northeast with some deviations to both sides, through a forest of scattered pines, walnut trees, grapevines, common oaks and evergreen oaks among which are four *arroyuelos*. Having travelled nine leagues we came to a large plain surrounded by trees, in whose center are two large lakes and nearby was a copious arroyo where we stopped. That evening, Indians numbering ninety-six, who had not yet visited us came in the following manner: They assembled at a place near the camp and arranged themselves into three files. The middle one was led by Don Louis, followed by all the chiefs and leaders. The two side lines were composed of the remainder of the people who accompanied them. Besides these, the Indians who on the preceding day had come to meet us, were advancing at a short distance with their firearms in order to give a salute. We, on our part, reciprocated, the Captain bearing a standard on which were painted the images of Christ Crucified and of Our Lady of Guadalupe. We, the Religious, took our places on both sides in a wing, with the soldiers in two files, and thus advanced towards them. Our Captain delivered the standard into my hands, and kneeling venerated and kissed the Holy Images and we embraced each other. All the others did likewise. When this ceremony ended, we went in procession singing the *Te Deum Laudamus*, to which the firearms made response. Upon arriving at the encampment all knelt for the conclusion of the hymn. Then we seated ourselves with the Indians on the carpets of the preceding day. The Indians conversed among themselves for a little while, and each chief bringing a handful of ground tobacco they mixed it together to show the unity of their wills, then handed it to the Captain. Afterwards they brought their gifts of ears of corn, watermelons, tomales and cooked beans with corn and nuts. To them were distributed, in the name of His Majesty, the blankets, sombreros, tobacco and flannel for undergarments. And that night they demonstrated their joy with dances.

June 29—Monday. High Mass . . . was attended by a multitude of Indians. . . . Clothing was distributed to them as to the others, and they also celebrated their coming with dances.

June 30—Tuesday. Three Masses were said for the success of their conversion, and again . . . we proceeded northeast through an open forest until we came to a plain which seemed to our Captain to be a suitable place, for the time being, to establish his presido, which was at the margin of a very large lake and not far from a medium sized river. The Religious went with the Captain and some Indians to choose a place for the first mission, and finding one that seemed the best for our purposes we returned to the encampment, having on the way appeased our hunger with cooked Indian corn, with nuts and other fruits of the earth, which the Indians gave us. The expedition travelled this day three leagues.

July 1—Wednesday. The Indians, who were still together, remained to construct a dwelling house for the Captain. It was begun this day, as well as the transferring of the implements and other things pertaining to the four missions.

July 2—Thursday. The house was covered with hay. Meanwhile . . . we wrote some of the language of the Asinai. The Indians reasoned and computed and apportioned among themselves the four prospective missions, Don Luis serving as interpreter. Having recourse to a learned Indian woman of this tribe, reared in Coahuila, we gave them to understand, as best we could, the object of our coming; and from that time forth they advised us that they could not assemble until they had gathered their harvest.

July 3—Friday. All the Religious with the Captain came to a spring of water which we had previously found and soon the Indians began to construct the house for the first mission. . . .

July 4—Saturday. . . . The house was finished although poorly [constructed] like a field shanty. We moved to it and distributed what appertained to each mission.

July 5—Sunday. The captain named *Alcaldes, Regidores,* and an *Alguacil,* and then came to give me, as President, possession of the mission in the name of His Majesty, . . . with the usual ceremonies. I appointed for Minister of the first mission, named "Nuestro Padre San Francisco de los Tejas," the Reverand Father Fray Francisco Hidalgo, who for so many years solicited this conversion. The Apostolic Preacher, Father Manuel Castellano, was appointed his companion and to him I entrusted the spiritual care of the assistants at the presidio. The greater part of the clothing and other things which we brought for the Indians was distributed. This day our Captain, with the Apostolic Preachers, Fathers Fray Matias Sans de San Antonio and Fray Pedro de Santa Maria y Mendoza went in search of the place occupied by the Nacocdochi in order to establish their first mission on behalf of the College of Our Lady of Guadalupe of Zacatecas.

July 6—Monday. Towards northeast a quarter to east-northeast through an open forest, we crossed a stream of water which runs to the first mission. . . . We crossed three small streams and came to the first wigwam of Hinai Indians where we passed the intense heat of the day and took some ears of green corn for refreshment. After midday we went eastward through a sparse forest, and having travelled about two more leagues, we came

to an arroyo with plenty of water. Further on there were poplars, walnut trees and oaks, and in the valleys many pines. Approaching other ranches of the Hinai, we met our Captain with the Fathers from Guadalupe of Zacatecas, who had not yet gone ahead. That evening we looked for a site for the Conception Mission, which we found, although it has a great deal of woodland. We travelled eight leagues this day.

July 7—Tuesday. . . . The Captain gave me possession in the name of His Majesty as is customary. He then, with the Fathers of Zacatecas went to establish their mission. . . .

July 8—Wednesday. The erection of the straw house was begun, though rather late, and the Father Fray Benito Sanchez went to the rancheria of the Nasoni, where he was appointed to establish the third mission on behalf of the College of Querétaro.

July 9—Thursday. Captain Francis Don Luis de San Dionisio and I went to the rancheria of the Nasoni, where we arrived after midday. It is located seven leagues northeast from the Conception Mission. There are on the way many ranches of Indians and arroyos of water with good places for settling. Father Fray Benito and I went out to make a survey, and our Captain, who this day gave possession of the Mission of Our Lady of Guadalupe to the Fathers of Zacatecas, came from the Nacadochi.

July 10—Friday. The Captain gave me possession of the Mission of San Jose, among the Nasoni and Nacono Indians, near a good-sized arroyo which runs to the north. I appointed as their Minister the Apostolic Preacher, Father Benito Sanchez. Thus three Missions were founded, which number about three thousand souls according to what we have seen. I returned to the Mission of the Conception which I attend.

Note: The particular traits which we have observed in this people are their loyalty to their lands and the skill with which they construct their houses. These have high beds for everyone, and compartments of wood where large baskets of nuts and beans are stored for the whole year. They are very charitable among themselves and assist one another in their necessities.

They recognize a superior head, who directs them when they have to work, and there is one who gives them orders, and punishes them harshly when they do not go to work or if they are lazy. They have all the earthenware that is necessary for their service, and curious seats of wood for those who come to their houses. From what we have observed it will require solicitude and labor to eradicate a number of abuses to which they are addicted, since they hardly ever take a step that is not directed by some particular abuse. Time will reveal minutely the good qualities as well as the evil propensities of this people, . . .

# 8. LA HARPE'S ATTEMPT TO ESTABLISH TRADE WITH THE SPANIARDS

## March 1, 1719—May 1, 1720

From Ralph Smith (trans. and ed.), "Account of the Journey of Bénard de la Harpe: Discovery Made by Him of Several Nations Situated in the West," *The Southwestern Historical Quarterly* LXII (July, 1958-April, 1959), from La Harpe's journal and accompanying letters printed in Pierre Margry (comp.), *Découvertes et établissements des Français dans le sud de l'Amérique Septentrional* (1614-1754). *Mémoires et documents Originaux* (6 vols.; Paris, 1875-1886), VI, 241-306.

The plans of St. Denis to introduce French trade into Texas having failed, the authorities in Louisiana determined to make another effort. For that purpose Bénard de la Harpe was commissioned in the latter part of 1718 to establish a post on the Red River among Indians who had deserted their Spanish mission in East Texas, and to enter into trade with Texas, New Mexico, and Nuevo León. The following account of that effort is from La Harpe's journal.

The Council of Louisiana, which consisted, at that time, of MM. de Bienville and Hubert, charged me with the command of the troops and of the post of the Nassonites, Cadodaquious, Nadsoos, and Nagodoches, savage nations above the Natchitoches, about whom we had yet little knowledge; to this end they ordered M. Blondel, lieutenant of the company, commanding at Natchitoches, to give to me, in passing, a detachment of six soldiers from his garrison with a senior sergeant to be under my orders. These gentlemen solicited me to do my utmost in order to succeed at entering into trade with the Spaniards of the province of Texas, the Kingdom of Leon, and New Mexico and to spare nothing in order to make discoveries in the western part of Louisiana, assuring me that I should be reimbursed by the Company [John Law's Company of the West] for any money that I should advance and expense that I should incur. . . .

The little island of Natchitoches, on which we have only a parapet of stakes, without cannon or mortar gun, . . . is a pistol shot from the big island, and at the same distance from Spanish territory, on which it would be better to have our fort, the terrain being beautiful and healthy. The place where the fort is at present is subject to several maladies, the island being very wet, the water bad, the mists continual, and the air penetrating there with difficulty because of the thickness of the timber.

It does not fail, however, to be very fertile as well as the big island, producing many beans, corn, potatoes, tobacco, cotton, and an abundance of different roots and vegetables. . . .

March 1st [1719], Father Manuel, head of the mission of Adayes, came to say mass at Natchitoches; it was through him that I learned that Don Martín de Alarcón had given the order to settle the Nassonites, on the Red River, at two leagues above the Cadodaquious; that hastened my voyage.

I got the necessary supplies and took as guide the war chief of the Natchitoches with twelve of his warriors. . . .

The 6th, we departed from Natchitoches and made the way to the north, . . . [by way of Red River until April 5;] we arrived at three o'clock in the afternoon at the dwelling of the chief of the Nassonites, at that time more than seventy years old. This chief, with those of the Cadodaquious, Nadsoos, and Natchitoches, was awaiting me at this dwelling, outside of which, under an *antichon*, they had prepared a feast, consisting of bread and boiled corn, prepared in different ways, and some bear meat and buffalo meat and fish. . . .

My design being to establish myself at the deserted place of the chief of the Nassonites, I proposed to him . . . to cede to me his ground with its cabin and his *antichon*. He consented, in consideration of a present of the value of thirty pistoles [300 francs] in merchandise . . . .

The 25th, the savages commenced to bring much cypress timber to me. I employed my men similarly at this work, and we laid the foundations for a house of a hundred ten feet long by twenty wide [in present Red River County, Texas], which has been finished only in the end of the month of July.

The 26th, I sent the corporal of the garrison to the Assinais [Hasinai] to carry the letter of M. de Bienville to Don Martín Alarcón, governor of the province of Texas. . . . I wrote on the same occasion to . . . the Reverend Father Marsillo, of the Order of the Recollects, Superior of the Missions of the province of Texas, for the Assinais.

> . . . Our proximity redoubles in me the desire that I have for seeing you and of serving you. . . . Your fervor is great; but you have need of assistance. Touched by these reflections, I have the honor of offering to you a singular and certain means for succeeding there; write to your friends in New Mexico, in Paral and in the Kingdom of New Leon that they will find at the Nassonites or at Natchitoches all the merchandise of Europe, of which they could have need, at a reasonable price, upon which they will make undoubtedly considerable profits. I am setting the prices for them, with the proviso that you shall receive from me five per cent of the total sales. Here is, my reverend Father, a singular means for opening commerce, for rendering service to many persons, who are in need of merchandise and whom the distance from Europe does not permit to have such for a long time. Receive them, my reverend Father, a sure means of establishing your missions with solidity and the offers which come from a heart truly devoted to your Reverence, in which charity has a greater part than all other interest. . . .

The 6th [of May], Saint-François, corporal of the garrison, whom I had sent to the Assinais, arrived with . . . two letters to me, one from Don Martín de Alarcón, governor of the province of Texas, and the other from Father Marsillo. . . .

The governor expressed himself thus:

> . . . The orders that I have from the King, my master, are to maintain a good union with the French of Louisiana; . . .

but I can not keep myself from telling you that your arrival at the Nassonites surprises me very greatly. It must be that your honored Governor ignored that the post that you occupy belongs to my Government and that all the lands situated to the west of the Nassonites are the dependance of New Mexico. Thus, Sir, I counsel you as a friend to give such advice to M. de Bienville; if not, I shall find myself forced to compel you to abandon the lands that the French have no right to settle upon. . . .

In his letter Father Marsillo said:

. . . This correspondence, that you propose to me, being founded on the principles of charity and of esteem, I accept with joy. I shall write to my friends according to your intentions; however, as it is not becoming to a friar to participate in commerce, it is *à propos* that our correspondence be secret, not only because of the consequences which could come from it, but because we are not strong friends with Don Martín de Alarcón; he would be able to thwart our designs. I believe, nevertheless, that he shall not remain long in this province. . . .

The 8th, the chiefs of the Nadaco nation celebrated with me four Calumets; they promised to maintain a good union with the French; I made some presents to them and charged them with a letter for Don Martín Alarcón, of which the following is the tenor:

. . . Permit me, Sir, to have the honor of saying to you that M. de Bienville, instructed perfectly on the limits of his Government, is certain that the post of Nassonites is not of the dependence of His Catholic Majesty. He knows even that the province of Texas, of which you have been named Governor, is a part of Louisiana. M. de La Salle took possession of it in the year 1684; and, since that time, it has been renewed by M. de Saint-Denis. In regard to the lands which are to the west of the Nassonites, I am unable to comprehend by what right you claim that they may be made a part of New Mexico. That which I may have the honor of telling you in this regard, is that all the rivers which flow into the Mississippi belong to the King, my master, and consequently, all the lands that they enclose between them. . . .

The 1st of August, the corporal arrived from the Assinais with . . . [news] that we had war with the Spaniards, and that M. Blondel, commander at Natchitoches, had driven the Recollect Fathers from the mission of the Adayes, which left me very puzzled, so much the more since these good fathers performed the functions of chaplain at Natchitoches. . . .

Seeing that this war was an obstacle to the commerce which I had undertaken to carry on with the Spaniards, and that I had nothing to fear from them for the present in my post, I believed that it was to the interest of the king to go to the discovery of the nations, which had been made mention of in the northwestward, to the end of making an alliance with them for facilitating means of penetrating into New Mexico and the nation of the Padoucas [Comanches], from where the Spaniards draw considerable wealth. . . .

## 9. AGUAYO'S RECOVERY OF EAST TEXAS

### 1719-1722

From "Diario del Viaje del Marquez de San Miguel de Aguayo Escrito por el B. D. Juan Antonio de la Peña, Capellan Mayor del Batallón de San Miguel de Aragón," in *Documentos para la Historia Eclesiastica y Civil de la Provincia de Texas* (Archivo General de la Nación, Mexico, Vol. XXVIII; transcript, Archives, University of Texas Library, Austin).

Spain's second occupation of eastern Texas ended with the retreat of the missionaries in 1719 upon the appearance of the French. The Marquis de Aguayo, resident of Coahuila, offered his services and treasure for the reconquest of the area. The King accepted, appointing him Governor and Captain General of the provinces of Coahuila and Texas. With over five hundred men and five thousand horses, Aguayo crossed the Rio Grande at San Juan Bautista on March 20, 1721, arriving at the Trinity by July 9, where he began to contact Indians. Meeting St. Denis, commandant of Natchitoches, he learned that the French had been entering the East Texas area, but St. Denis agreed to withdraw to the Red River. Aguayo re-established all the abandoned Spanish missions and the presidio in East Texas, established a new presidio at Los Adaes, in spite of St. Denis' protests, and returned to San Antonio late in the year. While awaiting supplies from Coahuila, he proceeded to La Bahía del Espíritu Santo in the spring of 1722, where he founded the La Bahía settlement on the site of Fort St. Louis. Having completed his task, he then returned to Coahuila where he disbanded his expedition on May 31, 1722.

The following selection, from the diary of Juan Antonio de la Peña, the vicar-general of the battalion, gives an account of Aguayo's meeting with St. Denis and the refounding of the mission of San Francisco de los Tejas.

. . . Thursday July 31 . . . This same day Captain Luis de San Dionis [St. Denis] arrived, swimming his horse through the river. The Governor [the Marquis de Aguayo] received him with the proper grace and seriousness; and the latter having said that he was fatigued from the sun and the road, the Governor granted him his request to rest and to spend the night with the Priests.

Friday 1 August. After having heard mass, the Governor had Captain Luis called, and having received him with the Lieutenant General and the Captains, he conferred with him asking that the Captain state the reason for his coming. He responded that he was the commander of the armed forces on the whole frontier, and that if the Governor would concur, he would observe the treaties that were published in Spain between the two crowns, believing from letters he had received from France, that peace was in all likelihood already established. His Lordship replied that under his orders he would abide by the treaties, with the provision that the French evacuate all the Province of Texas, returning to Natchitoches with all their people; and not impeding nor trying to impede directly or indirectly, the re-establishment that his Lordship must accomplish at all costs with the arms of the King our Lord in all the territory in his possession as far as Los Adaes inclusive. To these terms

St. Denis agreed entirely, even though he had the feeling which he dissembled that the French might keep Los Adaes. It was a district the French had ever aspired to since it would be helpful to them as a communication with the Caudodaches, and whose presidio would facilitate the passage to New Mexico. He exaggerated the unhealthliness of the district of Los Adaes, and the uselessness of its fields, where we could not help but know, we having had the Mission of San Miguel that they invaded, so we could not be ignorant of the good condition or quality of the land. And he left, promising to leave for Natchitoches without delay with his people.

Saturday, August 2. The Governor despatched a detachment with the Padre Predicator Fray José Guerra, whose horses swam the river to the mission of San Francisco, and another with the Padres Predicadores Fray Gabriel Vergara and Fray Bentito Sánchez to the mission of Concepción, to rebuild the churches and living quarters at both missions. Until this day when the Fathers were divided, they have celebrated in all the trip seven masses, and eight feast days, and a mission Sermon on all Sundays, the two Presidents of the two colleges alternating, . . .

Sunday, 3. The bridge finished, all the people, equipment, and animals passed easily, moving toward the east-northeast, and the expedition camped very near the mission of San Francisco, where the presidio of the second time that had been moved in the year, '16 had been; and the journey was only 2 leagues.

Monday 4. The Governor despatched a new force of people to complete the work of the Mission of San Francisco and it was possible the next day to celebrate the feast of the re-establishment of the Holy Catholic Faith that had been discontinued in the country of Texas.

Tuesday 5. Seeing that the church and the living quarters for the missionaries was finished, the Governor passed with all the Battalion to re-establish the Mission of San Francisco de los Neches, commonly called the Texas. This was done with the solemn function of a High Mass sung by the R. P. Fray Antonio Margil de Jesus, with a general salute to all the companies in the ceremony, accompanied by the pealing of bells, trumpets, and drums. The function was attended by admiring Indians, who kneeled at the slightest suggestion of the P. President of the Missions of the Santo Colegio de la Santa Cruz de Querétaro, the R. P. Fr. Ysidro Felix de Espinosa. While they were thus congregated in the living quarters of the Padres, and in their presence and in the presence of all the captains and officers of the batallion, he appointed, in the name of Our Lord the King (whom, God protect) as captain of the Neches, the one whom all the Indians acclaimed, giving him a bastion, and an entire suit of clothes of the Spanish style. He dressed entirely, also, one hundred and eighty-eight men and women, who were greatly pleased, since they had never received as much. The P. president told them that the purpose of this appearance (*venida*) was principally for His Majesty's zeal for the salvation of their souls, and that he would bring them under his Royal protection and shelter, to defend them from all their enemies, making them see that the presents that the French, presumably had made them is for their interest in the Indians' deerskins, buffalo hides, horses, and principally their women and children as slaves; and that our Lord the King (whom God protect) not only did not make demands upon them, but instead gave them with such abundance, as they have just seen, the Governor not wanting even one deerskin, because (not wishing even this thing a sign of recompense) he wished only that they enter the pale of the church, as His Highness made them understand. For this purpose it was necessary that they be congregated, and near to the aforesaid mission of San Francisco, forming a Pueblo after the method of the Spaniards, to be named San Francisco de Valero, and that it would not be as it had been before, when they were not congregated. They . . . unanimously responded . . . that they would do this as soon as the harvest; for they had corn in the field. So that they could accomplish this during the interim that his Lordship was at Los Adaes, they asked the Governor to grant them possession of all the lands and water necessary for their keep. He agreed, assigning them in the name of His Majesty and performing all the acts of possession. He left here, as the missionary, Padre Fray José Guerra of the Colegio de la Santa Cruz; and after the President of the College of Santa Cruz had presented that missionary, and after having told him that he trusted his zeal to reduce the souls in all haste, the Governor continued the march, proceeding on a route between northeast and east-northeast, among light forests of mulberry and oak. . . .

## 10. RUBI'S REPORT ON THE SAN SABA ESTABLISHMENT

### August, 1767

From "A copy of the report sent to his Excellency the viceroy, Marquis de Croix regarding the advantages of the maintaining or removing the presidio of San Saba, August, 1767" (Archivo General de Indias, Audiencia de Guadalajara, 1768-1772, 104-61-13, Sevilla; Dunn transcripts, Archives, University of Texas Library, Austin).

The establishment of the mission and presidio on the San Saba (properly, San Sabás) River grew out of appeals from the religious in San Antonio to the *junta de guerra y hacienda,* advisory body to the Viceroy. On May 18, 1756, orders were issued for the removal of the failing San Xavier missions to the San Saba country. The philanthropic offer of Don Pedro Romero de Terreros to undertake the expense of the enterprise was accepted and approved on August 24. After many difficulties, the Spaniards, on April 18, 1757, established Mission San Sabá de la Santa Cruz on the south bank of the San Saba River and Presidio San Luis de las Amarillas about three miles upstream (near present Menard). Shortly, there were six missionaries, a guard of five soldiers, and a few Indian servants in the mission, and one hundred troops and some three or four hundred people, including 237 women and children, in the presidio settlement.

But the work never prospered. The Apaches were reluctant converts; the presidio commander was convinced that the whole project was impossible, and three missionaries departed in despair. In March, 1758, a force of Comanches and their allies, variously estimated from seven hundred to two thousand, appeared. Under the guise of friendship, they entered and pillaged the mission, killing ten of the thirteen people there, including two priests. Father Molina, who gave an account of what happened, escaped from the burning buildings. The presidio commander watched helplessly, since he was undermanned and felt the necessity of maintaining his post. The mission was never re-activated, though the presidio held out for another ten years. Finally, the Marquis of Rubí, when making his inspection in 1767, advised that the presidio be withdrawn because of its unfavorable situation, despite the pressure such a withdrawal would place upon the presidio of San Antonio de Béxar. Of special interest in the document is Rubí's refutation of the arguments the religious used in their effort to have the mission maintained, arguments which the civilian authorities considered to be based not upon the reality of the situation, but on their wishes to maintain the mission regardless of cost.

Most Excellent Sir Dear Sir: In obedience to the repeated orders of your Excellency . . . that I should inform you of my opinion concerning the advantages or disadvantages offered by the present location of the San Saba Presidio for the purpose of a proper solution being made of the question pending in this captaincy general regarding its maintainance or removal to a more suitable place, I report to your Excellency the following:

There are various considerations that one must have in mind in order to form an opinion of the usefulness of a fort. The following are the principal ones. (1) Its situation and location in the most suitable terrain (2) Its construction and the skill used in the placing of its works and defenses so as to make it as strong as possible, foreseeing the disadvantages of the ground according to the strength with which it can be attacked (3) The principal avenues of trouble (attack) (4) The country to cover in case of a retreat and the shelter of towns in case of an invasion (5) The proximity of help in case of a blockade (6) and lastly, as a consideration of importance regarding the disposition and object of these presidios, the opportunity it affords for towns, extending the dominions of the king, and for the converting of the natives. I shall deal particularly with each one of these points.

1st. Regarding the first, that of the location; nothing could better inform your Excellency than the attached plan, outline, and explanation made by the captain of engineers Dn. Nicolas de la F Fora [sic]. The examination of these will show your Excellency that the presidio is located between two ravines which lie open in unequal distances to the north and south. The enemy can come and station themselves in these under cover for the purpose of attacking this presidio. Especially may this be done through that of the river on the southern side. From there they can make, as they do, a great deal of trouble helped by their proximity and the shelter of the underbrush. The thickness of this and the fertility of the soil which allows it to grow back so quickly prevents its being kept cleared away by so small a garrison. . . .

2nd. Concerning the second point . . . your Excellency will be informed of the great mistakes that have

been recognized in both. The same is seen from the named plain and the contour and by the opinion which I include of the before mentioned engineer, who treats this subject as a professor giving all the information that one would want, except that in one particular it occurs to me to add more than that naturally thought. Even a simple examination of the one map provokes one to think how far this work is from the value of 26 (thousand) pesos which it cost as stated by the captain in the proceedings, . . . Its generous transfer to the king in his name and that of the troops will always be useless to his majesty regardless of whether he abandons or maintains the presidio, because in the first circumstance there would remain the represented 26 (thousand) pesos and in the second nothing will be saved by that already done because of what he will need to spend to make a new fortification according to scientific laws and principles.

3rd. Regarding the third point . . . , it should be ordered that these be assigned to the best defenders and those most anxious to protect them [, . . . b]ecause of this country being so large and open in all direction with no important ridge of mountains to block any of the entrances. From whatever direction they come it will make no difference to the enemy; but when they do the enemy does not care to attack. This is well proved by the repeated attacks made at the foot of the presidio, on the villages of the Lipan Apaches, our faithless allies, and on the mission of San Lorenzo del Cañon in the valley of San Joseph. They forced the abandonment of Candelaria and its incorporation with San Lorenzo before it had been founded a year. The same is proved by the repeated raids made on the horses of this presidio on seven or eight occasions. These resulted in a total loss of the horses and the death of many of their defenders, even though the horses were kept immediately beside the presidio, on the Janes and Trancas rivers during the time that these same Lipan Apaches lived near the presidio; and their natural fear and hatred for the enemy of the north made them work ceaselessly to spy on them and keep the presidio posted so that with the horses, which today they no longer have, they could operate against them. This cannot now be done under present circumstances, but they could then go as far as the walls of the villa and presidio of San Antonio de Bexar. There is a recent case of the enemy's having invaded this territory and this they can do whenever they like for who can oppose them, on the Guadalupe, San Marcos, and Los Almagres rivers and all the uninhabited areas of 70 leagues lying between these two presidios? And what will happen in the meantime in San Saba, El Paso del Rio del Norte, and Santa Fe in New Mexico, which lies to the northwest at a still unknown distance? Will it be said, perhaps, that this presidio is located in front of the villages of the savages and will therefore cause them to respect it because of its nearness? Well, nothing is less correct, for if speaking of the Comanches, who are they to be considered as closest to this presidio, they have no fixed homes and it is very strange to face a fort a hundred leagues from our frontiers against a wandering nation which changes its location with all ease according to necessity and convenience. . . . So neither in case of their moving their present good location nor of an expedition they might want to make against the enemy would this presidio be of any assistance; nor would it serve as an assembly quarters in case of an expedition such as that made by Colonel Don Diego Parrilla in 1759 against the savages. . . . Against one nation or many combined the force of one lone presidio cannot hold.

4th. Let us now see what kind of a country shelters this for the purpose of protection or of a retreat in case of an invasion. This is another point with which I have charged myself. The thought already observed is easily seen, that is that being at a distance of over 100 leagues from the south bank of the Rio Grande del Norte, the recently established town of the villa of San Fernando de Austria, in the lands of Coahuyla, considers itself far enough away to not be attacked by the Comanches and other northern tribes and not needing the protection of the forces of this presidio. The chief and most natural barrier and protection for that town must always be considered as the Rio Grande itself, fourteen leagues distant from the village, which until now the enemy has not attacked.

Neither can it be said that it protects the mission of San Lorenzo in the Cañon or valley of San Joseph, this, too, being 50 leagues distant from the presidio of San Saba. This mission has suffered several attacks from which the presidio has been unable to protect it, and it could do far less today since it is without cavalry. . . .

The advancing of presidios with the certainty of their being kept up by the towns which follow them or more properly with the present opportunity of building them, is truly to extend the dominions of the king and facilitate the progress of spiritual conquest which is always to be desired. But to establish presidios 100 leagues distant from these towns with the pretences which always accompany these projects such as that of fertility of the soil, the abundance and ease of securing water, rich mineral wealth which is disproved by experience, only results in bringing expense to the public exchequer and discredit to the arms of the king.

By all of this it is proved that no land or possession of the Spaniards or Indians reach within 100 leagues of the said presidio, that being its distance from the villa of San Fernando. The proofs of the 5th point . . . should be carefully examined as they relate to the failure to ever receive help in the frightful event of a blockade or the cutting of communications.

5th. That this presidio could be blockaded or the introduction of its supplies from Coahuyla stopped is made evident by that already stated. The ease with which the enemy has been seen to maintain himself in its vicinity without being molested, added to the opportunities offered for their maintainance by the numbers of creeks and flowing springs, the abundance of buffalo which is their principal food, deer, wild turkeys and other animals will someday suggest to them the ease with which this presidio can be surrounded, and they maintain themselves in its vicinity to intercept its provisions. Their numbers in this case will not be small; the captain states that at times as many as three thousand savages have come to attack the presidio. How then could they be forced to raise the blockade and leave open the lines of

communication? . . . This makes it plain, these being the only and nearest towns which could send help to San Saba in the event of a possible blockade as has been shown, that the result of such would be very bad, because of the difficulty in securing any help as well as in its small supply of all kinds of war provisions and food, and the scarcity of water which has not yet been brought inside of the enclosure.

6th. Although as a necessary result of that already shown, it could be considered that the total lack of fitness which this presidio offers has been proved, due to its inconsiderate distance from all towns. . . . There has been much contradiction and difference of opinion regarding the objects and purposes as to the establishment of this presidio. Dating from the year 1751 it was established with a force of 50 enlistments on the San Javier river between the presidio of San Antonio de Bexar and that of Los Adays. Here it uselessly remained until 1756 when because of the hard weather in that location and of the disaster of the death of one of the religious and a citizen, and of its total uselessness and inability to accomplish the desired ends, the superiors determined to decide on a new proposal, that of moving it to the region of the San Saba river and giving it an additional 50 men, making a force of 100 in all. This is kept up at the present. Here the purpose of the presidio was again different from that it formerly had. The reduction of the Apache nation a different one from those surrounding the missions of San Javier was proposed. There were various enemies to combat and a location so different and so far away, since it is more than 100 leagues between the two places. In order that this place might be considered as the very best there was not lacking, as usual, a beautiful description of the fertility of the country, its abundance of water, wood, the ease with which dams could be built, and even the usual incentives of minerals of red earth. They would be much closer to the homes of the enemy so the extravagant idea of granting an additional 50 men to the presidio to make it 100 in all was carried out. It was proposed to assure without fail the captains of the possession of a good mine. The reduction of the Lipan Apaches was lost sight of, and these soon proved that the not giving of food to them without denying them their savage liberties and that avenging them on their enemies were costly mistakes. This was done at a great expense to the Royal Hacienda and at the sacrifice of the lives of many soldiers and two missionaries. Because of this they did not attempt another reduction. . . . And so inspired by the fear of losing a part of their 100 soldiers because of their failure they began to make new plans and appearances to insure their remaining. They represented as bordering on this presidio the settlements of the English and French nations and told of how the French were planning to soon make an invasion. They told of conditions which no one recognized and which in truth did not exist. They predetermined exact invasions which never occurred. . . . They proposed that the lands lying between there and New Mexico be peopled. . . . They attempted at El Cañon and at San Saba the boasted dams, and these they were unable to construct. And lastly all of the success which they had promised from the building of San Saba are being contradicted by the facts and the experience gained in the more than ten years of its unhappy existence during which they have sadly failed to establish one single mission; . . . [Y]ou might provisionally order it to withdraw (should this meet the approval of your Excellency) as a post to the new villa of San Fernando del Austria. . . .

Lastly there remains for me to tell your Excellency of the only risk to be guarded against in case of the removal of the presidio of San Saba. It is that the enemy, having already penetrated as far as the banks of the Rio Grande del Norte in pursuit of the Lipan Apaches, who are now having to seek protection; could perhaps with the threat offered by this presidio of San Saba removed as well as that of the military post of El Cañon, plan the destruction of the presidio and town of San Antonio de Bexar. Should they attack it with all their forces, the actual population of the villa and its small presidio of only 29 men, of whom 15 are assigned to the missions and the remaining 8 are needed for guards for the mails and envoys they must send to the presidio of La Bahia del Espiritu Santo, would be unable to withstand the attack. Before the founding of the presidio of San Saba that of San Antonio de Bexar had at first 54 enlistments and later 44. To these was added the town made by the islanders at his majesty's expense. These were thought to be sufficient to defend it under those conditions, but I should advise you that in them we did not have as many people as the northern Indian nations now have. It should be clearly realized that at the present time these can make war; and on the other hand the Lipan Apaches themselves, who will be little pleased with these new arrangements, can do likewise. For these reasons I consider it absolutely necessary for us to restore the presidio to the number of 51 soldiers including 3 officers and a sergeant and making the captains strictly responsible for the slovenly condition of this town, which lacks arms and horses which they should have for their own defense. . . .

## 11. THE RUBI RECOMMENDATIONS ON TEXAS

### April 10, 1768

From "Digttamen, que de orden del Exmo señor Marques de Croix, Virrey de este Reyno expone el Mariscal de Campo Marques de Rubi, en orden a la mejor Sittuazion de los Presidios, para la defensa, y exttension de su Fronttera a la Genttilidad en los Confines al Nortte de este Virreynatto," Tacubaya, April 10, 1768 (Archivo General de Indias, Audiencia de Guadalajara, 1768-1772, 104-6-13, Sevilla; Dunn transcripts, Archives, University of Texas Library, Austin).

By the end of the Seven Years' War it was apparent to King Charles III of Spain that the whole structure of the Spanish colonial system must be overhauled. For one phase of this he sent José de Gálvez as *visitor-general* to New Spain in 1765 to make sweeping reforms, including among others the improvement of the defenses of the northern frontier. To effect the latter, Gálvez determined on an inspection of the region, choosing for the purpose the Marquis de Rubí. The latter began his two-year, 7,000-mile journey from Mexico City on March 18, 1766, accompanied by an able engineer, Nicolás de Lafora, and a military escort. His tour took him from California to Louisiana. He entered Texas from the southwest, crossed the Rio Grande near San Juan Bautista on July 14, 1767, and visited the Spanish installations in Texas before returning to Mexico on February 23, 1768.

Rubí made his observations and recommendations in a lengthy *dictamen*, or report, later used as the basis for the reorganization of the frontier. In general, he recommended a withdrawal to a shorter line of defense. The following selections from this report illustrate his recommendations with respect to Texas: the formation of a new Indian policy; the retention of San Antonio as a frontier outpost, re-enforcing its garrison and making it the capital of Texas; and the suppression of the East Texas and San Saba establishments.

. . . [T]he injuries and expenses that the unfaithful Lipanes directly and indirectly have occasioned the possessions and treasure of the King, enticing us with their false friendliness and supposed desire for conversion and settlement never realized, cause me to take under consideration the remedy for such urgent damage. The desire for their punishment and correction, which is surely the only means to attract them to some [missionary] district which would be best for the religion and for the state, can well beguile me; but I confess that what I now propose seems to me, effortless and safe.

With this vile nation of Lipanes (incapable of resisting our presidios in an open war) placed as a buffer between our frontier and their enemy nations of the north, suffering on their front and rear a war which they cannot sustain, and it will be seen how they will be forced to admit the agreements that their demonstrated malice has made them recognize as inevitable. While the Comanches and their allies are finishing with them (which should not be difficult for them), it is probable that they will seek asylum in our missions and presidios; but this should not be permitted them except to intern them and divide them, extinguishing or confounding, as has been done with other nations whose names are lost to memory, the idea of one nation whose sagacity, capacity, and industry are always lamentable and indecorous to the progress of the arms of the King and the tranquility of his possessions.

One day undoubtedly we will have for neighbors the nations of the north, that are already nearing us; but these, because of their generosity and valor, do not need to be our enemies. Perhaps they will not be, since they are not so in our new colony of Louisiana, nor at our present presidio at Los Adaes, which they live near; nor were they at San Xavier, nor did they so indicate in New Mexico, where in the Valley of Taos they came annually to celebrate their fairs with us. Capable of some formality in their treaties (they have sufficient understanding to observe them), and, no longer embarrassed by the closeness of the abhorred Lipans, who pillage them as they do us, they will live (I judge) quiet in their own areas, without crossing our frontier, enjoying their peaceful possession of the buffalo hunt, which is all their sustenance, cultivation, and ambition.

These advantages . . . make me view as necessary the complete extermination of the Lipanes or at least their entire reduction. . . .

How painful and repugnant for many was the proposition that I now make, to abandon the villa and the five very rich missions located on the banks of the river of that name, bringing them back to this side of the Rio del Norte [Rio Grande] to the protection of the line of presidios, such as are those of San Juan and San Bernardo, and that of San Juan Bautista of the same Rio Grande to which I have just referred. This move that undoubtedly would cause many difficulties, could be justified by many examples of those executed in other, larger colonies, to gain their advancement or security. But I did not dare, nor do I have that much faith in my own opinions, to advise a change of such consideration. Let the presidio and the villa of San Antonio de Béjar, then, remain in their present and original positions, since many expenditures have been made from the Royal treasury in the movement of the families from the Canary Isles; in the erection of a temple, which must be sumptuous; in the gratuities distributed among the settlers, to provide the necessaries for their fields, which they do not take care of, and arms for the Service, that are not made without new costs to the account of the King. And permit also the five missions to remain; composed as they are, not of native Indians of that district, but of those brought from the coast of the colony of Nuevo Santander, and from other districts farther to the interior, where the missionaries go to get their spiritual recruits. But since this settlement will remain more than one degree farther toward the north than the latitude of the rest of the presidios placed in the cordon at the banks of the Rio Grande, it is necessary to guard in all possible ways against the risks that its location, a distance of more than 50 leagues from the Presidio of San Juan Bautista del Rio Grande, present.

When San Saba is evacuated, as I have advised; and the presidio of Los Adaes and its settlement, which is ending its unhappiness, suppressed or incorporated into the jurisdiction of New Orleans; and when the useless presidio of Orcoquiza has been retired at the proper time to this villa or other district in its vicinity, the villa of San Antonio will remain as our most advanced frontier in the province of Texas. . . . [It is necessary, therefore,] to keep this villa in a respectable state of defense until its security can be affirmed by a growth of its population and by those settlements that spring up in its vicinity owing to this same protection. . . .

For the further increase in forces, commerce, and the circulation and consumption of money and goods, it will be convenient for the governor, unhampered by the troublesome charge of Los Adaes, to reside in this settlement . . .

## 12. A NEW DEFENSE POLICY FOR THE NORTHERN FRONTIER

### June 9-15, 1778

From Report on Council of War held in Chihuahua convened by the Commandant General of the Interior Provinces (Archivo General de la Nación, Provincias Internas, Mexico, Vol. LXIV; transcript, Archives, University of Texas Library, Austin).

The Marquis de Rubí's recommendation calling for a reversal of Spain's Indian policy on her northern frontier was difficult to effect. The Spaniards were unable to contact all the Comanches, nor could they wage successful war against them and the Apaches for lack of forces. Meanwhile, both the Apaches and the Comanches raided the Spanish settlements from Texas to Taos. The Apaches, seeking protection from the Comanches, pressed against the Spanish settlements, stealing and killing with increasing intensity. To remedy the situation, the King created a military jurisdiction on the northern frontier, known as the Interior Provinces, under a commandant general, the first of whom was El Caballero de Croix. Croix began his work in Mexico City in 1777, and confronted by a vast number of reports narrating the appalling conditions in the provinces under his command, he decided to examine the frontier at first hand. At Monclova, San Antonio, and Chihuahua he held councils, attended by ranking officers in the respective areas, to analyze the defense problem on the basis of sixteen points he had prepared. The result was a new Indian policy, the essence of which called for an alliance with the Comanches and Nations of the North (Norteños) against the Apaches as Rubí had recommended. The following selection, from the report on the Chihuahua Council, June 9-15, 1778, concurring with the findings and opinions of the two previous councils, clearly defines the Indian problem on the northern frontier, discusses the advantages and disadvantages of an alliance or war with the Apaches and with the Indians of the North, and reveals Spain's dire military weakness.

The voting members of the council having the proper reports and finding themselves now sufficiently instructed with the necessary antecedents giving their opinions on the points of inquiry as follow:

1. How long the Apache nation has been known on these frontiers, and since when have they made war on us.

Opinion: The voters agreeing with what was reported in the councils celebrated in Coahuila and Texas, they declared that they have known the Apache Indians as declared enemies since they have been serving on these frontiers, and that from what they have heard generally and seen in various documents, reports, and files, they have made war on us for more than forty years without intermission.

2. What progress have we achieved against them, and especially in the last five years.

Opinion: They agreed to what was expressed in the cited councils of Coahuila and Texas, affirming that the Apaches have made progressively more war, especially in the last five years; that the placement of the presidios on the present line of the frontier had occasioned major dangers; that they would not experience that danger if they had made the line closer than the very considerable distance in which the presidios are situated from the settlements, and that the presidios should have been situated in more appropriate regions, since many of them cannot subsist on the terrain they occupy owing to the scarcity or lack of water, pasture, or wood, or because the presidio is vary rarely located where there are the commodities to establish a settlement; that with the moving of the presidios to distances sometimes as much as one hundred and fifty leagues from the settlements, the latter are left unprotected, and, as a consequence, neither they nor the presidios have been able to defend themselves from the continual hostilities of the Apaches; that these Indians, with their increasing number of victories, make themselves daily more odious, prideful, feared, and expert in operations of war; that what now generally all the provinces suffer is a harsher and bloodier war than was suffered in earlier times, which accounts for the infinitely greater extent of deaths that the Indians have caused among the faithful vassals of the King; the captivity of the children of both sexes, that cannot accord themselves with the sacred character they have received in the Holy Baptism, being souls that are perverted involuntarily and that add to the number of barbarians, and perhaps the ones that offer us the most damage; in the notable abandonment of towns, haciendas, and farms, and the despoilage of the products of the field. One is able to assure himself that these fertile provinces are becoming the most horrible deserts, and that they are the open door, unless the Indians are contained, through which [these Indians] will be introduced in a very few years to the immediate vicinity of the capital of New Spain. . . .

3. How many warriors (men of arms), by prudential count, compose each of the branches or bands of the Apache people (*Apacheria*), which we now recognize as Lipan Apaches of Above, Lipan Apaches of Below, Mescaleros, Natagés or Lipillanes, Faraones, Nabajó, and Gileños; and what friendship and relationships these Indians have among themselves.

Opinion: The members of the council agreed with that expressed in the council of Coahuila, except as to the number in the *Apacheria,* for Brigadier Don Pedro Fermín de Mendinueta and Lieutenant Colonel Don Juan Bautista de Anza [governor and ex-governor of New Mexico] were of the opinion that the number is much larger than the 5,000 men, and that to these should be added a similar number of women, since, if they do not make war in the same way as the men, they assist them in many actions begun by the Apaches. As has been observed, they usually form the reserve corps, hold the horses while the men commit themselves against our troops, and finally, that although they do not serve more than to swell the parties, the enemies succeed in their object, the well founded idea of making themselves more feared. The fact is that until this day there is not a

person in the province that would dare categorically to determine more or less the number of the Apaches that make war at one time in the various districts in numerous parties. . . .

5. What declared enemies the Apaches have in the gentile nations fronting their lands, settlements, or bands.

Opinion: They reported that the Eastern Apaches had as irreconcilable enemies the Taguayazes and the remainder of the Nations of the North; and all the *Apacheria* had the Comanches as enemies, whom they fear much for the rigor with which they make war. . . .

6. What opinion should the treaties of peace with Lipanes of this province merit; in what terms were they celebrated; what good has come from them and what advantages or disadvantages would be produced by the conservation of these treaties of peace or the declaration of war.

Opinion: The voters were in agreement with all that was expressed in the Council at Monclova, feeling that in none of the provinces should peace be permitted the Apaches, for experience showed that their friendship always produced the most deplorable results, and that councils for the purpose would have no other advantage than to spend money fruitlessly in giving presents to the enemies with little honor to the arms of the king, for the grave damages that the barbarians execute . . . in the same districts where they are soliciting peace; for at the same time they are asking for it, they are robbing what they can and kill the unhappy one that accepts confidence in them that he should never have, because of the bad faith of these barbarians. As a consequence the war must be maintained against the branches of the *Apacheria,* delaying the break with the Lipanes until there are sufficient troops in the provinces to conduct operations of war, considering very urgently the augmentation of force to prevent the Lipanes, who are the right arm of the *Apacheria,* from effecting shortly the ruination of these provinces. . . .

8. Concerning the Comanches, Taguayazes, Taguacanes, Texas, Vidais, Orcoquisac, Atacapas, and other Indians, and what we know as the Nations of the North, each voter will state what . . . [10.] benefits would be obtained by making war on said nations, or allying ourselves with the Lipanes, or the contrary.

Opinion: The voters conformed to that concurred in at the councils in Coahuila and Texas, and thought an alliance with the Indians of the North against the Lipanes and other sectors of the *Apacheria* safer and more advantageous, basing this decision first in that the proved bad faith of this nation gives no hopes that they ever would receive nor maintain the friendships thus promoted; secondly, forced to maintain their villages against our frontier to assure themselves against eruptions of their enemies, the Indians of the North, they cannot subsist without the incessant robberies that they commit; thirdly, that the great knowledge that they have of our territories facilitate the success of their hostilities, to which also the great number of captives that they have made contribute, having accommodated themselves to live happily with the Apaches and, though being less than these in war actions, do serve as guides and work with greater impiety than the savages; fourthly, in the most solid, convincing reasons that are read in . . . the opinions of the . . . Marqués de Rubí concerning the character of the Lipan Apaches, and the Nations of the North, for at the same time that he recommends the latter saying:  That for their generosity and bizarreness they are less inclined to be our enemies, and that perhaps they will not be, as they are not of our colony of Louisiana, etc.  The perfidy of the Lipanes is exposed, and the necessity to divide and confound that nation, whose wisdom, rapacity and industry are always dismal and indecorous to the progress of the arms of the king and the tranquility of these possessions.  Fifthly, . . . the New Regulation of Presidios  that prohibits treaties of peace or agreements that are not sealed and certain, with the Apaches who hostilize the frontiers, demonstrating the desire for peace or containment when their forces are inferior or when they are fearing for their success, and abusing afterward the first at the first opportunity, interpreting as weakness the clemency with which they have been treated and admitted.  For this is the same that they are experiencing in Coahuila and Texas with the Lipanes . . . that live at the present time on both banks of the Rio Grande del Norte in the shelter not only of the Presidio of San Juan Bautista, but also of that of Monclova and Santa Rosa.  Finally, in support of the useful alliance with the Nations of the North, it must be borne in mind that these Indians live in open and fertile lands, abundant with deer and buffalo, which are their delicacies and foodstuffs; that accustomed to living on them, and making war on the plains country, it is with difficulty that they accommodate . . . themselves in a territory of rugged mountains, arid, and scarce of all types of foodstuffs, for which cause the Apaches eat for the most part mules and horses that they steal.  Even when pressed by their enemies the Guaras, the Nations of the North see themselves obligated to come near our frontiers, where they will remain for a time, and this will be enough to protect them from these new enemies. For all these fundamental considerations, the voters approved the alliance with the Indians of the North.

11. If the present number of troops guarding our frontier will be sufficient to  begin  war operations, whether against the Lipanes and the other groups of the *Apachería*, or against the Indians of the North.

Opinion:  The voters agreed that there is not nor can there be sufficient force according to the present state of the provinces and the number of troops that garrison

it, nor can it be possible that a frontier of more than 900 leagues, from California to Texas, be defended by 1,900 men; nor can a general or special campaign be begun usefully against the *Apachería*. This assertion was founded on the fact that each presidial company was composed of fifty-six men including officers divided into several details. . . .

In order to clarify these views, the voters made the following chart:

| Detail of the Service of a Presidial Company | |
|---|---|
| Guarding the horse herd | 15 |
| Foraging | 20 |
| Escort duty, despatch duty . . . , etc. | 15 |
| Post guard | 6 |
| Total | 56 |

*Notes*

There are presidios situated in locations of major danger where 30 men are insufficient to guard the horse herd. . . .

16. Finally, what provisions can be made with the present troops, for the defense of each of the provinces, and what operations will be the most useful to that end, and to the general pacification of the territory, if the hoped-for enlargement of the forces is not realized.

Opinion:  On the last point, the voters had the following opinion:  With respect to the province of Texas, that it, during peace with the Indians of the North and the Lipanes, is not suffering incursions the other provinces are, peace and friendship should be maintained as long as possible, preventing as much as feasible the meeting of these nations at the same time at San Antonio de Béxar.  Much care must be taken to prohibit the citizens of that province trading or bartering firearms and munitions to the Apache, and the greatest caution be exercised to suppress this type of trade between them and the Vidais and Texas. . . . And if the increase in troops is realized, they must be divided among the necessary districts for best use to assure the success of the proposed general campaign, to defend the country, and aid the present and contemplated settlements. . . .

Finally, . . . if the King cannot increase the forces for the general campaign, that [he] permit the seven presidios [including San Saba to] . . . be returned to their original positions, and others, pointed out by the commandant general, be placed close to the existing settlements to protect them.

## 13. THE FOUNDING OF NACOGDOCHES

### January-May, 1779

From Antonio Gil Ybarbo to Commandant-General Teodoro de Croix, Nacogdoches, May 13, 1779, Letter, in Charles W. Hackett (trans.), *Pichardo's Treatise on the Limits of Louisiana and Texas* (4 vols.; Austin, 1946), IV, 209-211.  By permission of the publisher, the University of Texas Press.

On September 10, 1772, the King issued a decree implementing in the main the recommendations for changes on the northern frontier made by the Marquis de Rubí.  Don Hugo O'Conor, who was made responsible for effecting the changes, issued orders on May 6, 1773, to Governor Juan María, Baron de Ripperdá, of Texas, who was residing at San Antonio at the time, to proceed immediately with the suppression of the East Texas settlements in accordance with Rubí's recommendation. The Governor went in person to East Texas and on June 25 began the evacuation to San Antonio, reaching that place on September 26. Mourning their lost homes and not welcome among the San Antonio citizens, the East Texans on December 7, 1773, obtained Ripperdá's approval to send Antonio Gil Ybarbo and Gil Flores as their agents to Mexico to seek permission to return to their old homes. Only partially successful, they were granted approval on May 17, 1774, to move as far as the Trinity River where they established a pueblo which they named Nuestra Señora del Pilar de Bucareli (commonly known as Bucareli) in honor of the Viceroy. The settlement was located at a point called Paso Tomás (identified by modern historians as the present Robbins' Ferry in Madison County) on the old San Antonio-Nacogdoches Road. There they lived until a series of misfortunes overtook them, plaintively expressed by their leader and appointed captain, Gil Ybarbo, and by January 25, 1779, they were moving back to East Texas and settling around "the old mission of the Nacogdoches." Seeking recognition of this unauthorized action, Ybarbo wrote the following letter to the new military authority of the northern frontier, the Commandant-General Teodoro de Croix, depicting the hardships of the East Texans and relating the story of the third and last move of the settlers of Nacogdoches.

Señor commandant-general. Señor: The entire body of inhabitants and militia presented itself in my house on the first and eighth of January, 1779, and I granted them permission to move with their families to the vicinity of the pueblo of the Texas Indians, since they had become terrified by the hostile Comanches to such an extent that the families were suffering, the men being unable to go out to butcher meat, because of not wishing to leave their families exposed to the Indians' barbarities. [These hostilities] also have left them practically afoot and with little time, what with the constant agitation over defenses and guards, to support themselves, and with no hope of being able to plant crops for the same reason, and also because their fields are scattered and at a distance, and because of the scarcity of arms and ammunition for defending them. They believe that there [at the Texas pueblo] they could plant crops and support themselves until, your lordship being informed by my governor and by me, you may decide what you consider best with regard to the matter. Therefore, since all the arguments they advanced were obvious to me; and considering that, if I did not give them the permission, I exposed them to a serious risk and that if I did permit them to move farther away, to a greater one, and that the friendly nations would feel hurt; and in view of the grave necessity and danger as well as the long delay [occasioned] by applying to your lordship's superiority, particularly with the lack of means that I have for doing so, notwithstanding the amount of work that we have done in our pueblo—I decided to allow them to move and to give an account of it to my governor at once. They began to do this on January 25, while I remained with twenty men until these could return with their baggage and belongings. It was found that their fears had not been groundless, for it happened that on the night of February 14, the river went out of its banks and inundated everything on both sides, drowning most of the few horses and cattle that remained. Its waters rose to about the middle of the houses of the pueblo, endangering the domestic animals there and causing the loss of the poor things that the sudden flood gave no time to free, because of the necessity of attend-

ing to the women and children who remained. These were got out on boards and doors and taken to the highest point in the vicinity, where a few days later the Comanches fell upon us. They displayed their courage by surrounding our camp throughout the night. Being unable to kill us, on the following day (at about six in the morning) they carried off thirty-eight horses which had been saved from the waters in canoes with a great deal of trouble, and which could not be defended because we were unable to leave the families unprotected. Thus we were left entirely on foot. They [the Indians] went without taking leave, and encountered not very far away eight friendly Indians of whom they killed six. Two escaped and in fleeing came to our camp. When the crossing of the families to the other side of the river was begun in canoes on the wide-spreading, flooded waters (which on occasion lasted for eighty days at a time), there was heard, between seven and eight in the evening of the day on which the crossing was completed, a volley of shots from the direction of the place which we had left. Consequently, on the following day, when some people were sent to see what it had been, there were visible only a great many footprints of the enemy, who had left the said place after firing their shots. It must be added that if most of the families had not left on the said 25th of January, there is no doubt, señor, but that there would have been a greater loss because of the flood, for many children as well as some invalids disabled by disease would have been drowned. Continuing with all of them to the vicinity of the pueblo of the Texas Indians, two days' journey distant, more than a hundred days were spent on the road in getting the people together, and because of the many floods, which were general. There they suffered unspeakable hardships, until we saw the place of Los Texas and the old mission of the Nacogdoches, which is three leagues farther inland. Since there was a small chapel in it, where the reverend missionary father could administer the holy sacraments, and a house in which he lived, as well as sufficient water, lands, and building materials, I took advantage of these things to enable us to raise crops and sustain ourselves while awaiting your lordship's superior decision. I humbly beg your lordship to think well of my decision, it being impossible to return to the old site or to the banks [of the Trinity] below or above it, because they are lowlands, or to go farther inland because of the greater risk. No better place can be found here than this one and the one that was granted us by the most excellent señor viceroy. This place is situated conveniently for watching the movements and operations of the friendly nations and for controlling the traders, as well as for acquiring information from the coast, a matter with which I have been charged by my governor.

For this reason, in behalf of this entire pueblo as well as myself, I beg your lordship to be pleased to take pity on us for the hardships that we have been suffering since the suppression of Los Adaes, where we so obediently abandoned our belongings and our houses. We continue in this obedience and offer ourselves for whatever we have been ordered to do in the service of his Majesty, as we have done [hitherto] at our expense. After having had to move three times, we are now hoping that your lordship's piety will look upon us with your paternal love and will order us what you may consider best with regard to our settlement, for which purpose we beg that your lordship will bear us in mind in giving your orders. With regard to them, I do not omit telling your lordship that of the two places this one has more advantages.

May our Lord keep your lordship's life many years. Nacogdoches, May 13, 1779. Your most attentive and grateful subject kisses your lordship's hand. Antonio Gil Ybarbo. To Señor Commandant-general Don Teodoro de Croix.

## 14. A CENSUS OF SPANISH TEXAS
### December 31, 1783

From Governor Domingo Cabello, "Estado que manifiesta el Numero de Vasalles, y Habitantes que tiene el Rey en esta Probincia, con distincion de Clazes, Estados, y Castas de todas las Personas de Ambos Sexos Ynclusos los Parbulos," December 31, 1783 (Odie B. Faulk, trans.; Béxar Archives, University of Texas Library, Austin).

After their occupation of Texas was well established, the Spaniards normally took an annual census of the province. Of the available reports, that of 1783 appears to be best representative of the period between the zenith and nadir of Spanish power in Texas.

## PROVINCE OF TEXAS

Statement that manifests the number of vassals and inhabitants which the King has in this province, with distinction as to class, condition and race of all the persons of both sexes, including the children.

| Names of the Populations | Men | Women | Boys | Girls | Male Slaves | Female Slaves |
|---|---|---|---|---|---|---|
| Presidio of San Antonio de Béxar and Village of San Fernando | 331 | 311 | 321 | 264 | 8 | 13 |
| Mission of: | | | | | | |
| San José | 41 | 31 | 26 | 25 | | |
| San Juan Capistrano | 53 | 26 | 13 | 7 | | |
| San Francisco de la Espada | 32 | 28 | 30 | 6 | | |
| Nuestra Señora de la Concepción | 32 | 29 | 18 | 8 | | |
| San Antonio de Valero | 49 | 35 | 36 | 29 | | |
| Presidio of La Bahía del Espíritu Santo | 193 | 147 | 68 | 45 | 1 | |
| Mission of La Bahía del Espíritu Santo | 75 | 66 | 33 | 40 | | |
| Mission of Nuestra Señora del Rosario | | | | | | |
| Town of Nuestra Señora del Pilar de los Nacogdoches | 129 | 104 | 52 | 50 | 8 | 6 |
| Totals of the present year | 935 | 777 | 597 | 474 | 17 | 19 |
| Totals for last year | 947 | 786 | 597 | 474 | 17 | 19 |
| Decrease | 12 | 9 | | | | |
| General summary: | | | | | | |
| Of Spaniards | 488 | 373 | 376 | 340 | | |
| Of Indians | 290 | 241 | 70 | 76 | | |
| Of Mestizos | 43 | 38 | 32 | 12 | | |
| Of Mulattos [*de Color Quebrado*] | 114 | 125 | 119 | 46 | | |
| Of Slaves | | | | | 17 | 19 |
| Totals | 935 | 777 | 597 | 474 | 17 | 19 |
| General summary: | | | | | | |
| Of secular ecclesiastics | 3 | | | | | |
| Of regular clergy | 8 | | | | | |
| Of those married | 655 | 655 | | | | |
| Of widows and widowers | 61 | 122 | | | | |
| Of single persons | 208 | | | | | |
| Totals | 935 | 777 | 597 | 474 | 17 | 19 |

Royal Presidio of San Antonio de Béxar, December 31, 1783.

[Signed] Domingo Cabello [rubric]

## 15. THE TEXAS MISSIONS
### 1785

From Fray José Francisco López, "Report and Account That the Father President of the Missions in the Province of Texas or New Philippines Sends to the Most Illustrious Señor Fray Rafael José Verger of the Council of His Majesty, The Bishop of the New Kingdom of León, in Accordance with the Royal Order that, on January 31, 1781, Was Issued at El Pardo and Was Sent to His Illustrious Lordship, the Bishop, by the Most Excellent Viceroy Count of Gálvez, on August 4, 1785, filed [for Permanent Record] in the Archives of this Presidency" (photostat, University of Texas Library, Austin), in J. Autry Dabbs (trans.), "The Texas Missions in 1785," *Mid-America*, XXII, New Series XI (January, 1940), 38-58. By permission of the publisher, the Institute of Jesuit History.

The Spanish mission system, designed as a frontier institution to Christianize and civilize the Indians and to hold the frontier against the possible intrusion of foreigners, was a joint enterprise of both church and state. The state approved the location of the missions, bore the initial expense of the founding, and paid the stipend of the priests. In Texas, Spain had a well-developed mission field in three distinct areas: eastern Texas, extending from the upper Neches River eastward to Los Adaes, La Bahía (Goliad), and San Antonio. The Texas missionaries were Franciscans, coming from the seminary, or college, of the Propagation of the True Faith either of Querétara or Zacatecas. San Antonio de Valero (the Alamo) and the three missions moved from East Texas to San Antonio in 1731 (commonly called thereafter Concepción, San Juan, and Espada) were Querétaran; Guadalupe at Nacogdoches, Dolores at present San Augustine, and San Miguel at Los Adaes, Espíritu Santo (at Goliad after 1749), and San José at San Antonio were Zacatecan. In 1773 the Queréterans turned over their four missions at San Antonio to the Zacatecans.

The following account of the Texas missions is from the translation of a report, practically *in extenso*, written by Father Fray José Francisco López, the President of the Zacatecan order having authority over Texas missions. It is included at great length because of its acute observations and insights into the physical as well as the spiritual and intellectual conditions of the missions on which it touches.

### Mission San Antonio de Valero

This mission is situated across the [San Antonio] river from San Antonio de Béxar. It is built to form almost a square, surrounded by a single stone and mud wall that stands about 300 paces from the center. The same rampart serves as a wall for most of the fifteen or sixteen houses, with ample capacity for lodging the Indians. Nearly all the houses are covered with wood and mortar, as a protection against the rain, and have hand-carved, wooden doors with locks and iron keys. Within the square is the granary, made of stone and lime, which has enough room to hold two thousand *fanegas* [4000 bushels] of corn, two hundred or more *fanegas* of beans, etc. Next is the house or living quarters, adequate for the missionary and the officers of the community, made of stone and lime, with good roofs, doors, windows, and locks. Adjoining this building is the sacristy (which serves today as the church), while another room now serves as the sacristy. Both structures are of stone and mortar and are built with arched roofs. This mission has under construction a church with a very large nave, whose walls are built as high as the cornices, but the latter have been built only in the dome of the presbytery. In the front, its beautiful façade of wrought stone has been completed to the same height as the walls. At this point the construction stopped many years ago for lack of qualified workmen. For this and other reasons . . . it cannot now be carried on to completion. The lowest

evaluation that may be placed upon the church and sacristy is twenty thousand *pesos*, with an additional eight thousand for the furnishings and ornaments. . . . In personnel [*lo formal*] this mission consists of

Married couples, 12, from 20 to 50 years of age......24
Widowers and bachelors, from 25 to 40 years of age ........ 8
Boys, from 1 to 10 years and one girl ........20
Total number of persons ........52

This mission was founded with Indians of various nations, such as the Hierbipiames, Pataguas, Scipxames, Xaranames, Samas, Payatas (these last two were the principal ones), Yutas, Kiowas, Tovs, and Tamiques; but all these may be considered as Samas and Payas, whose language is in general use. Spanish is now more commonly used, the Indians having married mulattoes and mestizoes (who are called *Coyotes* in this country). Also it should be noted that although this mission was founded in the year 1716 [The mission was formally established in 1718 by Father Francisco Buenaventura de Olivares and Captain Martín de Alarcón, Governor of Texas.], most of the Indians in it, and there are more than fifty, are sons of uncivilized natives; and, further, they were baptized as adults when some were as much as forty years of age.

### Mission La Purísima Concepción de Acuna

This mission is situated on the bank of the River of San Antonio de Béxar, at a distance of one league from the presidio and from the mission already described. It stands on a clearing, protected by the woods along the river. The mission is square in shape and enclosed by a stone and mud wall, low in parts, and provided with three ample openings, one on the east, another on the west, and a third on the south. These have gates of carved wood with good locks. This rampart serves as a wall for houses of the same material. These furnish ample shelter for the Indians. In fact, there are twenty-three rooms, with flat roofs; and although some of them are in a ruinous state, they are not difficult to restore or repair. In the present year all or nearly all will be rebuilt. On the east side stands the roomy house of the missionaries, and the offices of the community, all made of stone and lime, nearly all provided with arched roofs. This is a one-story building except for one room built above. The sacristy and the church adjoin the main stone and lime structure; they are both very notable for this country because of the two towers and the beautiful cupola. The church and sacristy together are valued at 30,000 *pesos*, and their furnishings and ornaments at three or four thousand. East of the church is a spacious granary about fifteen or twenty *varas* in length, and eight or nine *varas* in width, with walls of stone and lime, and a flat, wooden roof. This building may be valued at not less than one thousand *pesos*. The mission consists of

Married couples, 17, from 25 to 60
    years of age ........................................34
Widowers and one widow, from 30 to 80
    years of age ........................................13
Bachelors, about 20 years of age ................. 2
Children ...............................................22
Total number of persons ..........................71

Although these people are descendents of the various nations for whom this mission was founded, . . . they are now reduced to and generally called Paxalaches . . . and although nearly all speak Spanish, it is with notable imperfection. It should be noted that most of the Indians were baptized after they were fullgrown and that those over forty years of age are children of uncivilized Indians.

### Mission San José de Aguayo

This mission, like the preceding ones, is situated on the west bank of the San Antonio River, south (downstream) of those already described, at a distance of about one league from Mission Concepción and two from that of San Antonio and the Royal Presidio. Situated on a broad plain, rather sparsely wooded, its grounds and buildings, surrounded by a rampart of stone-and-mud houses, offer an attractive sight. All the houses have hand-carved wooden doors, some with good locks. The rampart has four gates, each suitable for its purpose and directly facing one point of the compass. All have good strong locks. In addition to these main entrances there are two other smaller ones at places where they were deemed necessary on account of the growth of the pueblo, which from end to end may be said to be about 200 *varas*. These houses are built next to each other and have ample room, with kitchen for each family. They are sufficiently protected against rain, wind, and other inclemencies of the weather. On the west corner along the wall, separated from the habitations of the Indians by a street, stand the missionary's house, the church, and the sacristy. The first contains not only rooms for housing the missionaries, but also a kitchen, and the offices of the community. It is all of stone and lime and flat-roofed; the quarters for the missionary form a second story, and every part is in good taste. The church, with the sacristy, is contiguous to the other house so that through the latter one may enter a comparatively good pulpit in the presbytery. The church and the sacristy, because of their architecture, are the most beautiful structures to be seen anywhere this side of Saltillo. They may be valued without hesitation at 30,000 *pesos*, and their furnishings at eight or ten thousand. The numerous ornaments, some of them of silver, include a frontal, a throne, and a baldaquin. It is evident that the lack of other ornaments is due to the notable decline suffered by the mission as a result of influences which will be explained and discussed in the general report. The same happened to the other missions already referred to, and, in fact, to all of them, as will be seen when their funds are discussed. The mission consists of

#### Christians

Married couples, 24, from 18 to 60
    years of age ........................................48
Widowers and widows, from 40 to 80
    years of age ........................................11
Bachelors, between 15 and 20 years of age ......... 9
Children, from 1 to 10 years of age ..............38

#### Gentiles

Barrados, from 6 to 50 years of age ..............32
(Five of these have been baptized *in articulo mortis*.)
Total number of persons ..........................138

With the exception of the Gentile Barrados who came last year (1784) from the coast, the personnel is made up of the Pampopas and Postitos; and their language is the usual one in this mission, although most of them speak Spanish less incorrectly than in the other missions. Finally, this mission has always been the most populous in spite of having been the most affected by the plague of buboes; and furthermore it has been the richest, because the Indians are less indolent in the cultivation of the fields and the care of the herds.

### Mission San Juan de Capistrano

This mission is situated about one and a quarter or one and a half leagues from San José, two leagues from Concepción, and three or little more from San Antonio and the Royal Presidio de Béxar. It stands on the banks of the San Antonio River, in a small valley [*vega*], covered everywhere by woods. It is square in shape, with a wall like the others and with three entrances, one somewhat larger than the others. Adjoining this wall are the houses or Indians' lodgings, for the most part of the usual materials. Near one corner of the wall is a large house, with sufficient space for the missionary and with rooms for the usual offices. Joined to this house is the granary, also of ample space, and of a similar construction. Near the house, but not joining it, is the church and sacristy now in use. The structure is valued at fifteen hundred *pesos* and its furnishings and ornaments at that same amount or more. Another was being built, but it was left about half-finished; up to that time about 3,000 *pesos* had been spent, not counting the work of the Indians. The reason for stopping work was the same as in the case of San Antonio, that is, the lack of Indians. In addition, and more important perhaps, is the penury into which this mission has fallen, the reason for which will be explained in the general discussion of the condition of all the missions. The mission consists of

Married couples, 21, from 18 to 60 years of age ....42
Widowers and widows, from
    20 to 70 years of age ........................... 5
Bachelors and children, from 1 to 20
    years of age ........................................11
Total number of persons ......................... 58

These people, for the most part, are descended from the nations of the Pamaques, Orejones, and Marahuiayos; and they usually speak their own languages. They are children of recently converted and baptized adult Indians and are known as Marahuitos, the name given to all members of this mission.

## Mission San Francisco de la Espada

The site of this mission is on the west bank of the river, one half league from that of San Juan de Capistrano, one and a half leagues from San José, two and a half from Concepción. It lies between three and a fourth and four leagues down the river from San Antonio and the Royal Presidio, on a plain that is on the watershed, and is thickly covered with woods. The mission is square in shape and is surrounded by a stone and mud wall. Contiguous to these walls are the houses, mostly of stone and mud, where the Indians live. The missionary's house, the church, and the sacristy, which adjoin each other, take up half of the west side. They are of stone and lime and have sufficient room for all purposes. The church and sacristy, on account of their superior construction and their ornaments and furnishings, are valued at three or four thousand *pesos*. On the south side stands the granary, which is of stone and mud, but which has enough room to meet its requirements. This mission, like the others, was very populous, but, ... its population has fallen very much, as will be shown by the list of the persons now living in it:

Married couples, 14, from 40 to 80 years of age......28

Widowers and widows, from 40 to 80 years of age ................................13

Bachelors and children, from 1 to 15 years of age ................................16

Total number of persons ................................57

These are descendents of the Pacao nation (which was fairly numerous when the mission was founded for its benefit, their language being the one most commonly used) and the Barrados Marahuitos. Many of the latter were brought from the south coast, to which some returned and died, while others of this nation died in the mission during the small [pox?] epidemic in the recent year of 1780. No small number have died and are dying of buboes.

## Mission El Espíritu Santo de la Bahía

This mission is forty leagues downstream from the others, and is very near the southern seacoast. It is situated on an elevated spot accessible to the edge of the river, which runs between it and the Royal Presidio, usually called *La Bahía*. The mission, rectangular in shape, is completely surrounded by the corresponding wall. Next to this are the houses of the Indians, some of which, as in the other missions, have flat and others hay or grass roofs. The office and quarters of the missionary are in a house adjoining the church and sacristy. All are of stone and lime, have wooden roofs, and offer more than ample room. These, with their furnishings and ornaments, may be valued at twelve thousand *pesos*. The mission consists of

Married couples, 31, from 20 to 60 years of age ................................62

Widowers and widows, from 30 to 80 years of age ................................15

Bachelors and children, from 1 to 20 years of age ................................39

Total number of persons ................................116

Nearly as many natives have fled to the coast and woods, both from among those who were brought from there, and from those who, born in the mission, were induced by the bad example of the coastal Indians, to follow them. Neither the clamor nor the supplications of the missionaries have been successful in obtaining repressive measures from the Governor of the Province to put a stop to the almost daily escapes (even when these occur in his presence). Consequently, unless it be by the Grace of Heaven, that is, unless a remedy is found in the form of a particular or special intercession of Providence, this mission and all the others will be depopulated, abandoned, and destroyed within a few years. As a result of the pressing need felt for the labor necessary to support the missions, they are experiencing great scarcity, while the renegades, like fierce brutes, scare and seduce the other civilized Indians, who may be inclined to listen to the Evangelical Word. To this situation it must be added that since for this reason the wealth of these missions is diminishing, it is easy to understand the lack of ability to effect new conversions or to support those who are converted or may be converted. NOTE: Here it is necessary to state that the only wealth that this mission has enjoyed since its erection has been that derived from the herds of cattle (for on account of the bad weather and drought and the impossibility of irrigating, there has been no assistance furnished by agriculture as in the other missions). With only this wealth the mission was able to sustain and even grow and perpetuate itself without difficulty; even having had to buy grain for its consumption, it still had enough income for its members to dress more decently than is common among Indians, though they were more numerous than they are today; nor were the means lacking to spend considerable sums annually on public worship, as is evidenced by the value of the church, its furnishings, and its ornaments, none of which are very old; for on account of the strong south winds from the salt marshes, an almost constant replacement is necessary for the images and other ornaments. . . .

## New Settlement at Nacogdoches

By order of His Excellency the Viceroy there have been at this settlement two missionaries since the year 1775, principally for the purpose of bringing about the reduction of the Orqoquisac, Vidai, Texas, and the other tribes of that region. Its distance from here [San Antonio de Valero] is about two hundred leagues; the intervening land is entirely unpopulated but very suitable for being settled because of its natural beauty and rich resources, and its many promising sites or places that, if they were colonized, would be very profitable to the Crown and to the Kingdom. This would also be the most expeditious means of achieving the civilization of many tribes and peoples, who, influenced by the proximity of the settlements, or attracted by reasonable and polite dealings with the Spaniards, might without much difficulty, abandon their wild habits, become inclined to a more sociable life, and accept the catechism and Christian instruction. In addition to this primary purpose the two missionaries are there to administer spiritually to the settlers without charging them fees or parish dues of any kind, or making any sort of collection, even for things that may appear most just, such as the expense for the maintenance of a sacristan, etc. . . .

General Discussion or Summary of What Has Been Said
Concerning Each of the Missions

These missions, as stated in the title of this report, are in the Province of Texas, which belongs in its secular aspects to the Command [*Comandancia*] of the Internal Provinces of New Spain, and in its ecclesiastical affairs to the Bishopric of Nuevo León. The missions consist of towns protected by walls, with houses for inhabitants, each house roofed with timber and mud, and provided with a good floor. Some, according to the facilities of each mission, have façades of carved wood, and iron locks in the houses as well as in the ramparts. In this protective wall there are three or four doors for varying purposes and on different sides. In the center and at the most advantageous place in these missions are the houses for the missionaries, with sufficient room for living quarters and the other needs. Adjoining this house, or not far away from it, is the church and sacristy as described in the individual reports.

These missions were . . . founded, organized, and developed by the Apostolic Missionaries of the Order of Saint Francis, who have kept and tended them, as sons of the College of the Holy Cross of Querétaro and of Our Lady of Guadalupe of Zacatecas, in the seven pueblos as already described. These are San Antonio de Valero, La Purísima Concepción de Acuña, San José de Aguayo, San Juan de Capistrano, Nuestro Padre San Francisco de la Espada (which are in an area of three or four leagues along the banks of the San Antonio River), El Espíritu Santo de La Bahía, and Nuestra Señora del Rosario, which, as already stated, is abandoned and in ruins today as a result of the flight of its Indians to the coast from where they were brought. These missions in the beginning were founded for and organized with Indians of the most diversified nations, . . . nearly all . . . reduced to one language, which is common or uniform in meaning and differs only in the greater or less stress or speed with which some Indians, called Bozales, because they use and understand very little Spanish, are being instructed. In spite of what has been said, Spanish is generally and commonly spoken among both Spaniards and Indians, although, in the case of the latter, with noticeable imperfection or (in the common expressions) with stones in their mouths.

As already stated, these missions were organized and founded by the Apostolic Franciscan Missionaries, some by the sons of the Apostolic College of la Santísima Cruz de Querétaro, and others by those of Nuestra Señora de Guadalupe de Zacatecas. Today the latter have charge of the administration of all the missions. In them there are employed nine missionaries as follows: six resident, one in each mission, one supernumerary who substitutes for the sick or unavoidably absent, and two in the new settlement of Nacogdoches, as mentioned in the discussion of that establishment. . . . The precision and punctuality with which these missionaries discharge the duties of their ministry may be inferred by remembering that they are continually under the supervision of a Father President, who with the authority of a legitimate prelate granted and delegated to him by the Reverend Guardian of his College, resides in the locality of the missions. . . . And from time to time when it is deemed necessary and opportune, the College designates by a unanimous vote of its Senior Council a serious-minded missionary as an Inspector. . . . He makes a very careful examination of every phase of life pertinent to the missions and missionaries; but especially he inquires if they comply well with the duties of the ministry to which they have been assigned and if they manage the property of the Indians with the greatest personal disinterestedness, legality, and exactness. Likewise he examines whether the missionaries properly look after the needs of their indigent constituents. They remove at once those who have fallen into serious fault, acting in this matter with more asperity than leniency. Page by page he inspects the records of income and expenses, in which very punctilious note is made of each item. As soon as these missionaries reach their respective assignments, they make the most diligent attempt to learn, through use and daily intercourse, the language of their charges. This is the only means they have for communication, although usually the missionaries insist that the Indians understand and use Spanish, as is ordered by the laws of the kingdom. This order is compiled with by speaking often with the adults and by teaching the children usually or always to read, and, if it is deemed practical (which is not always the case) to write and figure. The piety of our Lord the King (May God keep Him) has appropriated for the missionaries the prebend or annual *sínodo* of 450 *pesos*. This amount is paid from His royal treasury and is drawn by the Apostolic Treasurer, acting as representative of the missionaries, with certificates from the royal judges of the region and by order of the Commandant of these Interior Provinces. Neither now nor ever have the missionaries demanded or received any compensation or fees, large or small, from either the Indians or the Spaniards. On the contrary they added the prebend to the products from the missions, limiting themselves to a most meager allowance, and leaving the balance for the Church expenses and the Divine Cult. In these churches and towns there are no confraternities or brotherhoods, for there is barely time for more than the teaching of the Faith and the administration of baptism.

In temporal matters these missions are governed and administered in the style and fashion of a family, by a common father who, being the spiritual head, also looks after their interests and wants with as much careful exactness and punctuality as the best father could do (because their Excellencies the Viceroys, who thought it best, provided that it should be done in that way). Nevertheless, an effort is made to instruct the Indians in civil and political life; and in accord with that purpose and the laws of the kingdom, the custom of electing annually two justices, who are called *governor* and *alcalde*, has been introduced. This is done in the presence of the missionary, and thus there have been Indian governors in the towns. If the pueblos are lacking in men, married couples vote. The voting is done by secret ballot; and those who are elected by a plurality vote have their names submitted to the governor of the Province, who confirms them by a written order [*auto inscriptis*]. During that year these men govern the town according to the established customs of most of the towns in the

Province, under the direction and with the advice of the missionary.

The wealth of these missions is derived from the cultivation of corn, beans, chile, or pimentos, and fruits like watermelons, cantaloups, pumpkins, and garden produce, as well as from the breeding of sheep, goats, and cattle. Concerning the latter there is something that needs to be said here.

Note: Sheep increase very slowly in this country for many reasons, but especially because the land, being thickly wooded, abounds in wild animals that destroy them. Also many are lost in the brush; and when we add to these reasons first, the indolence of the Indian shepherds and the misfortune of not having reliable herders, and second, the fact that these herds cause some Indians to run away lest greater carefulness be demanded of them, it is plainly impossible, generally speaking, to increase the flocks or even do more than keep them as large as they are. The herds of cattle increase rapidly, and they constitute the principal wealth. All the missions had considerable property of this kind. With these herds they maintained themselves without enduring many hardships or privations; and could they but be restored, the missions would regain their former prosperity. But the Commandant General added to the royal treasury (as mentioned in the note in the description of the Mission of El Espíritu Santo de la Bahía) all the unbranded cattle, which included nearly all of them. The cruel hostility of the Comanches, who at every opportunity killed many persons in the vicinity of the presidio and the missions, and also the numerous and inpenetrable forests, where even the gentlest sheep might become so entangled that only with the greatest difficulty could it be extricated, have contributed to the destruction of these herds. Moreover, the herders often ran into ambushes of the Comanches, from which they rarely escaped. Finally, these enemies left the missions without a brood of horses, tame or untamed, with the result that nearly all the herds were unbranded. But the Commandant, disregarding these reasons and many others equally serious, adjudged and declared in his proclamation (although I doubt its wisdom) all the unbranded cattle roaming in the royal domain the property of the royal treasury. But the king's minister did not consider that, in the event of judging them ownerless, he was supposed to safeguard them, to give public notice of the act, to hear the allegations of interested parties, to establish the case by law [calificar derechos], etc.; much less did he consider the grave and very prejudicial results that may be feared from such action. As a result these unfortunate missions have been reduced to such penury and want that even in order for them to eat what is unquestionably theirs, that is, the cattle born of their own branded herds and in their pastures or ranches (I call the pastures or ranches theirs whether they were assigned by the regional judge or were possessed in good faith), it is necessary for them to pay like any stranger the stipulated fee of four reales per head. And whereas in the past the income from the herds and missionaries' allowance alone was enough to clothe the Indians and pay the expenses of the Divine Cult, now without them [the herds], there is not enough

for either. As a result of the policy adopted, these wretches are made to suffer and endure great sorrow, while they observe that the Apaches are allowed, through cunning dissimulation and the Spaniards' tolerance, to cause excessive damages to their cattle, and that the soldiers and citizens are permitted to slaughter them. Both the Apaches and soldiers drive off substantial herds, mostly cows, to distant regions. Therefore it seems that these poor neophytes, in imitation of the Prophet Jeremiah, might . . . say: "Remember O Lord, what is come upon us. Consider and behold our reproach. Our inheritance is turned to aliens; our houses to strangers."

They are ignorant of our law and faith, who have driven it [our wealth] away in large and countless herds taken from our lands and ranches even by newcomers, such as the Apaches, who have destroyed greater numbers still, but who, in the guise of friendship, also carry on the most cruel, continuous, and wasting war against us, depriving us of human sustenance by the frightful destruction of our herds. Seeing these enemies masquerading under pretense, we are at a loss to understand what your royal will may be in retaining these presidial troops for our protection and support at such excessive cost. Not only is the enemy not punished, repressed, and taught a lesson, as in the past, but we behold, O Sorrow! these very troops so poorly governed that they turn in large part against us; and, leaving immune the former enemies, they even add to the damages caused by them [the Apaches], killing and destroying our cattle in one endless slaughter. While pretending to protect us, these troops serve only to inflict terrible punishment and reprisals upon us on the least provocation occasioned by our branding our own unbranded cattle or our eating them. As a result it is very possible that there might be imprinted upon our humble minds an impression very distinct from our former conception that in Your Majesty we have not so much a king and master who dominates us, as a very loving father who favors, protects, and defends us. We see many manifestations of your royal and benign protection in the law, particularly when it is stipulated that the royal interests are to be subordinated to ours. But we bemoan ourselves as orphans bereft of such a good father, if the common reasoning founded on such simple tests of your royal will and desires do not satisfy us, that these ministers work against your good intentions, when they tell us that what was plainly ours is not ours. They assign our property to your royal treasury which, no doubt, will profit as much as heretofore; but although the Bureau of Herds [Ramo de Mesteño] of this province should have produced over 25,000 pesos, we hear that there are hardly six or seven thousand in the treasury controlled by the judge of this territory. It is not known that a single real has been taken out to be sent to your treasury. Moreover, we do actually consider ourselves orphans because, while we know that our good father lives, protects, and assists us in every way that is within his command, still, on account of the distance and other hindrances, we see that neither our pleadings nor those of the ones who, like pious mothers under the protection of Your Majesty, assist, care for, and look after our needs, reach your pious ears, and this causes our hope for a remedy to waver. Finally, for these reasons we and our children see ourselves turned out to perish from hunger and even to desert the law and the faith in order to seek in the woods the sustenance of which we are deprived. . . .

With respect to the good order and style in which these missions were founded and have been maintained, in agreement with both human and divine laws, pagan customs are found to be almost completely exterminated. The evil habits that remain are only those that seem to have been inherent. Among these is the slightness of their inclination to do the work necessary for raising corn. In some missions and in some years (like the present one) there is a shortage sometimes, because of the combination of this disinclination and the Indians' susceptibility to the contagion of buboes or *Nanaguates*, a kind of leprous venereal disease (which has become common in the country). Some are excused from work on account of this ailment, and others pretend to have it in order not to have to work. Since there are so many to feed and be clothed, and so few to work, two grave problems arise in acquiring the necessary means: first, the absolute necessities are lacking; second, those who work are so burdened that many try to escape and some succeed in running away permanently to join the *gentiles*, whose life and customs they soon copy. These troubles are inevitable for anyone who administers the practical affairs of the town, for he can neither force a sick man to work nor be sure that those who use that pretext are really ill. He cannot exempt the healthy men from work nor fail to care for the sick. It seems that the only remedy for this situation is that one of the towns near the presidio should be designated as a common sick-ward, and to it each of the other missions should contribute, in proportion to its means, the necessary provisions for the sick. . . .

Concerning the products of the country, something was said in the discussion of the wealth of the missions. Here it need only be noted that wheat is not sown, although it does well, because the Indians hold it in very low regard in comparison with corn, which is the daily bread of this land, as well as because its cultivation would interfere with that of the latter, which is here considered absolutely necessary for human life. Although there are some wild berries that the Indians eat readily, they are not as abundant or as appetizing as the bananas, guanavas, *cherimolas, otes, chicos, mameys*, cocoanuts, Brazilian nuts, and other fruits that grow on some coasts or along the sea shore. Nevertheless, there is cultivation of vegetables, fruits, etc., which would give a good, large yield if the weather were not so changeable and if there were fewer of the locusts, grasshoppers, ants, beetles, plant lice, etc., that abound here. All the planting done in these missions, as well as the cultivation and distribution of the crops, is by communal labor. Those, however, who are considered most apt are assigned plots of land to cultivate with delicacies, such as vegetables, watermelons, cantaloups, and cucumbers. But here, just as in the case of the corn and beans that are gathered, no scruples are spared to divide them equally among all, even though, to do this, it is necessary to act with thorough forethought and prudence. Although the Indians in every other way are very limited in comprehension and lacking in reasoning ability, in the matter of concealing idleness or laziness by unostentatious excuses and the appearance of pious sanctity, which they do with consummate hypocrisy, they are very skillful. Thus they avail themselves of the assignment to the gardens or private work, only to slip away from the task and very shamelessly profit from the toil of the others, regardless of whether the latter be their fathers, sons, or brothers.

The tools for this work are provided as follows: Those of iron are acquired through the missionaries from the Apostolic Treasury [*sínodo apostólico*], and those of wood or other material either are made by the Indians who know how to fashion them or by some Spaniard who gets paid for his work. The farms are enclosed within strong, wooden fences that are repaired annually. In all of this work the missionaries, like fathers of a family, or tutors, or instructors of the Indians, determine everything that has to be done, even down to the very smallest details, such as adding to the fence rails that are needed, cleaning the fields by removing the stalks of the previous year, or the roots that sprout, digging, cleaning, or deepening the ditches and irrigation canals, etc.

The accounts of incomes and expenses are carried in a special book in each mission and are reported very punctually and clearly to the Father President, as well as to the Inspector when one comes around. The latter carries a very exact report to the College, where it is examined by the whole venerable council in order to avoid the censure that might otherwise fall upon the missionaries later on.

The present state of these missions, and also that for the last twelve or fifteen years, may well be compared in personnel and property with that of the Kingdom of the Indies [New Spain] during the fifties and sixties—particularly as regards the Interior Provinces. At that time there flourished several rich mines; the farms were all rich estates; and, with the exception of one or two years when they suffered setbacks, they were very fertile and abundant, whereas in these years all is poverty and want. Most of the mines have been depopulated on account of their extreme destitution, and those that persist do so in the face of indescribable hardships and work. Many of the most prosperous ranches have become wildernesses, deserted by man and beast. In short, decay and dissolution continue. . . . For the Indians scarcely have enough to eat and wear, while previously they had enough to adorn their temples and lived in relative comfort.

Likewise these missions suffer a great decrease in personnel, for there are less than half as many individuals as there were in the past. The principal reasons may be reduced to the following: many have died on account of the plague of buboes or *Nanaguates*, as has already been mentioned, and many others from smallpox. Moreover (nor is this less important than the other), in reclaiming the fugitives and preventing the escape of others, though using the most prudent and suitable methods possible, there has been the very greatest negligence on the part of the heads of the province. Therefore (as was said in speaking of the Indians of El Espíritu Santo) many fled from the other missions, impelled by their inclination to the wild, lazy life of the woods. Now many others have joined them. But here lies a great change. In the past the apostolic missionaries went out to the heathen, converted them by means of their enthusiasm and preaching, and brought them to the missions; then they taught them the catechism and instructed them in the mysteries of the Faith. Later, if they wished to be baptised, and stay in the mission, they were added to that group. This is no longer done, because that avenue has been closed by lack of cooperation from the heads of the province in not furnishing the necessary escorts. Moreover, not only through the lack of cooperation but much more because of their actions the missions have suffered, as, for example, in the sequestration of the cattle already mentioned, a loss that has reduced them to great poverty and need. . . . How, then, could we maintain a greater number of newly converted Indians who learn the faith through the mouth rather than through their ears, and are moved more by gifts than by the strongest and clearest reasoning? This the heads of the province should have kept in mind and given much thought to before adopting the resolution of applying to the royal treasury that which, in all justice, belonged to the missions. By going beyond the limits of the laws concerning pastures and cattle, they unquestionably acted against the royal will and intention, which looks primarily to, and orders by just regulations, the conservation and conversion of the Indians into the ranks of the Holy Church. . . .

Written in this mission of San Antonio de Valero, May 5, 1789. Fray José Franco López.

## 16. PHILIP NOLAN'S FILIBUSTERING EXPEDITION
### 1800-1801

From Ellis P. Bean, "Memoir of Ellis P. Bean" (written about 1816), in Henderson Yoakum, *History of Texas* (2 vols.; New York, 1855), I, 405-415.

At the beginning of the nineteenth century, Anglo-American intruders entered Texas in defiance of Spanish authority and appropriated much of the Indian trade. One of the earliest and best known of the filibusters was Philip Nolan, bookkeeper for General James Wilkinson from 1789 to 1791, who first came to Texas supposedly in 1791. Nolan drove horses out of Texas on several occasions, but his activities eventually aroused the suspicion of the Spanish authorities, who on August 8, 1800, issued orders for his arrest should he re-enter the province. Nolan returned, nevertheless, in December with a party of armed men. In March of the next year, he was killed near the site of present Waco in a battle with a superior Spanish force which had been sent out to intercept him. His followers, who had not deserted, were captured, imprisoned in Mexico, and finally required to cast dice to determine which one of the survivors should be executed.

The best known member of the party was Ellis P. Bean, who later served as an officer in the Mexican army and afterwards returned to Texas to live near Nacogdoches on a land grant he had acquired from the Mexican government. The following account of the activities and fate of the expedition was written by Bean.

. . . There being now but eighteen of us, seven of whom were Spaniards, we continued our journey, and, after five days, came to Red river at the old Caddo town, where we built a raft and crossed, swimming our horses. In about four miles we came to some large prairies, where we found a large quantity of buffalo-meat and some Indians. These were called Twowokanaes. They were very friendly to us, and sold us some fresh horses, of which they had very fine ones.

In about six days' journey we came to Trinity river, and, crossing it, we found the big, open prairies of that country. We passed through the plains till we reached a spring, which we called the *Painted spring*, because a rock at the head of it was painted by the Camanche and Pawnee nations in a peace that was made there by these two nations. In the vast prairie there was no wood, or any other fuel than buffalo-dung, which lay dry in great quantities. But we found that the buffalo had removed, and were getting so scarce, that, in three days after passing the spring, we were forced, in order to sustain life, to eat the flesh of wild horses, which we found in great quantities. For about nine days we were compelled to eat horseflesh, when we arrived at a river called the Brasos. Here we found elk and deer plenty, some buffalo, and wild horses by thousands.

We built a pen, and caught about three hundred of those wild horses. After some days, the Camanche nation came to see us. They were a party of about two hundred men, women, and children. We went with them to the south fork of Red river, to see their chief, by the name of Nicoroco, where we stayed with them a month. A number of them had arrows pointed, some with stone, and others with copper. This last they procure in its virgin state in some mountains that run from the river Missouri across the continent to the gulf of Mexico.

During our stay with this chief, four or five nations that were at peace with him came to see us, and we were great friends. We then thought of returning to our old camp, where we had caught our horses, and taking some more; for a great many of those we had taken had died, for want of being well taken care of. In about five days we arrived at our old camp. Those Indians stayed with us but a few days, and then went on in search of buffalo.

These red men have no towns, but roam over these immense plains, carrying with them their tents and clothing made of buffalo-skins. They raise no corn, but depend alone on the chase. Once a year they meet with their head chief on the Salt fork of the Colorado river, where he causes all the fire to be extinguished, and then makes new fire for the new year; and the bands also severally change their hunting-grounds. This meeting takes place in the new moon in June. At the place where they meet are lakes of salt water, so covered with salt, that they can break up any quantity they want.

When they left, a party of them stole from us eleven head of horses. They were our gentle horses, and all we had for running wild horses; so that we were left unable to do anything. We concluded to pursue the robbers; but this was to be done on foot. Philip Nolan, Robert Ashley, Joseph Reed, David Fero, a negro man called Caesar, and myself, were the volunteers of our small party. We pursued them nine days, and came upon them, encamped on a small creek. They did not see us till we were in fifty yards of them, when we went up in a friendly manner. There were but four men, and some women and children: the rest had gone out to kill buffalo. They were twelve men in number. I saw four of our horses close by, feeding. I pointed to them, and told them we had come for them, and that they must bring the others they had stolen, to us. An old man said the one who had stolen them had taken the others out hunting; that he would be in that evening; and that the rogue who stole them had but one eye, by which we could know him when he came. They gave us meat, of which they had a large quantity drying; and then we were glad to lie down and rest.

In the evening, as the old man said, One-Eye came up with our horses. We took him and tied him, the others saying nothing, and kept him tied till morning. His wife then gave us all our horses; and we took from the thief all the meat we could conveniently carry. We then told them all that there were but few of us, but we could whip twice their number, and they were of the same opinion. We then returned safely to our camp, and found all in readiness to run horses, and the pen in good repair. But we concluded to let our horses rest a few days before we began to run them, as we had travelled to our camp in four days.

In four days more it was our misfortune to be attacked by a hundred and fifty Spaniards sent by the commandant at Chihuahua. He was general-commandant of the five northeastern internal provinces, and called Don Nimesio de Salcedo. The troops that came were piloted by Indians from Nacogdoches that came with them. They surrounded our camp about one o'clock in the morning, on the 22d of March, 1801. They took the five Spaniards and one American that were guarding our horses, leaving but twelve of us, including Caesar. We were all alarmed by the tramping of their horses; and, as day broke, without speaking a word, they commenced their fire. After about ten minutes, our gallant leader Nolan was slain by a musket-ball which hit him in the head. In a few minutes after they began to fire grape-shot at us: they had brought a small swivel on a mule. We had a pen that we had built of logs, to prevent the Indians from stealing from us. From this pen we returned their fire until about nine o'clock. We then had two men wounded and one killed. I told my companions we ought to charge on the cannon and take it. Two or three of them agreed to it, but the rest appeared unwilling. I told them it was at most but death; and if we stood still, all would doubtless be killed; that we must take the cannon, or retreat. It was agreed that we should retreat. Our number was eleven, of which two were wounded. The powder that we could not put in our horns was given to Caesar to carry, while the rest were to make use of their arms. So we set out through a prairie, and shortly crossed a small creek. While we were defending our-selves, Caesar stopped at the creek and surrendered himself with the ammunition to the enemy. Of the two wounded men, one stopped and gave himself up, the other came on with us. There were then nine of us that stood the fire of the enemy, on both sides of us, for a march of half a mile. We were so fortunate, that not a man of us got hurt, though the balls played around us like hail.

In our march we came to a deep ravine. Here we took refuge, and stopped some time. They then began to come too close to us, when we commenced firing afresh. They then retreated; and about three o'clock in the afternoon they hoisted a white flag, and (through an American that was with them) told us that the commander wanted us to return to our own country, and not remain there with the Indians. We quickly agreed to go as companions with them, but not to give up our guns. It was granted, and we went back and buried our gallant leader Nolan.

The next day we started in company with the Spanish soldiers for Nacogdoches. In our journey we had to cross the Trinity which we found running over its banks. My companions and I, in a short time, made a small canoe out of a dry cottonwood, which answered very well to carry the soldiers all over. Their arms and their commander were still on the west side. I told my companions that we had it in our power to throw all their guns in the river, take what ammunition we wanted, and return. Some of them were willing; others said it would be very wrong now we were to be sent home. These last were unfortunate men who put confidence in Spanish promises. These are a people in whom you should put no trust or confidence whatever.

In some days after we arrived at Nacogdoches, the commandant told us he was waiting for orders from Chihuahua to set us at liberty and send us home. We waited in this hope for about a month, when, instead of our liberty, we were seized and put in irons, and sent off under a strong guard to San Antonio. Here we lay in prison three months. Then we were started to Mexico, but were stopped at San Luis Potosi, where we were confined in prison one year and four months. By this time we were getting bare of clothes. I told them I was a shoemaker, and would be very thankful if they would permit me, in the daytime, to sit at the door of my prison, and work at my trade. This was granted to me, and also to young Charles King. We made some money; but, in a short time afterward, orders came that we should be sent to Chihuahua. This order was quickly obeyed; and we started on horseback, with heavy irons. Yet it was cheering to think that we were going to change our prisons, hoping that in some change we might be able, some day or other, to escape. . . .

I must inform my reader that we had passed five years, in all, in Mexico; that our cases in this time had gone to Spain; and had also been sent to the United States, and laid before Mr. Jefferson, at that time president — who said he knew nothing of us, and that we should be tried according to the Spanish law. . . . The next day the parsons came again, and brought with them a colonel, who read to us the king's order — which was, that every fifth man was to be hung, for firing on the king's troops. But, as some were dead, there were but nine of us, and, out of the nine, but one had to die. This was to be decided by throwing dice on the head of a drum. Whoever threw lowest, was to be executed.

It was then agreed that the oldest must throw first. I was the youngest, and had to throw last. The first was blindfolded, and two dice put in a glass tumbler. He was led to the drum which was put in the room, and there cast the dice on the head of the drum. And so we went up, one by one, to cast the awful throw of life or death. All of my companions, except one, threw high: he threw four. As I was the last, all his hopes were that I should throw lower than he. As for my part, I was indifferent about it, for I had resigned myself to fortune. I took the glass in my hand, and gained the prize of life, for I threw five. My poor companion, who threw four, was led away from us, surrounded by the clergy, to be executed the next day. This was done in the presence of many sorrowful hearts that beheld it.

The rest of us were returned back to prison, without any other notice; and we so remained three or four days, when orders came that some of us were to be sent away, and I was one of them. The next day the governor came and told us that I and four of my companions were to be sent to the South sea, to a place called Acapulco, and that we had first to go to Mexico. . . .

## 17. THE NEUTRAL GROUND AGREEMENT

### October 29 and November 4, 1806

From the correspondence of General James Wilkinson to Governor Anthony [Antonio] Cordero [y Bustamente], October 29, 1806, and General Symon de Herrera to General James Wilkinson, November 4, 1806 (MSS, United States War Department Records, W-211, WD-3, National Archives, Washington).

No agreement on a boundary between Texas and Louisiana had been reached when Napoleon in 1803 sold Louisiana "with the same extent that it now has in the hands of Spain, and that it had when France possessed it" to the United States. President Thomas Jefferson asserted that Texas was a part of the purchase, but Spain protested the transaction and sent troops to the border for the purpose of maintaining her jurisdiction at least to the Arroyo Hondo, a small stream between the Sabine River and Natchitoches marking the eastern limit of Spanish occupation. To avoid an armed clash, General James Wilkinson, in command of United States forces in the West, agreed to occupy the territory no farther west than the Arroyo Hondo, and General Simón de Herrera, in command of the Spanish forces, agreed to remain west of the Sabine River, until their respective governments negotiated a permanent boundary settlement or issued further instructions. The land between the Arroyo Hondo and the Sabine River, sheltering lawless elements from both Spanish and American possessions, came to be known as the Neutral Ground. General Wilkinson's proposal to establish the Neutral Ground and General Herrera's acceptance (written in English) follow.

### 1. JAMES WILKINSON TO GOVERNOR ANTHONY [ANTONIO] CORDERO [Y BUSTAMENTE]

#### Octr. 29th, 1806

Sir, . . . In my letter to your Excellency the 24th ultimo, . . . I emphatically remarked to your Excellency, "that the ultimate decision of the competent authority had been taken, that my orders were absolute, and my determination first to assert and, under God, to sustain the jurisdiction of the United States to the Sabine River, against any force which may be opposed to me." . . .

Your Excellency appears to lay much stress on the letter of the Captain General Salcedo [Don Nemecio Salcedo, commandant-general of the Interior Provinces] to Governor [William] Claiborne [Governor of Louisiana Territory], but as that letter treats generally on subjects of civil import, and as my functions are purely Military, it does not fall within my province to take particular cognizance of it. I will however beg leave to observe that His Excellency's exposition of the grounds on which he asserts the Arroyo Honda [sic] to be the line of provincial demarcation, carries with it an air of much plausibility, but being diametrically opposed to the sense of Expression of my Government, I cannot respect it; . . .

Your Excellency is sensible to the extreme delicacy with which a Military man may exercise his discretion, when shackled by specific orders, yet such instances have occurred even on the field of Battle, and must frequently become necessary, where operations are at issue a thousand miles from the source of authority. Believing that the controversy in which we are engaged presents a case precisely in point, I am willing to risque the approbations of my Government to perpetuate the tranquility of the inhospitable wilds, where waving the point of Honor, the subject of our test is scarcely worth the blood of one brave man.

Permit me then in the true spirit of conciliation to propose to your Excellency, without yielding a Pretension, ceding a right, or interfering with the discussions which, belong to our superiors, to restore the "Status quo" at the delivery of the Province of Lousiana [sic] to the United States, by the withdrawal of our troops from the points they at present occupy to the post of Nacogdoches and Natchitoches respectively; your Excellency's assent to this proposition shall be conclusive on my conduct, and I will commence my retrograde, on the day you break up your Camp on the right bank of the Sabine; under the joint stipulation that the troops of my Command shall not cross the Arroyo Honda, so long as those under your orders are restrained from crossing the Sabine, or until we may receive further instruction from our respective Governments. . . .

I pray God to keep your Excellency in his Holy protection an Hundred Years. I am yr

James Wilkinson

His Excel.
  Governor Cordero
    Commander-in-chief

## 2. SYMON DE HERRERA TO JAMES WILKINSON

### Nov. 4th, 1806

Sir. Lieutenant Hughen, Aid de Camp to Y. E. delivered to me yesterday your favorable letter of same day, and another sealed for Colonel Anthony Cordero, Y. E.'s goodness having also sent me the Copy of the contents relative to Y. E., having determined to retire with the troops of Y. E.'s orders to the quarters of Natchitoches; Demanding that whilst Spain and the U. S. settle the differences suscitated on the property of the land 'till this River of Sabinas, H. M.'s troop do not cross it, and that those of the U.S. will not come further than Arroyo hondo.

Your E. manifesting by these operations, the peaceful ideas that posesses you, I wishes to conserve the reciprocal good Harmony that is to exist between the two Nations, these proceedings oblige me to retire also to Nacogdoches those troops that I have the honor to Command, leaving them the Order not to cross the River.

That in this point nor in any other that may occur henceforth, there may be no motives of disgust [regret], passes to that camp the Adjutant Inspector Francis Viana, second commander of these troops, in order to agree with Y. E. and on his return I will remit to the Colonel Anthony Cordero Y. E.'s letter.

I am happy of this occasion to offer my respects to Y. E. praying to the Almighty to conserve Y. E.'s life. Sabinas 4th Nov. 1806

(Signed), Symon de Herrera

The day after tomorrow 6th Inst. I will leave this camp, with the first divition [sic] of troops under my Command, of which I give Y. E. notice————

(Signed),        Herrera

To His Excellency James Wilkinson

## 18. THE GOVERNMENT OF TEXAS

### November 7, 1811

From Miguel Ramos Arizpe, *Report that Dr. Miguel Ramos de Arizpe Priest of Borbon, and Deputy in the Present General and Special Cortes of Spain for the Province of Coahuila One of the Four Eastern Interior Provinces of the Kingdom of Mexico Presents to the August Congress on the Natural, Political, and Civil Condition of the Provinces of Coahuila, Nuevo León, Nuevo Santander, and Texas of the Four Eastern Interior Provinces of the Kingdom of Mexico* (introduction, annotations, and translation by Nettie Lee Benson; Austin, 1950), 8-12. By permission of the publisher, The University of Texas Press.

In 1808 Napoleon Bonaparte invaded Spain and placed his brother Joseph on the throne. With the kingship thus usurped, Spaniards loyal to the rightful, but "captive," King Ferdinand VII organized councils or *juntas* in defiance of the French and kept open the kingship for him. The Seville *junta* in 1809 accepted the American colonies on a basis approaching equality with Spain and invited them to send representatives to the Cortes, the representative body reinstituted at that time at Cádiz. Among the delegates to the Cortes from America was Dr. Miguel Ramos de Arizpe, of Coahuila, who rendered to that body on November 7, 1811, a report describing conditions in and making recommendations for the governance of the Eastern Interior Provinces, consisting of Texas, Coahuila, Nuevo León, and Nuevo Santander (present Tamaulipas). The report gives an excellent survey of conditions in the province of Texas on the eve of Anglo-American colonization. The following extract describes the Spanish government of Texas at the time.

. . . In the town of Chihuahua resides a commandant general who is independent of the viceroyalty of Mexico and who has the same and even greater powers than the viceroy. The provinces of Coahuila and Texas, from two hundred and forty to seven hundred leagues distant from his residence, are subject to him in every way. Each one of these provinces has a provincial chief with the title of military and political governor, who, by inherent and delegated powers, has jurisdiction in all cases, being dependent in cases of war and general welfare on the com-

mandant general. In fiscal affairs, he is subject to the intendant of San Luis Potosí, who is from one hundred to six hundred leagues distant, with final recourse to the supreme council of finance in Mexico City; and in appeals for justice, the military and political governor is subject to the audiencia of New Galicia, which is as far away as the commandancy general [in Chihuahua]. . . .

Texas was discovered and settlements begun there by the inhabitants of Coahuila by the middle of the seventeenth century. It was subject to the governor of Coahuila until 1720. At that time the viceroy, the Marquis of Valero, named as governor of both provinces, the Marquis of San Miguel de Aguayo, who, with five hundred soldiers from Coahuila, re-established the presidios and missions of Texas, which several times had been destroyed by the Indians and one time threatened by the French. At the present, Texas has its military and political governor, and, after so many years of abandonment, contains in all its vast territory only three towns, which are most commonly known by the names of presidios. . . . They are:

San Fernando or Real Presidio de San Antonio de Véjar [San Antonio]
La Bahía del Espíritu Santo [Goliad]
Nacogdoches . . .

San Antonio de Véjar, which is today the capital, has for its local government a municipal council of two alcaldes, an attorney, all three elected, and six aldermen. La Bahía and Nacogdoches are commanded by lieutenants of the governor, assigned and replaced at his will; and the missions are governed by a corporal. In each town a company of cavalry is stationed. Since 1806, military detachments of not fewer than fifty men have been posted on the Guadalupe and Trinity Rivers on the road to the frontier of Louisiana and another at the port of Arcokisas [evidently a place on Galveston Bay], under whose protection some families have gathered. San An-

tonio and La Bahía are administered spiritually by parish priests, Nacogdoches and the missions by Recollect Franciscans of Guadalupe de los Zacatecas, and all are subject to the bishop of Nuevo León. As a result of the pretensions of the Anglo-Americans on the borders between Louisiana and Texas, the troops of Coahuila, aided by seven hundred militiamen of Nuevo León and Tamaulipas, all under the command of Colonel Antonio Cordero, governor of Coahuila, marched to Texas and to its frontier at the end of 1805. These men, having remained there until the present, have augmented the population of the province to seven thousand souls. . . .

## 19. TEXAS' FIRST DECLARATION OF INDEPENDENCE AND FIRST CONSTITUTION

### April 6 and 17, 1813

Mexico began its long struggle for independence in 1810. The revolution shortly spread to Texas. The initial revolt in 1811 at San Antonio was premature, but a more formidable movement, led by José Bernardo Gutiérrez de Lara, developed the next year. Gutiérrez, as an envoy of the Mexican revolutionists, had failed to gain official recognition by the United States, but he had found public sentiment in Natchitoches, New Orleans, and Washington highly favorable toward Mexican independence. Thereupon, he set up headquarters in the Neutral Ground, flooded Texas with propaganda advocating a new order along the lines of the current liberal philosophies, and got an ex-United States Army officer, Augustus W. Magee, to join him in raising the "Republican Army of the North" for the purpose of liberating Texas. Entering Texas on August 8, 1812, the revolutionists advanced to Nacogdoches, where they were received with great enthusiasm, the royalist troops deserting to their forces. They captured San Fernando de Béxar (San Antonio) without difficulty on April 1, 1813, where five days later the leaders issued a Declaration of Independence, a document obviously inspired by that of the United States.

On April 17 Gutiérrez and the *junta* at San Antonio issued the first constitution of Texas. The constitution provided for a Spanish-type government for "the State of Texas, forming a part of the Mexican Republic." Disappointed over this reactionary development, the liberals lost interest, and, shortly afterwards, when the Republican forces were defeated by General Joaquín de Arredondo, commandant of the Eastern Interior Provinces, on the Medina River near San Antonio, the first independent Texas movement collapsed. Gutiérrez sent a manuscript copy (in Spanish) of his "Constitution of the State of Texas" to William Shaler, Special Agent of the United States stationed at Natchitoches to observe developments in Texas, who in turn enclosed it in his report of May 14, 1813, to Secretary of State James Monroe. It is from this copy that the English translation reproduced here is taken.

### 1. THE DECLARATION OF INDEPENDENCE

#### April 6, 1813

From H. Niles (ed.), *The Weekly Register*, IV (July 17, 1813).

We, the people of the province of Texas, calling on the Supreme Judge of the Universe to witness the rectitude of our intentions, declare, that the ties which held us under the domination of Spain and Europe, are for-

ever dissolved; that we possess the right to establish a government for ourselves; that in future all legitimate authority shall emanate from the people to whom alone it rightfully belongs, and that henceforth all allegiance or subjection to any foreign power whatsoever, is entirely renounced.

A relation of the causes which have conduced to render this step necessary, is due to our dignity, and to the opinion of the world. A long series of occurrences, originating in the weakness and corruption of the Spanish rulers, has converted that monarchy into the theatre of a sanguinary war, between two contending powers, itself destined the prize of the victor; a king in the power and subject to the authority of one of them, the miserable wreck of its government in the possession of the other, it appears to have lost the substance and almost the form of sovereignty.—Unable to defend itself on the Peninsula, much less to protect its distant colonies; those colonies are abandoned to the caprice of wicked men, whilst there exists no power to which they may be made responsible for the abuse of their authority, or for the consequence of their rapacity. Self preservation, the highest law of nature, if no other motive, would have justified this step. But, independent of this necessity, a candid world will acknowledge that we have had cause amply sufficient, in the sufferings and oppression which we have so long endured.

Governments are established for the good of communities of men, and not for the benefit and aggrandisement of individuals. When these ends are perverted to a system of oppression, the people have a right to change them for a better, and for such as may be best adapted to their situation. Man is formed in the image of his Creator: he sins who submits to slavery. Who will say that our sufferings were not such as to have driven us to the farthest bounds of patience, and to justify us in establishing a new government, and in choosing new rulers to whom we may intrust our happiness?

We were governed by insolent strangers, who regarded their authority only as the means of enriching themselves by the plunder of those whom they were sent to govern, while we had no participation either in national or municipal affairs.

We feel, with indignation, the unheard of tyranny of being excluded from all communication with other nations, which might tend to improve our situation, physical and moral. We were prohibited the use of books, of speech, and even of thought—our country was our prison.

In a province which nature has favored with uncommon prodigality, we were poor. We were prohibited from cultivating those articles which are suitable to our soil and climate, and of pressing necessity. The commerce of our country was sold to the favorites of the court; and merchandise were supplied under the enormous exactions of the monopolists. A barbarous and shameful inhospitality was manifested to strangers, even to our nearest neighbors.

The product of our soil and of our country were alike denied exportation. Our trade consisted in a trifling system of smuggling.

Every path which led to fame or honor was closed upon us. We were denied participation in public employments; we had no rank in the army maintained in the bosom of our country. We expected no promotion in a church to which we have ever been faithful and obedient sons.

We saw the mighty monarchy of Spain threatened with destruction, and our oppressions were forgotten; we flew to her assistance like faithful and submissive vassals. As a reward for our faithful services, a sanguinary vagrant, distinguished in his own country by no honorable action, is sent amongst us, and his government exhibited only acts of cruelty, insatiable avarice and augmented oppression. Nothing but the specious promise that a general assembly of the Cortes would be convened, could have restrained us. Experience has shown this hope to be illusory. Some miserable wretches, styling themselves the rulers of Spain, have sold us to a foreign power, for a term of years, in order to procure the means of consigning us forever to the most ignominious servitude.

The Spanish colonies of South America, have long since declared and maintained their independence; the United States prove to us, by an experience of thirty years, that such a separation may be attended with national and individual prosperity.

We conceive it a duty we owe as well to ourselves as to our posterity, to seize the moment which now offers itself, of shaking off the yoke of European domination, and of laboring in the cause of the independence of Mexico; taking the authority into our own hands, forming laws, and of placing the government of our country upon a sure and firm basis, and by these means assure a rank among the nations of the world.

## 2. THE CONSTITUTION OF THE STATE OF TEXAS

### April 17, 1813

From "The Constitution of the State of Texas" (Special Agents: Shaler, 1810, II, MS, State Department, National Archives, Washington; microfilm copy, University of Texas Library, Austin); Julia Kathryn Garret, "The First Constitution of Texas, April 17, 1813," *The Southwestern Historical Quarterly*, XL (1936-37), 290-308.

1. The province of Texas shall henceforth be known only as the State of Texas, forming part of the Mexican Republic, to which it remains inviolably joined.

2. Our Holy Religion will remain unchanged in the way it is now established, and the laws will be duly executed unless they are expressly and publicly revoked or altered in the manner herein prescribed.

3. Private property and possessions will be inviolable, and will never be taken for public use except in urgent cases of necessity, in which instances the proprietor will be duly recompensed.

4. From today henceforward personal liberty will be held sacred. No man will be arrested for any crime without a formal accusation made in the proper form under oath being first presented. No man will be placed before the Tribunal without first having been examined by the witnesses. Neither will any man be deprived of life without having been heard completely [in court], an exception being made from this rule during the time of the present War in the case of criminals of the Republic, whose punishments will be decided by the Junta in accord with the Governor in order to assure the firmness of an Establishment and to protect the people.

5. The Governor selected by the Junta will be Commander-in-Chief of the military forces of the State, but he will undertake no campaign personally without having received the order of the Junta. In such a case, the Governor will provide the necessary means for maintaining the obligations of the Government during his absence. Also under his charge will be the establishment of laws pertaining to the organization of the Army, the naming of military officials, and the ratifying of the commissions and ranks of those already employed. He shall be intrusted with the defense of the Country, foreign relations, execution of the laws, and preservation of order. He will have a right to one secretary, two aides-de-camp, three clerks for the Spanish language and one for English.

6. The Salaries of the Governor and the other Civil and Military officials will be fixed as promptly as possible and will be assured by law.

7. There shall be a Treasurer whose function shall be to receive and to preserve intact the Public Funds, keeping them at the disposal of the Government.

8. The City of San Fernando will be the seat of government and the residence of all public officials. It will be governed by two mayors and four District Commissioners selected by the Junta.

9. The Cabildo will be entrusted with the policing of the interior of the city, and will have all the authority necessary to fulfill its purpose. The mayors shall each have power to judge cases in their jurisdiction and shall appoint the necessary officials and indicate the days for the hearing. Their judgments shall be governed by the established law on the individual cases [Blurs in this article make translation difficult.]

10. Each town in the State will be governed by a military officer named by the Governor, and this officer will be required to follow whatever rules are deemed necessary by the Junta.

11. It shall be the obligation of the Cabildo and the military commandants [of the towns] to present to the Governor an exact census of the population of their respective districts and to establish schools in each city or town.

12. The Junta shall have the power to dismiss any officials it has nominated should it deem such a procedure necessary.

13. There shall be a Superior Audiencia which will be composed of a Judge well versed in law appointed by the Junta. He will have the functions of taking the necessary measures for maintaining peace and good order, of trying all criminal cases, of deciding cases in which the sentence or amount in controversy exceeds 1000 pesos. This tribunal will name its officials, fixing the time and place of its session, and its emoluments will be determined by laws set up for that purpose. It will be the duty of the tribunal in trying persons accused of murder to name five of the most discreet and intelligent citizens of the district who shall swear to perform their duty in justice both to the State and to the defendant, and to assist the Judge in reaching a fair verdict. It shall also be the duty of the tribunal to establish a code of criminal law and methods of procedure, so that all crimes might have their respective punishments and might be clearly and promptly defined. Once approved by the Junta, this will be the law of the Land, and will be published for the benefit of the People. No one shall be punished for hav-

ing committed any crime or offense which the law has not provided for.

14. Any change or alteration in the laws in force at present will be effected by the Junta and will be made known to the People.

15. The Junta will meet to hold its sessions in the capital one day each week, or oftener if some matter is urgent. It shall preserve all powers granted it by the people, and will have as its obligation to keep close watch and care diligently for the welfare of the State, to alter or amend these regulations that becomes necessary, to preside in matters dealing with war and the various branches of foreign relations, and finally, to do everything in its power for the benefit of the great cause of Mexican independence.

16. The Junta will take notice of any enemy property found within its jurisdiction and will resolve whatever it deems fitting with regard to it.

17. The Commander-in-Chief, Governor-elect, of this State, will use every available means and will do everything in his power to facilitate the carrying out of all obligations contracted by him in the name of the Mexican Republic.

18. The Junta and Governor of the State, by common accord will proceed to the election of the necessary delegates to the general Mexican congress and to foreign countries.

City of San Fernando, April 17, 1813

## 20. TREATY ESTABLISHING THE BOUNDARY BETWEEN TEXAS AND THE UNITED STATES

### February 22, 1819

From *U. S. Statutes at Large*, VIII, 252-273.

By the terms of the agreement in 1806 between the Spanish and United States military commanders on the Louisiana-Texas frontier, the disputed territory between the Arroyo Hondo and the Sabine River became a neutral ground pending diplomatic settlement. Diplomatic efforts to settle the controversy broke down in 1808, when Napoleon interfered with the Spanish government, and were not renewed until 1815. Meanwhile, the United States had annexed West Florida on the basis that it was a part of the Louisiana purchase and demanded that Spain restrain her Indians in East Florida from raiding in the United States. A voluminous amount of correspondence between the two countries followed, culminating in the Adams-de Onís or Florida Purchase Treaty of February 22, 1819. By the terms of the treaty the United States acquired the Floridas and in return relinquished her doubtful claim to Texas. The boundary as established in the treaty placed the Neutral Ground within the United States. Final ratifications of the treaty were completed on February 19, 1821.

TREATY OF AMITY, SETTLEMENT, AND LIMITS, Between the United States of America and his Catholic Majesty

. . . Article 2. His Catholic Majesty cedes to the United States, in full property and sovereignty, all the territories which belong to him, situated in the eastward of the Mississippi, known by the name of East and West

Florida. The adjacent islands dependent on said provinces, all public lots and squares, vacant lands, public edifices, fortifications, barracks, and other buildings, which are not private property, archives and documents, which relate directly to the property and sovereignty of said provinces, are included in this article. The said archives and documents shall be left in possession of the commissioner or officers of the United States, duly authorized to receive them.

Article 3. The boundary line between the two countries, west of the Mississippi, shall begin on the Gulph of Mexico, at the mouth of the river Sabine, in the sea, continuing north, along the western bank of that river, to the 32d degree of latitude; thence, by a line due north, to the degree of latitude where it strikes the Rio Roxo of Nachitoches, or *Red River;* then following the course of the Rio Roxo westward, to the degree of longitude 100 west from London and 23 from Washington; then, crossing the said Red River, and running thence, by a line due north, to the river Arkansas; thence, following the course of the southern bank of the Arkansas, to its source, in latitude 42 north; and thence, by that parallel of latitude, to the South Sea. The whole being as laid down in Melish's map of the United States, published at Philadelphia, improved to the first of January, 1818. But if the source of the Arkansas River shall be found to fall north or south of latitude 42, then the line shall run from the said source due south or north, as the case may be, till it meets the said parallel of latitude 42, and thence, along the said parallel, to the South Sea: All the islands of the Sabine, and the said Red and Arkansas rivers, throughout the course thus described, to belong to the United States; but the use of the waters, and the navigation of the Sabine to the sea, and of the said rivers Roxo and Arkansas, throughout the extent of the said boundary, on their respective banks, shall be common to the respective inhabitants of both nations.

The two high contracting parties agree to cede and renounce all their rights, claims, and pretensions, to the territories described by the said line, that is to say: The United States hereby cede to His Catholic Majesty, and renounce forever, all their rights, claims, and pretensions, to the territories lying west and south of the above described line; and, in like manner, His Catholic Majesty cedes to the United States all his rights, claims, and pretensions to any territories east and north of the said line, and for himself, his heirs, and successors, renounces all claim to the said territories forever. . . .

Article 5. The inhabitants of the ceded territories shall be secured in the free exercise of their religion, without any restriction; and all those who may desire to remove to the Spanish dominions shall be permitted to sell or export their effects, at any time whatever without being subject, in either case, to duties. . . .

Article 11. The United States, exonerating Spain from all demands in the future, on account of the claims of their citizens to which the renumerations herein contained extend, and considering them entirely cancelled, undertake to make satisfaction for the same, to an amount not exceeding five millions of dollars. . . .

Article 16. . . . In witness whereof we, the underwritten Plenipotentiaries of the United States of America and His Catholic Majesty, have signed, by virtue of our powers, the present treaty of amity, settlement, and limits, and have hereunto affixed our seals, respectively.

Done at Washington this twenty-second day of February, one thousand eight hundred and nineteen.

John Quincy Adams    [L.S.]
Luis De Onis         [L.S.]

# 21. JAMES LONG: THE LAST OF THE FILIBUSTERS

## 1819

From Henry Stuart Foote, *Texas and Texans* (2 vols.; Philadelphia, 1841), I, 202-212.

Dissatisfaction along the lower Mississippi with the "surrender of Texas" to Spain by the Adam-de Onís Treaty of 1819 inspired the last filibustering expedition across the Sabine. Angry citizens at a public mass meeting at Natchez, Mississippi, that year organized an expedition, commanded by Dr. James Long, a merchant of Natchez, for the purpose of taking Texas from Spain and establishing an independent republic. The following extract, written by Mirabeau B. Lamar from information obtained from Mrs. Long, describes the final effort of the Americans to take Texas from the Spaniards by force.

. . . The Citizens of Natchez . . . resolved to make one more effort in behalf of the liberties of that oppressed and bleeding province [Texas]. A meeting was accordingly held by the inhabitants of that place, and arrangements entered into for an immediate and vigorous assault upon the country. General Adair, of Kentucky, was to have been the leader of the expedition; but from some cause unknown to us, he declined the proffered honour, and the command was tendered to General [James] Long, who, . . . accepted the responsibility with pride and pleasure, and entered at once upon the duties of the station with his characteristic energy and enthusiasm. His activity and zeal, as well as his acknowledged military talents, soon rendered the project quite popular. He pledged the whole of his private fortune in the enterprise; in which he was joined by some of the choicest spirits of the day. With the best wishes for his welfare, he left Natchez with about seventy-five of the most hardy and intrepid followers, on the 17th of June, 1819. As he pushed from the shore, a shot from the cannon

was fired to his success. It was evident, however, that an expedition so publicly gotten up and openly conducted, could not be permitted to pass off without the notice of the government. Attempts were accordingly made by the proper authorities to arrest the leader; but the officers not being over-active and vigilant, their efforts were easily eluded, and General Long moved off in triumph with his Spartan band, awakening the spirit of war in his march, and gathering strength as he moved along. He pushed for Natchitoches, where he had means of his own, and many friends; thence to the Sabine and on to Nacogdoches, where in a short time after his arrival he was able to muster about three hundred strong. . . . Long's designs were by many either misunderstood or misrepresented. Even some of his own followers looked upon the project as one which was entered upon merely because of its perils, and the individual glory to which it might lead. . . . The expedition was founded in neither private speculation nor a desire of personal aggrandizement. It was known to the intelligent portion of the people both of Natchez and New Orleans, that its sole design and intention were to get possession of the country, to rescue it from the grasp of tyranny, and, by establishing good government, order and security, to invite to its settlement by North Americans. General Long hoped to achieve by military operations what the two Austins had the ability and address to accomplish by peaceful negotiation. To show that . . . his views were liberal and comprehensive, directed solely to the freedom and independence of the country, we have only to give a plain statement of his proceedings on his arrival at Nacogdoches, . . .

In taking possession of this place, the first thing to which he directed his attention, was the establishment of civil government. If power or speculation had been his object, he might have made his *will* the law, . . . but instead of this we find a *"Supreme Council"* elected, invested with unlimited and controlling powers of legislation. . . . The council was to be composed of twenty-one members, but from some cause . . . eleven only were chosen, . . . General Long himself was chosen President. The Council met on the twenty-second of June, eighteen hundred and nineteen; and on the succeeding day declared the province a free and Independent Republic. Various laws were now enacted for the organization of the country, and the raising of revenue. The public domain, as a matter of course, was the chief dependence for means. A bill was accordingly passed for the survey and sale of lands on the Attoyac and Red Rivers; the minimum price of those on the first named being fixed at one dollar per acre, payable one-fourth down, and the residue in three equal annual instalments; whilst the lands lying on the latter stream were to be sold at various prices, according to quality, ranging from twelve and a half to fifty cents per acre. Major Cook was commissioned, on the twenty-ninth of July, to proceed to Pecan Point [in present northeastern Red River County, Texas], and invite to the settlement of that section, by offering bounty lands to soldiers, and head-rights to actual settlers. . . . Whilst these arrangements were going on in the civil department, the disposition of the military force stood thus. David Long, the General's youngest brother, was stationed at the upper crossing of the Trinity with a large quantity of merchandise to barter with the Indians for mules and horses. Johnson was sent on a similar expedition; whilst Major Smith, who had brought into the country a company of forty men by way of Galveston, was stationed at the Cochattee village. On the twenty-second of September, Walker was ordered with twenty-three men to fortify on the Brazos, which he did, at the old Labahia crossing, meeting on his way five of Johnson's men, who uniting with him increased his force to twenty-eight. Matters being thus arranged, General Long makes preparations to go to Galveston for the purpose of establishing a small post at Bolivar Point, and also to obtain, if possible, some munitions of war from the celebrated lord of that island—John La Fitte. He had already opened a correspondence with this bold rover of the seas, who says in one of his letters, that having devoted the last eight years of his life in a struggle against Spanish cruelty and despotism, he could not do otherwise than wish well to the General. . . . Persuaded by this manifestation of friendly regard, that some as-

sistance might be obtained from the pirate by a personal interview, the General . . . departed for the Island, taking with him thirteen men. He had scarcely turned his back, however, before Cook relapsed into his old habits of dissipation and drunkenness; and the garrison fell into uproar and confusion. And now commenced the calamities of the whole expedition; and never was a longer train of misfortunes and disasters crowded into a briefer space. On arriving at the Cochattee village, the very first thing that saluted his ears was the unexpected tidings of the enemy's approach. The intelligence . . . represented the Spaniards as rapidly advancing, seven hundred strong. Orders were immediately despatched to Cook, Walker, and David Long, to repair forthwith to this village, a point most favourable for the concentration of his forces, and where he intended to give the invaders battle; and then . . . he hastened with all possible speed to Galveston Island; but not receiving the desired and expected assistance from that quarter, he returns without delay to the village, where he is greeted with a letter from his lady, dated a day or two after his departure from Nacogdoches, apprising him of the approach of the enemy, and of the disorganized condition of that post. Exasperated at the conduct of Cook, he mounts his horse and dashes for Nacogdoches. On the way he meets his wife flying from the place, who tells him that it is useless to proceed—that all is lost—the garrison has dispersed and the families are evacuating the town as fast as possible. . . . Leaving his lady . . . he put the rowels to his horse, and after riding all night, reached Nacogdoches just in time to assist some of the poorer families who had been left behind, and were struggling to escape.

The town was now entirely deserted; with no human being in it except himself. He commenced gathering the public arms and ammunition; and whilst he was busily engaged in concealing them in an old dry well, he heard his name articulated in a feeble voice that scarcely rose above a whisper. He seized his sword—but on turning . . . beheld a pale and emaciated being . . . so worn down and altered by hunger and fatigue, that Long did not recognize his faithful Lieutenant. "My name," said the wretched being, "is Lightle." . . . This brave and suffering Lieutenant was attached to Johnson's party; and from him Long now received an account of the fate of that gallant and unfortunate company. They had been surprised, defeated, and dispersed. Lightle himself had been taken prisoner, but making his escape, had fled to Nacogdoches in hopes of finding that place strongly garrisoned. He found it deserted. "And what of Walker and my brother David?" inquired the General. "Of them," said Lightle, "I know nothing." This news fell heavily on the heart of Long; he read in it the ruin of his expedition. . . .

# 22. THE MOSES AUSTIN FAMILY

## 1765-1837

From Moses Austin, Stephen F. Austin, and Emily M. B. Austin (Mrs. James F. Perry), "Record of Moses Austin and Family," in Eugene C. Barker (ed.). *The Austin Papers* (3 vols.; Washington, 1924, 1928; Austin, 1927), I, 1-6.

After efforts of the filibusters to open Texas to Americans had failed repeatedly, the planting of an Anglo-American population in Texas was accomplished by peaceful, lawful colonization by Moses Austin and his son Stephen. "Of all the men who figured in American history," wrote Professor George P. Garrison, "there are no other two who have attracted so little attention from their contemporaries and have yet done things of such vast and manifest importance, as Moses Austin and his son Stephen. Their great work consisted in the making of Anglo-American Texas, an enterprise planned and begun by the one and carried into execution by the other." The history of Maryland, Pennsylvania, and Georgia without Lord Baltimore, William Penn, and James Oglethorpe would still be the story of Englishmen wresting the territory from nature and the Indians and becoming Americans. But without the Austins the boundary laid down in the Adams-de Onís Treaty, in all probability, would still mark the western limits of the United States, and "There is no reason to believe," Professor Eugene C. Barker asserts, "that Texas would differ today from the Mexican states south of the Rio Grande."

The following extract from the family record, written by Moses Austin while he lived, then by Stephen until his death, and after that by Stephen's sister, traces the genealogy and records the major activities of this remarkable family.

## RECORD OF MOSES AUSTIN AND FAMILY

Ocbr. 4*th*. Moses Austin was born in 1765 State of Connecticutt County Of New Haven and Town of Durham the Youngest Child of the family of Elias Austin

In 1783 Moses Austin removed from New Havin to Philadelphia and opened a Dry goods store in Markett Street between front and Second street, and in Feb*y*. 1784 formed a partnership with Maning Merril and Commenced the Importation of Dry Goods from England, and in May Opened a whole sale store in front Street between Walnut and Chesnutt and in Aug*t*. of the same Year extended the House to Richmond in Virginia and Moses Austin removed to that City in Sep*t*. and took charge of the business.

In 1785 Sep*t*. 29 Moses Austin Was Married unto Maria Brown Daughter of Abia Brown in New Jersey,
. . .

Jan*y*. 1*st*. Maria Austin Was born in the County of Sussex New Jersey the 1 Day of Jan*ry*. 1768 and, the first Daughter of Abia Brown.

Moses Austin and Maria his Wife left Philadelphia the 30 Day of Sep*t*. 1785 on board the Richmond Packett Capt. Tillinghast for Richmond Virginia and arrived on the 15 Day of Octbr.

Anna Maria Austin first Daughter of Moses and Maria Austin was born the 29 Day June 1787 and departed this life the 1 Day Aug*t*. following.

Eliza Fuller Austin Second Daughter of Moses Austin and Maria His Wife was born the 14 Day of April 1790 And departed this life 4*th*. Day of December following in Richmond Virginia.

Stephen Fuller Austin first son of Moses and Maria Austin Was born the 3 Day of November 1793 at Austin Ville, Virginia.

In 1791 Moses Austin and Maria his Wife Removed from Richmond Virginia to the Lead Mines in Wythe County and made Purchase of said Estate in Companey with his Brother Stephin Austin and Established the Village of Austin Ville.

Emely Margarett Brown Austin third Daughter of Moses and Maria Austin was born on 22 Day of June 1795. a[t] Austin Ville Virginia.

In december 1796 Moses Austin made a Visit to Louisiana then under the Spanish Government and in May obtained a Grant of Land from the said Government of three miles sqr. including the Mine a Burton and in June 1797 relinquished his interest in the Mines in Virginia to his Brother Stephen Austin and in December of the same Year Judather Kendle and Elias Bates Nephew of the said Austin, left Austin Ville to take possession of said Grant and Arrived in March following and took possession of the Mine A Burton for and in the name of Moses Austin. On 8*th*. Day of June 1798 Moses Austin and Family Consisting of Maria his Wife Stephen F. Austin his son and Emely M. B. Austin his Daughter together with Moses Bates and family and Others Whites and blacks to the number of Forty persons, and Nine Loaded Wagons, and a Coach and four Horses, All left Austin Ville and took the Road for Morrises Boat Yard on the Great Kanhawa and on 4*th*. Day July intered the Ohio and arrived at Kaskaskaia on 8*th*. Day Sep*t*. Sick and debilitated to such a degree, that out of 17 persons that arrived, two only could walk on Shore from the Barge, at Kaskaskia Mrs Bates and Mr. Parson Bates paid the debt of Nature and Henry Bates unhappily was Drowned passing the falls of Ohio the first Wife of Moses Bates was my Sister, She died in Middleton Connecticutt Parson and Henry Bates was her Children as Also Elias Bates who arrived in the Provence of Louisiana the Spring before.

On 20 Sepr. Moses Austin and Family passed the Mississippia and took up a residence in the Little Village of Saint Genevieve Until July 1798 [1799] when his family removed to the Mine a Burton.

At this time the Mine a Burton, as, well as all the District of Saint Genevieve [was] a Wilderness Except the village of Saint Genevieve which contained about 120 families and on the Saline four, or five, American families had commenced a Settlement with in 8 Miles of the Village

On 12*th* Day May 1802 The House of Moses Austin was Attacked by a Party of 30 Indians but they were repu[l]sd by the Americans 10 in Number and Driven from the Village of the Mines, the french gave No assistance, . . .

In May 1804 Stephen Fuller Austin left Saint Genevieve in Company with Daniel Phelps to Obtain his Education a[t] Colchester Academy where he remained three years and returned to the Academy at Lexington Kentucky and remained two Years.

Emily M. B. Austin left the Mines in Octbr. 1804 and remained at Mrs Becks boarding School in Lexington Kentucky untill December 1808

In May 1811 Mrs. Maria Austin Miss Emily M B Austin and Master James Elijah B Austin left Saint Genevieve On board a barge for New Orleans Under the Protection of Elish[a] Lewis, bound for New York Mrs. Maria Austin for her health and Miss Emily M B Austin to finish her Education at the Hermitage Academy, where she remained untill Octbr. 1812, James Elijah B. Went on to Connecticutt and Was put to the Revd. Mr. Whitteley of the Town of Washington.

1816 April 20 Moses Austin and Family removed from Mine A Burton and Gave up Durham Hall Negroes and Plantation together [with] Lead Mines and furnaces to his son Stephen F Austin.

1818 James Elijah Brown son of Moses Austin returned from Connecticut, remained at Home untill June 1819 when he went to Kentucky Near Nicholas Ville to finish his education under a Mr Wilson.

1819 Stephen F Austin left the Territory of Missouri and went to reside in the Territory of Arkansas. Red River at Long Bran[ch]

1820 Moses Austin left Missouri about the 1st. of May 1820 and went to the Little Rock in the Territory Of Arkansas where he remained Some Months after which he Proceeded on to San Antonio where he Arrived (after a journey through a perfect wilderness and attended with much fatigue) about the 10th. of Decemr. Same Year, he there pe[ti]tioned the Supreme Authorities of New Spain, through his Excellency Don Antonio Martinez (then Govr. and Political Chief Of this Province of Texas) for a grant of Land and Permission to Settle 300 American families in that Province. The petition was forwarded on to his Excellency Don Aredondo then Govr. Genl. of the Internal Eastern Provinces of New Spain who confirmed the Grant after a Previous decree of the Provincial Deputation (then assembled at the City of Monterrey) to that affect, and the necessary papers were forwarded on to San Antonio immediately. Moses Austin left San Antonio on the 29th. of Decemr. (previous to the confirmation of the Grant) and after a tedious and distressing journey he reached the Settlements on the Sabine River not having tasted any kind of Nourishment for 8 Days. Their Provisions having failed and the powder they supplied themselves with proved to be so damaged they could not kill any Game altho the Country abounded in Game of all Kinds. his hardships were so severe that he was taken with the Fever and confined to his bed 3 weeks at the house of Mr. Hugh McGuffin 20 Miles west of Natchitoches, at this place he was met by his Nephew Elias Bates who had left Herculam, Mo. Some time in Decemr. in pursuit of him. As soon as he could travel they started together, descended Red River to the Missispi and Arrived at Herculanium some time in March 1821. The journey proved to great for his Constitution which was much impaired Nevertheless he commenced Settleing his affairs in Mo. with the intention of returning to Texas in August following, but unfortunately he took a cold when at the

Mine a Burton, but reached his daughter's Mrs. Emily M. Bryans on Hazel Run; in a few days the cold terminated in an inflemation on the lungs and after lingering in much pain for 10 days which he bore with Christian fortitude, he resigned his Soul to his Maker without a groan on the 10th. of June 1821 in the 57 year of his age.

Stephen Fuller Austin son of Moses Austin left the Territory of Arkansas in 1820 and decended to New Orleans where he remained until his Father returned from St. Antonio — he then proceeded to Natchitoches to meet his Father and Share with the dangers and fatigues of the enterprize he was about commencing in the Province of Texas. When he arrived at Natchitoches he met the Commissioners (Don Erasmo Seguin and Don Juan Berimendi) dispatched by the Government of New Spain with a confirmation of the grant and orders to conduct Moses Austin to the District allotted to him to form his Colony. — but receiving intelligence of the sudden death of his Father he proceeded on to San Antonio in company with the commissioners and 16 Americans who attended him on the expedition — on his arrival at San Antonio he was immediately acknowledged as the legal heir and representative of his Father Moses Austin, by Don Antonio Martinez then Govr. and Political Chief of that Province and fully empowered to carry into effect the original disign of his Father.

Accordingly he left San Antonio with his party of Americans and proceeded to explore the Country and Select the part he might deem most desirable to form his Colony — after having Explored the Country bordering on the sea or Gulph of Mexico from the Bay of Matagorda to the Colorado and Brazos Rivers, he selected the Country lying on and between those two rivers extending from the San Antonio road leading to Nacogdoches down to the Sea as the most desireable for the formation of a flourishing Colony. He then returned to the United Sts. to complete his enterprize and introduce the number of families Stipulated, he proceeded to New Orleans and by the assistance of a Friend he fitted out a Schooner (called the Lively) and embarked on board of her 18 men with provisions, arms, ammunition, and farming tools with directions to proceed to the Mouth of the Colorado and ascend that river untill a suitable place offered where they were to plant corn, erect a Stockade, and put up dwelling houses etc.

The Lively left N. Orleans about the 20th. of November 1821 and Stephen F. Austin left there the day after by land to meet her at the Mouth of the Colorado. In Natchitoches he collected a party of 10 men to accompany him and proceed through the wilderness to the Mouth of the Colorado where he arrived sometime in the Month of January — after waiting nearly 3 weeks at that place and vicinity subsisting on catfish and wild onions — without bread or salt he dispaired of meeting his Vessel and ascended the river to the la Bahia Crossing — there he met his Brother Jas. E. B. Austin and they proceeded on together with 20 men to San Antonio where he arrived on the 15 of March 1822 much fatigued and reduced in flesh. The Govr. recd. him with a cordial welcome and advised him (as a material change had taken place in the Political aspect of the country) to proceed on to the City of Monterrey where the Govr. Genl. resided and if he could not get his business satisfactorily arranged to continue on to Mexico and lay his business before Congress. He left San Antonio on the 20th. March 1822 in company with an interpreter and D*r*. Rob. Andrews and arrived in Mexico on the 29 of April following — immediately on his arrival he presented a memorial to Congress praying that the Grant made to his Father by the former Government might be confirmed after Spending nearly a Year in Mexico attended with much labor and expence he succeeded in obtaining a complete confirmation of his Grant from Congress, and returned to San Antonio sometime in July after an Absence of 15 months and at a period when some of the most important events transpired in the Mexican History. immediately after his arrival at San Antonio he proceeded on to his Colony where he Found about 100 hundred families already Settled and commenced the organization of the Colony which he has nearly completed — the Government Commissioned him Lt Coronel and Supreme Judge of his Colony he Settled himself on the River Brazos where he now resides. July 1824.

James E. B. Austin second son of Moses Austin returned from Kentucky about the 1*st* of October 1821 and remained in Missouri until December following when he left it and went on to join his brother in the Province of Texas, he remained at the City of San Antonio de Bexar until his brother returned from the City of Mexico, he returned with him to the Colony where he remained until May 1824 then returned to Missouri to remove his Mother and Sister to that Province — but the death of his Mothar (who had died previous to his return and the marriage of his Sister with M*r*. James Perry Compelled him to return to the Province without her — accordingly he left Herculanium Missouri on the third day of November following 1824.

James E. B. Austin Died in New Orleans on the 24 of August 1829 with the Yellow fever after 63 hours sickness. . . .

Gen*l*. Stephen F. Austin Died at Judge McKinstry near Columbia Texas on the 27*th* December 1836 and was intered at James F Perrys Peach Point place on the 29th aged forty three years 1 month 24 days.

Moses Austin departed this life 10*th*. June 1821 in the 57*th*. year of his age at Hazel Run St. Francis Cty Missouri

Mary [Maria] Austin departed this life 8*th*. January 1824 in the 53 year of her age at Hazel Run St. Francis County State of Missouri 5 Oclock in the Morning.

James Bryan and Emily M. B. Austin were Married on the 31*st*. August 1813—at Mine A Burton Washington C. . . .

James Bryan departed this life 16*th*. July 1822 in the 33*rd*. year of his age in the town of Herculanium nine Oclock in the Morning.

M*rs*. E. M. Bryan with her family consisting of her Mother and four Children moved back to Hazel Run in August 1822 where she remained until her Marriage with James F. Perry.

James Franklen Perry was Born on the 19*th* of September 1790 in the state of Pensylvania in Allegheny County.

James F. Perry and Emily M. B. Bryan were Married by the Rev*d*. Thomas Donnell on the 23*rd* of September 1824 at Hazel Run S*t*. Francis C*y* State of Missouri. . . .

1831 June 7*th*. James F. Perry and Family left Potosi Missouri for the Province of Texas and arrived at San Felipe de Austin the Capatal of Austins Colonies on the 14th of August. . . .

# 23. THE MEXICAN COLONIZATION LAWS

## January 4, 1823, August 18, 1824, and March 24, 1825

From Stephen F. Austin, *Translation of the Laws, Orders, and Contracts on Colonization* (official trans.; Columbia, Texas, 1837), 40-45, 56-67.

On January 17, 1821, the Spanish officials at Monterrey granted Moses Austin permission to introduce as many as three hundred families into Texas. On his death shortly afterwards, the task of carrying out the project fell to his son, Stephen F. Austin, who established the first settlements early in 1822 and in March reported the fact to the Governor of Texas at San Antonio. But since Mexico had recently obtained its independence, he was advised to seek confirmation of his grant by the new government in Mexico City.

Arriving in Mexico City on April 29, 1822, he found Congress strongly divided upon the question of whether to establish a monarchy or a republic. A few days later a "revolution" made Iturbide emperor, and when Congress showed an unwillingness to submit to his will, Iturbide replaced it with a *junta* of forty-five favorites; whereupon Austin was unable to get action on his application until the *junta* passed the Imperial Colonization Law on January 4, 1823, and confirmed his application in accordance with its provisions on February 18. But by that time a reaction against

Iturbide was developing and Austin did not dare leave the capital. Fortunately, when in March the Emperor was forced to abdicate, the Congress, resuming power, ratified the concessions granted to Austin, although it then revoked the Imperial Colonization Law without approving any other application. The new executive authority approved Austin's contract on April 14, and fourteen days later Austin left the capital for Texas.

To provide for further colonization contracts, the Mexican Congress, on August 18, 1824, passed a new law which retained most of the liberal principles of the imperial law. The new law simply enumerated a few general provisions to which colonization contracts must conform and left the details of colonization regulations to the state legislatures. Consequently, the legislature of Texas and Coahuila (the two provinces having been united as one state on May 7, 1824, with the capital at Saltillo) enacted a colonization law on March 24, 1825, sponsored by Baron de Bastrop, a member of the legislature and a friend of the Austins, which supplemented the general law. Except for Austin's original contract, all colonization contracts while Texas was a part of Mexico were made in accordance with the laws of 1824 and 1825.

The following extracts are from Austin's official translation of the three laws.

## 1. THE IMPERIAL COLONIZATION LAW

### January 4, 1823

. . . Art. 1. The government of the Mexican nation will protect the liberty, property and civil rights, of all foreigners, who profess the Roman Catholic apostolic religion, the established religion of the empire.

Art. 2. To facilitate their establishment, the executive will distribute lands to them, under the conditions and terms, herein expressed.

Art. 3. The empresarios, by whom is understood those who introduced at least two hundred families, shall previously contract with the executive, and inform it what branch of industry they propose to follow, the property or resources they intend to introduce for that purpose, and any other particulars they may deem necessary, in order that with this necessary information, the executive may designate the province to which they must direct themselves, the lands which they can occupy with right of property, and the other circumstances which may be considered necessary.

Art. 4. Families who emigrate, not included in a contract, shall immediately present themselves to the ayuntamiento of the place where they wish to settle, in order that this body, in conformity with the instructions of the executive, may designate the lands corresponding to them, agreeably to the industry which they may establish.

Art. 5. The measurement of land shall be the following — establishing the *vara*, at three geometrical feet; a straight line of five thousand *varas* shall be a league; a square, each of whose sides shall be one league, shall be called a sitio; . . . five sitios shall compose one hacienda.

Art. 6. In the distribution made by government, of lands to the colonists, for the formation of villages, towns, cities, and provinces, a distinction shall be made between grazing lands, destined for the raising of stock, and lands suitable for farming or planting, on account of the facility of irrigation.

Art. 7. One labor shall be . . . one thousand varas on each side, . . .

Art. 8. To the colonists whose occupation is farming, there cannot be given less than one labor, and those whose occupation in stock raising cannot be given less than one sitio.

Art. 9. The government of itself, or by means of the authorities for that purpose, can augment [sic] said portions of land as may be deemed proper, agreeably to the conditions and circumstances of the colonists.

Art. 10. Establishment made under the former government which are now pending, shall be regulated by this law in all matters that may occur, . . .

Art. 13. Care shall be taken in the formation of said new town, that, so far as the situation of the ground will permit, the streets shall be laid off straight, running north and south, east and west. . . .

Art. 15. As soon as a sufficient number of families may be united to form one or more towns, their local government shall be regulated, and the constitutional ayuntamientos and other local establishments formed in conformity with the laws.

Art. 16. The government shall take care, in accord with the respective ecclesiastical authority, that these new towns are provided with a sufficient number of spiritual pastors, and in like manner, it will propose to congress a plan for their decent support.

Art. 17. . . . As a general rule, the colonists who arrive first, shall have the preference in the selection of land.

Art. 18. Natives of the country shall have a preference in the distribution of land; . . .

Art. 19. To each empresario who introduces and establishes families in any of the provinces designated for colonization, there shall be granted at the rate of three haciendas and two labors, for each two hundred families so introduced by him, but he will lose the right of property over said lands, should he not have populated and cultivated them in twelve years from the date of concession. The premium cannot exceed nine haciendas, and six labors, whatever may be the number of families he introduces.

Art. 20. At the end of twenty years the proprietors of the lands, acquired in virtue of the foregoing article, must alienate two thirds part of said lands, either by sale, donation, or in any other manner he pleases. . . .

Art. 23. If after two years from the date of the concession, the colonist should not have cultivated his land, the right of property shall be considered as renounced; in which case, the respective ayuntamiento can grant it to another.

Art. 24. During the first six years from the date of the concession, the colonists shall not pay tithes, duties on their produce, nor any contribution under whatever name it may be called.

Art. 25. The next six years from the same date, they shall pay half tithes, and the half of the contributions, whether direct or indirect, that are paid by the other citizens of the empire. After this time, they shall in all things relating to taxes and contributions, be placed on the same footing with the other citizens.

Art. 26. All the instruments of husbandry, machinery, and other utensils, that are introduced by the colonists for their use, at the time of their coming to the empire, shall be free, as also the merchandise introduced by each family, to the amount of two thousand dollars.

Art. 27. All foreigners who come to establish themselves in the empire, shall be considered as naturalized, should they exercise any useful profession or industry, by which, at the end of three years, they have a capital to support themselves with decency, and are married. Those who with the foregoing qualifications, marry Mexicans, will acquire particular merit, for the obtaining letters of citizenship.

Art. 28. Congress will grant letters of citizenship to those who solicit them, in conformity with the constitution of the empire.

Art. 29. Every individual shall be free to leave the empire, and can alienate the lands over which he may have acquired the right of property, agreeably to the tenor of this law, and he can likewise take away from the country, all his property, by paying the duties established by law.

Art. 30. After the publication of the law, there can be no sale or purchase of slaves which may be introduced into the empire. The children of slaves born in the empire shall be free at fourteen years of age.

Art. 31. All foreigners who may have established themselves in any of the provinces of the empire, under a permission of the former government, will remain on the lands which they may have occupied, being governed by the tenor of this law, in the distribution of said lands. . . .

Signed by the Emperor.———— To Don Jose Manuel de Herrera, Minister of Interior and Exterior Relations.

## 2. THE NATIONAL COLONIZATION LAW

### August 18, 1824

### (Decree No. 72)

The Supreme Executive Power, provisionally appointed by the General Sovereign Constituent Congress—To all who shall see and understand these presents: know ye—that the said Congress, has decreed as follows:

Art. 1. The Mexican nation offers to foreigners, who come to establish themselves within its territory, security for their persons and property, provided, they subject themselves to the laws of the country.

Art. 2. This law comprehends those lands of the nation, not the property of individuals, corporations, or towns, which can be colonized.

Art. 3. For this purpose the Legislature of the States, will, as soon as possible, form colonization laws, or regulations for their respective states, conforming themselves in all things, to the constitutional act, general constitution, and the regulations established in this law.

Art. 4. There cannot be colonized any lands, comprehended within twenty leagues of the limits of any foreign nation, nor within ten leagues of the coasts, without the previous approbation of the general supreme executive power.

Art. 5. If for the defence and security of the nation, the federal government should deem it necessary to use any portion of these lands, for the construction of warehouses, arsenals, or other public edifices, they can do so, with the approbation of the general congress, or in its recess, of the council of government.

Art. 6. Until after four years from the publication of this law, there shall not be imposed any tax whatever, on the entrance of foreigners, who come to establish themselves for the first time, in the nation.

Art. 7. Until after the year 1840, the general congress shall not prohibit the entrance of any foreigner, as a colonist, unless imperious circumstances should require it, with respect to the individuals of a particular nation.

Art. 8. The government, without prejudicing the objects of this law, shall take such precautionary measures as it may deem expedient, for the security of the confederation, as respects the foreigners who come to colonize.

Art. 9. A preference shall be given in the distribution of lands, to Mexican citizens, and no other distinction shall be made in regard to them except that which is founded on individual merit, or services rendered the country, or under equal circumstances, a residence in the place where the lands to be distributed are situated.

Art. 10. The military who in virtue of the offer made on the 27th March, 1821, have a right to lands, shall be attended to by the states, in conformity with the diplomas which are issued to that effect, by the supreme executive power.

Art. 11. If in virtue of the decree alluded to, in the last article, and taking into view the probabilities of life, the supreme executive power should deem it expedient to alienate any portion of land in favor of any officer, whether civil or military of the federation, it can do so from the vacant lands of the territories.

Art. 12. It shall not be permitted to unite in the same hands with the right of property, more than one league square of land, suitable for irrigation, four square leagues in superficie, of arable land without the facilities of irrigation, and six square leagues in superficie of grazing land.

Art. 13. The new colonists shall not transfer their property in mortmain (*manus muertos.*)

Art. 14. This law guarantees the contracts which the empresarios make with the families which they bring at their own expense, provided they are not contrary to the laws.

Art. 15. No person who by virtue of this law, acquires a title to lands, shall hold them if he is domiciliated out of the limits of the republic.

Art. 16. The government in conformity with the provisions established in this law, will proceed to colonize the territories of the republic.

Mexico, 18th. August, 1824.

Cayetano Ibarra, President.

## 3. THE COAHUILA-TEXAS STATE COLONIZATION LAW

### March 24, 1825

The Governor provisionally appointed by the Sovereign Congress of this state————to all who shall see these presents; know,————that the said congress, have decreed as follows:————

Decree No. 16. The constituent congress of the free, independent and sovereign State of Coahuila and Texas, desiring by every possible means, to augment the population of its territory; promote the cultivation of its fertile lands; the raising and multiplication of stock, and the progress of the arts, and commerce; and being governed by the constitutional act, the federal constitution, and the basis established by the national decree of the general congress, No. 72, have thought proper to decree the following LAW OF COLONIZATION:

Art. 1. All foreigners, who in virtue of the general laws of the 18th. August, 1824, which guarantees the security of their persons and property, in the territory of the Mexican nation, wish to remove to any of the settlements of the state of Coahuila and Texas, are at liberty to do so; and the said state invites and calls them.

Art. 2.  Those who do so instead of being incommoded, shall be admitted by the local authorities of said settlements, who shall freely permit them to pursue any branch of industry, that they may think proper, provided they respect the general laws of the nation, and those of the state. . . .

Art. 5.  Foreigners of any nation, or a native of any of the Mexican states, can project the formation of new towns on any lands entirely vacant, or even on those of an individual, in the case mentioned in the 35th article; but the new settlers who present themselves for admission, must prove their christianity, morality, and good habits, by a certificate from the authorities where they formerly resided. . . .

Art. 7.  The government shall take care, that within the twenty leagues bordering on the limits of the United States of the North, and ten leagues in a straight line from the coast of the Gulph of Mexico, within the limits of this state, there shall be no other settlements, except such as merit the approbation of the supreme government of the Union, for which object, all petitions on the subject, whether made by Mexicans or foreigners, shall be passed to the superior government, accompanied by a corresponding report.

Art. 8.  The projects for new settlements in which one or more persons offer to bring at their own expense, one hundred or more families shall be presented to the government, and if found comfortable with this law, they will be admitted; and the government will immediately designate to the contractors, the land where they are to establish themselves, and the term of six years, within which, they must present the number of families they contracted for, under the penalty of losing the rights and privileges offered in their favor, in proportion to the number of families which they fail to introduce, and the contract totally annulled if they do not bring at least one hundred families.

Art. 9.  Contracts made by the contractors or undertakers, *Empresarios*, with the families brought at their expense, are guaranteed by this law, so far as they are conformable with its provisions. . . .

Art. 11.  A square of land, which on each side has one league or five thousand varas, or what is the same thing, a superficie of twenty-five million varas, shall be called a sitio, and this shall be the unity for counting one, two, or more sitios; and also the unity for counting one, two, or more labors, shall be one million square varas, or one thousand varas on each side which shall compose a labor. The vara for this measurement shall be three geometrical feet.

Art. 12.  Taking the above unity as a basis, and observing the distinction which must be made, between grazing land, or that which is proper for raising of stock, and farming land, with or without the facility of irrigation; this law grants to the contractor or contractors, for the establishment of a new settlement, for each hundred families which he may introduce and establish in the state, five sitios of grazing land, and five labors at least, the one half of which, shall be without the facility of irrigation, but they can only receive this premium for eight hundred families, although a greater number should be introduced, and no fraction whatever,

less than one hundred shall entitle them to any premium, not even proportionally.

Art. 13.  Should any contractor or contractors in virtue of the number of families which he may have introduced, acquire in conformity with the last article, more than eleven square leagues of land, it shall nevertheless be granted, but subject to the condition of alienating the excess, within twelve years, and if it is not done, the respective political authority shall do it, by selling it at public sale, delivering the proceeds to the owners, after deducting the costs of sale.

Art. 14.  To each family comprehended in a contract, whose sole occupation is cultivation of land, one labor shall be given, should he also be stock raiser, grazing land shall be added to complete a sitio, and should his only occupation be raising of stock, he shall only receive a superficie of grazing land, equal to twenty-four million square varas [a sitio less one labor].

Art. 15.  Unmarried men shall receive the same quantity when they enter the matrimonial state, and foreigners who marry native Mexicans, shall receive one fourth more; those who are entirely single, or who do not form a part of some family whether foreigners or natives, shall content themselves with the fourth part of the above mentioned quantity, which is all that can be given them until they marry.

Art. 16.  Families or unmarried men who, entirely of their own accord, have emigrated and may wish to unite themselves to any new towns, can at all times do so, and the same quantity of land shall be assigned them, which is mentioned in the two last articles, but if they do so in the first six years from the establishment of the settlement, one labor more shall be given to families, and single men in place of the quarter designated in the 15th article, shall have the third part.

Art. 17.  It appertains to the government to augment the quantity indicated in the 14, 15, and 16th. articles, in proportion to the family, industry, and activity of the colonists, agreeably to the information given on these subjects by the Ayuntamientos and Commissioners; the said government always observing the provisions of the 12th. article, or the decree of the general congress on the subject.

Art. 18.  The families who emigrate in conformity with the 16th article shall immediately present themselves to the political authority of the place which they may have chosen for their residence, who finding in them the requisites, prescribed by this law for new settlers, shall admit them, and put them in possession of the corresponding lands, and shall immediately give an account thereof to the government; who of themselves, or by means of a person commissioned to that effect, will issue them a title.

Art. 19.  The Indians of all nations, bordering on the state, as well as wandering tribes that may be within its limits, . . . after having first declared themselves in favor of our religion and institutions wish to establish themselves in any settlements that are forming, they shall be admitted, and the same quantity of land given them, as to the settlers, spoken of in the 14th. and 15th. articles, always preferring native Indians to strangers. . . .

Art. 22.  The new settlers as an acknowledgment, shall pay to the state, for each sitio of pasture land, thirty dollars; two dollars and a half, for each labor without the facility of irrigation, and three dollars and a half, for each one that can be irrigated, and so on proportionally according to the quantity and quality of the land distributed; but the said payments need not be made, until six years after the settlement, and by thirds; the first within four years, the second within five years, and the last within six years, under the penalty of losing the land, for a failure, in any of said payments; . . .

Art. 24.   The government will sell to Mexicans, and to them only, such lands as they may wish to purchase, taking care that there shall not be accumulated in the same hands more than eleven sitios; and under the condition, that the purchaser must cultivate what he acquires by this title within six years from its acquisition, under the penalty of losing them; the price of each sitio, subject to the foregoing condition, shall be one hundred dollars, if it be pasture land; one hundred and fifty dollars, if it be farming land without the facility of irrigation; and two hundred dollars if it can be irrigated.

Art. 25.   Until six years after the publication of this law, the legislature of this state, cannot alter it as regards the acknowledgment, and price to be paid for land, or as regards the quantity and quality, to be distributed to the new settlers, or sold to Mexicans.

Art. 26.   The new settlers, who within six years from the date of the possession, have not cultivated or occupied the lands granted them, according to its quality, shall be considered to have renounced them, and the respective political authority, shall immediately proceed to take possession of them, and recall the titles. . . .

Art. 29.   Lands acquired by virtue of this law, shall not by any title whatever, pass into mortmain. . . .

Art. 31.   Foreigners who in conformity with this law, have obtained land, and established themselves in any new settlement, shall be considered from that moment, naturalized in the country; and by marrying a Mexican, they acquire a particular merit to obtain letters of citizenship of the state, subject however to the provisions which may be made relative to both particulars, in the constitution of the state.

Art. 32.   During the first ten years, counting from the day on which the new settlements may have been established, they shall be free from all contributions, of whatever denomination, with the exception of those which, in case of invasion by any enemy, or to prevent it, are generally imposed, and all the produce of agriculture or industry of the new settlers, shall be free from excise duty *Alcabala,* or other duties, throughout every part of the state, with the exception of the duties referred to in the next article; after the termination of that time, the new settlements shall be on the same footing as to taxes, with the old ones, and the colonists shall also in this particular, be on the same footing with the other inhabitants of the state.

Art. 33.   From the day of their settlement, the new colonists shall be at liberty to follow any branch of industry, and can also work mines of every description, communicating with the supreme government of the confederation, relative to the general revenue appertaining to it, and subjecting themselves in all other particulars, to the ordinances or taxes, established or which may be established on this branch.

Art. 34.   Towns shall be founded on the sites deemed most suitable, by the government, or the person commissioned for this effect, and for each one, there shall be designed four square leagues, whose area may be in a regular or irregular form, agreeably to the situation. . . .

Art. 36.   Building lots in the new towns shall be given gratis, to the contractors of them, and also to artists of every class, as many as are necessary for the establishment of their trade; and to the other settlers they shall be sold at public auction, after having been previously valued—under the obligation to pay the purchase money by instalments of one third each; the first in six months, the second in twelve months, and the third in eighteen months; but all owners of lots, including contractors and artists, shall annually pay one dollar for each lot, which, together with the produce of the sales, shall be collected by the Ayuntamientos, and applied to the building of churches in said towns. . . .

Art. 40.   As soon as at least forty families are united in one place, they shall proceed to the formal establishment of the new towns, and all of them shall take an oath, to support the general and state constitutions; which oath will be administered by the commissioner, they shall then, in his presence proceed for the first time, to the election of their municipal authority.

Art. 41.   A new town, whose inhabitants shall not be less than two hundred, shall elect an Ayuntamiento, provided there is not another one established within eight leagues, in which case, it shall be added to it. The number of individuals which are to compose the Ayuntamiento, shall be regulated by the existing laws.

Art. 42.   Foreigners are eligible, subject to the provisions which the constitution of the state may prescribe, to elect the members of their municipal authorities, and to be elected to the same. . . .

Art. 44.   For the opening and improving of roads, and other public works in Texas, the government will transmit to the chief of that department, the individuals, who in other parts of the state, may have been sentenced to public works as vagrants, or for other crimes, these same persons may be employed by individuals for competent wages, and as soon as the time of their condemnation is expired, they can unite themselves as colonists, to any new settlement, and obtain the corresponding lands, if their reformation shall have made them worthy of such favor in the opinion of the chief of the department, without whose certificate, they shall not be admitted.

Art. 45.   The government in accord with the respective ordinary ecclesiastics, will take care to provide the new settlements with the competent number of pastors, and in accord with the same authority, shall propose to the legislature for its approbation, the salary which the said pastors are to receive, which shall be paid by the new settlers. . . .

Art. 46.   As regards the introduction of slaves, the new settlers shall obey the laws already established, and which hereafter may be established on the subject. . . .

Saltillo, 24th March, 1825. — Signed,
Rafael Ramos Y Valdez, President

The Old Three Hundred 51

# 24. THE OLD THREE HUNDRED

## 1824-1828

From Lester G. Bugbee, "The Old Three Hundred," *The Quarterly* of the Texas State Historical Association, I (October, 1897), 108-117.

The colonists settled under the terms of Stephen F. Austin's first contract with the Mexican government became known as "The Old Three Hundred," because the contract was for the introduction of three hundred families. Austin returned to his colony in August, 1823, accompanied from San Antonio by Baron de Bastrop, whom the governor had authorized to issue land titles for him. By August 24, 1824, when he was called away, Bastrop had issued 272 titles to settlers. The remainder, issued in 1827 and 1828 after the arrival of a new land commissioner, brought the total number of families introduced, including "families" of single men who formed partnerships to meet the requirements of the law, to 297. Nine families, not including Austin, received two titles each, and special grants were made to a few men as compensation for substantial services or improvements.

The limits of the colony were not set by the terms of the contract, but the colonists, for the most part, selected the rich bottom lands along the Brazos and Colorado rivers. Others, however, were scattered over the entire territory between the San Jacinto and Lavaca rivers and between the Gulf and the San Antonio-Nacogdoches Road.

The following table, adapted from one compiled from the records of the Land Office at Austin, Texas, by Lester G. Bugbee, gives the names of the colonists, the amount of land each received, the present county in which the land is located, and the date the title was issued. A *sitio* of land is approximately 4428.4 acres, and a *labor* approximately 177.12 acres.

| NAME | AMOUNT Sitios | Labors | LOCATION Present County | Date of Title |
|------|------|------|------|------|
| Allcorn, Elijah | 1/2 | | Washington | July 10, 1824 |
| | 1 | | Fort Bend | July 10, 1824 |
| | | 1 | Waller | July 10, 1824 |
| Allen, Martin | 1 | | Wharton | July 19, 1824 |
| | | 1 | Austin | July 19, 1824 |
| Alley, John | 1 | | Jackson and Lavaca | May 14, 1827 |
| Alley, John | 1 | | Fayette | May 16, 1827 |
| Alley, Rawson | 1 1/2 | | Colorado | Aug. 3, 1824 |
| Alley, Thomas | | | | |
| Alley, William | 1 | | Brazoria | July 29, 1824 |
| Alsbury, Charles G. | 1 1/2 | | Brazoria | Aug. 3, 1824 |
| Alsbury, Harvey | | | | |
| Alsbury, Horace | | | | |
| Alsbury, Thomas | 2 | | Fort Bend and Brazoria | July 8, 1824 |
| | | | Brazoria | July 8, 1824 |
| | 1 1/2 | | Waller | |
| Anderson, S. A. | 1 | | Fayette | Aug. 10, 1824 |

| NAME | AMOUNT Sitios | Labors | LOCATION Present County | Date of Title |
|------|------|------|------|------|
| Andrews, John | 1 | | Fayette and Colorado | July 7, 1824 |
| | | 1 | Waller | July 7, 1824 |
| Andrews, William | 1 | | Fort Bend | July 15, 1824 |
| | | 1 | Fort Bend | July 15, 1824 |
| Angier, Samuel T. | 1 | | Brazoria | Aug. 16, 1824 |
| Angier, Samuel T. | | 1 | Brazoria | Aug. 24, 1824 |
| Austin, John | | 2 | Harris | July 21, 1824 |
| Austin, John | 1 | | Brazoria | Aug. 24, 1824 |
| Austin, Santiago E. B. | 3 | | Brazoria | Aug. 19, 1824 |
| | | | Brazoria | Aug. 19, 1824 |
| Austin, Santiago B. | 1 | | Waller | Aug. 24, 1824 |
| | 5 | | Brazoria | Sept. 1, 1824 |
| | | 7 1/2 | Brazoria | Sept. 1, 1824 |
| | | 1/3 | Brazoria | Sept. 1, 1824 |
| | | 1/2 | Brazoria | Sept. 1, 1824 |
| Austin, Estevan F | | 1/4 | Brazoria | Sept. 1, 1824 |
| | | 1 3/4 | Brazoria | Sept. 1, 1824 |
| | | 2 1/6 | Brazoria | Sept. 1, 1824 |

| NAME | Sitios | Labors | Present County | Date of Title |
|---|---|---|---|---|
| Austin, Estevan F. | 3 1/6 | | Wharton | Sept. 1, 1824 |
| | 2 | | Wharton | Sept. 1, 1824 |
| | 3 | | Brazoria | Sept. 1, 1824 |
| Baily, James B. | 1 | | Brazoria | July 7, 1824 |
| Balis, Daniel E. | 1 | | Matagorda | April 14, 1828 |
| Baratt, William | 1 | | Fort Bend | June 4, 1827 |
| Barnet, Thomas | 1 | | Fort Bend | July 10, 1824 |
| Battle, M. M. | 1 | | Matagorda | Aug. 10, 1824 |
| Battle, Mills M. | 1 | | Fort Bend | May 31, 1827 |
| Beard, James | 1 | | Fort Bend | Aug. 10, 1824 |
| Beason, Benejani | 1 | | Colorado | Aug. 7, 1824 |
| Belknap, Charles | 1 | | Fort Bend | May 22, 1827 |
| Bell, Josiah H. | 1 1/2 | | Brazoria | Aug. 7, 1824 |
| Bell, Thomas B. | 1 | | Brazoria | Aug. 16, 1824 |
| Berry, M. | | | (Partner of M. M. Battle) | |
| Best, Isaac | 1 | | Waller | Aug. 19, 1824 |
| Betts, Jacob | 1 | | Matagorda | Aug. 19, 1824 |
| Biggam, Fras | 1 | | Wharton | July 10, 1824 |
| | 1 | | Brazoria | July 10, 1824 |
| | | | Waller | July 10, 1824 |
| Bloodgood, Wm. | 1 | | Chambers and Harris | Aug. 10, 1824 |
| Boatwright, Thomas | 1 | | Austin | July 27, 1824 |
| Borden, Thos. | 1 | | Brazoria | July 29, 1824 |
| Bostwick, Caleb R. | 1 | | Matagorda | July 24, 1824 |
| Bowman, John T. | 1 | | Matagorda | Aug. 21, 1824 |
| Bradley, Edward R. | 1 | | Brazoria | Aug. 10, 1824 |
| Bradley, John | 1 | | Brazoria | July 8, 1824 |
| Bradley, Thomas | | | (Partner of S. T. Angier) | |
| Breen, Charles | 1 | | Brazoria | May 24, 1824 |

| NAME | Sitios | Labors | Present County | Date of Title |
|---|---|---|---|---|
| Brias, Patrick | 1 | | Harris | May 1, 1827 |
| Bridges, Wm. B. | 1 | | Jackson | July 21, 1824 |
| Bright, David | 1 | | Fort Bend | July 15, 1824 |
| | | 1 | Austin | July 15, 1824 |
| Brinson, Enoch | 1 | | Harris | Aug. 7, 1824 |
| Brooks, Bluford | 1 | | (Forfeited) | Aug. 10, 1824 |
| Brotherington, Robt. | | | (Partner of Caleb R. Bostwick) | |
| Brown, George | | | (Partner of Charles Belknap) | |
| Brown, John | 1 | | Harris | Aug. 19, 1824 |
| | | 1 | Waller | Aug. 19, 1824 |
| Brown, William S. | 1 | | Washington | July 29, 1824 |
| Buckner, Aylett C. | 1 | | Matagorda | July 24, 1824 |
| Buckner, Aylett C. | 2 | | Matagorda | Aug. 24, 1824 |
| Burnet, Pumphrey | 1 | | Matagorda | July 24, 1824 |
| Burnam, Jesse | 1 | | Fayette | Aug. 16, 1824 |
| | | 1 | Colorado | Aug. 16, 1824 |
| Byrd, Micajah | 1 | | Washington | July 16, 1824 |
| Calliham, Mosis A. | 1 | | Harris | Aug. 3, 1824 |
| Calvit, Alexr. | 1 | | Brazoria | Aug. 3, 1824 |
| | | 1 | Waller | Aug. 3, 1824 |
| | | 1 | Brazoria | Aug. 3, 1824 |
| Carpenter, David | 1 | | Harris | Aug. 16, 1824 |
| Carson, Wm. C. | 1 | | Brazoria | May 15, 1827 |
| Carter, Saml. | 1 | | Brazoria | July 8, 1824 |
| Cartwright, Jesse H. | 1 | | Fort Bend | Mar. 31, 1828 |
| | | 1 | Lavaca | Mar. 31, 1828 |
| Cartwright, Thomas | 1 | | Colorado | Aug. 10, 1824 |
| | | 1 | Austin | Aug. 10, 1824 |
| Castleman, Sylvenus | 2 | | Wharton | July 7, 1824 |
| | 1/2 | | Fayette | July 7, 1824 |
| | | 2 | Austin | July 7, 1824 |
| Chance, Samuel | 1 | | Brazoria | July 27, 1824 |

| NAME | Sitios | Labors | Present County | Date of Title |
|---|---|---|---|---|
| Charles, Isaac N. | 1 | | Brazoria | May 21, 1827 |
| Chriesman, Horatio | 1 | | Fort Bend | July 8, 1824 |
| | 2 | | Austin | July 8, 1824 |
| Clarke, Antony R. | 1 | | Brazoria | Aug. 24, 1824 |
| Clark, John C. | 1 | | Wharton | July 16, 1824 |
| Coats, Merit M. | 1 | | Waller | July 19, 1824 |
| Coles, Jno. P. | 7 1/2 | | Burleson and Washington | Aug. 19, 1824 |
| | 1/2 | | Washington | Aug. 19, 1824 |
| | 1/2 | | Brazoria | Aug. 19, 1824 |
| Cooke, Jno. | | | (Partner of Isaac Hughes) | |
| | 1 | | Harris | Aug. 10, 1824 |
| Cook, James | 1 | | Colorado | Aug. 3, 1824 |
| Cooper, William | 1 | | Matagorda | July 24, 1824 |
| Cooper, William | 1 1/2 | | Waller | Aug. 10, 1824 |
| | 2 | | Austin | Aug. 10, 1824 |
| Crier, John | 1 | | Matagorda | June 6, 1827 |
| Crownover, John | 1 | | Wharton and Matagorda | Aug. 3, 1824 |
| | 1 | | Austin | Aug. 3, 1824 |
| Cummings, James | 1 | | Brazoria | Aug. 16, 1824 |
| | 5 | | (Forfeited) | Aug. 16, 1824 |
| Cummings, John | 1 | | Brazoria | July 21, 1824 |
| Cummings, Rebecca | 1 | | Brazoria | July 21, 1824 |
| | 2 | | Waller | July 21, 1824 |
| Cummings, William | 1 | | Brazoria | July 21, 1824 |
| Cummins, James | 1 | | Colorado | July 7, 1824 |
| | 5 | | Austin | July 7, 1824 |
| | 1 | | Colorado | July 7, 1824 |
| Curtis, James, Sr. | 1 | | Burleson | Aug. 3, 1824 |
| Curtis, James, Jr. | 1 | | Brazos | Aug. 19, 1824 |
| Curtis, Hinton | 1 | | Matagorda | Aug. 10, 1824 |
| Davidson, Samuel | 1 | | Brazos | July 21, 1824 |

| NAME | Sitios | Labors | Present County | Date of Title |
|---|---|---|---|---|
| Davis, Thomas | 1 | | Austin | July 29, 1824 |
| Deckrow, D. | 1 | | Matagorda | July 24, 1824 |
| Demos, Charles | 1 | | Matagorda | Aug. 3, 1824 |
| Demos, Peter | 1 | | Matagorda | |
| Dewees, Wm. B. | | | (Partner of James Cook) | |
| Dickinson, John | 1 | | Galveston and Harris | Aug. 19, 1824 |
| Dillard, Nicholas | 1 | | Brazoria | Aug. 16, 1824 |
| Duke, Thomas M. | 1 | | Matagorda | July 24, 1824 |
| Duty, George | 1 | | Fayette | July 19, 1824 |
| Duty, Joseph | 1 | | Colorado | July 19, 1824 |
| Dyer, Clement C. | 1 | | Colorado | Aug. 10, 1824 |
| Dyer, Clement C. | 1 1/2 | | Waller | Aug. 24, 1824 |
| Earle, Thos. | 1 | | Harris | July 7, 1824 |
| | | 1 | Harris | July 7, 1824 |
| Edwards, G. E. | 1 | | Wharton | Aug. 19, 1824 |
| Elam, John | 1 | | (Forfeited) | Aug. 7, 1824 |
| Elder, Robert | | 1 | Waller | Aug. 24, 1824 |
| Falenash, Charles | 1 | | Burleson | Aug. 19, 1824 |
| Fenton, David | 1 | | Matagorda | July 29, 1824 |
| Fields, John F. | | 1 | Brazoria | Aug. 24, 1824 |
| Fisher, James | 1 | | Burleson | July 19, 1824 |
| Fitzgerald, David | 1 | | Fort Bend | July 10, 1824 |
| Flanakin, Isaiah | | 2 | Austin | July 19, 1824 |
| Flowers, Elisha | 1 | | Matagorda | July 19, 1824 |
| | | 1 | Colorado | July 19, 1824 |
| Foster, Isaac | 1 | | Matagorda | Aug. 10, 1824 |
| Foster, John | 2 1/2 | 3 | Fort Bend | July 15, 1824 / July 15, 1824 |

| NAME | AMOUNT Sitios | Labors | LOCATION Present County | Date of Title |
|---|---|---|---|---|
| Foster, Randolph | 1 | | Waller and Fort Bend | July 16, 1824 |
| Frazier, James | 1 | | Austin and Fort Bend | July 24, 1824 |
| Fulshear, Charles | 1 | | Fort Bend | July 16, 1824 |
| Garret, Charles | 1 | 1 | Brazoria / Waller | July 15, 1824 / July 15, 1824 |
| Gates, Samuel | 1/2 / 1/2 | | Washington / Washington | July 8, 1824 / July 8, 1824 |
| Gates, William | 1 / 1 | | Washington / Washington | July 16, 1824 / July 16, 1824 |
| George, Freeman | 1 | 1 | Matagorda / Waller | July 7, 1824 / July 7, 1824 |
| Gilbert, Preston | 1 | | Colorado | June 4, 1827 |
| Gilbert, Sarah | 1 | | Wharton and Fort Bend | May 11, 1827 |
| Gilleland, Daniel | 1 | | Austin | Aug. 3, 1824 |
| Gorbet, Chester S. | 1 | | Brazoria | July 19, 1824 |
| Gouldrich, Michael | 1 | | Galveston | Aug. 24, 1824 |
| Gray, Thos. | 1 / 1 | | Brazoria / Colorado | Aug. 16, 1824 / Aug. 16, 1824 |
| Groce, Jared E. | 5 / 2 / 3 | | Brazoria / Waller / Grimes | July 29, 1824 / July 29, 1824 / July 29, 1824 |
| Guthrie, Robert | 1 | | Jackson | July 19, 1824 |
| Haddan, John | 1 | | Colorado | July 29, 1824 |
| Hady, Samuel C. | 1 | | Waller | Aug. 19, 1824 |
| Hall, Geo. B. | | | (Partner of Samuel T. Angier) | |
| Hall, John W. | 2 | 2 | Brazoria / Waller | July 10, 1824 / July 10, 1824 |
| Hall, W. J. | 1 | | Fort Bend | July 10, 1824 |
| Hamilton, David | 1 | | Wharton | May 9, 1827 |
| Harris, Abner | | | (Partner of William Baratt) | |

| NAME | AMOUNT Sitios | Labors | LOCATION Present County | Date of Title |
|---|---|---|---|---|
| Harris, David | 1 | | Harris | Aug. 19, 1824 |
| Harris, John R. | 1 | | Harris | Aug. 16, 1824 |
| Harris, William | | | (Partner of David Carpenter) | |
| Harris, William | 1 | | Brazoria | July 10, 1824 |
| Harris, William J. | | 1 | Harris | July 21, 1824 |
| Harrison, George | 1 | | Brazoria | Aug. 16, 1824 |
| Harvey, William | 1 | | Austin | July 20, 1824 |
| Haynes, Thomas S. | 1 | | Brazos | Aug. 16, 1824 |
| Hensley, James | 1 | 1 | Brazoria / Austin | Aug. 3, 1824 / Aug. 3, 1824 |
| Hodge, Alexander | 1 | | Fort Bend | April 12, 1828 |
| Holland, Francis | 1 | | Grimes | Aug. 10, 1824 |
| Holland, William | 1 | | Grimes | Aug. 10, 1824 |
| Holliman, Kinchen | 1 | | (Forfeited) | Aug. 10, 1824 |
| Hope, James | 1 / 1/4 | 2 | Brazos / Brazos | July 10, 1824 / July 10, 1824 / July 10, 1824 |
| Hudson, C. S. | 1 | | Wharton | July 29, 1824 |
| Huff, John | 1 | | Wharton | July 10, 1824 |
| Huff, George | 1 1/2 | | Wharton and Fort Bend | Aug. 19, 1824 |
| Hughes, Isaac | | | (Partner of John Cooke) (Forfeited) | |
| Hunter, Eli | 1 | | Wharton | July 24, 1824 |
| Hunter, Johnson | 1 | | Harris | Aug. 10, 1824 |
| Iiams, John | 1 | | Chambers | Aug. 7, 1824 |
| Ingram, Ira | | 1 | Waller | Aug. 24, 1824 |
| Ingram, Seth | 2 | 1 | Wharton / Austin | July 29, 1824 / July 29, 1824 |
| Irons, John | 1 | | Waller | July 16, 1824 |
| Isaacks, Samuel | 1 | | Fort Bend | July 15, 1824 |

| NAME | Sitios | Labors | Present County | Date of Title |
|---|---|---|---|---|
| Jackson, Alexander | 2 | | Wharton | July 16, 1824 |
| Jackson, Humphrey | 1 | | Harris | Aug. 16, 1824 |
| | | 1 | Harris | Aug. 16, 1824 |
| Jackson, Isaac | 1 | | Grimes | Aug. 7, 1824 |
| Jamison, Thomas | 1 | | Matagorda and Brazoria | July 24, 1824 |
| Johnson, Henry W. | | | (Partner of Thos. H. Borden) | |
| Jones, Henry | 1 | | Fort Bend | July 8, 1824 |
| Jones, J. W. | 1 | | Wharton | Aug. 10, 1824 |
| | | 1 | Fort Bend | Aug. 10, 1824 |
| Jones, Oliver | 1 | | Brazoria | Aug. 10, 1824 |
| | | 1 | Austin | Aug. 10, 1824 |
| Jones, R. | 1/2 | | Wharton | July 15, 1824 |
| Jones, R. (Cont'd.) | 1/2 | | Fort Bend | July 15, 1824 |
| | | 1 | Fort Bend | July 15, 1824 |
| Keep, Imla | 1 | | Brazoria | July 24, 1824 |
| Keller, John C. | 1 | | Matagorda | June 4, 1827 |
| Kelly, John | 2 | | Brazos | July 19, 1824 |
| Kennedy, Sam'l. | | 1 | Fort Bend | July 7, 1824 |
| | | | Austin | July 7, 1824 |
| Kennon, Alfred | 1 | | Burleson | July 19, 1824 |
| Kerr, James | 1 | | Jackson | May 6, 1827 |
| Kerr, Peter | 1 | | Washington | Aug. 10, 1824 |
| Kerr, William | | | | |
| Kincheloe, William | 1 | | Wharton | July 8, 1824 |
| | | 1 | Wharton | July 8, 1824 |
| Kingston, William | 1 | | Matagorda | May 8, 1827 |
| Knight, James | 1 | | Fort Bend | July 15, 1824 |
| | | 1 | Fort Bend | July 15, 1824 |
| Kuykendall, Abner | 1 | | Fort Bend | July 7, 1824 |
| | 1/2 | | Washington | July 7, 1824 |
| | | 2 | Austin | July 7, 1824 |
| Kuykendall, Brazilla | 1 | | Austin | Aug. 7, 1824 |

| NAME | Sitios | Labors | Present County | Date of Title |
|---|---|---|---|---|
| Kuykendall, Robert | 1 | | Wharton | |
| | | 1 | Wharton | |
| Kuykendall, Joseph | 1 | | Fort Bend | July 8, 1824 |
| League, Hosea H. | 1 | | Matagorda | May 25, 1827 |
| Leakey, Joel | 1 | | Washington and Austin | May 28, 1827 |
| Linsey, Benjamin | 1 | | (Forfeited) | Aug. 19, 1824 |
| Little, John | 1 | | Austin | May 21, 1828 |
| | | 1 | Fort Bend | May 21, 1828 |
| Little, William | 1 | | Fort Bend | July 10, 1824 |
| | | 1 | Fort Bend | July 10, 1824 |
| Long, Jane H. | 1 | | Fort Bend | April 30, 1827 |
| | | 1 | Waller | May 1, 1827 |
| Lynch, James | 1 | | Washington | July 16, 1824 |
| Lynch, Nathanael | 1 | | Harris | Aug. 19, 1824 |
| McCroskey, John | 1 | | Brazoria | Aug. 16, 1824 |
| | | 1 | Austin | Aug. 16, 1824 |
| McCormick, Arthur | 1 | | Harris | Aug. 10, 1824 |
| McCormick, David | 1 | | Brazoria | July 21, 1824 |
| McCormick, John | | | (Partner of James Frazier) | |
| McCoy, Thomas | | | (Partner of Daniel Deckrow) | |
| McFarlan, Aechilles | 1 | | Brazoria | July 10, 1824 |
| | | 1 1/2 | Waller | July 10, 1824 |
| McFarlan, John | 1 1/4 | | Waller | Aug. 10, 1824 |
| | | 1 | Waller | Aug. 10, 1824 |
| McKenney, Thos. F. | 1 | | Brazos | Aug. 16, 1824 |
| McKinsey, Hugh | 1 | | Wharton and Matagorda | Aug. 3, 1824 |
| McClain, A. W. | 1 | | Colorado | July 24, 1824 |
| McNair, James | | | | |
| McNeel, Daniel | 1 | | Brazoria | Aug. 3, 1824 |
| McNeel, George W. | 1/2 | | Brazoria | Aug. 10, 1824 |
| McNeel, John G. | 1/2 | | Brazoria | Aug. 10, 1824 |

| NAME | Sitios | Labors | LOCATION Present County | Date of Title |
|---|---|---|---|---|
| McNeel, John | 1 | | Brazoria | Aug. 3, 1824 |
| McNeel, Pleasant D. | 1 | | Brazoria | Aug. 7, 1824 |
| McNeel, Sterling | 1 | | Brazoria | Aug. 19, 1824 |
| McNutt, Elizabeth | 1 | | Jackson | July 21, 1824 |
| McWilliams, William | 1 | | Burleson | July 19, 1824 |
| Marsh, Shubael | 1 | | Brazoria | July 8, 1824 |
| Martin, Wily | 1 | | Brazoria | July 29, 1824 |
| Mathis, William | 1 | | Brazos | July 19, 1824 |
| Milburn, David H. | | | (Partner of Thomas Davis) | |
| Miller, Samuel | 1 | | Washington | Aug. 19, 1824 |
| Miller, Samuel R. | 1 | | Washington | Aug. 19, 1824 |
| Miller, Simon | 1 | | Fort Bend | Aug. 7, 1824 |
| Millican, James D. | 1 | | Brazos | July 16, 1824 |
| Millican, Robert | 2 1/2 | | Brazos | July 16, 1824 |
| Millican, William | 1 | | Brazos | July 16, 1824 |
| Minus, Joseph | 1 | | Brazoria | Aug. 19, 1824 |
| Mitchell, Asa | 1 | 1/2 | Brazoria | Aug. 7, 1824 |
| | | | Brazoria | Aug. 7, 1824 |
| Mitchell, Asa | 1 | | Brazoria | Aug. 24, 1824 |
| Monks, John L. | 1 | | (Forfeited) | Aug. 16, 1824 |
| Moore, John H. | | | (Partner of Thomas Gray) | |
| Moore, Luke | 1 | | Harris | Aug. 3, 1824 |
| Morrison, Moses | | | (Partner of William Cooper) | |
| Morton, William | 1 1/2 | 1 | Fort Bend | July 15, 1824 |
| | | | Fort Bend | July 15, 1824 |
| Mouser, David | 1 | | Waller | Aug. 19, 1824 |
| Nelson, James | 1 | | Colorado | Aug. 7, 1824 |
| Newman, Joseph | 1 | 1 | Wharton | Aug. 10, 1824 |
| | | | Austin | Aug. 10, 1824 |

| NAME | Sitios | Labors | LOCATION Present County | Date of Title |
|---|---|---|---|---|
| Nuckols, M.B. | 1 | | Matagorda and Brazoria | Aug. 3, 1824 |
| | | 1 | Brazoria | Aug. 3, 1824 |
| Orrick, James | 1 | | Austin | Aug. 10, 1824 |
| Osborn, Nathan | 1 | | Colorado | July 24, 1824 |
| Parks, Wm. | 1 | | Wharton | July 24, 1824 |
| Parker, Joshua | | | | |
| Parker, William | 1 | | Brazoria | July 8, 1824 |
| | | 1 | Waller | July 8, 1824 |
| Pennington, Isaac | 1 | | Fort Bend | Aug. 3, 1824 |
| Pentecost, George S. | 1 | | Matagorda | Aug. 19, 1824 |
| Pettus, Freeman | 1 | | Colorado and Fayette | Aug. 3, 1824 |
| | | 1 | Matagorda and Brazoria | Aug. 3, 1824 |
| | | | Colorado | Aug. 3, 1824 |
| Pettus, William | 1 | | Wharton | July 10, 1824 |
| | | 1 | Fort Bend | July 10, 1824 |
| | | | Waller | July 10, 1824 |
| Petty, John | 1 | | Fayette | Aug. 10, 1824 |
| Peyton, J. C. | 1 | | Matagorda | Aug. 25, 1827 |
| Phelps, James A. E. | 1 | 2 | Brazoria | Aug. 16, 1824 |
| | | | Brazoria | Aug. 16, 1824 |
| Phillips, I. B. | 1 | | Wharton | May 9, 1827 |
| Phillips, Zeno | 1 | | Brazoria | July 19, 1824 |
| Picket, Pamelia | 1 | | Matagorda | July 21, 1824 |
| | | 1 | Austin | July 21, 1824 |
| Polley, Joseph H. | | | (Partner of Samuel Chance) | |
| Polley, Joseph H. | 1 | | Fort Bend | Aug. 16, 1824 |
| Powell, Peter | | | (Partner of William Kingston) | |
| Prater, William | 1 | | Brazoria | July 19, 1824 |
| | | 1 | Austin | July 19, 1824 |
| Pruitt, Pleasant | 1 | | Matagorda | July 24, 1824 |

| NAME | Sitios | Labors | Present County | Date of Title |
|---|---|---|---|---|
| Pryor, William | 1 | | Waller | Aug. 24, 1824 |
| Rabb, Andrew | 1 1/2 | | Wharton | Aug. 10, 1824 |
| Rabb, John | 1 | | Fort Bend | July 8, 1824 |
| | | 2 | Austin | July 8, 1824 |
| Rabb, Thomas J. | 1 | | Wharton | July 24, 1824 |
| Rabb, William | 3 | | Fayette | July 19, 1824 |
| | 2 | | Matagorda | July 19, 1824 |
| Rabb, William | 2 | | Fayette | Aug. 24, 1824 |
| Raleigh, William | 1 | | Burleson | Aug. 16, 1824 |
| Ramey, L. | 1 | | Matagorda | May 23, 1827 |
| Randon, David | | | (Partner of Isaac Pennington) | |
| Randon, John | 1 | | Fort Bend | Aug. 19, 1824 |
| Rankin, Frederic H. | 1 | | Harris | July 7, 1824 |
| | | 1 | Harris | July 7, 1824 |
| Rawls, Amos | 1 | | Matagorda | July 24, 1824 |
| Rawls, Benjamin | 1 | | Matagorda | Aug. 3, 1824 |
| Rawls, Daniel | 1 1/4 | | Matagorda | July 24, 1824 |
| Richardson, Stephen | 1 | | Brazoria | July 10, 1824 |
| Roark, Elijah | 1 | | Fort Bend | July 10, 1824 |
| | | 1 | Waller | July 10, 1824 |
| Robbins, Earle | 1 | | Austin | July 19, 1824 |
| Robbins, William | 1 | | Brazoria | July 19, 1824 |
| | | 1 | Austin | July 19, 1824 |
| Roberts, Andrew | 1 | | Fort Bend | May 10, 1827 |
| Roberts, Noel F. | 1 1/4 | | Fort Bend | July 15, 1824 |
| Roberts, William | 1 | | Brazoria | July 8, 1824 |
| Robertson, Edward | 1 | | Fort Bend | Mar. 31, 1828 |
| Robinson, A. | 1 1/2 | | Brazoria | July 8, 1824 |
| | 1/2 | | Washington | July 8, 1824 |
| | | 1 | Waller | July 8, 1824 |
| Robinson, Geo. | 1 | | Brazoria | July 8, 1824 |

| NAME | Sitios | Labors | Present County | Date of Title |
|---|---|---|---|---|
| Ross, James | 1 | | Colorado | July 19, 1824 |
| San Pierre, Joseph | 1 | | Fort Bend | Aug. 24, 1824 |
| Scobey, Robert | 1 | | Wharton | Aug. 3, 1824 |
| Scott, James | 1 | | Fort Bend | Aug. 7, 1824 |
| Scott, Wm. | 1 | | Harris | Aug. 19, 1824 |
| | | | Harris | Aug. 19, 1824 |
| | | 1 | Harris | Aug. 19, 1824 |
| Selkirk, William | 1 | | Matagorda | Aug. 10, 1824 |
| Shelby, David | | | (Partner of John McCormick) | |
| Shipman, Daniel | | | (Partner of Isaac N. Charles) | |
| Shipman, Moses | 1 | | Fort Bend | July 19, 1824 |
| | | 1 | Austin | July 19, 1824 |
| Sims, Bartlet | 1 | | Wharton | Aug. 7, 1824 |
| Singleton, G. W. | 1 | | Wharton | May 14, 1827 |
| Singleton, Phillip | 1 | | Burleson and Washington | Aug. 19, 1824 |
| Smith, Christian | 1 | | Harris and Chambers | July 19, 1824 |
| Smith, Cornelius | 1 | | Brazoria | Aug. 10, 1824 |
| Smith, John | | | (Partner of Hugh McKinsey) | |
| Smeathers, William | 1 | | Austin | July 16, 1824 |
| Snider, Gabriel S. | 1 | | Colorado | Aug. 7, 1824 |
| Sojourner, Albert L. | | | (Partner of Pumphrey Burnet) | |
| Spencer, Nancy | 1 | | Fort Bend | Aug. 19, 1824 |
| Stafford, Adam | | 1 | Waller | Aug. 24, 1824 |
| Stafford, William | 1 1/2 | | Fort Bend | Aug. 16, 1824 |
| | | 1 | Waller | |
| Stevens, Thomas | 1 | | Waller | Aug. 7, 1824 |
| Stout, Owen H. | | | (Partner of Benjamin Rawls) | |
| Strange, James | | 1 | Harris | Aug. 24, 1824 |
| Sutherland, Walter | 1 | | Brazos | Aug. 10, 1824 |

| NAME | AMOUNT Sitios | Labors | LOCATION Present County | Date of Title |
|---|---|---|---|---|
| Tally, David | 1 | | Brazoria | Aug. 16, 1824 |
| | | 1 | Austin | Aug. 16, 1824 |
| Taylor, John I. | 1 | | Harris | Aug. 10, 1824 |
| Teel, George | 1 | | Fort Bend | Aug. 3, 1824 |
| Thomas, Ezekiel | 1 | | Harris | Aug. 19, 1824 |
| Thomas, Jacob | | 1 | Waller | Aug. 24, 1824 |
| Thompson, Jesse | 1 | | Brazoria | Aug. 7, 1824 |
| Tone, Thomas J. | | | (Partner of Thomas Jamison) | |
| Tong, James F. | 1 | | Brazoria | Aug. 19, 1824 |
| Toy, Samuel | 1 | | Austin | May 7, 1827 |
| Trobough, John | | | (Partner of Patrick Brias) | |
| Tumlinson, Elizabeth | 1 | | Colorado | Aug. 16, 1824 |
| | 1 | | Colorado | Aug. 16, 1824 |
| Tumlinson, James | 1 | | Colorado | Aug. 19, 1824 |
| | 1/2 | | Wharton | Aug. 19, 1824 |
| | 1 | | Colorado | Aug. 19, 1824 |
| Vandorn, Isaac | | | (Partner of Daniel E. Baylis) | |
| Varner, Martin | 1 | | Brazoria | July 8, 1824 |
| | | 1 | Waller | July 8, 1824 |
| Vince, Allen | | | (Partner of M. A. Calliham) | |
| Vince, Richard / Vince, Robt. | 1 | | Harris | Aug. 21, 1824 |
| Vince, Wm. | 1 | | Harris | July 21, 1824 |
| Walker, James | 1 | | Washington | July 21, 1824 |
| Walker, Thomas | | | (Partner of Thomas H. Borden) | |
| Wallice, Caleb | 1 | | Grimes | May 14, 1828 |
| Wells, Francis F. | 1 | | Jackson | July 21, 1824 |
| | | 1 | Brazoria | July 21, 1824 |
| Westall, Thomas | 1 | | Wharton | July 19, 1824 |
| | 1 | | Fort Bend | July 19, 1824 |
| | 2 | | Austin | July 19, 1824 |
| White, Amy | 1 | | Harris | Aug. 16, 1824 |
| White, Joseph | 1 | | Brazoria | Aug. 16, 1824 |
| White, Reuben | 1 | | Harris | Aug. 19, 1824 |
| White, Walter C. | | | (Partner of James Knight) | |
| White, William C. | 1 | | Austin | Aug. 19, 1824 |
| Whitesides, Boland / Whitesides, Henry | 1 | | Brazos and Grimes | Aug. 10, 1824 |
| Whitesides, James | 1 | | Grimes and Brazos | July 16, 1824 |
| | | 1 | Waller | July 16, 1824 |
| Whitesides, William | 1 | | Waller | July 19, 1824 |
| Whiting, Nathl. | | | (Partner of Nathan Osborn) | |
| Whitlock, William | 1 | | Harris | Aug. 16, 1824 |
| Wightman, Elias D. | 1 | | Matagorda | May 25, 1827 |
| Wilkins, Jane | 1 | | Fort Bend | May 26, 1827 |
| Williams, George I. | 1 | | Matagorda | Aug. 19, 1824 |
| Williams, Henry | | | (Partner of John J. Bowman) | |
| Williams, John | | | (Partner of Mills M. Battle) | |
| Williams, John | | 1 | Waller | Aug. 24, 1824 |
| Williams, John R. | | 1 | (Forfeited) | July 29, 1824 |
| | | | (Forfeited) | July 29, 1824 |
| Williams, Robt. H. | 1 | | Matagorda | Aug. 19, 1824 |
| Williams, Samuel M. | | | Brazoria | Aug. 10, 1824 |
| | | | Brazoria | Aug. 10, 1824 |
| | | 1 | Waller | Aug. 10, 1824 |
| | | 1 | Austin | Aug. 10, 1824 |
| | | 1 | Brazoria | Aug. 10, 1824 |
| Williams, Solomon | 1 | | Matagorda | Aug. 7, 1824 |
| | | 1 | Waller | Aug. 7, 1824 |
| Williams, Thomas | 1 | | Matagorda | Aug. 16, 1824 |
| Woods, Zadock | | 1 | Matagorda | May 15, 1827 |

## 25. DE WITT'S EMPRESARIO CONTRACT
### April 15, 1825

From Ethel Ziveley Rather, "De Witt's Colony," *The Quarterly* of The Texas State Historical Association, VIII (October, 1904), 173-175.

Next to Austin, Green De Witt was the most successful of the *empresarios* who contracted to bring settlers to Texas under the terms of the colonization law of 1825. De Witt petitioned the state authorities at Saltillo on April 7, 1825, for permission "to colonize with four hundred industrious Catholic families" in accordance with the colonization law the lands between the Lavaca River and a line two leagues west of and parallel to the Guadalupe River and between the San Antonio-Nacogdoches Road and the ten-league reservation adjacent to the Gulf. The contract, signed by De Witt and the state officials on April 15, 1825, follows.

Conditions upon which is allowed the projected introduction by Green De Witt, a citizen of the United States of North America, of four hundred families as colonists into the department of Texas.

1st. Inasmuch as the plan presented in the preceding memorial by the person concerned conforms to the colonization law of the honorable congress of the state, adopted March 24, the government consents to it, and, therefore, in fulfillment of article 8 [of this colonization law], and in consideration of his petition, assigns to him the land for which he asks, contained within these limits: Beginning on the right bank of the Arroyo de la Vaca at a distance of the reserved ten leagues from the coast, adjoining the colony of Stephen Austin, the line shall go up this *arroyo* as far as the Béjar-Nacogdoches road; it shall follow this road toward the west until it reaches a point two leagues west of the Guadalupe River; from there it shall run parallel with the river south toward the coast until it reaches the ten-league coast reservation; thence it shall run along the inner edge of this reservation toward the east to the place of beginning.

2nd. The *empresario* shall respect the rights of individuals legally possessed of lands within this district.

3rd. In accordance with the above-mentioned colonization law of March 24, the *empresario*, Green De Witt, shall be obliged under penalty of losing the rights and privileges guaranteed by article 8 of this law, to introduce the four hundred families within the term of six years beginning from to-day.

4th. The families that shall compose this colony, besides being Catholic, as the *empresario* promises in his petition, must also be able to prove, by certificates from the authorities of the localities from which they come, their good moral character.

5th. The *empresario* shall not introduce into his colony criminals, vagrants, or persons of bad morals, and if such be found there he shall cause them to leave the republic, by force of arms if necessary.

6th. To this end he shall organize, in accordance with law, the national militia, and he shall be commanding officer of it until other arrangements shall be made.

7th. When he shall have introduced at least one hundred families he must advise the government, in order that a commissioner may be sent to put the colonists in possession of their lands according to law, and to establish towns, for which he shall carry competent instructions.

8th. Official correspondence with the government or with the state authorities, legal instruments, and other public documents must be written in Spanish, and when towns shall have been formed, it shall be the duty of the *empresario* to establish schools in that language.

9th. It shall also be his duty to erect churches in the new towns; to provide them with ornaments, sacred vessels, and other adornments dedicated to divine worship; and to apply in due time for the priests needed for the administration of spiritual instruction.

10th. In all matters not here referred to he shall be governed by the constitution, the general laws of the nation, and the special laws of the state which he adopts as his own. . . .

## 26. THE FREDONIAN DECLARATION OF INDEPENDENCE
### December 21, 1826

From H. P. N. Gammel (comp.), *The Laws of Texas*, 1822-1897 (10 vols.; Austin, 1898), I, 107-110.

On April 15, 1825, Haden Edwards secured an *empresario* grant to settle eight hundred families on the unoccupied lands covering a large area in the vicinity of Nacogdoches. Within the limits of the grant were descendants of the old Spanish settlers; a number of Anglo-Americans and Mexicans who had obtained land grants from the Mexican government; a group of about thirty families who, having started for Austin's colony but having stopped on the San Jacinto, had been incorporated into "The Old Three Hundred;" and finally, the squatters, some of whom had arrived before 1819 under the illusion that they would be within the United States when the boundary was established.

Edwards, asserting more power than his contract conferred upon him, charged a higher fee for the lands than the government price, and threatened to expel those who already held legal title unless they paid the difference. Both the squatters and those claiming rights under Spanish and Mexican grants hastened to obtain or perfect their titles, and Edwards, discovering evidences of fraud, announced that all titles must be brought to him for approval. When he questioned the validity of some, the political chief held that his action was unwarranted.

The issue became involved in the election for an alcalde. Edwards' son-in-law received the majority of votes, but the political chief threw out those cast by the squatters residing within the twenty-league prohibited zone adjacent to the United States and installed in office the anti-Edwards candidate who proceeded to decide most title controversies against Edwards. In Haden Edwards' absence, his brother, Benjamin W., wrote complaining about the situation to the governor, who took offense at the tone of the letter and on October 2, 1826, cancelled Edwards' contract. Feeling that he had been dealt with unjustly and standing to lose a heavy capital investment, Edwards rebelled and negotiated a treaty with the Cherokees, who were resentful toward Mexico for having refused them a land grant. The treaty, signed at Nacogdoches on December 21, 1826, provided that in return for their aid in the insurrection the Cherokees were to have the territory lying north of an east-west line drawn a short distance north of Nacogdoches, and embodied a declaration of independence of Texas. The document follows.

Whereas, the Government of the Mexican United States, have by repeated insults, treachery and oppression, reduced the White and Red emigrants from the United States of North America, now living in the Province of Texas, within the Territory of the said Government, into which they have been deluded by promises solemnly made, and most basely broken, to the dreadful alternative of either submitting their freeborn necks to the yoke of an imbecile, faithless, and despotic government, miscalled a Republic; or of taking up arms in defence of their unalienable rights and asserting their Independence; They —viz:—The White emigrants now assembled in the town of Nacogdoches, around the Independent Standard, on the one part, and the Red emigrants who have espoused the same Holy Cause, on the other, in order to prosecute more speedily and effectually the War of Independence, they have mutually undertaken, to a successful issue, and to bind themselves by the ligaments of reciprocal interests and obligations, have resolved to form a Treaty of Union, League and Confederation.

For the illustrious object, BENJAMIN W. EDWARDS and HARMAN B. MAYO, Agents of the Committee of Independence, and RICHARD FIELDS and JOHN D. HUNTER, the Agents of the Red people, being respectively furnished with due powers, have agreed to the following Articles.

1. The above named contracting parties, bind themselves to a solemn Union, League and Confederation, in Peace and War, to establish and defend their mutual independence of the Mexican United States.

2. The contracting parties guaranty, mutually, to the extent of their power, the integrity of their respective Territories, as now agreed upon and described, viz: The Territory apportioned to the Red people, shall begin at the Sandy Spring, where Bradley's road takes off from the road leading from Nacogdoches to the Plantation of Joseph Dust, from thence West, by the Compass, without regard to variation, to the Rio Grande, thence to the head of the Rio Grande, thence with the mountains to the head of Big Red River, thence north to the boundary of the United States of North America, thence with the same line to the mouth of Sulphur Fork, thence in a right line to the beginning.

The territory apportioned to the White people, shall comprehend all the residue of the Province of Texas, and of such other portions of the Mexican United States, as the contracting parties, by their mutual efforts and resources, may render Independent, provided the same shall not extend further west than the Rio Grande.

3. The contracting parties mutually guaranty the rights of Empressarios to their premium lands only, and the rights of all other individuals, acquired under the Mexican Government, and relating or appertaining to the above described Territories, provided the said Empresarios and individuals do not forfeit the same by an opposition to the Independence of the said Territories, or by withdrawing their aid and support to its accomplishment.

4. It is distinctly understood by the contracting parties, that the Territory apportioned to the Red people, is intended as well for the benefit of the Tribes now settled within the Territory apportioned to the White people, as for those living in the former Territory, and that is incumbent upon the contracting parties for the Red people to offer the said Tribes a participation in the same.

5. It is also mutually agreed by the contracting parties, that every individual, Red and White, who has made improvement within either of the Respective Allied Territories and lives upon the same, shall have a fee simple of a section of land including his improvement, as well as the protection of the government under which he may reside.

6. The contracting parties mutually agree, that all roads, navigable streams, and all other channels of conveyance within each Territory, shall be open and free to the use of the inhabitants of the other.

7. The contracting parties mutually stipulate that they will direct all their resources to the prosecution of the Heaven-inspired cause which has given birth to this solemn Union, League and Confederation, firmly relying upon their united efforts, and the strong arm of Heaven, for success.

In faith whereof the Agents of the respective contracting parties hereunto affix their names. Done in the Town of Nacogdoches, this twenty-first day of December, in the year of our Lord one thousand eight hundred and twenty-six.

[Signed.]

> B. W. EDWARDS,
> H. B. MAYO,
> RICHARD FIELDS,
> JOHN D. HUNTER,

We, the Committee of Independence, and the Committee of Red People, do ratify the above Treaty, and do pledge ourselves to maintain it in good faith. Done on the day and date above mentioned.

[Signed.]

> MARTIN PARMER, President
>
> RICHARD FIELDS,
> JOHN D. HUNTER,
> NE-KO-LAKE,
> JOHN BAGS,
> CUK-TO-KEH,
> HADEN EDWARDS,
> W. B. LEGON,
> JNO. SPROW,
> B. P. THOMPSON,
> JOS. A. HUBER,
> B. W. EDWARDS,
> H. B. MAYO.

## 27. THE CONSTITUTION OF THE STATE OF
## COAHUILA AND TEXAS

### March 11, 1827

From the *Political Constitution of the Free State of Coahuila* & *Texas*, Sanctioned by the Constitutive Congress of the Said State, on the 11th of March, 1827 (Natchitoches, Louisiana, 1827). It is believed that this very rare copy of the Constitution in the Library of Congress, Washington, D. C., is the first edition in English.

The Mexican National Constitution of 1824 created a federal republic. The Province of Texas by an act of the Mexican Congress on May 7, 1824, was united with Coahuila as one state of the new republic until such time as it should have sufficient population to justify a separate state government. The Constituent Congress of Coahuila and Texas, which convened on August 15, 1824, at Saltillo, on March 11, 1827, promulgated a constitution, making Texas one of the three departments of the new state. The following extracts from the Constitution, an elaborate document of 225 articles, illustrate the nature of the fundamental government of Texas during the decade preceding the Revolution.

. . . In the name of the omnipotent God, author and Supreme Legislator of the universe, The Constitutive Congress of the State of Coahuila and Texas, desiring to comply with the will of the People their Constituents, and for the purpose of duly fulfilling the grand and magnificent object of promoting the glory and prosperity of the same State, decree, for its administration and government, the following: . . .

Art. 6. The Territory of the State, embraces those Provinces formerly known under the name of the Provinces of Coahuila and Texas. . . .

Art. 9. The Roman Catholic Apostolick Religion is the Religion of the State. The State protects it by wise and just laws, and prohibits the exercise of any other.

Art. 10. The State will regulate all the expenses necessary to the preserving of this Religion, according to the Concordates which the nation will celebrate with the Apostolical Seal, and to the laws which the said Nation will pass concerning the exercise of the *Patronato* in the whole confederation.

Art. 11. Every man who inhabits the territory of the State, although he may be but a traveller, enjoys the imprescriptible rights of *Liberty*, *Security*, *Property* and *Equality*, and it is the duty of the said State, to preserve and protect by wise and equitable laws, these universal rights of men.

Art. 12. The State is also obliged to protect all its inhabitants, in the exercise of that right which they have, of writing, printing and publishing freely, their political ideas and opinions, without the necessity of any examination, revision or censure, anterior to the publication, under the restrictions and responsability [sic] established, or which may hereafter be established by the general laws on that subject.

Art. 13. From and after the promulgation of this Constitution in the principal town of each District, no body can be born a slave, and the introduction of slaves under any pretext after six months from said publication is prohibited. . . .

Art. 22. The exercise of these rights [of citizenship] is suspended: . . . fifthly, for not having any employment, office, or known means of living; sixthly, for not knowing how to read or write: but this disposition

shall take effect only after the year 1850, and with respect to those who then may enter upon the exercise of the rights of Citizens. . . .

Art. 27. The officers of the Government invested with any species of authority, are nothing but mere agents or commissioners of the State, responsible to it for their public conduct.

Art. 28. The Government of the State is, Popular, Representative and Federal, . . .

Art. 29. The supreme power of the State is divided, for its exercise, into Legislative, Executive and Judicial, and these three powers, or any two of them, can never be united in any corporation or person, nor can the Legislature ever be deposited in one individual alone.

Art. 30. The exercise of the Legislative power shall reside in a Congress composed of Deputies named by the people.

Art. 31. The exercise of the Executive power shall reside in a Citizen, who shall be styled the Governor of the State, and who shall also be elected by the people.

Art. 32. The exercise of the Judicial power shall reside in Tribunals and Courts, established by this Constitution.

Art. 33. Congress . . . shall consist of twelve land holders and six suppletories until the year 1833. . . .

Art. 37. Persons born out of the Territory of the Confederation, must in order to be Deputies, have lived eight years in it, possess real property to the amount of eight thousand dollars, or an occupation which yields one thousand each year, and the qualifications mentioned in the preceding Article. . . .

Art. 78. Congress shall meet every year . . . Whenever they may think it necessary to remove it to another place, they can do so should two thirds of the whole number of deputies agree to it. . . .

Art. 84. Congress shall open their ordinary session on the first day of January of each year, and on the first day of September of all the years following that of the renewal of said Congress. . . .

Art. 97. The following are the exclusive powers of Congress: . . .

17th. To promote and advance, by laws, literature, public education and the progress of the sciences, arts and useful establishments; removing the obstacles which tend to paralyse such commendable objects.

18th. To protect the political liberty of the press. . . .

Art. 121. For the better discharging of his duties, the governor shall have a consulting body, to be called the council of government; and it shall be comprised of three deputies and two suppletories, of all of whom only one can be a priest.

Art. 122. In order to be a member of the council, the same qualifications are necessary as to be deputies. . . .

Art. 145. In the chief town of each department of the State, there shall be a functionary, in whose charge the political government of the same shall be placed, and he shall be called, Chief of Police of the department.

Art. 146. In order to be chief of police of a department, one must be a citizen in the exercise of his rights, of twenty-five years of age, a citizen of the State and a resident in it for three years, one of which immediately before his election.

Art. 147. The governor, on the proposition of three of the counsillors [sic], together with the petition of the ayuntamientos of each department, shall nominate the chiefs of departments, except that of the capital.

Art. 148. The chiefs of the departments shall be immediately subject to the governor of the State, . . .

Art. 155. The duty of the ayuntamientos is to watch over the interior government of the *pueblos* of the State, and to this end each *pueblo* that heretofore possessed one, shall continue to do so.

Art. 156. In those *pueblos* which have no *ayuntamiento,* and which have a right to one, there shall be one; and they cannot avoid having them in the chief towns of the district, no matter what may be their population, nor in those *pueblos* which by themselves or with the neighboring one, amount to one thousand souls, unless these latter be joined to some other municipality, . . .

Art. 159. The *ayuntamientos,* shall be composed of the Alcalde or Alcaldes, Snydic or Snydics and Regidors, the number of whom shall be settled by the regulations already mentioned.

Art. 160. In order to be a member of the *ayuntamiento* one must be a citizen in the exercise of his rights, of the age of twenty-five years, or if married, of the age of twenty-one, a resident of the district to which the *ayuntamiento* belongs, and have three years of residence in it, and one of them immediately before the election, have some capital or trade, by which he can make a living and know how to read and write. . . .

Art. 164. The members of the *ayuntamiento* shall be nominated through the medium of electoral municipal assemblies, . . .

Art. 188. Criminal cases shall be public, . . .

Art. 192. One of the principal duties of Congress will be, to establish in criminal cases the mode of trial by jury, to extend it gradually, and even to adopt it in civil cases, in proportion as they go on proving the advantages of this precious institution.

Art. 193. Inferior courts shall be formed, in the manner pointed out by the law, until the revenue of the State, in the opinion of Congress, permits the establishment of learned judges who shall be appointed in each district.

Art. 194. There shall be in the capital of the State, a supreme court of justice, . . .

Art. 211. In every *pueblo* of the State there shall be established bodies of civic militia, and these shall compose the military force of the same.

Art. 212. The formation of these bodies, their organization, discipline and internal government, shall be regulated by Congress, comformably to the general laws of the Union on that subject.

Art. 213. The same Congress shall regulate the service of this militia, so that it shall be conformably to the objects of its institution and the best interests of the State, and also as little grievous as possible to the citizens.

Art. 214. No citizen of Coahuila and Texas can be excused from this service, when required and in the form disposed of by law. . . .

Art. 215. In all the *pueblos* of the State there shall be a competent number of elementary schools, in which youth shall be taught reading, writing and arithmetic, the catechism of the Christian religion, a brief and plain explanation of this constitution and the general constitution of the Republic, the rights and duties of men in society, and whatever may be conducive to the best education of youth.

Art. 216. In proper places also, in proportion as circumstances permit it, there shall be established for those branches of education most necessary to public instruction, the sciences and arts useful to the State, and the above mentioned constitution shall likewise be explained with the greatest attention.

Art. 217. The method of education shall be uniform all through the State, and to this end Congress shall, in order to facilitate it, form a general plan of public instruction, and shall regulate by means of statutes and laws, every thing appertaining to this very important business. . . .

Art. 221. Any proposition made, concerning alterations, reforms or repeals of any part or parts of the articles of this constitution, must be made in writing, and seconded and signed by the third part of the deputies.

Art. 222. Congress, at the time in which any of these propositions may be made, shall do nothing for the two succeeding years relative to them, except to read, print and publish them, with the reasons for such publications.

Art. 223. The following Congress shall permit the discussion of these propositions, or shall reject them. Should they be admitted, they shall be published again and printed; and they shall be circulated by the governor, in order to be read in the next electoral assemblies before electing deputies to Congress.

Art. 224. In the following Congress, the alterations, reformations or repeals proposed, shall be discussed, and should they be approved of, they shall immediately be published as constitutional articles. . . .

Given in Saltillo, on the 11th March, 1827.

Santiago del Valle, president — Juan Vincente Campos, vice president — . . .

## 28. SAN FELIPE DE AUSTIN: THE ANGLO-AMERICAN
## COLONIAL CAPITAL OF TEXAS

### 1828-1831

From Noah Smithwick, *The Evolution of a State* (Austin, 1900; facsimile reproduction, Austin, 1935), 55-72.

On July 26, 1823, the governor ordered the establishment of the town of San Felipe de Austin at the Atascosito crossing on the Brazos River, in present Austin County, and designated it as the seat of government for the Anglo-American colonies. The new town, the headquarters of Stephen F. Austin, continued to be the capital and political center for the Anglo-American colonists until 1836. The following selection describes San Felipe as Noah Smithwick, a resident blacksmith from 1828 to 1831, many years later remembered it.

. . . San Felipe de Austin! . . . Though not one of the Three Hundred, the writer was but a few years behind them, and knew them all by repute, many of them personally. The town was still in its swaddling clothes when the writer made his advent therein in 1827. Twenty-five or perhaps thirty log cabins strung along the west bank of the Brazos River was all there was of it, while the whole human population of all ages and colors could not have exceeded 200. Men were largely in the majority, coming from every state in the Union, and every walk in life.

There seeming to be a good opening for my trade in San Felipe, I bought a set of tools from George Huff on the San Bernard and set up business in the parent colony in the year 1828. In the absence of a more comprehensive view, a pen picture of the old town may not be uninteresting. The buildings all being of unhewn logs with clapboard roofs, presented few distinguishing features. Stephen F. Austin had established his headquarters something like half a mile back from the river on the west bank of a little creek — Palmito — that ran into the Brazos just above the main village. Just above Austin's house was the farm of Joshua Parker. Austin's house was a double log cabin with a wide "passage" through the center, a porch with dirt floor on the front with windows opening upon it, and chimney at each end of the building.

In this vicinity the Ingram brothers, Seth and Ira, had a store, with them being associated Hosea N. League, a lawyer by profession, who with his wife lived near by. League later formed a law partnership with David G. Burnet, their office being in the immediate vicinity. . . . Seth Ingram, a surveyor, laid off the town of San Felipe. William Pettus, better known as "Buck" Pettus, who was later elected a member of the Ayuntamiento, also resided in a suburban villa on the "west end." Going on down to the town proper, which lay along the west bank of the Brazos, the first house on the left was my bachelor abode, and near it, on the same side, stood the "village smithy" over which I presided. Then came the Peyton tavern, operated by Jonthan C. Peyton and wife; the house was the regulation double log cabin. The saloon and billiard hall of Cooper and Chieves, the only frame building in the place, was next below the Peyton's. The first house on the right as you entered the town from above was Dinsmore's store, and next it the store of Walter C. White. The office of the "Cotton Plant," the first newspaper in the colonies, and near it the residence of the genial proprietor, Godwin B. Cotton, filled the space between White's store and the Whiteside Hotel, which differed from its companion buildings, only in point of elevation, it being a story and a half in height; through the center ran the regulation "passage," and at either end rose a huge stick and mud chimney.

It must not be understood that these rows of buildings presented an unbroken or even regular line of front; every fellow built to suit himself, only taking care to give himself plenty of room, so that the town was strung along either side of the road something like half a mile — . . .

The alcalde's office was in a large double log house standing back some distance from the main thoroughfare almost immediately in the rear of the Whiteside Hotel, which building it much resembled. . . . The walls of hewn logs were roofed in and abandoned at that stage. It was here the ayuntamiento held its sittings, and this windowless, floorless pen, through the unchinked cracks of which the wild winds wandered and whistled at will, was presumably the Faneuil Hall of Texas. . . .

Hearing loud talking in the alcalde's office one night, I concluded there must be something interesting going on, though there was no light save that which the bright moon poured in through the cracks and open door. Approaching warily, expecting every moment to hear the bullets begin to sing, I got near enough to make out that it was some one apparently delivering a speech. Curious to learn what it was all about, I quietly drew nearer, and, peering through a crack, perceived Whiteside, junior, a boy of sixteen, rehearsing the address of the Scythian ambassador to Alexander the Great to an appreciative audience composed of the negro boy Will; . . .

Ludicrous as the incident was, there was something pathetic in it, occurring in that schoolless land, a relic of civilization which as yet had made but little progress there. . . .

Stephen F. Austin, the father of Texas, was of course, the central figure. He was at that time about thirty-six years of age, though care had left an added weight of years to his appearance. Dark hair and eyes, sparely built, and unassuming in manner, there was little in Austin's outward appearance to indicate the tremendous energy of which he was possessed. Though only mortal, he was far above the average of the mould, and his patience and perseverance under trials and difficulties that would have driven an ordinary man to despair abundantly testify.

His character often maligned, his motives impugned, the compact he had entered into with the Mexican government disregarded, thus impeaching his integrity, he yet extended his protecting care over the colonies, . . .

Godwin B. Cotton, the pioneer newspaper man in Texas, launched the "Cotton Plant," as he facetiously christened his paper, at San Felipe in '29. He was a genial old bachelor of fifty or thereabouts, his aldermanic proportions making him a conspicuous figure. . . .

Judge Williamson was associated with him in the Cotton Plant, which after struggling about four years against conditions unfavorable to its perfect development, finally succumbed. The press was moved down to Brazoria and used to print the Texas Republic, the publication of which continued only about eighteen months; . . .

Gail Borden whose name is more widely known than any of them and will perhaps outlive them all, had a blacksmith shop next door to me in San Felipe. He had an inventive genious, but strange to say it did not lean toward mechanics. His first venture was the soup biscuit which took quite a run, being very popular with seafaring men. He next embarked in the newspaper business, bringing out the fourth paper in the state at San Felipe in 1835. The Telegraph, as it was called, was devoted to the cause of independence, therefore when Santa Anna's invasion necessitated the evacuation of San Felipe, Borden thought it advisable to go along. . . .

An important personage was Padre Muldoon, not only in San Felipe where he made his home, but throughout the colonies, he being the only authorized agent of Cupid east of San Antonio. The father made a tour of the colonies occasionally when in need of funds, tying the nuptial knot and pocketing the fees therefor, $25 being the modest sum demanded for his services. But his visits were so much like an angel's, and his charges so much on the opposite extremity that the colonists had recourse to a plan of their own combining in itself the essential features of both marriage and divorce, the latter unknown in Catholic countries. When a couple concluded to join their fortunes they forthwith repaired to the alcalde's office and had him draw up a bond to avail themselves of the priest's services whenever he came around; both parties signed the bond and went on their way as man and wife. The plan had this advantage; that if they changed their minds before the priest got around, they had only to go together to the alcalde and demand the bond, which they tore to pieces and were free again. . . .

The first preacher to venture into this stronghold of Satan was Thomas J. Pilgrim, a Baptist; but as the colonists were supposed to be Catholics, Colonel Austin did not deem it advisable to establish a Protestant church, so the preacher, willing to make himself useful, turned

dominie, teaching the first English school in Texas, 1829. Comparatively few families resided in town, most of them going out on farms. On the farms, too, were to be found the wealthier portion of the colonists, who, having brought out slaves, were opening up cotton plantations.

Thus while there was a scarcity of ladies of any kind in San Felipe, single ladies were indeed few and far between. Occasionally one ventured into town to be almost immediately captured by some aspirant for matrimonial honors. . . .

So great was the dearth of female society in San Felipe that during my whole residence there — '28 to '31 — there was not a ball or party of any kind in which ladies participated. There being so little opportunity for social intercourse with the gentler sex, the sterner element should not be too severely censured if they sought diversion of a lower order. And if our stag parties were a bit convivial, they would probably compare favorably in that regard with the swell club dinners in the cities. . . .

Some sang, some told stories and some danced. Luke La Sascie, a Louisiana Frenchman, and by the way a brilliant lawyer, was our champion story teller; with Cotton and Doctor Peebles worthy competitors. I, being reckoned the most nimble footed man in the place, usually paid my dues in jigs and hornpipes, . . . The biggest time we ever had was on the occasion of a double wedding, the brides being a couple of grass widows who were domiciled together just out of town, their comfortable home and reputed bank account proving an irresistible attraction to a couple of good-looking young scamps who were hanging about; hence the wedding. The boys all got together and went out to charivari them. It was my first experience in that kind of a performance; and was unquestionably the most outrageous din I ever heard; cowbells, cowhorns, tin pans and in fact everything that contained noise were called into requisition; and with their discordant sounds mingled hoots, howls and caterwaulings enough to make the hair rise on one's head. But all our efforts to bring out the happy quartette proved abortive. We overdid the thing and frightened them out of their wits; so after exhausting every device short of breaking in the door and dragging them forth, we adjourned to town to wind up. Austin never participated in these jamborees, nor did the Bordens. Sam Williams sometimes looked in, took a glass and cracked a joke. . . .

## 29. THE LAW OF APRIL 6, 1830

Mexico, in an effort to define her boundary between Texas and the United States, commissioned Manuel Mier y Terán in 1827 to survey the existing limits inherited from the Spanish regime and to investigate seemingly the need of new military posts in Texas. In a letter from Nacogdoches to the President of Mexico and in his official report, dated June 30 and July 7, 1828, respectively, Mier y Terán among other observations noted the waning power of Mexico in East Texas owing to the rapid influx of Anglo-Ameri-

cans, and included recommendations for strengthening Mexican sovereignty. The Mexican government responded with the Law of April 6, 1830, incorporating his proposals with those of Minister of Foreign Relations Lucas Alamán, who was responsible for the provisions most objectionable to the Texans, particularly Article Eleven prohibiting further immigration from the United States. Mier y Terán's letter to the President, describing at length conditions in East Texas, and the unpopuar decree of April 6, 1830, follow.

## 1. MANUEL MIER Y TERAN'S LETTER TO PRESIDENT GUADALUPE VICTORIA

### June 30, 1828

From Alleine Howren, "Causes and Origin of the Decree of April 6, 1830," *The Southwestern Historical Quarterly*, XVI (April, 1913), 395-398.

. . . As one covers the distance from Béjar to this town [Nacogdoches], he will note that Mexican influence is proportionately diminished until on arriving in this place he will see that it is almost nothing. And indeed, whence could such influence come? Hardly from superior numbers in population, since the ratio of Mexicans to foreigners is one to ten; certainly not from the superior character of the Mexican population, for exactly the opposite is true, the Mexicans of this town comprising what in all countries is called the lowest class — the very poor and very ignorant. The naturalized North Americans in the town maintain an English school, and send their children north for further education; the poor Mexicans not only do not have sufficient means to establish schools, but they are not of the type that take any thought for the improvement of its public institutions or the betterment of its degraded condition. Neither are there civil authorities or magistrates; one insignifcant little man — not to say more — who is called an *alcalde,* and an *ayuntamiento* that does not convene once in a lifetime is the most that we have here at this important point on our frontier; yet, wherever I have looked, in the short time that I have been here, I have witnessed grave occurrences, both political and judicial. It would cause you the same chagrin that it has caused me to see the opinion that is held of our nation by these foreign colonists, since, with the exception of some few who have journeyed to our capital, they know no other Mexicans than the inhabitants about here, and excepting the authorities necessary to any form of society, the said inhabitants are the most ignorant of negroes and Indians, among whom I pass for a man of culture. Thus, I tell myself that it could not be otherwise than that from such a state of affairs should arise an antagonism between Mexicans and foreigners, which is not the least of the smoldering fires which I have discovered. Therefore, I am warning you to take timely measures. Texas could throw the whole nation into revolution.

The colonists murmur against the political disorganization of the frontier, and the Mexicans complain of the superiority and better education of the colonists; the colonists find it unendurable that they must go three hundred leagues to lodge a complaint against the petty pickpocketing that they suffer from a venal and ignorant *alcalde,* and the Mexicans with no knowledge of the laws of their own country, nor those regulating colonization, set themselves against the foreigners, deliberately setting nets to deprive them of the right of franchise and to exclude them from the *ayuntamiento.* Meanwhile, the incoming stream of new settlers is unceasing; the first news of these comes by discovering them on land already under cultivation, where they have been located for many months; the old inhabitants set up a claim to the property, basing their titles of doubtful priority, and for which there are no records, on a law of the Spanish

government; and thus arises a lawsuit in which the *alcalde* has a chance to come out with some money. In this state of affairs, the town where there are no magistrates is the one in which lawsuits abound, and it is at once evident in Nacogdoches and its vicinity, being most distant from the seat of the general government, the primitive order of things should take its course, which is to say that this section is being settled up without the consent of anybody.

The majority of the North Americans established here under the Spanish government — and these are few — are of two classes. First, those who are fugitives from our neighbor republic and bear the unmistakable earmarks of thieves and criminals; these are located between Nacogdoches and the Sabine, ready to cross and recross this river as they see the necessity of separating themselves from the country in which they have just committed some crime; however, some of these have reformed and settled down to an industrious life in the new country. The other class of early settlers are poor laborers who lack the four or five thousand dollars necessary to buy a *sitio* of land in the north, but having the ambition to become landholders — one of the strong virtues of our neighbors — have come to Texas. Of such as this latter class is Austin's colony composed. They are for the most part industrious and honest, and appreciate this country. Most of them own at least one or two slaves. Unfortunately the emigration of such is made under difficulties, because they lack the means of transportation, and to accomplish this emigration it has become necessary to do what was not necessary until lately; there are empresarios of wealth who advance them the means for their transportation and establishment.

The wealthy Americans of Louisiana and other western states are anxious to secure land in Texas for speculation, but they are restrained by the laws prohibiting slavery. If these laws should be repealed — which God forbid — in a few years Texas would be a powerful state which could compete in productions and wealth with Louisiana. The repeal of these laws is a point toward which the colonists are directing their efforts. They have already succeeded in getting from the Congress of Coahuila a law very favorable to their prosperity; the state government has declared that it will recognize contracts made with servants before coming to this country, and the colonists are thus assured of the employment of ample labor, which can be secured at a very low price in the United States. This law, according to the explanation made to me by several, is going to be interpreted as equivalent to permission to introduce slaves.

In spite of the enmity that usually exists between the Mexicans and the foreigners, there is a most evident uniformity of opinion on one point, namely the separation of Texas from Coahuila and its organization into a territory of the federal government. This idea, which was conceived by some of the colonists who are above the average, has become general among the people and does not fail to cause considerable discussion. In explaining the reasons assigned by them for this demand, I shall do no more than relate what I have heard with no addition of my own conclusions, and I frankly state that I have been commissioned by some of the colonists to explain to you their motives, notwithstanding the fact that I should have done so anyway in the fulfillment of my duty.

They claim that Texas in its present condition of a colony is an expense, since it is not a sufficiently prosperous section to contribute to the revenues of the state administration; and since it is such a charge it ought not to be imposed upon a state as poor as Coahuila, which has not the means of defraying the expenses of the corps of political and judicial officers necessary for the maintenance of peace and order. Furthermore, it is impracticable that recourse in all matters should be had to a state capital so distant and separated from this section by deserts infected by hostile savages. Again, their interests are very different from those of the other sections, and because of this they should be governed by a separate territorial government, having learned by experience that the mixing of their affairs with those of Coahuila brings about friction. The native inhabitants of Texas add to the above other reasons which indicate an aversion for the inhabitants of Coahuila; also the authority of the *comandante* and the collection of taxes is disputed.

That which most impressed me in view of all these conditions is the necessity of effective government in Nacogdoches at least, since it is the frontier with which the Republic is most in contact. Every officer of the federal government has immense districts under his jurisdiction, and to distribute these effectively it is necessary to give attention to economy as well as to government and security. The whole population here is a mixture of strange and incoherent parts without parallel in our federation; numerous tribes of Indians, now at peace, but armed and at any moment ready for war, whose steps toward civilization should be taken under the close supervision of a strong and intelligent government; colonists of another people, more progressive and better informed than the Mexican inhabitants, but also more shrewd and unruly; among these foreigners are fugitives from justice, honest laborers, vagabonds and criminals, but honorable and dishonorable alike travel with their political constitution in their pockets, demanding the privileges, authority and officers which such a constitution guarantees. The most of them have slaves, and these slaves are beginning to learn the favorable intent of the Mexican law toward their unfortunate condition and are becoming restless under their yoke, and the masters, in the effort to retain them, are making that yoke even heavier; they extract their teeth, set on the dogs to tear them in pieces, the most lenient being he who but flogs his slaves until they are flayed.

In short, the growing population, its unusual class, the prosperity and safety of the nation, all seem to me to demand the placing at this point of a *jefe politico* subordinate to the one at Béjar, and also a court of appeals. This done, I do not believe so radical a step as the separation of Texas from Coahuila, now desired by the inhabitants, would be necessary.

I must ask your forbearance for this long letter, but I desire to forward to you at once my observations of this country and not withhold them until the day when I make full report to the government, for fear the time for remedy will be past.

## 2. THE LAW OF APRIL 6, 1830

From the *Texas Gazette*, July 3, 1830; also translated in Alleine Howren, "Causes and Origin of the Decree of April 6, 1830," *The Southwestern Historical Quarterly*, XVI (April, 1913), 415-417.

The Vice President of the Mexican United States, to the inhabitants of the Republic, KNOW YE, that the General Congress has decreed, as follows: —

Article 1.  Cotton goods excluded in the Law of May 22, 1829, may be introduced through the ports of the Republic until January 1, 1831, and through the ports of the South Sea until June 30, 1831.

Art. 2.  The duties received on the above mentioned goods shall be used to maintain the integrity of Mexican territory, to form a reserve fund against the event of Spanish invasion, and to promote the development of national industries in the branch of cotton manufacturers.

Art. 3.  The government is authorized to name one or more commissioners who shall visit the colonies of the frontier states and contract with the legislatures, of said states for the purchase, in behalf of the federal government, of lands deemed suitable for the establishment of colonies of Mexicans and other nationalities; and the said commissioners shall make with the existing colonies whatever arrangements seem expedient for the security of the Republic. The said commissioners shall supervise the introduction of new colonists and the fulfilling of their contracts for settlement, and shall ascertain to what extent the existing contracts have been completed.

Art. 4.  The chief executive is authorized to take such lands as are deemed suitable for fortifications or arsenals and for the new colonies, indemnifying the states for same, in proportion to their assessments due the federal government.

Art. 5.  The government is authorized to transport the convict-soldiers destined for Vera Cruz and other points to the colonies, there to establish them as is deemed fit; the government will furnish free transportation to the families of the soldiers, should they desire to go.

Art. 6.  The convict-soldiers shall be employed in constructing the fortifications, public works and roads which the commissioners may deem necessary, and when the time of their imprisonment is terminated, if they should desire to remain as colonists, they shall be given lands and agricultural implements, and their provisions shall be continued through the year of their colonization.

Art. 7.  Mexican families who voluntarily express a desire to become colonists will be furnished transportation, maintained for one year, and assigned the best of agricultural lands.

Art. 8.  All the individuals above mentioned shall be subject to both the federal and state colonization laws.

Art. 9.  The introduction of foreigners across the northern frontier is prohibited under any pretext whatever, unless the said foreigners are provided with a passport issued by the agents of this Republic at the point whence the said foreigners set out.

Art. 10.  No change shall be made with respect to the slaves now in the states, but the federal government and the government of each state shall most strictly en-

Galveston Bay and Texas Land Company

67

force the colonization laws and prevent the further introduction of slaves.

Art. 11. In accordance with the right reserved by the general congress in the seventh article of the Law of August 18, 1824, it is prohibited that emigrants from nations bordering on this Republic shall settle in the states or territory adjacent to their own nation. Consequently, all contracts not already completed and not in harmony with this law are suspended.

Art. 12. Coastwide trade shall be free to all foreigners for the term of four years, with the object of turning colonial trade to the ports of Matamoras, Tampico, and Vera Cruz.

Art. 13. Frame houses and all classes of foreign food products may be introduced through the ports of Galveston and Matagorda, free of duty, for a period of two years.

Art. 14. The government is authorized to expend five hundred thousand dollars (*pesos*) in the construction of fortifications and settlements on the frontier, in the transportation of the convict-soldiers and Mexican families to same and their maintenance for one year, on agricultural implements, on expenses of the commissioners, on the transportation of troops, on premiums to such farmers among the colonists as may distinguish themselves in agriculture, and on all the other expedients conducive to progress and security as set forth in the foregoing articles.

Art. 15. To obtain at once one-half of the above sum, the government is authorized to negotiate a loan on the customs proceeds which will be derived from the ordinary classes of cotton goods, said loan to pay a premium of three per cent monthly, payable at the expiration of the periods fixed in the tariff schedule.

Art. 16. One-twentieth of the said customs receipts shall be used in the promotion of cotton manufactures, such as in the purchase of machines and looms, small sums being set aside for the installing of the machinery, and any other purpose that the government shall deem necessary; the government shall apportion these funds to the states having this form of industry. The said funds shall be under the control of the Minister of Relations for the purpose of promoting industries of such importance.

Art. 17. Also three hundred thousand dollars (*pesos*) of the above mentioned customs receipts shall be set aside as a reserve fund on deposit in the treasury, under the strict responsibility of the government, which shall have power to use the same only in the case of Spanish invasion.

Art. 18. The government shall regulate the establishment of the new colonies, and shall present to Congress within a year a record of the emigrants and immigrants established under the new law, with an estimate of the increase of population on the frontier. . . .

Anastacio Bustamente

## 30. THE GALVESTON BAY AND TEXAS LAND COMPANY AND THE SALE OF LAND SCRIP
### 1831

Some *empresarios* proceeded with colonization plans in disregard of the Law of April 6, 1830, prohibiting further immigration from the United States. Lorenzo de Zavala, Joseph Vehlein, and David G. Burnet on October 16, 1830, pooled their extensive grants in eastern Texas with the Galveston Bay and Texas Land Company, although *empresario* contracts were not transferable. The Company sold land scrip certificates, aggregating millions of acres for as much as ten cents an acre, to prospective settlers or over-eager speculators, some of whom were unaware that Texas had been closed to immigrants from the United States. The scrip merely gave the Company's consent for the purchaser to settle on lands originally granted to the above named contractors and to acquire the number of acres designated in accordance with the provisions of the colonization laws. Many purchasers erroneously believing that they had bought the land, subsequently contributed to the growing tension between the Anglo-American colonists and the Mexicans. The first extract which follows is from the trust deed establishing the Galveston Bay and Texas Land Company and includes a copy of a scrip certificate; the second is a letter of a Company official offering scrip for sale with comments by a purchaser who came from New York to Texas early in 1831 to locate the twenty thousand acres which he believed he had bought.

### 1. TRUST DEED OF THE GALVESTON BAY AND TEXAS LAND COMPANY

#### January 1, 1831

From "Trust Deed," *Address to the Reader of the Documents relating to the Galveston Bay*

*and Texas Land Company* (New York, 1831), 1-49.

. . . *And whereas* the said Lorenzo de Zavala, Joseph Vehlein and David G. Burnet and the several associates, by their several and separate deeds of indenture made between each of the three several persons above named, the several associates, and the said Anthony Dey, William H. Sumner and George Curtis, and bearing even date with these presents have covenanted and agreed to and with the several parties thereto that they and their several associates would put and place their stock to be held in trust, to and for the use of all the parties interested therein in the proportion in said instruments named, irrevocably in the hands and under the control of the said Anthony Dey, William H. Sumner and George Curtis, and their successors, for the purpose of surveying, locating and setting off the said territories and lands into settlements, villages and towns; and of giving, granting, selling, colonizing, and otherwise disposing of, and managing the same in such way and manner as they or the majority of them shall deem best for the interest of all the parties concerned. . . .

And the parties of the first and third parts do hereby further agree to and with the said Anthony Dey, William H. Sumner and George Curtis, the parties of the second part, that they in their capacity of trustees to all the parties these presents shall issue scrip themselves respectively, or to such persons as they shall severally appoint to the amount authorized and limited in the three tripartite indentures of agreements, this day made and herein before referred to, and also certificates of the number of shares in the stock of this association to which they are respectively entitled according to their several subscriptions therefor, and proportions therein; . . .

They shall compromise, if the same can be done on reasonable terms, with settlers upon the land who come within the contemplation of the laws, and give their consent to such settlers receiving their titles from the land commissioner of the government for such a quantity of land on such terms as shall be agreed on, and if no reasonable compromise can be made, shall remove such of them as have no right to remain, as well as all persons of bad character, not being Mexicans, from the land, according to the provisions of the laws; . . . They shall empower and substitute proper attorneys, and employ suitable agents, surveyors and persons, and invest them with proper authority and power, and give them suitable instructions to go upon the land for the foregoing purposes, as well as for receiving the new colonists as they arrive, and locating them upon land of the company, according to their occupation and the quantity or extent of land to which they may be entitled, by the scrip certificate they hold, or the agreements for labour or services in the company's behalf they may enter into with them. They shall have power to grant scrip, with or without consideration, to settlers intending actually to locate themselves on the land, and to persons who will contract to bring and place the number of settlers on the land which is now or at any time hereafter may be allowed and required to colonize the whole of said tracts and premises, . . . They are empowered to furnish the settlers with the means of transporting themselves and their families into the colony, and with subsistence from the time of their arrival until after the first harvest, or such other period, not exceeding one year, as they may deem advisable. They are empowered to provide barracks or other shelter for the colonists on their first landing, and supply them with agricultural and other implements necessary for their use in the infancy of their settlements, and with seeds of the common articles of export and consumption for the first year, upon trust or otherwise as they find it expedient and useful. They may also purchase horses, mules, cattle, waggons [sic], boats, and other vehicles for transporting the provisions and utensils of the first colonists, if it should, from the rapidity of the settlements, become necessary and expedient . . . and in case the directors shall at any time be of the opinion that the affairs of the company are not conducted with honesty and probity, or that the proceeds of the Scrip which the trustees have power to sell for the purpose of raising funds, are not faithfully appropriated to the objects of the company, or that more Scrip is sold or pledged for the purpose of raising funds for said objects, or at a price or rate greater than the interests of the company required, or . . .

Art. 7. It is agreed that the stock and property of the company shall be devided into one thousand shares, and that certificates of the number of shares set against the names of the subscribers thereto by themselves, or their attorneys . . . and notwithstanding the agreement prescribing the form of the three tripartite indentures this day made shall be in the following form:

Art. 8. It is agreed that the dividends of the company which shall be made by the directors in the manner pointed out in the provision of the third article (unless hereafter otherwise ordered) shall be made in scrip denominated "Sitios" and "Labors," which shall be signed by the trustees and attornies of the empresarios and the clerk or secretary of the company, and issued to each proprietor according to the number of his shares on demand, as soon after the same shall be declared as the said scrip can be made out; which scrip shall be transferable by the indorsement of the original proprietor's name thereon, and delivery afterwards. Said scrip giving the consent of the company to the location of the quantity of land therein named by the holder thereof within the company limits upon the terms and conditions therein named according to law, and such general regulations as shall be made respecting the colonization of the grants shall be in the form following:

"No.                              Acres."

"Galveston Bay and Texas Land Company."

This certifies that the subscribers as the Trustees and Attornies of Lorenzo de Zavala, Joseph Vehlein and David G. Burnet have given and do hereby give to _____ and _____, legal representatives, the bearer hereof, their consent to the location of and holding in severalty one _____ of land within the limits of four adjoining tracts of Land in Texas, heretofore severally granted to the said Lorenzo de Zavala on the 12th March, 1829; Joseph Vehlein on the 21st December 1826, and 17th November, 1828, and David G. Burnet, on the 22d December 1826, as empresarios for colonizing the same according to the terms of the said grants and the laws of the United States of Mexico, and the state of Coahuila and Texas which said several tracts are now united in one common interest, and placed under the direction and management of the subscribers as the Attornies and Trustees of the said Empresarios by virtue of and according to their several deeds of indenture dated the sixteenth day of October 1830, and to the articles of association of said company.

The four tracts of land aforesaid comprehend all the lands not settled according to law, and the terms of said grants, lying within the following limits, (excepting the town of Nacogdoches.) Beginning at the westerly boundary of the United States of America, on the Gulf of Mexico, thence running northerly, on the westerly side of the Sabine river to the road leading from Nachitoches to Nacogdoches, thence running westerly along said road, a distance of twenty Spanish leagues, from the boundary line to the suburbs or vicinity of Nacogdoches, then proceeding from said town of Nacogdoches, northwardly, a distance of fifteen Spanish leagues, where, leaving free on one side the twenty boundary leagues in a parallel with the river Sabine, and the dividing line of the United States of the north, shall be placed a land mark, and from which a right line shall be drawn to the west, until it strikes the rivulet named Navasoto; from thence the line shall descend upon the left margin of the said rivulet, following its course until it meets the road leading from Bexar to Nacogdoches; thence running along said road till it comes to a point thereon lying due north of the source of the waters of the rivulet St. Jacinto; thence running due south to the source of the waters of the said river; thence it shall follow the left bank of the St. Jacinto, to Galveston Bay; thence by the westerly side of said bay to the Gulf of Mexico, excluding the island of St. Louis; and thence by the said Gulf of Mexico, to the place of beginning.

The location of said land is to be made under the supervision, and direction of the agents of the trustees and attorneys of the Empresarios aforesaid, residing on the land, who, after making a record of the same, shall make report thereof to the commissioner appointed by the government to the intent that the holder of this Scrip, upon the surrender thereof, may have his land surveyed, and receive his title thereto, in severalty, from said commissioner according to law, subject to the payments required by the laws of the state. This Scrip being indorsed by the original holder, is transferable by delivery. Copies of the original grants and subsequent conveyances, and articles of association of the company, as well as the colonization laws before referred to, will be exhibited upon application to either of the subscribers hereto.

New York,                                    183-.
[Signatures of company officials to be affixed]

Art. 9. No scrip shall be issued for less quantity than a "Labor," nor for a larger quantity than a "Sitio" of land, and the Scrip for Sitios may at any time be surrendered to the clerk, who shall divide the same into Labors, and issue certificates therefor; . . .

## 2. LETTER OFFERING LAND SCRIP FOR SALE AND COMMENTS BY A PURCHASER

### 1831

From *A Visit to Texas*: *Being the Journal of a Traveller* (New York, 1834), 130-141.

. . . That they [the Galveston Bay and Texas Land Company officials] did and do profess to sell land, however, I presume will not be doubted. The letter of which the following is a copy, was addressed by one of the Trustees of the Company to a gentleman I know.

"My Dr. Sir, If you wish some of the Texas Lands, you can *now* have some at 10 cents — you can have one share in the *Company* of 10,000 acres, at $1000, at 6 months with interest; or if you desire it, you can have a less quantity in scrip, at the same rate. It appears to me whether purchased to sell again, or with a view to actual settlement, it cannot be otherwise than a most profitable investment. You can consider this offer as made to *you*, and if not disposed to avail yourself of it, you will of course be silent on the subject of it. Let me hear from you this morning." . . .

We had received our letters by ship from New York when the writer arrived at Point Bolivar in April, 1831 in the meantime; and in one of mine I found one of the most beautiful little pieces of scrip ever purchased. The design and execution showed the skill of an artist; and I could not but compare its value with that of twenty thousand acres of land. . . .

## 31. TRAVEL ACCOMMODATIONS AND CUSTOMS IN COLONIAL TEXAS

### March-May, 1831

From *A Visit to Texas*: *Being the Journal of a Traveller* (New York, 1834), 31-48, 204-211, 230-231, 117-118.

After the settlement of Stephen F. Austin's first colony, a considerable number of visitors came to Texas, particularly prospective colonists who usually travelled into the interior in search of a desirable location to settle. For several years the most travelled road followed the Brazos River from Brazoria northward through San Felipe. The traveller could find accommodations in over-crowded hotels at Brazoria and San Felipe, but elsewhere along the well-settled route he likely spent the night as a welcome guest in the home of a hospitable colonist. The following excellent description of travel accommodations and customs along the road was written by a New York purchaser of land scrip certificates who came to Texas in 1831 for the purpose of locating the land which he believed he owned.

. . . [The Brazoria Hotel in which] I took lodging [was] . . . a pretty fair specimen of most of the best houses in the country. I shall therefore be excused for introducing here a description of such a house, with a brief account of the manner in which we were accommodated. Two square houses, about fifteen feet apart, are constructed of logs, well fitted together by deep mortices cut at their ends, where they meet to form the corners. Each of these buildings has a door in the middle, on the side facing inwards; and the space between them being covered over by a roof, a broad passage is left, sheltered indeed above, but quite open at both ends. Add floors to the two houses, or apartments, a few windows closing with wooden shutters and destitute of glass, with a place for a fire in the northern one, and a hole through the roof for the smoke, and you have a description of the principal hotel in Brazoria. The furniture was of the plainest description, and such as barely to serve the most necessary purposes of thirty boarders: for that was the number with whom I found myself associated on entering the mansion. The regular price was four dollars a week; and for transient travellers a dollar a day. . . .

The company were cheerful, conversation was lively, our arrival brought new subjects of attraction and enquiry to all, and the time passed very pleasantly. The wife of our host, I found, was an intelligent lady from New-York; and her care furnished us with excellent food considering the disadvantages of the place, while her arrangements afforded us more comfort and convenience than we could have expected, in a habitation so disproportioned to our numbers. Our table was set on the ground, in the open passage of the house; while our mattresses were spread at night on the floor of the southern apartment. In order to place thirty men in a horizontal position, on a space about twenty feet square, and each upon a separate bed, required no small care and calculation; yet there we laid ourselves down, as on the floor of a steamboat, and slept soundly till morning. . . .

Our companion who remained at Mr. McNeil's afterwards informed me, that he set up a great part of the night conversing with his host. Every well behaved stranger, on account of the news he brings, is a welcome visitor in such families as these; and this fact, in connection with the general prosperity of the people, and the kind dispositions of a large portion of them, renders their hospitality very sincere. To be received at the house of strangers with cheerfulness and pleasure, and welcomed with every favor in their power, is doubly agreeable when you feel that your society is regarded as a rich reward for all you receive; and this we often found to be the case when we engaged in cheerful conversation, and readily imparted what information we possessed on subjects interesting to those about us. . . .

The route we were on, between Brazoria and San Felipe, is the most travelled in Texas, and is pretty well settled, with houses kept as regular inns. There is of course less danger of hurting the feelings of any body by offering to pay for food and lodging. The uncertainty we had often been in, on leaving our stopping places, whether to pay or not, we had found embarrassing [sic]; and we had resorted to different devices to ascertain the humor of our hosts. Sometimes we would put a piece of money into the hands of a child, to see how the parent regarded it, and if we found it not likely to be well received, we could easily reclaim it. Now we regularly called for our bills on departing, as we freely asked for such things as we needed during our stay. . . . [We] found them always well supplied with various and ex-

cellent food, and of such descriptions as might be looked for in such a country. We had plenty of fresh bread, venison, wild turkey, beef, fowl, eggs, milk and good coffee; and usually slept well on comfortable beds. The customary price for supper, lodging and breakfast was one dollar, including the feed of our horses: though we chose to take care of them ourselves. At some of these houses, as in many of those in Texas generally, we found one or more negroes, held as slaves, although the laws of Mexico forbid it. They are ignorant, the whites are generally in favor of slavery and ready to sustain the master in his usurped authority: the province is so distant from the capital, and had been for some time so little attended to by the government, that the laws on this subject were ineffectual.

Negroes are even publicly sold; . . . others evaded the Mexican law of emancipation: viz. by getting his negroes to sign a bond promising to serve him for ninety nine years. . . .

We spent the night at the house of a colonist [north of San Felipe] evidently of the poorer class. Flour was there but little known; but we were furnished with cakes made of Indian meal, which were very good, though unaccompanied by the variety of meats which we had found at the inns of San Felipe and on the road thither. Here I tasted the first good water I had found in Texas: that in the lower country being inferior, and almost without exception obtained from brooks or rivers. . . .

The farmers of Texas commonly make some butter and cheese, at least enough for their own families, and have abundance of milk: but these things engross but few of their thoughts. They churn daily, and therefore are always supplied with butter milk. They often regret it if they have no "sour milk" to offer a visiter [sic], and generally regale him with it—which, whether denominated "bonny clabber," or anything else, I had ere this become fond of, though in the endeavor to like it I had to overcome a strong prejudice. . . .

## 32. LIFE IN COLONIAL TEXAS

### December, 1831

From Mrs. Mary Austin Holley, *Texas* (Baltimore, 1833), 115-129.

One of the best reporters on social life in Texas for the period just prior to the Revolution was Mrs. Mary Austin Holley, a cousin of Stephen F. Austin, from Connecticut. Mrs. Holley, well educated and a keen observer, wrote a series of letters about everyday, commonplace life which she observed about her. The following extracts are from letters X, XI, and XII, headed "Bolivar, Texas, December, 1831."

. . . The people of Texas, as yet have little time for trade. Every body is occupied with his domestic arrangements and plans for supplying his immediate wants. It is found to be easier to raise or manufacture such articles as are needed in the family, or to do without, than to obtain them from abroad, or to employ an individual to scour the country, in search of such as may be desired. People live too far apart, to beg or borrow often, and

few trouble themselves to send any thing to market, though they have ever so much to spare. They had rather give to you of their abundance, if you will send to their doors. The towns are too distant to obtain supplies from them; while some are too proud, some too lazy, and most too indifferent, to trouble themselves about the matter. If they want any article of first necessity, coffee, for instance, which is much used, they will send some of their chickens, butter, and eggs, to a neighboring family newly arrived, and propose an exchange, as most new comers bring with them some stores. There is much of this kind of barter, provisions being so much more plenty than money. Nobody, however, fares very sumptuously; the new comers have not the articles, and the older residents have grown indifferent to the use of them. Besides, they are rich enough; without depending upon the sale of small matters for an income.

There is a peculiar feeling among them about game. No one will receive money for any thing taken by his gun, but will cheerfully give you as much as you will take, and feel insulted, if you offer him money in return. As the chief supplies are of this description, there is, of course, little for sale. It would be better for the public, if this feeling did not prevail, as provisions of this sort, could be furnished at so easy and cheap a rate.

Hence, there is some ground for reasonable complaint against the living in Texas. But it is not the fault of the country. It is an evil, which persons suitably disposed, who would open farms, gardens, and poultry yards, in the vicinity of the settlements, could very soon remedy, which they would not, themselves, be the persons least benefitted. In no country, with the usual attention to the arts of life, could more luxuries for the table be furnished. At present, vegetables, fruits, eggs, butter, and chickens, sell very high in Brazoria; though they are yielded in every season of the year, in a profusion unexampled in any part of the world. The new comer has but to plant his seeds in the ground, and collect a first supply of live stock to begin with. They need but little or no care afterwards, and the increase is astonishing. He brands his cattle and hogs, and lets them run. They require no attention, but to see that they do not stray too far from home, and become wild. A field once planted in pumpkins, seldom needs planting again. The scattered seed sow themselves, and the plants are cultivated with the corn. These pumpkins, as large, often, as a man can lift, have a sweet flavour, and are very palatable. A field of them is a curiosity, they are in such numbers and so large. Sweet potatoes, also, are cultivated with almost equal ease, and yield, at times, five hundred bushels to the acre. Some of these potatoes weigh from four, to seven pounds. Yet they sell, at Brazoria, at the enormous price of seventy-five cents a bushel. Corn is obtained in the prairie cane-brakes, the first year, when there is no time to prepare the land, with the plough, by merely making a hole for the seed, with a hoe. Cows and horses get their own living. The trees at this moment, (17th December,) are loaded with rich clusters of grapes, not very large, but of a delicious flavour. . . .

During my stay at Bolivar, we might have had, every day, the finest of game; could any one have been spared to take the field, with his gun. Our neighbour at one hunt, brought in three bears, a Mexican hog, a rabbit and two bee-trees. Our carpenter, without leaving his bench five minutes, killed several wild ducks, the finest I ever tasted. . . . .

House-keepers should bring with them all indispensable articles for household use, together with as much common clothing (other clothing is not wanted) for themselves and their children, as they, conveniently, can. Ladies in particular, should remember, that in a new country, they cannot get things made at any moment, as in an old one, and that they will be sufficiently busy, the first two years, in arranging such things as they have, without occupying themselves in obtaining more. It should also be done as a matter of economy. Where the population increases, beyond the increase of supplies, articles of

necessity, as well as of luxury, are dear. If, on arrival, they find a surplus on hand, it can be readily disposed of to advantage; for trade, by barter, is much practiced, and you buy provisions, with coffee, calico, tea-kettles, and saucepans, instead of cash.

Those who *must* have a feather-bed, had better bring it, for it would take too long to make one; and though the air swarms with live geese, a feather-bed could not be got for love or money. Everybody should bring pillows and bed linen. Mattresses, such as are used, universally, in Louisiana, and they are very comfortable, are made of the moss, which hangs on almost every tree. They cost nothing but the case and the trouble of preparing the moss. The case should be brought. Domestic checks are best, being cheap and light, and sufficiently strong. The moss is prepared, by burying it in the earth, until it is partially rotten. It is then washed very clean, dried and picked; when it is fit for use. These mattresses should be made very thick: and for those who like a warmer bed in winter, can put some layers of wool, well carded, upon the moss, taking care to *keep this side up.*

Every immigrant should bring musqueto [sic] bars. Since the middle of October, I have not found them necessary. They are indispensable in the summer season, and are made of a thin species of muslin, manufactured for the purpose. Furniture, such as chairs and bureaus, can be brought in separate pieces and put together, cheaper and better, after arrival, than they can be purchased here, if purchased at all. But it must be recollected, that very few articles of this sort, are required, where houses are small, and buildings expensive. Think of the Vicar of Wakefield's picture. Tables are made by the house carpenter, which answer the purpose as well, where nobody has better, and the chief concern is, to get something to put upon them. The maximum here, is, nothing for show, but all for use. . . .

With regard to the state of society here, as is natural to expect, there are many incongruities. It will take some time for people gathered from the north, and from the south, from the east, and from the west, to assimilate, and adapt themselves to new situations. The people are universally kind and hospitable, which are redeeming qualities. Every body's house is open, and table spread, to accommodate the traveller. There are no poor people here, and none rich; that is, none who have much money. The poor and the rich, to use the correlatives, where distinction, there is none, get the same quantity of land on arrival, and if they do not continue equal, it is for want of good management on the one part, or superior industry and sagacity on the other. All are happy, because busy; and none meddle with the affairs of their neighbors, because they have enough to do to take care of their own. They are bound together, by a common interest, by sameness of purpose, and hopes. As far as I could learn, they have no envyings, no jealousies, no bickerings, through politics or fanaticism. There is neither masonry, anti-masonry, nullification nor court intrigues.

The common concerns of life are sufficiently exciting to keep the spirits buoyant, and prevent every thing like ennui. Artificial wants are entirely forgotten, in the view of real ones, and self, eternal self, does not alone, fill up the round of life. Delicate ladies find they can be useful, and need not be vain. Even privations become pleasures: people grow ingenious in overcoming difficulties. Many latent faculties are developed. They discover in themselves, powers, they did not suspect themselves of possess-ing. Equally surprised and delighted at the discovery, they apply to their labours with all that energy and spirit, which new hope and conscious strength, inspire. . . .

## 33. WHY THE COLONISTS ATTACKED BRADBURN AT ANAHUAC

### June, 1832

From Mrs. Mary Austin Holley, *Texas* (Baltimore, 1833), Appendix, 147-151.

A number of factors contributed to the outbreak of hostilities between the Anglo-American colonists and the Mexicans in the summer of 1832. The tariff exemption ended in 1830 and the government took steps to collect the duties. George Fisher, the first collector, made some arbitrary and unreasonable rulings in violation of his instructions, and refused to name a deputy collector for the port of Brazoria, thereby causing the colonists considerable inconvenience.

Furthermore, in keeping with the provisions of the Law of April 6, 1830, additional soldiers were sent to Texas to strengthen existing garrisons and to establish others. Although the commanders generally adhered to their orders to be cautious in their relations with the citizens, the Anglo-American colonists deeply resented the presence of the soldiers and particularly the excesses of Colonel John Davis Bradburn, commander of the garrison at Anahuac. Led by Frank W. Johnson of San Felipe, 160 armed and irate Texans in June, 1832, confronted the commander at Anahuac with a demand that he respect their legal rights. Bradburn had arbitrarily imprisoned Commissioner Francisco Madero for issuing land titles to squatters in the prohibited zone adjacent to the Gulf and the United States on the ground that his instructions had been superseded by the Law of April 6, 1830, had placed the reserve zone under martial law, had requisitioned both slaves and supplies without compensation to the owners, and, finally, had arrested some prominent citizens of the town. The following explanation of the causes precipitating the attack was written shortly after it occurred by Mrs. Mary Austin Holley.

. . . On the 22d. April, 1828, concessions of land were made in conformity with the colonization laws by the president of the nation, Don Guadalupe Victoria, and the governor of this state, to the inhabitants established east of the San Jacinto, and in the district of Nacogdoches. In the year 1830, Don Jose Francisco Madero was appointed by the governor, commissioner to survey the said land, and issue the titles, in due form of law to said settlers. He arrived on the Trinity river in the month of January, 1831, and had made some progress in the discharge of his duties, when he and his surveyor, Jose Maria Carbajal, were arrested by Col. Juan Davis Bradburn, military commandant of Anahuac, and conducted to that post, as prisoners. The only reason given by said commandant for this direct and insulting attack upon the constitution and sovereignty of the state of Coahuila and Texas, was, that the arrest of Madero was made in obedience to the orders of his excellency the commandant Gen. Don Manuel de Mier y Teran. Similar orders were issued for the arrest of Madero to Col. Don Jose de las Piedras, commandant of the frontier of Nacogdoches. His excellency the governor of the state speaks of this affair in his message to the legislature at the opening of the session on the 2d January last, in the following words, as translated:

"The public tranquility has not been disturbed in any part of the state, although Col. Davis Bradburn assumed the power without knowledge of this government, to arrest a commissioner appointed by it, to survey vacant lands and issue titles, — which act might have caused a commotion; but nothing of the kind occurred, owing to the prudence of the arrested person, and of citizens who were to have received titles for lands, and who by this event were deprived for the time being from obtaining legal possession of their property. This government endeavored to ascertain the cause of this interference, and for that purpose entered into continued communications with the commandant general of the states, and so learned, that said general thinks, that agreeably to the commission conferred upon him by the supreme government of the union, under the 3d article of the national law of 6th April, 1830, the commission of said arrested commissioner was in opposition to the 11th article of said general law; and notwithstanding he has been assured that such is not the case, he still persists in his opinion. For these reasons, this matter is in such a situation, that to remove the obstacles it would be necessary to adopt measures that *might compromit the state to the highest degree.*"

*Second* — On the 10th December last, the commandant general, by a laconic military order annulled the Ayuntamiento of liberty [sic], which was legally established by the commissioner Madero, and established a new Ayuntamiento at Anahuac, without any authority from the state government, and without even consulting it.

*Third* — The commandant general has without any authority from the state, taken possession of, and appropriated such lands as he deemed proper; thus totally disregarding the rights and sovereignty of the state. Speaking of this subject, the governor, in the before mentioned message, says, (as translated.) "Although this government, in the message of last year, expressed a hope, that under the provisions of the law of 6th April, 1830, a considerable colonization of the vacant lands in the department of Bexar might be expected, nothing has been done up to the present time. The commissioner of the general government, notwithstanding the instructions he has received, to purchase from the state a portion of vacant lands, has not entered into the necessary contracts for this purpose, nor made any propositions to do so; but has, without any authority, occupied many points with garrisons. This government is ignorant of the causes of this strange mode of proceeding, and therefore cannot state what they are." . . .

In the month of May last, he [Bradburn] imprisoned seven citizens, and attempted to arrest George M. Patrick, the first regidor, and acting Alcalde of Anahuac, and Jas. Lindsey, another regidor of the Ayuntamiento of that place, who, in consequence, left Anahuac, and fled to Austin's colony for security.

These repeated and continued acts of despotism, added to the highly abusive manner in which Col. Bradburn expressed himself against the citizens, and his threats against the constitutional authorities of the state, finally exhausted the patience of all, and caused an excitement which spread through every part of the country. The quiet and peaceful citizens had looked on in silence, with their eyes and hopes directed to the state government, as the only constitutional authority competent to remedy evils of such magnitude, but unfortunately the state government was then borne down by the same iron rod that was held over Texas. . . .

The last and only remedy left to an oppressed people, was then resorted to, and without any previous combinations, or organized plans, a large number of citizens, moved by a common and simultaneous influence, took up arms, and marched to Anahuac, to release the prisoners whom Bradburn had illegally confined, to re-establish the Ayuntamiento of liberty, and to prove to him that the state of Coahuila and Texas, could not any longer be trampled upon with impunity by the military power.

## 34. THE TURTLE BAYOU RESOLUTIONS

### June 13, 1832

From "Address Setting Forth Grievances to Col. J. A. Mexia," July 18, 1832, Charles A. Gulick, Jr., and Katherine Elliott (eds.), *The Papers of Mirabeau Buonaparte Lamar* (6 vols.; Austin, 1920-1927), No. 157, I, 142-143.

As a result of his illegal and despotic acts, John Davis Bradburn, commandant of the garrison at Anahuac, created considerable excitement in every part of Texas. It was his announcement that the imprisoned Patrick C. Jack and William B. Travis must stand military trial, however, that finally incited the colonists to armed resistance. Upon receipt of this news, a number of prominent men, including William H. Jack, brother of Patrick C., Frank W. Johnson, R. M. Williamson, and Wiley Martin of San Felipe and John Austin of Brazoria, formed a company of irate citizens under the command of Johnson for the purpose of compelling Bradburn to release the prisoners and to respect the constitutional rights of civilians. The colonists, numbering 160 men by the time they reached Anahuac on June 10, camped on Turtle Bayou a few miles from the garrison to await the outcome of negotiations with Bradburn for an exchange of prisoners. Bradburn agreed to the exchange, but after some parleying refused to keep his agreement. Discovering that he had used the time to strengthen his position, the Texans sent John Austin to Brazoria for two cannon to use in an assault on the fort.

While waiting for Austin's return, the Texans on Turtle Bayou, cognizant of the seriousness of their action, prepared a formal statement of the causes which had impelled them to resist. They had very little understanding of Mexican politics, but they knew that Bradburn was in the service of the Anastacio Bustamente administration, and that President Bustamente had flagrantly violated the constitution; furthermore, they were aware that Santa Anna, who was heading a revolution against Bustamente, was posing as a liberal and as a champion of the Constitution of 1824. Thus, they asserted their loyalty to the constitution and declared that they were supporting Santa Anna and the liberals. The document, known as "The Turtle Bayou Resolutions," was included in the "Address Setting Forth Grievances to Col. J. A. Mexia" at Brazoria on July 18, 1832.

RESOLVED That we view with feelings of the deepest regret, the manner in which the Gover't of the Republic of Mexico is administered by the present dynasty — The repeated violations of the constitution — the total disregard of the law — the entire prostration of the civil authority; and the substitution in the stead of a military despotism, are grievances of such a character, as to arouse the feelings of every freeman, and impel him to resistance —

RESOLVED That we view with feelings of the deepest interest and solicitude, the firm and manly resistance, which is made by the highly talented and distinguished Chieftain — General Santa Anna, to the numberless Incroachments and infractions, which have been made by the present administration, upon the constitution and law of our adopted and beloved country.

RESOLVED That as freemen devoted to a correct interpretation, and enforcement of the Constitution, and laws, according to their true Spirit — We pledge our lives and fortunes in support of the same, and of the distinguished leader, who is now so gallantly fighting in defence of Civil liberty.

RESOLVED That the people of Texas be invited to cooperate with us, in support of the principles incorporated in The foregoing resolutions. — 13th June 1832. . . .

## 35. THE CONVENTION OF 1833

### April 1-13, 1833

A liberal revolution in Mexico in 1832 under Santa Anna overthrew the conservative government of Anastacio Bustamente that had precipitated the crisis at Anahuac and, as a result, the troops throughout East Texas were withdrawn. Hopeful that Santa Anna, whose cause they had supported, would be receptive to their requests for reforms, the Texans met in convention in October, 1832, and April, 1833, at San Felipe to draw up formal petitions for that purpose.

The first convention, consisting of fifty-six delegates representing sixteen districts, addressed memorials to the national and state governments, the two most important calling for the repeal of the Law of April 6, 1830, and for separation of Texas from Coahuila. Its petitions were never presented, however, possibly because Santa Anna had not yet won control of the government, but more probably because the Mexican officials in Texas and Coahuila considered the action extra-legal. But early in 1833 when it was apparent that Santa Anna would become president, the Central Committee of Safety and Correspondence at San Felipe called the second convention for April 1. A larger number of discontented delegates were in attendance this time, evidenced by the selection of William H. Wharton rather than Stephen F. Austin as president of the convention. Petitions similar to those of 1832 were prepared, but with greater emphasis on separate statehood.

The three documents which follow explain this sentiment clearly and provide the organic type of state government desired. The first was written by Austin at the request of the Central Committee of Safety and Correspondence to explain why the convention had been called; the second was written by David G. Burnet, chairman of the committee appointed by the convention to explain to Congress why Texas should have a separate state government; the third was the work of a committee, headed by Sam Houston, appointed by the convention to prepare a proposed constitution for the State of Texas.

### 1. AUSTIN'S ADDRESS EXPLAINING WHY THE CONVENTION WAS CALLED

#### April 1, 1833

From Eugene C. Barker (ed.), *The Austin Papers* (3 vols.; Washington, 1924, 1928; Austin, 1927), II, 934-940.

#### GENTLEMEN OF THE CONVENTION,

The central committee of safety and correspondence which was established by the late convention, and by whose request the present convention has assembled, beg leave to offer their sincere congratulations on your arrival at the theatre where you are to exercise the high and important duties which devolve upon you as the representatives of the people of your several districts.

Believing that your deliberations will be fraught with important results to the interests of our common country, the committee deem it a duty they owe you, as the delegates of the people to make a brief exposition of the reasons which have operated on them in calling this convention, and in doing this, they wish it to be understood, not as attempting to dictate to this convention the course it should pursue in the least degree, nor to prescribe limits to its action, but to give a satisfactory explanation to you, and through you to the great body of the people of Texas, of the causes which have impelled them to the exercise of this responsible duty.

The situation of Texas, is such as to give rise to great anxiety and even alarm in the heart of every person who inhabits it, or feels any interest for its prosperity or welfare.

The whole of this country, with the exception of the small towns of Bexar and Goliad, has been settled and redeemed from the wilderness within a few years by the enterprise of immigrants who removed to it in consequence of the express and earnest invitation of the Government, contained in the national and state colonization laws. Those immigrants have uniformly evinced their gratitude to the government and nation of their adoption for all the acts of kindness and liberality that have been extended towards them, and they have faithfully performed their duty as Mexican citizens, and fulfilled the intention and spirit of the colonization laws, by settling the country, defending it from hostile indians, or other enemies, and developing its resources, thus giving value and character to a large section of the Mexican territory which was before wild and almost unknown. They have introduced agriculture and the usefull arts and commerce, and if as has been said by a celebrated author "that man deserves well of his country who makes a blade of grass grow where none grew before," how much more do the people of Texas deserve from their country who have so materially added to the national grandeur, phisical force and resources. The people of Texas ought therefore to rely with confidence on the government for protection, and to expect that an adequate remedy will be applied to the many evils that are afflicting them.

The invitations in virtue of which they came here, and the guarantees of the constitution and laws, evidently contain a pledge on the part of the government, that they should be governed in accordance with the spirit of the free political institutions of the Mexican republic, and in the manner best adapted to the local situation and necessities of Texas. The *right* of the people of Texas to represent their wants to the government, and to explain in a respectfull manner the remedies that will relieve them cannot therefore be doubted or questioned. It is not merely a right, it is also a sacred and bounden duty which they owe to themselves and to the whole Mexican nation, for should evils of great and desolating magnitude fall upon Texas for the want of competent remedies, the people here would have cause to accuse themselves of neglect for not making an effort to procure such remedies, and the government would also have cause to complain, that a full and frank and timely representation had not been made and a remedy solicited.

It is very evident that these considerations have influenced the people of Texas in all they have done up to the present time. They have been governed by the desire to do their duty faithfully to the Mexican nation and to themselves. In the discharge of this duty the people and civil authorities of Austins Colony made a respectfull and humble petition to the General and State governments on the 18 day of Feby 1832 setting forth the evils that were afflicting this country. The inhabitants and civil authorities of Bexar, the ancient and present capital of Texas, also made a very able and energetic representation on the same subject on the 19th of December last. Numerous other representatives have been made at various times by all the Ayuntamientos of Texas, and on the first of October last delegates of the people of Texas met in convention at this Town and unanimously resolved that it was expedient that the political union between Coahuila and Texas should be dissolved and that Texas should be organised as a separate State of the Mexican confederation as soon as the approbation of the General government to that effect could be obtained. That convention accordingly memorialised congress on the subject, and elected an agent to go to Mexico in order to forward the views of the people of Texas in obtaining the sanction of the general government. But the continuation of the intestine commotions which have raged within the bosom of the Mexican republic for more than twelve months past, and which threaten'd a total overthrow of the established institutions of the country, prevented the memorial from being presented in accordance with the intentions of the October convention.

That convention adopted many other memorials and resolutions, amongst the most important of which was the provisional organization of the militia, as a precaution against contemplated attacks upon our exposed frontier by the many tribes of hostile indians who inhabit the northern and western parts of Texas; and the establishment of the central and sub-committees of safety and correspondence throughout the country all of which were rendered inoperative by the decree of the governor of the state of Coahuila and Texas, who declared the proceedings of the convention null and void, and ordered the several committees to dissolve.

At the time when this committee determined to convoke the present convention, they took an impartial survey of our federal relations and of our local affairs.

They beheld the Mexican confederation torn and broken asunder by political parties each of which sustained its pretentions to the supreme executive power of the nation by force of arms. Civil war raged in every part of the Mexican territory and in looking upon the face of the nation nothing was to be seen but confusion and bloody discord—Brother contending with brother in deadly strife for mastery in political power. They saw that the constitution of the republic, that instrument which they had been taught to look upon as the sacred charter of their liberties was alternately violated and set aside by all parties, and that all the constitutional guarantees were merged for the time being in military power. They saw the constitutional period for the election of President and vice President of the nation and of members of Congress, pass by, and at least one third of the states refuse or neglect to hold the elections. The future presented the gloomy prospect that the days of constitutional freedom had been numbered to the Mexicans, and that we should ere long see the waves of anarchy and confusion close forever over the wreck of that Mexican republic. The disorganization of the government was so extream, that even the leaders of the liberal party who have been contending for the restoration of constitutional liberty, and whose cause was espoused by the people of Texas, and generously defended with their blood

and treasure, found themselves compelled to lay aside all the established forms, and to renovate the constitution by violent and unconstitutional means.

The committee turned from this view of our national affairs to that of the local internal situation of Texas which has not materially changed since the last convention. The political system under which Texas has heretofore been governed, tends to check the growth of the country, and to produce confusion and insecurity, rather than to extend protection to lives liberty and property. The unnatural annexation of what was formerly the province of Texas to Coahuila by the constituent congress of the Mexican nation, has forced upon the people of Texas a system of laws which they do not understand and which cannot be administered so as to suit their condition or to supply their wants.

The Alcaldes who are the highest judicial officers in Texas and have unlimited jurisdiction in all cases, are elected annually by the people, and those who are ignorant and corrupt and without responsibility are as liable to be chosen as the wise, the virtuous and the responsible. This remark is justified by the fact that the office is without emolument and is extreemly burdensome, and will therefore seldom be sought by those who are best qualified to fill it. In all civil cases there is an appeal to the supreme tribunal of the state at Saltillo a distance of near seven hundred miles from the inhabited parts of Texas. There are but few men in Texas who are qualified to prepare cases for the supreme court and when appeals have been taken they have generally been sent back several times to be reformed so that decissions in such cases are seldom had. It has become proverbial in Texas, that an appeal to Saltillo is a payment of the debt. It amounts to a total denial of justice especially to the poor, and this is the frail tenure by which the most important rights of the people of Texas are suspended.

The manner of trying culprits for high criminal offences is such that it amounts to no tryal at all. The tryal by jury is not sanctioned by law, and the rights of the accused are committed to an alcalde who is ignorant of the formulas of the laws, and of the language in which they are written who prepares the cause for the judgment of the supreme tribunal in Saltillo, thus the lives, liberty and honor of the accused are suspended upon the tardy decission of a distant tribunal which knows not nor cares not for his suffering, and the rights of the community to bring offenders to speedy and exemplary punishment are sacrificed to forms equally uncertain and unknown. The formula required by law in the prosecution of criminals is so difficult to be pursued that most of the courts in Texas have long since ceased to attempt its execution. The tryal by jury has been attempted in some of the municipalities, but being unsupported by the sanction of law it also has failed of success. A total interegnum in the administration of justice in criminal cases may be said to exist. A total disregard of the laws has become so prevalent, both amongst the officers of justice, and the people at large, that reverence for laws or for those who administer them has almost intirely disappeared and contempt is fast assuming its place, so that the protection of our property our persons and lives is circumscribed almost exclusively to the moral honesty or virtue of our neighbor.

The people and authorities of Bexar in their representation in December last speaking of the judiciary system in Texas use the following strong and conclusive language.

"In the judiciary department there never has been any adequate organization and it may be said with just cause that in this department there is not and never has been any government in Texas."

Besides the evils which menace Texas for the want of a judiciary there are others of no less appalling effects. This country is in danger of being inundated by bands of northern indians who are removing from the east side of the Mississippi to Arkansas on our borders. Also the Comanche, Tahuacana and other tribes of native Texas indians have recently become hostile and are committing depredations on the frontiers. But [it] is unnecessary to enter into details—enough is said in the representation of Bexar by the declaration that there is not and never has been any adequate gov*t* in Texas.

Judging from the past, it must be considered a vain hope to look to the State government of Coahuila and Texas for a redress of grievances, or a remedy of wrongs. We have twice beheld the mortifying spectacle of the corrupt mob of the Capital driving the legislature by force to. adopt measures, unconstitutional in themselves, insulting to the inhabitants of Texas, and disregardful of their rights. The general neglect of the state Legislature of all the important interests and rights of Texas and their repeated violations of the constitution are very clearly and energetically set forth in the Bexar remonstrance of last December. There seems to be no cause to expect any favourable change towards Texas in the politics of Coahuila. But even supposing there were the legislature that would suit Coahuila would be pernicious in Texas. No organization can be devised under the constitution of the State of Coahuila and Texas that would suit the two extremes, separated as they are more than 400 leagues, a great part through a wilderness that cannot be passed without imminent danger from hostile indians. The dissimilarity of habits occupation and language also present still greater difficulties than the distance. These difficulties are hard to reconcile for the reason that the state constitution requires that all general laws shall be the same throughout the whole state. There cannot therefore be any organization of the judiciary for Texas materially different from that of Coahuila.

In this state of things the committee considered themselves bound by a solemn duty to call on the people of Texas through their representatives to meet in general convention with full powers to deliberate on the present distracted situation of our infant country and to adopt such constitutional measures as in their wisdom they may deem necessary. In exercising this highly responsible duty the committee did not act unadvisedly or without the most mature deliberation, and they did not call this convention untill they were satisfied that a large majority of the people of Texas were in favor of applying for a well organized state Gov*t* as the only remedy for existing evils.

The law of the constituent Congress of 7 May 1824 evidently contemplates that Texas should form a separate State. The 2*d* article of that law is in the following words as translated "Coahuila and Texas shall also form another state, but so soon as the latter is in a situation to figure as a separate state, it shall inform congress thereof for its resolution."

The right which this law confers upon the people of Texas to inform congress when they are in a situation to figure as a State, and to apply for admission into the Union is certainly very clear and unequivocal.

What method may be the best to obtain a remedy for the many evils which afflict Texas, can only be determined by the wisdom of the convention. Trusting that your deliberations will be conducted with that zeal for the public welfare which the common good of our adopted country requires and that they will tend to that happy issue which all so confidently anticipate, the central committee take leave of the convention by depositing the power which they have exercised for a time in the hands of those who gave it.

## 2. THE MEMORIAL TO CONGRESS REQUESTING SEPARATE STATEHOOD

### April, 1833

From H. Yoakum, *A History of Texas* (2 vols.; New York, 1855; facsimile, Austin, 1935), I, 469-482.

The inhabitants of Texas, by their representatives elect, in convention assembled, would respectfully approach the national Congress, and present this their memorial, praying that the union which was established between Coahuila and Texas, whereby the two ancient provinces were incorporated into one free and independent state, under the name of "COAHUILA AND TEXAS," may be dissolved, abrogated, and perpetually cease; and that the inhabitants of Texas may be authorized to institute and establish a separate state government, which will be in accordance with the federal constitution and the constitutive act; and that the state so constituted shall be received and incorporated into the great confederation of Mexico, on terms of equality with the other states of the Union.

To explain the grounds of this application, your memorialists would respectfully invite the attention of the general Congress to the following considerations:

The consolidation of the late provinces of Coahuila and Texas was, in its nature, provisional, and, in its intention, temporary. The decree of the sovereign constituent Congress, bearing date the 7th of May, 1824, contemplates a separation, and guaranties to Texas the right of having a state government whenever she may be in condition to ask for the same. That decree provides that, "so soon as Texas shall be in a condition to figure as a state of itself, it shall inform Congress thereof, for its resolution." The implication conveyed by this clause is plain and imperative; and vests in Texas as perfect a right as language can convey. . . .

By the *Constitutive Act*, adopted on the 31st of January, 1824, Coahuila, New Leon, and Texas, were joined together, and denominated "the internal eastern state."

By a law passed by the constituent Congress on the 7th of May, 1824, that union was dissolved, and the province of New Leon was admitted into the confederacy as an independent state. It is on the *second* article of this law that the people of Texas now predicate their right to a similar admission. The constitutive act, above mentioned, consolidated the late provinces of Chihuahua, Durango, and New Mexico, under the style of "the internal northern state;" and on the 22d of May, 1824, a summary law decreed that "Durango should form a state of the Mexican confederation," and she was admitted accordingly. The same privilege was extended to Chihuahua by a decree of the 6th of July of the same year. These conjunct provinces stood, at the period of their separation, in precisely the same relation to the federal government that Texas and Coahuila now occupy. . . .

The general Congress may possibly consider the mode of this communication as informal. To this suggestion we would, with great deference, reply, that the events of the past year have not only violated the established forms and etiquette of the government, but have suspended, at least, its vital functions; and it would appear exceedingly rigorous to exact from the inhabitants of Texas, living on a remote frontier of the republic, a minute conformity to unimportant punctilios. The ardent desire of the people is made known to the Congress through their select representatives, the most direct and unequivocal medium by which they can possibly be conveyed; and surely the enlightened Congress will readily concur with us in the sentiment that the wishes and wants of the people form the best rule for legislative guidance. The people of Texas consider it not only an absolute right, but a most sacred and imperative duty to themselves, and to the Mexican nation, to represent their wants in a respectful manner to the general government, and to solicit the best remedy of which the nature of their grievances will admit. Should they utterly fail in this duty, and great and irremediable evils ensue, the people would have reason to reproach themselves alone; and the general Congress, in whom the remedial power resides, would also have reason to censure their supineness and want of fidelity to the nation. Under this view, we trust the Congress will not regard with excessive severity any slight departure which the good people of Texas may in this instance have made from the ordinary formalities of the government.

And we would further suggest to the equitable consideration of the federal Congress that, independent of and anterior to the express guaranty contained in the decree of the 7th of May, 1824, the right of having a separate state government was vested in and belonged to Texas, by the fact that she participated as a distinct province in the toils and sufferings by which the glorious emancipation of Mexico was achieved, and the present happy form of government was established. The subsequent union with Coahuila was a temporary compact, induced by a supposed expediency, arising from an inadequate population on the part of Texas "to figure as a state of itself." . . . The obvious design of the union between Coahuila and Texas was, on one part at least, the more effectually to secure the peace, safety, and

happiness, of Texas. That design has not been accomplished, and facts piled upon facts afford a melancholy evidence that it is utterly impracticable. Texas never has and never can derive from the connection benefits in any wise commensurate with the evils she has sustained, and which are daily increasing in number and in magnitude.

But our reasons for the proposed separation are more explicitly set forth in the subjoined remarks. . . . The two territories are disjunct in all their prominent respective relations.

In point of locality, they approximate only by a strip of sterile and useless territory, which must long remain a comparative wilderness, and present many serious embarrassments to that facility of intercourse which should always exist between the seat of government and its remote population. In respect to commerce and its various intricate relations, there is no community of interests between them. The one is altogether *interior*; is consequently abstracted from all participation in maritime concerns; and is naturally indifferent, if not adverse, to any system of polity that is calculated to promote the diversified and momentous interests of commerce. The other is blest with many natural advantages for extensive commercial operations, which, if properly cultivated, would render many valuable accessions to the national marine, and a large increase to the national revenues. The importance of an efficient national marine is evinced, not only by the history of other and older governments, but by the rich halo of glory which encircles the brief annals of the Mexican navy. In point of climate and of natural productions, the two territories are equally dissimilar. Coahuila is a pastoral and a mining country; Texas is characteristically an agricultural district. The occupations incident to these various intrinsic properties are equally various and distinct; and a course of legislation that may be adapted to the encouragement of the habitual industry of the one district, might present only embarrassment and perplexity, and prove fatally deleterious to the prosperity of the other.

It is not needful, therefore—neither do we desire—to attribute any sinister or invidious design to the legislative enactments or to the domestic economical policy of Coahuila (whose ascendency in the joint councils of the state gives her an uncontrolled and exclusive power of legislation), in order to ascertain the origin of the evils that affect Texas, and which, . . . whether those evils have proceeded from a sinister policy in the predominant influences of Coahuila, or whether they are the natural results of a union . . . are equally repugnant and injurious, whether emanating from the one other source.

Bexar, the ancient capital of Texas, presents a faithful but a gloomy picture of her general want of protection and encouragement. Situated in a fertile, picturesque, and healthful region, and established a century and a half ago (within which period populous and magnificent cities have sprung into existence), she exhibits only the decrepitude of age—sad testimonials of the absence of that political guardianship which a wise government should always bestow upon the feebleness of its exposed frontier settlements. A hundred and seventeen years have elapsed since Goliad and Nacogdoches assumed the distinctive names of towns, and they are still entitled only to the diminutive appellation of villages. Other military and missionary establishments have been attempted, but, from the same defect of protection and encouragement, they have been swept away, and scarcely a vestige remains to rescue their locations from oblivion.

We do not mean to attribute these specific disasters to the union with Coahuila, for we know they transpired long anterior to the consummation of that union. But we do maintain that the same political causes, the same want of protection and encouragement, the same malorganization and impotency of the local and minor faculties of the government, the same improvident indifference to the peculiar and vital interests of Texas, exist *now* that operated then. Bexar is still exposed to the depredations of her ancient enemies; the insolent, vindictive, and faithless Camanches. Her citizens are still massacred, their cattle destroyed or driven away, and their very habitations threatened, by a tribe of erratic and undisciplined Indians, whose audacity has derived confidence from success, and whose long-continued aggressions have invested them with a fictitious and excessive terror. Her schools are neglected, her churches desolate, the sounds of human industry are almost hushed, and the voice of gladness and festivity is converted into wailing and lamentation, by the disheartening and multiplied evils which surround her defenceless population. Goliad is still kept in constant trepidation; is paralyzed in all her efforts for improvement; and is harassed on all her borders by the predatory incursions of the Wacoes, and other insignificant bands of savages, whom a well-organized local government would soon subdue and exterminate.

These are facts, not of history merely, on which the imagination must dwell with an unwilling melancholy, but they are events of the present day, which the present generation feel in all their dreadful reality. And these facts, revolting as they are, are as a fraction only in the stupendous aggregate of our calamities. Our misfortunes do not proceed from Indian depredations alone; neither are they confined to a few isolated, impoverished, and almost-tenantless towns. They pervade the whole territory—operate upon the whole population—and are as diversified in character as our public interests and necessities are various. Texas at large feels and deplores an utter destitution of the common benefits which have usually accrued from the worst system of internal government that the patience of mankind ever tolerated. She is virtually without a *government;* and if she is not precipitated into all the unspeakable horrors of anarchy, it is only because there is a redeeming spirit among the people, which still infuses some moral energy into the miserable fragments of authority that exist among us. We are perfectly sensible that a large portion of our population, usually denominated "the colonists," and composed of Anglo-Americans, have been greatly calumniated before the Mexican government. But could the honorable Congress scrutinize strictly into our real condition—could they see and understand the wretched confusion in all the elements of government, which we daily feel and deplore—our ears would no longer be insulted, nor our feelings mortified, by the artful fictions of hireling emissaries from abroad, nor by the malignant aspersions of disappointed military commandants at home.

Our grievances do not so much result from any positive misfeasance on the part of the present state authorities, . . . We complain more of the *want* of *all* the important attributes of government, than of the abuses of any. . . .

It is equally obvious that the happiness of the people is more likely to be secured by a local than by a remote government. In the one case, the governors are partakers, in common with the governed, in all the political evils which result to the community, and have therefore a personal interest in so discharging their respective functions as will best secure the common welfare. In the other supposition, those vested with authority are measurably exempt from the calamities that ensue [upon] an abuse of power, and may very conveniently subserve their own interests and ambition, while they neglect or destroy "the welfare of the associated."

But, independent of these general truths, there are some impressive reasons why the peace and happiness of Texas demand a local government. Constituting a remote frontier of the republic, and bordering on a powerful nation, a portion of whose population, in juxtaposition to hers, is notoriously profligate and lawless, she requires, in a peculiar and emphatic sense, the vigorous application of such laws as are necessary, not only to the preservation of good order, the protection of property, and the redress of personal wrongs, but such also as are essential to the prevention of illicit commerce, to the security of the public revenues, and to the avoidance of serious collision with the authorities of the neighboring republic. That such a judicial administration is impracticable under the present arrangement, is too forcibly illustrated by the past to admit of any rational hope for the future.

It is an acknowledged principle in the science of jurisprudence, that the prompt and certain infliction of mild and humane punishment is more efficacious for the prevention of crime than a tardy and precarious administration of the most sanguinary penal code. Texas is virtually denied the benefit of this benevolent rule by the locality and the character of her present government. Crimes of the greatest atrocity may go unpunished, and hardened criminals triumph in their iniquity, because of the difficulties and delays which encumber her judicial system, and necessarily intervene [between] a trial and conviction, and the sentence and the execution of the law. Our "supreme tribunal of justice" holds its sessions upward of seven hundred miles distant from our central population; and that distance is greatly enlarged, and sometimes made impassable, by the casualities incident to a *"mail"* conducted by a single horseman through a wilderness, often infested by vagrant and murderous Indians. Before sentence can be pronounced by the local courts on persons charged with the most atrocious crimes, a copy of the process must be transmitted to an assessor, resident at Leona Vicario (Saltillo), who is too far removed from the scene of guilt to appreciate the importance of a speedy decision, and is too much estranged from our civil and domestic concerns to feel the miseries that result from a total want of legal protection in person and property. But our difficulties do not terminate here. After the assessor shall have found leisure to render his opinion, and final judgment is pronounced, it again becomes necessary to resort to the capital to submit the tardy sentence to the supreme tribunal for "approbation revocation, or modification," before the judgment of the law can be executed. Here we have again to encounter the vexations and delays incident to all governments where those who exercise its most interesting functions are removed by distance from the people on whom they operate, and for whose benefit the social compact is created.

These repeated delays, resulting from the remoteness of our courts of judicature are pernicious in many respects. They involve heavy expenses, which, in civil suits, are excessively onerous to litigants, and give to the rich and influential such manifold advantages over the poor as operate to an absolute exclusion of the latter from the remedial and protective benefits of the law. They offer seductive opportunities and incitements to bribery and corruption, and endanger the sacred purity of the judiciary, which, of all the branches of the government, is most intimately associated with the domestic and social happiness of man, and should therefore be, not only sound and pure, but unsuspected of the venal infection. They present insuperable difficulties to the exercise of the corrective right of recusation, and virtually nullify the constitutional power of impeachment. In criminal actions they are no less injurious. They are equivalent to a license to iniquity, and exert a dangerous influence on the moral feelings at large. Before the tedious process of the law can be complied with, and the criminal—whose hands are perhaps imbrued in a brother's blood—be made to feel its retributive justice, the remembrance of his crime is partially effaced from the public mind; and the righteous arbitrament of the law, which, if promptly executed, would have received universal approbation, and been a salutary warning to evil doers, is impugned as vindictive and cruel. The popular feeling is changed from a just indignation of crime into an amiable but mistaken sympathy for the criminal; and an easy and natural transition is converted into disgust and disaffection toward the government and its laws.

These are some of the evils that result from the annexation of Texas to Coahuila, and the exercise of legislative and judicial powers by the citizens of Coahuila over the citizens of Texas. The catalogue might be greatly enlarged, but we forbear to trespass on the time of the honorable Congress (confiding to the worthy citizens, who shall be charged with the high duty of presenting this memorial, and the protocol of a constitution, which the people of Texas have framed, as the basis of their future government, the more explicit enunciation of them). Those evils are not likely to be diminished, but they may be exceedingly aggravated by the fact that that political connection was formed without the cordial approbation of the people of Texas, and is daily becoming more odious to them. . . .

The idea may possibly occur, in the deliberations of the honorable Congress, that a territorial organization would cure our political maladies, and effectuate the great purposes which induce this application; and plausible reasons may be advanced in favor of it. But the wisdom of Congress will readily detect the fallacy of these reasons, and the mischief consequent to such vain sophistry. In this remote section of the republic, a territorial government must, of necessity, be divested of one essential and radical principle in all popular institutions—the immediate responsibility of public agents to the people whom they serve. . . .

And we would further present with great deference, that the institution of a territorial government would confer upon us neither the form nor the substance of our high guaranty. It would, indeed, diversify our miseries, by opening new avenues to peculation and abuse of power; but it would neither remove our difficulties nor place us in the enjoyment of our equal and vested rights. The only adequate remedy that your memorialists can devise, and which they ardently hope the collective wisdom of the nation will approve, is to be found in the establishment of a *local state government*. We believe that if Texas were endowed with the faculties of a state government, she would be competent to remedy the many evils that now depress her energies, and frustrate every effort to develop and bring into usefulness the natural resources which a beneficent Providence has conferred upon her. We believe that a local legislature, composed of citizens who feel and participate in all the calamities which encompass us, would be enabled to enact such conservative, remedial, and punitive laws, and so to organize and put into operation the municipal and inferior authorities of the country, as would inspire universal confidence; would encourage the immigration of virtuous foreigners—prevent the ingress of fugitives from the justice of other countries—check the alarming accumulations of ferocious Indians, whom the domestic policy of the United States of the North is rapidly translating to our borders; would give impulse and vigor to the industry of the people—secure a cheerful subordination and a faithful adhesion to the state and general governments; and would render Texas what she ought to be—a strong arm of the republic, a terror to foreign invaders, and an example of peace and prosperity—of advancement in the arts and sciences, and of devotion to the Union—to her sister-states. We believe that an executive chosen from among ourselves would feel a more intense interest in our political welfare, would watch with more vigilance over our social concerns, and would contribute more effectually to the purposes of his appointment. We believe that a local judiciary, drawn from the bosom of our own peculiar society, would be enabled to administer the laws with more energy and promptitude—to punish the disobedient and refractory—to restrain the viciousness of the wicked—to impart confidence and security, of both person and property, to peaceable citizens—to conserve and perpetuate the general tranquillity of the state—and to render a more efficient aid to the coordinate powers of the government, in carrying into effect the great objects of its institution. We believe that, if Texas were admitted to the Union as a separate state, she would soon "figure" as a brilliant star in the Mexican constellation, and would shed a new splendor around the illustrious city of Montezuma. We believe she would contribute largely to the national wealth and aggrandizement

—would furnish new staples for commerce, and new materials for manufactures. The cotton of Texas would give employment to the artisans of Mexico; and the precious metals, which are now flowing into the coffers of England, would be retained at home, to reward the industry and remunerate the ingenuity of native citizens. . . .

For these and other considerations, your memorialists would solemnly invoke the magnanimous spirit of the Mexican nation, concentrated in the wisdom and patriotism of the federal Congress. And they would respectfully and ardently pray that the honorable Congress would extend their remedial power to this obscure section of the republic; would cast around it "the sovereign mantle of the nation," and adopt it into a free and plenary participation of that "constitutional *regime*" of equal sisterhood which alone can rescue it from the miseries of an ill-organized, inefficient, internal government, and can reclaim this fair and fertile region from the worthlessness of an untenanted waste, or the more fearful horrors of barbarian inundation.

DAVID G. BURNET, *Chairman of the Committee.*

## 3. THE PROPOSED CONSTITUTION FOR THE STATE OF TEXAS

### April 13, 1833

From *Constitution or Form of Government of the State of Texas* (Made in General Convention, in the Town of San Felipe de Austin, in the Month of April, 1833; New Orleans, 1833; photostat copy, Archives, Texas State Library, Austin).

### CONSTITUTION OF TEXAS.

In the name of God, Omnipotent Author, and Supreme Legislator of the Universe! We, the People of Texas, being capable of figuring as a State in the manner contemplated in the second article of the Decree of the General Congress of the Nation, of the 7th of May, 1824, DO ORDAIN THE FOLLOWING CONSTITUTION, and do mutually agree with each other, to form ourselves into a Free and Independent State of the Mexican Confederacy, by the name of the STATE OF TEXAS.

### GENERAL PROVISIONS

ARTICLE 1. All power is inherent in the people; and all free governments are founded on their authority, and established for their peace, safety, and happiness: for the advancement of these ends, they have at all times an undeniable right to alter, reform, or abolish the government, in such manner as they may think proper.

Art. 2. Government being instituted for the protection and common benefit of all persons, the slavish doctrine of non-resistance against arbitrary power and oppression is discarded, as destructive of the happiness of mankind, and as insulting to the rights, and subversive of the liberties of any people.

Art. 3. All elections shall be free and equal.

Art. 4. The right of trial by jury, and the privilege of the *Writ of Habeas Corpus* shall be established by law, and shall remain inviolable.

Art. 5. The people shall be secure in their persons, houses, papers, and possessions, from unreasonable searches and seizures: and general warrants, whereby an officer may be commanded to search suspected places, without evidence of the fact committed, or to seize any person, or persons, not named, whose offences are not particularly described, and supported by evidence, are dangerous to liberty, and *shall not be granted.*

Art. 6. No citizen shall be taken, or imprisoned, or disseized of his freehold, liberties or privileges, or outlawed, or exiled, or in any manner distrained, or deprived of his life, liberty, or property, but by the law of the land.

Art. 7. In all criminal prosecutions, the accused hath a right to be heard by himself and his counsel, to demand the nature and cause of the accusation against him, and to have a copy thereof: he shall be confronted by his accusers and the witnesses, he shall have compulsory processes for obtaining witnesses in his favor, and in prosecutions by indictment or presentment, a speedy public trial, by an impartial jury of the municipality or district, in which the crimes shall have been committed; and shall not be compelled to give evidence against himself.

Art. 8. No person shall, for the same offence, be twice put in jeopardy of life or limb.

Art. 9. No retrospective law, or law impairing the obligation of contracts shall be made.

Art. 10. No conviction shall work corruption of blood, or forfeiture of estate.

Art. 11. No person arrested, or confined in jail, shall be treated with unnecessary rigour.

Art. 12. No person shall be compelled to answer any criminal charge but by presentment, indictment, or impeachment, or by a concurrent vote of both houses of the legislature, as provided by the constitution.

Art. 13. All persons shall be bailable by sufficient sureties, unless for capital crimes, when the proof is evident, or the presumption strong; and the privelege of the Writ of Habeas Corpus shall not be suspended, except when in cases of rebellion, or invasion, the public safety may require it.

Art. 14. Excessive bail shall not be required, nor excessive fines imposed: or cruel or unusual punishment inflicted: all courts shall be open, and every man, for an injury done him in his lands, goods, person, or reputation, shall have remedy by due course of law, and right and justice administered, without sale, denial, or delay.

Art. 15. The person of a debtor, where there is not strong presumption of fraud, shall not be continued in prison after delivering up his estate for the benefit of his creditor, or creditors, in such manner as shall be prescribed by law.

Art. 16. The free communication of thoughts and opinions, is one of the inviolable rights of man; and every person may freely speak, write, print, and publish, on any subject, being responsible for the abuse of that liberty; but in prosecutions for the publication of papers investigating the official conduct of men in public capacity, the truth thereof may be given in evidence, as well as in personal actions of slander; and in all indictments for libles, the jury shall have the right to determine the law and the facts, under the direction of the court as in other cases.

Art. 17. No man's particular service shall be demanded, nor property taken, or applied to public use, without the consent of himself, or his, representative; or without just compensation being made therefor, according to law.

Art. 18. The people have a right to assemble together, in a peaceable manner, for their common good: to instruct their representatives and to apply to those invested with the powers of government, for redress of grievances, or for other proper purposes, by address or remonstrance.

Art. 19. Perpetuities and monopolies are contrary to the genius of a free government, and shall not be allowed.

Art. 20. The sure and certain defence of a free people, is a well regulated militia: and it shall be the duty of the legislature to enact such laws, as may be necessary to the organization of the militia of this State.

Art. 21. No soldier, in the time of peace, shall be quartered in the house, or within the inclosure of any individual, without the consent of the owner; nor in time of war, but in a manner prescribed by law.

Art. 22. No property qualifications shall be required to entitle a citizen to vote, or hold any office, in the gift of the people of this State.

Art 23. All persons residing in Texas, at the date of this Constitution, except bonded servants, and other persons not liable to taxation by virtue of laws enacted under this Constitution, shall be regarded as citizens, and as being entitled to all the benefits of persons who emigrated to the country under the Colonization Law of 1825, and shall be acknowledged and admitted to all the rights and privileges of such immigrants.

Art. 24. All contracts and transfers of property, by will or otherwise, as well in relation to real as personal estate, which have been made in Texas heretofore, or which hereafter may be made, in good faith, by the parties, shall not be void for any want of form or technicality, but shall be construed and enforced according to the true intention of the parties.

Art 25. Treason against the State shall consist only in levying war against it, or adhering to its enemies, giving them aid and comfort.—No person shall be convicted of treason, unless on the testimony of two witnesses to the same overt act.

Art. 26. The benefits of education, and of useful knowledge, generally diffused through a community, are essential to the preservation of a free government. The protection and advancement of these great objects are given in special and solemn charge to the legislature.—It shall be a particular duty of the government to patronize and cherish the interests of literature, of science, and the arts; and as soon as practicable, to establish schools, where the poor shall be taught gratis.

Art. 27. All elections in this State, shall be by ballot: and the manner thereof shall be prescribed by law.

Art. 28. All lands in this state, liable to taxation, held by deed, grant, concession, colonization law, or otherwise, shall be taxed according to their valuation.

Art. 29. The right of suffrage shall not be exercised by any person of insane mind, or who shall be a pauper, or supported by public or private charity, nor by any non-commissioned officer, soldier, seaman, or marine, in the service of the United Mexican States; nor by any person convicted of an infamous offence, hereafter committed.

Art. 30. No bank nor banking institution, nor office of discount and deposite, nor other monied corporation, nor private banking establishment, shall ever exist during the continuance of this constitution.

Art. 31. All lands within the limits of Texas, at this date vacant, or not held agreeable to law, or to be located under genuine and bonifide grants, now issued and received by the grantee, or grantees, or otherwise provided for by this constitution, shall belong and constitute a fund for the use of the state; and be subject to the disposal of the legislature: Provided, that nothing contained in this article shall be so construed, as to prejudice the rights of citizens, colonists or settlers, who hold, or are entitled to acquire, under this constitution, lands by deed, grant, concession, or settlement right.

## LEGISLATURE

Art. 32. The legislative authority of this State, shall be vested in a Legislature, which shall consist of a Senate and House of Representatives, both dependent on the people.

Art. 33. The members of the legislature shall be chosen by the qualified electors, and shall serve for the term of two years from the day of commencement of the general election, and no longer.

Art. 34. The senators and representatives shall be chosen every two years, on the first Monday of August, and the day following.

Art. 35. Within three years from the meeting of the first legislature under this constitution, an enumeration of the population of the state shall be made agreeably to the mode which shall be prescribed by the legislature, and the apportionment and representation shall be regulated by law.

Art. 36. The number of senators shall, at the several periods of making the enumeration before mentioned, be fixed by the legislature, and apportioned among the precincts, formed as hereinafter directed, according to the number of taxable inhabitants in each, and shall never be less than one third, nor more than one half of the whole number of representatives.

Art. 37. Elections for representatives for the several precincts entitled to representation, shall be held at the places of holding their respective courts, or at such other places as the legislature may prescribe.

Art. 38. The senators shall be chosen by districts, to be formed by the legislature according to the number of taxable inhabitants in each, provided that no precinct shall be divided in forming a senatorial district.

Art 39. The first three years after the adoption of this constitution, the legislature shall meet annually, on the first Monday of November; and thereafter it shall meet biennially, on the same day, and be held at such place as the legislature shall prescribe.

Art. 40. No person shall be eligible to a seat in the senate until he has arrived to the age of twenty-five years, nor in the house of representatives until he shall have arrived to the age of twenty-one years; he shall be a citizen of the state, and shall have resided within the same twelve months, and six months within the precinct, or district for which he is elected, immediately preceding the time of his election.

Art. 41. Every male inhabitant of the age of twenty-one years, who shall be a citizen of the state, and shall have resided for the last six months, immediately preceding the day of election, within the precinct, or district, shall enjoy the right of an elector.

Art. 42. the senate, at its meeting, shall elect a president protempore: and the house of representatives shall elect its speaker. Each house shall elect its own officers, and be judges of the qualifications and election of its members.

Art. 43. Each house may determine the rules of its proceedings; punish its members for disorderly behaviour, and with the concurrence of two-thirds, expel a member; but not a second time for the same offence; and shall have all other powers necessary for the legislature of a state.

Art. 44. Senators and representatives shall, in all cases except treason, felony, or breach of the peace, be priviledged from arrest during the session of the legislature, and in going to and returning from the same.

Art. 45. Each house may punish, by imprisonment, any person not a member, who shall be guilty of disrespect to the house, by any disorderly or contemptuous behavior in their presence;—Provided, that such imprisonment shall not be for a longer time than thirty days.

Art. 46. Bills may originate in either house, but may be afterwards amended or rejected by the other.

Art. 47. Every bill shall be read on three different days, and signed by the president of the senate, and speaker of the house [of] representatives, before it becomes a law, unless the public safety should be endangered by delay.

Art. 48. After a bill has been rejected, no bill containing the same substance shall be passed into a law during that session.

Art. 49. The style of the laws of this state shall be—"Be it enacted by the Senate and House of Representatives of the State of Texas."

Art. 50. Each house shall keep a journal of its proceedings, and publish them, except such parts as the welfare of the state may require to be kept secret; and the yeas and nays of the members, on any question, shall at the request of one-fourth of the members present, be entered on the journal.

Art. 51. The legislature shall have power to establish, from time to time, the salaries of all the officers of the state; and to regulate the compensation of its own members.

Art. 52. The doors of each house, and committees of the whole, shall be kept open, unless when the business before them require secrecy.

Art. 53. No money shall be drawn from the treasury but in pursuance of appropriation by law.

Art. 54. No person, who heretofore hath been, or hereafter may be a collector, or holder of public monies, shall have a seat in either house of the legislature of the state, until such person shall have accounted for, and paid into the treasury, all sums for which he may be liable.

Art. 55. No judge of any court of law, or equity, secretary of state, attorney general, register, clerk of any court of record, or person holding any office under the authority of the Mexican United States, shall have a seat in the legislature of this state, nor shall any person in this state hold more than one lucrative office at one and the same time; Provided, that no appointment in the militia, or to the office of justice of the peace, so long as no salary is attached thereto, shall be considered a lucrative office.

Art. 56. If any member of the legislature is appointed to, or elected to, or accepts any other office than that of justice of the peace, trustee of a literary society, or commission in the militia, such appointment and acceptance shall be a vacation of his seat in the legislature, and no member thereof shall be eligible to hold any office, created by the legislature, during his term of service as a member.

Art. 57. Any member of either house of the legislature shall have liberty to dissent from, and protest against, any act or resolve which he may think injurious to the public, or to any individual, and have the reasons of his dissent entered on the journals.

Art. 58. The legislature shall have power to establish such a system of internal improvement as they may think proper.

Art. 59. The legislature shall have power to enact laws to impose taxes, and collect money for the use of the state; but no currency shall ever be made lawful tender, except gold, silver and copper coin.

## EXECUTIVE

Art. 60. The Executive power shall be vested in a Chief Magistrate, who shall be styled the Governor of the State of Texas.

Art. 61. The Governor shall be elected by the qualified electors, at the time and place of choosing representatives for the legislature. — He shall hold his office for the term of two years from the time of his installation, and until a successor be duly appointed and qualified; but shall not be eligible for more than four years in any term of six years. He shall be a citizen of the United States of Mexico; shall be at least twenty-seven years of age, and shall have resided in Texas at least three years, next preceeding his election.

Art. 62. The returns of every election for governor and lieutenant governor shall be sealed up, and transmitted to the president of the senate pro tem. who shall open and publish them, in presence of both houses of the legislature. The person having the highest number of votes shall be governor. Should two or more have been candidates for the office, and two or more persons be equal and highest in number one of those who are equal and highest shall be chosen governor, by joint ballot of both houses; and in like manner, under similar circumstances, shall the lieutenant governor be chosen.

Art. 63. The governor shall, at stated times, receive for his services a compensation which shall be neither increased nor reduced during the term for which he shall have been elected.

Art. 64. The governor shall be commander in chief of the militia of the state; except when they shall be called into the service of the Mexican United States; but he shall not command personally in the field, unless he shall be advised so to do by resolution of the legislature; shall take care that the constitution of this state, the constitutive act, and the constitution of the Mexican United States, and the laws be faithfully executed; shall communicate to the legislature at every session the condition of the state; and recommend such measures as he may deem expedient; he shall have power to convene the legislature, when, in his opinion, the interest of the state may require it; to grant reprieves and pardons, except in case of impeachment; to conduct all correspondence, or intercourse, with other states, and with the general government; and during the recess of the legislature, to fill, pro tempore, until the end of the next succeeding session, all vacancies in those offices which it may be the duty of the two houses, or of the executive and senate, to fill permanently.

Art. 65. Every bill which shall have passed both houses of the legislature, shall be presented to the governor; if he approve he shall sign it, but if not, he shall return it, with his objections, to the house in which it shall have originated, who shall enter the objections at large upon the journals, and proceed to reconsider it; if, after such reconsideration, a majority of the whole number elected to that house shall agree to pass the bill, it shall be sent, with the objections, to the other house, by whom it shall likewise be reconsidered; if approved by a majority of the whole number elected to that house, it shall become a law; but in such cases, the votes of both houses shall be determined by yeas and nays, and the names of the members voting for or against the bill, shall be entered on the journals of each house, respectively. If any bill shall not be returned by the governor within five days, Sundays excepted, after it shall have been presented to him, the same shall be a law in like manner, as if he had signed it, unless the legislature by their adjournment, prevent its return, in which case it shall not be a law.

Art. 66. Every order, resolution, or vote to which the concurrence of both houses may be necessary, except on questions of adjournment, shall be presented to the governor, and before it shall take effect be approved by him; or being disapproved, shall be repassed by both houses, according to the rules and limitation prescribed in the case of a bill.

Art. 67. There shall be a Lieutenant Governor, who shall be elected at the same time, in the same manner, for the same term, and shall possess the same qualifications as the governor. The electors shall designate for whom they vote as governor, and for whom as lieutenant governor.

Art. 68. The lieutenant governor shall, exoficio, be president of the senate, and when there is an equal division in the senate, shall give the casting vote; and also, in joint voting of both houses.

Art. 69. When the office of governor shall become vacant by death, resignation, absence from the state, removal from office, refusal to qualify, impeachment, or otherwise, the lieutenant governor, or in case of the disability on his part, the president of the senate pro tempore; or if there be no president of the senate pro tem. the speaker of the house of representatives shall possess all the powers and discharge all the duties of governor; and shall receive for his services the like compensation to the end of the term, or until the disability of the governor be removed. Provided, that should the office become permanently vacant, within ten months from the beginning of the term, the person exercising the powers of governor, for the time being, shall, as may be, cause an election to be held to fill such vacancy, giving three months notice thereof.

Art. 70. There shall be a Secretary of State, appointed by the governor, with the advice and consent of the senate. He shall hold his office three years, and shall keep a register of all the official acts and proceedings of the governor, and perform such duties as may be enjoined upon him by law. He shall, as soon as may be, procure and keep a seal of state, with such emblems and devices as shall be directed by law, which shall not be subject to change.

Art. 71. A state treasurer shall be elected by joint vote of both houses who shall also discharge the duties of Auditor, until otherwise provided by law.

Art. 72. There shall be an ayuntamiento in each municipality. The powers and duties of the ayuntamientos, the number of members who are to compose them, and the mode of their election, shall be prescribed by law.

Art. 73. All commissions shall be in the name of "The State of Texas," be sealed with the state seal, signed by the governor, and attested by the secretary of state.

Art. 74. Sheriffs and Coroners shall be elected every two years, by the qualified electors; at the time and place of choosing representatives. Their duties shall be regulated by law, and they shall hold their office for two years, and until a successor shall be duly appointed and qualified, unless sooner removed for misdemeanor in office.

Art. 75. The governor shall nominate and appoint, with advice and consent of the senate, all officers whose offices are established by this constitution, and whose appointments are not herein otherwise provided for: Provided, however that the legislature shall have the right to prescribe the mode of appointment of all other officers to be established by law.

Art. 76. The governor shall make use of his private seal until a seal of the state shall be provided.

## JUDICIARY

Art. 77. The judicial power shall be vested in a supreme court, and inferior courts.

Art. 78. The State of Texas shall be divided into four judicial districts, in each of which there shall be appointed a district judge.

Art. 79. The said district judges shall compose the supreme court; a majority of whom shall form a quorum. The said judges shall hold their courts as district judges, and judges of the supreme court, at the time and places prescribed by law.

Art. 80. The legislature shall create and establish such inferior courts as may be convenient for the administration of justice.

Art. 81. The judges of the district and supreme courts, who shall be elected at the first session of the legislature, shall hold their offices for the term of three years, eligible for re-electon; and their successors in office shall hold their office for the term of six years, eligible to re-election by the legislature every six years.

Art. 82. The judges, by virtue of their office, shall be conservators of the peace through the state. The style of all processes shall be, "The State of Texas;" all prosecutions shall be carried on "In the name, and by the authority of the State of Texas," and conclude, "against the peace and dignity of the State."

Art. 83. There shall be an attorney general for the state, and as many prosecuting attornies as may hereafter be found necessary.—Their duties, salaries, perquisites, and terms of service shall be determined by law.

Art. 84. The clerks of the districts and supreme courts shall be appointed by the judges of the respective courts.

Art. 85. The judges of the district and supreme courts shall receive fixed and adequate salaries, which shall be established by law.

Art. 86. The judges may be removed from office by a concurrent vote of both houses of the legislature: but two-thirds of the number present, must concur in such vote, and the causes of removal shall be entered on the journal of each. The judge against whom the legislature may be about to proceed, shall receive notice thereof, accompanied with a copy of the causes alleged for his removal, at least thirty days before the day on which either house of the legislature shall sit thereupon.

Art. 87. The judges may also be removed by impeachment.

Art. 88. The power of impeachment shall be vested in the house of representatives.

Art. 89. All impeachments shall be tried by the Senate: when acting for that purpose, the members shall be upon oath, and no person shall be convicted without the concurrence of two-thirds of the members present.

Art. 90. The governor, and all civil officers shall be liable to impeachment for all misdemeanors in office; but judgment in such cases, shall not extend further than removal from office, and disqualification to hold any office of trust or profit, in this state. But the parties shall nevertheless, be liable and subject to indictment, trial and punishment according to law.

Art. 91. The judges of the district and supreme courts, and the attorney general, shall be at least twenty-five years of age, and shall be learned in the law.

Art. 92. Alcaldes and Comisarios shall be elected by the people; their duties, jurisdiction, number in each municipality, and fees, shall be determined by law.

Art. 93. The legislature is authorised to increase the number of judicial districts and district judges, whenever the necessity of the country requires it.

Art. 94. The legislature shall establish a separate supreme court, so soon as the condition of the state may require it.

Art. 95. The interpretation of the constitution and laws of this state shall belong exclusively to the judiciary.

## SCHEDULE

Art. 96. The state of Texas shall include all the country formerly known as the province of Texas.

Art. 97. That no invonvenience may arise in our separation from Coahuila, it is declared that all rights, actions, prosecutions, and contracts, shall continue as if no change had taken place, except in cases provided for in the body of this constitution.

Art. 98. All dues, fines, penalties, and forfeitures due and owing to the State of Coahuila and Texas, shall be collectable in the name, and for the use of Texas. All bonds for the performance of duties, shall be passed over to the first Governor of Texas, and his successors in office, for the use and benefit of the parties interested.

Art. 99. The authorities of the State of Coahuila and Texas shall fill their offices within the limits of Texas, and shall continue in the exercise of their respective duties until suspended under this constitution.

Art. 100. Until the first enumeration, as provided for by this constitution, the apportionment of representation to the legislature, shall be regulated by a resolution to be adopted by this constitution.

Art. 101. All officers or persons elected, or appointed to any office or place of trust, profit, or honor, in this state, before entering upon the duties of his office, or station, shall take the following oath:—"I A. B.. do solemnly swear, that I will support the constitution of the United Mexican States, the constitutive act, and the constitution of this state, and that I will faithfully discharge the duties of the office of————, according to law, to the best of my abilities.—So help me God."

Art. 102. The election of Senators and Representatives to the general congress, shall take place agreeably to the provisions of the Federal constitution of the United Mexican States; and laws to that effect, shall be passed by the legislature.

Art. 103. Whenever a majority of both houses of the legislature, may deem it necessary to amend this constitution, they shall recommend to the electors at the next election of members of the legislature, to vote for or against a convention, and if it shall appear, that a majority of all the electors of the state, voting for the members of the legislature, shall have voted for a convention, the legislature shall, at their next session, call a convention to consist of at least as many members as there may be in the legislature, to be elected at the same places, and in like manner as prescribed for the election of members of that body.

Art. 104. Until the first enumeration shall be made as described by this constitution, the senatorial districts shall be composed of the following precincts:

Bexar, shall be entitled to one senator.
Nueces, Goliad and Guadalupe Victoria, one senator.
Labaca, Matagorda, and Santa Anna, one senator.
Victoria, and Bolivar, one senator.
San Felipe, one senator.
Magnolia, San Jacinto, [west side] and precinct of San Jacinto, one senator.
New-Holland, Hidalgo, and Tenoxticlan, one senator.
Anahuac, Liberty and Cow Bayou, one senator.
Nacogdoches, one senator.
Ayish and Snow River, one senator.
Tennahaw and Sabine, one senator.

Art. 105. The number of representatives that each of the precincts, above enumerated, shall have in the first legislature, shall be determined by the number of votes given in at the first election, on the basis of one representative for every hundred voters, without counting fractions under one hundred. Provided, that each precinct shall have one representative, whatever may be the number of its voters. After all the votes are taken, and the polls are closed, the judges of the election shall declare the persons who have received the highest number of votes for representatives, to be duly elected, agreeably to the basis above established, and shall issue certificates to such persons accordingly. In case of a tie between two or more, it shall be decided by lot, by the judges.

Art. 106. All powers, or grants of power, rights, or privileges, and immunities, not expressly given or granted by this constitution, are reserved *to,* and shall remain *with,* the People of the State, and can only be divested, or delegated, by amendment of this Constitution.

DONE in the Town of San Felipe de Austin, in Convention of the People of Texas, by means of their chosen Delegates, on the thirteenth day of April, in the Year of our Lord, eighteen hundred and thirty-three.

WILLIAM H. WHARTON.

Member and President of the Convention.

[Signed]

### EXPLANATION.

The paragraph following has been omitted at the proper place. It should be article 60, and follow article 59, under the head of LEGISLATURE. In the copy it stood as 85.

Art. 85. The existing law of the State of Coahuila and Texas, when this constitution goes into effect, shall continue in force until altered, or abolished, by the legislature; Provided, however, that the legislature shall never adopt any system of code of laws by general reference to said system or code, but in all cases shall specify the several provisions of the laws it may enact.

## 36. AUSTIN'S LETTER DESCRIBING HIS IMPRISONMENT

### May 10, 1834

From Stephen F. Austin, Ex-inquisicion Mexico May 10th 1834, Letter to James F. Perry, in Eugene C. Barker (ed.), *The Austin Papers* (3 vols.; Washington, 1924, 1928; Austin, 1927), II, 1049-1054.

Delegated by the Convention of 1833 to present its petitions to the federal government, Austin set forth at once and arrived in Mexico City on July 18. While waiting for President Santa Anna and Congress to return to the capital, he bluntly told Vice-President Gómez Farías on October 1 "that if the evils which threatened that country [Texas] with ruin were not remedied by the Govt, the people of Texas would remedy them of themselves without waiting any longer." Gómez Farías interpreted the statement as a threat, and the two separated in anger. The next day, in a "moment of irritation and impatience," Austin wrote the ayuntamiento of Béxar, suggesting that it take the initiative in *organizing a state government.* Nevertheless, by December 10 he had obtained Santa Anna's consent to almost every request of the Convention except that for separate statehood. While en route home, he was arrested at Saltillo on January 3, 1834, returned to Mexico City, and imprisoned on the basis of his "unfortunate letter" of October 2.

In the following letter from his cell to his brother-in-law, James F. Perry, Austin described his prison life and defended his own principles in the conflict with Mexico.

### Dr BROTHER.

I improve the first moment that I could write to you since I arrived here which was on the 13 Feby — on that day I was locked up in one of the dungeons of this vast building *incomunicado,* that is I was not allowed to speak to, or communicate with any person whatever except the officer of the guard. I remained in this situation untill yesterday when I was permitted to communicate with persons outside, receive books, writing materials, visits etc and to mix with the other prisoners — there are about 60 of them, all officers except two clergymen (Padres) and all men of good families and respectability confined for political opinions in the revolution of the past year. The occupant of my dungeon before me was a Col. who was banished. General Busta-mante former vice-President occupied one in July and August last near mine, as I am informed.

You may have some curiosity to know how I am lodged and what sort of a place an inquisicion prison is, about which so many horrid things are said all over the world, and which are no doubt true and probably much worse.

My room is about 16 feet by 13—very high ceiling—two doors, one flush with the outside surface of the wall, the other near the inside surface and within the wall which is about 3 feet thick of large hewn stone—the latter door has an oblong hole large enough to admit a plate—the other is solid, both were always locked and bolted untill yesterday—no windows—a very small skylight in the roof which barely afforded light to read on very clear days when the sun was high, say from 10 to 3 o'clock—quite free from damp except such as would naturally result from the want of a free circulation of air. There are 19 similar dungeons in this range with the difference that some of them are a little larger than mine, tho most are the same size—they are in the interior of this extensive building and the doors open into an oblong *patio* or open court about 120 by 60 feet which has a varanda or gallery all round it supported by pillars and arches—a fountain of good water from the acqueduct in the centre. This part of the building is one story but is surrounded on every side by other parts of the same building that are two stories and present a solid wall above our range without windows that look into this patio. On two sides of the base of the two story wall before mentioned there are *solederos* or sunning places which are spaces about 14 feet square (one is much larger) ranged along the back of the dungeons and between them and the before mentioned two story wall—they are separated from each other by high walls—each has a door, locks etc—open above for the sun—they communicate with the patio by arched passages.

When I came in each dungeon had its occupant and all were *incomunicado* the same as myself. All the doors were locked and bolted no one came into the patio except the sentinel—all was silent—each one was taken out about two hours the middle of the day and put into one of the *solederos* or sunning places, alone and locked in. In time of the inquisicion the prisoners were covered with a kind of sack or over garment with a mask at the top to cover the head and face, so that they could not be known, even by the guard in going through the patio to and from the *solederos,* nothing of the kind was done with us, we saw each other but could not salute or speak. I am told that in the time of the inquisicion there were four other patios or open courts that belonged to the part of the building that was used as a prison—they formerly communicated with each other by obscure passages which are now closed. The entrance into each from the street was always separate as they still are so that if the friend of a prisoner saw him enter one of the outside doors, he could not from that circumstances form any idea of the patio or part of the building where he was confined. The *patio* I am in communicates with the street by a narrow dark passage about 150 feet long.

Padre Servando Mier a very distinguished patriot was confined in the same dungeon I am in by the tribunal of the inquisicion in its time, and also by the emperor Iturbide. I visited him here in this room in October 1822, he was a member of congress and was arrested the 20 of August with 14 other members. General Morelos the most distinguished of the generals in the beginning of the revolution, was confined in a dungeon near mine in this range from which he was taken to be shot. In short each of these dungeons has some tradition of the sufferings of some victim of the inquisicion or of the revolution. Since the Independence this building has been used as a prison for political opinions or offences—no one accused of felonious crimes is confined here. The prisoners are well treated.

The first of April all the prisoners were put in communication except myself and four others we remained shut up untill yesterday—our doors are now open from sun rise to 9 o'clock at night—we have the free use of the *patio* and can visit another extensive range of dungeons in the 2d story of the main building which communicates with this patio by a dark passage and much darker stone staircase. From this range there is a passage onto the *asotea* or roof of our range of dungeons which is flat so that we can walk over our dungeons and all around our patio and have sufficient room for exercise I was shewn a dungeon in the 2d story where a man from Guatamala was confined by the inquisicion 30 years he is now living in a hospital of this city and has given some account of the treatment of prisoners in those days of superstition and despotism

I have received no personal ill treatment from any of the officers or guards who have had charge of me since my first arrest up to this day I received such provisions as I needed them through the guard—they were handed in at the hole in the inside door. When I left Monterey the officer of the guard, Cap Manuel Barragan, told me that he would put no guard over me except my word that I would not attempt to escape nor speak or write to any one without his permission. I gave it of course, for I would have returned to Mexico on the simple order of the Govt my conscience told me that I had committed no crime. I was imprudent in urging the claims of Texas that were confided to me as an agent with more determination and obstenancy than was consistent with my personal security or wellfare, but nothing more. I accepted the agency with reluctance, but in good faith and conformed to what I had every right to believe was the general wish of the people so far as the convention expressed that wish. Much good will result to Texas from my sufferings. The state government have been stimulated to apply proper remedies in many things and some of those who would have ruined the country and thrown it into confusion merely from personal feelings and low mean jealousies towards me, are now satisfied and rejoicing and are in favor of peace and quietness, because they think I am suffering—others who were restless and dissatisfied with me and with every thing without knowing why, are more calm and reasonable, and others who were my enemies a year ago, have no doubt had the magninimity to do me justice— this conduct (if it be true as I am told it is) will do them honor and be remembered to their advantage at some future day when all personal feelings have passed away. My own personal friends (and the mass of the honest and laboring farmers are so) have always been in favor of peace and quietness and opposed to turbulence. They have no doubt blamed me for suffering violent men to involve me as I have been. They have seen that I have permitted myself to be thrown into the mire by others whose sole object was my ruin. I was unsuspicious and acted in good faith—the fact is that when a few persons combine to ruin another who is unsuspicious and acts in good faith and with honest intentions, it is very difficult for him to escape.

Thus it is, that those who a year ago were the most anxious for a state and the most turbulent, are now for peace—they have in fact adopted my own principles which allways have been *peace quietness, patience and submission to the laws and no revolutions.* If I ever wandered from those principles, it was because the public feeling was so disordered and things were so disjointed that my opposition would have increased the evils and in all probability caused a great deal of confusion. I yielded from this motive, *and yielded in good faith,* and not to undermine or counteract. Thus my own principles of peace and quietness are now predominant, when had I attempted to have made them prevail by direct opposition to violent measures the reverse would have been the case.

It is very evident that Texas must become a state at some future day and not very distant—all will be in favor of it— the attempt that has been made was premature and totally wrong as to the manner. The particular act that involved me in all this, was the calling of the convention in my absence. I yielded after my return. So far as I am to blame in agreeing to those measures I am ready to be censured—they grew out of the situation of public feelings at the time—it would have been worse than useless for me to have opposed them—the only way I could have done it was to enter into the thing in bad faith so as to defeat and counteract. Such a course I did not think was correct or honorable— on my arrival here I could have put the state question to sleep. If I had done so those who now blame me for an excess of zeal would have been vociferous on the opposite extreem. All those things are mere matters of course—in short it is mankind. The only substantial manner in this business that is worthy of consideration is *that much substantial good will result to Texas from my sufferings* and I am content—as to office or public employ you know that I have always been averse to it—I am more so now than ever— I am no office hunter nor no demagogue seeking popularity— I have tryed in good faith to do all the good I could to everybody—as to enemies and friends—the common acceptation of those words amongst mankind in general conveys to the mind the same idea of change, that the word *clouds*, does— not so with true personal friends— of these I shall never want. Such men for example as T. F. McKinney. These are the only kind of friends I wish for.

I have no idea when I shall be at liberty. I think that all depends on the report of Almonte, who has been sent to Texas and I presume is now there or on his way back. It is much in my favor that all remains quiet in Texas I was confident that no friend of mine would try to get up an excitement but I feared that my enemies would. Such a thing would have increased my difficulty, for I would have been blamed for it all. My confinement has been very rigid but I am in good health and have borne it with tolerable patience. I had no books the first month, and it was solitary enough—after that I prevailed on the sergeant to go to D. Victor Blanco who sent them—he and Padre Muldoon have been firm and unwavering in their friendship to me in all this business, so has Ramon Musquis and many others in Bexar who have written here in my favor I have never complained of the Vice President Farias—he has been deceived—he has been made to believe, as I am told, that my object was to separate Texas from Mexico and deliver it to the United States of the north, which is absolutely false and without the shadow of foundation besides being a great absurdity. In a moment of irritation I said to the vice President that if the evils of Texas were not remedied the public there would remedy them of themselves this irritated him very much and my difficulties commenced. The truth is I lost patience and was imprudent and of course to blame, for patience is necessary in such cases. I hope that no friend of mine will blame the vice President or complain of him. I put on one side all considerations of personal safety or consequences to myself and thought only of suffering Texas and the fevered and excited situation of my constituents — had I erred from a want of zeal or industry or dilligence in the discharges of my duty as an agent, all would have had cause to censure me and my own conscience would have been the first to do it, for nothing can be more sacred than a public agency. My conscience is at rest — as an agent I did my duty, or, only erred from excess of zeal to do it — good has resulted even from that error if it was one. I am suffering but the evils of Texas are remedied — this idea consoles me for my misfortunes and enables me to bear them firmly. Remember me to McKinney and show him this letter also H. Austin and if Mason and Hotchkiss are there remember me to them.

Love to Emily and all the family

S. F. Austin

## 37. ALMONTE'S DESCRIPTION OF TEXAS

### 1834

From William Kennedy, *Texas: The Rise, Progress, and Prospects of the Republic of Texas* (2d ed.; London, 1841; reprinted, Fort Worth, 1925), 435-441.

In the spring of 1834 Colonel Juan N. Almonte was commissioned by Vice-President Gómez Farías to make a tour of inspection through Texas, and report his observations upon its condition. The following translated selection from his report published in 1835 describes Texas as Almonte saw it on the eve of the Revolution.

### 1. THE DEPARTMENT OF BEXAR

In 1806 the department of Bexar contained two municipalities; San Antonio de Bexar, with a population of 5,000 souls, and Goliad, with 1,400; total 6,400. In 1834 there were four municipalities, with the following population respectively: — San Antonio de Bexar, 2,400; Goliad, 700; Victoria, 300; San Patricio, 600; total 4,000. Deducting 600 for the municipality of San Patricio (an Irish settlement), the Mexican population had declined from 6,400 to 3,400 between 1806 and 1834.

This is the only district of Texas in which there are no negro labourers. Of the various colonies introduced into it, only two have prospered; one of Mexicans, on the river Guadalupe, by the road which leads from Goliad to San Felipe; the other of Irish, on the river Nueces, on the road from Matamoros to Goliad. With the exception of San Patricio, the entire district of Bexar is peopled by Mexicans. . . .

Extensive undertakings cannot be entered on in Bexar, as there is no individual capital exceeding 10,000 dollars. All the provisions raised by the inhabitants are consumed in the district. The wild horse is common, so as rarely to be valued at more than 20 rials [about $2.50] when caught. Cattle are cheap; a cow and a calf not being worth more than 10 dollars, and a young bull or heifer from 4 to 5 dollars. Sheep are scarce, not exceeding 5,000 head. The whole export trade is confined to from 8,000 to 10,000 skins of various kinds, and the imports to a few articles from New Orleans, which are exchanged in San Antonio for peltry or currency.

There is one school in the capital of the Department supported by the municipality, but apparently the funds are so reduced as to render the maintenance of even this useful establishment impossible. . . . In the whole department there is but one curate; the vicar died of cholera morbus in September last.

## 2. THE DEPARTMENT OF THE BRAZOS

The capital of the Department of the Brazos is San Felipe de Austin, . . .

The following are the municipalities and towns of the Department, with the population: — San Felipe, 2,500; Columbia, 2,100; Matagorda, 1,400; Gonzalez, 900; Mina, 1,100: total, 8,000. Towns: Brazoria, Harrisburg, Velasco, Bolivar. In the population are included about 1,000 negroes, introduced under certain conditions guaranteed by the State Government; and although it is true that a few African slaves have been imported into Texas, yet it has been done contrary to the opinion of the respectable settlers, who were unable to prevent it. It is to be hoped that this traffic has already been stopped; and it is desirable that a law of the General Congress and of the State should fix a *maximum* period for the introduction of negroes into Texas, as servants to the empresarios, which period ought not, in my opinion, to exceed 10 or 12 years, at the end of which time they should enjoy absolute liberty.

The most prosperous colonies of this Department are those of Austin and Dewitt. Towards the northwest of San Felipe there is now a new colony under the direction of Robertson; the same that was formerly under the charge of Austin.

In 1833, upwards of 2,000 bales of cotton, weighing from 400 to 500 lbs. each, were exported from the Brazos; and it is said that in 1832 not less than 5,000 bales were exported. The maize [corn] is all consumed in the country, though the annual crop exceeds 50,000 barrels. The cattle, of which there may be about 25,000 head in the district, are usually driven for sale to Natchitoches. The cotton is exported regularly from Brazoria to New Orleans, where it pays 2½ per cent. duty, and realises from 10 to 10½ cents per lb. for the exporter, after paying cost of transport, &c. The price of cattle varies but little throughout Texas, and is the same in the Brazos as in Bexar. There are no sheep in this district; herds of swine are numerous, and may be reckoned at 50,000 head.

The trade of the Department of the Brazos has reached 600,000 dollars. Taking the estimate for 1832 (the settlements having been ravaged by the cholera in 1833), the exports and imports are estimated thus: 5,000 bales of cotton, weighing 2,250,000 lbs., sold in New Orleans, and producing at 10 cents. per lb. 225,000 dollars net; 50,000 skins, at an average of 8 rials each, 50,000 dollars. Value of exports, 275,000 dollars (exclusive of the sale of live stock). The imports are estimated at 325,000 dollars.

In this Department there is but one school, near Brazoria, erected by subscription, and containing from 30 to 40 pupils. The wealthier colonists prefer sending their children to the United States; and those who have not the advantages of fortune care little for the education of their sons, provided they can wield the axe and cut down a tree, or kill a deer with dexterity.

## 3. THE DEPARTMENT OF NACOGDOCHES

The Department of Nacogdoches contains four municipalities and four towns. Nacogdoches municipality has a population of 3,500; that of San Augustine, 2,500; Liberty, 1,000; Johnsburg, 2,000; the town of Anahuac, 50; Bevil, 140; Teran, 10; Tanaha, 100: total population, 9,000, in which is included about 1,000 negroes, introduced under special arrangements. . . .

The settlements of this district have not prospered, because speculators have not fulfilled their contracts, and the scattered population is composed of individuals who have obtained one or more leagues of land from the State, and of others who, in virtue of the law of colonization inviting strangers, have established themselves wherever it appears most convenient. But the latter have not even the titles to their properties, which it would be only fair to extend for them, in order to relieve them from that cruel state of uncertainty in which some have been placed for several years, as to whether they appertain to the United States or to Mexico. And as these colonists have emigrated at their own expense, it seems just that the contractors on whose lands they have settled, and who were not instrumental to the introduction of their families, should not receive the premium allowed by law. . . .

There are three common schools in this department: one in Nacogdoches, very badly supported, another at San Augustine, and the third at Johnsburg. Texas wants a good establishment for public instruction, where the Spanish language may be taught; otherwise the language will be lost: even at present, English is almost the only language spoken in this section of the Republic.

The trade of this Department amounts for the year to 470,000 dollars. The exports consist of cotton, skins of the deer, otter, beaver, &c., Indian corn, and cattle. There will be exported during this year about 2,000 bales of cotton, 90,000 skins, and 5,000 head of cattle, equal in value to 205,000 dollars. The imports are estimated at 265,000 dollars; the excess in the amount of imports is occasioned by the stock which remains on hand in the stores of the dealers.

There are about 50,000 head of cattle in the whole Department, and prices are on a level with those in the Brazos. There are no sheep, nor pasturage adapted to them. There are above 60,000 head of swine, which will soon form another article of export.

There are machines for cleaning and pressing cotton in the Departments of Nacogdoches and the Brazos. There are also a number of saw-mills. A steam-boat is plying on the Brazos river, and the arrival of two more is expected; one for the Neches, the other for the Trinity.

The amount of the whole trade of Texas for the year 1834 may be estimated at 1,400,000 dollars. . . .

Money is very scarce in Texas; not one in ten sales are made for cash. Purchases are made on credit, or by barter; which gives the country, in its trading relations, the appearance of a continued fair. Trade is daily increasing, owing to the large crops of cotton, and the internal consumption, caused by the constant influx of emigrants from the United States. . . .

# 38. AUSTIN'S ADDRESS AT BRAZORIA ON THE NECESSITY OF A CONSULTATION

## September 8, 1835

From Eugene C. Barker (ed.), *The Austin Papers* (3 vols.; Washington, 1924, 1928; Austin, 1927), III, 116-119.

After having allowed Vice-President Gómez Farías to exercise the executive power for the greater part of a year, Santa Anna reassumed the presidency in April, 1834. Shortly, he had sent Gómez Farías into exile, dissolved Congress, and disbanded state legislatures and ayuntamientos, and by the summer of 1835 the Centralist trend was apparent. Most states rebelled against his program, and the Texans in May, 1835, began organizing local committees of safety and correspondence. By July 4 the committees were considering the advisability of a convention. The committee at Columbia, acting upon the instructions of a gathering of citizens on August 15, called upon all municipalities to send delegates to a consultation to be held at Washington on October 15. The people, still divided as to its propriety, turned immediately to Austin for advice on what course to pursue when he returned from Mexico on September 1 after an absence of twenty-eight months, of which more than sixteen were spent in prison or under bond. At a public dinner given in his honor on September 8 at Brazoria, Austin delivered a keynote address in which he gave his opinion of Mexican politics and unequivocally declared in favor of a consultation and resistance to Santa Anna's attempt to overthrow the constitution. The address follows.

I cannot refrain from returning my unfeigned thanks for the flattering sentiments with which I have just been honored, nor have I words to express my satisfaction on returning to this my more than native country, and meeting so many of my friends and companions in its settlement.

I left Texas in April, 1833, as the public agent of the people, for the purpose of applying for the admission of this country into the Mexican confederation as a state separate from Coahuila. This application was based upon the constitutional and vested rights of Texas, and was sustained by me in the city of Mexico to the utmost of my abilities. No honorable means were spared to effect the objects of my mission and to oppose the forming of Texas into a territory, which was attempted. I rigidly adhered to the instructions and wishes of my constituents, so far as they were communicated to me. My efforts to serve Texas involved me in the labyrinth of Mexican politics. I was arrested, and have suffered a long persecution and imprisonment. I consider it my duty to give an account of these events to my constituents, and will therefore at this time merely observe that I have never, in any manner, agreed to any thing, or admitted any thing, that would compromise the constitutional or vested rights of Texas. These rights belong to the people, and can only be surrendered by them.

I fully hoped to have found Texas at peace and in tranquility, but regret to find it in commotion; all disorganized, all in anarchy, and threatened with immediate hostilities. This state of things is deeply to be lamented; it is a great misfortune, but it is one which has not been produced by any acts of the people of this country: on the contrary, it is the natural and inevitable consequence of the revolution that has spread all over Mexico, and of the imprudent and impolitic measures of both the general and state governments, with respect to Texas. The people here are not to blame, and cannot be justly censured. They are farmers, cultivators of the soil, and are pacific from interest, from occupation, and from inclination. They have uniformly endeavored to sustain the constitution and the public peace by pacific means, and have never deviated from their duty as Mexican citizens. If any acts of imprudence have been committed by individuals, they evidently resulted from the revolutionary state of the whole nation, the imprudent and censurable conduct of the state authorities, and the total want of a local government in Texas. It is, indeed, a source of surprise and creditable congratulation, that so few acts of this description have occurred under the peculiar circumstances of the times. It is, however, to be remembered that acts of this nature were not the acts of the people, nor is Texas responsible for them. They were, as I before observed, the natural consequences of the revolutionary state of the Mexican nation; and Texas certainly did not originate the revolution, neither have the people, as a people, participated in it. The consciences and hands of the Texians are free from censure, and clean.

The revolution in Mexico is drawing to a close. The object is to change the form of government, destroy the federal constitution of 1824, and establish a central or consolidated government. The states are to be converted into provinces.

Whether the people of Texas ought or ought not to agree to this change, and relinquish all or a part of their constitutional and vested rights under the constitution of 1824, is a question of the most vital importance; one that calls for the deliberate consideration of the people, and can only be decided by them, fairly convened for the purpose. As a citizen of Texas I have no other right, and pretend to no other. In the report which I consider it my duty to make to my constituents, I intend to give my views on the present situation of the country, and especially as to the constitutional and natural rights of Texas, and will, therefore, at this time, merely touch this subject.

Under the Spanish government, Texas was a separate and distinct local organization. It was one of the unities that composed the general mass of the nation, and as such participated in the war of the revolution, and was represented in the constituent congress of Mexico, that formed the constitution of 1824. This constituent congress, so far from destroying this unity, expressly recognized and confirmed it by the law of May 7th, 1824, which united Texas with Coahuila *provisionally*, under the especial guarantee of being made a state of the Mexican confederation, as soon as it possessed the necessary elements. That law and the federal constitution gave to Texas a specific political existence, and vested in its inhabitants special and defined rights, which can only be relinquished by the people of Texas, acting for themselves as a unity, and not as a part of Coahuila, for the reason that the union with Coahuila, was *limited*, and only gave power to the state of Coahuila and Texas to govern Texas for the time being, but *always subject to the vested rights of Texas*. The state, therefore, cannot relinquish those vested rights, by agreeing to the change of government, or by any other act, unless expressly authorized by the people of Texas to do so; neither can the general government of Mexico legally deprive Texas of them without the consent of this people. These are my opinions.

An important question now presents itself to the people of this country.

The federal constitution of 1824 is about to be destroyed, the system of government changed, and a central or consolidated one established. Will this act annihilate all the rights of Texas, and subject this country to the uncontrolled and unlimited dictation of the new government?

This is a subject of the most vital importance. I have no doubts the federal constitution will be destroyed, and a central government established, and that the people will soon be called upon to say whether they agree to this change or not. This matter requires the most calm discussion, the most mature deliberation, and the most perfect union. How is this to be had? I see but one way, and that is by a general consultation of the people by means of delegates elected for that purpose, with full powers to give such an answer, in the name of Texas, to this question, as they may deem best, and to adopt such measures as the tranquility and salvation of the country may require.

It is my duty to state that general Santa Anna verbally and expressly authorized me to say to the people of Texas, that he was their friend, that he wished for their prosperity, and would do all he could to promote it; and that, in the new constitution, he would use his influence to give to the people of Texas a special organization, suited to their education, habits, and situation. Several of the most intelligent and influential men in Mexico, and especially the Ministers of Relations and War, expressed themselves in the same manner. These declarations afford another and more urgent necessity for a general consultation of all Texas, in order to inform the general government, and especially general Santa Anna, what kind of organization will suit the education, habits, and situation of this people.

It is also proper for me to state that, in all my conversation with the president and ministers and men of influence, I advised that no troops should be sent to Texas, and no cruisers along the coast. I gave it as my decided opinion, that the inevitable consequence of sending an armed force to this country would be war. I stated that there was a sound and correct moral principle in the people of Texas, that was abundantly sufficient to restrain or put down all turbulent or seditious movements, but that this moral principle could not, and would not unite with any armed force sent against this country; on the contrary, it would resist and repel it, and ought to do so. This point presents another strong reason why the people of Texas should meet in general consultation. This country is now in anarchy, threatened with hostilities; armed vessels are capturing every thing they can catch on the coast, and acts of piracy are said to be committed under cover of the Mexican flag. Can this state of things exist without precipitating the country into a war? I think it cannot, and therefore believe that it is our bounden and solemn duty as Mexicans, and as Texians, to represent the evils that are likely to result from this mistaken and most impolitic policy in the military movement.

My friends, I can truly say that no one has been, or is now, more anxious than myself to keep trouble away from this country. No one has been, or now is more faithful to his duty as a Mexican citizen, and no one has personally sacrificed or suffered more in the discharge of this duty. I have uniformly been opposed to have any thing to do with the family political quarrels of the Mexicans. Texas needs peace, and a local government: its inhabitants are farmers, and they need a calm and quiet life. But how can I, or any one, remain indifferent, when our rights, our all, appear to be in jeopardy, and when it is our duty, as well as our obligation as good Mexican citizens, to express our opinions on the present state of things, and to represent our situation to the government? It is impossible. The crisis is such as to bring it home to the judgment of every man that something must be done, and that without delay. The question will perhaps be asked, what are we to do? I have already indicated my opinion. Let all personalities, or divisions, or excitements, or passion, or violence, be banished from among us. Let a general consultation of the people of Texas be convened as speedily as possible, to be composed of the best, and most calm, and intelligent, and firm men in the country, and let them decide what representations ought to be made to the general government, and what ought to be done in future.

With these explanatory remarks I will give a toast— *The constitutional rights and the security and peace of Texas—they ought to be maintained; and jeopardized as they now are, they demand a general consultation of the people.*

## 39. THE TEXAS DECLARATION OF CAUSES FOR TAKING UP ARMS AGAINST SANTA ANNA

### November 7, 1835

From "Declaration of the People of Texas in General Convention Assembled," *Journals of the Consultation Held at San Felipe De Austin, October 16, 1835* (Published by Order of Congress; Houston, 1838), 21-22.

A "consultation" of the delegates representing the municipalities of Texas was assured when Stephen F. Austin upon his return from Mexico publicly declared for it and accepted the leadership of the Central Committee of Safety and Correspondence. Because of the outbreak of fighting on October 2, the delegates met at San Felipe on November 1 rather than at Washington on October 15 as originally instructed. A quorum was obtained on November 3, when fifty-five delegates representing twelve municipalities appeared. Branch T. Archer, who was elected president of the Consultation, foreshadowed the decision of the majority in his keynote address with the statement that Texas was "laying the corner stone of liberty in the great Mexican republic," and was not "battling alone for her rights and liberties."

John A. Wharton, who favored a declaration of independence, was named chairman of a committee of twelve — one from each municipality represented — to draft a declaration "setting forth to the world the causes that impelled us to take up arms, and the objects for which we fight." Opinion, however, was sharply divided, and until November 6 the delegates hotly debated the question of whether Texas was fighting for independence or for its rights under the Constitution of 1824 before voting 33 to 14 in favor of a "provisional government, upon the principles of the constitution of 1824," and then 33 to 15 against a declaration of independence. The next day the Consultation accepted Wharton's committee report reflecting the majority view. The declaration follows.

### DECLARATION OF THE PEOPLE OF TEXAS IN GENERAL CONVENTION ASSEMBLED.

*Whereas*, General Antonio Lopez de Santa Anna and other Military Chieftains have, by force of arms, overthrown the Federal Institutions of Mexico, and dissolved the Social Compact which existed between Texas and the other Members of the Mexican Confederacy—Now, the good People of Texas, availing themselves of their natural rights,

### SOLEMNLY DECLARE

1st. That they have taken up arms in defence of their rights and Liberties, which were threatened by the encroachments of military despots, and in defence of the Republican Principles of the Federal Constitution of Mexico of eighteen hundred and twenty-four.

2d. That Texas is no longer, morally or civilly, bound by the compact of Union; yet, stimulated by the generosity and sympathy common to a free people they offer their support and assistance to such Mexicans of the Mexican Confederacy as will take up arms against their military despotism.

3d. That they do not acknowledge, that the present authorities of the nominal Mexican Republic have the right to govern within the limits of Texas.

4th. That they will not cease to carry on war against the said authorities, whilst their troops are within the limits of Texas.

5th. That they hold it to be their right, during the disorganization of the Federal System and the reign of despotism, to withdraw from the Union, to establish an independent Government, or to adopt such measures as they may deem best calculated to protect their rights and liberties; but that they will continue faithful to the Mexican Government so long as that nation is governed by the Constitution and Laws that were formed for the government of the Political Association.

6th. That Texas is responsible for the expenses of her Armies now in the field.

7th. That the public faith is pledged for the payment of any debts contracted by her Agents.

8th. That she will reward by donations in Land, all who volunteer their services in her present struggle, and receive them as Citizens.

These *Declarations* we solemnly avow to the world, and call GOD to witness their truth and sincerity; and invoke defeat and disgrace upon our heads should we prove guilty of duplicity.

[P. B. Dexter], *Secretary*    B. T. Archer, *President*

## 40. PLAN AND POWERS OF THE PROVISIONAL GOVERNMENT OF TEXAS

### November 13, 1835

From *Ordinances and Decrees of the Consultation, Provisional Government of Texas and the Convention, Which Assembled at Washington March 1, 1836* (Printed by Order of the Secretary of State; Houston, 1838), 4-13.

Having declared that it was the right of Texas to resist Santa Anna's attempt to overthrow federalism, the Consultation then had the responsibility of establishing a temporary government for Texas until the Constitution of 1824 was restored. The delegates, guided by the traditional Anglo-American view that legal government must be contractual, named a committee with Henry Millard as chairman to draft a plan for a provisional state government. The plan which follows was adopted by the Consultation on November 13.

Plan and Powers of the Provisional Government of Texas.

Article I.    That there shall be, and there is hereby created, a Provisional Government for Texas, which shall consist of a Governor, a Lieutenant-Governor, and a General Council, to be elected from this body, one member from each Municipality, by the majority of each separate Delegation present; and the Governor and Lieutenant-Governor shall be elected by this body.

Article II.    The Lieutenant-Governor shall be President of the Council, and perform the duties of Governor in case of death, absence, or from other inability of the Governor, during which time a President "pro tem." shall be appointed to perform the duties of the Lieutenant-Governor in Council.

Article III.    The duties of the General Council shall be, to devise ways and means, to advise and assist the Governor in the discharge of his functions: they shall pass no laws except such as, in their opinion, the emergency of the country requires—ever keeping in view the Army in the field, and the means necessary for its comfort and support: they shall pursue the most effective and energetic measures to rid the country of her enemies, and place her in the best possible state of defence: two-thirds of the members elect of the General Council shall form a quorum to do business; and in order that no vacancy shall happen in the Council, if any member, from death or other casualty, shall be incapacitated to act, the Governor shall immediately, on information thereof, notify the member elected to fill the place; and on his default, any member who has been elected to this body from the same jurisdiction. The Governor and Council shall be authorized to contract for loans, not to exceed one million of Dollars, and to hypothecate the Public Lands and pledge the faith of the Country for the security of the payment: that they have power to impose and regulate Impost and Tonnage Duties, and provide for their collection under such regulations as may be most expedient. They shall have power, and it is hereby made the duty of the Governor and Council, to treat with the several tribes of Indians concerning their Land Claims, and if possible, to secure their friendship.

They shall establish Post-Offices and Post-Roads and regulate the rates of postage, and appoint a Postmaster-General, who shall have competent power for conducting this Department of the Provisional Government, under such rules and regulations as the Governor and Council may prescribe: they shall have power to grant pardons, remit fines, and to hear and judge all cases usual in high Courts of Admiralty, agreeably to the Law of Nations.

They shall have power to appoint their own Secretary and other officers of their own body; also, that they have the power to create and fill such offices as they may deem proper: *provided, nevertheless,* that this power does not extend to officers heretofore rejected by this House.

That the Governor and Council have power to organize, reduce, or increase the regular forces, as they may deem the emergencies of the Country require.

Article IV. The Governor, for the time being, and during the existence of the Provisional Government, shall be clothed with full and ample executive powers, and shall be Commander-in-Chief of the Army and Navy, and of all the military forces of Texas, by sea and land; and he shall have full power by himself, by and with the consent of the Council, and by his proper commander or other officer or officers, from time to time, to train, instruct, exercise and govern the Militia and Navy; and for the special defence and safety of the country, to assemble in martial array, and put in warlike attitude the inhabitants thereof; and to lead and conduct them by his proper officers, and with them to encounter, repel, resist and pursue by force of arms, as well by sea and by land, within or without the limits of Texas; and, also, to destroy, if necessary, and conquer by all proper means and enterprises whatsoever, all and every such person or persons as shall, at any time, in a hostile manner attempt or enterprise the destruction of our liberties, or the invasion, detriment, or annoyance of the country; and by his proper officers, use and exercise over the Army and Navy, and the Militia in actual service, the Law Martial in time of war, invasion or rebellion; and to take and surprise by all honorable ways and means consistent with the Law of Nations, all and every such person or persons, with their ships, arms, ammunition and goods as shall, in a hostile manner, invade or attempt the invading or annoying our adopted country; and that the Governor be clothed with all these and all other powers which may be thought necessary by the Permanent Council, calculated to aid and protect the country from her enemies.

Article V.    There shall be constituted a Provisional Judiciary in each jurisdiction represented, or which may hereafter be represented in this House, to consist of two judges, a first and second, the latter to act only in the absence or inability of the first, and be nominated by the Council and commissioned by the Governor.

Article VI.    Every Judge, so nominated and commissioned, shall have jurisdiction over all crimes and misdemeanors recognized and known to the common law of England: he shall have power to grant writs of "habeas corpus" in all cases known and practised, to and under the same laws; he shall have power to grant writs of sequestration, attachment, or arrest, in all cases established by the "Civil Code" and "Code of Practice" of the State of Louisiana, to be regulated by the forms thereof; shall possess full testamentary powers in all cases; and shall also be made a Court of Records for conveyances which may be made in English, and not on stamped paper; and that the use of stamped paper be, in all cases, dispensed with; and shall be the "Notary Public" for their respective Municipalities: all office fees shall be regulated by the Governor and Council. All other civil proceedings at law shall be suspended until the Governor and General Council shall otherwise direct. Each Municipality shall continue to elect a sheriff, alcalde and other officers of Ayuntamientos.

Article VII.    All trials shall be by jury, and in criminal cases the proceedings shall be regulated and conducted upon the principles of the common law of England; and the penalties prescribed by said law, in case of conviction, shall be inflicted, unless the offender shall be pardoned, or fine remitted; for which purpose a reasonable time shall be allowed to every convict to make application to the Governor and Council.

Article VIII. The officers of the Provisional Government, except such as are elected by this House, or the people, shall be appointed by the General Council, and all officers shall be commissioned by the Governor.

Article IX.  All Commissions to officers shall be, "in the name of the People, free and sovereign," and signed by the Governor and Secretary; and all pardons and remissions of fines granted, shall be signed in the same manner.

Article X.  Every officer and member of the Provisional Government, before entering upon the duties of his office, shall take and subscribe the following oath of office: "I, A. B., do solemnly swear, (or affirm) that I will support the republican principles of the Constitution of Mexico of 1824, and obey the Declarations and Ordinances of the Consultation of the chosen Delegates of all Texas in General Convention assembled, and the Ordinances and Decrees of the Provisional Government; and I will faithfully perform and execute the duties of my office agreeably to law, and to the best of my abilities, so help me God."

Article XI.  On charges and specifications being made against any officer of the Provisional Government for malfeasance or misconduct in office, and presented to the Governor and Council, a fair and impartial trial shall be granted, to be conducted before the General Council; and if, in the opinion of two-thirds of the members, cause sufficient be shown, he shall be dismissed from office by the Governor.

Article XII.  The Governor and Council shall organize and enter upon their duties immediately after the adjournment of this House, and hold their sessions at such times and places as, in their opinion, will give the most energy and effect to the objects of the people, and to the performance of the duties assigned to them.

Article XIII.  The General Council shall appoint a Treasurer, whose duties shall be clearly defined by them, and who shall give approved security for their faithful performance.

Article XIV.  That all Land Commissions, Empressarios, Surveyors, or persons in anywise concerned in the location of Land, be ordered, forthwith, to cease their operations during the agitated and unsettled state of the country,  and continue to desist from further locations until the Land Offices can be properly systematized by the competent authorities which may be hereafter established; that fit and suitable persons be appointed to take charge of all the archives belonging to the different Land Offices, and deposite the same in safe places, secure from the ravages of fire or devastations of enemies; and that the persons so appointed be fully authorized to carry the same into effect, and be required to take and sign triplicate schedules of all the books, papers and documents found in the several Land Offices, one of which shall be given to the Governor and Council, one left in the hands of the officers of the Land Office, the other to be retained by the said persons: and they are enjoined to hold the said papers and documents in safe custody, subject only to the orders of the Provisional Government, or such competent authority as may hereafter be created. And the said persons shall be three from each Department as Commissioners to be forthwith appointed by this House, to carry this Resolution into full effect, and report thereof to the Governor and Council; that the political chiefs immediately cease their functions. The different Archives of the different primary Judges, Alcaldes and other municipal officers of the various jurisdictions shall be handed over to their successors in office, immediately after their election and appointment; and the archives of the several Political Chiefs of Nacogdoches, Brazos, and Bexar shall be transmitted forthwith to the Governor and Council, for their disposition.

Article XV.  All persons, now in Texas, and performing the duties of citizens, who have not acquired their quantum of land, shall be entitled to the benefit of the Laws on Colonization under which they emigrated; and all persons who may emigrate to Texas during her conflict for Constitutional Liberty, and perform the duties of Citizens, shall also receive the benefits of the Law under which they emigrated.

Article XVI. The Governor and Council shall continue to exist as a Provisional Government until the re-assembling of this Consultation, or until other Delegates are elected by the people and another Government established.

Article XVII. This Convention, when it may think proper to adjourn, may stand adjourned, to meet at the town of Washington on the first day of March next, unless sooner called by the Executive and Council.

Article XVIII. All grants, sales and conveyances of lands, illegally or fraudulently made by the legislature of the State of Coahuila and Texas, located, or to be located, within the limits of Texas, are hereby solemnly declared null, void and of no effect.

Article XIX. All persons who leave the country in its present crisis, with a view to avoid a participation in its present struggle, without permission from the Alcalde, or Judge of their Municipality, shall forfeit all or any lands they may hold, or may have a claim to, for the benefit of this Government: *provided*, nevertheless, that widows and minors are not included in this provision.

Article XX. All monies now due or that may hereafter become due, on lands lying within the limits of Texas, and all public funds or revenues, shall be at the disposal of the Governor and General Council, and the receipt of the Treasurer shall be a sufficient voucher for any and all persons who may pay monies into the Treasury; and the Governor and Council shall have power to adopt a system of Revenue to meet the exigencies of the country.

Article XXI.  Ample powers and authority shall be delegated, and are hereby given and delegated to the Governor and General Council of the Provisional Government of all Texas, to carry into full effect the provisions and resolutions adopted by "the Consultation of the chosen Delegates of all Texas in General Convention assembled," for the creation, establishment and regulation of said Provisional Government.

## 41. THE RESOLUTION CALLING FOR THE CONVENTION
## OF MARCH 1, 1836
### December 10, 1835

From *Ordinances and Decrees of the Consultation, Provisional Government of Texas and the Convention, Which Assembled at Washington March 1, 1836* (By Order of the Secretary of State; Houston, 1838), 76-78.

Having created a provisional government (a governor, a lieutenant governor, and a council composed of one member from each municipality), the Consultation adjourned on November 14, 1835, until March 1 unless the Council called it into session sooner or ordered an election for new delegates. Since sentiment for independence was crystallizing, however, the Council on December 10 passed a resolution calling for the election on February 1 of delegates to convene on March 1 at Washington to form a new government, on condition that there would be a referendum on any proposed constitution. The resolution, which follows, is significant because of its recognition of the need for a new government that would reflect the changing attitude toward independence, and because of its assertion of the right of revolution.

By the laws of Creation and Nature, all men are free and equal, of these natural rights no man can be forcibly deprived of the principles of immutable justice: a desire for domination and power in man over his fellowman, subjects the weak and unambitious to the machinations of the more subtle and strong — to avoid such evils social compacts or Governments are formed for mutual and individual protection:— to this end each member of a community surrenders certain of his natural rights for common security; — thus, of necessity, all the legitimate powers of any Government are immediately derived from the governed. The people are sovereign, and all the officers designated for the execution of their civil compact are agents and accountable for their fidelity:— when such agents assume the character of principals or dictators, and attempt of their own will to subvert the form and true principles of the Governmental Compact and substitute another without the consent of the people [resistance] is necessary and a virtue: in this situation are the citizens of Texas and a considerable portion of the Mexican Republic of which Texas is a part— resistance is, therefore, a duty. The protection of our liberties— one natural and reserved right to make it so:— arms are the resort, and in arms the people will find their only security from the oppression of ambitious tyrants, whose chains are forged to manacle our citizens and subdue them to their will: courage and bravery in resistance, and prudence in council will restore to us the natural sovereignty of all Governments: — one civil compact or constitution is destroyed and another must be formed to guarantee the purposes and ends of political associations: a Provisional or temporary Government, however wisely formed or prudently administered, is at best uncertain and insecure— permanency and strength should be the basis of all Governments— therefore,

*Be it resolved*, That in virtue of the powers vested in the "Provisional Government of Texas" by the Representatives of the people in convention assembled, and it is hereby *resolved*, by the General Council of the Provisional Government aforesaid, that a Convention of Delegates of the people for each Municipality of the three departments of Texas shall be called, to assemble on the first day of March next, at the town of Washington.

Sec. 2. *Be it further resolved*, That the Delegates elected by the people clothed with ample, unlimited, or plenary powers as to the form of government to be adopted: *provided*, that no Constitution formed shall go into effect, until the same be submitted to the people and confirmed by a majority thereof, in such manner as shall be prescribed by a provision in such instrument.

Sec. 3. *Be it further resolved*, That the acting Judge, or in case there be no acting Judge, the Alcalde of each Municipality be required, and it is hereby made his duty to issue writs of election to some competent and respectable citizen of each election district, to hold the election in the said district on the first day of February, 1836, to be conducted in the same manner that elections have heretofore been conducted— allowing all free white males *and* Mexicans opposed to a Central Government a vote: *provided*, that no proxy votes shall be received— excepting, nevertheless, all the Citizen Volunteers in the Army, each of whom shall have a right to his vote, which he shall write upon paper over his own signature, and send to the Judge or Alcalde of his respective Municipality, to be received on or before the day of the election aforesaid; also *provided*, that the said Judge or Alcalde shall appoint the several places for holding said elections; of which time and place for holding the same, reasonable notice shall be given in the best manner for informing the people thereof; and duplicate returns of each election shall be made to the Judge or Alcalde aforesaid, one of which shall be filed on the archives of his office, the other to be presented at the Convention as evidence of the election of the members.

Sec. 4. *Be it further resolved*, That with a view to as just an equalization of representatives as can be at present determined, that the Municipality of Austin shall elect three delegates, Brazoria four, Washington four, Mina three, Gonzales two, Viesca two, Harrisburg two, Jasper two, Matagorda two, Jackson two, Tenehaw two, Jefferson two, Refugio two, Goliad two, San Patricio two, Bexar four, Guadaloupe Victoria two, and the citizens of Pecan Point two.

Sec. 5. *Be it further resolved*, That the Governor shall, and it is hereby made his duty, as soon as may be, to issue his proclamation for carrying into effect the preceding Resolutions.

Passed at San Felipe de Austin, Dec. 10, 1835. . . .

This was vetoed by the Governor but it passed by a constitutional majority on the 13th December, 1835.

HENRY SMITH, Governor

## 42. TREATY WITH THE CHEROKEE INDIANS

### February 23, 1836

From Ernest William Winkler (ed.), *Secret Journals of the Senate, Republic of Texas,* 1836-1845 (Austin, 1911), 35-39.

Cherokee Indians from the United States in 1819 began settling the lands north of the San Antonio road between the Neches and Sabine rivers. Although the territory they occupied had been parcelled out among *empresarios* and the central government never sanctioned the concessions, the Mexican officials generally respected the Cherokee claim.

Realizing the precariousness of the Texas situation and the justice of the Cherokee position, the Consultation on November 13, 1835, resolved that the Provisional Government recognize those claims, and establish with the Indians a definite boundary, secure their confidence and friendship, and guarantee them the peaceable enjoyment of their lands. Accordingly, in December Sam Houston and John Forbes were commissioned to negotiate with the Indians, and on February 23, 1836, they concluded such a treaty. More pressing matters developed, however, and it was not until December 20, 1836, that President Houston sent the treaty to the Senate with a recommendation that it be ratified. That body a year later declared the treaty null and void on the basis that the Consultation overstepped its authority, that the Mexican government had never actually granted the Indians titles to the lands, and that the Cherokees by their hostility had forfeited any rights they may have had. Houston thereupon took the position that the treaty was valid since the Convention of 1836 had confirmed the acts of the Provisional Government, and proceeded in the autumn of 1838 to have the boundary surveyed. President Mirabeau B. Lamar, who succeeded Houston in December, nevertheless, energetically enforced the opinion of the Senate. The treaty follows.

Art. 1. The parties declare, that there shall be a firm and lasting peace forever, and that a friendly intercourse shall be preserved by the people belonging to both parties.

Art. 2. It is agreed and declared that the before named Tribes, or Bands, shall form one community, and that they shall have and possess the lands within the following bounds, towit, — laying West of the San Antonio road, and beginning on the West, at the point where the said road crosses the River Angeline, and running up said river, until it reaches the mouth of the first large creek (below the Great Shawanee village) emptying into the said River from the north east, thence running with said creek to its main source, and from thence a due north line to the Sabine River, and with the said river west— then starting where the San Antonio road crosses the Angeline river, and with the said road to the point where it crosses the Naches river and thence running up the east side of said river, in a north west direction.

Art. 3. All lands granted or settled in good faith previous to the settlement of the Cherokees, within the before described bounds, are not conveyed by this treaty, but excepted from its operation. All persons who have once been removed and returned shall be considered as intruders and their settlements not be respected.

Art. 4. It is agreed by the parties aforesaid that the several Bands or Tribes named in this Treaty, shall all remove within the limits or bounds as before described.

Art. 5. It is agreed and declared, by the parties aforesaid, that the Land, lying and being within the aforesaid limits shall never be sold or alienated to any person or persons, power or Government, whatsoever else than the Government of Texas, and the Commissioners on behalf of the Government of Texas bind themselves, to prevent in future all persons from intruding within the said bounds. And it is agreed upon the part of the Cherokees, for themselves and their Younger Brothers, that no other tribes or Bands of Indians whatsover shall settle within the limits aforesaid, but those already named in this Treaty, and now residing in Texas.

Art. 6. It is declared that no individual person, member of the Tribes before named, shall have power to sell or lease land to any person or persons, not a member or members of this community of Indians, nor shall any citizen of Texas be allowed to lease or buy land from any Indian or Indians.

Art. 7. That the Indians shall be governed by their own Regulations and Laws, within their own territory, not contrary to the Laws of the Government of Texas. All property stolen from the citizens of Texas, or from the Indians shall be restored to the party from whom it was stolen, and the offender or offenders shall be punished by the party to whom he or they may belong.

Art. 8. The Government of Texas shall have power to regulate Trade and intercourse, but no Tax shall be levied on the Trade of the Indians.

Art. 9. The parties to this Treaty agree that one or more agencies, shall be created and at least one agent shall reside, specially, within the Cherokee Villages, whose duty it shall be to see that no injustice is done them, or other members of the community of Indians.

Art. 10. The parties to this Treaty agree that . . . all the Lands and improvements now occupied by any of the before named Bands or Tribes, not lying within the limits before described shall belong to the Government of Texas and subject to its disposal.

Art. 11. The parties to this Treaty agree and stipulate that all the Bands or Tribes . . . shall remove within the before described limits, within eight months from the date of this Treaty.

Art. 12. The parties to this Treaty agree that nothing herein contained shall effect [sic] the relations of the Saline, on the Naches nor the settlers in the neighbourhood thereof until a General Council of the Several Bands shall take place and the pleasure of the Convention of Texas be known.

Art. 13. It is also declared, that all Titles issued to Lands, not agreeably to the declaration of the General Consultation of the People of Texas, dated the thirteenth day of November, eighteen hundred and thirty five, within the before recited limits, are declared void, as well as all orders and surveys made in relation to the same.

Done at Colonel Bowls Village on the Twenty third day of February, Eighteen hundred and thirty six, and the First Year of the Provisional Government of Texas. . . . [signatures affixed]

# 43. THE FALL OF THE ALAMO

On February 12, 1836, Santa Anna with an army of about six thousand crossed the Rio Grande to crush the rebellion in Texas. He ordered General José Urrea to move from Matamoros against Texas forces stationed at San Patricio and Goliad, while he led the main army directly to San Antonio.

San Antonio was a frontier post defended by a small group of Texans. In January, Colonel James C. Neill, commander at San Antonio, reported that he had only one hundred men and was badly in need of supplies, and the efforts during the next few weeks to enlist volunteers were almost futile. General Sam Houston ordered Colonel James Bowie to San Antonio to destroy the fortifications and then to retreat, but once there with about twenty-five volunteers Bowie was convinced that it was a strategic post and he chose to defy his orders and remain with the defenders. On February 3 William Barrett Travis with thirty men of the regular army, in compliance with Governor Henry Smith's order, joined the garrison. A few days later Neill went home on account of illness in his family and left Travis in command of the garrison. Though at first Bowie refused to accept the arrangement, illness forced his acquiescence.

Santa Anna surprised the garrison by arriving about one month before he was expected. On the afternoon of February 23 Travis dispatched a hasty note to the alcalde of Gonzales calling for assistance: "The enemy in large force is in sight. We want men and provisions. Send them to us. We have 150 men and are determined to defend the Alamo to the last. Give us assistance." The next day he wrote a stirring appeal for aid that has been called "the most heroic document in American history." In response to the appeals, Captain Albert Martin and thirty-one men of Gonzales slipped through the Mexican line into the Alamo on the night of March 1. Two days later, after the arrival of the remainder of Santa Anna's army, Travis sent out his final appeal for aid.

The first of the following documents is Travis' letter of February 24; the second is his final appeal for aid; the third is the report of Colonel Francisco Ruíz, the alcalde of San Antonio, who was ordered by Santa Anna to dispose of the dead.

## 1. TRAVIS' LETTER OF FEBRUARY 24, 1836

From William Barrett Travis, Bejar, To the People of Texas & All Americans in the world, Feby. 24th, 1836 (MS; Archives, Texas State Library, Austin).

Commandancy of The Alamo

Bejar, Feby. 24th, 1836

To the People of Texas & All Americans in the world — Fellow Citizens & compatriots —

I am besieged, by a thousand or more of the Mexicans under Santa Anna — I have sustained a continual Bombardment & cannonade for 24 hours & have not lost a man — The enemy has demanded a surrender at discretion, otherwise, the garrison are to be put to the sword, if the fort is taken — I have answered the demand with a cannon shot, & our flag still waves proudly from the walls — *I shall never surrender or retreat.* Then, I call on you in the name of Liberty, of patriotism & everything dear to the American character, to come to our aid, with all dispatch — The enemy is receiving reinforcements daily & will no doubt increase to three or four thousand in four or five days. If this call is neglected, I am determined to sustain myself as long as possible & die like a soldier who never forgets what is

due to his own honor & that of his country — VICTORY OR DEATH.

William Barrett Travis,
Lt. Col. comdt.

P. S. The Lord is on our side — When the enemy appeared in sight we had not three bushels of corn — We have since found in deserted houses 80 or 90 bushels and got into the walls 20 or 30 heads of Beeves.

Travis

## 2. TRAVIS' LAST APPEAL FOR AID

March 3, 1836

From Mary Austin Holley, *Texas* (Lexington, Ky., 1836), 351-353.

Commandancy of the Alamo,
Bejar, March 3, 1836.

Sir, — In the present confusion of the political authorities of the country, and in the absence of the commander-in-chief, I beg leave to communicate to you the situation of this garrison. You have doubtless already seen my official report of the action of the 25th ult., made on that day to Gen. Sam. Houston, together with the various communications heretofore sent by express. I shall therefore confine myself to what has transpired since that date.

From the 25th to the present date, the enemy have kept up a bombardment from two howitzers, (one a five and a half inch, and the other an eight inch,) and a heavy cannonade from two long nine pounders, mounted on a battery on the opposite side of the river, at the distance of four hundred yards from our walls. During this period the enemy have been busily employed in encircling us with entrenched encampments on all sides, at the following distances, to wit: —in Bejar, four hundred yards west; in Lavilleta, three hundred yards south; at the powder house, one thousand yards east by south; on the ditch, eight hundred yards northeast, and at the old mill, eight hundred yards north. Notwithstanding all this, a company of thirty-two men, from Gonzales, made their way into us on the morning of the 1st inst., at 3 o'clock, and Col. J. B. Bonham (a courier from Gonzales) got in this morning at 11 o'clock, without molestation. I have so fortified this place, that the walls are generally proof against cannon balls; and I still continue to intrench on the inside, and strengthen the walls by throwing up the dirt. At least two hundred shells have fallen inside of our works without having injured a single man: indeed, we have been so fortunate as not to lose a man from any cause; and we have killed many of the enemy. The spirits of my men are still high, although they have had much to depress them. We have contended for ten days against an enemy whose numbers are variously estimated at from fifteen hundred to six thousand men, with Gen. Ramier Siesma and Col. Batres, the aids-de-camps of Santa Anna, at their head. A report was circulated that Santa Anna himself was with the enemy, but I think it was false. A reinforcement of about one thousand men is now entering Bejar from the west, and I think it more than probable that Santa Anna is now in town, from the rejoicing we hear. Col. Fannin is said to be on the march to this place with reinforcements; but I fear it is not true, as I have repeatedly sent to him for aid without receiving any. Colonel Bonham, my special messenger, arrived at La Bahia fourteen days ago, with a request for aid; and on the arrival of the enemy in Bejar ten days ago, I sent an express to Col. Fannin, which arrived at Goliad on the next day, urging him to send us reinforcements— *none have yet arrived*. I look to the *colonies alone* for aid: unless it arrives soon, I shall have to fight the enemy on his own terms. I will, however, do the best I can under the circumstances; and I feel confident that the determined valor, and desperate courage, heretofore evinced by my men, will not fail them in the last struggle: and although they may be sacrificed to the vengeance of a gothic enemy, the victory will cost the enemy so dear, that it will be worse for him than a defeat. I hope your honourable body will hasten on reinforcements, ammunition, and provisions to our aid, as soon as possible. We have provisions for twenty days for the men we have— our supply of ammunition is limited. At least five hundred pounds of cannon powder, and two hundred rounds of six, nine, twelve, and eighteen pound balls— ten kegs of rifle powder, and a supply of lead, should be sent to this place without delay, under a sufficient guard.

If these things are promptly sent and large reinforcements are hastened to this frontier, this neighborhood will be the great and decisive battle ground. The power of Santa Anna is to be met here, or in the colonies; we had better meet them here, than to suffer a war of desolation to rage in our settlements. A blood red banner waves from the church of Bejar, and in the camp above us, in token that the war is one of vengeance against rebels: they have declared us as such, and demanded that we should surrender at discretion, or that this garrison should be put to the sword. Their threats have had no influence on me, or my men, but to make all fight with desperation, and that high souled courage which characterizes the patriot, who is willing to die in defence of his country's liberty and his own honor.

The citizens of this municipality are all our enemies except those who have joined us heretofore; we have but three Mexicans now in the fort; those who have not joined us in this extremity, should be declared public enemies, and their property should aid in paying the expenses of the war.

The bearer of this will give your honorable body, a statement more in detail, should he escape through the enemies lines— *God and Texas—Victory or Death!*

Your obedient servant,

W. BARRETT TRAVIS,

Lieut Col. Comm.

P.S. The enemies troops are still arriving, and the reinforcement will probably amount to two or three thousand.　　　　T.

## 3. COLONEL RUIZ'S REPORT OF THE SCENE AFTER THE FALL OF THE GARRISON

### March 6, 1836

From Francisco Ruíz, "Report," trans. in Amelia Williams, "A Critical Study of the Siege of the Alamo and the Personnel of Its Defenders," *The Southwestern Historical Quarterly*, XXXVII (July, 1933), 39-40. Another translation by J. H. Quintero was published in the *Texas Almanac* (Galveston, 1860), 80-81.

On the 6th of March 1836, at 3 a.m., General Santa Anna at the head of 4,000 men advanced against the Alamo. The infantry, artillery and cavalry had formed about 1000 varas from the walls of the same fortress. The Mexican army charged and were twice repulsed by the deadly fire of Travis's artillery, which resembled a constant thunder. At the third charge the Toluca battalion commenced to scale the walls and suffered severely. Out of 830 men only 130 of the battalion were left alive.

When the Mexican army entered the walls, I with the political chief, Don Ramon Musquiz and other members of the corporation, accompanied by the curate, Don Refugio de la Garza, who by Santa Anna's orders had assembled during the night at a temporary fortification on Protero Street, with the object of attending the wounded, etc. As soon as the storming commenced we crossed the bridge on Commerce Street, with this object in view and about 100 yards from the same a party of Mexican dragoons fired upon us and compelled us to fall back on the river to the place that we had occupied before. Half an hour had elapsed when Santa Anna sent one of his aides-de-camp with an order for us to come before him. He directed me to call on some of the neighbors to come with carts to carry the (Mexican) dead to the cemetary and to accompany him, as he desired to have Colonels Travis, Bowie, and Crockett shown to him.

On the north battery of the fortress convent, lay the lifeless body of Col. Travis on the gun carriage, shot only through the forehead. Toward the west and in a small fort opposite the city, we found the body of Colonel Crockett. Col. Bowie was found dead in his bed in one of the rooms on the south side.

Santa Anna, after all the Mexican bodies had been taken out, ordered wood to be brought to burn the bodies of the Texans. He sent a company of dragoons with me to bring wood and dry branches from the neighboring forests. About three o'clock in the afternoon of March 6, we laid the wood and dry branches upon which a pile of dead bodies was placed, more wood was piled on them, then another pile of bodies was brought, and in this manner they were all arranged in layers. Kindling wood was distributed through the pile and about 5 o'clock in the evening it was lighted.

The dead Mexicans of Santa Anna were taken to the graveyard, but not having sufficient room for them, I ordered some to be thrown into the river, which was done on the same day.

The gallantry of the few Texans who defended the Alamo was really wondered at by the Mexican army.

Even the generals were astonished at their vigorous resistance, and how dearly victory was bought.

The generals under Santa Anna who participated in the storming of the Alamo, were Juan Amador, Castrillon, Ramirez y Sesma, and Andrade.

The men (Texans) burnt were one hundred and eighty-two. I was an eyewitness, for as alcalde of San Antonio, I was with some of the neighbors, collecting the dead bodies and placing them on the funeral pyre.

Francis Antonio Ruiz

# 44. THE TEXAS DECLARATION OF INDEPENDENCE

## March 2, 1836

From *Laws of the Republic of Texas* (Printed by Order of the Secretary of State, 2 vols.; Houston, 1838), I, 3-7.

A quarrel between Governor Henry Smith and the Council in January, 1836, paralyzed the Provisional Government of Texas. Fortunately, the Council had called for an election on February 1 to select delegates to a convention at Washington on March 1 to form a new government. Public sentiment, reflected by the attitude of the forty-one delegates on hand for the opening session, favored a declaration of independence. After the Convention had been organized, the first act of President Richard Ellis was to appoint a committee consisting of George C. Childress, chairman, James Gaines, Bailey Hardeman, Edward Conrad, and Collin McKinney to draft a declaration of independence. The following report of the committee, supposedly written by Childress and closely paralleling the United States Declaration of 1776, was unanimously adopted the next day.

THE DECLARATION OF INDEPENDENCE Made by the Delegates of The People of Texas in General Convention, at Washington, ON MARCH 2nd, 1836.

When a government has ceased to protect the lives, liberty and property of the people, from whom its legitimate powers are derived, and for the advancement of whose happiness it was instituted; and so far from being a guarantee for their inestimable and inalienable rights, becomes an instrument in the hands of evil rulers for their suppression. When the federal republican constitution of their country, which they have sworn to support, no longer has a substantial existence, and the whole nature of their government has been forcibly changed, without their consent, from a restricted federative republic, composed of sovereign states, to a consolidated central military despotism, in which every interest is disregarded but that of the army and the priesthood, both the eternal enemies of civil liberty, the ever ready minions of power, and the usual instruments of tyrants. When, long after the spirit of the constitution has departed, moderation is at length so far lost by those in power, that even the semblance of freedom is removed, and the forms themselves of the constitution discontinued, and so far from their petitions and remonstrances being regarded, the agents who bear them are thrown into dungeons, and mercenary armies sent forth to enforce a new government upon them at the point of the bayonet.

When, in consequence of such acts of malfeasance and abduction on the part of the government, anarchy prevails, and civil society is dissolved into its original elements, in such a crisis, the first law of nature, the right of self-preservation, the inherent and inalienable right of the people to appeal to first principles, and take their political affairs into their own hands in extreme cases, enjoins it as a right towards themselves, and a sacred obligation to their posterity, to abolish such government, and create another in its stead, calculated to rescue them from impending dangers, and to secure their welfare and happiness.

Nations, as well as individuals, are amenable for their acts to the public opinion of mankind. A statement of a part of our grievances is therefore submitted to an impartial world, in justification of the hazardous but unavoidable step now taken, of severing our political connection with the Mexican people, and assuming an independent attitude among the nations of the earth.

The Mexican government, by its colonization laws, invited and induced the Anglo American population of Texas to colonize its wilderness under the pledged faith of a written constitution, that they should continue to enjoy that constitutional liberty and republican government to which they had been habituated in the land of of their birth, the United States of America.

In this expectation they have been cruelly disappointed, inasmuch as the Mexican nation has acquiesced to the late changes made in the government by General Antonio Lopez de Santa Anna, who, having overturned the constitution of his country, now offers, as the cruel alternative, either to abandon our homes, acquired by so many privations, or submit to the most intolerable of all tryanny, the combined despotism of the sword and the priesthood.

It hath sacrificed our welfare to the state of Coahuila by which our interests have been continually depressed through a jealous and partial course of legislation, carried on at a far distant seat of government, by a hostile majority, in an unknown tongue, and this too, notwithstanding we have petitioned in the humblest terms for the establishment of a separate state government, and have, in accordance with the provisions of the national constitution, presented to the general congress a republican constitution, which was, without a just cause, contemptuously rejected.

It incarcerated in a dungeon, for a long time, one of our citizens, for no other cause but a zealous endeavor to procure the acceptance of our constitution, and the establishment of a state government.

It has failed and refused to secure, on a firm basis, the right of trial by jury, that palladium of civil liberty, and only safe guarantee for the life, liberty, and property of the citizen.

It has failed to establish any public system of education, although possessed of almost boundless resources, (the public domain,) and although it is an axiom in political science, that unless a people are educated and enlightened, it is idle to expect the continuance of civil liberty, or the capacity for self government.

It has suffered the military commandants, stationed among us, to exercise arbitrary acts of oppression and tyranny, thus trampling upon the most sacred rights of the citizens, and rendering the military superior to the civil power.

It has dissolved, by force of arms, the state congress of Coahuila and Texas, and obliged our representatives to fly for their lives from the seat of government, thus depriving us of the fundamental political right of representation.

It has demanded the surrender of a number of our citizens, and ordered military detachments to seize and carry them into the interior for trial, in contempt of the civil authorities, and in defiance of the laws and the constitution.

It has made piratical attacks upon our commerce, by commissioning foreign desperadoes, and authorizing them to seize our vessels, and convey the property of our citizens to far distant parts for confiscation.

It denies us the right of worshiping the Almighty according to the dictates of our own conscience, by the support of a national religion, calculated to promote the temporal interest of its human functionaries, rather than the glory of the true and living God.

It has demanded us to deliver up our arms, which are essential to our defence—the rightful property of freemen—and formidable only to tyrannical governments.

It has invaded our country both by sea and by land, with the intent to lay waste our territory, and drive us from our homes; and has now a large mercenary army advancing, to carry on against us a war of extermination.

It has, through its emissaries, incited the merciless savage, with the tomahawk and scalping knife, to massacre the inhabitants of our defenceless frontiers.

It has been, during the whole time of our connection with it, the contemptible sport and victim of successive military revolutions, and hath continually exhibited every characteristic of a weak, corrupt, and tyrannical government.

These, and other grievances, were patiently borne by the people of Texas, until they reached that point at which forbearance ceases to be a virtue. We then took up arms in defence of the national constitution. We appealed to our Mexican brethren for assistance: our appeal has been made in vain; though months have elapsed, no sympathetic response has yet been heard from the interior. We are, therefore, forced to the melancholy conclusion, that the Mexican people have acquiesced in the destruction of their liberty, and the substitution therefor of a military government; that they are unfit to be free, and incapable of self government.

The necessity of self-preservation, therefore, now decrees our eternal political separation.

WE, *therefore, the delegates, with plenary powers, of the people of Texas, in solemn convention assembled, appealing to a candid world for the necessities of our condition, do hereby resolve and declare, that our political connection with the Mexican nation has forever ended, and that the people of Texas do now constitute a* FREE, SOVEREIGN, *and* INDEPENDENT REPUBLIC, *and are fully invested with all the rights and attributes which properly belong to independent nations; and, conscious of the rectitude of our intentions, we fearlessly and confidently commit the issue to the supreme Arbiter of the destinies of nations.*

In witness whereof we have hereunto subscribed our names.

RICHARD ELLIS,
*President and Delegate from Red River.*

ALBERT H. S. KIMBLE, *Secretary.*

C. B. Stewart,
James Collingsworth,
Edwin Waller,
A. Brigham,
John S. D. Byrom,
Francis Ruis,
J. Antonio Navarro,
William D. Lacy,
William Menifee,
John Fisher,
Matthew Caldwell,
John S. Roberts,
Robert Hamilton,
Collin McKinney,
A. H. Latimore,
James Power,
Sam. Houston,
Edward Conrad,
Martin Palmer,
James Gaines,
William Clark, jun.,
Sydney O. Pennington,
William Motley,
Lorenzo de Zavala,
George W. Smyth,
Stephen H. Everett,
Elijah Stepp,
Claiborne West,

William B. Leates,
M. B. Menard,
A. B. Hardin,
John W. Bunton,
Thomas J. Gazley,
R. M. Coleman,
Sterling C. Robertson,
George C. Childress,
Baily Hardiman,
Robert Potter,
Charles Taylor,
Samuel P. Carson,
Thomas J. Rusk,
William C. Crawford,
John Turner,
Benjamin Briggs Goodrich,
James G. Swisher,
George W. Barnet,
Jesse Grimes,
E. O. Legrand,
David Thomas,
S. Rhoads Fisher,
John W. Bower,
J. B. Woods,
Andrew Briscoe,
Thomas Barnett,
Jesse B. Badgett,
Stephen W. Blount.

## 45. THE CONSTITUTION OF THE REPUBLIC OF TEXAS

### March 17, 1836

From *Laws of the Republic of Texas* (Printed by Order of the Secretary of State, 2 vols.; Houston, 1838), I, 9-26.

Having adopted a declaration of independence on March 2, the Convention, on the same day, appointed a committee to draft a constitution for the Republic of Texas. The following constitution in its final form was adopted by the Convention shortly after midnight on the morning of March 17. The framers drew heavily from the Constitution of the United States and those of several of its states, but in one respect there was a basic difference in that there was to be only one state, rather than a federal system, in the Republic of Texas.

We, the people of Texas, in order to form a government, establish justice, ensure domestic tranquility, provide for the common defence and general welfare; and to secure the blessings of liberty to ourselves, and our posterity, do ordain and establish this constitution.

### ARTICLE I.

Section 1. The powers of this government shall be divided into three departments, viz: legislative, executive and judicial, which shall remain forever separate and distinct.

Sec. 2. The legislative power shall be vested in a senate and house of representatives, to be styled the congress of the republic of Texas.

Sec. 3. The members of the house of representatives shall be chosen annually, on the first Monday of September each year, until congress shall otherwise provide by law, and shall hold their offices one year from the date of their election.

Sec. 4. No person shall be eligible to a seat in the house of representatives until he shall have attained the age of twenty-five years, shall be a citizen of the republic, and shall have resided in the county or district six months next preceding his election.

Sec. 5. The house of representatives shall not consist of less than twenty-four, nor more than forty members, until the population shall amount to one hundred thousand souls, after which the whole number of representatives shall not be less than forty, nor more than one hundred: *Provided,* however, that each county shall be entitled to at least one representative.

Sec. 6. The house of representatives shall choose their speaker and other officers, and shall have the sole power of impeachment.

Sec. 7. The senators shall be chosen by districts, as nearly equal in free population (free negroes and Indians excepted,) as practicable; and the number of senators shall never be less than one third nor more than one half the number of representatives, and each district shall be entitled to one member and no more.

Sec. 8. The senators shall be chosen for the term of three years, on the first Monday in September; shall be citizens of the republic, reside in the district for which they are respectively chosen at least one year before the election; and shall have attained the age of thirty years.

Sec. 9. At the first session of congress after the adoption of this constitution, the senators shall be divided by lot into three classes, as nearly equal as practicable; the seats of the senators of the first class shall be vacated at the end of the first year; of the second class, at the end of the second year; the third class, at the end of the third year, in such a manner that one third shall be chosen each year thereafter.

Sec. 10. The vice president of the republic shall be president of the senate, but shall not vote on any question, unless the senate be equally divided.

Sec. 11. The senate shall choose all other officers of their body, and a president pro tempore, in the absence of the vice president, or whenever he shall exercise the office of president; shall have the sole power to try impeachments, and when sitting as a court of impeachment, shall be under oath; but no conviction shall take place without the concurrence of two thirds of all the members present.

Sec. 12. Judgment in cases of impeachment shall only extend to removal from office, and disqualification to hold any office of honor, trust or profit under this government; but the party shall nevertheless be liable to indictment, trial, judgment and punishment according to law.

Sec. 13. Each house shall be the judge of the elections, qualifications and returns of its own members. Two thirds of each house shall constitute a quorum to do business, but a smaller number may adjourn from day to day, and may compel the attendance of absent members.

Sec. 14. Each house may determine the rules of its own proceedings, punish its members for disorderly behavior, and with the concurrence of two thirds, may expel a member, but not a second time for the same offence.

Sec. 15. Senators and representatives shall receive a compensation for their services, to be fixed by law, but no increase of compensation, or diminution, shall take effect during the session at which such increase or diminution shall have been made. They shall, except in case of treason, felony, or breach of the peace, be privileged from arrest during the session of congress, and in going to and returning from the same; and for any speech or debate in either house they shall not be questioned in any other place.

Sec. 16. Each house may punish, by imprisonment, during the session, any person not a member, who shall be guilty of any disrespect to the house, by any disorderly conduct in their presence.

Sec. 17. Each house shall keep a journal of its proceedings, and publish the same, except such parts as in its judgment require secrecy. When any three members shall desire the yeas and nays on any question, they shall be entered on the journals.

Sec. 18. Neither house, without the consent of the other, shall adjourn for more than three days, nor to any other place than that in which the two houses may be sitting.

Sec. 19. When vacancies happen in either house, the executive shall issue writs of election to fill such vacancies.

Sec. 20. No bill shall become a law until it shall have been read on three several days in each house, and passed by the same, unless, in cases of emergency, two thirds of the members of the house where the bill originated shall deem it expedient to dispense with the rule.

Sec. 21. After a bill shall have been rejected, no bill containing the same substance shall be passed into a law during the same session.

Sec. 22. The style of the laws of the republic shall be, "Be it enacted by the senate and house of representatives of the republic of Texas, in congress assembled."

Sec. 23. No person holding an office of profit under the government shall be eligible to a seat in either house of congress, nor shall any member of either house be eligible to any office which may [be] created, or the profits of which shall be increased during his term of service.

Sec. 24. No holder of public monies or collector thereof, shall be eligible to a seat in either house of congress, until he shall have fully acquitted himself of all responsibility, and shall produce the proper officer's receipt thereof. Members of either house may protest against any act or resolution, and may have such protest entered on the journals of their respective houses.

Sec. 25. No money shall be drawn from the public treasury but in strict accordance with appropriations made by law; and no appropriations shall be made for private or local purposes, unless two thirds of each house concur in such appropriations.

Sec. 26. Every act of congress shall be approved and signed by the president before it becomes a law; but if the president will not approve and sign such act, he shall return it to the house in which it shall have originated, with his reasons for not approving the same, which shall be spread upon the journals of such house, and the bill shall then be reconsidered, and shall not become a law unless it shall then pass by a vote of two thirds of both houses. If any act shall be disapproved by the president, the vote on the reconsideration shall be recorded by ayes and noes. If the president shall fail to return a bill within five days (Sundays excepted) after it shall have been presented for his approval and signature, the same shall become a law, unless the congress prevent its return within the time above specified by adjournment.

Sec. 27. All bills, acts, orders, or resolutions, to which the concurrence of both houses may be necessary, (motions or resolutions for adjournment excepted,) shall be approved and signed by the president, or being disapproved, shall be passed by two thirds of both houses, in manner and form as specified in section twenty.

## ARTICLE II.

Sec. 1. Congress shall have power to levy and collect taxes and imposts, excise and tonage duties; to borrow money on the faith, credit, and property of the government, to pay the debts and to provide for the common defence and general welfare of the republic.

Sec. 2. To regulate commerce, to coin money, to regulate the value thereof and of foreign coin, to fix the standard of weights and measures, but nothing but gold and silver shall be made a lawful tender.

Sec. 3. To establish post offices and post roads, to grant charters of incorporation, patents and copy rights, and secure to the authors and inventors the exclusive use thereof for a limited time.

Sec. 4. To declare war, grant letters of marque and reprisal, and to regulate captures.

Sec. 5. To provide and maintain an army and navy, and to make all laws and regulations necessary for their government.

Sec. 6. To call out the militia to execute the law, to suppress insurrections, and repel invasion.

Sec. 7. To make all laws which shall be deemed necessary and proper to carry into effect the foregoing express grants of power, and all other powers vested in the government of the republic, or in any officer or department thereof.

## ARTICLE III.

Sec. 1. The executive authority of this government shall be vested in a chief magistrate, who shall be styled the president of the republic of Texas.

Sec. 2. The first president elected by the people shall hold his office for the term of two years, and shall be ineligible during the next succeeding term; and all subsequent presidents shall be elected for three years, and be alike ineligible; and in the event of a tie, the house of representatives shall determine between the two highest candidates by a vive voce vote.

Sec. 3. The returns of the elections for president and vice president shall be sealed up and transmitted to the speaker of the house of representatives, by the holders of elections of each county; and the speaker of the house of representatives shall open and publish the returns in presence of a majority of each house of congress.

## ARTICLE IV.

Sec. 1. The judicial powers of the government shall be vested in one supreme court, and such inferior courts as the congress may, from time to time, ordain and establish. The judges of the supreme and inferior courts shall hold their offices for four years, be eligible to re-election, and shall, at stated periods, receive for their services a compensation, not to be increased or diminished during the period for which they were elected.

Sec. 2. The republic of Texas shall be divided into convenient judicial districts, not less than three, nor more than eight. There shall be appointed for each district a judge, who shall reside in the same, and hold the courts at such times and places as congress may by law direct.

Sec. 3. In all admiralty and maritime cases, in all cases affecting ambassadors, public ministers or consuls, and in all capital cases, the district courts shall have exclusive original jurisdiction, and original jurisdiction in all civil cases when the matter in controversy amounts to one hundred dollars.

Sec. 4. The judges, by virtue of their offices, shall be conservators of the peace, throughout the republic. The style of all process shall be, "the republic of Texas;" and all prosecutions shall be carried on in the name and by the authority of the same, and conclude, "against the peace and dignity of the republic."

Sec. 5. There shall be a district attorney appointed for each district, whose duties, salaries, perquisites, and term of service shall be fixed by law.

Sec. 6. The clerks of the district courts shall be elected by the qualified voters for members of congress, in the counties where the courts are established, and shall hold their offices for four years, subject to removal by presentment of a grand jury, and conviction of a petit jury.

Sec. 7. The supreme court shall consist of a chief justice and associate judges; the district judges shall compose the associate judges, a majority of whom, with the chief justice, shall constitute a quorum.

Sec. 8. The supreme court shall have appellate jurisdiction only, which shall be conclusive, within the limits of the republic; and shall hold its sessions annually, at such times and places as may be fixed by law: *Provided,* that no judge shall sit in a case in the supreme court tried by him in the court below.

Sec. 9. The judges of the supreme and district courts shall be elected by joint ballot of both houses of congress.

Sec. 10. There shall be in each county a county court, and such justices' courts as the congress may, from time to time, establish.

Sec. 11. The republic shall be divided into convenient counties, but no new county shall be established, unless it be done on the petition of one hundred free male inhabitants of the territory sought to be laid off and established; and unless the said territory shall contain nine hundred square miles.

Sec. 12. There shall be appointed for each county, a convenient number of justices of the peace, one sheriff, one coroner, and a sufficient number of constables, who shall hold their offices for two years, to be elected by the qualified voters of the district or county, as congress may direct. Justices of the peace and sheriffs shall be commissioned by the president.

Sec. 13. The congress shall, as early as practicable, introduce, by statute, the common law of England, with such modifications as our circumstances, in their judgment, may require; and in all criminal cases, the common law shall be the rule of decision.

## ARTICLE V.

Sec. 1. Ministers of the gospel being, by their profession, dedicated to God and the care of souls, ought not to be diverted from the great duties of their functions: therefore, no minister of the gospel, or priest of any denomination whatever, shall be eligible to the office of the executive of the republic, nor to a seat in either branch of the congress of the same.

Sec. 2. Each member of the senate and house of representatives shall, before they proceed to business, take an oath to support the constitution, as follows;
"I, A. B., do solemnly swear [or affirm, as the case may be] that, as a member of this general congress, I will support the constitution of the republic, and that I will not propose or assent to any bill, vote, or resolution, which shall appear to me injurious to the people."

Sec. 3. Every person who shall be chosen or appointed to any office of trust or profit shall, before entering on the duties thereof, take an oath to support the constitution of the republic, and also an oath of office.

## ARTICLE VI.

Sec. 1. No person shall be eligible to the office of president who shall not have attained the age of thirty-

five years, shall be a citizen of the republic at the time of the adoption of this constitution, or an inhabitant of this republic at least three years immediately preceeding his election.

Sec. 2. The president shall enter on the duties of his office on the second Monday in December next succeeding his election, and shall remain in office until his successor shall be duly qualified.

Sec. 3. The president shall, at stated times, receive a compensation for his services, which shall not be increased or diminished during his continuance in office; and before entering upon the duties of his office, he shall take and subscribe the following oath or affirmation: "I, A. B., president of the republic of Texas, do solemnly and sincerely swear (or affirm, as the case may be) that I will faithfully execute the duties of my office, and to the best of my abilities preserve, protect, and defend the constitution of the Republic."

Sec. 4. He shall be commander-in-chief of the army and navy of the republic, and militia thereof, but he shall not command in person without the authority of a resolution of congress. He shall have power to remit fines and forfeitures, and to grant reprieves and pardons, except in cases of impeachment.

Sec. 5. He shall, with the advice and consent of two-thirds of the senate, make treaties; and with the consent of the senate, appoint ministers and consuls, and all officers whose offices are established by this constitution, not herein otherwise provided for.

Sec. 6. The president shall have power to fill all vacancies that may happen during the recess of the senate; but he shall report the same to the senate within ten days after the next congress shall convene; and should the senate reject the same, the president shall not re-nominate the same individual to the same office.

Sec. 7. He shall, from time to time, give congress information of the state of the republic, and recommend for their consideration such measures as he may deem necessary. He may, upon extraordinary occasions, convene both houses, or either of them. In the event of a disagreement as to the time of adjournment, he may adjourn them to such time as he may think proper. He shall receive all foreign ministers. He shall see that the laws be faithfully executed, and shall commission all the officers of the republic.

Sec. 8. There shall be a seal of the republic, which shall be kept by the president, and used by him officially; it shall be called the great seal of the republic of Texas.

Sec. 9. All grants and commissions shall be in the name, and by the authority of the republic of Texas, shall be sealed with the great seal, and signed by the president.

Sec. 10. The president shall have power, by and with the advice and consent of the senate, to appoint a secretary of state and such other heads of executive departments as may be established by law, who shall remain in office during the term of service of the president, unless sooner removed by the president, with the advice and consent of the senate.

Sec. 11. Every citizen of the republic who has attained the age of twenty-one years, and shall have resided six months within the district or county where the election is held, shall be entitled to vote for members of the general congress.

Sec. 12. All elections shall be by ballot, unless congress shall otherwise direct.

Sec. 13. All elections by joint vote of both houses of congress shall be viva voce, shall be entered on the journals, and a majority of the votes shall be necessary to a choice.

Sec. 14. A vice president shall be chosen at every election for president, in the same manner, continue in office for the same time, and shall possess the same qualifications of the president. In voting for president and vice president, the electors shall distinguish for whom they vote as president, and for whom as vice president.

Sec. 15. In cases of impeachment, removal from office, death, resignation, or absence of the president from the republic, the vice president shall exercise the powers and discharge the duties of the president until a successor be duly qualified, or until the president, who may be absent or impeached, shall return or be acquitted.

Sec. 16. The president, vice president, and all civil officers of the republic, shall be removable from office by impeachment for, and on conviction of, treason, bribery, and other high crimes and misdemeanors.

## SCHEDULE.

Sec. 1. That no inconvenience may arise from the adoption of this constitution, it is declared by this convention that all laws now in force in Texas, and not inconsistent with this constitution, shall remain in full force until declared void, repealed, altered, or expire by their own limitation.

Sec. 2. All fines, penalties, forfeitures and escheats, which have accrued to Coahuila and Texas, or Texas, shall accrue to this republic.

Sec. 3. Every male citizen, who is, by this constitution, a citizen, and shall be otherwise qualified, shall be entitled to hold any office or place of honor, trust, or profit under the republic, any thing in this constitution to the contrary notwithstanding.

Sec. 4. The first president and vice president that shall be appointed after the adoption of this constitution, shall be chosen by this convention, and shall immediately enter on the duties of their offices, and shall hold said offices until their successors be elected and qualified, as prescribed in this constitution, and shall have the same qualifications, be invested with the same powers, and perform the same duties which are required and conferred on the executive head of the republic by this constitution.

Sec. 5. The president shall issue writs of election directed to the officers authorized to hold elections of the several counties, requiring them to cause an election to be held for president, vice president, representatives, and senators to congress, at the time, and mode prescribed by this constitution, which election shall be conducted in the manner that elections have been heretofore conducted. The president, vice president, and members of congress, when duly elected, shall continue to discharge the duties of their respective offices for the time and manner prescribed by this constitution, until their successors be duly qualified.

Sec. 6. Until the first enumeration shall be made, as directed by this constitution, the precinct of Austin shall be entitled to one representative; the precinct of Brazoria to two representatives; the precinct of Bexar two representatives; the precinct of Colorado one representative; Sabine one; Gonzales one; Goliad one; Harrisburg one; Jasper one; Jefferson one; Liberty one; Matagorda one; Mina two; Nacogdoches two; Red River three; Victoria one; San Augustine two; Shelby two; Refugio one; San Patricio one; Washington two; Milam one; and Jackson one representative.

Sec. 7. Until the first enumeration shall be made, as described by this constitution, the senatorial districts shall be composed of the following precincts: Bexar shall be entitled to one senator; San Patricio, Refugio and Goliad one; Brazoria one; Mina and Gonzales one; Nacogdoches one; Red River one; Shelby and Sabine one; Washington one; Matagorda, Jackson and Victoria one; Austin and Colorado one; San Augustine one; Milam one; Jasper and Jefferson one; and Liberty and Harrisburg one senator.

Sec. 8. All judges, sheriffs, commissioners, and other civil officers shall remain in office, and in the discharge of the powers and duties of their respective offices, until there shall be others appointed or elected under the constitution.

## GENERAL PROVISIONS.

Sec. 1. Laws shall be made to exclude from office, from the right of suffrage, and from serving on juries, those who shall hereafter be convicted of bribery, perjury, or other high crimes and misdemeanors.

Sec. 2. Returns of all elections for officers who are to be commissioned by the president, shall be made to the secretary of state of this republic.

Sec. 3. The presidents and heads of departments shall keep their offices at the seat of government, unless removed by the permission of congress, or unless in cases of emergency in time of war, the public interest may require their removal.

Sec. 4. The president shall make use of his private seal until a seal of the republic shall be provided.

Sec. 5. It shall be the duty of congress, as soon as circumstances will permit, to provide by law, a general system of education.

Sec. 6. All free white persons who shall emigrate to this republic, and who shall, after a residence of six months, make oath before some competent authority that he intends to reside permanently in the same, and shall swear to support this constitution, and that he will bear true allegiance to the republic of Texas, shall be entitled to all the privileges of citizenship.

Sec. 7. So soon as convenience will permit, there shall be a penal code formed on principles of reformation, and not of vindictive justice; and the civil and criminal laws shall be revised, digested, and arranged under different heads; and all laws relating to land titles shall be translated, revised and promulgated.

Sec. 8. All persons who shall leave the country for the purpose of evading a participation in the present struggle, or shall refuse to participate in it, or shall give aid or assistance to the present enemy, shall forfeit all rights of citizenship, and such lands as they may hold in the republic.

Sec. 9. All persons of color who were slaves for life previous to their emigration to Texas, and who are now held in bondage, shall remain in the like state of servitude: *provided,* the said slave shall be the bona fide property of the person so holding said slave as aforesaid. Congress shall pass no laws to prohibit emigrants from bringing their slaves into the republic with them, and holding them by the same tenure by which such slaves were held in the United States; nor shall congress have power to emancipate slaves; nor shall any slave holder be allowed to emancipate his or her slave or slaves without the consent of congress, unless he or she shall send his or her slave or slaves without the limits of the republic. No free person of African descent, either in whole or in part, shall be permitted to reside permanently in the republic, without the consent of congress; and the importation or admission of Africans or negroes into this republic, excepting from the United States of America, is forever prohibited, and declared to be piracy.

Sec. 10. All persons (Africans, the descendants of Africans, and Indians excepted,) who were residing in Texas on the day of the declaration of independence, shall be considered citizens of the republic, and entitled to all the privileges of such. All citizens now living in Texas, who have not received their portion of land, in like manner as colonists, shall be entitled to their land in the following proportion and manner: Every head of a family shall be entitled to one league and labor of land; and every single man of the age of seventeen and upwards, shall be entitled to the third part of one league of land. All citizens who may have previously to the adoption of this constitution, received their league of land as heads of families, and their quarter of a league of land as single persons, shall receive such additional quantity as will make the quantity of land received by them equal to one league and labor, and one third of a league, unless by bargain, sale, or exchange, they have transferred or may henceforth transfer their right to said land, or a portion thereof, to some other citizen of the republic: and in such case, the person to whom such right shall have been transferred shall be entitled to the same, as fully and amply as the person making the transfer might or could have been.—No alien shall hold land in Texas, except by titles emanating directly from the government of this republic. But if any citizen of this republic should die intestate or otherwise, his children or heirs shall inherit his estate, and aliens shall have a reasonable time to take possession of and dispose of the same, in a manner hereafter to be pointed out by law. Orphan children whose parents were entitled to land under the colonization laws of Mexico, and who now reside in the republic, shall be entitled to all the rights of which their parents were possessed at the time of their death. The citizens of the republic shall not be compelled to reside on the land, but shall have their lines plainly marked.

All orders of survey legally obtained by any citizen of the republic, from any legally authorized commissioner, prior to the act of the late consultation closing the land offices, shall be valid. In all cases the actual settler and occupant of the soil shall be entitled, in locating his land, to include his improvement, in preference to all other claims not acquired previous to his settlement, according to the law of the land and this constitution—*provided,* that nothing herein contained shall prejudice the rights of any other citizen from whom a settler may hold land by rent or lease.

And whereas, the protection of the public domain from unjust and fraudulent claims, and quieting the people in the enjoyment of their lands, is one of the great duties of this convention; and whereas the legisture of Coahuila and Texas having passed an act in the year 1834, in behalf of general John T. Mason of New York, and another on the 14th day of March, 1835, under which the enormous amount of eleven hundred leagues of land has been claimed by sundry individuals, some of whom reside in foreign countries, and are not citizens of the republic,—which said acts are contrary to articles fourth, twelfth, and fifteenth of the laws of 1824 of the general congress of Mexico, and one of said acts, for that cause has, by said general congress of Mexico, been declared null and void: It is hereby declared that the said act of 1834, in favor of John T. Mason, and of the 14th of March, 1835, of the said legislature of Coahuila and Texas, and each and every grant founded thereon, is, and was from the beginning, null and void; and all surveys made under pretence of authority derived from said acts, are hereby declared to be null and void: and all eleven league claims, located within twenty leagues of the boundary line between Texas and the United States of America, which have been located contrary to the laws of Mexico, are hereby declared to be null and void. And whereas many surveys and titles to lands have been made whilst most of the people of Texas were absent from home, serving in the campaign against Bexar, it is hereby declared that all the surveys and locations of land made since the act of the late consultation closing the land offices, and all titles to land made since that time, are, and shall be null and void.

And whereas the present unsettled state of the country and the general welfare of the people demand that the operations of the land office, and the whole land system shall be suspended until persons serving in the army can have a fair and equal chance with those remaining at home, to select and locate their lands, it is hereby declared, that no survey or title which may hereafter be made shall be valid, unless such survey or title shall be authorized by this convention, or some future congress of the republic. And with a view to the simplification of the land system, and the protection of the people and the government from litigation and fraud, a general land office shall be established, where all the land titles of the republic shall be registered, and the whole territory of the republic shall be sectionized, in a manner hereafter to be prescribed by law, which shall enable the officers of the government or any citizen, to ascertain with certainty the lands that are vacant, and those lands which may be covered with valid titles.

Sec. 11. Any amendment or amendments to this constitution, may be proposed in the house of representatives or senate, and if the same shall be agreed to by a majority of the members elected to each of the two houses, such proposed amendment or amendments shall be entered on the journals, with the yeas and nays thereon, and referred to the congress then next to be chosen, and shall be published for three months previous to the election; and if the congress next chosen as aforesaid, shall pass said amendment or amendments by a vote of two-thirds of all the members elected to each house, then it shall be the duty of said congress to submit said proposed amendment or amendments to the people, in such manner and at such times as the congress shall prescribe; and if the people shall approve and ratify such amendment or amendments by a majority of the electors qualified to vote for members of congress voting thereon, such amendment or amendments shall become a part of this constitution: *Provided*, however, that no amendment or amendments be referred to the people oftener than once in three years.

## DECLARATION OF RIGHTS.

This declaration of rights is declared to be a part of this constitution, and shall never be violated on any pretence whatever. And in order to guard against the transgression of the high powers which we have delegated, we declare that every thing in this bill of rights contained, and every other right not hereby delegated, is reserved to the people.

First. All men, when they form a social compact, have equal rights, and no men or set of men are entitled to exclusive public privileges or emoluments from the community.

Second. All political power is inherent in the people, and all free governments are founded on their authority, and instituted for their benefit; and they have at all times an inalienable right to alter their government in such manner as they may think proper.

Third. No preference shall be given by law to any religious denomination or mode of worship over another, but every person shall be permitted to worship God according to the dictates of his own conscience.

Fourth. Every citizen shall be at liberty to speak, write, or publish his opinions on any subject, being responsible for the abuse of that privilege. No law shall ever be passed to curtail the liberty of speech or of the press; and in all prosecutions for libels, the truth may be given in evidence, and the jury shall have the right to determine the law and fact, under the direction of the court.

Fifth. The people shall be secure in their persons, houses, papers, and possessions, from all unreasonable searches and seizures, and no warrant shall issue to search any place or seize any person or thing, without describing the place to be searched or the person or thing to be seized, without probable cause, supported by oath or affirmation.

Sixth. In all criminal prosecutions the accused shall have the right of being heard, by himself, or counsel, or both; he shall have the right to demand the nature and cause of the accusation, shall be confronted with the witnesses against him, and have compulsory process for obtaining witnesses in his favor. And in all prosecutions by presentment or indictment, he shall have the right to a speedy and public trial, by an impartial jury; he

shall not be compelled to give evidence against himself, or be deprived of life, liberty, or property, but by due course of law. And no freeman shall be holden to answer for any criminal charge, but on presentment or indictment by a grand jury, except in the land and naval forces, or in the militia when in actual service in time of war or public danger, or in cases of impeachment.

Seventh. No citizen shall be deprived of privileges, outlawed, exiled, or in any manner disfranchised, except by due course of the law of the land.

Eighth. No title of nobility, hereditary privileges or honors, shall ever be granted or conferred in this republic. No person holding any office of profit or trust shall, without the consent of congress, receive from any foreign state any present, office, or emolument of any kind.

Ninth. No person, for the same offence, shall be twice put in jeopardy of life or limbs. And the right of trial by jury shall remain inviolate.

Tenth. All persons shall be bailable by sufficient security, unless for capital crimes, when the proof is evident or presumption strong; and the privilege of the writ of "habeas corpus" shall not be suspended, except in case of rebellion or invasion the public safety may require it.

Eleventh. Excessive bail shall not be required, nor excessive fines imposed, or cruel or unusual punishments inflicted. All courts shall be open, and every man for any injury done him in his lands, goods, person, or reputation, shall have remedy by due course of law.

Twelfth. No person shall be imprisoned for debt in consequence of inability to pay.

Thirteenth. No person's particular services shall be demanded, nor property taken or applied to public use, unless by the consent of himself or his representative, without just compensation being made therefor according to law.

Fourteenth. Every citizen shall have the right to bear arms in defence of himself and the republic. The military shall at all times and in all cases be subordinate to the civil power.

Fifteenth. The sure and certain defence of a free people is a well regulated militia; and it shall be the duty of the legislature to enact such laws as may be necessary to the organizing of the militia of this republic.

Sixteenth. Treason against this republic shall consist only in levying war against it, or adhering to its enemies, giving them aid and support. No retrospective or ex-post facto law, or laws impairing the obligation of contracts, shall be made.

Seventeenth. Perpetuities or monopolies are contrary to the genius of a free government, and shall not be allowed; nor shall the law of primogeniture or entailments ever be in force in this republic.

The foregoing constitution was unanimously adopted by the delegates of Texas, in convention assembled, at the town of Washington, on the seventeenth day of March, in the year of our Lord one thousand eight hundred and thirty-six, and of the Independence of the Republic, the first year.

In witness whereof, we have hereunto subscribed our names.

RICHARD ELLIS,
*President and Delegate from Red River.*

ALBERT H. S. KIMBLE, *Secretary,*

C. B. Stewart,
James Collinsworth,
Edwin Waller,
A. Brigham,
John S. D. Byrom,
Francis Ruis,
J. Antonio Navarro,
William D. Lacy,
William Menifee,
John Fisher,

Matthew Caldwell,
William Motley,
Lorenzo de Zavala,
George W. Smyth,
Stephen H. Everett,
Elijah Stepp,
Claiborne West,
John S. Roberts,
Robert Hamilton,
Collin McKinney,

A. H. Latimore,
James Power,
Sam. Houston,
Edward Conrad,
Martin Palmer,
James Gaines,
William Clark, jun.,
Sydney O. Pennington,
Samuel P. Carson,
Thomas J. Rusk,
William C. Crawford,
John Turner,
Benjamin Briggs Goodrich,
James G. Swisher,
William B. Leates,
M. B. Menard,
A. B. Hardin,
John W. Bunton,

Thomas J. Gazley,
R. M. Coleman,
Sterling C. Robertson,
George C. Childress,
Baily Hardiman,
Robert Potter,
Charles Taylor,
George W. Barnet,
Jesse Grimes,
E. O. Legrand,
David Thomas,
S. Rhoads Fisher,
John W. Bower,
J. B. Woods,
Andrew Briscoe,
Thomas Barnett,
Jesse B. Badgett,
Stephen W. Blount.

## 46.   THE GOLIAD CAMPAIGN AND MASSACRE

### MARCH, 1836

From Henry S. Foote, *Texas and the Texans* (2 vols.; Philadelphia, 1841; facsimile, Austin, 1935), II, 227-248.

After the Mexican forces had been driven from Texas in December, 1835, the Provisional Government authorized Frank W. Johnson and James W. Fannin to lead separate expeditions against Matamoros. When Fannin learned that General José Urrea was concentrating forces at Matamoros preparatory to an invasion of Texas, he marched to Goliad, where he assembled between 450 and 500 volunteers. On March 14 he received orders from General Sam Houston, commander-in-chief of all Texas forces since March 4, to blow up the fortress and fall back to Victoria. Meanwhile, he learned that the expedition under Johnson was annihilated by Urrea at San Patricio on February 27 and March 2. Having sent a detachment of about 180 men to aid the settlers at Refugio to escape Urrea's forces, Fannin waited for the return of his men until March 19 before beginning his retreat.

It was then too late. About seventeen miles out and near the crossing on Coleto Creek, the Texans were surrounded by Urrea's lancers, which had been augmented by five or six hundred troops detached from Santa Anna's command after the fall of the Alamo, and in the resulting engagement suffered seven killed and sixty wounded. Realizing the futility of further resistance, Fannin surrendered the next day "subject to the disposition of the Supreme Government," but the survivors insisted that they capitulated as prisoners of war or to be returned to the United States. The prisoners were returned to Goliad, kept in confinement for a week, and then, on orders of Santa Anna, about 350 (including some captured elsewhere) were shot. The lives of the four physicians and a few needed workers were spared, and a few escaped the firing squads.

Two of the physicians, Dr. Jack Shackelford, Captain of the Alabama "Red Rovers," and Dr. Joseph H. Barnard, afterwards published very similar accounts; a third was written by J. C. Duval who escaped the firing squad. The following account is that of Dr. Shackelford, whose son and two nephews were among the unfortunate victims.

### SOME FEW NOTES UPON A PART OF THE TEXAN WAR. — By JACK SHACKELFORD

. . . Some time in the early part of March, 1836, Col. Fannin had under his command, at Goliad, upwards of 400 men, consisting of Ward's battalion from Georgia, and the . . . command of Major Wallace of the Texan army, who had recently been elected Major of the 2d Battalion, . . . The companies were all small, excepting the Red Rovers, which numbered nearly seventy. About the 12th of March, Captain King's company was sent to the Mission of Refugio for the purpose of bringing off some families that were in a state of alarm. At the Mission, King encountered a large force of the enemy. Having taken protection in the church, he despatched a message to Fannin, and with his little band of 28 men, maintained himself against a large party of the enemy. About midnight, on the 14th, King's express reached Goliad, and Col. Fannin immediately despatched Col. Ward's Battalion to his relief. This was the beginning of our trouble; and the only act for which I ever blamed Fannin. Those families should have left the Mission before they did, and Fannin should not have divided his forces; but that he was actuated by the best feelings, none can deny. Ward reached the Mission on the evening following, and cut his way through a large force; against which, King had been gallantly contending all day. The next day the enemy withdrew some distance across a small stream, and were pursued by Ward and King, who unfortunately separated. This event led to the capture of King and his company, who were, as I have been informed by one present, marched a short distance and massacred in a cold-blooded manner; King meeting his fate with the intrepidity of a soldier. Ward returned to the church, and after having expended the greater part of his ammunition, retreated silently, and under cover of the night, and made his way to the East in the direction of the Guadaloupe. This manoeuvre eluded the vigilance of the Mexicans, as they had laid an ambuscade for him in the direction of Goliad. He reached Victoria on the 21st, after great suffering and being four or five days without anything to eat. At this place he expected to find the Texan army, and was not apprised of his mistake until surrounded by a large force of Mexicans under General Urea. . . .

On the morning after Ward left Goliad for the Mission, to relieve King, Col. Fannin received Gen. Houston's order to evacuate Goliad and fall back on Victoria. He took immediate steps in making preparation to *obey this order,* by dismounting several guns and burying them, sending out one or two parties of men, accompanied by officers, to procure teams and carts, and making other arrangements for an immediate retreat. An express was likewise forthwith sent to Ward, commanding him to return with as little delay as possible, and stating to him the nature of Gen. Houston's order. This express was followed by another, and yet another, who were all taken prisoners by the enemy; and it was not until the evening of the 18th that we received any intelligence from Ward, and that not of a satisfactory character. I have mentioned this circumstance, if possible, to dissipate an unworthy prejudice which has been created in the minds of many, that Fannin wished to forestall Houston in the command of the army, and therefore *disobeyed his orders.* I have said, that he committed an error in separating his forces. Had he not done this, we should have been prepared to fall back on Victoria, as ordered, with a force sufficient to contend with every Mexican we might have encountered. Fannin's great anxiety alone, for the fate of Ward and King, and their little band, delayed our march. This delay, I feel assured, was not the result of any wish to *disobey orders.*

On the 16th of March, Colonel Albert C. Horton, of Matagorda, with twenty-seven men under his command, arrived at Goliad, bringing with them some oxen, to enable us to take off our stores and munitions. A fourth messenger was despatched to Col. Ward, urging his immediate return, while we were busied in making preparation for a retreat. On the 17th, Horton was ordered to examine the country towards San Antonio, and keep scouts out in every direction. On his return, Horton reported a large force, a few miles from the fort, moving on slowly and in good order. We immediately dug up our cannon, which had been buried, and re-mounted them, expecting an attack that night, or early the next morning. During the night, the guard was doubled, and every arrangement made by the commanding officer, to prevent surprise. On the 18th, the enemy was still roving about the neighborhood of the fort, and during the day a large reconnoitring party showed themselves on the opposite side of the river, in the vicinity of the old Mission. Horton was immediately sent over with his company, and a few others who could procure horses. I posted myself on a commanding bastion of the fort, where I had a full view of the encounter that ensued. *Horton behaved in a very gallant manner,* and made a furious charge upon the enemy, drove them into the timber, and after encountering a very large force of infantry, fell back and formed his company in good order, immediately in front of the Mission. In this rencontre, young Fenner, of my company, shot a spy-glass from the hands of an officer. When I saw Horton in the midst of such peril, contending against such fearful odds, I ob-

tained Col. Fannin's permission to go with my company to his relief. Such was the enthusiasm of the men, that they waded the river up to their arm-pits, although by taking a little more time, we could have availed ourselves of the benefit of a flat which was at the ford. So soon as we reached the Mission, and were about to flank the enemy, they made a precipitate retreat into the woods; although they outnumbered us ten to one. This was, no doubt, in part, the result of a cannonading from the fort, which unfortunately commenced about this time. . . .

On the morning of the 19th, we commenced the retreat very early, the Red Rovers leading the van, and Duval's company covering the rear. The lower road had been well examined by Horton's videttes, who reported all clear. At the lower ford of the San Antonio, much time was consumed in consequence of the inability of the team to draw our cannon up the bank. I waded into the river myself, with several of my company, assisting the artillerists by putting our shoulders to the wheels, and forcing the guns forward. We then moved on briskly and in good order, Horton's scouts examining the country in front and rear. We had advanced about six miles, when our scouts came in with a report that the route was still clear. As our teams had become somewhat weary, and very much in want of food, from having been kept in the fort for the last twenty-four hours, Col. Fannin determined to halt and graze them, and that we also might have time to take a little refreshment. I remonstrated warmly against this measure, and urged the necessity of first reaching the Coleta, then about five miles distant. In this matter I was overruled, . . . Col. Fannin and many others could not be made to believe that the Mexicans would dare follow us. He had too much contempt for their prowess, and too much confidence in the ability of his own little force. That he was deficient in that *caution* which a prudent officer should always evince, must be admitted; but that he was a brave, gallant, and intrepid officer, none who knew him can doubt.

We halted near an hour, and then took up our march. Horton's Company was sent in advance, to examine the pass on the Coleto. We had advanced about four miles, when a large force of cavalry were seen emerging from the timber, about two miles distant, and to the West of us. About one half of this force (350 men) were detached and thrown in front of our right flank, with the intention of cutting us off from a skirt of timber, about one mile and a half in front. Our artillery was ordered to open upon them and cover our rear. Several cannon were fired at them, but without effect. About this time, we discovered a large force of infantry emerging from the same skirt of woodland, at which their cavalry had first been seen. Our guns were then ordered to be limbered; and we had purposed to reach the timber in front, but the enemy approached so rapidly, that Col. Fannin determined to make an immediate disposition for battle. The prairie, here, was nearly in the form of a circle. In front was the timber of the Coleto, about a mile distant; in the rear, was another strip of timber, about six miles distant; whilst on our right and left, equi-distant, four or five miles from us, there were, likewise, bodies of timber. The order of battle was that of a hollow square.

But, unfortunately for us, in endeavouring to reach a commanding eminence in the prairie, our ammunition-cart broke down, and we were compelled to take our position in a valley, six or seven feet below the mean base, of about one fourth of a mile in area. I have said the order, of battle was that of a hollow square; I should more properly say, an oblong square. We had several pieces of artillery, which were judiciously posted. The Red Rovers and New Orleans' Greys formed the front line of the square; the Red Rovers being on the extreme right. Colonel Fannin took a commanding position, directly in rear of the right flank. Our orders were, not to fire until the enemy approached in point blank shot. The cavalry on our right dismounted, about 350 strong, and when within about a quarter of a mile of us, gave a volley with their scopets, which came whizzing over our heads. They still continued to advance, and from the proximity of the second volley of balls to our heads, I ordered my company to sit down, which example was followed by all, excepting the artillerists. The third volley from their pieces wounded the man on my left, and several others. About this time, Colonel Fannin had the cock of his rifle shot away by a ball, and another buried in the breech. He was still standing erect, a conspicuous mark, giving orders, "not to fire yet," in a calm and decided manner. The enemy had now advanced within about one hundred yards of us; they halted and manifested a determination to give us a regular battle. At this moment we opened our fire on them, rifles, muskets, and artillery. Colonel Fannin, at the same time, received a severe wound in the fleshy part of the thigh, the ball passing obliquely over the bone, carrying with it a part of his pocket-handkerchief. At this crisis, the enemy's infantry, from about ten to twelve hundred strong, advanced on our left and rear. Those on our left were the celebrated "Tampico permanent Regiment," of which Santa Anna said:—"They were the best troops in the world." When at a convenient distance, they gave us a volley and charged bayonet. So soon as the smoke cleared away, they were received by a piece of artillery, Duval's riflemen, and some other troops, which mowed them down with tremendous slaughter. Their career being thus promptly stopped, they contented themselves with falling down in the grass and occasionally raising up to fire; but whenever they showed their heads, they were taken down by the riflemen. The engagement now became general; and a body of cavalry, from two to three hundred strong, made a demonstration on our rear. They came up in full tilt, with gleaming lances, shouting like Indians. When about sixty yards distant, the whole of the rear division of our little command, together with a piece or two of artillery, loaded with double canister filled with musket-balls, opened a tremendous fire upon them, which brought them to a full halt and swept them down by scores. The rest immediately retreated, and chose to fight on foot the balance of the day. Our guns had now become hot—we had no water to sponge them —many of our artillerists had been wounded, and we had to rely alone on our small-arms. These were industriously handled, as all our men were kept busy during the balance of the day. The action commenced about one o'clock, and continued, without intermission, until after sunset. Our whole force did not exceed *two hundred and*

*seventy-five effective men.* That of the enemy, (from all the information we could get) was reckoned at *seven hundred Cavalry and twelve hundred Infantry!* Our loss was seven killed, besides several mortally wounded, and sixty *badly* wounded. We had many others slightly wounded. Out of the number killed, four belonged to my company; and more than *one half* of my company were struck with balls during the battle.

The courage of all was of that character which would have done honour to veterans. . . .

During the night, the enemy occupied the strip of wood-land in front of us; and we entrenched ourselves on the ground where we fought. It has been often asked, as a matter of surprise, why we did not retreat in the night. A few reasons, I think, ought to satisfy every candid man on this point. During the engagement our teams had all been killed, wounded, or had strayed off; so that we had no possible way of taking off our wounded companions. Those who could have deserted them under such circumstances, possess feelings which I shall never envy. I will mention another reason, which may have more weight with some persons, than the one already given. We had been contending for five hours, without intermission, with a force more than *seven times* larger than our own; had driven the enemy from the field with great slaughter; and calculated on a reinforcement in the morning, from Victoria, when we expected to consummate our victory. The morning of the 20th came; but instead of a reinforcement, as we had anticipated, the reverse was the fact. The enemy had an accession to their remaining number of about *five hundred* men.

Their whole force was then displayed in the most imposing and pompous manner; together with about three hundred pack mules; keeping, however, concealed, some pieces of artillery. These, being masked, were placed upon an elevated piece of ground, and were poured upon us; but without any effect. They took care to keep without the range of our rifles. Our cannon had become cool and we could have returned their fire; but perhaps with no effect, and therefore reserved all for close quarters. Here let me remark, that I have read Gen. Urea's pamphlet on this subject, in which he says the firing of the artillery was only the signal for a general charge. On this point, as well as his denial of any capitulation, I never read a more villanous *falsehood* from the pen of any man, who aspired to the rank of General. After they had fired a few rounds at us, they raised a white flag which was soon taken down. We then had a consultation of officers, a majority of whom believed that we could not save our wounded without a capitulation; and but *one* solitary man in the ranks would have surrendered at discretion. We then raised a white flag, which was responded to by the enemy. Major Wallace was then sent out together with one or two others who spoke the Mexican language. They shortly returned, and reported that the Mexican General could capitulate with the commanding officer only. Col. Fannin, although quite lame, then went out with the flag. When he was about to leave our lines, the emotions of my mind were intense, and I felt some anxiety to hear the determination of the men. I remarked to him, that I would not oppose a surrender, provided we could obtain an *honourable capitulation*; one, on which he could rely: that if he could not obtain such,—come back—our graves are already dug—let us all be buried together. To these remarks the men responded in a firm and determined manner; and the Colonel assured us, that he never would surrender on any other terms. He returned in a short time thereafter, and communicated the substance of an agreement entered into by Gen. Urea and himself. Col. Holsinger, a German, and an engineer in the Mexican service, together with several other officers, then came into our lines to consummate the arrangement. The first words Col. Holsinger uttered after a very polite bow, were: "WELL GENTLEMEN, IN EIGHT DAYS, LIBERTY AND HOME!" I heard this distinctly. The terms of the Capitulation were then written in both the English and Mexican languages, and read two or three times by officers who could speak and read both languages. The instruments which embodied the terms of Capitulation as agreed on, were then signed and interchanged in the most formal and solemn manner; and were in substance, as follows: "1st. That we should be received and treated as prisoners of war according to the *usages of the most civilized nations*. 2d. That private property should be respected and restored: that the side arms of the officers should be given up. 3d. That the men should be sent to Copano, and thence to the United States in eight days, or so soon thereafter as vessels could be procured to take them. 4th. That the officers should be paroled and return to the United States in like manner." I assert most positively, that this Capitulation was entered into, without which a surrender never would have been made. . . . After our arms had been given up and the necessary arrangements made, all who were not so badly wounded as to prevent their marching, were posted off to Goliad under a strong guard. We reached there a little after sunset, and were driven into the church like so many swine. We were compelled to keep a space open in the centre for the guard to pass backward and forward, under the penalty of having it kept open by a discharge of guns. To avoid this, we had literally to lie one upon another. Early in the morning, their soldiery commenced dragging the blankets from our wounded. I resisted an attempt of this sort near me, and had a bayonet drawn and thrust at me.

So soon as it was sufficiently light to see well, I commenced (with what little means I could procure,) dressing and attending our wounded; but I was soon summoned by some Mexican officers, who came to the church door, to attend them. From that moment I found that I had to labour in the Hospital, and that scarcely an hour in the day would be allowed me to attend to my wounded companions.

On the second day after our arrival, Col. Fannin and the wounded who were left behind arrived at the Fort; the men having scarcely any water, being compelled to bring it from the river in canteens; nor had we any other food than a scanty pittance of beef without bread or salt. Col. Fannin was then under the protection of Col. Holsinger. On passing from one part of their wounded to another, I made it convenient to see Fannin, and stated to him how badly we were treated. . . . The next day Col. Fannin went in company with Col. Holsinger, on their way to Copano for the purpose of chartering a vessel, then said to be there, to take himself and

men to the United States. When they reached that place, however, the vessel had departed. This, I afterwards learned, was a stratagem to get possession of one of the vessels belonging to Uncle Sam's folks. . . . On the 23d, Major Miller and about seventy men were brought in, having been taken at Copano; and on the 25th, Col. Ward and command, taken, as I before said, near Victoria.

Our treatment did not vary much during the week, except that the men were marched into an area of the Fort, without any protection or covering; and the Church filled with a part of their wounded; ours occupying the barracks, or rather one room. On the 26th, Col. Fannin returned. That night I slept in a small room with him and some other officers. This room was in one corner of the Church, and was where we kept our medicines, instruments, bandages, &c. Col. Fannin was quite cheerful, and we talked pleasantly of the prospect of our reaching the United States. I cannot, here, resist an inclination to mention one more incident of that evening — the last evening of many, very many gallant spirits. . . . Many of our young men had a fondness for music, and could perform well, particularly on the flute. In passing by . . . on the outside of the Fort, my ear caught the sound of music, as it rolled in harmonious numbers from several flutes in concert. The tune was *"Home, Sweet Home."* . . . Poor fellows! It was their last earthly evening. . . .

27th March, — Palm Sunday. — . . . At dawn of day we were awakened by a Mexican officer calling us up, and saying he "wanted the men to form a line, that they might be counted." On hearing this, my impression was, that in all probability some poor fellows had made their escape during the night. After leaving the Church, I was met by Colonel Guerrear, said to be the Adjutant General of the Mexican army. This officer spoke the English language as fluently as I did myself; and to his honour be it said, he seemed a gentleman and a man of feeling. He requested that I would go to his tent in company with Major Miller and men; and that I would take my friend and companion, Dr. Joseph H. Bernard, with me. We accordingly went over to his tent, about one hundred yards off, in a south-westerly direction. On passing the gate of the Fort, I saw Ward's men in line, with their knapsacks on. I inquired of them where they were going; some of them stated that they were to march to Copano, and from thence to be sent *home!* After reaching Colonel Guerrear's tent (to attend to some wounded, as we expected,) we sat down and engaged in familiar conversation with a little Mexican officer who had been educated at Bardstown, Ky. In about half an hour, we heard the report of a volley of small-arms, towards the river, and to the east of the Fort. I immediately inquired the cause of the firing; and was assured by the officer that he "did not know, but expected it was the guard firing off their guns." In about fifteen or twenty minutes thereafter, another such volley was fired, directly south of us, and in front. At the same time, I could distinguish the heads of some of the men through the boughs of some peach trees, and could hear their screams. It was then, for the first time, the awful conviction seized upon our minds — that *Treachery* and *Murder* had begun their work. Shortly afterwards, Col. Guerrear appeared at the mouth of the tent. I asked him if it could be possible they were murdering our men? He replied that "it was so" — but that he "had not given the order; neither had he executed it." He further said, he had done all in his power to save as many as he could; and that if he could have saved more, he would have done so.

The men were taken out in four divisions, and under different pretexts; such as, making room in the Fort for the reception of Santa Anna,—going out to slaughter beef,—and being marched off to Copano, to be sent home. In about an hour, the closing scene of this base and treacherous tragedy was acted in the Fort; and the cold-blooded murder of all the wounded, who were unable to be marched out, was its infernal catastrophe. I learned from the interpreter, that Col. Fannin was the last doomed captive of vengeance; ... and that Fannin met his fate in a calm and soldier-like manner: that he handed his watch to the officer who superintended his *murder,* with a request that he would have him decently interred; and that he should be shot in the *breast,* and not in the *head;* with all of which the officer *solemnly promised* to comply; that Fannin was then placed in a chair, tied the handerchief over his eyes with his own hands, and then opened his *bosom* to receive their balls. Major Miller, who knew Fannin, informed me that the next day he saw him lying in the prairie among a heap

of wounded; and that he was shot in the *head!* We were marched into the Fort about 11 o'clock, and ordered to the Hospital.—Had to pass close by our butchered companions, who were stripped of their clothes, and their naked, mangled bodies thrown in a pile. The wounded were all hauled out in carts that evening; and some brush thrown over the different piles, with a view of burning their bodies. A few days afterwards, I accompanied Major Miller to the spot where lay those who were dear to me whilst living; ... and Oh! what a spectacle! The flesh had been burned from off the bodies; but many hands and feet were yet unscathed—I could recognize no one.—The bones were all still knit together, and the vultures were feeding upon those limbs which, one week before, actively played in battle.

I will here relate an incident which I received from the lips of one of my company who made his escape. When the division of the army to which he belonged was brought out and made ready for the work of destruction, the men were ordered to sit down with their backs to the Guard. Young Fenner (the same who had shot the spy-glass from the hands of the officer, as before mentioned), rose on his feet, and exclaimed: "Boys, they are going to kill us—die with your faces to them, like men!" At the same moment, two other young men, flourishing their caps over their heads, shouted at the top of their voices: "Hurra for Texas!" ...

## 47. THE RUNAWAY SCRAPE

### March-April, 1836

From "The Reminiscences of Mrs. Dilue Harris," *The Quarterly* of the Texas State Historical Association, IV (January, 1901), 160-179.

On March 26, 1836, General Sam Houston broke camp on the Colorado River and began moving eastward, abandoning the country to the advancing Mexican forces. Probably as many as a thousand families lived along the Colorado and the Brazos at the time. The news that the army was retreating, coupled with that of the fate of the defenders of the Alamo and Goliad, created panic not only among the inhabitants of the abandoned territory but among those east of the Brazos as well. The people fled in confusion toward the Sabine where they hoped to find safety within the United States, most of the group encountering great suffering in the course of their flight. The following account of the "Runaway Scrape," written by Mrs. Dilue Harris who was one of the refugees, is based on a journal kept by Dr. Pleasant W. Rose, the father of Mrs. Harris. In copying the journal, Mrs. Harris added her own recollections in a manner that makes the two accounts almost indistinguishable.

... By the 20th of February [1836] the people of San Patricio and other western settlements were fleeing for their lives. Every family in our neighborhood was preparing to go to the United States. Wagons and other vehicles were scarce. Mr. [Adam] Stafford [a cripple], with the help of small boys and negroes, began gathering cattle. All the large boys had gone to the army. ...

Father finished planting corn. He had hauled away a part of our household furniture and other things and

hid them in the bottom. Mother had packed what bedding, clothes, and provisions she thought we should need, ready to leave at a moment's warning. Father had made arrangements with a Mr. Bundick to haul our family in his cart; but we were confident that the army under General Houston would whip the Mexicans before they reached the Colorado river. ...

On the 12th of March came the news of the fall of the Alamo. A courier brought a dispatch from General Houston for the people to leave. ...

Then began the horrors of the "Runaway Scrape." We left home at sunset, hauling clothes, bedding, and provisions on the sleigh with one yoke of oxen. Mother and I were walking, she with an infant in her arms. Brother drove the oxen, and my little sisters rode in the sleigh. We were going ten miles to where we could be transferred to Mr. Bundick's cart. Father was helping with the cattle, but he joined us after dark and brought a horse and saddle for brother. He sent him to help Mr. Stafford with the cattle. He was to go a different road with them and ford the San Jacinto. Mother and I then rode father's horse.

We met Mrs. M——. She was driving her oxen home. We had sent her word in the morning. She begged mother to go back and help her, but father said not. He told the lady to drive the oxen home, put them in the cow pen, turn out the cows and calves, and get her children ready, and he would send assistance. . . .

It was ten o'clock at night when we got to Mrs. Roark's. We shifted our things into the cart of Mr. Bundick, who was waiting for us, and tried to rest till morning. . . .

Early the next morning we were on the move, mother with her four children in the cart, and Mr. Bundick and his wife and negro woman on horseback. . . . He brought with him two slaves, the woman already mentioned and a man who was driving the cart; and, as Mr. Bundick had no children, we were as comfortable as could have been expected. . . .

Mr. Cotie would not go to the army. He hauled five families in the big blue wagon with his six yoke of oxen, besides negroes, provisions, bedding, and all the plunder the others could not carry.

We camped the first night near Harrisburg, about where the railroad depot now stands. Next day we crossed Vince's Bridge and arrived at the San Jacinto in the night. There were fully five thousand people at the ferry. The planters from Brazoria and Columbia with their slaves were crossing. We waited three days before we crossed. Our party consisted of five white families: father's, Mr. Dyer's, Mr. Bell's, Mr. Neal's, and Mr. Bundick's. Father and Mr. Bundick were the only white men in the party, the others being in the army. There were twenty or thirty negroes from Stafford's plantation. They had a large wagon with five yoke of oxen, and horses, and mules, and they were in charge of an old negro man called Uncle Ned. Altogether, black and white, there were about fifty of us. Everyone was trying to cross first, and it was almost a riot.

We got over on the third day, and after travelling a few miles further to the next timber and water, some of our party wanted to camp; but others said that the Trinity river was rising, and if delayed we might not get across. So we hurried on.

When we got about half across the prairie Uncle Ned's wagon bogged. The negro men driving the carts tried to go around the big wagon one at a time until the four carts were fast in the mud. Mother was the only white woman that rode in a cart; the others travelled on horseback. Mrs. Bell's four children, Mrs. Dyer's three, and mother's four rode in the carts. All that were on horseback had gone on to the timber to let their horses feed and get water. They supposed their families would get there by dark. The negro men put all the oxen to the wagon, but could not move it; so they had to stay there until morning without wood or water. Mother gathered the white children in our cart. They behaved very well and went to sleep, except one little boy, Eli Dyer, who kicked and cried for Uncle Ned and Aunt Dilue till Uncle Ned came and carried him to the wagon. He slept that night in Uncle Ned's arms.

Mother with all the negro women and children walked six miles to the timber and found our friends in trouble. Father and Mr. Bundick had gone to the river and helped with the ferry boat, but late in the evening the boat grounded on the east bank of the Trinity and didn't get back until morning. While they were gone the horses had strayed off and they had to find them before

they could go to the wagons. Those that travelled on horseback were supplied with provisions by other campers. We that stayed in the prairie had to eat cold corn bread and cold boiled beef. The wagons and carts didn't get to the timber till night. They had to be unloaded and pulled out.

At the Trinity river men from the army began to join their families. . . . The Texas army was retreating and the Mexicans were crossing the Colorado, Col. Fannin and his men were prisoners, there were more negroes than whites among us and many of them were wild Africans, there [were] . . . the Cherokee Indians in Eastern Texas at Nacogdoches, and there were tories, both Mexicans and Americans, in the country. It was the intention of our men to see their families across the Sabine river, and then to return and fight the Mexicans. I must say for the negroes that there was no insubordination among them; for they were loyal to their owners.

Our hardships began at the Trinity. The river was rising and there was a struggle to see who should cross first. Measles, sore eyes, whooping cough, and every disease that man, woman, or child is heir to, broke out among us. . . . The horrors of crossing the Trinity are beyond my power to describe. One of my little sisters was very sick, and the ferryman said that those families that had sick children should cross first. When our party got to the boat the water broke over the banks above where we were and ran around us. We were several hours surrounded by water. Our family was the last to get to the boat. We left more than five hundred people on the west bank. Drift wood covered the water as far as we could see. The sick child was in convulsions. It required eight men to manage the boat.

When we landed the lowlands were under water, and everybody was rushing for the prairie. Father had a good horse, and Mrs. Dyer let mother have her horse and saddle. Father carried the sick child, and sister and I rode behind mother. She carried father's gun and the little babe. All we carried with us was what clothes we were wearing at the time. The night was very dark. We crossed a bridge that was under water. As soon as we crossed, a man with a cart and oxen drove on the bridge, and it broke down, drowning the oxen. That prevented the people from crossing, as the bridge was over a slough that looked like a river.

Father and mother hurried on, and we got to the prairie and found a great many families camped there. A Mrs. Foster invited mother to her camp, and furnished us with supper, a bed, and dry clothes.

The other families stayed all night in the bottom without fire or anything to eat, and the water up in the carts. The men drove the horses and oxen to the prairies, and the women, sick children, and negroes were left in the bottom. The old negro man, Uncle Ned, was left in charge. He put the white women and children in his wagon. It was large and had a canvas cover. The negro women and their children he put in the carts. Then he guarded the whole party until morning.

It was impossible for the men to return to their families. They spent the night making a raft by a torch light. As the camps were near a grove of pine timber, there was no trouble about lights. It was a night of terror. Father and the men worked some distance from the camp cutting down timber to make the raft. It had to be put together in the water. We were in great anxiety about the people that were left in the bottom; we didn't know but they would be drowned, or killed by panthers, alligators, or bears.

As soon as it was daylight the men went to the relief of their families and found them cold, wet, and hungry. . . . When the men on the raft got to those who had stayed all night in the Trinity bottom they found that the negroes were scared, and wanted to get on the raft; but Uncle Ned told them that his young mistress and the children should go first. It was very dangerous crossing the slough. The men would bring one woman and her children on the raft out of deep water, and men on horseback would meet them. It took all day to get the party out to the prairies. . . .

The second day they brought out the bedding and clothes. Everything was soaked with water. They had to take the wagons and carts apart. . . . It took four days to get everything out of the water.

The man whose oxen had drowned sold his cart to father for ten dollars. He said he had seen enough of Mexico and would go back to old Ireland.

It had been five days since we crossed the Trinity, and we had heard no news from the army. The town of Liberty was three miles from where we camped. The people there had not left their homes, and they gave us all the help in their power. My little sister that had been sick was buried in the cemetery at Liberty. After resting a few days our party continued their journey, but we remained in the town. Mother was not able to travel; she had nursed an infant and the sick child until she was compelled to rest.

A few days after our friends had gone a man crossed the Trinity in a skiff bringing bad news. The Mexican army had crossed the Brazos and was between the Texas army and Harrisburg. Fannin and his men were massacred. President Burnet and his cabinet had left Harrisburg and gone to Washington on the bay and were going to Galveston Island. The people at Liberty had left.

We had been at Liberty three weeks. . . . One Thursday evening all of a sudden we heard a sound like distant thunder. When it was repeated father said it was cannon, and that the Texans and Mexicans were fighting. . . . The cannonading lasted only a few minutes, and father said that the Texans must have been defeated, or the cannon would not have ceased firing so quickly. We left Liberty in half an hour. . . .

We travelled nearly all night, sister and I on horseback and mother in the cart. . . . We were as wretched as we could be; for we had been five weeks from home, and there was not much prospect of our ever returning. . . .

We continued our journey through mud and water and when we camped in the evening fifty or sixty young men came by who were going to join General Houston. One of them was Harvey Stafford, our neighbor, who was returning from the United States with volunteers. . . . He said also that General Gaines of the United States army was at the Neches with a regiment of soldiers to keep the Indians in subjection, but didn't prevent the people from crossing with their slaves. General Gaines said the boundary line between the United States and Mexico was the Neches.

The young men went a short distance from us and camped. Then we heard some one calling in the direction of Liberty. We could see a man on horseback waving his hat; and, as we knew there was no one left at Liberty, we thought the Mexican army had crossed the Trinity. The young men came with their guns, and when the rider got near enough for us to understand what he said, it was "Turn back! The Texas army has whipped the Mexican army and the Mexican army are prisoners. No danger! No danger! Turn back!" . . . When the young men began to understand the glorious news they wanted to fire a salute, but father made them stop. He told them to save their ammunition, for they might need it.

[The courier] . . . showed a despatch from General Houston giving an account of the battle and saying it would be safe for the people to return to their homes. The courier had crossed the Trinity River in a canoe, swimming his horse with the help of two men. . . .

The good news was cheering indeed. The courier's name was McDermot. He was an Irishman and had been an actor. He stayed with us that night and told various incidents of the battle. There was not much sleeping during the night. . . . We were on the move early the next morning. The courier went on to carry the glad tidings to the people who had crossed the Sabine, but we took a lower road and went down the Trinity. . . .

We crossed the San Jacinto the next morning and stayed until late in the evening on the battle field. Both armies were camped near. . . . I had lost my bonnet crossing Trinity Bay and was compelled to wear a table cloth again. It was six weeks since we had left home, and our clothes were very much dilapidated. I could not go to see the Mexican prisoners with a table cloth tied on my head for I knew several of the young men. I was on the battle field of San Jacinto the 26th of April, 1836. . . .

We stayed on the battle field several hours. Father was helping with the ferry boat. We visited the graves of the Texans that were killed in the battle, but there were none of them that I knew. The dead Mexicans were lying around in every direction. . . .

We left the battle field late in the evening. We had to pass among the dead Mexicans, and father pulled one out of the road, so we could get by without driving over the body, since we could not go around it. The prairie was very boggy, it was getting dark, and there were now twenty or thirty families with us. We were glad to leave the battle field, for it was a grewsome [sic] sight. We camped that night on the prairie, and could hear the wolves howl and bark as they devoured the dead. . . .

Early the next morning we were on the move. We had to take a roundabout road, for the burning of Vince's bridge prevented us from going directly home. We could hear nothing but sad news. San Felipe had been burned, and dear old Harrisburg was in ashes. There was nothing left of the Stafford plantation but a crib with a thousand bushels of corn. . . .

Burning the sawmill at Harrisburg and the buildings on Stafford's plantation was a calamity that greatly affected the people. On the plantation there were a sugar-mill, cotton-gin, blacksmith-shop, grist-mill, a dwelling-house, negro houses, and a stock of farming implements. The Mexicans saved the corn for bread, and it was a great help to the people of the neighborhood. . . .

We stayed one day on Sim's Bayou. There were more than one hundred families, and all stopped to rest and let the stock feed. . . . It was only fifteen miles home. . . .

Early in the morning we broke camp. . . . The weather was getting warm, and we stopped two hours in the middle of the day at a water hole. When the sun set we were still five miles from home. . . . It was ten o'clock when we got home. We camped near the house. . . .

As soon as it was light enough for us to see we went to the house, and the first thing we saw was the hogs running out. Father's bookcase lay on the ground broken open, his books, medicines, and other things scattered on the ground, and the hogs sleeping on them. . . . Through the joy and excitement since the battle of San Jacinto, we had forgotten our sad bereavement.

The first thing that father did after breakfast was to go to the corn field. He had planted corn the first of March, and it needed plowing. He did not wait for Monday, or to put the house in order, but began plowing at once. His field was in the bottom, and he had hidden his plow. . . .

Father had hid some of our things in the bottom, among them a big chest. Mother had packed it with bedding, clothes, and other things we could not take when we left home. After a few days, Uncle and brother hauled it to the house, and that old blue chest proved a treasure. When we left home we wore our best clothes. Now our best clothes were in the chest, among them my old sunbonnet. I was prouder of that old bonnet than in after years of a new white lace one that my husband gave me.

By the middle of May our neighbors that we had parted from came home. They had got to the Sabine River before they heard of the battle of San Jacinto. . . .

## 48.   THE BATTLE OF SAN JACINTO

### April 21, 1836

#### 1. HOUSTON'S OFFICIAL REPORT
April 25, 1836

From Sam Houston, Commander-in-Chief, San Jacinto, To his Excellency D. G. Burnett [sic], President of the Republic of Texas, April 25th, 1836 (MS; Archives, Texas State Library, Austin).

Headquarters of the Army
San Jacinto, April 25th, 1836

Sir — I regret extremely that my situation since the battle of the 21st has been such as to prevent my rendering you my official report of the same, previous to this time.

I have the honor to inform you that, on the evening of the 18th inst., after a forced march of fifty-five miles, which was effected in two days and a half, the army arrived opposite Harrisburg. That evening a courier of the enemy was taken, from whom I learned that General Santa Anna, with one division of his choice troops, had marched in the direction of Lynch's ferry, on the San Jacinto—burning Harrisburg as he passed down. The army was ordered to be in readiness to march early on the next morning. The main body effected a crossing over Buffalo Bayou, below Harrisburg, on the morning of the 19th, having left the baggage, the sick, and a sufficient camp-guard, in the rear. We continued to march throughout the night, making but one halt in the prairie for a short time, and without refreshments. At daylight we resumed the line of march, and in a short distance our scouts encountered those of the enemy, and we received information that General Santa Anna was at New Washington, and would that day take up the line of march for Anahuac, crossing at Lynch's ferry. The Texan army halted within half a mile of the ferry, in some timber, and were engaged in slaughtering beeves,

when the army of Santa Anna was discovered to be approaching in battle array, having been encamped at Clopper's point, eight miles below. Disposition was immediately made of our forces, and preparation for his reception. He took a position with his infantry, and artillery in the centre, occupying an island of timber, his cavalry covering the left flank. The artillery, consisting of one double-fortified medium brass twelve-pounder, then opened on our encampment. The infantry, in column, advanced with the design of charging our lines, but were repulsed by a discharge of grape and canister from our artillery, consisting of two six-pounders. The enemy had occupied a piece of timber within rifle-shot of the left wing of our army, from which an occasional interchange of small-arms took place between the troops, until the enemy withdrew to a position on the bank of the San Jacinto, about three quarters of a mile from our encampment, and commenced fortification.

A short time before sunset, our mounted men, about eighty-five in number, under the special command of Colonel Sherman, marched out for the purpose of reconnoitring the enemy. While advancing, they received a volley from the left of the enemy's infantry, and, after a sharp rencounter with their cavalry, in which ours acted extremely well, and performed some feats of daring chivalry, they retired in good order, having had two men severely wounded, and several horses killed. In the meantime, the infantry under the command of Lieut.-Col. Millard, and Col. Burleson's regiment, with the artillery, had marched out for the purpose of covering the retreat of the cavalry if necessary. All then fell back in good order to our encampment about sunset, and remained without ostensible action until the 21st, at half-past three o'clock, taking the first refreshment which they had enjoyed for two days. The enemy in the meantime extended the right flank of their infantry, so as to occupy the extreme point of a skirt of timber on the bank of the San Jacinto, and secured their left by a fortification about five feet high, constructed of packs and baggage, leaving an opening in the centre of the breastwork, in which their artillery was placed, their cavalry upon their left wing.

About 9 o'clock on the morning of the 21st, the enemy were reinforced by five hundred choice troops, under the command of Gen. Cos, increasing their effective force to upward of 1500 men, while our aggregate force for the field numbered 783. At half-past three o'clock in the evening, I ordered the officers of the Texan army to parade their respective commands, having in the meantime ordered the bridge on the only road communicating with the Brazos, distant eight miles from our encampment, to be destroyed, thus cutting off all possibility of escape. Our troops paraded with alacrity and spirit, and were anxious for the contest. Their conscious disparity in numbers seemed only to increase their enthusiasm and confidence, and heightened their anxiety for the conflict. Our situation afforded me an opportunity of making the arrangements preparatory to the attack without exposing our designs to the enemy. The 1st Regiment, commanded by Col. Burleson, was assigned to the centre. The 2d. Regiment, under the command of Col. Sherman, formed the left wing of the army. The artillery, under the special command of Col. George W. Hockley, inspector-general, was placed on the right of the 1st Regiment; and four companies of Infantry, under the command of Lieut.-Col. Henry Millard, sustained the artillery upon the right. Our cavalry, sixty-one in number, commanded by Col. Mirabeau B. Lamar (whose gallant and daring conduct on the previous day had attracted the admiration of his comrades, and called him to that station), placed on our extreme right, completed our line. Our cavalry was first despatched to the front of the enemy's left, for the purpose of attracting their notice, while an extensive island of timber afforded us an opportunity of concentrating our forces, and deploying from that point, agreeably to the previous design of the troops. Every evolution was performed with alacrity, the whole advancing rapidly in line, through an open prairie, without any protection whatever for our men. The artillery advanced and took station within two hundred yards of the enemy's breastwork, and commenced an effective fire with grape and cannister [sic]. Col. Sherman, with his regiment, having commenced the action upon our left wing, the whole line, at the centre and on the right, advancing in double quick time, raised the war-cry, "Remember the Alamo," received the enemy's fire, and advanced within point-blank shot, before a piece was discharged from our lines. Our line advanced without a halt, until they were in possession of the woodland and the enemy's breastwork —the right wing of Burleson's and the left of Millard's taking possession of the breastwork; our artillery having gallantly charged up within seventy yards of the enemy's cannon, when it was taken by our troops.

The conflict lasted about eighteen minutes from the time of close action until we were in possession of the enemy's encampment, taking one piece of cannon (loaded), four stand of colours, all their camp-equipage, stores, and baggage. Our cavalry had charged and routed that of the enemy upon the right, and given pursuit to the fugitives, which did not cease until they arrived at the bridge which I have mentioned before—Captain Karnes, always among the foremost in danger, commanding the pursuers. The conflict in the breastwork lasted but a few moments; many of the troops encountered hand to hand, and, not having the advantage of bayonets on our side, our riflemen used their pieces as war-clubs, breaking many of them off at the breech. The rout commenced at half-past four, and the pursuit by the main army continued until twilight. A guard was then left in charge of the enemy's encampment, and our army returned with their killed and wounded. In the battle, our loss was two killed and twenty-three wounded, six of them mortally. The enemy's loss was 630 killed, among whom was 1 general officer, 4 colonels, 2 lieutenant-colonels, 5 captains, 12 lieutenants; wounded 208, of which were 5 colonels, 3 lieutenant-colonels, 2 second lieutenant-colonels, 7 captains, 1 cadet; prisoners 730—President-General Santa Anna, Gen. Cos, 4 colonels, aides to Gen. Santa Anna, and the Colonel of the Guerrero Battalion, are included in the number. Gen. Santa Anna was not taken until the 22d, and Gen. Cos yesterday, very few having escaped. About 600 muskets, 300 sabres, and 200 pistols, have been collected since the action; several hundred mules and horses were taken, and near twelve thousand dollars in specie.

For several days previous to the action, our troops were engaged in forced marches, exposed to excessive rains, and the additional inconvenience of extremely bad roads, illy supplied with rations and clothing; yet, amid every difficulty, they bore up with cheerfulness and fortitude, and performed their marches with spirit and alacrity—there was no murmuring.

Previous to and during the action, my staff evinced every disposition to be useful, and were actively engaged in their duties. In the conflict I am assured that they demeaned themselves in such a manner as proved them worthy members of the army of San Jacinto. Col. T. J. Rusk, Secretary of War, was on the field. For weeks his services had been highly beneficial to the army; in battle, he was on the left wing, where Col. Sherman's command first encountered and drove in the enemy: he bore himself gallantly, and continued his efforts and activity, remaining with the pursuers until resistance ceased.

I have the honor of transmitting herewith a list of all the officers and men who were engaged in the action, which I respectfully request may be published, as an act of justice to the individuals. For the Commanding General to attempt discrimination as to the conduct of those who commanded in the action, or those who were commanded, would be impossible. Our success in the action is conclusive proof of their daring intrepidity and courage; every officer and man proved himself worthy of the cause in which he battled, while the triumph received a lustre from the humanity which characterized their conduct after victory, and richly entitles them to the admiration and gratitude of their General. Nor should we withhold the tribute of our grateful thanks from that Being who rules the destinies of nations, and has in the time of greatest need enabled us to arrest a powerful invader whilst devasting [sic] our country.

> I have the honor to be,
> With high consideration,
> Sam Houston, Commander-in-Chief

## 2. COLONEL PEDRO DELGADO'S ACCOUNT

From "Mexican Account of the Battle of San Jacinto," *Texas Almanac* (Galveston, 1870), 41-53.

The following account, written in 1837 by Pedro Delgado who was a colonel on Santa Anna's staff, is the most vivid description of the Battle of San Jacinto by a Mexican participant.

On the 14th of April, 1836, His Excellency the President [Santa Anna] ordered his Staff to prepare to march, with only one skiff, and leaving his own and the officers' baggage with General Ramirez y Sesma, who was instructed to remain at the crossing of the Brazos, . . . started for Harrisburg, with the force above mentioned. . . .

On the 15th, . . . at about noon, we reached a plantation abundantly supplied with corn, meal, sheep and hogs; it had a good garden and a fine cotton-gin. We halted to refresh men and beasts.

At 3 o'clock P. M., after having set fire to the dwelling and gin-houses, we resumed our march. Here, His Excellency started ahead with his Staff and escort, leaving General Castrillon in command of the infantry. We travelled, at a brisk trot, at least ten leagues, without halting, until we reached the vicinity of Harrisburg, at about 11 o'clock at night. His Excellency, with an Adjutant and fifteen dragoons, . . . succeeded in capturing two Americans, who stated that Zavala and other members of the so-called Government of Texas, had left the morning before for Galveston. . . .

On the 16th, we remained at Harrisburg, to await our broken-down stragglers, who kept dropping in till 2 or 3 o'clock P. M.

On the opposite side of the bayou, we found two or three houses well supplied with wearing apparel, mainly for women's use, fine furniture, an excellent piano, jars of preserves, chocolate, fruit, &c., all of which were appropriated for the benefit of His Excellency and his attendants. I and others obtained only what they could not use. After the houses had been sacked and burnt down, a party of Americans fired upon our men from the woods; it is wonderful that some of us . . . were not killed. . . .

On the 17th, at about 3 o'clock P. M., His Excellency, after having instructed me to burn the town, started for New Washington with the troops. It was nearly dark when we had finished crossing the bayou. . . .

At noon [the 18th], we reached New Washington, where we found flour, soap, tobacco, and other articles, which were issued to the men. His Excellency instructed me to mount one of his horses, and, with a small party of dragoons, to gather beeves for the use of the troops. In a short time I drove in more than one hundred head of cattle, so abundant are they in that country. . . .

On the 19th, His Excellency ordered Captain Barragan to start with a detachment of dragoons to reconnoitre Houston's movements. We halted at that place, all being quiet.

On the 20th, [we] . . . had burnt a fine warehouse on the wharf, and all the houses in the town, when Captain Barragan rushed in, at full speed, reporting that Houston was close on our rear, and that his troops had captured some of our stragglers, and had disarmed and dispatched them. . . .

It was two o'clock P. M. when we descried Houston's pickets at the edge of a large wood, in which he concealed his main force. Our skirmishers commenced firing; they were answered by the enemy, who fell back in the woods. His Excellency reached the ground with our main body, with the intention, as I understood, of attacking at once; but they kept hidden, which prevented him from ascertaining their position. He, therefore, changed his dispositions, and ordered the company of Toluca to deploy as skirmishers in the direction of the woods. . . .

Then His Excellency went to look for a camping ground, and established his whole force along the shore of San Jacinto Bay, at least one mile from the place where I had been left. About one hour later, I received orders, through Colonel Bringas, to come into camp immediately with the ordnance stores and the piece of artillery. . . .

At length, at 5 o'clock P. M., my duty was performed, and, as I entered the camp with the last load, I was closely followed by the enemy's cavalry. His Excellency, noticing it, . . . commanded our cavalry, to face the enemy, without gaining ground. This movement checked the enemy for a few moments; but, soon after, they dashed upon our dragoons, and were close enough to engage them with the sword without, however, any material result. Then, His Excellency, deploying several companies as skirmishers, forced the enemy back to his camp, on which he retired sluggishly and in disorder.

This last engagement took place after sun-down.

At daybreak on the 21st, His Excellency ordered a breastwork to be erected for the cannon. It was constructed with pack-saddles, sacks of hard bread, baggage, etc. A trifling barricade of branches ran along its front and right. . . .

At 9 o'clock a. m. General Cos came in with a reinforcement of about 500 men. His arrival was greeted with the roll of drums and with joyful shouts. As it was represented to His Excellency that these men had not slept the night before, he instructed them to stack their arms, to remove their accoutrements, and to go to sleep quietly in the adjoining grove.

No important incident took place until 4:30 p. m. At this fatal moment, the bugler on our right signaled the advance of the enemy upon that wing. His Excellency and staff were asleep; the greater number of the men were also sleeping; of the rest, some were eating, others were scattered in the woods in search of boughs to prepare shelter. Our line was composed of musket stacks. Our cavalry were riding, bareback, to and from water.

I stepped upon some ammunition boxes, the better to observe the movements of the enemy. I saw that their formation was a mere line in one rank, and very extended. In their center was the Texas flag; on both wings, they had two light cannons, well manned. Their cavalry was opposite our front, overlapping our left.

In this disposition, yelling furiously, with a brisk fire of grape, muskets, and rifles, they advanced resolutely upon our camp. There the utmost confusion prevailed. General Castrillon shouted on one side; on another, Colonel Almonte was giving orders; some cried out to commence firing; others, to lie down to avoid grape shots. Among the latter was His Excellency.

Then, already, I saw our men flying in small groups, terrified, and sheltering themselves behind large trees. I endeavored to force some of them to fight, but all efforts were in vain — the evil was beyond remedy; they were a bewildered and panic stricken herd. . . .

Then I saw His Excellency running about in the utmost excitement, wringing his hands, and unable to give an order. General Castrillon was stretched on the ground, wounded in the leg. Colonel Treviño was killed, and Colonel Marcial Aguirre was severely injured. I saw also the enemy reaching the ordnance train, and killing a corporal and two gunners who had been detailed to repair cartridges which had been damaged on the previous evening.

Everything being lost, I went — leading my horse, which I could not mount, because the firing had rendered him restless and fractious — to join our men, still hoping that we might be able to defend ourselves, or to retire under the shelter of night. This, however, could not be done. It is a known fact that Mexican soldiers, once demoralized, can not be controlled, unless they are thoroughly inured to war.

On the left, and about a musket-shot distance from our camp, was a small grove on the bay shore. Our disbanded herd rushed for it, to obtain shelter from the horrid slaughter carried on all over the prairie by the blood-thirsty usurpers. Unfortunately, we met on our way an obstacle difficult to overcome. It was a bayou, not very wide, but rather deep. The men, on reaching it, would helplessly crowd together, and were shot down by the enemy, who was close enough not to miss his aim. It was there that the greatest carnage took place.

Upon reaching that spot, I saw Colonel Almonte swimming across the bayou with his left hand, and holding up his right, which grasped his sword.

I stated before that I was leading my horse, but, in this critical situation, I vaulted on him, and, with two leaps, he landed me on the opposite bank of the bayou. To my sorrow I had to leave the noble animal, mired, at that place, and to part with him, probably forever. As I dismounted, I sank in the mire waist deep, and I had the greatest trouble to get out of it, by taking hold of the grass. Both my shoes remained in the bayou. I made an effort to recover them, but I soon came to the conclusion that, did I tarry there, a rifle shot would certainly make an outlet for my soul, as had happened to many a poor fellow around me. Thus I made for the grove, barefooted.

There I met a number of other officers, with whom I wandered at random, buried in gloomy thoughts upon our tragic disaster. We still entertained a hope of rallying some of our men, but it was impossible.

The enemy's cavalry surrounded the grove, while his infantry penetrated it, pursuing us with fierce and blood-thirsty feelings. . . .

Thence they marched us to their camp. I was barefooted; the prairie had recently been burnt up, and the blades of grass, hardened by fire, penetrated like needles the soles of my feet, so that I could hardly walk. . . .

After having kept us sitting in camp about an hour and a half, they marched us into the woods, where we saw an immense fire, . . . I and several of my companions were silly enough to believe that we were about to be burnt alive, in retaliation for those who had been burnt in the Alamo. We should have considered it an act of mercy to be shot first. Oh! the bitter and cruel moment! However, we felt considerably relieved when they placed us around the fire to warm ourselves and to dry our wet clothes. We were surrounded by twenty-five or thirty sentinels. You should have seen those men, or, rather, phantoms, converted into moving armories. Some wore two, three, and even four brace of pistols; a cloth bag of very respectable size filled with bullets, a powder horn, a sabre or a bowie knife, besides a rifle, musket, or carbine. Everyone of them had in his hand a burning candle. . . . Was this display intended to prevent us from attempting to escape? The fools! Where could we go in that vast country, unknown to us, intersected by large rivers and forests, where wild beasts and hunger, and where they themselves would destroy us? . . .

At 2 o'clock P. M. [the 22d] His Excellency the General-in-Chief, Don Antonio Lopez de Santa Anna, arrived, under the charge of a mounted soldier. He wore linen trousers, a blue cotton jacket, a cap, and red worsted slippers. His leader did not know him, but, noticing a motion of curiosity amongst us as he approached, he became satisfied that he was conducting no common officer, and reported at once with him to General Houston. The latter sent two of his Adjutants to inquire of us whether Santa Anna had lost any teeth; some answered that they did not know, but others, with more candor, or, perhaps, less discretion, said: "Yes, gentlemen; and you may, further say to your General, that the person just brought before him is President Santa Anna himself." The news spread over the whole camp, and the inquisitive fellows who surrounded us ran to strike up an acquaintance with His Excellency. Some of them proposed to fire salutes, and to make other demonstrations to celebrate the capture of so lofty a person. But Houston courteously forbade it. From this time we were left alone, His Excellency having become the centre of attraction.

On the 23d, seventy or eighty loads of ordnance stores had already been brought in, and deposited, together with piles of loaded muskets and of cartridge-boxes, in close proximity to our camp. . . .

On the 24th, . . . a steamboat arrived, having on board the Texan President, Vice-President Zavala, and other members of the administration. . . .

## 49. THE TREATY OF VELASCO

### May 14, 1836

From Henry Yoakum, *History of Texas*, 1685-1845 (2 vols.; New York, 1855), I, 526-528.

After his capture at San Jacinto Santa Anna agreed with General Sam Houston on an armistice pending negotiations for peace. Upon receipt of the news, President David G. Burnet and other members of the government with him on Galveston Island proceeded to San Jacinto and took charge of negotiations. Finding a strong sentiment among the soldiers in favor of executing Santa Anna, however, Burnet took the captive president of Mexico for safety to Velasco which had been selected as the temporary seat of government because of its better accommodations. There on May 14 the two presidents signed the Treaty of Velasco, consisting of a "Public Agreement" and a "Secret Agreement." The treaty, which follows, was rejected a few days later by the Mexican Senate.

### PUBLIC AGREEMENT.

*Articles of Agreement entered into between His Excellency* DAVID G. BURNET, *President of the Republic of Texas, of the one part, and His Excellency General* ANTONIO LOPEZ DE SANTA ANNA, *President-General-in-Chief of the Mexican Army, of the other part:*—

ARTICLE 1. General Antonio Lopez de Santa Anna agrees that he will not take up arms, nor will he exercise his influence to cause them to be taken up, against the people of Texas, during the present war of independence.

ARTICLE 2. All hostilities between the Mexican and Texan troops will cease immediately, both on land and water.

ARTICLE 3. The Mexican troops will evacuate the territory of Texas, passing to the other side of the Rio Grande del Norte.

ARTICLE 4. The Mexican army, in its retreat, shall not take the property of any person without his consent and just indemnification, using only such articles as may be necessary for its subsistence, in cases where the owners may not be present, and remitting to the commander of the army of Texas, or to the commissioners to be appointed for the adjustment of such matters, an account of the value of the property consumed, the place where taken, and the name of the owner, if it can be ascertained.

ARTICLE 5. That all private property, including horses, cattle, negro slaves, or indentured persons of whatever denomination, that may have been captured by any portion of the Mexican army, or may have taken refuge in the said army, since the commencement of the late invasion, shall be restored to the commander of the Texan army, or to such other persons as may be appointed by the government of Texas to receive them.

ARTICLE 6. The troops of both armies will refrain from coming into contact with each other; and, to this end, the commander of the army of Texas will be careful not to approach within a shorter distance of the Mexican army than five leagues.

ARTICLE 7. The Mexican army shall not make any other delay on its march than that which is necessary to take up their hospitals, baggage, &c., and to cross the rivers. Any delay, not necessary to these purposes, to be considered an infraction of this agreement.

ARTICLE 8. By express, to be immediately despatched, this agreement shall be sent to General Filisola, and to General T. J. Rusk, commander of the Texan army, in order that they may be apprized of its stipulations; and, to this end, they will exchange engagements to comply with the same.

ARTICLE 9. That all Texan prisoners now in possession of the Mexican army, or its authorities, be forthwith released, and furnished with free passports to return to their homes; in consideration of which a corresponding number of Mexican prisoners, rank and file, now in possession of the government of Texas, shall be immediately released. The remainder of the Mexican prisoners, that continue in possession of the government of Texas, to be treated with due humanity: any extraordinary comforts that may be furnished them to be at the charge of the government of Mexico.

ARTICLE 10. General Antonio Lopez de Santa Anna will be sent to Vera Cruz, as soon as it shall be deemed proper.

The contracting parties sign this instrument for the above-mentioned purposes, by duplicate, at the port of Velasco, this the 14th day of May, 1836.

DAVID G. BURNET,
ANT°. LOPEZ DE SANTA ANNA.

### SECRET AGREEMENT.

ANTONIO LOPEZ DE SANTA ANNA, *General-in-Chief of the Army of Operations, and President of the Republic of Mexico, before the Government established in Texas, solemnly pledges himself to fulfil the Stipulations contained in the following Articles, so far as concerns himself:*—

ARTICLE 1. He will not take up arms, nor cause them to be taken up, against the people of Texas, during the present war for independence.

ARTICLE 2. He will give his orders that, in the shortest time, the Mexican troops may leave the territory of Texas.

ARTICLE 3. He will so prepare matters in the cabinet of Mexico, that the mission that may be sent thither by the government of Texas may be well received, and that by means of negotiations all differences may be settled, and the independence that has been declared by the convention may be acknowledged.

ARTICLE 4. A treaty of commerce, amity, and limits, will be established between Mexico and Texas, the territory of the latter not to extend beyond the Rio Bravo del Norte.

ARTICLE 5. The present return of General Santa Anna to Vera Cruz being indispensable for the purpose of effecting his solemn engagements, the government of Texas will provide for his immediate embarkation for said port.

ARTICLE 6. This instrument, being obligatory on one part as well as on the other, will be signed in duplicate, remaining folded and sealed until the negotiations shall have been concluded, when it will be restored to his excellency General Santa Anna; no use of it to be made before that time, unless there should be an infraction by either of the contracting parties.

PORT OF VELASCO, *May the 14th*, 1836.
ANT°. LOPEZ DE SANTA ANNA,
DAVID G. BURNET.

## 50.  AN ABOLITIONIST'S EXPLANATION OF THE CAUSE OF THE TEXAS REVOLUTION

### 1836

From Benjamin Lundy, *The War in Texas* (Philadelphia, 1836), 3-15.

New Jersey born, Quaker Benjamin Lundy was one of the early crusaders for the complete abolition of slavery in the United States. He undertook his task almost single-handed and became the link between the earlier anti-slavery and the later radical abolitionist movements. He opposed the efforts of the earlier societies to deport negroes to Africa, but used his pen, fluently if not always accurately, in behalf the cause to which he gave his full devotion. In 1821 he established in Ohio the first paper devoted exclusively to emancipation, and later published it in Tennessee, Baltimore, and Washington before merging it in 1836 with the *National Inquirer* at Philadelphia. Before his death in 1839, he had travelled thousands of miles, lecturing and promoting the organization of abolitionist societies.

Lundy was at San Felipe, Texas, shortly after the Convention of April, 1833, and afterwards in his book, *The War in Texas,* set forth his thesis as to the causes of the Texas Revolution. Although naive and inaccurate, Lundy's major contention probably influenced enough people to delay the annexation of Texas to the United States, and it continues to draw the attention of some students of pre-Civil War history. The following extracts articulately illustrate Lundy's view.

. . . . But the prime cause, and the real objects of this war [the Texas Revolution], are not distinctly understood by a large portion of the honest, disinterested, and well-meaning citizens of the United States. . . . They have been induced to believe that the inhabitants of Texas were engaged in a legitimate contest for the maintenance of the sacred principles of Liberty, and the natural, inalienable Rights of Man: — whereas, the motives of its instigators, and their chief incentives to action, have been, from the commencement, of a directly opposite character and tendency. *It is susceptible of the clearest demonstration, that the immediate cause and the leading object of this contest originated in a settled design, among the slaveholders of this country, (with land-speculators and slave-traders,) to wrest the large and valuable territory of Texas from the Mexican Republic, in order to re-establish the SYSTEM OF SLAVERY; to open a vast and profitable SLAVE-MARKET therein; and, ultimately, to annex it to the United States.* And further, it is evident — nay, it is very generally acknowledged — that the insurrectionists are principally citizens of the United States, who have preceeded thither *for the purpose* of revolutionizing the country; and that they are dependant [sic] upon this nation, for both the physical and pecuniary means, to carry the design into effect. We have a still more important view of the subject. *The Slaveholding Interest is now paramount in the Executive branch of our national government; and its* influence operates, *indirectly, yet powerfully, through that medium, in favor of this Grand Scheme of Oppression and Tyrannical Usurpation.* Whether the national *Legislature* will join hands with the Executive, and lend its aid to this most unwarrantable, aggressive attempt, will depend on the VOICE OF THE PEOPLE, expressed in their primary assemblies, *by their petitions,* and through the ballot-boxes.

The writer of this has long viewed, with intense anxiety, the clandestine operations of this unhallowed scheme, and frequently warned the public of the danger to be apprehended, in case of its success. He has carefully noted the preparatory arrangements for its consummation — the combination of influence — the concentration of physical power — the organization of various means — and, finally, the undissembled prosecution of it, by overt acts of violence and bloodshed: . . .

In this state of things, propositions were made by the government of the U. States to that of Mexico, for the purchase of the Texas country, with a view of incorporating it into the Union. The overture was instantly rejected by the Mexican authorities, . . . Many of the newspapers in the United States now teemed with essays and remarks, tending to urge the acquisition of Texas by any practicable means; and the agent of the government was charged with intriguing for the purpose at the Mexican capital. The idea was also held out by the colonists, that the laws prohibiting the introduction of slaves could be easily evaded, and that they would soon be strong enough to declare and enforce the perpetuation of slavery (although it was abolished by the general and state governments) in that part of the country. — The emigration from the slaveholding States to Texas was thus accelerated, in the hope of eventually accomplishing this object. In order to counteract these efforts, the operations of the colonization system were suspended by law in the year 1830. A few troops were then sent to Texas, in addition to a small number previously stationed there, to prevent the illicit and contraband trade, the introduction of slaves, and to enforce obedience to the laws generally; but their number was insufficient for the purpose; and the regulations of the government were daringly and continually violated with impunity. . . . For some length of time thereafter, the political affairs of the Republic were somewhat unsettled, and the colonists in Texas were permitted to pursue their own course, subject only to the civil authority of the State.

This they heeded no further than it suited their whims or their interests; and the laws, forbidding the introduction of slaves, the trade with the Indians in arms, etc., and the swindling speculations in land, were considered by them as mere blank leaves in the statute book.

Among the settlers in the colonies, at this period, were some ambitious aspirants from the United States of the North, who having lost the confidence of the people of their own country, here sought a new theatre where they might press their claims to public favor and political distinction. These, with the large slave-holders, land-speculators, etc., were claimants for the speedy adoption of measures to form a State government for Texas. . . . All hopes of a voluntary cession of Texas to the United States by the Mexican government, were now at an end. Therefore, unless the measure of establishing an independent State, separate from any district containing a large native population could be carried into effect, their views of political aggrandizement would be thwarted, and it would also be impossible to carry out their schemes of slave-holding, etc., when the government should determine to enforce obedience to the laws. The idea was entertained, that an "independent State," under the confederated system, might stand upon its "sovereignty" and nullify the decrees of the general government, to suit its purposes. This doctrine was promulgated throughout the Texas country, and embraced by a considerable portion. . . . The office-seekers were principally men of little or no capital; engaged in no business enterprises; would be subject to slight taxation, if any; and, of course, they had nothing to lose, but every thing to gain, from the success of the proposed measure. And by their clamorous efforts, with the aid of the speculators and extensive slave proprietors, they succeeded at length in calling a convention, to draft a State Constitution for Texas, in the early part of the year 1833.

The Convention assembled without having been legally authorized to enter upon the performance of the duties which it assumed. . . . Although the then existing Constitution of Coahuila-Texas contained an express prohibition of slavery, as before mentioned, the subject was not even adverted to in this one proposed for Texas. . . .

From the commencement of their [Anglo-Americans] settlement in that province, we must bear in mind, the most of them anticipated its eventual separation from the government of Mexico, and attachment to the Northern Union. This was early resolved on by them, unless indeed other measures could be adopted for the perpetuation of slavery. A full and complete understanding existed between them and the advocates of the system in this country and elsewhere. A very active and extensive private correspondence was kept up for this purpose. Their plans were all deeply laid; and the rejection, by the Mexican government of the proposition to cede the territory in question to the United States, had no other effect than temporarily to frustrate their operations and occasion a modification of their arrangements. A vast combination was then entered into (though not *formally organized*). . . . [The] immediate object now is the establishment of an "Independent" government in Texas, to promote its grand ulterior designs.

As I have said before, the great land speculators, in New York and elsewhere, (consisting of individuals and companies) have covered with their "grants" almost the whole area of the unsettled parts of Coahuila-Texas, and the Territory of Santa Fe. These "grants" will nearly all soon be forfeited, as it will be impossible to introduce a sufficient number of settlers in season to comply with the terms upon which they were issued by the government. A recent act of the State Legislature prohibits the renewal of them in Coahuila-Texas; and no further hope is entertained that the general Congress will further tolerate such unlimited schemes of swindling speculation.

In case the Independence of Texas shall be established, all grants and claims, as aforesaid, are legalized, (particularly if the claimants take an active part in the revolution). . . .

It was not considered sound policy, to declare the Texas country entirely independent of Mexico, while the hope of continuing the Federal form of government existed. The colonists still felt themselves too weak to compete with the power of the republic; and it was doubtful whether the auxiliary force from the United States, which they expected to co-operate with them, would be sufficient to ensure success. Besides, they were somewhat divided in opinion among themselves as to the measures that should be adopted, and the *men* who should be entrusted with the authority to direct the operations of the scheme. The most of those who marshalled as political and military leaders, were upstarts in whom they had little confidence — some of them broken down politicians and mere adventurers from the United States — persons in fact of very doubtful character and capacity. When the change in the form of government was proposed, therefore, they declared for the Constitution of 1824, hoping that the native citizens of the State of Coahuila-Texas, as well as those of several contiguous States, would unite with them. This would give them time at least, if successful to acquire more numerical strength to carry out their main design at a future period. But in the result of these calculations, they were totally disappointed. When it was ascertained that a majority of the States readily sanctioned the proposition to alter the Constitution, and that every one, except Coahuila-Texas, finally acquiesced, without attempting forcible resistance, the native inhabitants of this State also gave in the adhesion, or refused to join the colonists in an insurrection . . . it was now "neck or nothing" with the speculators and advocates of slavery. They could not even stand upon the basis of "State sovereignty," as a great majority of the *citizens* of Coahuila and Texas itself had agreed, tacitly at least, to the new order of things. A factional part only, and that almost entirely composed of foreigners, were disposed to resist for any considerable length of time, the decree of the General Congress. A meeting of some of the colonists and adventurers was held, and the incipient steps were taken to proclaim the Independence and sovereignty of Texas. . . .

## 51.    A DESCRIPTION OF THE TOWNS IN TEXAS

### 1836

From Mary Austin Holley, *Texas* (Lexington, Ky., 1836), 109-125.

The settled portion of the new Republic of Texas in 1836 extended inland to the San Antonio-Nacogdoches Road and from the Sabine River westward to San Antonio and Copano Bay. Within those limits there were more than thirty towns which Mrs. Mary Austin Holley deemed worthy of including in her description of Texas. The following selection from the pen of the talented cousin of Stephen F. Austin is the best contemporary over-all description of the towns.

*San Felipe de Austin* was founded in 1824 by Gen. Austin and the commissioner, Baron de Bastrop. It is the capital of Austin's colony, and situated on the right bank of the Brazos river, eighty miles from the gulf by land, and one hundred and eighty by the meanders of the river, at the head of boat navigation. The site of this town is exceedingly beautiful. It is a high prairie bluff which strikes the river, at the upper or northern limit of the level region, about forty feet above the level of the stream: an elevation which is unusual in this section. It is the residence of Gen. Austin. The State and municipal officers of the jurisdiction hold their offices here; and this was the capital designated for Texas, when its separation from Coahuila and its reception as an independent State of the Mexican confederacy, should take place. Here, likewise, all the land and judicial business of the colony is transacted. It contains several stores, and presents altogether the appearance of a busy and pleasant little village.

*Brazoria* is thirty miles from the mouth of the Brazos by the meanders of the river, and fifteen by land. It is not located in a prairie, where nothing was to be done to prepare the foundation of the rising city, but to mark off its lines with compass and chain; but upon a wooded elevation of peach land, as it is called. This spot was chosen as the most commanding and healthful, besides combining other advantages. . . . One street stretches along the banks of the Brazos, and there is one parallel with it further back, while other streets are laid out to intersect these at right angles.

In 1831, Brazoria gave promise of being a large and populous town. From several causes, however, it has not fulfilled the expectations of its sanguine inhabitants. In 1833, that scourge, the cholera, took off some of its most enterprising population, and since that time other towns have sprung up to direct the channel of trade. Columbia, one mile and a half back from Bell's landing was made the seat of the new courts, thereby drawing off the lawyers and others from Brazoria. It was found however to be a bad arrangement, and they are now returned to their first location. A regular mail route is established between it and San Felipe, once a week.

Brazoria, besides being well situated, will always be important as the first stopping place for emigrants. . . . Here may be found those necessaries which the newly arrived, and those wishing to penetrate into the interior, have need of. Such persons having heard of Brazoria as a considerable place, will feel disappointment at the sight of it. It contained, in 1831, fifty families, and now,

1836, it has not many more, though it numbers more houses. Nor have any of the then existing towns in Texas increased much. Most people, mechanics and all, choose to settle on their own estates, or are attracted by some boasted advantage to some new settlement. It is however looking up; business is increasing, and its favorable situation, being easy of access and convenient to the sea, combined with other advantages, will inevitably render it one of the most important towns in Texas.

*Nacogdoches.*—The old Spanish military post and village of Nacogdoches, is situated in the eastern section of Texas, in latitude 31° 40', sixty miles west of the Sabine river. In 1819 or 1820 it was totally broken up by the revolution and abandoned. . . .

Nacogdoches remained without population until the year 1822-3, when many of the emigrants who left the United States with the view of joining Austin's colony, stopped at this place. A number of the ancient inhabitants, also, returned to their former possessions, and thus the town has been gradually repeopled and is now a respectable village. A garrison of Mexican troops, before the late war for independence, was stationed here under the command of a colonel of the army. There is, also, a custom house establishment, for the collection of duties on the inland trade from Louisiana. The country on the road between this place and the Sabine, is thinly settled by emigrants from the United States. This place is the great throughfare of emigrants to Texas.

*San Antonio de Bexar.* — The ancient town of Bexar is situated in the western part of the undulating region on the San Antonio river, which flows through it, and is remarkably pleasant and healthy. This place is in latitude 29° 25', one hundred and forty miles from the coast, and contains two thousand five hundred inhabitants, all native Mexicans, with the exception of a very few American families who have settled there. A military outpost was established at this spot by the Spanish government in 1718. In the year 1731, the town was settled by emigrants sent out from the Canary Islands by the king of Spain. It became a flourishing settlement, and so continued till the revolution in 1812. Since which period the Comanche and other Indians have greatly harassed the inhabitants, producing much individual suffering, and totally destroying for a season, at least, the prosperity of the town. It is the capital of the province, and has been rendered a place of considerable notice, as the seat of the late war, . . .

*Columbia,* on the league of Mr. Bell, is a place of considerable business, and was, for a while, the seat of justice. It contains a hotel kept by Bell, new and spacious —the largest building there. There is besides a building or two, constructed while it was the seat of the courts, for a court house, and offices, &c. and a few dwelling houses. This town is on the edge of the prairie, and the scenery about it is pretty. A broad road through timber is cut to the landing, which is very muddy in wet weather. It was thought by many that this place was not so convenient for the court as Brazoria, which was formerly the seat of justice, and it was, accordingly again removed thither. Columbia is more central than Brazoria, but has less accommodation, and is too far from the river for convenience.

*Marion, or Bell's Landing,* two miles distant from Columbia, since 1831, has had an increase of a number of dwelling houses, and several large warehouses, one of which was built by an extensive dealer in cotton, many bales of which I have observed in going up the river, lying on the shore ready to be shipped. Some of the fine trees have been cut away, and in some places the banks have caved in, which with the business-like air of the place, have destroyed much of the picturesque effects observed on my former visit.

*Anahuac.*—This was formerly a military post town established by order of Gen. Teran, on the northeast corner of Galveston Bay, opposite the mouths of the Trinity river in Vehlein's grant. Its situation is very pleasant, on the borders of a prairie, at an elevation of thirty feet above the waters of the bay which is spread before it. This town was at first known by the name of Perry's Point, until the ancient title of the city of Mexico was bestowed upon it, at the time it was occupied by a Mexican garrison of about an hundred soldiers under the command of Col. Bradburn. It contains about thirty houses besides the building erected as barracks for the soldiery. This is about one hundred and fifty feet long and twenty wide, with the colonel's quarters at one end, and the guard house on the other.

*Goliad.*—This village formerly called La Bahia is situated on the right bank of the San Antonio river, about one hundred and ten miles southeast of Bexar, and thirty miles from the coast. It contains about eight hundred inhabitants, all Mexicans. It was garrisoned by Mexican troops, and was one of the first places signalized by a triumph of the Texan arms in their struggle for liberty.

*San Patrick*—This is an Irish colony situated in McMullen's and McGloin's grant, on the right bank of the Nueces. A number of Irish families have settled here, and many others will probably find an asylum, with the certain prospect of plenty and independence. The settlement of Irish colonies in this grant is the great object of the Empresarios who are, themselves, "exiles of Erin." . . .

*Gonzales*—the capital of DeWitt's colony, is built on the left bank of the Guadalupe river, at the point where the direct road from San Felipe de Austin intersects that river. The site of the town is elevated, pleasant, and healthful, and possesses many natural advantages. It contains about three hundred inhabitants; and is distinguished as being the opening scene of the late war, where the first blow was struck against the despot Santa Anna and Centralism— the *Lexington* of Texas.

*Bastrop or Mina,* lies on the left bank of the Colorado, at the intersection of the road leading from Bexar to Nacogdoches with the river. It was laid out in 1830 by the Empresario, General Austin, in his contract of 1827, and is already a considerable place, and continues to grow rapidly. It is a favorite spot for new settlers, and is quite the rage at present; no sickness of any kind having ever been known there. It is situated on a bend of the river, sloping beautifully down to the water, with ranges of timber—first oak, then pine, then cedar, rising in regular succession behind it.

*Bolivar* is at the head of tide water on the Brazos, sixty miles from the river's mouth by water and forty-five by land. It is an important point, as any vessel that can pass the bar can ascend to this place in the lowest stage of water, but not farther. The road via Bolivar to San Felipe is fifteen miles nearer than the road from Brazoria to San Felipe direct, and is much better. The distance from Bolivar to the navigable waters of Galveston bay, is but fifteen miles over a high, dry prairie, with the exception of six miles through timber land, where the road is good. The land in and about Bolivar is the best in the colony; clothed with heavy timber, with peach and cane undergrowth, to the distance of six miles from the river. The bank of the river in front of the town, is a high bluff of stiff red clay. About fifty acres are cleared and under cultivation.

Bolivar, though selected as an advantageous location for a commercial town, and laid off for that purpose before Brazoria, is as yet a town only in name. Its location, for purposes of trade as well as on account of the fertility of the adjacent country, has doubtless many advantages. But it was neglected for that which was regarded, upon the whole, as a more eligible position, on account of its easier access from the sea. At some future day however it will, in all probability, become one of the most flourishing emporiums in Texas. We are warranted in this belief by the fact, that it is, even now, the great point for the embarkation of cotton, from the rich plantations which every where surround it. There is not a wealthier or better settled district in the colony, than that which surrounds Bolivar, in the raising and sale of cotton, particularly. It possesses, likewise, all the other advantages, which one of the best positions on a large and commercial river can bestow.

*Cox's Point.*—The new town at Cox's Point will eventually rival Matamoras, inasmuch as it has a better harbor, and is equally near to all the great mining districts. The facility of getting goods to the interior is at this time greater; and it is preferred as a market by almost all the interior traders. There are already heavy capitalists located there, and one *conducta* has arrived from Chihuahua with three hundred thousand dollars. It is situated at the mouth of the La Baca, and contains about two hundred inhabitants.

*Matagorda* is an older and a larger town than its rival Cox's Point, at the mouth of the Colorado. It contains five hundred inhabitants and is a place of great business, trading with the interior and New Orleans. Before the existence of the settlement at Cox's Point, it was the only place of depot of the Colorado river, and of an extensive fertile country which found its natural market at this point.

*Washington* is situated on the Brazos, in one of its bends, about fifty miles above San Felipe, and on the San Antonio road. It is quite a new town, but is increasing very rapidly, and already numbers fifty houses. It was designated by the Provisional Government as the future seat of government in Texas; and the sessions of the convention were removed there, in March of the present year. It is pleasantly and healthfully situated;

and, with the numerous advantages which it enjoys, cannot fail to become an important point in Texas.

*San Augustine* is beautifully situated on the verge of a prairie, forty-five or fifty miles east of Nacogdoches, on a branch of the Angelina, in Zavala's grant. It is on the direct road from Nachitoches; and is the first town that the traveller meets, within the limits of Texas, in going from the United States. It is a prosperous place, though new; and is about the size of the capital, Washington.

*New Washington.*—This is as yet a small place, laid out a short time since by Col. Morgan, a resident and associated with a New York company. It is at the mouth of the San Jacinto river, at the head of Galveston bay, in Austin's colony. Several well laden vessels have already gone there; and it promises to be a place of great commercial importance. A large warehouse and a hotel for accommodation of visiters [sic] are now being built there. It is generally known by the name of Clopper's point, and probably will continue to be its common appellation, on account of there being another town of the same name— Washington, the capital of the State.

*Cole's Settlement.*—This place is situated in a rich and romantic country, and is a prosperous and populous neighborhood. It lies near the Brazos above San Felipe, is increasing fast, and is especially noted for a young ladies school, kept there by Miss Trask.

*Orozembo and Montezuma* are located on the Brazos river, opposite to Bolivar. They are as yet but "castles in the air," and were laid out on two contiguous leagues of land, by their respective proprietors. The situation of both of these rival *towns* is pleasant, and favorable for trade. Which of them, however, is to be the most flourishing, or whether both of them will be entirely abandoned for some other more advantageous and popular position— are questions which require more of the prophetic "unction" than we possess, to answer definitely.

*Fort Settlement* on the Brazos, a little higher up than the two last mentioned, contains a considerable population. It is not a thickly settled village, but a section of country containing many farms: such as we would call, in this country, a well settled neighborhood.

*Harrisburgh.*—This town has its name from Mr. Harris, the owner of a steam saw-mill at this place. There are now extensive steam saw-mills here, belonging to the Harrisburgh Saw Mill Company; and large quantities of lumber are constantly made and disposed of. Vessels are frequently loaded at these mills with lumber, destined for the Mexican ports of the Gulf, and any quantity may be sold, at good prices, either for domestic or foreign consumption. The timber, consisting of yellow pine and oak, is abundant. The mills are on Buffalo Bayou about thirty miles from the Brazos river, and are accessible to vessels drawing five or six feet water. The price of lumber is at present twenty-five dollars per thousand feet. The town is irregularly built and contains only about twenty houses, mostly log, with two or three frame buildings. The situation is, probably, rather unhealthy, and the importance of the village can be sustained only by its valuable mills, which furnish more lumber, probably, than all the others in Texas.

*Tenoxticlan* is a military post and town established on the right bank of the Brazos, twelve miles above the upper road leading from Bexar to Nacogdoches, fifteen miles below the mouth of San Ardress river, and one hundred miles above San Felipe de Austin. It is very eligibly situated and abundantly supplied with excellent water. . . . The adjacent country for many miles around, is fertile and healthful, and the Brazos in seasons of freshets, is navigable some miles above this port.

*Galveston* is situated on the bay of that name in Vehlein's grant, and, as a commercial town, possesses one of the best locations on the Gulf. Indeed Galveston as a harbor is said to be much superior to any other on the Gulf between Pensacola and Vera Cruz; and her vicinity to the West Indies, the United States, and the Mexican ports, with the Gulf stream, the great river of the ocean, at hand to sweep her vessels, with its mighty and rapid current, to the eastern Atlantic, renders her position for foreign commerce highly felicitous.

*Velasco*, a small town at the mouth of the Brazos river in Austin's colony, is celebrated for its salt works which are very notable. It is a small town but is well situated, and is in a flourishing state. A collector of customs resides here.

Velasco is the resort, in summer, of great numbers of visiters from the north of the colony, who come to enjoy the delightful sea-breezes, sea bathing, and the comforts with which they are every where surrounded. Excellent accommodations can always be obtained at boarding houses, which, among other attractions, are always furnished with supplies of oysters and fish of the first quality. Musqutoe bars are not often needed here, and, altogether, it is one of the most delightful places in the country. . . .

*Quintana* is a town in embryo, containing a proprietor's house belonging to Mr. McKinney, and a large warehouse; but "farther the deponent saith not." It is situated on the Brazos opposite to Velasco.

*Powhatan* has been just laid out by Dr. Archer and Mr. Williams, at the mouth of Dickson's creek, on the western shore of Galveston bay. It possesses a first rate harbor.

*Tuscasito*, in the vicinity of Anahuac, instead of being a town or even a village, is a mere stopping place on the way to San Antonio with a single house and a blacksmith's shop. It is situated in a dreary and barren country, with scarce a sign of vegetation around it. The view from this place looking out upon the bay is very fine. The spot is important to travellers, who will receive good accommodation from the proprietor, Mr. Orr.

*Victoria*, named after the patriot Guadalupe Victoria, is situated on the east side of the Guadalupe, in DeLeon's grant, at the intersection of the road leading from San Felipe to Goliad with that river, and about twenty miles from the mouth of the La Baca. It is a small village, and its population is chiefly Mexican.

*Aransaso and Copano* are both located on Aransaso bay, in Power's grant, and are inconsiderable places at present. They are however favorably situated, and their future prospects are good. The region around them is one of the most valuable portions of Texas, and the bay is much deeper than either Galveston or Matagorda, and is the principal harbor for vessels, whose cargoes are destined for Goliad or Bexar, and for the Irish colonies of the Nueces. Aransaso was formerly a Mexican garrison-town, and Copans was the winter-quarters, this past season, of a part of the volunteer troops in the cause of Texas.

*Liberty.*— This is a small place on the east bank of the Trinidad river, in Vehlein's grant, at the intersection of that river by the road leading to San Felipe. It is a point in the weekly mail route, established between San Felipe and Belew's Ferry on the Sabine river. It is the capital of a jurisdiction, and its citizens have taken an active part in the war of Independence.

*Lynchburg* is a new town at the mouth of the San Jacinto and Buffalo Bayou, at the head of Galveston bay; it is a point in the eastern mail route from San Felipe.

*Houston,* in compliment to the General who so nobly volunteered in the Texan cause, has recently been laid out on the east side of the Trinity river, forty miles north of the San Antonio road. It contains between three and four hundred building lots and a large quantity of out land. The situation is said to be handsome, salubrious, and well watered; surrounded by fertile, well timbered

land, and is about six miles distant from a good steam-boat landing on the Trinity. The town is intended to be on the roads leading from Nacogdoches and Pecan Point, to the falls of the Brazos. Within a few miles of it there are two large and good salines.

*Bevil's Settlement* is situated on the Sabine, and forms one of the jurisdictions of the department of Nacogdoches. A mail arrives here weekly by the way of *Zavala*—a small place on the Neches river in Zavala's grant—from San Augustine. It is a populous neighborhood, but cannot be called a town. Bevil's mill is the point embraced in the mail route.

We have thus enumerated the principal towns and settlements in Texas, . . . which are worthy of notice; . . . There are many other *nominal* towns, and a number of good settlements, not included in our present sketch, and which, conceiving we had offered sufficient information for the emigrant, . . . we thought proper to omit. Towns in Texas, indeed, are of mushroom growth; they spring up in a day, and decay as soon, being abandoned for some more alluring spot, which has the charm of novelty for a roving and unsettled emigrant. . . .

## 52.   PRESIDENT HOUSTON'S FIRST INAUGURAL ADDRESS
### October 22, 1836

From Amelia W. Williams and Eugene C. Barker (eds.), *The Writings of Sam Houston* (8 vols.; Austin, 1938-43), I, 448-452. This copy was taken from Texas *House Journal*, First Congress, First Session, 84-88.

On July 3, 1836, *ad interim* President David G. Burnet called an election for the first Monday in September, at which time the voters ratified the proposed constitution, expressed overwhelmingly their desire for annexation to the United States, and elected officers to serve under the constitutional government. For president they cast 5,110 votes for Sam Houston, 743 for Henry Smith, and 587 for Stephen F. Austin, and elected Mirabeau B. Lamar vice-president. Burnet convened the First Congress at Columbia on October 3, and on the next day delivered to it his message embodying recommendations for legislative consideration.

There was a growing demand, however, that Houston and Lamar assume office without waiting until the second Monday in December as provided in the constitution. On October 22 Burnet resigned, and Houston took the oath as the first constitutionally elected president of the Republic of Texas. In his impromptu inaugural address, which follows, Houston spoke briefly of his proposed program.

### Columbia, October 22, 1836.

MR. SPEAKER AND GENTLEMEN: Deeply impressed with a sense of responsibility devolving on me, I can not, in justice to myself, repress the emotion of my heart, or restrain the feelings which my sense of obligation to my fellow-citizens has inspired. Their suffrage was gratuitously bestowed. Preferred to others, possibly superior in merit to myself, called to the most important station among mankind by the voice of a free people, it is utterly impossible not to feel impressed with the deepest sensations of delicacy in my present position before the world. It is not here alone, but our present attitude before all nations has rendered my position, and that of my country, one of peculiar interest.

A spot of earth almost unknown to the geography of the age, destitute of all available resources, comparatively few in numbers, we modestly remonstrated against oppression, and, when invaded by a numerous host, we dared to proclaim our independence and to strike for freedom on the breast of the oppressor. As yet our course is onward. We are only in the outset of the campaign of liberty. Futurity has locked up the destiny which awaits our people.

Who can contemplate with apathy a situation so imposing in the physical and moral world? None! no not one. The relations among ourselves are peculiarly delicate and important; for no matter what zeal or fidelity I may possess in the discharge of my official duties, if I do not obtain co-operation and an honest support from the co-ordinate departments of the government, wreck and ruin must be the inevitable consequences of my administration.

If then, in the discharge of my duty, my competency should fail in the attainment of the great objects in view, it would become your sacred duty to correct my errors and sustain me by your superior wisdom. This much I anticipate—this much I demand. I am perfectly aware of the difficulties that surround me, and the convulsive throes through which our country must pass. I have never been emulous of the civil wreath—when merited it crowns a happy destiny. A country situated like ours is environed with difficulties, its administration is frought with perplexities. Had it been my destiny, I would infinitely have preferred the toils, privations, and perils, of a soldier, to the duties of my present station.

Nothing but zeal, stimulated by the holy spirit of patriotism, and guided by philosophy and wisdom, can give that impetus to our energies necessary to surmount the difficulties with which our political path is obstructed.

By the aid of your intelligence, I trust all impediments in our advancement will be removed; that all wounds in the body politic will be healed, and the Constitution of the Republic will derive strength and vigor equal to all opposing energies. I shall confidently anticipate the establishment of Constitutional liberty. In the attainment of this object, we must regard our relative situation to other countries.

A subject of no small importance is the situation of an extensive frontier, bordered by Indians, and open to their depredations. Treaties of peace and amity, and the maintenance of good faith with the Indians, present themselves to my mind as the most rational grounds on which to obtain their friendship. Let us abstain on our part from aggressions, establish commerce with the different tribes, supply their useful and necessary wants, maintain even-handed justice with them, and natural reason will teach them the utility of our friendship.

Admonished by the past, we can not, in justice, disregard our national enemies; vigilance will apprise us of their approach, a disciplined and valiant army will insure their discomfiture. Without discrimination and system, how unavailing would all the resources of an old and overflowing treasury prove to us. It would be as unprofitable to us in our present situation as the rich diamond locked in the bosom of the adamant.

We can not hope that the bosom of our beautiful prairies will soon be visited by the balmy breezes of peace. We may again look for the day when their verdure will be converted into dyes of crimson. We must keep all our energies alive, our army organized, desciplined, and increased agreeably to our present necessities. With these preparations we can meet and vanquish despotic thousands. This is the attitude we at present must regard as our own. We are battling for human liberty; reason and firmness must characterize our acts.

The course our enemies have pursued has been opposed to every principle of civilized warfare— bad faith, inhumanity, and devestation [sic] marked their path of invasion. We were a little band, contending for liberty; they were thousands, well appointed, munitioned, and provisioned, seeking to rivet chains upon us, or extirpate us from the earth. Their cruelties have incurred the universal denunciation of Christendom. They will not pass from their nation during the present generation.

The contrast of our conduct is manifest; we were hunted down as the felon wolf, our little band driven from fastness to fastness, exasperated to the last extreme; while the blood of our kindred and our friends was invoking the vengeance of an offended God, was smoking to high heaven, we met the enemies and vanquished them. They fell in battle, or suppliantly kneeled and were spared. We offered up our vengeance at the shrine of humanity, while Christendom rejoiced at the act and viewed with delightful pride the ennobling sacrifice. The civilized world contemplated with proud emotions conduct which reflected so much glory on the Anglo-Saxon race. The moral effect has done more towards our liberation, than the defeat of the army of veterans. When our cause has been presented to our friends in the land of our origin, they have embraced it with their warmest sympathies. They have rendered us manly and efficient aid. They have rallied to our standard, they have fought side by side with our warriors— they have bled, and their dust is mingling with the ashes of our heroes.

At this moment I discern numbers around me who battled in the field of San Jacinto, and whose chivalry and valor have identified them with the glory of the country, its name, its soil, and its liberty. There sits a gentleman within my view whose personal and political services to Texas have been invaluable. He was the first in the United States to respond to our cause. His purse was ever open to our necessities. His hand was extended in our aid. His presence among us and his return to the embraces of our friends will inspire new efforts in behalf of our cause. [The attention of the Speaker and that of Congress, was directed to Wm. Christy, Esq., of New Orleans, who sat by invitation within the bar.]

A circumstance of the highest import will claim the attention of the court at Washington. In our recent election the important subject of annexation to the United States of America was submitted to the consideration of the people. They have expressed their feelings and their wishes on that momentous question. They have with a unanimity unparalleled, declared that they will be reunited to the great Republican family of the North. The appeal is made by a willing people. Will our friends disregard it? They have already bestowed upon us their warmest sympathies. Their manly and generous feelings have been enlisted in our behalf. We are cheered by the hope that they will recive us to a participancy of their civil, political, and religious rights, and hail us welcome into the great family of freemen. Our misfortunes have been their misfortunes— our sorrows, too, have been theirs, and their joy at our success has been irrepressible.

A thousand considerations press upon me, each claiming attention; but the shortness of the notice of this emergency (for the speaker had had only four hours' notice of the inauguration, and all this time was spent in conversation) will not enable me to do justice to those subjects, and will necessarily induce their postponement for the present.

[Here the President paused for a few seconds and disengaged his sword.]

It now, Sir, becomes my duty to make a presentation of this sword— this emblem of my past office! [The President was unable to proceed further; but having firmly clinched it with both hands, as if with a farewell grasp, a tide of varied associations of ideas rushed upon him in the moment; his countenance bespoke the workings of the strongest emotions, his soul seemed to have swerved from the hypostatic union of the body, and to dwell momentarily on the glistening blade; and the greatest part of the auditory gave outward proof of their congeniality of feeling! It was in reality a moment of deep and exciting interest. After this pause, more eloquently impressive than the deepest pathos conveyed in language, the President proceeded]: I have worn it with some humble pretensions in defence of my country; and should the danger of my country again call for my services, I expect to resume it, and respond to that call, if needful, with my blood and life.

## 53.  THE BOUNDARY OF TEXAS ESTABLISHED

### December 19, 1836

From *Laws of the Republic of Texas* (Printed by Order of the Secretary of State, 2 vols.; Houston, 1838), I, 133-134.

On May 14, 1836, President David G. Burnet and Santa Anna signed the Treaty of Velasco which specified among other things that Mexican troops were "to evacuate the territory of Texas, passing to the other side of the Rio Grande" and that the boundary between Mexico and Texas was to be established by a later treaty, "the territory of the latter not to exceed beyond the Rio Bravo del Norte." The Mexican Congress, however, on May 20 declared that Santa Anna had no power to bind the nation in the Treaty of Velasco, notified the world that Mexico would recognize no action taken by him while a prisoner, and announced that it was making preparations to subdue the rebellious Texans. Since the possibility of a permanent settlement appeared rather remote and it was desirable to define the geographic extent of its jurisdiction, the Texas Congress on December 19, 1836, established a statutory boundary for the nation.

Sec. 1. *Be it enacted by the senate and house of representatives of the republic of Texas, in congress assembled,* That from and after the passage of this act, the civil and political jurisdiction of this republic be, and is hereby declared to extend to the following boundaries, to wit: beginning at the mouth of the Sabine river, and running west along the Gulf of Mexico three leagues from land, to the mouth of the Rio Grande, thence up the principal stream of said river to its source, thence due north to the forty-second degree of north latitude, thence along the boundary line as defined in the treaty between the United States and Spain, to the beginning: . . .

## 54.  PRESIDENT LAMAR'S POLICIES

From Charles A. Gulick, Jr., and Katherine Elliott (eds.), *The Papers of Mirabeau Buonaparte Lamar* (6 vols.; Austin, 1922), II, 316-323, 346-369.

Mirabeau B. Lamar, who had directed the opposition to Houston's policies, was elected president to succeed Houston in 1838. His program was almost the antithesis of his predecessor's for good reason. When Houston was elected, annexation to the United States seemed imminent; now, that possibility appeared remote, and it was necessary to establish a government on a permanent basis. Furthermore, Lamar had opposed annexation from the first.

In his inaugural address Lamar outlined his program, much of it being reminiscent of Jefferson's first inaugural address, and in a very lengthy message to Congress a few days later, he elaborated upon his policies and made specific recommendations for consideration. The following extracts from the two addresses clearly set forth Lamar's political ideology and reveal the character of his administration.

### 1. LAMAR'S INAUGURAL ADDRESS

#### December 10, 1838

. . . The character of my administration may be anticipated in the domestic nature of our government, and peaceful habits of the people. Looking upon agriculture, commerce and the useful arts, as the true basis of all national strength and glory, it will be my leading policy to awaken into vigorous activity, the wealth, talent and enterprise of the country; and, at the same time, to lay the foundation of those higher institutions for moral and mental culture, without which no government, on democratic principles, can prosper, nor [th]e people long preserve their liberties. In the management of our foreign intercourse, I would recommend that we deal justly with all nations, aggressively to none; preserve friendly and amicable relations with such as may be disposed to reciprocate the policy, and avoiding all protracted and perplexing negociations, court free and

unrestricted commerce wherever it may be to the interest of our people to carry the national flag. Perferring peace, but not averse to war, I shall be ever ready to adjust all differences with our enemies by friendly discussion and arrangement, at the same time be equally prompt to adopt either offensive or defensive operations, as their disposition and our own safety may render necessary. Unconscious of any selfish influences which are likely to draw me from the path of duty, I hope in the administration of our domestic affairs, to recommend by my example, the spirit of justice and moderation in the exercise of official functions. I shall . . . sustain the freedom of the press, the purity of elections, the right of opinion, and the freedom and sanctity of religion; maintain the integrity and independence of the judiciary as the great dispensary of justice, and the correction of civil, criminal and constitutional abuses; economize the public resources; protect the frontiers; recommend equality of taxation, burthening none of the branches of industry for the benefit of others; discourage multiplicity of legislation; patronize talents, integrity and sobriety; support wi[th] becoming liberality all laudable and patriotic institutions founded i[n] reason and tested by experience. . . .

There is, however, one question of the highest national concernment, on which I feel it a privilege and a duty to address myself to the great body of the people themselves. I mean the annexation of our country to the American union. Notwithstanding the almost undivided voice of my fellow-citizens at one time in favor of the measure, . . . I have never been able myself to perceive the policy of the desired connexion, or discover in it any advantage either c[i]vil, political or commercial, which could possibly result to Texas. But on the contrary . . .

the step once taken would produce a lasting regret, and ultimately prove as disastrous to our liberty and hopes, as the triumphant sword of the enemy. And I say this from no irreverence to the character and institutions of my native country, whose welfare I have ever desired, and do still desire above my individual happiness, but . . . the land of my adoption must claim my highest allegiance and affection; her glory and happiness must be my paramount consideration, and I cannot allow myself to speak in any other than the language of freedom and frankness on all matters involving her safety, dignity and honor.

When I reflect upon the invaluable rights which Texas will have to yield up with the surrender of her Independence — the right of making either war or peace; the right of controlling the Indian tribes within her borders; the right of appropriating her public domain to purposes of education and internal improvements; of levying her own taxes; regulating her own commerce and forming her own alliances and treaties — when I view her divested of the most essential attributes of free government; reduced to the level of an unfelt fraction of a giant power; or peradventure divided into Territorial districts, with Governors and judges and excise men appointed from abroad to administer laws which she had no adequate voice in enacting, and to gather imposts for the benefit of those who levy them — when I look upon her, as she soon will be, the cornucopia of the world, pouring her abundant treasures into the lap of another people than her own; a tributary vassal to remote and uncongenial communities; communities as widely separated from her in pursuits as in distance, who are known to be opposed to her peculiar and essential interests, and who are daily sending forth their denunciations against her from the fire-side, the pulpit and the council chamber; and when I bear in mind that all this sacrifice of rights and dignity and character is to be made, . . . for the privilege of going into a union in which she carries wealth without proportional influence — for the glory of identifying her fortunes with a government . . . embracing conflicting interests and irreconcilable prejudices with lasting causes of domestic quarrel, where Texas can . . . be the means perhaps of producing or accelerating an awful catastrophe which none could be more ready to avert or sincerely deplore than herself — when I reflect upon these, the inevitable and fatal consequences of the proposed connection, and then turn from the dark and dreary picture to the contemplation of the high destiny that awaits our country; . . . when I view her vast extent of territory, stretching from the Sabine to the Pacific and away to the South West as far as the obstinacy of the enemy may render it necessary for the sword to make the boundary; embracing the most delightful climate and the richest soil in the world, and behold it all in the state of high cultivation and improvement — her mountains of minerals yielding their vast treasures to the touch of industry; her luxuriant pastures alive with flocks and herds, and her wide fields whitening with a staple commodity, in the production of which she can have no rival; with the whole world for her market; and then consider the noble purposes to which this immense and exhaustless wealth

may be applied, in adorning and beautifying the country, providing for its safety and defence, endowing institutions for the spread of virtue, knowledge and the arts, and carrying to the door of every citizen of the Republic, peace, plenty, and protection — and when in addition to these glorious and grand results, I look still farther to the important improvements which she will be able to devise in government, and to the entire revolution which her example in free trade will effect in the commerce of other nations, emancipating it from the thralldom of tariff restrictions and placing it upon the high grounds of equitable reciprocity, . . . I cannot regard the annexation of Texas to the American Union in any other light than as the grave of all her hopes of happiness and greatness; and if, contrary to the present aspect of affairs, the amalgamation shall ever hereafter take place, I shall feel that the blood of our ma[r]tyred heroes had been shed in vain — . . .

That the people of Texas should have been in favor of *Annexation* at the time their votes were given on the question, is not a matter of surprise when we consider the then existing condition of the country. — She was left after the battle of San Jacinto feeble and exhausted; without means and without credit; her settlements broken up; her villages desolated by ruthless invasion; and amidst all still threatened in her defenceless situation with a return of the foe and a renewal of the sad calamaties of war. Under such a state of things, no wonder that the people, harrassed, and almost ruined, bleeding with present wounds and apprehe[nd]ing a farther accumulation of ills, should be willing to purchase momentary security by a surrender of their national Independence. Perhaps there was wisdom in the choice; but I am free to confe[ss] that even at that time, amidst the darkest period of our country's h[ist]ory, I never despaired of the Republic, but with unshaken confid[e]nce in the strength of our cause, and a full knowledge of what the [e]nergies of a free and determined people were capable of achieving, I raised my feeble voice against the sacrifice which we were about to make, . . .

But these imposing considerations which at one time rendered the proposed political connection seemingly desirable, . . . exist no longer. Our desolated plains have become green meadows and luxuriant fields. Where the iron car of war rolled with destroying energy, the ploughshare of the husbandman is driven in peace and safety; and instead of a sparse and suffering population, weighed down with poverty and blighted hopes, we behold a powerful and prosperous people, daily increasing in wealth and numbers happy in their present possessions and looking forward to still higher and more glorious results. Invasion too, has lost its terrors. Conscious of our own strength, we know very well that the enemy has greater reason to apprehend danger from us, than we from him. . . . And shall we now, in the midst of glori[ous] hopes and increasing vigor, persevere in a suicidal policy, origi[nal]ly founded in necessity rather than in choice? Would it not be far better for us, since the reasons which influenced our former verdict can have no further application, to re-consider that verdict, and no good and valid shewing, reverse the judgment? . . .

## 2. LAMAR'S MESSAGE TO CONGRESS

### December 21, 1838

. . . The achievement of a people's independence from the domination of an unjust and vacillating Government, is an event, which will always attract the warmest sympathies of the friends of human liberty throughout the world. . . . Let us . . . by a vigorous and persevering discharge of our respective duties, show that we are worthy of the sympathies bestowed, and can give fruition to the hopes excited. Let us maintain our sovereignty, preserve concord at home; faithfully observe all national obligations; and transmit to posterity the free institutions we have erected, unimpaired by selfishness, and untouched by vain and pernicious ambition. . . .

Our immediate relations with foreign powers, are necessarily circumscribed. The newness of our political existence will, for some time to come, cause them to be brief and simple, and it will be wise in us to preserve their simplicity as far as practicable, while we endeavor by all means compatable with national dignity, to extend their limits. The Government of the United States, always foremost in whatever tends to the advancement of liberty, continues to manifest towards us, the same just, and magnanimous spirit which prompted the early recognition of our Independence; and I entertain a profound hope, that other leading powers will shortly see the propriety of extending to us, and acquiring for themselves, the advantages of international fellowship. To Great Britain the Independence of Texas cannot be an indifferent event: — The advancement of her great manufacturing and commercial interests, is too deeply identified with our future prosperity as a nation, to permit us to believe, that she can view our present position with other than favorable regard. To France also, it presents inducements, which cannot fail to elicit that chivalrous liberality, which has heretofore so conspicuously characterized her National Councils. With Mexico, our posture is unchanged. — She still seems to cherish the illusory hope of conquest, without adopting any means for its realization. . . . It may become the duty and interest of Texas, to reduce the question of her right to Independence, to a more summary adjustment than our adversary seems inclined to give it. While we would meet with alacrity, the first indication of a desire, for a just and honorable peace, we should compel a more active prosecution of the war. If peace can be obtained only by the sword, let the sword do its work.

If we desire to establish a Republican Government on a broad and permanent basis, it will become our duty to adopt a comprehensive and well regulated system of mental and moral culture. Education is a subject in which every citizen, and especially every parent, feels a deep and lively concern. It is one in which no jarring interests are involved, . . . for its benefits are so universal that all parties can cordially unite in advancing it. It is admitted by all, that [a] cultivated mind is the guardian genius of Democracy, and while guided and controlled by virtue, the noblest attribute of man. It is the only dictator that freemen acknowledge, and the only security which freemen desire. The influence of Education in the moral world, is like light in the physical; rendering luminous, what before was obscure. It opens a wide field for the exercise and improvement of all the faculties of man, and imparts vigor and clearness to those important truths in the science of Government, as well as of morals, which would otherwise be lost in the darkness of ignorance. Without its aid, how perilous and insufficient would be the deliberations of a Government like ours? How ignoble and useless its legislation for all the purposes of happiness? How fragile and insecure its liberties? War would be conducted without the science necessary to insure success, . . . and peace would be joyless, because its train would be unattended by that civilization and refinement which can alone give zest to social and domestic enjoyments. . . . Cultivation is as necessary to the supply of rich intellectual and moral fruits, as are the labors of the husbandman to bring forth the valuable productions of the earth. . . . The present is a propitious moment, to lay the foundation of a great moral, and intellectual edifice, which will in after ages be hailed as the chief ornament and blessing of Texas. A suitable appropriation of lands to the purpose of general Education can be made at this time without inconvenience, to the Government, or the people, but defer it until the public domain shall have passed from our hands, and the uneducated youths of Texas, will constitute the living monuments of our neglect and remissness. To commence a liberal system of instruction a few years hence, may be attended with many difficulties. . . . A liberal endowment which will be adequate to the general diffusion of a good rudimental education in every district of the Republic, and to the establishment of a University where the highest branches of science may be taught, can now be effected without the expenditure of a single dollar — postpone it a few years, and millions will be necessary to accomplish the great design.

I must also invite the attention of Congress to the defects in the Municipal Code. Unfortunately for the Country, we have now in force many portions of two systems different in their origin, discordant in their provisions and calculated to lead to the most conflicting decisions. Of the cases that present themselves before the courts many are included in neither Code, many are indifferently provided for by both, leaving the parties without remedy in the first instance, and often wholly uncertain as to the proper remedy in the second. . . . Thus it may not unfrequently occur, that upon the same question of law, we shall have the most conflicting judicial decisions throughout the Republic. . . . We are the only people who have adopted a system of laws of which the great body of the people are entirely ignorant. It would be a task of extreme difficulty for the most learned in the science even to enumerate the various Mexican authorities now in force in this Government. Most of these authorities . . . are written in a foreign language unknown to our people; and to a large majority of the profession as well as to a majority of the legal tribunals appointed by Congress to interpret and administer them. Nor is there a reasonable hope, that at an early period we can be relieved from the painful preplexity; for it would be entirely impracticable for the government to procure at this time, the translation, publication, and general distribution of these authorities. — And until this is done, or the system changed, we shall be doomed to the painful necessity of having the titles to our property tried, and all our contracts interpreted by laws unknown to our Courts, and unknown to the community. . . . Congress is required by that sacred instrument [the Constitution] at a period as early as practicable to introduce by statute the Common Law of England with such modifications as the circumstances of the country may in their judgement require. The period here contemplated by the Constitution in the opinion of the Executive has now arrived; and the speedy execution of this provision, it is respectfully believed will save our country from much public disaster and individual ruin. . . .

But among the many subjects that unite the solemn and deliberate attention of the Congress of Texas at this moment, no one involves a more affecting interest, than the exposed and defenceless condition of our inland frontier. Since the memorable victory of San Jacinto, we have sustained but little annoyance from our principal enemy. Their spirits were daunted and their energies paralyzed by that signal defeat; and from that period they have been occupied with domestic disturbances, or difficulties growing out of their foreign relations. These causes of inaction on their part may be temporary, and we ought by no means to permit them to beguile us into negligence. . . .

Unhappily our frontier is suffering greater evils than result from these occasional and desultory incursions. Several native tribes of Indians, deriving confidence from our forbearance, have waged, and are waging, a petty, but in some instances, a disastrous and cruel warfare upon our neglected border settlements. The importance of chastising these savage offenders, and extending protection to our exposed and suffering fellow-citizens, cannot fail to attract your early and most serious notice. — Honor, humanity, and patriotism, conspire to enjoin this duty upon us. It is a cardinal principle in all political associations, that protection is commensurate with allegiance, and the poorest citizen whose sequestered cabin is reared on our remotest frontier, holds as sacred a claim upon the government for safety and security as does the man who lives in ease and wealth in the heart of our most populous city. I am by no means desirous of aggravating the ordinary and inevitable calamities of war, by inculcating the harsh doctrine of the *lex talionis* toward the debased and ignorant savages. War is in itself an evil, which all good people will strive to avoid; but when it cannot be avoided, it ought to be so met and pursued as will best secure a speedy and lasting peace. If that better mode consists in severity to the enemy, then severity to him, becomes clemency to all. The moderation hitherto extended to the Indians on our borders has been repeatedly retorted upon us, in all the atrocious cruelties that characterize their modes of warfare. . . . As long as we continue to exhibit our mercy without shewing our strength, so long will the Indian continue to bloody the edge of the tomahawk, and move onward in the work of rapacity and slaughter. . .

. . . It is thought by some, that the Indians have been encroached upon in the enjoyment of their landed rights. . . . But I am far from conceding that the Indians, either Native, or Emigrant, have any just cause of complaint. That the Emigrant Tribes have no legal or equitable claim to any portion of our territory is obvious, from a cursory examination of their history. Their emigration to Texas was unsolicited and unauthorized; and has always been a source of regret to its more enlightened population. The federal government of Mexico, neither conceded, nor promised them lands, or civil rights. They came as intruders; were positively forbid to make any permanent abidance; and have continued in the country up to the present period against the public wish, and at the sacrifice of the public tranquility. This is particularly the case with the Cherokees. The offer made to bordering Indians in the colonization law of Coahuila and Texas, carries with it precedent conditions which have in no instance been complied with by any one of these tribes. . . . Such promises (if ever made) under such circumstances can impose no moral obligations on us. But the pledge of the Consultation of Texas in 1835, and the treaty consequent upon it, are said to be regarded by the Indians, and their advocates, as the chief foundation of the claims which they set up for lands in Texas. It is not necessary to inquire into the nature and extent of the powers which originated and negotiated that treaty; for the treaty itself never was ratified by any competent authority, and therefore can in nowise be legally considered as binding or obligatory upon us. Had it been ratified however by all the solemnities of the constitution, still this government is now wholly absolved from the performance of its conditions, by the notorious and habitual violation of its principal stipulations by the Indians. . . . I would respectfully offer the following suggestions: — That there be established as early as practicable a line of military posts, competent to the protection of our frontier from the incursions of the wandering tribes that infest our borders; and that all intercourse between them and our citizens, be made under the eye, and subject to the control of the Government. In order to allay the apprehension of the friendly tribes, and prevent any collision between them and our own citizens, I would recommend that each Indian family be permitted to enjoy such improvements as they occupy, together with a suitable portion of land, without interruptions or annoyance, so long as they choose to remain upon it, and shall deport themselves in a friendly manner; being subordinate to our laws in all criminal matters, and in matters of contract, to the authorized agents of the Government. . . .

My great solicitude on the subject of frontier protection has partially overruled the repugnance I have always felt for standing armies. In the present disturbed condition of our foreign and Indian relations, the proper security of the country at large, and especially the peace and safety of our border settlements, seem imperatively to require the immediate organization of a regular, permanent and efficient force. The magnitude of that force must vary with circumstances; but until we shall have obtained a full acknowledgment of our Independence, and shall have either by treaties or chastisement secured our exposed fellow citizens from Indian aggression or the apprehension of hostilities, I should suppose that, that force could not, compatible with safety, be either small or inactive. Such a force when properly and judiciously disposed of would deter the Indian from his depredations — inspire a confidence which would lead to a rapid settlement of our present frontier, and at the same time form a nucleus around which the chivalric yeomanry of the land would rally in the event of another invasion from our national foe. . . . Free governments have always found their best defence against foreign and domestic enemies in the patriotism, the intelligence and the chivalry of the great body of the people. A well regulated militia is the strongest and the surest bulwark of liberty. . . . While recommending the organization of a sufficient regular force to insure the present protection of the Republic from temporary aggressions without calling the people from their various pursuits of industry, I would still prefer, in the hour which tries men's souls, to rest the nation's defence, upon the zeal, the valor, and the patriotism of the citizen soldier.

. . . [The] commercial intercourse of nations . . . now constitutes one of the most important and complicate branches of national policy. . . . Texas is happily situated in this respect, and can never reach the acme of her greatness until a well cherished commerce shall aid her agricultural faculties by distributing the surplus products of her soil to other nations. This distribution can be effected only by a suitable marine power; for unless commerce be protected from insult and depredation on the high seas, agriculture with all its concomitant interests will languish in its unprofitable abundance. To re-establish our navy on a respectable footing, is therefore of primary importance, and we cannot better serve our country, than by devoting a portion of her means to this purpose. . . .

As connected with the national defence, the finances will merit and receive your early attention. . . . To levy burdensome taxes on a people, many of whose farms and dwellings have been recently abandoned, and made desolate by an invading enemy, and who are still laboring under the embarrassments incident to a new settlement, and who are yet struggling for political existence, has an aspect of serverity and injustice, and ought by all possible means to be avoided. The only practical mode of doing this, is to anticipate the future abundant resources of the country, and to devolve upon our posterity, a portion of the burdens to which the perfecting our independence, and theirs has subjected, and is still subjecting us. . . .

So long as the resources of a country are permitted to lie dormant and intangible, without an effort on the part of the Government to bring them into activity, their intrinsic value, and positive abundance, are comparatively of little import. Laws tending to encourage agriculture, to foster commerce, to withdraw the rich minerals imbedded in the earth, will always exert a salutary influence on the national character and credit abroad, beside the many blessings they dispense at home. The far interior of our country abounds in mineral wealth. Not to secure that wealth from individual appropriation, would be . . . unwise and improvident. Hence, I would urge the passage of a general law, . . . reserving to the Republic all minerals of whatever description; and at the same time would respectfully suggest the policy of adopting suitable measures by which we may turn them to our early advantage. . . .

Notwithstanding my decided aversion to an onerous system of taxation, I am precluded by the actual necessities of the government from advising any abatement in the present rate; for I apprehend that the revenue as now realized, is scarcely sufficient to defray the current expenses. The increased expenditures which must result from the necessity of defending our frontiers will render it absolutely necessary that the tax on land if not augmented should at least be more equally and uniformly assessed. . . .

Besides other sources of revenue, I would invite the congress to the continuance of the tariff laws, with such alterations as reflection and experience may suggest. The decided bias of my mind is for the total abolition of all duties on imports, . . . [and] I look forward to a period, (I hope near at hand) when we shall be able, and will find it to be our interest, to invite the commerce of the world to our free and open ports. The radical policy of Texas is anti-tariff, because its commercial commodities are of the raw material, which fears no impost rivalry, and paying no contributions to manufactories. Yet the immediate adoption of free trade, . . . would in the present situation of our country, exhibit an apparent recklessness and imprudence, which could not fail to affect our credit abroad; for . . . the revenue collected through custom houses has been, and is still our chief dependence for sustaining the credit of our public issues, which must most certainly sink into a disastrous and degrading depreciation with the repeal of the imposts. . . . Under these circumstances I feel constrained to ask of the honorable congress a continuance of the tariff to meet the exigencies of the times, until other sources of wealth, and revenue, shall be opened for supplying the treasury, and defraying the necessary expenses of the government. . . .

To remedy the many inconveniencies incident to a cumbersome metalic currency and to furnish greater facilities to operations in money, banks have been incorporated in all countries where commerce has flourished, or agriculture has prospered beyond the immediate wants of a simple predial existence. The experiment of banking has been fully tested by experience, and the almost universal adoption of the expedient affords abundant and incontrovertible evidence of its general utility and adaptation to the wants and convenience of men. But great diversity of opinion exists in regard to the various modes of creating, and organizing, and managing such institutions. To my mind the objections to private incorporated banks far transcend in practical importance any useful purposes they may have, or are likely to fulfill. . . . That many of them have been extensively beneficial, is without doubt; that in general they have been productive of more evil than good, and have exerted a pernicious influence on society, is no less clear. . . .

In contemplation of these and many other reasons which might be added, I feel it my duty to recommend to you the early establishment of a strictly national Bank, which shall be the exclusive property, and under the exclusive control of the republic. An admixture of private interests would embarrass its operations, without bringing equivalent advantages to the institution. Such a bank incorporated for a suitable term of years, founded on a specific hypothecation of a competent portion of the public domain, which should be immediately appropriated to that purpose; with the additional guarantee of the plighted faith of the nation, and an adequate deposit of specie in its vaults, would, it is confidently believed, confer many eminent and continued blessings upon the country. It would furnish an immediate and complete remedy for the existing pecuniary difficulties, which result entirely from the insufficiency and depreciation of our present circulating medium. . . . And an institution having all the elements of usefulness and prosperity in itself, and sustained by the confidence and affections of an enlightened people, can scarcely be supposed capable of degenerating into an instrument of fraud, or of oppresion; or failing to realize the benefits expected from it. The triple security it would offer to its creditors, is of the highest character, of the most indubitable responsibility; for it is an approved maxim, that real-estate affords the best possible guarantee for

the ultimate payment of a debt. The pledge of the nation's faith will give peculiar solemnity and increased confidence to its obligations; and a competent deposit of specie will always be present, or presently attainable, to answer the contingent and occasional demands for that article. . . . It is evident, that a Bank so constituted, the exclusive property of a stable and popular government and combining the three guarantees, of land, specie, and the public faith, would not require to retain in its vaults as large a proportion of dormant capital as is acknowledged to be indispensable to the safe conduct of a private institution. . . . The profits and avails . . . might reasonably be expected to diminish, and ultimately to abolish the whole tariff of duties, and internal taxation. . . .

## 55.  THE HOMESTEAD LAW
### January 26, 1839

From H. P. N. Gammel (comp.), *The Laws of Texas*, 1822-1897 (10 vols.; Austin, 1898), II, 125-126.

In an effort to attract settlers and to make the Republic a nation of home owners, the Texans enacted two types of homestead laws. The first provided for liberal land grants; the second, passed by the Third Congress during President Lamar's administration, protected a household against seizure for debt. The latter was the first legislation of its kind passed by any country, and is particularly unique in that its property exemption provision was unknown in English common law and was in derogation thereof. Its origin possibly may have been influenced by Spanish-Mexican laws which left to a debtor a very limited amount of personal property. Extended by constitutional provision, legislative enactment, and judicial interpretation, it continues to be the most liberal property exemption law of any state in the United States. The law, as enacted originally, follows.

Be it enacted by the Senate and House of Representatives of the Republic of Texas in Congress assembled, That from and after the passage of this act, there shall be reserved to every citizen or head of a family in this

Republic, free and independent of the power of a writ of fire facias, or other execution issuing from any court of competent jurisdiction whatever, fifty acres of land or one town lot, including his or her homestead, and improvements not exceeding five hundred dollars in value, all house hold and kitchen furniture, (provided it does not exceed in value two hundred dollars,) all implements of husbandry, (provided they shall not exceed fifty dollars in value,) all tools, apparatus and books belonging to the trade or profession of any citizen, five milch cows, one yoke of work oxen or one horse, twenty hogs, and one year's provisions; and that all laws and parts of laws contravening or opposing the provisions of this act, be and the same are hereby repealed: Provided, The passage of this act shall not interfere with contracts between parties heretofore made.

## 56.  THE SELECTION OF A SITE FOR THE PERMANENT CAPITAL OF TEXAS
### April 13, 1839

From A. C. Horton, Chairman of the Commissioners Named to Select a Permanent Capital for the Republic of Texas, City of Houston, "Report," to His Excellency, Mirabeau B. Lamar, President of the Republic of Texas, April 13th A. D. 1839 (MS; Archives, Texas State Library, Austin).

One of the lasting features of President Mirabeau B. Lamar's administration was the location of a permanent capital for Texas. After the battle of San Jacinto, *ad interim* President David G. Burnet chose Columbia as a temporary seat of government, and it was there in October, 1836, that the First Congress assembled and Sam Houston was inaugurated president. Before adjourning, Congress voted to move the seat of government to the new town of Houston in May, 1837, with the stipulation that a permanent location would

be designated by 1840. On October 19, 1837, President Houston approved an act providing for the establishment of a commission to select the permanent location of the capital, but because of sectional rivalry the site had not been designated when Lamar became president. Prompted by Lamar, Congress on January 14, 1839, passed a resolution authorizing the appointment of a new commission to select the exact site for the capital between the Colorado and Brazos rivers and north of the "Old San Antonio Road," and that it should be named for Stephen F. Austin. Eastern and central Texas joined western Texas to block the selection of Houston.

On April 13 the commissioners reported to Lamar that they had chosen a site on the east bank of the Colorado River, at the straggling village of Waterloo, thirty miles west of the line of settlement. In their report, the commissioners, reflecting the influence of Lamar, gave an excellent description of the location and stated their reasons for the selection. The document follows.

The Commissioners appointed under the act of Congress dated January 1839, for locating the permanent site of the Seat of Government for the Republic, have the honor to report to your Excellency.

That they have selected the site of the Town of Waterloo on the East Bank of the Colorado River with the lands adjoining as per the Deed of the Sheriff of Bastrop County bearing date March 1839, and per the relinquishments of Logan Vandever, James Rogers, G. D. Handcock, J. W. Herrall, and Aaron Burleson by Edward Burleson all under date of 7th March 1839, as the site combining the greatest number of, and the most important advantages to the Republic by the location of the Seat of Government thereon, than any other situation which came under their observation within the limits assigned them, and as being therefore their choice for the location aforesaid.

We have the honor to represent to your Excellency that we have traversed and critically examined the country on both sides of the Colorado and Brazos Rivers from the Upper San Antonio road to, and about the falls, on both those rivers and that we have not neglected the intermediate country between them, but have examined it more particularly than a due regard to our personal safety did perfectly warrant. We found the Brassos River more central perhaps in reference to actual existing population, and found in it and its tributaries perhaps a greater quantity of fertile lands—than are to be found on the Colorado, but on the other hand we were of opinion that the Colorado was more central in respect to Territory, and this in connection with the great desideratums of health, fine water, stone, stone coal, water power &c, being more abundant and convenient on the Colorado than on the Brassos river, did more than counterbalance the supposed superiority of the lands as well as the centrality of position in reference to population, possessed by the Brassos river.

In reference to the protection to be afforded to the frontier by the Location of the Seat of Government, a majority of the Commissioners are of opinion that that object will be as well attained by the location upon one river as upon the other, being also of opinion that within a very short period of time following the location of the Seat of Government on the Frontier, the extensions of the settlements produced thereby, will engender other theories of defence, on lands now the homes of the Comanche and the Bisson.

The site selected by the Commissioners is composed of five thirds of leagues of lands and two labors, all adjoining and having a front upon the Colorado river somewhat exceeding three miles in breadth. It contains seven thousand seven hundred and thirty five acres land and will cost the Republic the sum of Twenty one thousand dollars or thereabouts, one tract not being Surveyed. Nearly the whole front is a Bluff of from thirty to forty feet elevation, being the termination of a Prairie containing perhaps two thousand acres, composed of a chocolate colored sandy loam, intersected by two beautiful streams of permanent and pure water, one of which forms at its debouche into the river a timbered rye bottom of about thirty acres. These rivulets rise at an elevation of from Sixty to one hundred feet on the back part of the site or tract, by means of which the contemplated city might at comparatively small expense be well watered, in addition to which are several fine bluff springs of pure water on the river at convenient distances from each other.

The site is about two miles distant from and in full view of the Mountains or breaks of the Table Lands which, judging by the eye, are of about three hundred feet elevation. They are of Limestone formation and are covered with Live Oak and Dwarf Cedar to their summits. On the site and its immediate vicinity, stone in inexhaustible quantities and great varieties is found almost fashioned by nature for the builders hands; Lime and Stone coal abound in the vicinity, timber for firewood and ordinary building purposes abound on the tract, though the timber for building in the immediate neighborhood is not of so fine a character as might be wished, being mostly Cotton wood, Ash, Burr Oak, Huckberry, Post Oak and cedar, the last suitable for shingles and small frames.

At the distance of eighteen miles west by South from the site, on Onion Creek, "a stream affording fine water power" is a large body of very fine cyprus, which is also found at intervals up the River for a distance of forty miles, and together with immense quantities of fine cedar might readily be floated down the stream, as the falls two miles above the site present no obstruction to floats or rafts, being only a descent of about five feet in one hundred and fifty yards over a smooth bed of limestone formation very nearly resembling colored Marble. By this rout also immense quantities of Stone Coal, building materials, and in a few years Agricultural and Mineral products for the contemplated city, as no rapids save those mentioned occur in the River below the San Saba, nor are they known to exist for a great distance above the junction of that stream with the Colorado.

Opposite the site, at the distance of one mile, Spring Creek and its tributaries afford perhaps the greatest and most convenient waterpower to be found in the Republic. Walnut Creek distance six miles, and Brushy creek distance sixteen miles both on the east side of the river, afford very considerable water power. Extensive deposits of Iron ore adjudged to be of very superior quality is found within eight miles of the location.

This section of the Country is generally well watered, fertile in a high degree and has every appearance of health and salubriety of climate. The site occupies and will effectually close the pass by which Indians and outlawed Mexicans have for ages past traveled east and west to and from the Rio Grande to eastern Texas, and will now force them to pass by the way of Pecan Bayou and San Saba above the Mountains and the sources of the Guadalupe river.

The Commissioners confidently anticipate the time when a great thoroughfare shall be established from Santa Fe to our Sea ports, and another from Red River to Matamoras, which two routs must almost of necessity intersect each other at this point. They look forward to the time when this city shall be the emporium of not only the productions of the rich soil of the San Saba, Puertenalis Hono and Pecan Bayo, but of all the Colorado and Brassos, as also of the Produce of the rich mining country known to exist on those streams. They are satisfied that a truly National City could at no other point within the limits assigned them be reared up, not that other sections of the Country are not equally fertile, but that no other combined so many and such varied advantages and beauties as the one in question. The imagination of even the romantic will not be disappointed on viewing the Valley of the Colorado, and the fertile and gracefully undulating woodlands and luxuriant Prairies at a distance from it. The most sceptical will not doubt it healthiness, and the citizens bosom must swell with honest pride when standing in the Portico of the Capitol of his Country he looks abroad upon a region worthy only of being the home of the brave and free. Standing on the juncture of the routs of Santa Fe and the Sea Coast, of Red River and Matamoras, looking with the same glance upon the green romantic Mountains, and the fertile and widely extended plains of his Country, can a feeling of Nationality fail to arise in his bosom or could the fire of patriotism lie dormant under such circumstances.

Fondly hoping that we may not have disappointed the expectations of either our Countrymen or your Excellency, we subscribe ourselves Your Excellency's Most obedient Servants.

A. C. Horton   Chairman
I. W. Burton
William Menefee
Isaac Campbell
Louis P. Cooke

# 57.  THE TREATY WITH FRANCE
## September 25, 1839

From H. P. N. Gammel (comp.), *The Laws of Texas*, 1822-1897 (10 vols.; Austin, 1898), II, 655-662.

France was the first European nation to recognize the independence of Texas. Without waiting for the United States to act on the offer of annexation, President Houston had commissioned J. P. Henderson as agent and minister plenipotentiary to Great Britain and France with instructions to secure recognition of independence and commercial treaties. Henderson went first to London, but, unable to interest the British, proceeded to Paris in April, 1838. Fifteen months later, after the outbreak of war between France and Mexico and the receipt of a favorable report from the French agent in Texas, Foreign Minister Marshall Soult, Duke of Dalmatia, agreed to negotiate. A treaty, signed by the two ministers on September 25, was ratified by the Texas Senate on January 14. The following extracts from the treaty include its most significant provisions.

Treaty of Amity, Navigation and Commerce, between the Republic of Texas and his Majesty the King of the French

ARTICLE 1.   There shall be perpetual peace and amity between his Majesty the King of the French, his heirs and successors, on the one part, and the Republic of Texas, on the other part; and between the citizens of the two states, without exception of persons or of places.

ARTICLE 2.   The French and Texians shall enjoy, in their persons and property, in the entire extent of their respective territories, the same rights, privileges, and exemptions, which are or may be granted to the most favored nation. They shall have the right of disposing freely of their property by sale, exchange, by deed of gift, will, or in any other manner, without any impediment or difficulty. In like manner, the citizens of each, inheriting property in either of the states, may become heirs, without any hindrance, . . . They shall be exempted from all military service, — from all war contributions, — forced loans, — military requisitions, and in every other case, their personal or real estate shall not be subject to any other charge or impost than that which shall be paid by the citizens of the country themselves.

ARTICLE 3.   If it should happen that one of the two contracting parties be at war with any other power whatever, the other power shall prohibit their citizens from taking or holding commissions or letters of marque to cruise against the other, or to molest the commerce or property of her citizens.

ARTICLE 4.   The two contracting parties adopt in their mutual relations, the principle "that the flag covers the goods."

If one of the two parties remains neuter when the other may be at war with a third power, the goods covered by the neutral flag shall also be considered to be neutral, even if they should belong to the enemies of the other contracting party.

It is equally understood, that the neutrality of flag protects also the freedom of persons, and that the individuals belonging to a hostile power, who may be found on board a neutral vessel, shall not be made prisoners, unless they are actually engaged in the service of the enemy. . . .

ARTICLE 5.   In case one of the contracting parties should be at war with another power, and her ships at sea should be compelled to exercise the right of search, it is agreed that if they meet a vessel belonging to the other, then neutral, party, they shall send their boat on board said vessel with two persons charged to enter on an examination of the nationality and cargo of said vessel. The commanders shall be responsible for all vexations, acts of violence, which they may either commit or tolerate on such occasion. The search shall not be permitted but on board vessels which navigate without convoy. . . .

ARTICLE 6.   In case one of the two countries should be at war with a third power, the citizens of the other country, shall have a right to continue their commerce and their navigation with the same power, with the exception of the towns or ports, before which there shall be established an actual and effective blockade. It is fully understood, that this liberty of commerce and navigation, shall not extend to articles reputed contraband of war, . . .

ARTICLE 8.  The two contracting parties shall have the right to appoint consuls, vice-consuls, and consular agents in all the cities or ports open to the foreign commerce: . . .

ARTICLE 9.  The respective consuls, vice consuls, consular agents, and their chancellors, shall enjoy in the two countries, the privileges which generally belong to their functions, such as . . . shall be granted in their places of residence, to the agents of the same rank of the most favored nation.

ARTICLE 10.  The archives, and in general all the papers of the offices of the respective consulates, shall be inviolable; and under no pretext, nor in any case, shall they either be seized or searched by the local authorities. . . .

ARTICLE 12.  The respective Consuls, Vice-Consuls, and Consular agents, shall be charged exclusively with the internal police of the commercial vessels of their nation; and the local authorities shall not interfere, except in cases of riot or disturbance of a nature calculated to affect the public peace, either on shore or on board other vessels.

ARTICLE 13.  The respective Consuls, Vice-Consuls, and Consular agents, shall have the right to arrest all sailors who shall have deserted from vessels of war, or merchant vessels belonging to their respective countries, and may send them on board, or to their own country. . . .

ARTICLE 14.  French vessels arriving in or sailing out of the ports of Texas, and Texian vessels on their entry in or leaving the ports of France, shall not be subject to other or higher duties, . . . than those which are paid, or shall be paid by the vessels of the country itself.

ARTICLE 15.  The products of the soil, and of the industry of either of the two countries, imported directly into the ports of the other, the origin of which shall be duly ascertained, shall pay the same duties whether imported in French or Texian vessels. In like manner, the products exported will pay the same duties, and will enjoy the same privileges, allocations and drawbacks, which are or shall be allowed on the exportation of the same articles in the vessels of the country from which they are exported.

ARTICLE 16.  The cottons of Texas, without distinction of quality, will pay on their entry into the ports of France, when they shall be imported directly in French or Texian vessels, a uniform duty of twenty francs on one hundred kilogrammes.

All reduction of duties which may hereafter be made in favor of the cottons of the United States, shall be equally applied to those of Texas, . . .

ARTICLE 17.  From the day of the exchange of the ratifications of the present treaty, the duties at present levied in Texas on all fabricks and other articles of silk, or of which silk shall be a chief component part, imported directly into Texas, the manufacture of France, in French or Texian vessels, shall be reduced one half. It is clearly understood, that if the Texian government reduce the duties upon similar products of other nations, to a rate inferior to one half of the duties now existing, France cannot be obliged, in any case, to pay higher duties than those paid by the most favored nation. The duties at present levied in Texas on the Wines and Brandies of France, also imported directly in French or Texian vessels, shall be reduced, the first two-fifths, and the second one fifth.

It is understood, that in case the Republic of Texas should hereafter think proper to diminish the present duties on Wines and Brandies, the production of other countries, a corresponding reduction shall be made on the Wines and Brandies of France, . . .

ARTICLE 18.  The inhabitants of the French colonies, their property and ships, shall enjoy in Texas, and reciprocally the citizens of Texas, their property and ships shall enjoy in the French colonies, all the advantages which are or shall be granted to the most favored nation.

ARTICLE 19.  The stipulations of the present treaty shall be prepetual, with the exception of the articles, the fourteenth, fifteenth, sixteenth, seventeenth, and eighteenth, the duration of which is fixed to eight years, counting from the day of the exchange of the ratifications. . . .

Done at Paris, the twenty-fifth day of September, in the year of our Lord, one thousand eight hundred and thirty-nine.

J. PINCKNEY HENDERSON,
MAL. DUC DE DALMATIE.

## ADDITIONAL ARTICLES

ARTICLE 1.  As the laws of France require, as conditions of the nationality of a vessel, — that it should have been built in France, — that the owner, the captain, and three-fourths of the crew, shall be citizens of France: and Texas, by reason of the particular circumstances in which she is placed, being unable to comply with the same conditions, the two contracting parties have agreed to consider as Texian vessels, those which shall be bona fide the exclusive and real property of a citizen or citizens of Texas, residents of the country for at least two years, and of which the captain and two-thirds of the crew, shall also be bona fide citizens of Texas.

ARTICLE 2.  It is understood, that if the Republic of Texas thinks proper, hereafter, to diminish the duties now in force on silk goods, they will maintain between the silk goods the produce of countries beyond the Cape of Good Hope, and similar goods of other countries, a difference of ten per cent. in favor of the latter. . . .

J. PINCKNEY HENDERSON,
MAL. DUC DE DALMATIE.

## 58. THE COUNCIL HOUSE FIGHT

### March 19, 1840

From Hugh McLeod, Adj. and Inspector General, San Antonio, To His Excellency M. B. Lamar, March 20, 1840, *Richmond* (Texas) *Telescope and Texas Register,* April 4, 1840 (Archives, Texas State Library, Austin; photocopy in possession of Ernest Wallace).

Disturbed by the westward advance of the whites, some Southern Comanches early in 1838 asked for peace with the Texans. President Houston, however, refused to accept their demand for a definite boundary, and when Lamar became president in December, they were waging a petty but disastrous war upon the exposed frontier. Congress; acting upon Lamar's recommendation, promptly provided for a system of frontier posts and punitive military forces.

Realizing that war would lead to their own destruction, the Comanches early in 1840 sent messengers to San Antonio to request a peace council. The overture was accepted when the Comanches agreed to cease their raids, give up their white prisoners, and restore all stolen property. Colonel Hugh McLeod and Colonel William G. Cooke, the Texas commissioners, were instructed to inform the Comanches at the peace council that they were only tenants-at-will on the Texas domain and that they must remain away from the frontier. They also were told to seize and hold as hostages those Comanches who came to the council for the safe return of all white captives still in their possession. Colonel William S. Fisher was ordered to San Antonio with three companies of his regiment to support the commissioners.

The remainder of the story, the Council House Fight, is best told by McLeod in his official report.

*San Antonio,* March 20, 1840.
To his Excellency M. B. Lamar:

Sir — On yesterday morning the 19th inst. two runners came into town and announced the arrival of the Comanches, who, about a month since, held a talk at this place, and promised to bring in the Texian prisoners in their camp. The party consisted of 65 — men, women, and children. The runners also informed us that they had with them but one prisoner (the daughter of Mr. Lockhart).

They came to town. The little girl was very intelligent, and told us that she had seen several of the other prisoners at the principal camp a few days before she left; and that they brought her in to see if they could get a high price for her, and if so, would bring in the rest, one at a time.

Having ascertained this, it became necessary to execute your orders, and take hostages for the safe return of our own people — and the order was accordingly given by Col. Wm. G. Cooke, acting Secretary of War.

Lieut. Col. Fisher, 1st infantry, was ordered to march up two companies, and place them in the immediate vicinity of the council room. The chiefs were then called together, and were asked "Where are the prisoners you promised to bring to this talk?" One of them, Muke-war-rab, the chief who held the last talk, and made the promise, replied — "We have brought in the only one we had; the others are with other tribes." A pause ensued, because, as this was a palpable lie, and a direct violation of the pledge given scarcely a month since, we had the only alternative left us. He oberved the pause, and asked quickly, "How do you like answer?"

The order was now given to march one company into the council room, and the other in the rear of the build-

ing, where the warriors were assembled. During the execution of this order, the talk was re-opened, and the terms of a treaty directed by your excellency to be made with them in the case the prisoners were restored, were discussed, and they were told the treaty would be made when they brought in the prisoners. They acknowledged that they had violated all their previous treaties, and yet tauntingly demanded that new confidence should be reposed in another promise to bring in the prisoners.

The troops being now posted, the chiefs and captains were told that they were *our* prisoners and would be kept as hostages for the safety of our people, then in their hands, and they might send the young men to the tribe, and as soon as our friends were restored they should be liberated.

Capt. Howard, whose company was stationed in the council house, posted sentinels at the doors and drew up his men across the room. We told the chiefs that the soldiers they saw were their guards, and descended from the platform. The chiefs immediately followed. One sprang to the door and attempted to pass the sentinel, who presented his musket, when the chief drew his knife and stabbed him. A rush was then made for the door. Capt. Howard collared one of them, and received a severe stab from him in the side. He ordered the sentinel to fire upon him, which he immediately did, and the Indian fell dead. They now all drew their knives and bows, and evidently resolved to fight to the last. Col. Fisher ordered "fire, if they resist." The Indians rushed on, attacked us desperately, and a general order to fire became necessary. The chiefs in the council house, twelve in number, were immediately shot.

The council house being cleared, Capt. Howard was ordered to form in front, to receive any who might attempt to retreat in that direction. He was subsequently relieved of command, in consequence of the severity of his wound, by Capt. Allen, who commanded the company during the rest of the action.

Capt. Redd, whose company was formed in rear of the council house, was attacked by the warriors in the yard, who fought with desperation. They were repulsed and driven into the stone houses, from which they kept up a galling fire with their bows, and a few rifles. Their arrows, when they struck, were driven to the feather.

A small party succeeded in breaking through, and gained the opposite bank of the river, but were pursued by Col. Wells, with a party of mounted men, and all killed but one, a renegade Mexican.

A single warror, who threw himself into a very strong stone house, refused every effort of his life, sent to him through the squaws, and after killing and wounding several of our men, was forced out by fire late at night, and fell as he passed the door.

In a melee action, and so unexpected, it was impossible to discriminate between the sexes, so similar in dress, and several women were shot; but when discovered, all were spared, and twenty-nine women and children remain our prisoners.

Our loss was as follows: killed — Lieut. W. M. Dunnington, 1st infantry; private Kaminski, of A. company; private Whitney, of E. company, Judge Thompson, of Houston; Judge Hood, of Bexar; Mr. Casey, of Matagorda county; and a Mexican (name unknown). Total killed 7.

### LIST OF WOUNDED.

Capt. George T. Howard, 1st infantry; Capt. Mathew Caldwell, 1st infantry; Lieut. Edward A. Thompson; private Kelly, company I; Judge Robinson; Mr. Higginbotham; Mr. Morgan; and Mr. Carson. Total wounded 8.

Capt. Howard, Lieut. Thompson, and private Kelly, very severely.

The loss of the enemy was total, with the exception of the renegade Mexican above mentioned — 35 killed, including three women and two children — and 27 women and children and two old men, captured. The Mexican was allowed to leave the quarters, and his departure was unobserved.

The regular troops did their duty, and the citizens rallied to our aid, as soon as the firing was heard.

Upwards of a hundred horses and a large quantity of buffalo robes and peltries were taken.

At the request of all the prisoners, a squaw has been liberated, and well mounted, to go to the main tribe and tell them we are willing to exchange prisoners. She promises to return in four days with our captive friends, and Col. Cooke and myself will wait here until her return. . . .

H. McLEOD,
Agt. and Inspector General.

## 59.  THE TREATIES WITH GREAT BRITAIN

From H. P. N. Gammel (comp.) *The Laws of Texas*, 1822-1897 (10 vols.; Austin, 1898), II, 880-898.

J. P. Henderson, Texas' first envoy to Britain and France, arrived in London in October, 1837, to seek recognition and commercial treaties, but he found Lord Palmerston, secretary of foreign affairs, unwilling to negotiate for a variety of reasons. He then went to Paris where he signed a treaty with France in September, 1839, and, after ascertaining that Palmerston's position was unchanged, sailed for Texas.

James Hamilton, who as a special agent to secure loans for Texas had assisted on the French treaty, was named by President Lamar as Henderson's successor. Since it no longer appeared that Texas would be annexed to the United States, Hamilton found the European diplomats more receptive to Texas advances. Completing a treaty with the Netherlands on September 18, 1840, Hamilton went to London, and in October obtained Palmerston's consent to discuss the Texas question. The negotiations led to three treaties: a treaty of commerce and navigation, containing the ordinary provisions included in commercial treaties; a "Convention," obligating Britain to mediate with Mexico in behalf of Texas; and a treaty for the suppression of the African slave trade.

The first two treaties were ratified by the Texas Senate early in 1841, but Palmerston, unwilling to take any chances on the treaty for the suppression of the African slave trade, insisted on exchanging ratifications of the three at the same time. The Texas Senate finally approved the third treaty on January 22, 1842, and ratifications of the three were exchanged in London on June 28, 1842. The extracts which follow contain the most significant provisions of the second and third treaties.

### 1. CONVENTION FOR BRITISH MEDIATION WITH MEXICO

#### November 14, 1840

#### CONVENTION

Whereas Her Majesty the Queen of the United Kingdom of Great Britain and Ireland, being desirous of putting an end to the hostilities which still continue to be carried on between Mexico and Texas, has offered Her Mediation to the Contending Parties, with a view to bring about a pacification between them; and whereas the Republic of Texas has accepted the mediation so offered; the Republic of Texas and Her Britannic Majesty have determined to settle, by means of a Convention, certain arrangements which will become necessary in the event of such pacification being effected, and have for this purpose . . . agreed upon and concluded the following Articles:

ARTICLE 1.  The Republic of Texas agrees that if, by means of the Mediation of Her Britannic Majesty, an unlimited Truce shall be established between Mexico and Texas, within thirty days after this present Convention shall have been communicated to the Mexican Government by her Britannic Majesty's Mission at Mexico; and if, within Six Months from the day on which that communication shall have been so made, Mexico shall have concluded a Treaty of Peace with Texas, then and in such case the Republic of Texas will take upon itself a portion, amounting to One Million Pounds Sterling, of the Capital of the Foreign Debt contracted by the Republic of Mexico before the 1st of January, One thousand Eight Hundred and Thirty-Five.

ARTICLE II.  The manner in which the Capital of One Million Pounds Sterling of Foreign Debt, mentioned in the preceding Article, shall be transferred from the Republic of Mexico to the Republic of Texas, shall be settled hereafter by special Agreement between the Republic of Texas and the Republic of Mexico, under the Mediation of Her Britannic Majesty.

ARTICLE III.  The present Convention shall be ratified, and the Ratifications shall be exchanged at London, as soon as possible within the space of Nine Months from this date.

In witness whereof, the respective Plenipotentiaries have signed the same, and have affixed thereto the Seals of their Arms.

Done at London, the Fourteenth day of November, in the Year of our Lord One Thousand Eight Hundred and Forty.

J. HAMILTON.
PALMERSTON.

## 2. TREATY BETWEEN THE REPUBLIC OF TEXAS AND GREAT BRITAIN FOR THE SUPPRESSION OF AFRICAN SLAVE TRADE

### November 16, 1840

Her Majesty, the Queen of the United Kingdom of Great Britain and Ireland, wishing to give fuller effect to the principles which form the basis of the Treaties which have been concluded between Great Britain and several other European powers, for the suppression of the African Slave Trade, and the Republic of Texas being likewise desirous of rendering effectual the fundamental article in her Constitution, which declares the said trade piracy, have determined to negotiate and conclude a Treaty for the more effectual extinction of this traffic. . . .

ARTICLE I. The Republic of Texas and Her Majesty, the Queen of the United Kingdom of Great Britain and Ireland, engage to prohibit African Slave Trade, either by their respective citizens or subjects, or under their respective flags, or by means of capital belonging to their respective citizens or subjects, and to declare such trade piracy. And the high contracting parties further declare, that any vessel attempting to carry on the slave trade shall, by that act alone, lose all right to claim the protection of their flag.

ARTICLE II. In order more completely to accomplish the object of the present treaty, the high contracting parties mutually consent that those ships of their respective navies which shall be provided with special warrants and orders, according to the form in Annex A, to this treaty, may visit such merchant vessels of either of the high contracting parties as may, upon reasonable grounds, be suspected of being engaged in the aforesaid traffic in slaves, or of having been fitted out for that purpose, or of having, during the voyage on which they are met with by the said cruisers, being engaged in the aforesaid traffic; and that such cruisers may detain, and send or carry away such vessels, in order that they may be brought to trial in the manner hereinafter agreed upon.

But the above mentioned right of searching merchant vessels of either of the high contracting parties, shall be exercised only by ships of war, . . . and the said right shall not be exercised within the Mediterranean sea, nor within those seas in Europe which lie without the Straits of Gibralter, and to the northward of the 37th parallel of north latitude, and within and to the eastward of the meridian of longitude, twenty degrees west of Greenwich; nor in the Gulf of Mexico, to the northward of the 25th parallel of north latitude, nor to the westward of the 90th degree of longitude, west of Greenwich.

ARTICLE III. Each of the high contracting parties reserves to itself the right to fix, according to its own convenience, the number of ships of its navy which shall be employed on the service mentioned in the second article of this treaty, and the stations on which such ships shall cruise. . . .

ARTICLE V. . . . The cruisers of the high contracting parties shall afford to each other mutual assistance, on all occasions when it may be useful that they should act in concert.

ARTICLE VI. Whenever a merchant vessel, navigating under the flag of either of the contracting parties, shall have been detained by a cruiser of the other, duly authorized to that effect, conformably to the provisions of this treaty, such merchant vessel, as also her master, her crew, her cargo, and the slaves who may be on board of her, shall be carried to such place as shall have been appointed to that end by the contracting parties, respectively; and they shall be delivered over to the authorities appointed for that purpose by the government within whose territory such place shall be, to be proceeded against before the proper tribunals, as hereinafter directed. . . .

ARTICLE VII. If the commander of a cruiser of either of the contracting parties shall have reason to suspect that a merchant vessel, navigating under convoy of, or in company with, a ship of war of the other contracting party, has been engaged in the slave trade or has been fitted out for the said trade, he is to make known his suspicions to the commander of the ship of war, who shall proceed alone to visit the suspected vessel; and if the last mentioned commander shall find that the suspicion is well founded, he shall cause the vessel, together with her master, her crew, and the cargo, and the slaves who may be on board of her, to be taken into a port of her own nation, to be proceeded against before the proper tribunals, as hereinafter directed.

ARTICLE IX. Any merchant vessel of either of the high contracting parties, which shall be visited and detained in pursuance of the provisions of this treaty, shall, unless proof be given to the contrary, be deemed to have been engaged in the African Slave Trade, or to have been fitted out for the purposes of such traffic, if any of the particulars hereinafter specified shall be found in her outfit or equipment, or to have been on board during the voyage on which the vessel was proceeding when captured, videlicet:

First: — Hatches with open gratings, instead of the close hatches which are usual in merchant vessels;

Secondly: — Divisions or bulk-heads in the hold or on deck, in greater number than are necessary for vessels engaged in lawful trade;

Thirdly: — Spare plank fitted for being laid down as a second or slave deck;

Fourthly: — Shackles, bolts, or handcuffs;

Fifthly: — A larger quantity of water in casks or in tanks, than is requisite for the consumption of the crew of the vessel, as a merchant vessel;

Sixthly: — An extraordinary number of water casks, or of other receptacles for holding liquid; unless the master shall produce a certificate from the custom-house at the place from which he cleared outwards, stating that sufficient security had been given by the owners of such vessel, that such extra quantity of casks or of other receptacles should only be used to hold palm-oil, or for other purposes of lawful commerce;

Seventhly: — A greater quantity of mess-tubs or kids, than are requisite for the use of the crew of the vessel, as a merchant vessel.

Eighthly: — A boiler, or other cooking apparatus, of an unusual size, and larger, and fitted for being made larger, than requisite for the use of the crew of the vessel as a merchant vessel; or more than one boiler, or other cooking apparatus of the ordinary size;

Ninthly: — An extraordinary quantity of rice, of the flour of Brazil manioc, or cassada, commonly called farina, of maize, or of Indian corn, or of any other article of food whatever, beyond what might probably be requisite for the use of the crew; such rice, flour, maize, Indian corn, or other articles of food, not being entered in the manifest, as part of the cargo for trade;

Tenthly: — A quantity of mats or matting, greater than is necessary for the use of the vessel as a merchant vessel.

Any one or more of these several things, if proved to have been found on board, or to have been on board during the voyage on which the vessel was proceeding when captured, shall be considered as prima facie evidence of the actual employment of the vessel in the African Slave Trade; and the vessel shall thereupon be condemned and be declared lawful prize, unless clear and incontestible evidence on the part of the master or owners shall establish, to the satisfaction of the court, that such vessel was, at the time of her detention or capture, employed in some legal pursuit; and that such of the several things, above enumerated, as were found on board her at the time of her detention, or which had been put on board her during the voyage on which she was proceeding when captured, were needed for legal purposes on that particular voyage.

ARTICLE X. A vessel detained as before mentioned, together with her master, crew, and cargo, shall be forthwith proceeded against before the proper tribunals of the country to which she belongs, and shall be tried and adjudged by, and according to, the established forms and laws in force in that country; and if, in consequence of such proceedings, the said vessel shall be found to have been employed in the African Slave Trade, or to have been fitted out for the purposes thereof, the vessel and her equipments, and her cargo of merchandize, shall be confiscated; and the master, the crew, and the accomplices shall be dealt with conformably to the laws by which they have been tried.

If the said vessel shall be confiscated, the proceeds arising from her sale shall, within six months from the date of such sale, be paid into the hands of the government of the country to which the captor belongs, to be distributed according to law among the officers and crew of the capturing ship.

ARTICLE XI. If any of the things specified in Article IX of this treaty shall be found on board, or to have been on board, of any merchant vessel, during the voyage, on which the vessel was proceeding when captured, no compensation for losses, damages, or expenses, consequent upon the detention of such vessel, shall, in any case, be granted, either to her master, or to her owner, or to any other person interested in her equipment or lading, even though sentence of condemnation

should not be pronounced against her, in consequence of her detention.

ARTICLE XII. In all cases in which a vessel shall, under this treaty, be detained as having been engaged in the African Slave Trade, or as having been fitted out for the purposes thereof, and shall be adjudged and confiscated accordingly, the government whose cruizer detained the vessel, or the government by whose tribunal the vessel may be condemned, may purchase the condemned vessel for the use of its navy, at a price to be fixed by a competent person, . . .

ARTICLE XIII. When a merchant vessel, detained under this treaty, shall, upon adjudication before the proper tribunal, be held not to have been engaged in the African Slave Trade, and not to be fitted up for the purposes thereof, she shall be restored to her lawful owner or owners; and if, in the course of adjudication, it shall be proved that she has been visited and detained illegally, or without sufficient cause of suspicion; or if it shall be proved that the visit and detention have been attended with any abuse, or with vexatious acts, the commander of the cruizer, . . . or the officer who shall have been appointed to bring her in, and under whom (as the case may be) the abuse or vexatious acts shall have been committed, shall be liable to costs and damages to be paid to the master and to the owners of the vessel and cargo. . . .

ARTICLE XIV. If in the visit or detention of a merchant vessel under this treaty, any abuse or vexation shall have been committed, and if the vessel shall not have been delivered over to the jurisdiction of her own nation, the master of the vessel shall make a declaration, on oath, of the abuses or vexations of which he has to complain, and of the costs and damages to which he lays claim; and . . . the Government of the country to which the officer so charged with abuses and vexations shall belong, shall forthwith institute an inquiry into the matter; and if the complaint be proved to be valid, the said government shall cause to be paid to the master or owner, or to any other person interested either in the vessel which has been molested, on in her cargo, the proper amount of costs and damages.

ARTICLE XVI. The high contracting parties agree to ensure the immediate freedom of slaves who shall be found on board vessels detained and condemned in virtue of the stipulations of the present treaty; and, for this purpose, it is agreed that all slaves found on board a Texian vessel detained in the West Indies, shall, if the vessels be condemned by the Texian tribunals, be delivered over by the Texian to the British authorities, to be conveyed, at the expense of the British government, to some one of the British colonies in the West Indies; and in regard to Texian vessels detained on the coast of Brazil, or on the coast of Africa, it is further agreed that, in order that any slave found of board such vessels may not be exposed to the sufferings which would attend a voyage to Texas, such slaves shall . . . be carried or sent, at once, by the commander of the capturing cruizer, to one of the British settlements on the coast of Africa, the vessel herself being sent on to Galveston for adjudication. . . .

J. HAMILTON.
PALMERSTON.

## 60.  LAMAR'S ADDRESS TO THE PEOPLE OF SANTA FE

### June 5, 1841

From Charles A. Gulick and Katherine Elliott (eds.), *The Papers of Mirabeau Buonaparte Lamar* (6 vols.; Austin, 1922), III, 488-495.

By an act of December 19, 1836, the Texas Congress designated the Rio Grande from its mouth to its source as the southern and western boundary of the Republic. Along the east side of the upper Rio Grande, centering around Santa Fe, were the major settlements that had long composed the old Spanish province and later the Mexican territory of New Mexico. Those settlements had never been united to Texas, nor had they showed any disposition to support the cause of Texas. President Houston, pre-occupied with more pressing problems, took no step to assert the jurisdiction of Texas over the region. By the time Lamar became president the United States had rejected the Texas offer of annexation, the possibility of a lucrative trade with Santa Fe via Texas was attracting attention, and reports from Santa Fe indicated that the Mexican hold on that territory was weak and that the people would welcome a union with Texas. Lamar, therefore, proposed to extend the jurisdiction of Texas to the Rio Grande, and when Congress refused to authorize an expedition for that purpose, he proceeded to send it on his own responsibility. He sent along with the expedition William G. Cooke, José Antonio Navarro, and Richard F. Brenham as commissioners to establish a government under the authority of Texas in accordance with his letter of June 5, 1841, addressed "To the Inhabitants of Santa Fe and of the other portions of New Mexico, to the East of the Rio Grande."

In the following extract from the letter, Lamar showed the advantages to be derived from a union with Texas, and set forth the conditions for bringing about unification.

#### Executive Department
#### Austin City June 5th, 1841

*To the Inhabitants of Santa Fe and of the other portions of New Mexico, to the East of the Rio Grande*

FELLOW CITIZENS

Very early after assuming the duties of this official station, the present executive felt it to be his obligation to assert the Jurisdiction of the Government over the inhabited portion of the Republic; and to admit its remotest citizens to an equal participation of the blessings which have been acquired by our late glorious revolution, and made secure by a wise and liberal constitution. . . .

Believing that you are the friends of liberty, and will duly appreciate the motives by which we are actuated, we have appointed commissioners to make known to you in a distinct and definite manner, the general desire of the citizens of this Republic to receive the people of Santa Fe, as a portion of the national family, and to give to them all the protection which they themselves enjoy. This union, however, to make it agreeable to this Government, must be altogether voluntary on your part; and based on mutual interest, confidence and affection. Should you, therefore, in view of the whole matter be willing to avail yourselves of this opportunity to secure your own prosperity, as well as that of your descendents, by a prompt, cheerful and unanimous adherence to the Government of this republic we invite you to a full and unreserved intercourse and communication with our commissioners, who are instructed to extend to you every assistance and co-operation to effectuate the object desired; and, at the same time, to assure you that your religion will in no wise be interfered with by this Government. The only change we desire to effect in your affairs, is such as we wrought in our own when we broke our fetters and established our freedom; a change which was well worth the price we paid; and the blessings of which we are ready now to extend to you at the sacrafice [sic] of our own lives and fortunes, if you are ready to receive them; and if not we have ordered our commissioners, not to interrupt you in any of your rights, nor to disturb your tranquility, but to establish with you, if possible such commercial relations as you may deem conducive to your own interests and then peacibly [sic] retire from your city.

MIRABEAU B. LAMAR.

## 61.  THE FIRST COLLEGE IN TEXAS

### 1841-42

Text: *Second Annual Catalogue of Rutersville College*, Rutersville, Fayette County, Texas, 1841 (Austin, 1842).

Protestant denominations pioneered the founding of colleges in Texas. The first "college" worthy of the designation was Rutersville College, a coeducational institution located in the new town of Rutersville some six miles northeast of La Grange, which officially opened its doors on February 1, 1840, with sixty-three students in attendance. The school was established in honor of the late Martin Ruter, superintendent of the Methodist mission in Texas and active advocate of a Methodist college, by a group of associates and friends who purchased the land for its location, solicited funds, and sought congressional approval of its charter. Congress approved the charter in 1840, after it had been amended to provide for the promotion of knowledge equally accessible to all religious denominations, and endowed the institution with four sitios of land. The first faculty consisted of President Chauncey Richardson and two assistants. The main building, a two-story wooden structure, was completed in 1842. By 1844 the enrollment had climbed to 194, and for a few years the community was the leading educational center of the Republic. The Mexican War, Indian troubles, and the opening of rival institutions caused a decline in the student body, however, and in 1856 its properties were merged with the Texas Monumental and Military Institute.

Its *Second Annual Catalogue*, the major portion of which follows, provides an excellent source for an understanding of higher education in Texas during the formative years.

TERMS OF ADMISSION. Candidates for the Classical Course must be acquainted with the rudiments of the English Language, Ancient and Modern Geography, Davies' Arithmetic, Davies' First Lessons in Algebra, Anthon's Greek Grammar, Andrews' & Stoddard's Latin Grammar, Anthon's Greek and Latin Prosody, Anthon's Cicero, Cooper's Virgil, the four Gospels, or Anthon's Jacob's Greek Reader.

Those who wish to take only the English and Scientific Course, must also be acquainted with the preceding branches, except the Greek and Latin.

In all cases, satisfactory testimonials of a good moral character will be required.

Beginners in science and literature will be admitted to the Preparatory and Female Departments.

CLASSIFICATION. All the studies pursued at the College are divided into Departments or General Classes, with a Professor at the head of each. These Departments will be modified or increased as the future prosperity of the College may require.

1.—Moral Science and Belles Lettres.
2.—Mathematics.
3.—Ancient Languages and Literature.
4.—Modern Languages.
5.—Natural Science.
6.—Preparatory Department.
7.—Female Department.

The students in each Department are divided into sections, so as to accommodate their different degrees of advancement in the particular Department, without any reference to their standing in the other Departments, or to the time they have been members of the College.

Any student may take a partial or an entire course, as may suit his circumstances; and when any one shall have completed the entire English and Scientific Course, he shall receive a degree of Bachelor of Science and English Literature. But no one will be entitled to the collegiate degree of Bachelor of Arts, except he pass a thorough and satisfactory examination in the entire Classical Course. Whenever he does this, he will be entitled to the degree, without regard to the time he may have been in the College.

COURSE OF STUDY I. *Department of Moral Science and Belles Lettres.*—Elocution, Porter's Analysis, Jamieson's Rhetoric, Hedge's Logic, Upham's Intellectual Philosophy, (2d edition), Wayland's Elements of Moral Science, Kame's Elements of Criticism, Paley's Evidences of Christianity, Wayland's Political Economy. Weekly exercises during the whole course in composition and declamation.

II. *Department of Mathematics.*—Davies' Algebra, Davies' Geometry, Davies' Plain and Spherical Trigonometry, Davies' Surveying, Navigation, Davies' Differential and Integral Calculus, Mahan's Civil Engineering, Norton's Astronomy, Natural Philosophy.

III. *Department of Ancient Languages and Literature.*—LATIN—Gould's Ovid, Anthon's Caesar, Folsom's Ovid, Anthon's Horace, Kingsley's Tacitus; Latin declamation and composition. GREEK—Graeca Majora, (vol. 1) Excerpta Historica, Excerpta Miscellanea, Excerpta Rhetorica, Excerpta Critica, Graeca Majora (vol. 2). Lyrics, &c., Aeschylus' Prometheus, Homer's Iliad (five books), Aeschines and Demosthenes de Corona, Greek composition and declamation, Eschenberg's Classical Manual, Anthon's Lempriere's Classical Dictionary, and an ancient Atlas used for reference through the whole course.

IV. *Department of Modern Languages.*—SPANISH—Neuman's and Baretti's Dictionary, José's Grammar, (by Sales), Brady's Guide, Traductor Español; Colmena Española, Estractos Españoles; FRENCH—Boyer's or Meadow's Dictionary, Levizac's Grammar, (Bolmar's Edition), Bolmar's Colloquial Phrases, Hent's Classical French Reader, Charles XII; ITALIAN—Evaglia's Dictionary, Bachi's Grammar, Bachi's Conversazione Italiane, Prose Italiane, Gerussalemme Liberatia; GERMAN—Kunst's Dictonary, Fosdick's German Introduction, Gueter's Phrase-Book, Fellen's German Reader.

V. *Department of Natural Science.*—Johnston's Turner's Chemistry, Chirography, Smith's Productive Grammar, Maltebrun's Geography, Worcester's Elements of History, Davies' Arithmetic, Davies' First Lessons in Algebra, Davies' Analytical and Descriptive Geometry, Anthon's Ancient Geography, Anthon's First Greek Lessons, Anthon's Greek Grammar, Anthon's Greek Prosody, Anthon's Greek Reader, Anthon's Cicero, Anthon's First Latin Lessons, Anthon's Latin Prosody, Andrew's & Stoddard's Latin Grammar, Cooper's Virgil, Comstock's Elements of Christianity, Comstock's Natural Philosophy, Comstock's Elements of Geology, Mineralogy and Botany, Guy's Astronomy and Burret's Geography of the Heavens.

VII. Female Department.—Students in this Department can pursue any of the studies embraced in either of the preceding Departments, and, in addition to these, may attend to Music on the Piano Forte, to Drawing and Painting.

TERMS. The Collegiate Year is divided into two Terms; the first commences on the third Monday of January, and closes on the second Thursday of June; the second commences on the third Monday of July, and closes on the second Thursday of December.

An Examination at the close of each Term. Annual Commencement on the second Thursday of December.

EXPENSES.

| | |
|---|---|
| Elementary Studies, per term, | $13.00 |
| Higher branches,      ” | 20.00 |
| ”      ”    including the languages, | 25.00 |
| Music on the Piano Forte, per quarter, | 15.00 |
| Board, including washing and fuel, per month, | 12.50 |

Tuition will be charged from the date of entrance to the close of the Term.

GENERAL INFORMATION. Daily bills of merit and demerit are kept of each student—the former denoting the excellencies, and the latter the delinquences of each, in his or her respective duties. An exhibit of these records will be furnished at the close of each term.

A College Library and Cabinet have been commenced. One of the permanent College buildings will be ready for occupancy next term. Other buildings will be erected soon.

The various professorships will be filled as the patronage of the College may require.

The College was chartered January, 1840, with University privileges.

LECTURES. Lectures will be delivered by the President semi-weekly on Moral Science and Natural Philosophy before all the students.

DONORS TO THE COLLEGE. The names of all the donors to the College will be carefully registered in a book, with the character and amount of their donations, to be kept in the College, for the inspection of visitors.

RUTERSVILLE—A SEAT OF EDUCATION. The local advantages, as a seat of education, are distinguished.

It occupies a central position in the Republic, and is as remarkable for the purity of its atmosphere, the healthfulness of its climate, and its picturesque scenery, as for the virtue, intelligence and enterprise of its society.

By a wise regulation, all establishments for the sale of intoxicating drinks, or for gaming of any description, are forever excluded from the corporation.

The public roads leading from the coast to Austin City, and from the Sabine to the Rio Grande, pass through Ruterville, giving it direct communication with every section of the Republic. . . .

## 62.  DRAWING THE BLACK BEANS: THE MIER PRISONERS

### March 25, 1843

From Thomas J. Green, *Journal of the Texian Expedition against Mier* (New York, 1845), 168-175.

Responding to the Santa Fe Expedition, the Mexicans made several raids into Texas. In September, 1842, General Adrian Woll occupied San Antonio for nine days and carried off several prominent Texans when he withdrew. Angry Texans hurriedly answered President Houston's reluctant call for volunteers to punish the raiders. General Alexander Somervell led them as far as the Rio Grande, but finding that the Mexicans had retired to the other side of the river, he ordered the expedition home. About three hundred of his men, however, refused to obey, chose Colonel W. S. Fisher as their leader, and started down the river toward Matamoros. On December 26 they lost a desperate battle at Mier to General Pedro Ampudia, and were started as prisoners toward Mexico City, but at Salado, south of Saltillo, they escaped. After nearly starving in the arid mountains, 176 of the 193 to escape were recaptured and returned to Salado. Only three reached Texas. Seventeen black and 159 white beans were placed in a vessel and each man required to draw out one. Those drawing black beans were summarily shot. Ewen Cameron, who had engineered the escape, drew a white bean but was afterwards executed by special order. The survivors were taken to Mexico City and imprisoned in Castle Perote with the prisoners of the Santa Fe Expedition and from San Antonio.

The following account of the drawing of the beans is from the pen of General Thomas J. Green, a participant.

Soon after they arrived [at the Salado on March 25, 1843], our men received the melancholy intelligence that they were to be decimated, and each tenth man shot.

It was now too late to resist the horrible order. Our men were closely ironed and drawn up in front of all their guards, with arms in readiness to fire. Could they have known it previously, they would have again charged their guards, and made them dearly pay for this last perfidious breach of national faith. It was now too late! A manly gloom and a proud defiance prevaded all countenances. They had but one alternative, and that was to invoke their country's vengeance upon their murderers, consign their souls to God, and die like men. . . .

The decimator, Colonel Domingo Huerta, who was especially nominated to this black deed after Governor Mexier refused its execution, had arrived at Salado ahead of our men. The *"Red-cap"* company were to be their executioners; those men whose lives had been so humanely spared by our men at this place on the 11th of February.

The decimation took place by the drawing of black and white beans from a small earthen mug. The white ones signified *exemption*, and the black *death*. One hundred and fifty-nine white beans were placed in the bottom of the mug, and seventeen black ones placed upon the top of them. The beans were not stirred, and had so slight a shake that it was perfectly clear they had not been mixed together. Such was their anxiety to execute Captain Cameron, and perhaps the balance of the officers, that first Cameron, and afterward they, were made to draw a bean each from the mug in this condition. . . .

He [Cameron] said, with his usual coolness, "Well, boys, we have to draw, let's be at it;" so saying, he thrust his hand into the mug, and drew out a white bean. Next came Colonel Wm. F. Wilson, who was chained to him; then Captain Wm. Ryan, and then Judge F. M. Gibson, all of whom drew white beans. Next came Captain Eastland, who drew the first black one, and then came the balance of the men. They all drew their beans with that manly dignity and firmness which showed them superior to their condition. Some of lighter temper jested over the bloody tragedy. One would say, "Boys, this beats raffling all to pieces;" another would say that "this is the tallest gambling scrape I ever was in," and such remarks. . . .

Poor Major Cocke, when he first drew the fatal bean, held it up between his forefinger and thumb, and with a smile of contempt, said, "Boys, I told you so; I never failed in my life to draw a prize;" . . .

Just previous to the firing they were bound together with cords, and their eyes being bandaged, they were set upon a log near the wall, with their backs to their executioners. They all begged the officer to shoot them in front, and at a short distance; that "they were not afraid to look death in the face." This he refused; and, to make his cruelty as refined as possible, fired at several paces, and continued the firing from ten to twelve minutes, lacerating and mangling these heroes in a manner too horrible for description. . . .

During the martyrdom of these noble patriots, the main body of our men were separated from them by a stone wall of some fifteen feet high, and heard their last agonized groans with feelings of which it would be mockery to attempt the description. The next morning, as they were marched on the road to Mexico, they passed the mangled bodies of their dead comrades, whose bones now lie bleaching upon the plains of Salado, . . .

# 63. TREATY OF BIRD'S FORT

## September 29, 1843

From E. W. Winkler (ed.), *Secret Journals of the Senate, Republic of Texas*, 1836-1845 (Austin, 1911), 288-293.

At the beginning of his second term as president of Texas, Houston considered the establishment of friendly relations with the Indians as one of the government's most pressing problems. In his message to Congress on December 20, 1841, he suggested that the Republic could secure peace and friendship with less expense by concluding treaties with the Indian tribes and establishing trading posts under proper regulations at suitable points. Congress concurred, and on July 5, 1842, Houston appointed a commission "to treat with any and all Indians on the Frontiers of Texas." Lamar's military offensive had convinced the Indians that negotiations might be more advantageous than the continuation of war, and in August they promised to attend a peace council at the Waco village on October 26, 1842. They failed to keep the appointment, but on March 31, 1843, chiefs of nine tribes agreed to attend a Grand Council for the purpose of concluding a permanent treaty of peace and friendship with the Republic of Texas.

The Grand Council convened six months later at Bird's Fort on the Trinity River, and, although the Comanches were not present, a treaty embodying the principles of Houston's peace policy was signed on September 29, 1843, and ratified by the Texas Senate on January 31, 1844. The treaty, which follows, illustrates Houston's concept of how peaceful relations between the two races might be maintained.

A Treaty of Peace and Friendship, between the Republic of Texas and the Deleware, Chickasaw, Waco, Tiwocano, Keachi, Caddo, Anadkah, Ionie, Biloxi and Cherokee tribes of Indians, concluded and signed at Bird's Fort, on the Trinity River, the 29th day of Sept 1843.

Whereas for some time past, hostilities have existed and war been carried on between the white and red men of Texas to the great injury of both parties; and whereas, a longer continuance of the same would lead to no beneficial result, but increase the evils which have so long unhappily rested upon both races; and whereas the parties are now willing to open the path of lasting peace and friendship and are desirious to establish certain solemn rules for the regulation of their mutual intercourse. Therefore, the Commissioners of the Republic of Texas and the Chiefs and headmen of the before mentioned tribes of Indians, being met in Council at Bird's Fort, on the Trinity River, the 29th Day of Sept 1843, have concluded, accepted, agreed to and signed the following articles of treaty:

Article 1. Both parties agree and declare, that they will forever live in peace, and always meet as friends and brothers. Also, that the war which may have heretofore existed between them shall cease and never be renewed.

Art. 2. They further agree and declare, that it is the duty of warriors to protect women and children, and that they will never make war upon them, or upon unarmed persons, but only upon warriors.

Art. 3. They further agree and declare, that the Indians will never unite with the enemies of Texas, nor make any treaty with them, which shall require of the Indians to take part against Texas; and that if any such proposals should ever be made to them that they will immediately communicate the same to an agent or to the President.

Art. 4. They further agree and declare, that when they learn that Texas is at war with any people, a chief will come to an agent and ask to be conducted to the President that they may commune with him.

Art. 5. They further agree and declare, that agents shall be appointed by the Government of Texas and be stationed at such places as may be deemed proper, for the purpose of hearing the complaints of the Indians and seeing that justice is done between them and the whites; and also to communicate the orders and wishes of the President to the various bands and tribes.

Art. 6. They further agree and declare, that no person shall go among the Indians to trade, except by the express authority of the Government of Texas.

Art. 7. They further agree and declare, that no white man or other person within the control of the laws of Texas shall introduce among any tribe or nation of Indians, or sell to any Indian or Indians ardent spirits or intoxicating liquors of any kind.

Art. 8. They further agree and declare, that no white man or other person, else than a regularly licensed trader shall purchase any property of an Indian or Indians without the consent of an agent of the Government of Texas.

Art. 9. They further agree and declare, that when any property is found among the whites, belonging to the Indians, it shall be the duty of the agent to see that the same is restored; and on the other hand, whenever property belonging to the whites is found among the Indians, the same shall be restored in like manner by the Chiefs on application of the owner or owners thereof through the agent.

Art. 10. They further agree and declare, that no trader shall furnish any warlike stores to the Indians, but by the express permission of the President.

Art. 11. They further agree and declare, that no person or persons shall pass the line of trading houses without the special permission of the President, and then only for friendly purposes; nor shall any person or persons reside or remain within the territory assigned to the Indians unless by express direction of the President.

Art. 12. They further agree and declare, that any person or persons who shall molest or attempt to molest the persons or property of the Indians while they remain peaceable under this treaty, shall be held guilty of felony and punished accordingly by the Government of Texas.

Art. 13. They further agree and declare, that any killing or outrage whatsoever committed by a white man, or other person within the control of the laws of Texas, upon an Indian in time of peace shall be punished by the Government of Texas in the same manner as though the Indian were a white man, and that the person so offending shall be liable to indictment and punishment in any county in the Republic.

Art. 14. They further agree and declare, that if any Indian or Indians shall kill any white person, he or they shall suffer death; and that if any Indian or Indians shall steal any property of the whites, he or they shall be punished by the tribe in presence of an agent with whipping or other punishment according to the offence.

Art. 15. They further agree and declare, that the Chiefs and Captains will not permit the Indians to cross the line for any purpose whatsoever without authority and a passport from an agent; nor sell any property to a white man unless authorized so to do by some agent.

Art. 16. They further agree and declare, that if any person or persons shall come among the Indians without authority from the President or agent, they will immediately seize and deliver him or them to some one of the agents.

Art. 17. They further agree and declare, that they will mutually surrender and deliver up all prisoners which they have of the other party for their own prisoners; and that they will not be friendly with any people or nation, or enter into treaty with them who will take prisoners from Texas, or do its citizens any injury.

Art. 18. They further agree and declare, that the President may send among the Indians such blacksmiths and other mechanics, as he may think proper for their benefit; and also that he may send schoolmasters and families for the purpose of instructing them in a knowledge of the English language and Christian religion.

Art. 19. They further agree and declare, that when the President shall send persons among the Indians, they will extend to them kind treatment and protect them from harm.

Art. 20. They further agree and declare, that the Chiefs and headmen of the Indians will cause their young men and warriors to behave themselves agreeably to the words of this treaty, or that they will punish them with death or in such other way as will compel them to keep peace and walk in the path made straight between the white and red brothers.

Art. 21. They further agree and declare, that should any difficulty or cause for war arise between the Government of Texas and the Indians, they will send their complaints to the President, and hear his answer, before they commence hostilities and the Government of Texas will do the same.

Art. 22. They further agree and declare, that the Government of Texas reserves to itself the right of working all mines, which have been, or may hereafter be discovered in the territory assigned the Indians.

Art. 23. They further agree and declare, that so soon as the Indians shall have shown that they will keep this treaty and no more make war upon the whites, nor steal horses from them, the President will authorize the traders of Texas to sell to them powder, lead, guns, spears and other arms, such as they may need for the purpose of killing game, and also make to them every year such presents as the Government of Texas may provide.

Art. 24. They further agree and declare, that the President shall make such arrangements and regulations with the several tribes of Indians, as he may think best for their peace and happiness. . . .

## 64. PRESIDENT TYLER PROPOSES ANNEXATION

### October 16, 1843

From United States, Twenty-eighth Congress, First Session, *Senate Document*, No. 341 (Washington, 1844), 37.

On September 1, 1836, the people of Texas by an overwhelming majority voted to seek annexation to the United States. The proposal was formally presented on August 4, 1837, but the United States refused to entertain the subject. When the question was introduced into congress early the next year, John Quincy Adams blocked a vote on it in the House by a filibuster. President Houston then withdrew the offer, and the congress of Texas ratified his action on January 23, 1839. There was no further negotiation until October 16, 1843, when President John Tyler, a Southern sympathizer out of harmony with his party and aroused by fear of the growing British interests in Texas and elsewhere in North America, officially proposed through Secretary of State A. P. Upshur to Isaac Van Zandt, the Texas minister at Washington, the annexation of Texas to the United States. Upshur's letter to Van Zandt follows.

Department of State
Washington, October 16, 1843

Sir: The subject of the annexation of Texas to the United States, by treaty, has engaged the serious attention of this Government, as well as of a large portion of our people. Recent occurrences in Europe, which have doubtless attracted your notice, have imparted to the subject a fresh interest, and presented it in new and important aspects. I cannot, as you will readily see, offer any positive assurance that the measure would be acceptable to all branches of this Government, but I have no difficulty of assuring you of the desire which is felt to present it, in the strongest manner, to the consideration of Congress. A treaty of annexation is considered the most proper form; and, unless the views of the Administration shall undergo a very great and unexpected change, I shall be prepared to make a proposition to that effect whenever you shall be prepared with proper powers to meet it. If you agree in this view, I respectfully suggest that no time ought to be lost, as it is highly desirable that the treaty should be presented to the Senate at as early a period as possible.

A. P. Upshur

## 65. THE TREATY OF ANNEXATION
### April 12, 1844

From United States, Twenty-eighth Congress, First Session, *Senate Document*, No. 341 (Washington, 1844), 10-13.

President John Tyler, fearful of growing British interest in America, on October 16, 1843, proposed annexing Texas by treaty as early as possible. In contrast to his earlier attitude, Houston assumed a position of indifference and caution lest Texas be placed in an awkward diplomatic situation with other nations should the treaty fail. Yet on January 29, 1844, he instructed Isaac Van Zandt, his minister at Washington, to proceed cautiously, demanding as a preliminary condition that the United States place her armed forces in position to protect Texas in the event of attack. United States Secretary of State, A. P. Upshur, who had been hesitant to give the assurances Houston demanded, was succeeded in March by John C. Calhoun, who was anxious to secure the annexation of Texas and thwart the British designs to promote the abolition of slavery. He agreed to the prerequisite, and on April 12, 1844, signed the following treaty with the Texas representatives, Van Zandt and J. P. Henderson. President Tyler urged its adoption, but the United States Senate rejected it on June 8, 1844, by a vote of thirty-five to sixteen.

*A treaty of annexation, concluded between the United States of America and the Republic of Texas, at Washington the 12th day of April, 1844.*

The people of Texas having, at the time of adopting their Constitution, expressed, by an almost unanimous vote, their desire to be incorporated into the Union of the United States, and being still desirous of the same with equal unanimity, in order to provide more effectually for their security and prosperity; and the United States, actuated solely by the desire to add to their own security and prosperity, and to meet the wishes of the Government and people of Texas, have determined to accomplish, by treaty, objects so important to their mutual and permanent welfare.

For that purpose, the President of the United States has given full powers to John C. Calhoun, Secretary of State of the said United States, and the President of the Republic of Texas has appointed, with like powers, Isaac Van Zandt and J. Pinckney Henderson, citizens of the said Republic; and the said plenipotentiaries, after exchanging their full powers, have agreed on and concluded the following articles:

Article I. The Republic of Texas, acting in conformity with the wishes of the people and every department of its Government, cedes to the United States all its territories, to be held by them in full property and sovereignty, and to be annexed to the said United States as one of their Territories, subject to the same constitutional provisions with their other Territories. This cession includes all public lots and squares, vacant lands, mines, minerals, salt lakes and springs, public edifices, fortifications, barracks, ports and harbors, navy and navy yards, docks, magazines, arms, armaments, and accoutrements, archives and public documents, public funds, debts, taxes and dues unpaid at the time of the exchange of the ratifications of this treaty.

Article II. The citizens of Texas shall be incorporated into the Union of the United States, maintained and protected in the free enjoyment of their liberty and property, and admitted, as soon as may be consistent with the principles of the Federal Constitution, to the enjoyment of all the rights, privileges, and immunities, of citizens of the United States.

Article III. All titles and claims to real estate, which are valid under the laws of Texas, shall be held to be so by the United States; and measures shall be adopted for the speedy adjudication of all unsettled claims to land, and patents shall be granted to those found to be valid.

Article IV. The public lands hereby ceded shall be subject to the laws regulating the public lands in other Territories of the United States, as far as they may be applicable; subject, however, to such alterations and changes as Congress may from time to time think proper to make. It is understood between the parties, that, if in consequence of the mode in which lands have been surveyed in Texas, or from previous grants or locations, the sixteenth section cannot be applied to the purpose of education, Congress shall make equal provision by grant of land elsewhere. And it is also further understood, that, hereafter, the books, papers, and documents of the General Land Office of Texas shall be deposited and kept at such place in Texas as the Congress of the United States shall direct.

Article V. The United States assume and agree to pay the public debts and liabilities of Texas, however created, for which the faith or credit of her Government may be bound at the time of the exchange of the ratifications of this treaty; which debts and liabilities are estimated not to exceed, in the whole, ten millions of dollars, to be ascertained and paid in the manner hereinafter stated.

The payment of the sum of three hundred and fifty thousand dollars shall be made at the Treasury of the United States, within ninety days after the exchange of the ratifications of this treaty, as follows: Two hundred and fifty thousand dollars to Frederick Dawson, of Baltimore, or his executors on the delivery of that amount of ten per cent. bonds of Texas; one hundred thousand dollars, if so much be required, in the redemption of the exchequer bills which may be in circulation at the time of the exchange of the ratifications of this treaty. For the payment of the remainder of the debts and liabilities of Texas, which, together with the amount already specified, shall not exceed ten millions of dollars, the public lands herein ceded, and the net revenue from the same, are hereby pledged.

Article VI. In order to ascertain the full amount of the debts and liabilities herein assumed, and the legality and validity thereof, four commissioners shall be appointed by the President of the United States, by and with the advice and consent of the Senate, who shall meet at Washington, Texas, within the period of six months after the exchange of the ratifications of this treaty, and may continue in session not exceeding twelve months, unless the Congress of the United States should prolong the time. They shall take an oath for the faithful discharge of their duties, and that they are not directly or indirectly interested in said claims at the time, and will not be during their continuance in office; and the said oath shall be recorded with their proceedings. In case of the death, sickness, or resignation of any of the commissioners, his or their place or places may be supplied by the appointment as aforesaid, or by the President of the United States during the recess of the Senate. They, or a majority of them, shall be authorized, under such regulations as the Congress of the United States may prescribe, to hear, examine, and decide on all questions touching the legality and validity of said claims, and shall, when a claim is allowed, issue a certificate to the claimant, stating the amount, distinguishing principal from interest. The certificates so issued shall be numbered, and entry made of the number, the name of the person to whom issued, and the amount, in a book to be kept for that purpose. They shall transmit the records of their proceedings and the book in which the certificates are entered, with the vouchers and documents produced before them, relative to the claims allowed or rejected, to the Treasury Department of the United States, to be deposited therein; and the Secretary of the Treasury shall, as soon as practicable after the receipt of the same, ascertain the aggregate amount of the debts and liabilities allowed; and if the same, when added to the amount to be paid to Federick Dawson and the sum which may be paid in the redemption of the exchequer bills, shall not exceed the estimated sum of ten millions of dollars, he shall, on the presentation of a certificate of the commissioners, issue, at the option of the holder, a new certificate for the amount, distinguishing principal from interest, and payable to him on order, out of the net proceeds of the public lands hereby ceded, or stock of the United States, for the amount allowed, including principal and interest, and bearing an interest of three per cent. per annum, from the date thereof; which stock, in addition to being made payable out of the net proceeds of the public lands hereby ceded, shall also be receivable in payment for the same cause. In case the amount of the debts and liabilities allowed, with the sums aforesaid to be paid to Frederick Dawson, and which may be paid in the redemption of the exchequer bills, shall exceed the said sum of ten millions of dollars, the said Secretary, before issuing a new certificate, or stock, as the case may be, shall make in each case such proportionable and ratable reduction on its amount as to reduce the aggregate to the said sum of ten millions of dollars; and he shall have power to make all needful rules and regulations necessary to carry into effect the powers hereby invested in him.

Article VII. Until further provision shall be made, the laws of Texas, as now existing, shall remain in force, and all executive and judicial officers of Texas, except the President, Vice-President, and heads of departments, shall retain their offices, with all power and authority appertaining thereto, and the courts of justice shall remain in all respects as now established and organized.

Article VIII. Immediately after the exchange of the ratifications of this treaty, the President of the United States, by and with the advice and consent of the Senate, shall appoint a commissioner, who shall proceed to Texas and receive the transfer of the territory thereof, and all the archives and public property, and other things herein conveyed, in the name of the United States. He shall exercise all executive authority in said territory necessary to the proper execution of the laws, until otherwise provided.

Article IX. The present treaty shall be ratified by the contracting parties, and the ratifications exchanged at the city of Washington, in six months, from the date hereof, or sooner if possible.

In witness whereof, we, the undersigned, plenipotentiaries of the United States of America and of the Republic of Texas, have signed, by virtue of our powers, the present treaty of annexation, and have hereunto affixed our seals, respectively.

Done at Washington, the twelfth day of April, eighteen hundred and forty-four.

J. C. Calhoun.
Isaac Van Zandt.
J. Pinckney Henderson.

# 66. THE TREATY OF TEHUACANA CREEK

## October 9, 1844

From the original manuscript (Archives, Texas State Library, Austin).

The Comanches, distrustful of the sincerity of Houston's peace overtures, had refused to attend the council at Bird's Fort in 1843. Since they were the most powerful and hostile Indians in Texas, President Houston sent a commission composed of J. C. Eldredge, Superintendent of Indian Affairs, Hamilton Bee, and Thomas Torrey to bring them into council. Finding the prominent Penateka chief, Paha-yuca, in present western Oklahoma, the commissioners on August 9, 1843, obtained a rather indifferent promise to attend a peace council the following April, but some of the powerful war chiefs sent word that they would negotiate with no less a person than the president of Texas.

Houston agreed to meet them, and the peace council finally got underway on October 7, 1844, on Tehuacana Creek, about nine miles east of present Waco, with representatives of the Penateka Comanches and ten other tribes in attendance. In addition to Houston, Texas was represented by Commissioners J. C. Neill, Thomas S. Smith, and E. Morehouse, Secretary of War G. W. Hill, and Attorney General G. W. Terrell; the principal spokesman for the Comanches was Chief Buffalo Hump. The major difficulty was the establishment of a mutually satisfactory boundary. Buffalo Hump insisted on a line far to the east of that proposed by Houston, and unable to reach any sort of compromise, Houston struck out the two articles establishing a boundary.

The treaty, which follows, was signed on October 9, and was ratified by the Texas Senate on January 24, 1845.

*Treaty of Peace, Friendship and Commerce,* Between the Republic of Texas and the Comanche, Keechie, Waco, Caddo, Anadahkah, Ionie, Delaware, Shawnee, Cherokee, Lepan & Tahwahkarro tribes of Indians, concluded and signed at Tahwahkarro Creek, on the 9th day of October, in the year one thousand eight hundred and forty-four.

Whereas, in time past, hostilities have existed and war been carried on between the white and red men of Texas, to the great injury of both; and whereas, a longer continuance of the same would lead to no beneficial result, but increase the evils which have so long unhappily rested upon the two races; and whereas, both parties are now willing to open the path of lasting peace, friendship and trade, and are desirous to establish certain solemn rules for the regulation of their mutual intercourse:

Therefore, the Commissioners of the Republic of Texas, and the Chiefs and Head men of the before mentioned tribes of Indians, being met in council at Tahwaccaro Creek on the ninth day of October, in the year of 1844, have concluded, accepted, agreed to and signed the following articles of treaty:

Article I. Both parties agree and declare, that they will forever live in peace, and always meet as friends and brothers. The tomahawk shall be buried, and no more blood appear in the path between them now made white. The Great Spirit will look with delight upon their friendship, and will frown in anger upon their enmity.

[Struck Out By Houston]
Art. II. They further agree and declare, that a line shall be run between them, separating the hunting grounds of the white and the red man; over which neither party shall cross without permission from the President or some agent on the line.
Art. III. They further agree and declare, that the said line shall be marked, and run from the Red River with the Upper Cross Timbers to the Camanche Peak — from thence to the old fort of San Saba, and from thence in a southwest direction to the Rio Grande. The chiefs of the Indians shall accompany those who mark the line.

Art. II. They further agree and declare, that the government of Texas shall permit no bad men to cross the line into the hunting grounds of the Indians; and that if the Indians should find any such among them,

they will bring him or them to some one of the agents, but not do any harm to his or their person or property.

Art. III. They further agree and declare, that the Indians will make no treaty with any nation at war with the people of Texas; and, also, that they will bring in and give up to some one of the agents of the Government of Texas, any and all persons who may go among them for the purpose of making or talking of war.

Art. IV. They further agree and declare, that if the Indians know of any other tribe who may be going to make war upon the people of Texas, or steal their property, they will notify the whites of the fact through some one of the agents, and prevent such tribe or tribes from carrying out their intentions.

Art. V. They further agree and declare, that the Indians shall no more steal horses or other property from the whites; and if any property should be stolen, or other mischief done by the bad men among any of the tribes, that they will punish those who do so and restore the property taken to some one of the agents.

Art. VI. They further agree and declare, that the Indians will not trade with any other people than the people of Texas, so long as they can get such goods as they need at the trading houses.

Art. VII. They further agree and declare, that the Government of Texas shall establish trading houses for the convenience and benefit of the Indians, and such articles shall be kept for the Indian trade as they may need for their support and comfort.

Art. VIII. They further agree and declare, that when peace is fully established between the white and red people, and no more war or trouble exists, the Indians shall be supplied with powder, lead, guns, spears and other arms to enable them to kill game and live in plenty.

Art. IX. They further agree and declare, that they will not permit traders to go among them, unless they are sent by the Government of Texas, or its officers.

Art. X. They further agree and declare, that the Indians will not sell any property to the whites, except such as are authorized to trade with them by the Government of Texas.

Art. XI. They further agree and declare, that the President shall appoint good men to trade with the Indians at the trading houses, so that they may not be cheated; and, also, that he shall appoint good men as agents who will speak truth to the Indians, and bear their talks to him.

Art. XII. They further agree and declare, that if the trading houses should be established below the line, to be run and marked, that the Indians shall be permitted to cross the line for the purpose of coming to trade.

Art. XIII. They further agree and declare, that no whiskey, or other intoxicating liquor, shall be sold to the Indians or furnished to them upon any pretext, either within their own limits or in any other place whatsoever.

Art. XIV. They further agree and declare, that the government of Texas shall make such presents to the Indians as the President from time to time shall deem proper.

Art. XV. They further agree and declare, that the President may send among the Indians such blacksmiths and other mechanics, as he may think best, for their benefit: and also that he may send schoolmasters and families for the purpose of instructing them in a knowledge of the English language and Christian Religion, as well as other persons to teach them how to cultivate the soil and raise corn.

Art. XVI.   They further agree and declare, that if the President should at any time send men among them to work mines, or agents to travel with them over their hunting grounds, the Indians will treat them with friendship and aid them as brothers.

Art. XVII.   They further agree and declare, that hereafter, if the Indians go to war they will not kill women and children, or take them prisoners, or injure them in any way; and that they will only fight against warriors who have arms in their hands.

Art. XVIII.   They further agree and declare, that they never will, in peace or war, harm any man that carries a white flag; but receive him as a friend and let him return again to his people in peace.

Art. XIX.   They further agree and declare, that they will mutually surrender and deliver up all the prisoners which they have of the other party for their own prisoners; and that they will not be friendly with any people or nation, or enter into treaty with them, who will take prisoners from Texas, or do its citizens any injury.

Art. XX.   They further agree and declare, that if ever hereafter trouble should grow up between the whites and Indians, they will immediately come with a white flag to some one of the agents and explain to him the facts; and he will send a messenger to the President, who will remove all trouble out of the path between the white and the red brothers.

Art. XXI.   They further agree and declare, that there shall be a general council held once a year, where chiefs from both the whites and the Indians shall attend. At the council presents will be made to the chiefs.

Art. XXII.   They further agree and declare, that the President may make such arrangements and regulations with the several tribes of Indians, as he may think best for their peace and happiness.

The foregoing articles having been read, interpreted, and fully understood by the parties, they agree to and confirm the same by sealing and signing their several names.

[The seal of the Republic of Texas and the signatures follow.]

# 67.   THE RESOLUTION ANNEXING TEXAS TO THE UNITED STATES

## March 1, 1845

From *United States Statutes at Large*, V, 797-798.

President Tyler interpreted the election of 1844 as a mandate to annex Texas, and in his message to Congress in December recommended a joint resolution, embodying the provisions of the rejected treaty, to be binding on the two countries when accepted by the government of Texas. Within a week such a resolution had been introduced in both the Senate and the House. The proposal encountered strong opposition, especially in the Senate, and was not adopted until February 28, 1845, and then in a form differing greatly from the treaty. Tyler signed the resolution, which follows, on the next day, and it was accepted by Texas on July 4.

*Resolved by the Senate and House of Representatives of the United States in Congress assembled,* That Congress doth consent that the territory properly included within, and rightfully belonging to the Republic of Texas, may be erected into a new State, to be called the State of Texas, with a republican form of government, to be adopted by the people of said republic, by deputies in convention assembled, with the consent of the existing government, in order that the same may be admitted as one of the States of this Union.

2.   *And be it further resolved,* That the foregoing consent of Congress is given upon the following conditions, and with the following guarantees, to wit: *First,* Said State to be formed, subject to the adjustment by this government of all questions of boundary that may arise with other governments; and the constitution thereof, with the proper evidence of its adoption by the people of said Republic of Texas, shall be transmitted to the President of the United States, to be laid before Congress for its final action, on or before the first day of January, one thousand eight hundred and forty-six. *Second,* Said State, when admitted into the Union, after ceding to the United States, all public edifices, fortifications, barracks, ports and harbors, navy and navy-yards, docks, magazines, arms, armaments, and all other property and means pertaining to the public defence belonging to said Republic of Texas, shall retain all the public funds, debts, taxes, and dues of every kind, which may belong to or be due and owning said republic; and shall also retain all the vacant and unappropriated lands lying within its limits, to be applied to the payment of the debts and liabilities of said Republic of Texas, and the residue of said lands, after discharging said debts and liabilities, to be disposed of as said State may direct; but in no event are said debts and liabilities to become a charge upon the Government of the United States. *Third,* New States, of convenient size, not exceeding four in number, in addition to said State of Texas, and having sufficient population, may hereafter, by the consent of said State, be formed out of the territory thereof, which shall be entitled to admission under the provisions of the federal constitution. And such States as may be formed out of that portion of said territory lying south of thirty-six degrees thirty minutes north latitude, commonly known as the Missouri compromise line, shall be admitted into the Union with or without slavery, as the people of each State asking admission may desire. And in

such State or States as shall be formed out of said territory north of said Missouri compromise line, slavery, or involuntary servitude, (except for crime,) shall be prohibited.

3. *And be it further resolved,* That if the President of the United States shall in his judgment and discretion deem it most advisable, instead of proceeding to submit the foregoing resolution of the Republic of Texas, as an overture on the part of the United States for admission, to negotiate with the Republic; then,

*Be it resolved,* That a State, to be formed out of the present Republic of Texas, with suitable extent and boundaries, and with two representatives in Congress, until the next appointment of representation, shall be admitted into the Union, by virtue of this act, on an equal footing with the existing States, as soon as the terms and conditions of such admission, and the cession of the remaining Texian territory to the United States shall be agreed upon by the Governments of Texas and the United States: And that the sum of one hundred thousand dollars be, and the same is hereby, appropriated to defray the expenses of missions and negotiations, to agree upon the terms of said admission and cession, either by treaty to be submitted to the Senate, or by articles to be submitted to the two houses of Congress, as the President may direct.

Approved, March 1, 1845.

## 68. A PRELIMINARY TREATY WITH MEXICO
### May 19, 1845

From United States, Twenty-ninth Congress, First Session, *House Executive Document,* No. II (Washington, 1845), 72-73. The official British translation is slightly different.

Upon learning that the United States had adopted a resolution to annex Texas, the British and French governments sent their ministers, Captain Charles Elliot and Count de Saligny respectively, in haste from Galveston to Washington-on-the-Brazos with an alternate proposal. Elliot and Saligny formally offered President Jones the good offices of their governments in obtaining an early and honorable settlement with Mexico on the basis of independence. After a conference with his cabinet President Jones accepted the offer of intervention, and instructed Ashbel Smith, Secretary of State, to draft conditions preliminary to a treaty of peace. Having secured Jones' promise not to accept any proposal, or to enter into any negotiations to annex Texas to any other country for a period of ninety days, Elliot hurried on a secret mission to Mexico to obtain the consent of that government to the conditions drafted by Texas. After the Mexican Congress had granted its approval, Luis G. Cuevas, Minister of Foreign Affairs, consented to the Texas proposal "as the preliminaries of a formal and definitive treaty," with the reservation that it would be void should Texas accept the offer made by the United States. His document follows.

The Minister of Foreign Affairs and Government of the Mexican Republic has received the preliminary propositions of Texas for an arrangement or definitive treaty between Mexico and Texas, which are of the following tenor: "*Conditions preliminary to a treaty of peace between Mexico and Texas.*

"1st. Mexico consents to acknowledge the independence of Texas.

"2nd. Texas engages that she will stipulate in the treaty not to annex herself or become subject to any country whatever.

"3rd. Limits and other conditions to be matter of arrangement in the final treaty.

"4th. Texas will be willing to remit disputed points respecting territory, and other matters, to the arbitration of umpires.

"Done at Washington (on the Brazos) the 29th of March, 1845.

ASHBLE SMITH,          [L. S.]
Secretary of State"

The government of the republic has asked, in consequence, of the national Congress, the authority which it has granted, and which is of the following tenor:

"The government is authorized to hear the propositions which Texas has made, and to proceed to the arrangement or celebration of the treaty, that may be fit and honorable to the republic, giving an account to Congress for its examination and approval."

In consequence of the preceding authority of the Congress of the Mexican republic, the undersigned, Minister of Foreign Affairs and Government, declares: That the supreme government receives the four articles above mentioned as the preliminaries of a formal and definitive treaty; and further, that it is disposed to commence the negotiations as Texas may desire, and to receive the commissioners which she may name for this purpose.

LUIS G. CUEVAS,          [L. S.]

Mexico, May 19, 1845.

### Additional Declaration.

It is understood that besides the four preliminary articles proposed by Texas, there are other essential and important points which ought also to be included in the negotiation, and that if this negotiation is not realized on account of circumstances, or because Texas, influenced by the law passed in the United States on annexation, should consent thereto, either directly or indirectly, then the answer which under this date is given to Texas, by the undersigned, Minister for Foreign Affairs, shall be considered as null and void.

LUIS G. CUEVAS,          [L. S.]

Mexico, May 19, 1845.

## 69.   THE ANNEXATION OFFER ACCEPTED

### July 4, 1845

From W. S. Oldham and G. W. White (comps.), *A Digest of the General Statutes Laws of the State of Texas* (Published by Authority of the Texas Legislature, February 15, 1858; Austin, 1859), 11.

On March 3, 1845, President Tyler instructed A. J. Donelson to proceed to Texas and get a prompt acceptance of the Joint Resolution of Congress. President Anson Jones, however, had signed an agreement with the British and French ministers, Charles Elliot and Count de Saligny, to delay action on annexation for ninety days while they endeavored to obtain from Mexico an immediate acknowledgement of Texas independence.

But throughout the Republic the people held mass meetings denouncing Jones for his inaction and demanding that he call a convention to consider the offer of annexation. Hoping to delay until Elliot returned from Mexico, Jones on April 15 issued a call for Congress to meet on June 16 to "consult and determine on such measures as in their wisdom may be deemed necessary for the welfare of Texas." Since the resolution specified that the offer must be accepted by the representatives of the people of Texas in convention assembled, Congress could only advise Jones whether to present the resolution to the convention or negotiate a treaty, and it could accept or reject the preliminary treaty with Mexico if Elliot were successful. On May 5 Jones called for a convention to meet on July 4 in Austin, and on June 3 Elliot returned with Mexican approval of the preliminary treaty. Jones presented both proposals to Congress when it met and promised that he would give immediate effect to its expressed will. Congress on June 21 voted unanimously to reject a Mexican treaty and two days later in favor of annexation. When the Annexation Convention assembled, it promptly passed the following ordinance by a vote of fifty-five to one.

### IN CONVENTION OF THE PEOPLE OF THE REPUBLIC OF TEXAS

#### July 4, 1845

#### An Ordinance

Whereas, the Congress of the United States of America has passed resolutions providing for the annexation of Texas to that Union, which resolutions were approved by the President of the United States on the first day of March, one thousand eight hundred and forty-five; and whereas the President of the United States has submitted to Texas the first and second sections of the said resolution as the basis upon which Texas may be admitted as one of the States of the said Union; and whereas the existing government of the Republic of Texas has assented to the proposals thus made, the terms and conditions of which are as follows:

*Resolved by the Senate and House of Representatives of the United States in Congress assembled,* That Congress doth consent that the territory properly included within, and rightfully belonging to the Republic of Texas, may be erected into a new State, to be called the State of Texas, with a republican form of government, to be adopted by the people of said republic, by deputies in convention assembled, with the consent of the existing government, in order that the same may be admitted as one of the States of this Union.

2. *And be it further resolved,* That the foregoing consent of Congress is given upon the following conditions, and with the following guarantees, to wit: *First,* Said State to be formed, subject to the adjustment by this government of all questions of boundary that may arise with other governments; and the constitution thereof, with the proper evidence of its adoption by the people of said Republic of Texas, shall be transmitted to the President of the United States, to be laid before Congress for its final action, on or before the first day of January, one thousand eight hundred and forty-six. *Second,* Said State, when admitted into the Union, after ceding to the United States, all public edifices, fortifications, barracks, ports and harbors, navy and navy-yards, docks, magazines, arms, armaments, and all other property and means pertaining to the public defence belonging to said Republic of Texas, shall retain all the public funds, debts, taxes, and dues of every kind, which may belong to or be due and owning said republic; and shall also retain all the vacant and unappropriated lands lying within its limits, to be applied to the payment of the debts and liabilities of said Republic of Texas, and the residue of said lands, after discharging said debts and liabilities, to be disposed of as said State may direct; but in no event are said debts and liabilities to become a charge upon the Government of the United States. *Third,* New States, of convenient size, not exceeding four in number, in addition to said State of Texas, and having sufficient population, may hereafter, by the consent of said State, be formed out of the territory thereof, which shall be entitled to admission under the provisions of the federal constitution. And such States as may be formed out of that portion of said territory lying south of thirty-six degrees thirty minutes north latitude, commonly known as the Missouri compromise line, shall be admitted into the Union with or without slavery, as the people of each State asking admission may desire. And in such State or States as shall be formed out of said territory north of said Missouri compromise line, slavery, or involuntary servitude, (except for crime,) shall be prohibited.

Now, in order to manifest the assent of the people of this Republic as required in the above-recited portions of the said resolutions; we, the deputies of the people of Texas in Convention assembled, in their name, and by their authority, do ordain and declare, that we assent to, and accept the proposals, conditions, and guarantees contained in the first and second sections of the resolution of the Congress of the United States aforesaid.

Done at the City of Austin, Republic of Texas, July 4th, 1845.

Tho. J. Rusk, *President.*

## 70. THE TEXAS CONSTITUTION OF 1845

### August 28, 1845

From United States, Twenty-ninth Congress, First Session, *House Executive Document*, No. XVI (Washington, 1845), 2-22.

The task of preparing a constitution for the new state was assigned to the Annexation Convention, a political body generally conceded to be the ablest ever assembled in Texas. Convention members included Thomas J. Rusk, president, a participant in the Convention of 1836 and former cabinet officer; J. Pinckney Henderson, also a former cabinet officer and once minister to England and France; Isaac Van Zandt, who had been a member of the Texas Congress and a minister to the United States; R. E. B. Baylor, who had represented Alabama in the United States Congress; an ex-governor of Mississippi, Hardin R. Runnels; Abner S. Lipscomb, a protégé of John C. Calhoun, who had served as chief justice of Alabama; N. H. Darnell, recent Speaker of the Texas House of Representatives; and José Antonio Navarro, a veteran of the Convention of 1836. Almost every member had already attained, or later achieved, a distinguished record of public service.

The Constitution of 1845, characterized by Daniel Webster as the best of all American state constitutions, was modeled after that of Louisiana. Completed on August 27 and adopted unanimously the next day, it was signed by Secretary J. H. Raymond, President Rusk, and sixty other members of the Convention. President Anson Jones then called an election for October 13 for the ratification of the Constitution and to permit the voters to express their "opinions for and against annexation." In a comparatively light vote (there was little opposition) the decisions were overwhelmingly affirmative, 4,174 to 312 and 4,254 to 267, respectively. The results, certified on November 10, were then sent to Washington with copies of the Constitution. Both houses of the United States Congress approved the Constitution, 141 to 56 in the House and 31 to 14 in the Senate; and when President Polk signed the act on December 29, Texas officially became a state of the United States.

We, the people of the republic of Texas, acknowledging with gratitude the grace and beneficence of God, in permitting us to make a choice of our form of government, do, in accordance with the provisions of the joint resolution for annexing Texas to the United States, approved March first, one thousand eight hundred and forty-five, ordain and establish this constitution.

### ARTICLE I.

#### *Bill of Rights.*

That the general, great, and essential principles of liberty and free government may be recognized and established, we declare that—

Sec. 1. All political power is inherent in the people, and all free governments are founded on their authority, and instituted for their benefit; and they have at all times the unalienable right to alter, reform, or abolish their form of government, in such manner as they may think expedient.

Sec. 2. All freemen, when they form a social compact, have equal rights; and no man or set of men is entitled to exclusive, separate public emoluments or privileges, but in consideration of public services.

Sec. 3. No religious test shall ever be required as a qualification to any office or public trust in this State.

Sec. 4. All men have a natural and indefeasible right to worship God according to the dictates of their own consciences; no man shall be compelled to attend, erect, or support any place of worship, or to maintain any ministry against his consent; no human authority ought, in any case whatever, to control or interfere with the rights of conscience in matters of religion; and no preference shall ever be given by law to any religious societies or mode of worship; but it shall be the duty of the legislature to pass such laws as may be necessary to protect every religious denomination in the peaceable enjoyment of their own mode of public worship.

Sec. 5. Every citizen shall be at liberty to speak, write, or publish his opinions on any subject, being responsible for the abuse of that privilege; and no law shall ever be passed curtailing the liberty of speech or of the press.

Sec. 6. In prosecutions for the publication of papers investigating the official conduct of officers, or men in a public capacity, or when the matter published is proper for public information, the truth thereof may be given in evidence; and in all indictments for libels, the jury shall have the right to determine the law and the facts, under the direction of the court, as in other cases.

Sec. 7. The people shall be secure in their persons, houses, papers, and possessions, from all unreasonable seizures or searches; and no warrant to search any place, or to seize any person or thing, shall issue, without describing them as near as may be; nor without probable cause, supported by oath or affirmation.

Sec. 8. In all criminal prosecutions, the accused shall have a speedy public trial, by an impartial jury; he shall not be compelled to give evidence against himself; he shall have the right of being heard by himself or counsel, or both; shall be confronted with the witnesses against him, and shall have compulsory process for obtaining witnesses in his favor; and no person shall be holden to answer for any criminal charge, but on indictment or information, except in cases arising in the land or naval forces, or offences against the laws regulating the militia.

Sec. 9. All prisoners shall be bailable by sufficient sureties, unless for capital offences, when the proof is evident, or the presumption great; but this provision shall not be so construed as to prohibit bail after indictment found, upon an examination of the evidence by a judge of the supreme or district court, upon the return of a writ of *habeas corpus,* returnable in the county where the offense is committed.

Sec. 10. The privileges of the writ of *habeas corpus* shall not be suspended, except when, in case of rebellion or invasion, the public safety may require it.

Sec. 11. Excessive bail shall not be required, nor excessive fines imposed, nor cruel or unusual punishment inflicted. All courts shall be open; and every person, for an injury done him in his lands, goods, person, or reputation, shall have remedy by due course of law.

Sec. 12. No person, for the same offense, shall be twice put in jeopardy of life or limb; nor shall a person be again put upon trial for the same offence, after a verdict of not guilty; and the right of trial by jury shall remain inviolate.

Sec. 13. Every citizen shall have the right to keep and bear arms in the lawful defence of himself or the State.

SEC. 14. No bill of attainder, *ex post facto* law, retroactive law, or any law impairing the obligation of contracts, shall be made; and no person's property shall be taken, or applied to public use, without adequate compensation being made, unless by the consent of such person.

SEC. 15. No person shall ever be imprisoned for debt.

SEC. 16. No citizen of this State shall be deprived of life, liberty, property, or privileges, outlawed, exiled, or in any manner disfranchised, except by due course of the law of the land.

SEC. 17. The military shall, at all times, be subordinate to the civil authority.

SEC. 18. Perpetuities and monopolies are contrary to the genius of a free government, and shall never be allowed; nor shall the law of primogeniture or entailments ever be in force in this State.

SEC. 19. The citizens shall have the right, in a peaceable manner, to assemble together for their common good; and to apply to those invested with the power of government for redress of grievances, or other purposes, by petition, address, or remonstrance.

SEC. 20. No power of suspending laws in this State shall be exercised, except by the legislature or its authority.

SEC. 21. To guard against transgressions of the high powers herein delegated, we declare that every thing in this "bill of rights" is excepted out of the general powers of government, and shall forever remain inviolate; and all laws contrary thereto, or to the following provisions, shall be void.

## ARTICLE II.

### *Division of the Powers of Government.*

SEC. 1. The powers of the government of the State of Texas shall be divided into three distinct departments, and each of them be confided to a separate body of magistracy, to wit: those which are legislative, to one; those which are executive, to another; and those which are judicial, to another; and no person, or collection of persons, being of one of those departments, shall exercise any power properly attached to either of the others, except in the instances herein expressly permitted.

## ARTICLE III.

### *Legislative Department.*

SEC. 1. Every free male person who shall have attained the age of twenty-one years, and who shall be a citizen of the United States, or who is, at the time of the adoption of this constitution by the Congress of the United States, a citizen of the republic of Texas, and shall have resided in this State one year next preceding an election, and the last six months within the district, county, city, or town in which he offers to vote, (Indians not taxed, Africans, and descendants of Africans, excepted,) shall be deemed a qualified elector; and should such qualified elector happen to be in any other county situated in the district in which he resides at the time of an election, he shall be permitted to vote for any district officer: *Provided,* That the qualified electors shall be permitted to vote anywhere in the State for State officers: *And provided further,* That no soldier, seaman, or marine, in the army or navy of the United States, shall be entitled to vote at any election created by this constitution.

SEC. 2. All free male persons over the age of twenty-one years, (Indians not taxed, Africans, and descendants of Africans, excepted,) who shall have resided six months in Texas immediately preceding the acceptance of this constitution by the Congress of the United States, shall be deemed qualified electors.

SEC. 3. Electors in all cases shall be privileged from arrest during their attendance at elections, and in going to and returning from the same; except in cases of treason, felony, or breach of the peace.

SEC. 4. The legislative powers of this State shall be vested in two distinct branches; the one to be styled the Senate, and the other the House of Representatives, and both together the legislature of the State of Texas. The style of all laws shall be, "Be it enacted by the legislature of the State of Texas."

SEC. 5. The members of the House of Representatives shall be chosen by the qualified electors, and their term of office shall be two years from the day of the general election; and the sessions of the legislature shall be biennial, at such times as shall be prescribed by law.

SEC. 6. No person shall be a representative unless he be a citizen of the United States, or at the time of the adoption of this constitution a citizen of the republic of Texas, and shall have been an inhabitant of this State two years next preceding his election, and the last year thereof a citizen of the county, city, or town for which he shall be chosen, and shall have attained the age of twenty-one years at the time of his election.

SEC. 7. All elections by the people shall be held at such time and places in the several counties, cities, or towns as are now, or may hereafter be, designated by law.

SEC. 8. The senators shall be chosen by the qualified electors for the term of four years; and shall be divided by lot into two classes, as nearly equal as can be. The seats of senators of the first class shall be vacated at the expiration of the first two years; and of the second class, at the expiration of four years; so that one half thereof shall be chosen biennially thereafter.

SEC. 9. Such mode of classifying new additional senators shall be observed as will as nearly as possible preserve an equality of number in each class.

SEC. 10. When a senatorial district shall be composed of two or more counties, it shall not be separated by any county belonging to another district.

SEC. 11. No person shall be a senator unless he be a citizen of the United States, or at the time of the acceptance of this constitution by the Congress of the United States a citizen of the republic of Texas, and shall have been an inhabitant of this State three years next preceding the election; and the last year thereof a resident of the district for which he shall be chosen, and have attained the age of thirty years.

SEC. 12. The House of Representatives, when assembled, shall elect a speaker and its other officers; and the Senate shall choose a president for the time being, and its other officers. Each house shall judge of the qualifications and elections of its own members; but contested elections shall be determined in such manner as shall be directed by law. Two-thirds of each house shall constitute a quorum to do business, but a smaller number may adjourn from day to day, and compel the attendance of absent members, in such manner and under such penalties as each house may provide.

SEC. 13. Each house may determine the rules of its own proceedings; punish members for disorderly conduct; and, with the consent of two-thirds, expel a member, but not a second time for the same offence.

SEC. 14. Each house shall keep a journal of its own proceedings, and publish the same; and the yeas and nays of the members of either house on any question shall, at the desire of any three members present, be entered on the journals.

SEC. 15. When vacancies happen in either house, the governor, or the person exercising the power of the governor, shall issue writs of election to fill such vacancies.

SEC. 16. Senators and representatives shall in all cases, except in treason, felony, or breach of the peace, be privileged from arrest during the session of the legislature; and, in going to and returning from the same, allowing one day for every twenty miles such member may reside from the place at which the legislature is convened.

SEC. 17. Each house may punish, by imprisonment during the session, any person, not a member, for disrespectful or disorderly conduct in its presence, or for obstructing any of its proceedings, provided such imprisonment shall not, at any one time, exceed forty-eight hours.

SEC. 18. The doors of each house shall be kept open.

SEC. 19. Neither house shall, without the consent of the other, adjourn for more than three days; nor to any other place than that in which they may be sitting, without the concurrence of both houses.

SEC. 20. Bills may originate in either house, and be amended, altered, or rejected by the other; but no bill shall have the force of a law until, on three several days, it be read in each house, and free discussion be allowed thereon, unless, in case of great emergency, four-fifths of the house in which the bill shall be pending may deem it expedient to dispense with this rule; and every bill, having passed both houses, shall be signed by the speaker and president of their respective houses.

SEC. 21. All bills for raising revenue shall originate in the House of Representatives, but the Senate may amend or reject them as other bills.

SEC. 22. After a bill or resolution has been rejected by either branch of the legislature, no bill or resolution containing the same substance shall be passed into a law during the same session.

SEC. 23. Each member of the legislature shall receive from the public treasury a compensation for his services, which may be increased or diminished by law; but no increase of compensation shall take effect during the session at which such increase shall be made.

SEC. 24. No senator or representative shall, during the term for which he may be elected, be eligible to any civil office of profit under this State which shall have been created, or the emoluments of which may have been increased, during such term; and no member of either house of the legislature shall, during the term for which he is elected, be eligible to any office or place the appointment to which may be made in whole or in part by either branch of the legislature; nor shall the members thereof be capable of voting for a member of their own body for any office whatever, except it be in such cases as are herein provided.

The president for the time being of the Senate and speaker of the House of Representatives shall be elected from their respective bodies.

SEC. 25. No judge of any court of law or equity, secretary of state, attorney general, clerk of any court of record, sheriff, or collector, or any person holding a lucrative office under the United States, or this State, or any foreign government, shall be eligible to the legislature, nor shall at the same time hold or exercise any two offices, agencies, or appointments of trust or profit under this State: *Provided,* That offices of the militia to which there is attached no annual salary, or the office of justice of the peace, shall not be deemed lucrative.

SEC. 26. No person who, at any time, may have been a collector of taxes, or who may have been otherwise intrusted with public money, shall be eligible to the legislature, or to any office of profit or trust under the State government, until he shall have obtained a discharge for the amount of such collections, and for all public moneys with which he may have been intrusted.

SEC. 27. Ministers of the gospel being, by their profession, dedicated to God, and the care of souls, ought not to be diverted from the great duties of their functions; therefore, no minister of the gospel, or priest of any denomination whatever, shall be eligible to the legislature.

SEC. 28. Elections for senators and representatives shall be general throughout the State, and shall be regulated by law.

SEC. 29. The legislature shall, at their first meeting, and in the years one thousand eight hundred and forty-eight and fifty, and every eight years thereafter, cause an enumeration to be made of all the free inhabitants (Indians not taxed, Africans, and descendants of Africans, excepted) of the State, designating, particularly, the number of qualified electors; and the whole number of representatives shall, at the several periods of making such enumeration, be fixed by the legislature, and apportioned among the several counties, cities, or towns, according to the number of free population in each, and shall not be less than forty-five, nor more than ninety.

SEC. 30. Until the first enumeration and apportionment under this constitution, the following shall be the apportionment of representatives amongst the several counties, viz:

The county of Montgomery shall elect four representatives; the counties of Red River, Harrison, Nacogdoches, Harris, and Washington, shall elect three representatives each; the counties of Fannin, Lamar, Bowie, Shelby, San Augustine, Rusk, Houston, Sabine, Liberty, Robertson, Galveston, Brazoria, Fayette, Colorado, Austin, Gonzales, and Bexar, two representatives each; the counties of Jefferson, Jasper, Brazos, Milam, Bastrop, Travis, Matagorda, Jackson, Fort Bend, Victoria, Refugio, Goliad, and San Patricio, one representative each.

SEC. 31. The whole number of senators shall, at the next session after the several periods of making the enumeration, be fixed by the legislature, and apportioned among the several districts to be established by law, according to the number of qualified electors, and shall never be less than nineteen nor more than thirty-three.

SEC. 32. Until the first enumeration, as provided for by this Constitution, the senatorial districts shall be as follows, to wit: The counties of Fannin and Lamar shall constitute the first district, and elect one senator; the counties of Red River and Bowie the second district, and elect one senator; the counties of Fannin, Lamar, Red River, and Bowie, conjointly, shall elect one senator; the county of Harrison, the third district, shall elect one senator; the counties of Nacogdoches, Rusk, and Houston, the fourth district, shall elect two senators; the counties of San Augustine and Shelby, the fifth district, shall elect one senator; the counties of Sabine and Jasper, the sixth district, shall elect one senator; the counties of Liberty and Jefferson, the seventh district, shall elect one senator; the counties of Robertson and Brazos, the eighth district, shall elect one senator; the county of Montgomery, the ninth district, shall elect one senator; the county of Harris, the tenth district, shall elect one senator; the county of Galveston, the eleventh district, shall elect one senator; the counties of Brazoria and Matagorda, the twelfth district, shall elect one senator; the counties of Austin and Fort Bend, the thirteenth district, shall elect one senator; the counties of Colorado and Fayette, the fourteenth district, shall elect one senator; the counties of Bastrop and Travis, the fifteenth district, shall elect one senator; the counties of Washington and Milam, the sixteenth district, shall elect one senator; the counties of Victoria, Gonzales, and Jackson, the seventeenth district, shall elect one senator; the county of Bexar, the eighteenth district, shall elect one senator; and the counties of Goliad, Refugio, and San Patricio, the nineteenth district, shall elect one senator.

Sec. 33. The first session of the legislature, after the adoption of this constitution by the Congress of the United States, shall be held at the city of Austin, the present seat of government, and thereafter until the year one thousand eight hundred and fifty; after which period the seat of government shall be permanently located by the people.

Sec. 34. The members of the legislature shall, at their first session, receive from the treasury of the State, as their compensation, three dollars for each day they shall be in attendance on, and three dollars for every twenty-five miles travelling to and from the place of convening, the legislature.

Sec. 35. In order to settle permanently the seat of government, an election shall be holden throughout the State, at the usual places of holding elections, on the first Monday in March, one thousand eight hundred and fifty, which shall be conducted according to law; at which time the people shall vote for such place as they may see proper, for the seat of government. The returns of said election to be transmitted to the governor by the first Monday in June. If either place voted for shall have a majority of the whole number of votes cast, then the same shall be the permanent seat of government until the year one thousand eight hundred and seventy, unless the State shall sooner be divided. But in case neither place voted for shall have the majority of the whole number of votes given in, then the governor shall issue his proclamation for an election to be holden in the same manner, on the first Monday in October, one thousand eight hundred and fifty, between the two places having the highest number of votes at the first election. The election shall be conducted in the same manner as at the first, and the returns made to the governor; and the place having the highest number of votes shall be the seat of government for the time herein before provided.

## ARTICLE IV.

### *Judicial Department.*

Sec. 1. The judicial power of this State shall be vested in one supreme court, in district courts, and in such inferior courts as the legislature may from time to time ordain and establish; and such jurisdiction may be vested in corporation courts as may be deemed necessary, and be directed by law.

Sec. 2. The supreme court shall consist of a chief justice and two associates, any two of whom shall form a quorum.

Sec. 3. The supreme court shall have appellate jurisdiction only, which shall be coextensive with the limits of the State; but in criminal cases, and in appeals from interlocutory judgments, with such exceptions and under such regulations as the legislature shall make; and the supreme court and judges thereof shall have power to issue the writ of *habeas corpus,* and, under such regulations as may be prescribed by law, may issue writs of *mandamus,* and such other writs as shall be necessary to enforce its own jurisdiction; and also compel a judge of the district court to proceed to trial and judgment in a cause; and the supreme court shall hold its sessions once every year, between the months of October and June inclusive, at not more than three places in the State.

Sec. 4. The supreme court shall appoint its own clerks, who shall hold their offices for four years, and be subject to removal by the said court for neglect of duty, misdemeanor in office, and such other causes as may be prescribed by law.

Sec. 5. The governor shall nominate, and, by and with the advice and consent of two-thirds of the Senate, shall appoint the judges of the supreme and district courts, and they shall hold their offices for six years.

Sec. 6. The State shall be divided into convenient judicial districts. For each district there shall be appointed a judge, who shall reside in the same, and hold the courts at one place in each county, and at least twice in each year, in such manner as may be prescribed by law.

Sec. 7. The judges of the supreme court shall receive a salary not less than two thousand dollars annually, and the judges of the district court a salary not less than seventeen hundred and fifty dollars annually; and the salaries of the judges shall not be increased or diminished during their continuance in office.

Sec. 8. The judges of the supreme and district courts shall be removed by the governor, on the address of two thirds of each house of the legislature, for wilful neglect of duty, or other reasonable cause, which shall not be sufficient ground for impeachment: *Provided, however,* That the cause or causes for which such removal shall be required shall be stated at length in such address, and entered on the journals of each house: *And provided further,* That the cause or causes shall be notified to the judge so intended to be removed; and he shall be admitted to a hearing in his own defence, before any vote for such address shall pass; and in all such cases the vote shall be taken by yeas and nays, and entered on the journals of each house respectively.

Sec. 9. All judges of the supreme and district courts shall, by virtue of their offices, be conservators of the peace throughout the State. The style of all writs and process shall be "the State of Texas." All prosecutions shall be carried on "in the name and by the authority of the State of Texas," and conclude "against the peace and dignity of the State."

Sec. 10. The district court shall have original jurisdiction of all criminal cases, of all suits in behalf of the State to recover penalties, forfeitures and escheats, and of all cases of divorce, and of all suits, complaints, and pleas whatever, without regard to any distinction between law and equity, when the matter in controversy shall be valued at or amount to one hundred dollars, exclusive of interest; and the said courts, or the judges thereof, shall have power to issue all writs necessary to enforce their own jurisdiction, and give them a general superintendence and control over inferior jurisdictions; and in the trial of all criminal cases, the jury trying the same shall find and assess the amount of punishment to be inflicted, or fine imposed; except in capital cases, and where the punishment or fine imposed shall be specifically imposed by law.

Sec. 11. There shall be a clerk of the district courts for each county, who shall be elected by the qualified voters for members of the legislature, and who shall hold his office for four years, subject to removal by information, or by presentment of a grand jury, and conviction by a petit jury. In case of vacancy, the judge of the district shall have the power to appoint a clerk until a regular election can be held.

Sec. 12. The governor shall nominate, and, by and with the advice and consent of two thirds of the senate, appoint an attorney general, who shall hold his office for two years; and there shall be elected by joint vote of both houses of the legislature a district attorney for each district, who shall hold his office for two years; and the duties, salaries, and perquisites of the attorney general and district attorneys shall be prescribed by law.

Sec. 13. There shall be appointed for each county a convenient number of justices of the peace, one sheriff, one coroner, and a sufficient number of constables, who shall hold their offices for two years, to be elected by the qualified voters of the district or county as the legislature may direct. Justices of the peace, sheriffs, and coroners, shall be commissioned by the governor. The sheriff shall not be eligible more than four years in every six.

Sec. 14. No judge shall sit in any case wherein he may be interested, or where either of the parties may be connected with him by affinity or consanguinity within such degrees as may be prescribed by law, or where he shall have been of counsel in the cause. When the supreme court, or any two of its members, shall be thus disqualified to hear and determine any cause or causes in said court, or when no judgment can be rendered in any case or cases in said court, by reason of the equal division of opinion of said judges, the same shall be certified to the governor of the State, who shall immediately commission the requisite number of persons learned in the law, for the trial and determination of said case or cases. When the judges of the district court are thus disqualified, the parties may, by consent, appoint a proper person to try the said case; and the judges of the said courts may exchange districts, or hold courts for each other when they may deem it expedient, and shall do so when directed by law. The dis-

qualifications of judges of inferior tribunals shall be remedied as may hereafter be by law prescribed.

Sec. 15. Inferior tribunals shall be established in each county for appointing guardians, granting letters testamentary and of administration; for settling the accounts of executors, administrators, and guardians, and for the transaction of business appertaining to estates; and the district courts shall have original and appellate jurisdiction and general control over the said inferior tribunals, and original jurisdiction and control over executors, administrators, guardians, and minors, under such regulations as may be prescribed by law.

Sec. 16. In the trial of all causes in equity in the district court, the plaintiff or defendant shall, upon application made in open court, have the right of trial by jury, to be governed by the rules and regulations prescribed in trials at law.

Sec. 17. Justices of the peace shall have such civil and criminal jurisdiction as shall be provided for by law.

Sec. 18. In all causes arising out of a contract, before any inferior judicial tribunal, when the amount in controversy shall exceed ten dollars, the plaintiff or defendant shall, upon application to the presiding officer, have the right of trial by jury.

Sec. 19. In all cases where justices of the peace, or other judicial officers of inferior tribunals, shall have jurisdiction in the trial of causes where the penalty for the violation of a law is fine or imprisonment, (except in cases of contempt,) the accused shall have the right of trial by jury.

## ARTICLE V.

### *Executive Department.*

Sec. 1. The supreme executive power of this State shall be vested in a chief magistrate, who shall be styled the governor of the State of Texas.

Sec. 2. The governor shall be elected by the qualified electors of the State at the time and places of elections for members of the legislature.

Sec. 3. The returns of every election for governor, until otherwise provided by law, shall be made out, sealed up, and transmitted to the seat of government, and directed to the speaker of the House of Representatives, who shall, during the first week of the session of the legislature thereafter, open and publish them in the presence of both houses of the legislature; the person having the highest number of votes, and being constitutionally eligible, shall be declared by the speaker, under the direction of the legislature, to be governor; but if two or more persons shall have the highest and an equal number of votes, one of them shall be immediately chosen governor by joint vote of both houses of the legislature. Contested elections for governor shall be determined by both houses of the legislature.

Sec. 4. The governor shall hold his office for the term of two years from the regular time of installation, and until his successor shall be duly qualified, but shall not be eligible for more than four years in any term of six years; he shall be at least thirty years of age, shall be a citizen of the United States, or a citizen of the State of Texas, at the time of the adoption of this constitution, and shall have resided in the same three years immediately preceding his election.

Sec. 5. He shall, at stated times, receive a compensation for his services, which shall not be increased or diminished during the term for which he shall have been elected. The first governor shall receive an annual salary of two thousand dollars, and no more.

Sec. 6. The governor shall be commander-in-chief of the army and navy of this State, and of the militia, except when they shall be called into the service of the United States.

Sec. 7. He may require information, in writing, from the officers of the executive department on any subject relating to the duties of their respective offices.

Sec. 8. He may, by proclamation, on extraordinary occasions, convene the legislature at the seat of government, or at a different place, if that should be in the actual possession of a public enemy. In case of disagreement between the two houses with respect to adjournment, he may adjourn them to such time as he shall think proper, not beyond the day of the next regular meeting of the legislature.

Sec. 9. He shall, from time to time, give to the legislature information in writing of the state of the government, and recommend to their consideration such measures as he may deem expedient.

Sec. 10. He shall take care that the laws be faithfully executed.

Sec. 11. In all criminal cases, except in those of treason and impeachment, he shall have power, after conviction, to grant reprieves and pardons; and under such rules as the legislature may prescribe, he shall have power to remit fines and forfeitures. In cases of treason, he shall have power, by and with the advice and consent of the Senate, to grant reprieves and pardons; and he may, in the recess of the Senate, respite the sentence until the end of the next session of the legislature.

Sec. 12. There shall also be a lieutenant governor, who shall be chosen at every election for governor, by the same persons and in the same manner, continue in office for the same time, and possess the same qualifications. In voting for governor and lieutenant governor, the electors shall distinguish for whom they vote as governor, and for whom as lieutenant governor. The lieutenant governor shall, by virtue of his office, be president of the Senate, and have, when in committee of the whole, a right to debate and vote on all questions, and when the Senate is equally divided, to giving the casting vote. In case of the death, resignation, removal from office, inability or refusal of the governor to serve, or of his impeachment or absence from the State, the lieutenant governor shall exercise the power and authority appertaining to the office of governor until another be chosen at the periodical election and be duly qualified, or until the governor impeached, absent, or disabled, shall be acquitted, return, or his disability be removed.

Sec. 13. Whenever the government shall be administered by the lieutenant governor, or he shall be unable to attend as president of the Senate, the Senate shall elect one of their own members as president for the time being. And if, during the vacancy of the office of governor, the lieutenant governor shall die, resign, refuse to serve, or be removed from office, or be unable to serve, or if he shall be impeached, or absent from the State, the president of the Senate for the time being shall in like manner administer the government until he shall be superseded by a governor or lieutenant governor; the lieutenant governor shall, whilst he acts as president of the Senate, receive for his services the same compensation which shall be allowed to the speaker of the House of Representatives, and no more; and during the time he administers the government as governor, shall receive the same compensation which the governor would have received had he been employed in the duties of his office, and no more. The president for the time being of the Senate shall, during the time he administers the government, receive in like manner the same compensation which the governor would have received, had he been employed in the duties of his office. If the lieutenant governor shall be required to administer the government, and shall, whilst in such administration, die, resign, or be absent from the State during the recess of the legislature, it shall be the duty of the secretary of State to convene the Senate for the purpose of choosing a president for the time being.

Sec. 14. There shall be a seal of the State, which shall be kept by the governor, and used by him officially. The said seal shall be a star of five points, encircled by an olive and live-oak branches, and the words "the State of Texas."

Sec. 15. All commissions shall be in the name, and by the authority, of the State of Texas, be sealed with the State seal, signed by the governor, and attested by the secretary of State.

Sec. 16. There shall be a secretary of State, who shall be appointed by the governor, by and with the advice and consent of the Senate, and shall continue in office during the term of service of the governor elect. He shall keep a fair register of all official acts and proceedings of the governor, and shall, when required, lay the same, and all papers, minutes, and vouchers relative thereto, before the legislature, or either house thereof; and shall perform such other duties as may be required of him by law.

Sec. 17. Every bill which shall have passed both houses of the legislature shall be presented to the governor; if he approve, he shall sign it; but if not, he shall return it, with his objections, to the house in which it shall have originated, who shall enter the objections at large upon the journals, and proceed to reconsider it; if, after such reconsideration, two-thirds of the members present shall agree to pass the bill, it shall be sent, with the objections, to the other house, by which it shall likewise be reconsidered; if approved by two-thirds of the members present of that house, it shall become a law; but in such cases, the votes of both houses shall be determined by yeas and nays, and the names of the members voting for or against the bill shall be entered on the journals of each house respectively; if any bill shall not be returned by the governor within five days (Sundays excepted) after it shall have been presented to him, the same shall be a law, in like manner as if he had signed it. Every bill presented to the governor one day previous to the adjournment of the legislature, and not returned to the house in which it originated before its adjournment, shall become a law, and have the same force and effect as if signed by the governor.

Sec. 18. Every order, resolution, or vote, to which the concurrence of both houses of the legislature may be necessary, except on questions of adjournment, shall be presented to the governor, and, before it shall take effect, be approved by him; or, being disapproved, shall be repassed by both houses according to the rules and limitations prescribed in the case of a bill.

SEC. 19. The governor, by and with the advice and consent of two-thirds of the Senate, shall appoint a convenient number of notaries public, not exceeding six for each county, who, in addition to such duties as are prescribed by law, shall discharge such other duties as the legislature may, from time to time, prescribe.

SEC. 20. Nominations to fill all vacancies that may have occurred during the recess, shall be made to the Senate during the first ten days of its session. And should any nomination so made be rejected, the same individual shall not again be nominated during the session to fill the same office. And should the governor fail to make nominations to fill any vacancy during the session of the Senate, such vacancy shall not be filled by the governor until the next meeting of the Senate.

SEC. 21. The governor shall reside, during the session of the legislature, at the place where their sessions may be held, and at all other times wherever, in their opinion, the public good may require.

SEC. 22. No person holding the office of governor shall hold any other office or commission, civil or military.

SEC. 23. A State treasurer and comptroller of public accounts shall be biennially elected by the joint ballot of both houses of the legislature; and in case of vacancy in either of said offices during the recess of the legislature, such vacancy shall be filled by the governor, which appointment shall continue until the close of the next session of the legislature thereafter.

## ARTICLE VI.

### *Militia.*

SEC. 1. The legislature shall provide by law for organizing and disciplining the militia of this State, in such manner as they shall deem expedient, not incompatible with the constitution and laws of the United States in relation thereto.

SEC. 2. Any person who conscientiously scruples to bear arms shall not be compelled to do so, but shall pay an equivalent for personal service.

SEC. 3. No licensed minister of the gospel shall be required to perform military duty, work on roads, or serve on juries in this State.

SEC. 4. The governor shall have power to call forth the militia to execute the laws of the State, to suppress insurrections, and to repel invasions.

## ARTICLE VII.

### *General provisions.*

SEC. 1. Members of the legislature, and all officers, before they enter upon the duties of their offices, shall take the following oath or affirmation: "I (A. B.) do solemnly swear, (or affirm,) that I will faithfully and impartially discharge and perform all the duties incumbent on me as _____, according to the best of my skill and ability, agreeably to the constitution and laws of the United States, and of this State; and I do further solemnly swear, (or affirm,) that since the adoption of this constitution by the Congress of the United States, I, being a citizen of this State, have not fought a duel with deadly weapons within

this State, nor out of it; nor have I sent or accepted a challenge to fight a duel with deadly weapons; nor have I acted as second in carrying a challenge, or aided, advised, or assisted any person thus offending—so help me God."

SEC. 2. Treason against this State shall consist only in levying war against it, or in adhering to its enemies—giving them aid and comfort; and no person shall be convicted of treason unless on the testimony of two witnesses to the same overt act, or his own confession in open court.

SEC. 3. Every person shall be disqualified from holding any office of trust or profit in this State, who shall have been convicted of having given or offered a bribe to procure his election or appointment.

SEC. 4. Laws shall be made to exclude from office, serving on juries, and from the right of suffrage, those who shall hereafter be convicted of bribery, perjury, forgery, or other high crimes. The privilege of free suffrage shall be supported by laws regulating elections, and prohibiting, under adequate penalties, all undue influence thereon from power, bribery, tumult, or other improper practice.

SEC. 5. Any citizen of this State who shall, after the adoption of this constitution, fight a duel with deadly weapons, or send or accept a challenge to fight a duel with deadly weapons, either within the State or out of it, or who shall act as second, or knowingly aid and assist in any manner those thus offending, shall be deprived of holding any office of trust or profit under this State.

SEC. 6. In all elections by the people, the vote shall be by ballot, until the legislature shall otherwise direct; and in all elections by the Senate and House of Representatives, jointly or separately, the vote shall be given *viva voce*, except in the election of their officers.

SEC. 7. The legislature shall provide by law for the compensation of all officers, servants, agents, and public contractors, not provided for by this constitution; and shall not grant extra compensation to any officer, agent, servant, or public contractor, after such public service shall have been performed, or contract entered into for the performance of the same; nor grant by appropriation or otherwise any amount of money out of the treasury of the State, to any individual, on a claim real or pretended, where the same shall not have been provided for by preexisting law: *Provided,* That nothing in this section shall be so construed as to affect the claims of persons against the republic of Texas, heretofore existing.

SEC. 8. No money shall be drawn from the treasury but in pursuance of specific appropriations made by law; nor shall any appropriation of money be made for a longer term than two years, except for purposes of education; and no appropriation for private or individual purposes, or for purposes of internal improvement, shall be made without the concurrence of two thirds of both houses of the legislature. A regular statement and account of the receipts and expenditures of all public money shall be published annually, in such manner as shall be prescribed by law. And in no case shall the legislature have the power to issue treasury warrants, treasury notes, or paper of any description intended to circulate as money.

SEC. 9. All civil officers shall reside within the State, and all district or county officers within their districts or counties; and shall keep their offices at such places therein as may be required by law.

SEC. 10. The duration of all offices not fixed by this constitution shall never exceed four years.

SEC. 11. Absence on the business of this State, or of the United States, shall not forfeit a residence once obtained, so as to deprive any one of the right of suffrage, or of being elected or appointed to any office under the exceptions contained in this constitution.

SEC. 12. The legislature shall have power to provide for deductions from the salaries of public officers who may neglect the performance of any duty that may be assigned them by law.

SEC. 13. No member of Congress nor person holding or exercising any office of profit or trust under the United States, or either of them, or under any foreign power, shall be eligible as a member of the legislature, or hold or exercise any office of profit or trust under this State.

SEC. 14. The legislature shall provide for a change of venue in civil and criminal cases, and for the erection of a penitentiary, at as early a day as practicable.

SEC. 15. It shall be the duty of the legislature to pass such laws as may be necessary and proper to decide differences by arbitration, when the parties shall elect that method of trial.

SEC. 16. Within five years after the adoption of this constitution, the laws, civil and criminal, shall be revised, digested, arranged, and published in such manner as the legislature shall direct; and a like revision, digest, and publication shall be made every ten years thereafter.

SEC. 17. No lottery shall be authorized by this State; and the buying or selling of lottery tickets within this State is prohibited.

SEC. 18. No divorce shall be granted by the legislature.

SEC. 19. All property, both real and personal, of the wife, owned or claimed by her before marriage, and that acquired afterwards by gift, devise, or descent, shall be her separate property; and laws shall be passed more clearly defining the rights of the wife in relation as well to her separate property as that held in common with her husband. Laws shall also be passed providing for the registration of the wife's separate property.

SEC. 20. The rights of property and of action, which have been acquired under the constitution and laws of the republic of Texas, shall not be divested; nor shall any rights or actions which have been divested, barred, or declared null and void by the constitution and laws of the republic of Texas, be re-invested, revived, or re-instated by this constitution; but the same shall remain precisely in the situation [in] which they were before the adoption of this constitution.

SEC. 21. All claims, locations, surveys, grants, and titles to land, which are declared null and void by the constitution of the republic of Texas, are and the same shall remain forever null and void.

SEC. 22. The legislature shall have power to protect by law, from forced sale, a certain portion of the property of all heads of families. The homestead of a family, not to exceed two hundred acres of land, (not included in a town or city, or any town or city lot or lots,) in value not to exceed two thousand dollars, shall not be subject to forced sale for any debts hereafter contracted; nor shall the owner, if a married man, be at liberty to alienate the same, unless by the consent of the wife, in such manner as the legislature may hereafter point out.

SEC. 23. The legislature shall provide in what cases officers shall continue to perform the duties of their offices, until their successors shall be duly qualified.

SEC. 24. Every law enacted by the legislature shall embrace but one object, and that shall be expressed in the title.

SEC. 25. No law shall be revised or amended by reference to its title; but in such case, the act revised, or section amended, shall be re-enacted and published at length.

SEC. 26. No person shall hold or exercise at the same time more than one civil office of emolument, except that of justice of the peace.

SEC. 27. Taxation shall be equal and uniform throughout the State. All property in this State shall be taxed in proportion to its value, to be ascertained as directed by law; except such property as two-thirds of both houses of the legislature may think proper to exempt from taxation. The legislature shall have power to lay an income tax, and to tax all persons pursuing any occupation, trade, or profession: *Provided,* That the term occupation shall not be construed to apply to pursuits either agricultural or mechanical.

SEC. 28. The legislature shall have power to provide by law for exempting from taxation two hundred and fifty dollars' worth of the household furniture, or other property belonging to each family in this State.

SEC. 29. The assessor and collector of taxes shall be appointed in such manner and under such regulations as the legislature may direct.

SEC. 30. No corporate body shall hereafter be created, renewed, or extended, with banking or discounting privileges.

SEC. 31. No private corporation shall be created, unless the bill creating it shall be passed by two thirds of both houses of the legislature; and two thirds of the legislature shall have power to revoke and repeal all private corporations, by making compensation for the franchise; and the State shall not be part owner of the stock or property belonging to any corporation.

SEC. 32. The legislature shall prohibit, by law, individuals from issuing bills, checks, promissory notes, or other paper, to circulate as money.

SEC. 33. The aggregate amount of debts hereafter contracted by the legislature shall never exceed the sum of one hundred thousand dollars, except in case of war, to repel invasions, or suppress insurrections; and in no case shall any amount be borrowed except by a vote of two-thirds of both houses of the legislature.

SEC. 34. The legislature shall, at the first session thereof, and may at any subsequent session, establish new counties for the convenience of the inhabitants of such new county or counties: *Provided,* That no new county shall be established which shall reduce the county or counties, or either of them, from which it shall be taken, to a less area than nine hundred square miles, (except the county of Bowie,) unless by consent of two-thirds of the legislature; nor shall any county be laid off of less contents. Every new county, as to the right of suffrage and representation, shall be considered as part of the county or counties from which it was taken, until entitled by numbers to the right of separate representation.

SEC. 35. No soldier shall, in time of peace, be quartered in the house or within the enclosure of any individual, without the consent of the owner; nor in time of war, but in a manner prescribed by law.

SEC. 36. The salaries of the governor and judges of the supreme and district courts are hereby fixed at the minimum established in the constitution, and shall not be increased for ten years.

### Mode of amending the Constitution.

SEC. 37. The legislature, whenever two thirds of each house shall deem it necessary, may propose amendments to this constitution; which proposed amendments shall be duly published in the public prints of the State, at least three months before the next general election of representives, for the consideration of the people; and it shall be the duty of the several returning officers, at the next election which shall be thus holden, to open a poll for, and make a return to the Secretary of State, of the names of all those voting for representatives, who have voted on such proposed amendments; and if, thereupon, it shall appear that a majority of all the citizens of this State, voting for representatives, have voted in favor of such proposed amendments, and two-thirds of each house of the next legislature shall, after such election and before another, ratify the same amendments by yeas and nays, they shall be valid to all intents and purposes as parts of this constitution: *Provided,* That the said proposed amendments shall, at each of the said sessions, have been read on three several days in each house.

## ARTICLE VIII.

### Slaves.

SEC. 1. The legislature shall have no power to pass laws for the emancipation of slaves without the consent of their owners, nor without paying their owners, previous to such emancipation, a full equivalent in money for the slaves so emancipated. They shall have no power to prevent emigrants to this State from bringing with them such persons as are deemed slaves by the laws of any of the United States, so long as any person of the same age or description shall be continued in slavery by the laws of this State: *Provided,* That such slave be the *bona fide* property of such emigrants: *Provided, also,* That laws shall be passed to inhibit the introduction into this State of slaves who have committed high crimes in other States or Territories. They shall have the right to pass laws to permit the owners of slaves to emancipate them, saving the rights of creditors, and preventing them from becoming a public charge. They shall have full power to pass laws which will oblige the owners of slaves to treat them with humanity; to provide for their necessary food and clothing; to abstain from all injuries to them, extending to life or limb; and, in case of their neglect or refusal to comply with the directions of such laws, to have such slave or slaves taken from such owner and sold for the benefit of such owner or owners. They may pass laws to prevent slaves from being brought into this State as merchandise only.

SEC. 2. In the prosecution of slaves for crimes of a higher grade than petit larceny, the legislature shall have no power to deprive them of an impartial trial by a petit jury.

SEC. 3. Any person who shall maliciously dismember, or deprive a slave of life, shall suffer such punishment as would be inflicted in case the like offence had been committed upon a free white person, and on the like proof, except in case of insurrection of such slave.

## ARTICLE IX.

### Impeachment.

SEC. 1. The power of impeachment shall be vested in the House of Representatives.

SEC. 2. Impeachments of the governor, lieutenant governor, attorney general, secretary of state, treasurer, comptroller, and of the judges of the district courts, shall be tried by the Senate.

SEC. 3. Impeachments of judges of the supreme court shall be tried by the Senate. When sitting as a court of impeachment the senators shall be upon oath or affirmation; and no person shall be convicted without the concurrence of two-thirds of the senators present.

SEC. 4. Judgment, in cases of impeachment, shall extend only to removal from office, and disqualification from holding any office of honor, trust, or profit, under this State; but the parties convicted shall, nevertheless, be subject to indictment, trial, and punishment according to law.

SEC. 5. All officers against whom articles of impeachment may be preferred, shall be suspended from the exercise of the duties of their office during the pendency of such impeachment. The appointing power may make a provisional appointment to fill the vacancy occasioned by the suspension of an officer, until the decision on the impeachment.

SEC. 6. The legislature shall provide for the trial, punishment, and removal from office, of all other officers of the State, by indictment or otherwise.

## ARTICLE X.

### Education.

SEC. 1. A general diffusion of knowledge being essential to the preservation of the rights and liberties of the people, it shall be the duty of the legislature of this State to make suitable provision for the support and maintenance of public schools.

SEC. 2. The legislature shall, as early as practicable, establish free schools throughout the State, and shall furnish means for their support by taxation on property; and it shall be the duty of the legislature to set apart not less than one-tenth of the annual revenue of the State derivable from taxation as a perpetual fund, which fund shall be appropriated to the support of free public schools; and no law shall ever be made diverting said fund to any other use; and, until such time as the legislature shall provide for the establishment of such schools in the several districts of the State, the fund thus created shall remain as a charge against the State, passed to the credit of the free common school fund.

SEC. 3. All public lands which have been heretofore, or may hereafter be granted for public schools, to the various counties, or other political divisions in this State, shall not be alienated in fee, nor disposed of otherwise than by lease, for a term not exceeding twenty years, in such manner as the legislature may direct.

SEC. 4. The several counties in this State which have not received their quantum of lands for the purposes of education shall be entitled to the same quantity heretofore appropriated by the Congress of the republic of Texas to other counties.

## ARTICLE XI.

SEC. 1. All certificates for head-right claims to lands, issued to fictitious persons, or which were forged, and all locations and surveys thereon, are, and the same were, null and void from the beginning.

SEC. 2. The district courts shall be opened until the first day of July, one thousand eight hundred and forty-seven, for the establishment of certificates for head-rights not recommended by the commissioners appointed under the act to detect fraudulent land certificates, and to provide for issuing patents to legal claimants; and the parties suing shall produce the like proof, and be subjected to the requisitions which were necessary, and were prescribed by law, to sustain the original application for the said certificates; and all certificates above referred to, not established or sued upon before the period limited, shall be barred; and the said certificates, and all locations and surveys thereon, shall be forever null and void; and all re-locations made on such surveys shall not be disturbed until the certificates are established, as above directed.

## ARTICLE XII.

### *Land Office.*

SEC. 1. There shall be one general land office in the State, which shall be at the seat of government, where all titles which have heretofore emanated, or may hereafter emanate, from government, shall be registered; and the legislature may establish, from time to time, such subordinate offices as they may deem requisite.

## ARTICLE XIII.

### *Schedule.*

SEC. 1. That no inconvenience may arise from a change of separate national government to a State government, it is declared that all process which shall be issued in the name of the republic of Texas prior to the organization of the State government under this constitution shall be as valid as if issued in the name of the State of Texas.

SEC. 2. The validity of all bonds and recognizances, executed in conformity with the constitution and laws of the republic of Texas, shall not be impaired by the change of government, but may be sued for and recovered in the name of the governor of the State of Texas; and all criminal prosecutions or penal actions which shall have arisen prior to the organization of the State government under this constitution, in any of the courts of the republic of Texas, shall be prosecuted to judgment and execution in the name of said State. All suits at law and equity which may be depending in any of the courts of the republic of Texas prior to the organization of the State government under this constitution shall be transferred to the proper court of the State which shall have jurisdiction of the subject-matter thereof.

SEC. 3. All laws or parts of laws now in force in the republic of Texas, which are not repugnant to the constitution of the United States, the joint resolutions for annexing Texas to the United States, or to the provisions of this constitution, shall continue and remain in force as the laws of this State, until they expire by their own limitation, or shall be altered or repealed by the legislature thereof.

SEC. 4. All fines, penalties, forfeitures and escheats, which have accrued to the republic of Texas under the constitution and laws, shall accrue to the State of Texas; and the legislature shall, by law, provide a method for determining what lands may have been forfeited or escheated.

SEC. 5. Immediately after the adjournment of this convention, the President of the republic shall issue his proclamation, directing the chief justices of the several counties of this republic, and the several chief justices and their associates are hereby required, to cause polls to be opened in their respective counties, at the established precincts, on the second Monday of October next, for the purpose of taking the sense of the people of Texas in regard to the adoption or rejection of this constitution; and the votes of all persons entitled to vote under the existing laws, or this constitution, shall be received. Each voter shall express his opinion by declaring by a *"viva voce"* vote for "the constitution accepted," or "the constitution rejected," or some words clearly expressing the intention of the voter; and at the same time the vote shall be taken in like manner for and against annexation. The election shall be conducted in conformity with the existing laws regulating elections; and the chief justices of the several counties shall carefully and promptly make duplicate returns of said polls, one of which shall be transmitted to the secretary of State of the republic of Texas, and the other deposited in the clerk's office of the county court.

SEC. 6. Upon the receipt of the said returns, or on the second Monday of November next, if the returns be not sooner made, it shall be the duty of the president, in presence of such officers of his cabinet as may be present, and of all persons who may choose to attend, to compare the votes given for the ratification or rejection of this constitution; and if it should appear from the returns that a majority of all the votes given is for the adoption of the constitution, then it shall be the duty of the president to make proclamation of that fact, and thenceforth this constitution shall be ordained and established as the constitution of the State, to go into operation and be of force and effect from and after the organization of the State government under this constitution; and the president of this republic is authorized and required to transmit to the President of the United States duplicate copies of this constitution, properly authenticated, together with certified statements of the number of votes given for the ratification thereof, and the number for rejection; one of which copies shall be transmitted by mail, and one copy by a special messenger, in sufficient time to reach the seat of government of the United States early in December next.

SEC. 7. Should this constitution be accepted by the people of Texas, it shall be the duty of the president, on or before the second Monday in November next, to issue his proclamation, directing and requiring elections to be holden in all the counties of this republic on the third Monday in December next, for the office of governor, lieutenant governor, and members of the Senate and House of Representatives of the State legislature, in accordance with the apportionment of representation directed by this constitution. The returns for members of the legislature of this State shall be made to the department of State of this republic; and those for governor and lieutenant governor shall be addressed to the speaker of the House of Representatives, endorsed "election returns of _____ county, for governor," and directed to the Department of State; and should, from any cause whatever, the chief justices of counties fail to cause to be holden any of the polls or elections provided for by this constitution, at the times and places herein directed, the people of the precincts where such failure exists are hereby authorized to choose managers, judges, and other officers, to conduct said elections.

SEC. 8. Immediately on the President of this republic receiving official information of the acceptance of this constitution by the Congress of the United States, he shall issue his proclamation convening, at an early day, the legislature of the State of Texas at the seat of government established under this constitution; and, after the said legislature shall have organized, the speaker of the House of Representatives shall, in presence of both branches of the legislature, open the returns of the elections for governor and lieutenant governor, count and compare the votes, and declare the names of the persons who shall be elected to the offices of governor and lieutenant governor, who shall forthwith be installed in their respective offices; and the legislature shall proceed, as early as practicable, to elect senators to represent this State in the Senate of the United States; and also provide for the election of representatives to the Congress of the United States. The legislature shall also adopt such measures as may be required to cede to the United States, at the proper time, all public edifices, fortifications, barracks, ports, harbors, navy and navy yards, docks, magazines, arms and armaments, and all other property and means pertaining to the public defence, now belonging to the republic of Texas; and to make the necessary preparations for transferring to the said United States all customhouses and other places for the collection of impost duties and other foreign revenues.

SEC. 9. It shall be the duty of the President of Texas, immediately after the inauguration of the governor, to deliver to him all records, public money, documents, archives, and public property of every description whatsoever, under the control of the executive branch of the government; and the governor shall dispose of the same in such manner as the legislature may direct.

SEC. 10. That no inconvenience may result from the change of government, it is declared that the laws of this republic relative to the duties of officers, both civil and military, of the same, shall remain in full force; and the duties of their several offices shall be performed in conformity, with the existing laws, until the organization of the government of the State under this constitution, or until the first day of the meeting of the legislature; that then, the offices of President, Vice President, of the President's cabinet, foreign ministers, chargés, and agents and others repugnant to this constitution, shall be superseded by the same; and that all others shall be holden and exercised until they expire by their own limitation, or be superseded by the authority of this constitution, or laws made in pursuance thereof.

SEC. 11. In case of any disability on the part of the President of the republic of Texas to act as herein required, it shall be the duty of the secretary of State of the republic of Texas, and in case of disability on the part of the secretary of State, then it shall be the duty of the attorney general of the republic of Texas, to perform the duties assigned to the President.

SEC. 12. The first general election for governor, lieutenant-governor, and members of the legislature, after the organization of the government, shall take place on the first Monday in November, one thousand eight hundred and forty-seven, and shall be held biennially thereafter on the first Monday in November, until otherwise provided by the legislature; and the governor and lieutenant-governor elected in December next shall hold their offices until the installation in office of the governor and lieutenant-governor to be elected in the year one thousand eight hundred and forty-seven.

SEC. 13. The ordinance passed by the convention on the fourth day of July, assenting to the overtures for the annexation of Texas to the United States, shall be attached to this constitution and form a part of the same.

Done in convention by the deputies of the people of Texas, at the city of Austin, this twenty-seventh day of August, in the year of our Lord one thousand eight hundred and forty-five.

In testimony whereof we have hereunto subscribed our names.

Tho. J. Rusk, *President.*

| | |
|---|---|
| John D. Anderson | Oliver Jones |
| James Armstrong | H. L. Kinney |
| Cavitt Armstrong | Henry R. Latimer |
| B. C. Bagby | Albert H. Latimer |
| R. E. B. Baylor | John M. Lewis |
| R. Bache | James Love |
| J. W. Brashear | P. O. Lumpkin |
| Geo. Wm. Brown | Sam. Lusk |
| Jas. M. Burroughs | Abner S. Lipscomb |
| John Caldwell | James S. Mayfield |
| William L. Cazneau | A. McGowen |
| Edward Clark | Archibald McNeill |
| A. S. Cunningham | J. B. Miller |
| Phil. M. Cuny | Francis Moore, jr. |
| Nicholas H. Darnell | J. Antonio Navarro |
| James Davis | W. B. Ochiltree |
| Lemuel Dale Evans | Isaac Parker |
| Gustavus A. Everts | James Power |
| Robert M. Forbes | Emery Rains |
| David Gage | H. G. Runnels |
| John Hemphill | James Scott |
| J. Pinckney Henderson | Geo. W. Smyth |
| A. W. O. Hicks | Israel Standefer |
| Jos. L. Hogg | Chas. Bellinger Stewart |
| A. C. Horton | E. H. Tarrant |
| Volney E. Howard | Isaac Van Zandt |
| Spearman Holland | Francis M. White |
| Wm. L. Hunter | George T. Wood |
| Van. R. Irion | G. W. Wright |
| Henry J. Jewett | Wm. Cock Young |

Attest:

JAMES H. RAYMOND,
*Secretary of the Convention*

## 71. "THE REPUBLIC OF TEXAS IS NO MORE"

### February 19, 1846

From Anson Jones, *Letters Relating to the History of Annexation* (2d ed.; Philadelphia, 1852), 25.

The convention that accepted the United States offer of annexation completed a state constitution on August 28, 1845. Because the outcome was certain, a referendum on annexation and the Constitution on October 13 aroused only half-hearted interest. The official *viva voce* vote as certified on November 10 was 4,174 to 312 for the Constitution, and 4,254 to 267 in favor of annexation. In the United States Congress, the House accepted the Constitution on December 16 by a vote of 141 to 56, and the Senate on December 22 gave its approval by a vote of 31 to 14. President Polk on December 29 signed the act, making Texas officially one of the United States.

A special election was held in Texas on December 15 for new state officers. In a public ceremony at noon on February 19, 1846, President Anson Jones relinquished executive authority to Governor J. P. Henderson. During the whole time of his valedictory address, delivered from a platform erected for the occasion in front of the capitol, according to the *Austin Democrat* for February 20, "the most intense emotion thrilled every bosom—tears crept unconsciously from the eyes of many a weather-beaten Texan, who had toiled and suffered and bled to establish an independent government—to win freedom for a people who were now being stricken from the roll of nations." A portion of the address follows.

*Gentlemen of the Senate and the House of Representatives:*

The great measure of annexation, so earnestly desired by the people of Texas, is happily consummated. The present occasion, so full of interest to us and to all the people of this country is an earnest of that consummation, and I am happy to tender to you my cordial congratulations on the event the most extraordinary in the annals of the world, and one which marks a bright triumph in the history of republican institutions. A government is changed both in its officers and its law; not by violence and disorder, but by the deliberate and free consent of its citizens.

I, as President of the Republic, with my officers, am now present to surrender into the hands of those whom the people have chosen, the power and the authority which we have some time held. This surrender is made with the most perfect cheerfulness. . . .

The lone star of Texas, which ten years since arose amid clouds over fields of carnage, and obscurely shone for a while, has culminated, and, following an inscrutable destiny, has passed on and become fixed forever in that glorious constellation which all freemen and lovers of freedom in the world must reverence and adore—the American Union. . . . Blending its rays with its sister stars long may it continue to shine, and may a gracious Heaven smile upon this consummation of the wishes of the two Republics, now joined together in one. "May the Union be perpetual, and may it be the means of conferring benefits and blessings upon the people of all the States," is my ardent prayer.

The final act in this great drama is now performed. The Republic of Texas is no more.

## 72. PRESIDENT POLK CLAIMS THE RIO GRANDE AS THE BOUNDARY BETWEEN TEXAS AND MEXICO

### November 10, 1845, and May 11, 1846

The annexation of Texas brought to a climax the increasingly bitter relations between Mexico and the United States. For years the Mexican government had been suspicious of the expansionist designs of the United States. In their eyes the sympathetic attitude of the American people for the Texans, during the Texas Revolution, was sufficient justification for their suspicions. The United States, on the other hand, was concerned by the continued refusal of the Mexican government to pay claims made against it by United States citizens. When the United States Congress passed the joint resolution annexing Texas, the Mexican government severed diplomatic relations on March 6, 1845. Obligated to protect Texas from an invasion by Mexican forces during the negotiations for annexation, President James K. Polk, in June, ordered General Zachary Taylor to take a position between the Nueces and the Rio Grande.

Since no further effort was made to prevent the annexation of Texas, Polk, under the impression that the Mexican government was favorable to an amicable solution, commissioned John Slidell of Louisiana, in November, as minister plenipotentiary with instructions to make proposals for the settlement of all grounds for controversy, including the boundary question as contained in the first document below.

By this time the major contention had shifted from annexation to the location of the southern boundary of Texas. The Mexican government claimed the Nueces River as the southernmost limit of Texas and the United States government insisted on the Rio Grande. When it became evident that the Mexican government could not come to terms with Slidell, Polk ordered Taylor, who had established his camp at Corpus Christi on the Nueces River, to move to the Rio Grande. Resulting skirmishes between contingents of American and Mexican troops north of the Rio Grande became the principal argument for Polk's request for war with Mexico. The portion of his message dealing with the boundary controversy is reproduced in the second document below.

### 1. POLK'S INSTRUCTIONS TO SLIDELL

#### November 10, 1845

From United States, Thirtieth Congress, First Session, *Senate Executive Document,* No. LII (Washington, 1847), 71-80.

Sir: . . . Fortunately, the joint resolution of Congress, approved 1st March, 1845, "for annexing Texas to the United States" presents the means of satisfying these claims [of citizens of the United States against the Mexican government discussed in the preceding section of these instructions], in perfect consistency with the interests, as well as the honor, of both republics. It has reserved to this government the adjustment "of all questions of boundary that may arise with other governments." This question of boundary may, therefore, be adjusted in such a manner between the two republics as to cast the burden of the debt to American claimants upon their own government, whilst it will do no injury to Mexico. . . .

In regard to the right of Texas to the boundary of the del Norte, from the mouth to the Paso, there cannot, it is apprehended, be any very serious doubt. It would be easy to establish, by the authority of our most eminent statesmen—at a time, too, when the question of the boundary of the province of Louisiana was better understood than it is at present—that is, to this extent, at least, the del Norte

was its western limit. Messrs. Monroe and Pinckney, in their communications of January 28, 1805, to Don Pedro Cevallos, then the Spanish minister of foreign relations, assert, in the strongest terms, that the boundaries of that province "are the River Perdido to the east, and the Rio Bravo to the west." They say, "the facts and principles which justify this conclusion are so satisfactory to our government, as to convince it that the United States have not a better right to the island of New Orleans under the cession referred to, (Louisiana) than they have to the whole district of territory which is above described." Mr. Jefferson was at that time President, and Mr. Madison Secretary of State; you well know how to appreciate their authority. In the subsequent negotiation with Mr. Cevallos, Messrs. Monroe and Pinckney conclusively vindicated the right of the United States as far west as the del Norte. . . .

It cannot be denied, however, that the Florida treaty of 22d February, 1819, ceded to Spain all that part of ancient Louisiana within the present limits of Texas; and the more important inquiry now is, what is the extent of the territorial rights which Texas has acquired by the sword in a righteous resistance to Mexico. In your negotiations with Mexico, the independence of Texas must be considered a settled fact, and is not to be called in question. . . .

Finally, on the 29th March, 1845, Mexico consented in the most solemn form, through the intervention of the British and French governments, to acknowledge the independence of Texas, provided she would stipulate not to annex herself or become subject to any country whatever.

It may, however, be contended on the part of Mexico, that the Nueces, and not the Rio del Norte, is the true western boundary of Texas. I need not furnish you arguments to controvert this position. You have been perfectly familiar with the subject from the beginning, and know that the jurisdiction of Texas has been extended beyond that river, and that representatives from the country between it and the del Norte have participated in the deliberations both of her congress and her convention. Besides, this portion of the territory was embraced within the limits of ancient Louisiana.

The case is different in regard to New Mexico. Santa Fe, its capital, was settled by the Spaniards more than two centuries ago; and that province has been ever since in their possession and that of the republic of Mexico. The Texans never have conquered or taken possession of it, nor have its people ever been represented in any of their legislative assemblies or conventions. . . .

Besides, it is greatly to be desired that our boundary with Mexico should now be established in such a manner as to preclude all future difficulties and disputes between the two republics. A great portion of New Mexico being on this side of the Rio Grande, and included within the limits already claimed by Texas, it may hereafter, should it remain a Mexican province, become a subject of dispute and a source of bad feeling between those who, I trust, are destined in future to be always friends.

On the other hand, if, in adjusting the boundary, the province of New Mexico should be included with the limits of the United States, this would obviate the danger of future collisions. . . .

Should the Mexican authorities prove unwilling to extend our boundary beyond the del Norte, you are, in that event, instructed to offer to assume the payment of all the just claims of citizens of the United States against Mexico, should she agree that the line shall be established along the boundary defined by the act of Congress of Texas, approved December 19, 1836, to wit: beginning at "the mouth of the Rio Grande; thence up the principal stream of said river to its sources; thence due north to the forty-second degree of north latitude."

I am, &c. James Buchanan.

John Slidell, Esq.

*Envoy Extraordinary and Minister Plenipotentiary from the United States to Mexico.*

### 2. POLK'S WAR MESSAGE

#### May 11, 1846

From James D. Richardson (ed.), *Messages and Papers of the Presidents, 1789-1897* (10 vols.; Washington, 1900), IV, 437-443.

The existing state of the relations between the United States and Mexico renders it proper that I should bring the subject to the consideration of Congress. . . .

In my message at the commencement of the present session I informed you that upon the earnest appeal both of the Congress and convention of Texas I had ordered an efficient military force to take a position "between the Nueces and the Del Norte." This had become necessary to meet a threatened invasion of Texas by the Mexican forces, for which extensive military preparations had been made. The invasion was threatened solely because Texas had determined, in accordance with a solemn resolution of the Congress of the United States, to annex herself to our Union, and under these circumstances it was plainly our duty to extend our protection over her citizens and soil.

This force was concentrated at Corpus Christi, and remained there until after I had received such information from Mexico as rendered it probable, if not certain, that the Mexican Government would refuse to receive our envoy.

Meantime Texas, by the final action of our Congress, had become an integral part of our Union. The Congress of Texas, by its act of December 19, 1836, had declared the Rio del Norte to be the boundary of that Republic. Its jurisdiction had been extended and exercised beyond the Nueces. The country between that river and the Del Norte had been represented in the Congress and in the convention of Texas, had thus taken part in the act of annexation itself, and is now included within one of our Congressional districts. Our own Congress had, moreover, with great unanimity, by the act approved December 31, 1845, recognized the country beyond the Nueces as a part of our territory by including it within our own revenue system, and a revenue officer to reside within that district has been appointed by and with the advice and consent

of the Senate. It became, therefore, of urgent necessity to provide for the defense of that portion of our country. Accordingly, on the 13th of January last instructions were issued to the general in command of these troops to occupy the left bank of the Del Norte. This river, which is the southwestern boundary of the State of Texas, is an exposed frontier. From this quarter invasion was threatened; upon it and in its immediate vicinity, in the judgment of high military experience, are the proper stations for the protecting forces of the Government. In addition to this important consideration, several others occurred to induce this movement. Among these are the facilities afforded by the ports at Brazos Santiago and the mouth of the Del Norte for the reception of supplies by sea, the stronger and more healthful military positions, the convenience for obtaining a ready and a more abundant supply of provisions, water, fuel, and forage, and the advantages which are afforded by the Del Norte in forwarding supplies to such posts as may be established in the interior and upon the Indian frontier.

The movement of the troops to the Del Norte was made by the commanding general under positive instructions to abstain from all aggressive acts toward Mexico or Mexican citizens and to regard the relations between that Republic and the United States as peaceful unless she should declare war or commit acts of hostility indicative of a state of war. He was specially directed to protect private property and respect personal rights.

The Army moved from Corpus Christi on the 11th of March, and on the 28th of that month arrived on the left bank of the Del Norte opposite to Matamoras, where it encamped on a commanding position, which has since been strengthened by the erection of fieldworks. A depot has also been established at Point Isabel, near the Brazos Santiago, 30 miles in rear of the encampment. The selection of his position was necessarily confided to the judgment of the general in command.

The Mexican forces at Matamoras assumed a belligerent attitude, and on the 12th of April General Ampudia, then in command, notified General Taylor to break up his camp within twenty-four hours and to retire beyond the Nueces River, and in the event of his failure to comply with these demands announced that arms, and arms alone, must decide the question. But no open act of hostility was committed until the 24th of April. On that day General Arista, who had succeeded to the command of the Mexican forces, communicated to General Taylor that "he considered hostilities commenced and should prosecute them." A party of dragoons of 63 men and officers were on the same day dispatched from the American camp up the Rio del Norte, on its left bank, to ascertain whether the Mexican troops had crossed or were preparing to cross the river, "became engaged with a large body of these troops, and after a short affair, in which some 16 were killed and wounded, appear to have been surrounded and compelled to surrender." . . .

Upon the pretext that Texas, a nation as independent as herself, thought proper to unite its destinies with our own, she has affected to believe that we have severed her rightful territory, and in official proclamations and manifestoes has repeatedly threatened to make war upon us for the purpose of reconquering Texas. In the meantime we have tried every effort at reconciliation. The cup of forbearance had been exhausted even before the recent information from the frontier of the Del Norte. But now, after reiterated menaces, Mexico has passed the boundary of the United States, has invaded our territory and shed American blood upon the American soil. She has proclaimed that hostilities have commenced, and that the two nations are now at war.

As war exists, and, notwithstanding all our efforts to avoid it, exists by the act of Mexico herself, we are called upon by every consideration of duty and patriotism to vindicate with decision the honor, the rights, and the interests of our country. . . .

In further vindication of our rights and defense of our territory, I invoke the prompt action of Congress to recognize the existence of the war, and to place at the disposition of the Executive the means of prosecuting the war with vigor, and thus hastening the restoration of peace. . . .

JAMES K. POLK.

## 73. A TEXAN'S VIEW OF THE WAR WITH MEXICO

### May 13, 1846

From the *Northern Standard* (Clarksville, Texas), May 13, 1846.

The news that the United States had declared war on Mexico was received in Texas with ecstatic approval. On the day after Congress declared war, Charles DeMorse, a highly talented and respected editor in the state, published the following editorial in the columns of his *Northern Standard*.

At last we have a real "sure enough" war on hand; something to warm the blood, and draw out the national enthusiasm. It seems that the "Magnanimous Mexican Nation" has at last come out of its chapparal of wordy diplomacy, treachery, meanness and bombast, and concluded for a little while, only a little while, to act like white people. There is at last—our pulses beat quickly with the thought—an opportunity to pay off a little of the debt of vengeance which has been accumulating since the massacre of the Alamo.

We trust that every man of our army, as he points his rifle and thrusts his bayonet, will think of his countrymen martyred at the Alamo, at Goliad, and at Mier, whose blood yet cries aloud from the ground for remembrance and vengeance, and taking a little closer aim or giving a little stronger thrust, will give his blow in his country's cause and an additional "God speed."

## 74. TREATY ESTABLISHING THE RIO GRANDE AS THE BOUNDARY BETWEEN TEXAS AND MEXICO

### February 2, 1848

From *United States Statutes at Large*, Vol. IX, 922-942.

The boundary between Texas and Mexico was finally settled by the Treaty of Guadalupe Hidalgo at the end of the Mexican War. The treaty was negotiated by Nicholas P. Trist. He was instructed to demand recognition of the Rio Grande boundary for which the United States would assume the claims of its citizens against the Mexican government, the sale of New Mexico and California to the United States, and a right of way across the Isthmus of Tehauntepec. When Trist's blundering negotiations hampered General Winfield Scott's progress, Scott asked for, and received, Trist's recall. But the Mexican commissioners soon became anxious to make peace, and Trist, disregarding his recall, concluded the Treaty of Guadalupe Hidalgo on February 2, 1848. The treaty, among other provisions, established the Rio Grande as the boundary from its mouth to the southern limits of New Mexico. Although Polk would have preferred more territory than ceded by Mexico in the treaty, he faced strong Whig opposition; the treaty, moreover, followed his instructions fairly closely. After some hesitation, he presented it to the Senate, where it was approved on March 10, 1848, by a vote of 38 to 14.

TREATY OF PEACE, FRIENDSHIP, LIMITS, AND SETTLEMENT BETWEEN THE UNITED STATES OF AMERICA AND THE MEXICAN REPUBLIC.

ARTICLE I. There shall be firm and universal peace between the United States of America and the Mexican republic, and between their respective countries, territories, cities, towns and people, without exception of places or persons. . . .

ARTICLE V. The boundary line between the two Republics shall commence in the Gulf of Mexico, three leagues from land, opposite the mouth of the Rio Grande, otherwise called Rio Bravo del Norte, or opposite the mouth of its deepest branch, if it should have more than one branch emptying directly into the sea; from thence up the middle of that river, following the deepest channel, where it has more than one, to the point where it strikes the southern boundary of New Mexico; thence, westwardly, along the whole southern boundary of New Mexico (which runs north of the town called *Paso*) to its western termination; thence, northward, along the western line of New Mexico, until it intersects the first branch of the River Gila; (or if it should not intersect any branch of that river, then to the point on the said line nearest to such branch, and thence in a direct line to the same;) thence down the middle of the said branch and of the said river, until it empties into the Rio Colorado; thence across the Rio Colorado, following the division line between Upper and Lower California, to the Pacific Ocean. . . . And, in order to preclude all difficulty in tracing upon the ground the limit separating Upper from Lower California, it is agreed that the said limit shall consist of a straight line drawn from the middle of the Rio Gila, where it united with the Colorado, to a point on the coast of the Pacific Ocean, distant one marine league due south of the southernmost point of the port of San Diego, . . .

ARTICLE VII. The River Gila, and the part of the Rio Bravo del Norte lying below the southern boundary of New Mexico, being, agreeably to the fifth article, divided in the middle between the two Republics, the navigation of the Gila and of the Bravo below said boundary shall be free and common to the vessels and citizens of both countries; and neither shall, without the consent of the other, construct any work that may impede or interrupt, in whole or in part, the exercise of this right; not even for the purpose of favoring new methods of navigation. . . .

ARTICLE VIII. Mexicans now established in territories previously belonging to Mexico, and which remain for the future within the limits of the United States, as defined by the present treaty, shall be free to continue where they now reside, or to remove at any time to the Mexican Republic, retaining the property which they possess in the said territories, or disposing thereof, and removing the proceeds wherever they please, without their being subjected, on this account, to any contribution, tax, or charge whatever.

Those who shall prefer to remain in the said territories may either retain the title and rights of Mexican citizens, or acquire those of citizens of the United States. But they shall be under the obligation to make their election within one year from the date of the exchange of ratifications of this treaty; and those who shall remain in the said territories after the expiration of that year without having declared their intention to retain the character of Mexicans, shall be considered to have elected to become citizens of the United States.

In the said territories, property of every kind, now belonging to Mexicans not established there, shall be in-

violably respected. The present owners, the heirs of these and all Mexicans who may hereafter acquire said property by contract, shall enjoy with respect to it guarantees equally ample as if the same belong to citizens of the United States. . . .

ARTICLE XII. In consideration of the extension acquired by the boundaries of the United States, as defined in the fifth article of the present treaty, the Government of the United States engages to pay to that of the Mexican Republic the sum of fifteen millions of dollars. . . .

ARTICLE XIII. The United States engage, moreover, to assume and pay to the claimants all the amounts now due them, and those hereafter to become due, by reason of the claims already liquidated and decided against the Mexican Republic, under the conventions between the two republics severally concluded on the eleventh day of April, eighteen hundred and thirty-nine, and on the thirtieth day of January, eighteen hundred and forty-three; so that the Mexican Republic shall be absolutely exempt, for the future, from all expense whatever on account of the said claims.

ARTICLE XIV. The United States do furthermore discharge the Mexican Republic from all claims of citizens of the United States, not heretofore decided against the Mexican Government, which may have arisen previously to the date of the signature of this treaty; which discharge shall be final and perpetual, whether the said claims be rejected or be allowed by the board of commissioners provided for in the following article, and whatever shall be the total amount of those allowed.

ARTICLE XV. The United States, exonerating Mexico from all demands on account of the claims of their citizens mentioned in the preceding article, and considering them entirely and forever cancelled, whatever their amount may be, undertake to make satisfaction for the same, to an amount not exceeding three and one-quarter millions of dollars. . . .

ARTICLE XXIII. This treaty shall be ratified . . . and the ratifications shall be exchanged in the city of Washington, or at the seat of Government of Mexico, in four months from the date of the signature hereof, or sooner if practicable.

In faith whereof we, the respective plenipotentiaries, have signed this treaty of peace, friendship, limits, and settlement, and have hereunto affixed our seals respectively. Done in quintuplicate, at the city of Guadalupe Hidalgo, on the second day of February, in the year of our Lord one thousand eight hundred and forty-eight.

N. P. Trist
Luis G. Cuevas
Bernardo Couto
Migl. Atristain

## 75. JOURNAL OF A PLANTATION

### 1848

From "Journal Kept by Stephen S. Perry during the Year 1848," published in *The Southwestern Historical Quarterly,* XXVI (October, 1922), 117-126.

The most important occupation in Texas, prior to the Civil War, was farming. The Census of 1850 showed that 25,000 persons, of the 43,000 who listed occupations, owned an aggregate of 639,111 acres of improved farmlands. The commercial crop was cotton. The most valuable food crops were corn, sweet potatoes, and sugar cane. There being 21,878 slaveowners in Texas in 1860, a slave economy existed, although only fifty-four owned one hundred slaves or more. Of these owners, more than half of the slaveholders owned five slaves or fewer. The influence of the large planters in the affairs of the state, however, was out of proportion to their numbers.

The following selection, illustrating plantation life, is from the 1848 journal of the operation of a small plantation called Peach Point, located a few miles above the mouth of the Brazos River and owned by James F. Perry, Stephen F. Austin's brother-in-law.

### JOURNAL KEPT BY STEPHEN S. PERRY DURING THE YEAR 1848

| Month & Day | Occupation | Delinquencys |
|---|---|---|
| January the 16 | Gin is runing Making rails thering down and rebuilding fences— | Allin Sick |
| 17 | Making fence, cleaning the gutters, shelling corn— Gin runing | Allen Sick 1 |
| 18 | Tearing down and rebuilding fences. Cut down the hedge in the Prairy field—Making rails Gin runing until nine oc at night | Bill Sick—1 Allen " 1 |
| 19 | Taring down and rebuilding fences. | Ben and Chaney sick 1 Allin " 1 |
| 20 | Taring down and rebuilding fences— | Allin Sick 1 |
| 21 22 | Finished rebuilding fences in the Prairy field. | Allin Sick 1 |
| 20 | Mrs. Jack's Tom commenced work | |
| 22 | Making cotton bailes, (made 16,) carryin Cotton into gin house | Allin sick 1 |
| 23 | Sunday— | Allen Sick 1 |
| 24 | Weighing cotton bailes, shelling corn | Allen sick 1 |
| 25 | Making Ben's chimley | Allin sick 1 |
| 26 | Finished Ben's chimley. Commenced rebuilding fence in the Bottom field | Allen sick Mary and Ben sick |
| 27 | Killed sixteen Hogs, cut them up and salted, part of the hands was occupied carrying cotton from the pens into the Gin Hous. Gin runing All savd and cured | Mary and Ben Allen sick Bill half a day sick— Silvey sick afternoon |
| 28 | Killed Fifteen Hogs. Cut them up and salted part of the hands was ocupied carrying cotton from the pens into the Gin House, Gin running all savd and cured | Allen sick |

| Month & Day | Ocupation | Delinquencys |
|---|---|---|
| 29 | Shelling corn all hands continued building fence. | Allen sick |
| 30 | Sunday | Allen sick |
| 31 | Taring down and rebuilding fences. Hunting sowes and pigs, put nine sowes with about forty young pigs in the Prairy field, | Allen sick |
| February the 1 | Kill'd Sixteen hogs this morning cut them and salted, continue making fence, with the women | Allen sick George " |
| 2 | Making fence and splitting railes Shiped to Aycock's landing fifteen sacks of corn, containing 40 bushels to be sent to Judge Low Galveston | George sick Allen sick |
| 3 | Making and splitting railes, continue building fence | Alen sick |
| 4 | Making cotten bails, made fifteen bailes carrying cotton in to the Gin, | Allen sick |
| 5 | Continued to bail Made seven bales, weighed, and shiped eleven to Mr Aycocks Landing Making fence, gin stoped today | Allen sick |
| 6 | Sunday | |
| 7 | Finished building the back string of fence in the Bottom field Shiped eleven bailes of cotton to Mr Aycocks Landing | Alen and Mary sick |
| 8 | Commenced pulling cotton stocks, and cleaning up the corn ground, | Allen and Mary sick, |
| 9 | Continued to pull and roll Cotton Stocks, And Cleaning up Corn Ground, | |
| 9 | Ploughes commenced today, the 9. of February | |
| 10 | Three Ploughs running, Cleaning up cotton stocks, | |
| 11 | Ploughing and cleaning up ground, | |
| 12 | Ploughing | |
| 13 | Ploughing | |
| 14 | Ploughing and braking down cotton stocks, | |
| 15 | Ploughing and braking down cotten stocks. Father with four of the men, has been repairing the Cotton press. Finished Gining today | Becksy commenced working in the field to day stoped working in the field the 7 of February |
| 16 | Ploughing and braking down cotton stocks &c &c | |
| 17 | Commenced planting corn, Continue to brake up land— | |
| 18 | Planting corn braking up land | |
| 19 | Planting corn | |
| 20 | Sunday | |

| Month & Day | Ocupation | Delinquencys |
|---|---|---|
| 21 | Planting corn and braking up land | |
| 22 | Planting corn and Ploughing | |
| 23 | Planting corn and Ploughing | |
| 24 | Planting corn and Ploughing | |
| 25 | Finished planting corn this morning Braking up land and braking down cotten stocks | George sick Silvy commenced work today having miss one week |
| 26 | Ploughing: throwing up cotten ridges in the bottom field, the ground is too hard to plough in the Prairy field, braking down cotton stocks Commence minding birds corn coming up | Ben sick Allen sick |
| 27 | Sunday | |
| 28 | Making cotton ridges braking down cotton stocks and minding birds | |
| 29 | Making cotton ridges cleaning up the suger cane ground minding birds— | Tom sick |
| March 1 | Braking up potatoe ground and making cotton ridges. Minding birds. Commenc planting cotton to day about twelve oc | Tom Sick |
| 2 | Ploughing up potato ground and making cotton ridges finished cleaning up the suger ground minding birds corn coming up very slow. | |
| 3 | Braking up cotton ridges planting cotton, Making Potato hills and cleaning out ditches in the bottom field west of the Gin, | |
| 4 | Making cotton ridges plowing cotton Making potato hills Minding birds | |
| 5 | Sunday | |
| 6 | Commenced Ploughing in the Prairy field, very good ploughing since the rain. Setting out Potato slipes Planting cotton in the bottom field— | Betsy sick this afternoon George absent to day— Westly absent Silvy working in the garden |
| 7 | Braking up cotton ground in the Prariy field. Planting Potatoes | Silvy absent |
| 8 | Braking up cotton ridges in the Prairy field Cutting up cotton stocks. Planting Potatoes | Silvy absent George absent |
| 9 | Braking up cotten ridges in the Prairy field Cutting up Cotten stocks. Commenced Planting Cotten in the Prairy field to day | Silvy absent to day George absent |
| 10 | Finished ploughing the Prairie field and also the bottom part, planting cotton in the Prairy part, finished planting sweet potatoes Minding birds corn not all up yet— | Clenon absent from the field Bob sick George absent |

| Month & Day | Ocupation | Delinquencys |
|---|---|---|
| 11 | Commenced ploughing on the north side of the turn row, next to the house in the bottom field Planting cotten in the prairy field | George absent |
| 12 | Sunday, no work don on Sunday | |
| 13 | Braking up cotton land on the west side of the turnrow next to the house Planting cotten now Cotten commince comming up | |
| 14 | Braking up cotten ridges in the Bottem field. Cotten coming up | |
| 15 | Planting cotten in the bottom field on the west side of the turnrow. Commenced braking out the midles Finished making cotten ridges | |
| 16 | Making cotten bales | Mary Ann Sick |
| 17 | Finished making cotten bales the last of this years crop Ploughing out the middles | |
| 18, 19 & 20, 21 | Absent from home Cotton coming in the Prairy field | |
| 22 | Braking out the middles in the Bottom field, Making a ditch the whole length of the string of fence in the Prairy runing East and West, cleaning out other Ditches, making fences in the around the paster— | John sick Mary Ann sick |
| 23 | Commence ploughing corn Cleaning out ditches | Mary Ann Sick John Sick |
| 24 | Ploughin corn, commence hoing corn to day, (we did not harrow our corn this year. I do not think we did right) We smothered down the ridges with the hoes | Mary Ann Sick John Sick Clenon Sick |
| 25 | Ploughing and hoing corn | John and Mary Ann Sick |
| 26 | Sunday | John & Mary Ann Sick |
| 27 | Ploughing and hoing corn | John Mary Ann Peter Sick |
| 28 | Finished Ploughing & hoing corn on the cut north of the Ditch | John Peter Mary Ann Sick Ben |
| 28 | Ploughing and hoing corn sourth of the ditch. A very good stand of corn on both cuts | John Peter Ben Mary Ann sick |
| 29 | Ploughing and hoing corn | John Mary Ann Beckey |
| 30 | Ploughing and hoing corn Sweet-Potatoes cuming up. | John Mary Ann & Beckey Tom all sick |
| 31 | Ploughing and hoing corn Commenced ploughing cotton | Beckey sick |

Synopsis of the months of January February and March,—

The months of January February and March have been exceedingly favorable to the Planters in this Latitude. Very little rain for the the last four or five years, the Winter and fall has been noted for dryness: The sun has been obscured the greater part of the months of February and March. Heavy clouds have constantly been threatening us with a deluge, the atmosphere; in consequence of this and the coold winds blowing almost constant from the north & south also the heavy dews at night with the few refreshing showers that have fallen. This keeps the earth moist & mellow & in a good condition too *moisten* the seed and bringing forth vegetation. The field is in good condition to work, all (except the prairy part which requires heavy rains being very stiff land the soil will not undergo filtering like the [bottoms] on account of the few rains and strong winds The atmosphere has become impure which has produced sickness among the negroes. They complain principally of pains in the breast and sides—rumatisoms &c &c &c— The months of February and March has been practically dry. We commenced Ploughing on the ninth of February. The ground was in an excellent condition and broke up well, we had very little rain during this month not sufficient to prevent the Ploughs from runing On the 22 of March we finished braking up the whole plantation (the middles in both cotten & corn ground) the ground was in excellent condition. Commence planting corn on the 17 day of February. Finished ploughing [planting] corn on the 25 *Feb.* Corn up on the 26. Commenced Minding birds on the 26 Febr—commenced planting cotton on the, 1, *of March* Commenced planting cotten in the Prairry field on the 9 of March. Finished planting cotton on the 26 March Cotton up on the 14 of March. Commence running round the cotten with a one horse plough on the 31 of March. hoes commenced on the 2 of

April.

Commenced ploughing corn on the 23 of March hoing corn on the 24, of March, Finished hoing and ploughing on the 31.

Planting potatoes on the seventh of March finished Planting on the 10 of March. Potatoes coming up on the 26 of March—

Stephen S. Perry

Delinquences during the months from the 17 January to the [first] of April.

Number of days sick—

| Allen |  | 24 |
|-------|------|----|
| Bill |  | Day and one-halfe |
| Silvey | Sick | 1 |
| George | " | 3 |
| May Ben | " | 4 |
| Ben | " | 3 |
| Tom | " | 3 |
| Clenen | " | 2 |
| Mary Ann | " | 11 |
| John | " | 9 |
| Peter | " | 2 |
| Bob | " | 1 |
| Beckey | " | 3 |

[On a slip of paper attached to the last sheet of the Synopsis was the following:]

Silvy absent from the field Days working at the house

|  | Days |
|--|------|
| Silvey | 11 |
| George absent | 4 |
| Becky working at the house | 14 |
| Wesly absent | 1 |

| April | Ocupation | Delinq |
|-------|-----------|--------|
| 1 | Ploughing cotten finished hoing | Beckey absent |
| 2 | Sunday | |
| 3 | Ploughing cotten and hoing cotten | Beckey Wesley Robert absent |
| 4 | Ploughing cotten and hoing cotten | George absent |
| 5 | Ploughing and hoing cotten | Mary sick |
| 6 | Ploughing and hoing cotten | George absent |
| 7 | Ploughing and hoing cotton The corn and Cotten want rain Corn wants rain worse than the cotten | George absent |
| 8 | Ploughin cotten and hoing cotten in the bottom field | George absent |
| 9 | Sunday No working to day | |
| 10 | Ploughing and hoing cotten Finished Ploughing Cotten in Bottom field. Commenced Ploughing in Bottom part of the Prairy field. | Beckey absent |
| 11 | Ploughing and hoing cotten Cleaning out the well in the pasture | Beckey Tom Simon absent from the field |

| April | Ocupation | Delinquences |
|:---:|---|---|
| 12 | Ploughing and hoing cotten finished in the Bottom field, hoing potatoes Finished Cleaning out the well in the pasture | Tom Simon Doctor cleaning out the well |
| 13 | Commenced scraping Cotton in the Prairy field. Ploughin cotten in the Prairy field | Beckey absent |
| 14 | Ploughing and hoing cotten | Beckey absent |
| 15 | Ploughing cane and hoing cotten First time the cane has been ploughed this year | Beckey absent |
| 16 | Sundy | |
| 17 | Finished hoing cotten, hoing and ploughing cane Need left this morning for Chocolet (Sam coming in his place) | Beckey absent Ben sick |
| 18 | Commenced ploughing corn hilling it up and ploughing out the middles. Corn looks very well indeed wants rain very much good stand in all of it except the cotten ground replant not all come up | Ben Beckey Betsey sick Silvey absent |
| 19 | Ploughing corn seven ploghs runing Commenc hoing this morning about 10 Oc Robert left for Choclet on the 17 of April With Need carryed two mules with him | Betsey Beckey Sick Silvey absent |
| 20 | Ploughing and hoing corn | Betsey Beckey sick Silvey absent |
| 21 | Very cloudy this morning Ploughing and hoing corn | Betsey Beckey sick Silvey absent |
| 22 | Ploughing and hoing corn | Betsey Beckey Allin Sick |
| 23 | Sundy | |
| 24 | Ploughing and hoing corn | |
| 25 | Ploughing and hoing corn | |
| 26 | Wednesday. Rained from 10 oc AM to one. Wet the ploughed ground about 2 inches. | |
| 27 | Thursday. fair (finished hoing corn 3 o'clock P.M.) | |
| 28 | Friday—Cloudy in the morning fair prospect for Rain Rained in the night' hard | |
| 29 | Saturday. Set out Sweet Potato Sprouts with 8 hands. 1 Hand Cooking old Sarah Sick 2 Hands Halling wood 2 hands Grinding in the afternoon driving up Cows & Calves 3 Hands work on the Road between Crosbys and Brazoria by order of Majr. J. P. Caldwell overseer | |
| May 1 | Monday May 1st. 4 ploughs started again in Cotten plowing Cotten on the cut N.E. of Gin. 12 Hoe Hands finished seting out potatoes before Breckfast, and went to replanting Cotten in the Prairie field—at least one third missing | |

| May | Ocupation | Delinquences |
|---|---|---|
| 2 | Tuesday 2 11 Hands finished Replanting Cotten in prairie field againt Breckfast and went to Hoeing Cotten in the Cut N.E. of Gin—1 Hand Bob with Caraige to Canney | |
| 3 | Wednesday 3 Ploughing Cotten with the shovl plogh and runing around with a one horse plough, hoing cotten cutting the Cotten out to a stand Ploughed the potatoes | |
| 4 | Thursday 4 Finished ploughing with the shovel plough to day in the bottom field. Commenced with the two shovel. Ploughes in the Prairy field. Ploughing with one horse plough. Cutting the Cotten out to a stand fine prospects for a good crop of cotten. corn tassoling | |
| 5 | Friday 5 Ploughing Cane and Cotten Finished ploughing cane to day | |
| 6 | Ploughing Cotten in the Prairy field hoing cotten out to a stand in the bottom field | |
| 7 | Sunday | |
| 8 | Ploughing cotten in the Prairy field Commenc Cutting the Cotten out to a stand in the Prairy field | Mary sick |
| 9 | Ploughing and hoing cotten in the Prairy field Cotten coming up in the prairy part since the rain in the hard places think that I will get a tollerable good stand | Mary sick |
| 10 | Finished Ploughing in the Prairy field to day. Commenc ploughing out the middles with the sweeps on that Cut next to the Corn on the south side of the gin, hoing the cotten out to a stand in the prairy field | May & Bill Sick |
| 11 | Ploughing cotten Finished hoing cotten in the prairy field. Commen hoing that Cut South of the Gin next to the Corn— | |
| 12 | Ploughing corn, Commenc hoing corn to day | |
| 13 | Sunday | |
| 14 | Ploughing and hoing Corn | Wesly Sick |
| 15 | Ploughing corn on the north side of the ditch, hoing Corn on the South side of the ditch | Wesly Sick |
| 16 | Ploughing and hoin corn | Wesly Sick |
| 17 | Ploughing and hoing corn | Wesly Sick |
| 18 | Finished Ploughing the Corn to day about 12 o.c Commenc braking out the Cotten Ground | Wesly Sick |
| 19 | hoing corn and Ploughing cotten | Wesly Sick |
| 20 | hoing Corn and Ploughing Cotten on the West side of the gin | Wesly Sick |
| 21 | Sunday | |
| 22 | Houing corn part of the day, commenc hoing potatoes about nine Oc Ploughing Cotten, on the west side of the gin, | Ben sick Bill sick Wesly sick |

| May | Ocupation | Delinquences |
|---|---|---|
| 23 | Hoing Potatoes and ploughing Cotten on the West side of the gin | Ben sick<br>Wesley sick |
| 24 | Ploughing cotten and hoing Potatoes until (nine) of (ten Oc) Making potatoe ridges in the corn | Tom sick<br>Wesly sick |
| 25 | Finished running around the Cotten on the north eist side of the gin  hoing Cotten on the North east side of the gin | Tom sick<br>Wesly sick |
| 26 | Ploughing cotten in the Prairy field hoing cotten on the east side of the gin | Wesly sick |
| 27 | Finished Ploughing the Cotten in the bottom part of the Prairy field—hoing Cotten on the east side of the Gin north of the midle turn row and south of the Potatoe patch Killed a beef this morning | |
| 28 | Sunday | |
| 29 | Ploughing cotten on the south east side of the gin north of the turn row hoing cotten there also (Cotten boles Cottin boles) | |
| 30 | Finished Ploughing the cut on the south side of the gine and north of the turnrow Commenc ploughing out the midles on the other side of the turnow | Tom run off |
| 31 | Ploughing out the middles on the same side of the turn row, Howing corn | Tom run off |
| | Absent from home untill the seventh of June | Tom run off |
| Month of June 7 | Ploughing cotten in the Prairy field, runing out the middles, hoing cotten, Ploughing cane with a double horse Plough— | Tom come in |
| 8 | Finished Ploughing and hoing the Prairy cottin to day about Twelve and one Oc Ploughing the slip potatoes also hoing the Potatoes, Commenc braking out the midles in the bottom field on the north side of the gin to the right of the middle turn row, | |
| 9 | having rained all night was too wet to hoe the potatoes or plough Cotten, spent part of the day hoing cane having rained halfe of the day assorting the corn from the shucks and shelling corn to grind | |
| 10 | Plough hands hoing cane until breakfast time, they then cut wood untill dinner time Doctor and Allen halling wood & cotten Bill's gang hoing cane all day. Ploughs commenc runing after dinner. | |
| 11 | Sunday | |
| 12 | Commenc ploughing out the midles north of the slue and on the right of the gin next to the corn hoing potatoes | |
| 13 | Finished Ploughing the cut of cotten on the right of the gine and north of the slue Ploughing the cut south of the gin and on the left of the turnrow going down Finished hoing potatoes and Commenc hoing the cotten following the Ploughs, Fine cotten nearly as high as my hand Bold hoed out the turnrow and as fare down as the gin | Becky sick |

| June | Ocupation | Delinquences |
|---|---|---|
| 14 | Ploughs stoped on account of the rain hands have been employed a variety of ways some carrying shuck some getting board timber and some hoing down the the large weeds in the fields Cleaned the ridge where the Bo dark is planted | |
| 15 | Four hands getting board timber Three of the hand gon halfe of the day after basket timber, Clenen and Allen halling board timber the other halfe Bob with John and Simon was together with Bill's gang hoing cotten very wet hoing | Carlin sick |
| 16 | Commenc ploughing this morning six ploughs runing and two sweeps Finished hoing the Cotten cut next to the corn and north of the slue | Carolin sick |
| 17 | Ploughing cotten hoing cotten south of the slew and next to the corn—Wesly has a sore shine which is nearly well, we have been doctering him by applying a plaster of fresh cow menure which is very good— | |
| 18 | Sunday  Sunday | |
| 19 | Ploughing and hoing cotten south of the gine hoing on the right hand side of the turnrow Ploughing on the other side— | John sick this morning |
| 20 | Finished Ploughing out the midles today about (—) Oc. I have Ploughed out all the middles on the Plantation all hands hoing the cut on the south side of the gin and west of the turnrow. Two sweeps runing on the cut West of the gin and South of the ditch | |
| 21 | Two sweps runing, all the rest of the hand hoing excep Ben who is making bords | |
| 22 | Two sweeps runing so the rest of the hands are hoing cotten, having finished that cut south and west of the gin, Commenced hoing on the west side and of the gin and north of the slue, | |
| 23 | Two swep runing after two Ploughs hoing cotten and Ben is making boards, Droped the sweep today about 12 Oc | |
| 24 | Droped the sweeps and commenced ploughing again, finished this cut to day about 12 Oc hoing cotten with the remainder of the hands in this same cut, | |
| 25 | Sunday | |
| 26 | Commenced ploughing out the middles in the cut south of the slew next to the corn and on the east side of the gin Hoing the cut north of the slew and east of the gin, Three sweeps runing in the Prairy field | |
| 27 | Three sweeps runing in the prairy field Sam, Tom, and Bob Finished hoing cotten Wednesday the 26 hoed out the turnrow hoing potatoes in the corn cutting down the weeds in the corn | |
| 28 | Sweep runing, Cutting down weeds in the corn | |
| 30 | Sweeps running in the Prairy field, Cutting out the weeds in the Prairy field— | |

| | |
|---|---|
| August the 17 | Picking cotten in the Bottom field Commenced yesterday on the cut south of the gin and east of the turn-row |
| 19 | All hands commenc picking cotten to day the first fair day we have had since I have commen[ced] picking— *Georg sick* |
| October the 11, 1848 | Stoped picking cotten We have picked, 154188 |
| November 1 | We had a light frost the first this year. |
| November the, 4, | We had frost quite heavy |
| November the 5 | Very heavy frost the suger cane was Killed on the fourth of November I commenced cutting cane on the 4 of November |
| November the 6 | Frost not quite so heavy as the night before cane all killed, |
| Nov the | Finished cutting cane |
| November the 21, 1848 | Finished diging potatoes The Potatoes turned out very well this year— |
| November the 24, | The gin commenced running— |

## 76. THE SONS OF TEMPERANCE: CONSTITUTION OF THE CHAPTER AT AUSTIN, TEXAS

### March 22, 1849

From *Constitution and Rules of Order of Metropolitan Division, No. 29, of the Sons of Temperance of Austin* (Austin, 1850; copy in the Archives, University of Texas Library, Austin), pamphlet.

One of the strongest and most emotion-charged of the social reform movements of the 1830's and 1840's in the United States was that directed toward the prohibition of the use of "Demon Rum." During the latter decade this movement spread to Texas, where prominent churchmen crusaded diligently for the cause, calling upon their congregations to take the "pledge." The Sons of Temperance, a national organization, became its most active advocate in Texas. First established in Texas in 1848, it combined mutual assistance welfare with temperance crusade, and by 1850 claimed a membership of three thousand, including a majority of the members of the State Legislature. A traveller in 1851 reported that local organizations of The Sons of Temperance were to be found in nearly every town and in many rural communities. Even Sam Houston, formerly a heavy imbiber, worked energetically in its behalf. The constitution of a local chapter established in March, 1849, in Austin sets forth the nature and objectives of the organization.

### PREAMBLE

We, . . . desirous of forming a Society to shield us from the evils of intemperance, afford mutual assistance in case of sickness, and elevate our character as men, do pledge ourselves to be governed by the following CONSTITUTION and BY-LAWS:

## CONSTITUTION

### Article I.—*Name.*

This Association shall be known as "METROPOLITAN DIVISION, No. 29, OF THE SONS OF TEMPERANCE," of Austin City, Texas.

### Article II.—*Pledge.*

No brother shall make, buy, sell, or use, as a beverage, any spirituous or Malt Liquors, Wine, or Cider.

### Article III.—*Officers*

The Officers shall consist of a W.P., W.A., R.S., A.R.S., F.S., T., C., I.S., and O.S., all of whom shall be elected by ballot every three months, viz: last regular meetings in September, December, March and June, and installed the first regular meetings in October, January, April and July. . . .

### Article V.—*Eligibility for Membership*

Sec. 1. No person shall be initiated into the Division under eighteen years of age, nor for a less sum than two dollars.

Sec. 2. No person shall be admitted into this Division, who does not possess a good moral character, or who is in any way incapacitated from earning a livelihood, or who has no visible means of support.

Sec. 3. The name of a person offered for membership, must be proposed by a member in writing—stating age, residence and business, which must be entered on the record, and the subject referred to three brothers for investigation, who shall report in writing at a succeeding meeting, when the candidate shall be ballotted for with ball ballots; and if not more than four black balls appear against him, he shall be declared elected; but if five or more black balls appear, he shall be rejected, and so declared. No person so rejected, shall be again proposed in any Division of the Order under six months.

Sec. 4. A proposition for membership shall not be withdrawn after it has been referred to a committee for investigation, without the consent of a majority of the members present.

Sec. 5. A vote of rejection may be re-considered within three meetings, exclusive of the meeting at which the vote was taken; but a vote which has resulted in an election, shall not be re-considered.

Sec. 6. The name of a candidate, or brother, constitutionally suspended, rejected, or expelled, shall not be published in any other manner than the usual notice to the Divisions.

Sec. 7. Any brother applying for membership by deposit of card, shall be subject to the same ballot as a new applicant.

### Article VI.—*Contributions and Benefits.*

Sec. 1. The regular dues of this Division shall not be less than six and a quarter cents per week.

Sec. 2. Every bona-fide member who shall be qualified, as required by the Constitution and By-Laws of this Division, shall, in case of sickness or disability, be entitled to, and receive weekly, not less than three dollars, except it be shown that such sickness or disability be brought on by his own improper conduct.

Sec. 3. No brother residing within five miles of the Division of which he is a member, shall be entitled to benefits for more than one week previous to his case being reported to such Division. No benefits shall be granted for a less time than one week. All arrears, either for dues or fines, shall, in every case, be deducted from the first payment.

Sec. 4. In case of the death of a brother entitled to benefits, the sum of thirty dollars shall be appropriated as a funeral benefit. The W.P., in the absence of competent relations or friends, shall take charge of the funeral, and keep an account of the disbursement.

Sec. 5. On the death of the wife of a brother, also, benefical, he shall be entitled to the sum of fifteen dollars as a funeral benefit.

### Article VII.—*Offence.*

Sec. 1. Any member who shall offend against these Articles or By-Laws, except Article 2, shall be subject to be fined, reprimanded, suspended, or expelled, as two-thirds of the members present, at any regular meeting, may determine.

Sec. 2. Every member shall be entitled to a fair trial for any offence involving reprimand, suspension, or expulsion; but no member shall be put on trial unless charges, duly specifying his offence, be submitted in writing by a member of the Division.

Sec. 3. When charges have been preferred against a brother in a proper manner, or any matters of grievance between brothers are brought before the Division, they shall be referred to a special committee of five members, who shall, with as little delay as the case will admit, summon the parties, and examine and determine the matter in question; and if their decision does not involve the suspension or expulsion of a member, and no appeal be taken from it to the Division, it shall be final without further action. Should the committee be convinced of the necessity of suspending or expelling a member, they shall submit a motion for the purpose to the Division for action.

Sec. 4. When a motion for the expulsion or suspension of a member shall have been submitted in due form, it shall be announced at one regular meeting previous to action being taken; and the accused shall be summoned to be in attendance at the Division, at the time when it may have been determined to consider the question—at which time, whether the implicated member be present or not, the Division may proceed to consider and determine it: two-thirds of the members present voting in favor of the motion, it shall be carried; but the Division shall be fully competent, while such motion is under consideration, to vary the penalty from the original motion.

Sec. 5. When the decision of a committee appointed under sec. 3, of this article, otherwise final, shall not be satisfactory to all parties, either of those interested shall have the privilege of an appeal to the Division; and at the time appointed for trying the appeal, the committee shall present to the Division, in writing, the grounds on which their decision was founded, and the parties shall have the privilege of being heard before the Division; and the Division shall determine the correctness of the decision of the Committee by a majority of votes present.

Sec. 6. Any member having been expelled, shall not be proposed for membership under six months from the date of expulsion.

## Article VIII.—*Terms.*

Regular quarterly terms shall commence on the first of October, January, April and July. Officers elected previous to the expiration of half the term, shall be entitled to the full honors of the term: those elected after half the term has expired, shall not count the honors, except when they may be elected to fill vacancies occasioned by resignation, suspension, expulsion, or death; in which case, the brother who serves the residue of the term, shall be entitled to the full honors; and he who resigns, or is suspended, or expelled, shall forfeit the claim.

## Article IX.—*Eligibility for Chief Officers.*

Sec. 1. After a Division has been instituted three terms, no brother shall be eligible to the office of W.P., unless he has served a regular quarterly term as W.A.; nor shall any brother be eligible to the office of W.A., unless he has served two terms in a subordinate office or offices.

Sec. 2. No brother shall serve two terms in the same office during the term of one year, except in the offices of R.S., F.S., and T.

Sec. 3. No brother shall be eligible to office, who is under twenty-one years of age.

## Article X.—*Violating Art. 2.*

Sec. 1. Any brother violating Art. 2 of the Constitution, shall forfeit his membership, and his name shall be erased from the books, after proceeding, in accordance with sections 2, 3, and 4 of Art. 7. Nevertheless, it shall be in the power of two-thirds of the members present, at a regular meeting, to reinstate him on his re-signing the Constitution, and paying a fine of one dollar; for the second offence, they shall have the power to reinstate him on his re-signing the Constitution and paying a fine of two dollars; for the third offence, he can be admitted as a newly proposed member only: *provided,* that the power to reinstate shall not extend over the term of one month from the time the offence was proven. The above fines must be paid to the F.S. on the night he is reinstated, or the member to stand suspended until they are paid.

Sec. 2. If a Division refuse to reinstate a brother, he shall be declared expelled, and the R.S. shall give the usual notice.

Sec. 3. An officer or representative violating Art. 2, shall not be eligible to fill such, or any office, for twelve months from the time he is reinstated, and shall forfeit all honors.

Sec. 4. Any member, knowing of a brother having violated Art. 2, and neglecting to prefer the charge to the Division, within three weeks after, shall be fined one dollar.

## Article XI.

No alteration or addition shall be made to this Constitution unless by a two-third vote of the National Division.

## 77. AN EARLY TEXAS HIGH SCHOOL

### December 31, 1849

From *Prospectus of the Guadalupe High School, at Seguin, Texas* (Victoria, 1850; copy in Archives, University of Texas Library, Austin).

Prior to 1854, when the Texas legislature first made provision for a public school system, many communities and private organizations had already established their own schools under state charters. Charters were granted to 117 schools between 1846 and 1861; in addition, nine so-called educational associations were incorporated. One of the nine in the group was the Guadalupe High School Association which was a joint stock company created on December 31, 1849. The Association opened at Seguin in 1850 with two teachers and one hundred students and operated until December, 1854, when it was declared insolvent. The "Address" by the trustees and the Constitution of this Association describe one type of school found in Texas prior to the adoption of a public educational system.

### 1. ADDRESS

THE TRUSTEES OF THE GUADALUPE HIGH SCHOOL ASSOCIATION, at Seguin, submit to the Public in Texas, and elsewhere, a statement showing the origin and progress of the Institution, and the future prospects thereof—and pledge themselves that no exertion shall be spared to render it one of the best that can be found in the Southern States.

The Institution was organized in December of last year by a Joint Stock Company of twenty-five members—since which time we have had to open the subscriptions and receive members and stock to the number of fifty, by the urgent application of those who had not the opportunity offered at the first organization.

An Act of Incorporation was obtained at the last session of the Legislature, which is herewith submitted, with the Constitution, and such Rules as the Association has had occasion to frame for their government, and that of the Board of Trustees.

Grounds have been secured by donation and purchase, and since our incorporation in January last, buildings have been erected of a superior order, and arrangements made to enlarge them when they may be required.

The locality of the school, the healthiness and salubrity of the climate around Seguin, and the beauty of the situation of their buildings, render it a most desirable location for the youth of the country; and those families who reside in more unfavorable sections could find no more eligible place to send their children in any part of the United States. The society of the village cannot be surpassed for intelligence, morality, and industry—and every attention will be paid by the Trustees to the morals of the youth intrusted to their care.

The principal building is of stone, sixty feet long by twenty-six wide, two stories high—and an observatory extending twenty-five feet above the upper walls; commanding a beautiful view of the Guadalupe river and surrounding country. Close by the grounds are numerous springs of water, and a lawn of ten acres south of the building, which is one quarter of a mile from the courthouse.

They have engaged the services of Mr. Wm. J. Glass to take charge of the male, and Mrs. Glass for the female Department, which will be in different wings of the building. And with the qualifications possessed by them, and the high recommendations he brings with him from Washington College, Pa., of which he is a graduate, they have no fears for the success of the Institution. They have adopted the very lowest rates of tuition which could be established, to aid in defraying the current expenses of the teachers, who will be paid a regular salary by the Association. And they have determined to educate at all times, orphans and fatherless children who have not the means to educate themselves, on the most perfect equality with all others, come from where they may, *free of charge*.

The sessions are formed with due regard to the seasons, and appropriate classes will be organized, and public examinations had at suitable intervals, to be hereafter determined.

The sessions will open on the first Mondays in March and September.

The first session will commence on the third Monday of September ensuing, (1850), and will continue two weeks later in the spring, to enable arrangements which are in progress to be completed before opening.

An extensive Library and Philosophical and Chemical Apparatus are secured, and now on the way, for the School—and all the necessary Class Books can be obtained by students at the Institution on the most favorable terms. . . .

## 2. CONSTITUTION

We, the undersigned, with a view to the great importance of establishing and perpetuating a High School in Guadalupe county, such as will best improve and develope the minds and elevate the morals of the youth of the country, do agree to form ourselves into an Association, to be known as the "Guadalupe High School Association." We further agree, to create a fund of five thousand dollars for the use of the Association, in erecting a suitable building, and procuring a suitable teacher: the fund so created, to be made up by shares of one hundred dollars each. We further agree, that so soon as the entire fund is subscribed, to hold a meeting in Seguin, at the courthouse, on as early a day as may be designated, and proceed to draft and adopt the style and dimensions of a building, to make choice of a locality for the same, to elect officers, and to do and perform all business necessary to the expeditious advancement of the purposes of the Association. We further agree to adopt the following Constitution, or Guide, for the Association, to wit:

ARTICLE 1. The Association shall not be composed of less than fifty members.

ART. 2. The School shall be located in the vicinity of the town of Seguin.

ART. 3. The officers of the Association shall be a President, Secretary, Treasurer, and four Trustees—offices to be honorary, until otherwise ordered by the majority of the Association.

ART. 4. It shall be the duty of the President to preside over the deliberations of the Association, and of the Board of Trustees, to sign all orders from either, to give the casting vote in case of a tie, to call meetings of the Association, or of the Trustees, when exigencies may require it, to order elections to fill vacancies, and to exercise a general supervision over the Association.

ART. 5. It shall be the duty of the Secretary to make and keep a record of the proceedings generally of the Association, to prepare and attest orders and advertisements for the President, and to do and perform such other duties as may be directed by the Association.

ART. 6. The Treasurer shall give bond in such amount with such security, payable to the President and his successors in office, as the Association may think right and proper; shall keep an account of all the receipts and disbursements of money, and make a yearly report of the same at the annual meeting of the Association.

ART. 7. The Trustees shall, under the direction of the Association, take measures for procuring teachers and shall judge of their qualifications, shall fix and determine the rates of tuition and the time and manner of its payment, and shall do and perform such other duties as the Association may from time to time direct for the better success of the institution.

ART. 8. All business of the Association shall be decided by a majority vote, except such as is hereinafter provided for.

ART. 9. The annual elections for officers shall take place on the first Tuesday in January of each year.

ART. 10. The subscription of one share or more will entitle the subscriber to one vote in the Association.

ART. 11. Two or more persons unitedly subscribing one share or more, shall be entitled to one vote in solido.

ART. 12. No member of the Association shall withdraw his subscription from the general fund under any circumstance.

ART. 13. No member shall alienate, transfer, or alter his relations to the Association, without its constitutional permission.

ART. 14. No person shall become a member of the Association by purchase, gift, devise or descent, except by the constitutional consent of its members.

ART. 15. A member may be expelled from the Association by a full vote of two-thirds of the members, for lawless or immoral conduct of sufficient magnitude—of which the members of the Association shall, in all cases, be competent judges.

ART. 16. Any member being expelled, shall have his pro rata interest in the institution refunded.

ART. 17. In case of vacancy by death or resignation, the President shall cause the Secretary to call a meeting of the members, by public advertisement posted on the court-house door in the town of Seguin, and at two other public places in the county, giving at least ten days notice, of an election to fill the vacancy; and in case the exigencies shall require it, the President may appoint; and in case of his death, absence, or resignation, the Secretary may appoint an incumbent pro tem.

ART. 18. Should the day of holding the annual elections be unfavorable, so as to prevent the attendance of the members, the President shall appoint another day, the earliest practicable, giving due notice of the same. The officers, in all cases, to act until their successors are installed.

ART. 19. If it should appear necessary to the greater utility of the institution, the fund may be enlarged by the further purchase of stock by the members of the Association.

ART. 20. The revenue arising from the institution shall be divided and paid at the end of each year, by the Treasurer, to the stockholders, on a pro rata basis.

ART. 21. This Constitution shall not be revised, altered, or amended in any particular, without the concurrent vote of two-thirds of all the members of the Association in favor of such alteration.

ART. 22. The Trustees shall have power to receive donations of money or property for the benefit of the Association; and when the donation consists of property, the title shall be taken in the name of the "President and Trustees of the Guadalupe High School Association."

ART. 23. The Association shall be composed of not more than fifty members, and no person shall be permitted to subscribe, except with the approbation and consent of the Board of Trustees.

### TERMS.
### PER SESSION OF FIVE MONTHS.

#### Preparatory Department.

Spelling, Reading, Writing, and
Mental Arithmetic, - - - - - - - - - $ 8.00

#### Second Department.

Arithmetic, Geography, English Grammar,
History, Natural Philosophy, &c., - - - - - 12.00

#### Third Department.

Higher branches of English Literature, Mathematics,
and Classics, - - - - - - - - - - - 15.00

Orphans and fatherless children who have not the means—educated free of charge.

Boarding, including all incidental expenses, can be obtained in families at the rates of from $8 to $10 per month.

## 78. ESTABLISHMENT OF THE TEXAS–NEW MEXICO BOUNDARY

### September 9, 1850

At the conclusion of the Mexican War, the government of Texas took steps to assert its authority over the area lying east of the Rio Grande above El Paso, claimed as part of Texas since 1836. When Federal occupation forces, responding to local and national sentiment, prevented this assertion, an impasse fraught with dangerous possibilities followed. Meanwhile, the country at large was becoming tense over other issues: the existence of slavery in the District of Columbia; the alleged laxness of enforcement of the Fugitive Slave laws; the question of the extension of slavery into the Mexican Cession; and finally, the petition of California for admission to the Union as a free state.

To resolve these problems, Henry Clay in January 1850 introduced several resolutions in Congress. They were referred to a Select Committee of Thirteen, chaired by Clay, for study. In May this group proposed a series of bills designed to reconcile the various factions and issues. Progress on the bills was slow owing to the steadfast opposition of President Zachary Taylor; but Millard Fillmore, who succeeded Taylor upon the latter's death, supported them, with the result that they passed as the Compromise of 1850.

The first of the following documents reflects the temper of Governor Peter H. Bell. The second and third respectively are the reports of the Committees regarding the Texas boundary question and the final act establishing the boundary. The location of the actual boundary was proposed by Senator James A. Pearce of Maryland, whose view finally prevailed.

### 1. GOVERNOR BELL'S MESSAGE TO THE LEGISLATURE

#### August 13, 1850

From Texas *House Journal*, Third Legislature, Extra Session (Austin, 1850), 6-18.

Executive Department,
Austin, August 13, 1850.

To the Honorable Senate
and House of Representatives
Gentlemen: . . .

Upon receiving the report of the Commissioner appointed under the authority of the act of the last Legislature, to provide for the civil organization of the counties of Presidio, El Paso, Worth and Santa Fe, and other information which subsequently came to my knowledge connected with the subject of that report, it occurred to me, that if the "occasion" contemplated by the constitution for the exercise of the power by the Executive of convening the Legislature in extraordinary session could ever exist, it was presented by the various facts and circumstances, in reference to a portion of the territory of our State, requiring in my judgment the most prompt and decisive action on the part of the Government; and . . . the oath

I had taken, faithfully to administer the duties of the station which I occupy, did not permit me to disregard the necessity of invoking the aid and assistance of the legislative wisdom of the country at a crisis in which the interest, honor, and character of the State were so deeply involved.

In accordance with the provision and requirement of the act of January 4, 1850, Robert S. Neighbors, Esq., was with the advice and consent of the Senate, appointed the Commissioner of the State, to carry into operation the objects contemplated by it, and after receiving such instruction and aid as it was in the power of the Executive to afford, he left the City of Austin on the 8th day of January for the region of country in which the duties of his mission required his presence and action.

Upon his arrival in the County of El Paso, he took the necessary measures for its immediate organization, and by his prudence, zeal, and activity, he succeeded to the fullest extent of our expectations. Within the space of a few weeks, he effected with a people heretofore unaccustomed to our Government and laws, and strongly imbued with prejudices against us as a race, a full recognition of the rights and of their relations to it, and inspired in them a desire to cultivate those relations in the performance of all the obligations of good citizens. . . .

The success of Major Neighbors in the County of El Paso gave rise to strong hopes of accomplishing the purposes of his mission in the County of Santa Fe, and these hopes were strengthened by assurances that he would meet with no opposition or obstacles on the part of the officers commanding the United States forces at that place. Previous to his departure from El Paso, he was furnished with a copy of an Official Order issued at Santa Fe on the 12th day of March, 1850, by Col. John Munroe, commanding the 9th Military Department, recognizing him as "a Commissioner of the State of Texas *for the purpose of establishing the civil jurisdiction of the State over this territory,*" and requiring from the military authorities under his command, a rigid non-interference with him in the exercise of his functions. This order . . . would have been sufficient to have enabled him to accomplish the object he had undertaken, had it been observed in good faith. I regret to be compelled to state however, that it was not observed in good faith—very far from it.

Your honorable body will perceive from the report of the Commissioner . . . that on his arrival at Santa Fe, he not only met with every discouragement on the part of the individual exercising the authority of civil and military Gov., but it was distinctly intimated to him, that if he succeeded in holding his elections, and in qualifying the officers elected, the jurisdiction of Texas would not be recognized.—Super added to this, he was threatened by a judge holding a commission from the President of the United States with imprisonment if he attempted to enforce the laws of the State over that territory. Appeals were made by the same Judge to the populace to resist the authority of the State. Public meetings were called and held with the same object which were presided over and comprised principally of the officers and other persons in the pay and employment of the United States Government—and all this under the immediate eye and observation of the commanding officer, who if not the projector of these proceedings, unquestionably yielded his assent to

them, and subsequently adopted them, by issuing his proclamation calling a convention to form a government adverse to, and independent of our own.

This course of conduct on the part of Col. Munroe would seem strange after his *order of March* the 12th, were we not able to account for it by a belief which scarcely admits a doubt, that subsequent to the date of the order, he received instructions to repudiate the rights and authority of Texas in that territory.— . . . I was anxious that the President should have one more opportunity of disclaiming such design, and hence it was, that I requested our Delegation in Congress to have an interview with him on the subject previous to the delivery of the protest.—No such disclaimer however, has been received, and facts which have since come to my knowledge, indicate most clearly that none such was made or intended to be made.

Having thus, gentlemen, placed before you, in a very plain and brief manner, the most prominent facts and circumstances connected with our relations with Santa Fe, . . . the question at once presents itself—what course does duty, honor, patriotism and a just appreciation of our solemn obligations to the country require us to adopt?

I am fully sensible, that this is a question involving the most serious considerations, and in its contemplation there is commingled much of hope and apprehension. But who will falter in the pathway of duty though the wrong-doer be there powerful and mighty? . . . So long as we were permitted to cherish the hope, that there existed no fixed or premeditated design, to deprive us of our acknowledged and essential rights, our language was that of entreaty and supplication—our course that of forbearance and moderation: but with the undeniable evidence now before us of a settled determination to despoil us, regardless of compacts and constitutional guaranties, of at least one-third of our territory—a continuance of such language and such a course, would be degradation and shame.

Difficult and embarrassing then, as the question undoubtedly is, and however fraught its contemplation with painful solicitude, we have left us no choice, but to meet it. It must be met boldly, and fearlessly and determined. Not by further supplications or discussion with Federal authorities; not by renewed appeals to their generosity and sympathy; not by a longer reliance on the delusive hope, that justice will yet be extended to us; but by action—manly and determined action on our part, by a prompt assertion of our rights and a practical maintenance of them with all the means we can command, *"at all hazards and to the last extremity."*

After deeply, and I trust maturely reflecting on this subject, . . . it is my deliberate and firm conviction that there is now left us but one course consistent with honor, and a just sense of what is due to ourselves as a sovereign community, and that is, the immediate adoption by your honorable body with perfect unanimity, of such measures as are necessary for the occupation of Santa Fe, with a force ample to quell the arrogant and rebellious spirit now prevailing there, and to enable us to extend and firmly establish the jurisdiction and laws of the State over it.

Should the adoption and unswerving enforcement of these measures lead to a conflict with those who, by Executive authority, are now unlawfully exercising the powers of a government adverse to our interests within our defined and acknowledged limits, . . . I should fearlessly meet it, trusting and feeling assured that Texas would stand exonerated before the world, even should that conflict shake, to its very centre, the most glorious confederacy upon which the sun has ever shone. . . .

In view, then, of the unpleasant and extraordinary position in which we are placed, and of the absolute necessity of immediate and decisive action on our part, I recommend that your honorable body authorize the Executive to raise, with as little delay as possible, *with power to supply,* at least two regiments of mounted volunteers for the contemplated move to and occupancy of Santa Fe. . . .

However willing Texas may have been, and may still be to *dispose* of a portion of her northwestern territory, upon fair, equitable and honorable terms, I cannot believe that any party respectable for its numbers or intelligence will be found amongst us who would be willing to accept a proposition so degrading to the character and dignity of the State, as the one contained in the bill reported by the Compromise Committee of the Senate. The right of the General Government to dispose of any portion of the territory of a sovereign State without its consent, cannot be admitted or acquiesced in by a free people, so long as they retain any just conception of the relative rights and obligations of the Federal and State Governments to each other; . . . If a proposition had been made founded *upon her acknowledged rights of territory,* to purchase from her that portion of it lying north of the 34th degree of north latitude, and accompanied with a sufficient guarantee that the provisions of the Joint Resolutions for annexation in respect to slavery should be observed, the most respectful consideration would have been given to it, and I risk but little in saying, that a large majority of our fellow citizens would have met such a proposition in the most liberal spirit and with a sincere desire to accord every thing reasonable and just that might have been asked in reference to it.

I have deemed it my duty to call your attention to this subject, because it may not be inappropriate for you, coming directly from the people, to give an expression of the public sentiment in regard to it. Such an expression may have a salutary influence elsewhere—if . . . clear and unequivocal. . . .

## 2. REPORT OF THE COMMITTEE OF THIRTEEN

### May 8, 1850

From United States, Thirty-first Congress, First Session, *Senate Reports, The Reports of Committees,* No. 123 (Washington, 1850), 6-7.

. . . The committee beg leave next to report on the subject of the northern and western boundary of Texas. On that question a great diversity of opinion has prevailed. According to one view of it, the western limit of Texas was the Nueces; according to another, it extended to the Rio Grande, and stretched from its mouth to its source. A majority of the committee, having come to the conclusion of recommending an amicable adjustment of the boundary with Texas, abstain from expressing any opinion

as to the true and legitimate western and northern boundary of that State. The terms proposed for such an adjustment are contained in the bill herewith reported, and they are, with inconsiderable variation, the same as that reported by the Committee on Territories.

According to these terms, it is proposed to Texas that her boundary be recognized to the Rio Grande, and up that river to the point commonly called El Paso, and running thence up that river twenty miles, measured thereon by a straight line, and thence eastwardly to a point where the hundredth degree of west longitude crosses Red river; being the southwest angle in the line designated between the United States and Mexico, and the same angle in the line of the territory set apart for the Indians by the United States.

If this boundary be assented to by Texas, she will be quieted to that extent in her title. And some may suppose that, in consideration of the concession by the United States, she might, without any other equivalent, relinquish any claim she has beyond the proposed boundary: that is, any claim to any part of New Mexico. But, under the influence of a sentiment of justice and great liberality, the bill proposes to Texas, for her relinquishment of any such claim, a large, pecuniary equivalent. As a consideration for it, and considering that a portion of the debt of Texas was created on a pledge to her creditors of the duties on foreign imports, transferred by the resolution of annexation to the United States, and now received and receivable in their treasury, a majority of the committee recommend that payment of the sum of _____ millions of dollars to Texas, to be applied in the first instance to the extinction of that portion of her debt for the reimbursement of which the duties on foreign imports were pledged as aforesaid, and the residue in such manner as she may direct. The said sum is to be paid by the United States in a stock, to be created, bearing five per cent. interest annually, payable half yearly, at the treasury of the United States, and the principal reimbursable at the end of fourteen years.

According to an estimate which has been made, there are included in the territory to which it is proposed that Texas shall relinquish her claim, embracing that part of New Mexico lying east of the Rio Grande, a little less than 124,933 square miles, and about 79,957.120 acres of land. From the proceeds of the sale of this land, the United States may ultimately be reimbursed a portion, if not the whole, of the amount of what is thus proposed to be advanced to Texas.

It cannot be anticipated that Texas will decline to accede to these liberal propositions; but if she should, it is to be distinctly understood that the title of the United States to any territory acquired from Mexico east of the Rio Grande will remain unimpaired, and in the same condition as if the proposals of adjustment now offered had never been made. . . .

## 3. THE TEXAS-NEW MEXICO BOUNDARY ACT

### September 9, 1850

From *United States Statutes at Large,* Vol. IX, 446-447.

*Be it enacted by the Senate and House of Representatives of the United States in Congress assembled,* That the following propositions shall be, and the same hereby are, offered to the State of Texas, which, when agreed to by the said State, in an act passed by the general assembly, shall be binding and obligatory, upon the United States, and upon the said State of Texas: *Provided,* The said agreement by the said general assembly shall be given on or before the first day of December, eighteen hundred and fifty:

First. The State of Texas will agree that her boundary on the north shall commence at the point at which the meridian of one hundred degrees west from Greenwich is intersected by the parallel of thirty-six degrees thirty minutes north latitude, and shall run from said point due west to the meridian of one hundred and three degrees west from Greenwich; thence her boundary shall run due south to the thirty-second degree of north latitude; thence on the said parallel of thirty-two degrees of north latitude to the Rio Bravo del Norte; and thence with the channel of said river to the Gulf of Mexico.

Second. The State of Texas cedes to the United States all her claim to territory exterior to the limits and boundaries which she agrees to establish by the first article of this agreement.

Third. The State of Texas relinquishes all claim upon the United States for liability of the debts of Texas, and for compensation or indemnity for the surrender to the United States of her ships, arsenals, custom-houses, custom house revenues, arms and munitions of war, and public buildings with their sites, which became the property of the United States at the time of the annexation.

Fourth. The United States, in consideration of said establishment of boundaries, cession of claim to territory, and relinquishment of claims, will pay to the State of Texas the sum of ten millions of dollars in a stock bearing five per cent. interest, and redeemable at the end of fourteen years, the interest payable half-yearly at the treasury of the United States. . . .

## 79. THE ESTABLISHMENT OF THE TEXAS SCHOOL SYSTEM

### January 31, 1854

From H. P. N. Gammel (comp.), *The Laws of Texas, 1822-1897* (10 vols.; Austin, 1898), III, 1461-1465.

In 1839 and 1840 a beginning was made toward establishing a public school system when Congress, acting upon President Lamar's recommendation, set aside four *sitios* of land in each county for the support of the public schools and fifty *sitios* for the endowment of two universities or colleges. Later, the Constitution of 1845 made the establishment of a system of schools mandatory and specified that one-tenth of the annual revenue of the state derived from taxation should be set apart for educational purposes. It was 1854, however, before the legislature, prodded by Governor E. M. Pease, passed an act establishing a public system of schools to implement the constitutional provision. The law is significant because it established a system that lasted, with only minor changes, well into the twentieth century, except for the short period when the radical reconstructionists were in power.

Section 1. Be it enacted by the Legislature of the State of Texas, That the sum of two millions of dollars of the five per cent bonds of the United States, now remaining in the treasury of the State, be set apart as a school fund, for the support and maintenance of Public Schools, which shall be called the Special School Fund, and the interest arising therefrom shall be apportioned and distributed for the support of the schools as herein provided.

Sec. 2. That the Chief Justice and County Commissioners shall constitute a board of School Commissioners for each county, whose duty it shall be, during the year eighteen hundred and fifty-four, to form their respective counties into school districts of convenient size and number the same, so that each district in a county shall be known by its appropriate number. Provided, however, that in forming said districts the convenience of neighborhoods shall be regarded as much as possible, and each school district shall contain a sufficient number of children for the maintenance of a school. They shall also, at the same time, order an election by the qualified voters of each school district, for three Trustees for each district, . . . stating fully the time and places of holding, and the object of said election. . . .

Sec. 5. That it shall be the duty of the Assessor and Collector of each county in the state, during the year eighteen hundred and fifty-four, and every year thereafter, to make out a list of all the free white population in his county, between the ages of six and sixteen years, particularly designating the number of persons between such ages in each school district, and transmit the same, under his hand and official signature, to the County Clerk of the county, and a certified copy thereof to the Treasurer of the State, on or before the first day of July, in each year and every year.

Sec. 6. That it shall be the duty of the Clerk of the County Court to file and preserve in his office the election returns and the list aforesaid furnished by the Assessor and Collector.—It shall be the duty of the Treasurer of the State to ascertain, from the abstracts transmitted to him by the Assessor and Collector, the aggregate population between the ages of six and sixteen years, and so much of the fund appropriated by this act as may be in the treasury shall be apportioned among the different counties in the State, according to the number of the population of scholastic age in each county, . . .

Sec. 7. That it shall be the duty of the District Trustees to fix the time and place for holding an election in their respective districts (for the location or selection of school houses within their respective districts) and to appoint a presiding officer.—That the chairman of the board of trustees shall cause written notices of said election to be posted up for at least five days next preceding the election, in three public places in each school district. That the returns of said election shall be made within five days to the chairman of the said board, who shall examine the same in presence of his co-trustees; and a majority of the votes polled in a district shall be necessary to the permanent location of a school house; and no change of the location of a school house thus located shall be made, except by a majority of two-thirds of those voting in such election, taken after due notice as above provided.

Sec. 8. That no money shall be drawn from the county Treasury for school purposes in any school district, until the people of such district shall have provided a good and substantial school house, with the necessary seats and other fixtures, and that the money appropriated by this act shall be applied only towards the payment of teachers for each school.

Sec. 9. That it shall be the duty of the school trustees for each district, as nearly as practicable after their election, by giving due notice, to call a meeting of all the patrons of the school in the district, and a majority of those present shall indicate to the trustees the length of time during the year they desire a school, the kind of teacher they want and the amount of salary they are willing to pay. It shall be the duty of said trustees, to observe, as far as possible, such instructions, to employ teachers of suitable moral character and qualifications, to visit from time to time the district school or schools under their charge, to expel a pupil for misconduct, to examine all complaints between teacher and pupil of a serious character, to discharge a teacher for incapacity or improper conduct, and generally to exercise supervision over the affairs of the school within their district.

Sec. 10. That the teacher of each school shall be required to keep a roll or day book and at the close of his term of service to furnish said school trustees with a tabular statement of the names of all the patrons and pupils of the school; the number of pupils sent by each patron, and the number of days attendance by each pupil, which statement shall be supported by his affidavit, made before some officer authorized to administer oaths, that the same is true and correct.

Sec. 11. That it shall be the duty of said trustees, upon receiving the shares of the school fund to which their school district is entitled, to apply the same towards the payment of the teacher's salary, and the remainder of said salary, if any, to apportion equally among the patrons of the School according to the number of pupils and the time sent by each to the school; and if any such patron should neglect or refuse to pay his share of the salary apportioned as aforesaid said trustees may institute suit against him or her for the amount of money due, and the tabular statement furnished them, under oath, by the teacher, and mentioned in the preceding section of this act, shall be prima facia evidence of such indebtedness.

Sec. 12. If any patron or patrons of the school are unable to pay their share of the salary apportioned as aforesaid, and the said trustees be satisfied of the fact, it shall be the duty of said trustees to make out a list of all such patrons in the district, together with the amount of money due from each for tuition, and forward the same under their own proper signatures to the Chief-Justice of the county.

Sec. 13. That the Chief-Justice of each county shall annually furnish the Treasurer of the State with a statement under his hand and seal of the county, of the amount of money due for tuition from all such patrons as are exempt under the preceding sections of this act, in the county, according to the list returned by the school trustees. And the Treasurer of the State is hereby authorised and required to pay said amounts of money due from the patrons so exempt, out of the school fund derivable from taxation and created by the Constitution of the State, and he shall distribute the same in manner and form as provided in the sixth section of this act.

Sec. 14. That the County Treasurer of each county shall give bond with two or more securities, payable to the county, in twice the amount of the school fund to which his county shall be entitled, . . . and faithfully keep an account for the money to him committed as a school fund for his county, and pay out the same only upon the order of the Chief-Justice of the county, under his hand and the seal of the County Court. He shall also enter into a bound book, to be kept by him for that purpose, all moneys received, all moneys paid out, and to whom and when paid, and register and number all orders by him paid or accepted to be paid, which book, together with such orders, shall be by him exhibited at his annual settlement with the County Court. . . .

Sec. 15. That the trustees of each school district shall be elected annually after the year eighteen hundred and fifty-four, on the first Monday in September, in the manner herein provided; that they shall be a body corporate and politic, by the corporate name of the Trustees of Common School District No. _____ , (filling the blank with the number of the District,) and for the purposes for which they are created, may sue and be sued, hold and dispose of property, and do such acts and things as are incidental and necessary to the performance of their duties.

Sec. 16. That the Treasurer of the State shall be ex-officio Superintendent of Common Schools in this State, and it shall be his duty immediately after the first day of September in each and every year, to record the abstracts of children of lawful age in the different counties, and apportion the moneys as herein contemplated, distributing to the several counties the amount to which each is entitled, according to its scholastic population, ascertained in the manner herein prescribed, and also the amount due for the tuition of children exempt from tuition fees; and it shall further be the duty of the Treasurer of the State, to provide the necessary record books, to be by him kept exclusively for recording abstracts, as herein contemplated, and keeping a full and perfect account of all investments and moneys belonging or in any wise appertaining to the Common School Fund of this State, and all apportionments and distribution of moneys by him made for common school purposes; and he shall report to the Governor annually, on or before the first day of October, the condition of the common school fund, and also make to each regular session of the Legislature such suggestions in regard to the Common School system as may be deemed advisable; that the fiscal scholastic year shall commence on the first day of September and end on the first day of August in each and every year from and after the first day of September next.

Sec. 17. That it shall be the duty of the chairman of

the board of trustees for each school district, to present, at least once a year, his application to the Chief-Justice of his county for such amounts of said fund as his district may be entitled to receive, according to the number of children between the ages heretofore prescribed within his district, and also present his application to the Chief-Justice annually for the amount of money due his district for the tuition of children exempt from tuition fees, and the said Chief-Justice, having duly informed himself that the same is correct, shall draw upon the County Treasurer an order, under his hand and seal of the County Court, for the amount or amounts so due and demanded.

Sec. 18. That nothing in this act shall prevent the trustees of any school district, after being instructed by a majority of the patrons of schools in such district, from employing the teacher of a primary department in any college or academy, and converting such primary department into a common school for such district; and that this act take effect from and after its passage.

Approved, January 31, 1854.

## 80. TEXAS BEFORE THE CIVIL WAR: A YANKEE'S DESCRIPTION

### December 1853—May 1854

From Frederick L. Olmsted, *A Journey through Texas; or, A Saddle-Trip on the Southwestern Frontier* (New York, 1860), 99-102, 113-114, 115-117, 140-147.

Frederick Law Olmsted, still recognized as the most famous landscape architect, and a distinguished journalist, was commissioned by the New York *Times* in 1852 to tour the southern states and write his impressions of the region for the newspaper. His trip took him to Texas in the winter and spring of 1853-1854. His observations there resulted in the publication in 1857 of *A Journey through Texas*. The following extracts, describing four scenes of pre-Civil War Texas that caught his attention, are from a slightly amplified 1860 edition of the work.

### 1. THE HOME OF AN EAST TEXAS CATTLEMAN

. . . At sunset, . . . we saw, about half a mile to the right of the road, a point of woodland, and a little beyond it, on a hill-top, was a house. We turned off, and with some difficulty made our way across the gullies between the hills, and approached the house. It proved to be deserted; but beyond it, on the top of the next and highest hill, there was another. We rode to it, and inquired if we could obtain corn for our horses, and shelter and food for ourselves. The proprietor "supposed we might," and our horses were led away, not to a stable, but to a pen or yard, on the windward side of the hill. We strapped blankets upon them, and left them before their corn, to weather it as they could, and betook ourselves to the house.

It was a log cabin, of one room, fourteen feet by fourteen, with another small room in a "lean-to" of boards on the windward side. There was no window, but there were three doors, and openings between the logs in all quarters. The door of the "lean-to" was barricaded, but this erection was very open; and as the inner door, from sagging on its wooden hinges, could not be closed at all, the norther had nearly free course through the cabin. A strong fire was roaring in the great chimney at the end of the room, and we all clustered closely around it, "the woman" alone passing through our semicircle, as she prepared the "pone" and "fry," and coffee for supper.

Our host seemed a man of thirty, and had lived in Texas through all the "trouble times." His father had moved his family here when Texas was still Mexican territory; and for years of the young man's life, Indians were guarded against and hunted just as wolves now are by the shepherd. They had always held their ground against them, however, and had constantly increased in wealth, but had retired for a few weeks before the Mexican invasion. His father had no property when he came here, but the wagon and horses, and the few household effects he brought with him. "Now," said the son, "he raises fifty bales of cotton"—equivalent to informing us that he owned twenty or thirty negroes, and his income was from two to three thousand dollars a year. The young man himself owned probably many hundred acres of the prairie and woodland range about him, and a large herd of cattle. He did not fancy taking care of a plantation. It was too much trouble. He was a regular Texan, he boasted, and was not going to slave himself looking after niggers. Any man who had been brought up in Texas, he said, could live as well as he wanted to, without working more than one month in the year. For about a month in the year he had to work hard, driving his cattle into the pen, and roping and marking the calves; this was always done in a kind of frolic in the spring—the neighboring herdsmen assisting each other. During the rest of the year he hadn't anything to do. When he felt like it he got on to a horse and rode around, and looked after his cattle; but that wasn't work, he said—'twas only play. He raised a little corn; sometimes he got more than he needed, and sometimes not as much; he didn't care whether it was enough or not—he could always buy meal, only bought meal wasn't so sweet as that was which they ground fresh in their own steel mill. When he wanted to buy anything, he could always sell some cattle and raise the money; it did not take much to supply them with all they wanted.

This was very evident. The room was, as I said, fourteen feet square, with battens of split boards tacked on between the broader openings of the logs. Above, it was open to the rafters, and in many places the sky could be seen between the shingles of the roof. A rough board box, three feet square, with a shelf in it, contained the crockery-ware of the establishment; another similar box held the store of meal, coffee, sugar, and salt, a log crib at the horse-pen held the corn, from which the meal was daily ground, and a log smoke or store-house contained the store of pork. A canopy-bed filled one quarter of the room; a cradle, four chairs seated with untanned deer-hide, a table, a skillet or bake-kettle, a coffee-kettle, a frying-pan, and a rifle laid across two wooden pegs on the chimney, with a string of patches, powder-horn, pouch, and hunting-knife, completed the furniture of the house. We all sat with hats and overcoats on, and the woman cooked in bonnet and shawl. As I sat in the chimney-corner I could put both my hands out, one laid on the other, between the stones of the fire-place and the logs of the wall.

A pallet of quilts and blankets was spread for us in the lean-to, just between the two doors. We slept in all our clothes, including overcoats, hats, and boots, and covered entirely with blankets. At seven in the morning, when we threw them off, the mercury in the thermometer in our saddle-bags, which we had used for a pillow, stood at 25 deg. Fahrenheit.

We contrived to make cloaks and hoods from our blankets, and after going through with the fry, coffee and pone again, and paying one dollar each for the entertainment of ourselves and horses, we continued our journey. . . .

## 2. THE HOME OF AN EAST TEXAS PLANTER

. . . We stopped one night at the house of a planter, now twenty years settled in Eastern Texas. He was a man of some education and natural intelligence, and had, he told us, an income, from the labor of his slaves, of some $4,000. His residence was one of the largest houses we had seen in Texas. It had a second story, two wings and a long gallery. Its windows had been once glazed, but now, out of eighty panes that originally filled the lower windows, thirty only remained unbroken. Not a door in the house had been ever furnished with a latch or even a string; when they were closed, it was necessary to *claw* or to ask some one inside to push open. (Yet we happened to hear a neighbor expressing serious admiration of the way these doors fitted.) The furniture was of the rudest description. . . .

On our supper-table was nothing else than the eternal fry, pone and coffee. Butter, of dreadful odor, was here added by exception. Wheat flour they never used. It was "too much trouble."

We were waited upon by two negro girls, dressed in short-waisted, twilled-cotton gowns, once white, now looking as though they had been drawn through a stove-pipe in spring. The water for the family was brought in tubs upon the heads of these two girls, from a creek, a quarter of a mile distant, this occupation filling nearly all their time.

This gentleman had thirty or forty negroes, and two legitimate sons. One was an idle young man. The other was already, at eight years old, a swearing, tobacco-chewing young bully and ruffian. We heard him whipping the puppy behind the house, and swearing between the blows, his father and mother being at hand. His tone was an evident imitation of his father's mode of dealing with his slaves.

"I've got an account to settle with you; I've let you go about long enough; I'll teach you who's your master; there, go now, God damn you, but I havn't got through with you yet."

"You stop that cursing," said his father, at length, "it isn't right for little boys to curse."

"What do *you* do when you get mad?" replied the boy; "reckon you cuss some; so now you'd better shut up." . . .

## 3. THE GERMANS OF NEW BRAUNFELS

. . . The first German settlers we saw, we knew at once. They lived in little log cabins, and had inclosures of ten acres of land about them. The cabins were very simple and cheap habitations, but there were many little conveniences about them, and a care to secure comfort in small ways evident, that was very agreeable to notice. So, also, the greater variety of the crops which had been grown upon their allotments, and the more clean and complete tillage they had received contrasted favorably with the patches of corn-stubble, overgrown with crab-grass, which are usually the only gardens to be seen adjoining the cabins of the poor whites and slaves. The people themselves were also to be seen, men, women, and children, busy at some work, and yet not so busy but that they could give a pleasant and respectful greeting to the passing traveler.

A few miles further on, we passed several much more comfortable houses, boarded over, and a good deal like the smaller class of farm-houses in New England, but some of them having exterior plaster-work, or brick, laid up between the timbers, instead of boards nailed over them. About these were larger inclosures, from which extensive crops of corn had been taken; and it caused us a sensation to see a number of parallelograms of COTTON—FREE-LABOR COTTON. These were not often of more than an acre in extent. Most of them looked as if they had been judiciously cultivated, and had yielded a fine crop, differing, however, from that we had noticed on the plantations the day before, in this circumstance—the picking had been entirely completed, and that with care and exactness, so that none of the cotton, which the labor of cultivation had produced, had been left to waste. The cotton-stalks stood rather more closely, and were of less extraordinary size, but much more even or regular in their growth than on the plantations.

We were entering the valley of the Guadalupe river, which is of the same general character as that of the San Marcos, and had passed a small brown house with a turret and cross upon it, which we learned was a Lutheran church, when we were overtaken by a good-natured butcher, who lived in Neu-Braunfels, whence he had ridden out early in the morning to kill and dress the hogs of one of the large farmers. He had finished his job, and was returning.

He had been in this country eight years. He liked it very much; he did not wish to go back to Germany; he much preferred to remain here. The Germans, generally, were doing well, and were contented. They had had a hard time at first, but they were all doing well now—getting rich. He knew but one German who had bought a slave; they did not think well of slavery; they thought it better that all men should be free; besides, the negroes would not work so well as the Germans. They were improving their condition very rapidly, especially within the last two years. It was sickly on the coast, but here it was very healthy. He had been as well here as he was in Germany—never had been ill. There were Catholics and Protestants among them; as for himself, he was no friend to priests, whether Catholic or Protestant. He had had enough of them in Germany. They could not tell him anything new, and he never went to any church.

We forded, under his guidance, the Guadalupe, and after climbing its high bank, found ourselves upon the level plateau between the prairie hills and the river on which Neu-Braunfels is situated. We had still nearly a mile to ride before entering the town, and in this distance met eight or ten large wagons, each drawn by three or four pairs of mules, or five or six yokes of oxen, each carrying under its neck a brass bell. They were all driven by Germans, somewhat uncouthly but warmly and neatly dressed; all smoking and all good-humored, giving us "good morning" as we met. Noticing the strength of the wagons, I observed that they were made by Germans, probably.

"Yes," said the butcher, "the Germans make better wagons than the Americans; the Americans buy a great many of them. *There are seven wagon-manufactories in Braunfels.*"

The main street of the town, which we soon entered upon, was very wide—three times as wide, in effect, as Broadway in New York. The houses, with which it was thickly lined on each side for a mile, were small, low cottages, of no pretensions to elegance, yet generally looking neat and comfortable. Many were furnished with verandahs and gardens, and the greater part were either stuccoed or painted. There were many workshops of mechanics and small stores, with signs oftener in English than in German, and bare-headed women, and men in caps and short jackets, with pendent pipes, were everywhere seen at work.

We had no acquaintance in the village, and no means of introduction, but, in hopes that we might better satisfy ourselves of the condition of the people, we agreed to stop at an inn and get dinner, instead of eating a cold snack in the saddle, without stopping at noon, as was our custom. "Here," said the butcher, "is my shop—indicating a small house, at the door of which hung dressed meat and beef sausages—and if you are going to stop, I will recommend you to my neighbor, there, Mr. Schmitz." It was a small cottage of a single story, having the roof extended so as to form a verandah, with a sign swinging before it, "Guadalupe Hotel, J. Schmitz."

I never in my life, except, perhaps, in awakening from a dream, met with such a sudden and complete transfer of associations. Instead of loose boarded or hewn log walls, with crevices stuffed with rags or daubed with mortar, which we have been accustomed to seeing during the last month, on staving in a door, where we have found any to open; instead, even, of four bare, cheerless sides of whitewashed plaster, which we have found twice or thrice only in a more aristocratic American residence, we were—in short, we were in Germany.

There was nothing wanting; there was nothing too much, for one of these delightful little inns which the pedestrian who has tramped through the Rhine land will ever remember gratefully. A long room, extending across the whole front of the cottage, the walls pink, with stenciled panels, and scroll ornaments in crimson, and with neatly-framed and glazed pretty lithographic prints hanging on all sides; a long, thick, dark oak table, with rounded ends, oak benches at its sides; chiseled oak chairs; a sofa, covered with cheap pink calico, with a small vine pattern, a stove in the corner; a little mahogany cupboard in another corner, with pitcher and glasses upon it; a smoky atmosphere; and finally, four thick-bearded men, from whom the smoke proceeds, who all bow and say "Good morning," as we lift our hats in the doorway.

The landlady enters; she does not readily understand us, and one of the smokers rises immediately to assist us. Dinner we shall have immediately, and she spreads the white cloth at an end of the table, before she leaves the room, and in two minutes time, by which we have got off our coats and warmed our hands at the stove, we are asked to sit down. An excellent soup is set before us, and in succession there follow two courses of meat, neither of them pork, and neither of them fried, two dishes of vegetables, salad, compote of peaches, coffee with milk, wheat bread from the loaf, and beautiful and sweet butter—not only such butter as I have never tasted south of the Potomac before, but such as I have been told a hundred times it was impossible to make in a southern climate. What is the secret? I suppose it is extreme cleanliness, beginning far back of where cleanliness usually begins at the South, and careful and thorough *working.* . . .

We went out to look at our horses; a man in cap and jacket was rubbing their legs—the first time they had received such attention in Texas, except from ourselves, or by special and costly arrangement with a negro. They were pushing their noses into racks filled with fine mesquit hay—the first they had had in Texas. They seemed to look at us imploringly. We ought to spend the night. But there is evidently no sleeping-room for us in the little inn. They must be full. But then we could sleep with more comfort on the floor here, probably, than we have been accustomed to of late. We concluded to ask if they would accommodate us for the night. Yes, with pleasure—would we be pleased to look at the room they could afford us? Doubtless in the cock-loft. No, it was in another little cottage in the rear. A little room it proved, with blue walls again, and oak furniture; two beds, one of them would be for each of us—the first time we had been offered the luxury of sleeping alone in Texas; two large windows with curtains, and evergreen roses trained over them on the outside—not a pane of glass missing or broken—the first sleeping-room we have had in Texas where this was the case; a sofa; a bureau, on which were a complete set of the *Conversations Lexicon;* Kendall's Santa Fe Expedition; a statuette in porcelain; plants in pots; a brass study lamp; a large ewer and basin for washing, and a couple of towels of thick stuff, full a yard and a quarter long. O, yes, it will do for us admirably; we will spend the night. . . .

As I was returning to the inn, about ten o'clock, I stopped for a few moments at the gate of one of the little cottages, to listen to some of the best singing I have heard for a long time, several parts being sustained by very sweet and well-trained voices. . . .

In the morning we found that our horses had been bedded, for the first time in Texas.

As we rode out of town, it was delightful to meet again troops of children, with satchels and knapsacks of books, and little kettles of dinner, all with ruddy, cheerful faces, the girls especially so, with their hair braided neatly, and without caps or bonnets, smiling and saluting us—*"guten morgen"*— as we met. Nothing so pleasant as that in Texas before, hardly in the South. . . .

## 4. THE LEGISLATURE AT WORK

. . . We visited, several times, the Texas Legislature in session, and have seldom been more impressed with respect for the working of Democratic institutions.

I have seen several similar bodies at the North; the Federal Congress; and the Parliament of Great Britain, in both its branches, on occasions of great moment; but none of them commanded my involuntary respect for their simple manly dignity and trustworthiness for the duties that engaged them, more than the General Assembly of Texas. There was honest eloquency displayed at every opportunity for its use, and business was carried on with great rapidity, but with complete parliamentary regularity, and all desirable gentlemanly decorum. One gentleman, in a state of intoxication, attempted to address the house (but that happens elsewhere), and he was quietly persuaded to retire. . . .

# 81. THE AMERICAN (KNOW-NOTHING) PARTY PLATFORM

## January 21-22, 1856

From E. W. Winkler (ed.), *Platforms of Political Parties in Texas* (*Bulletin* of the University of Texas; Austin, 1916), 68-71.

The American or Know-Nothing Party, a nativist movement, started originally as a series of secret societies. It was opposed to foreigners holding office; decidedly anti-Catholic; strongly pro-Union; and it was anxious to promote the reconciliation of the sections. Organized in 1852, the American Party became generally known as the Know-Nothing because when asked what they stood for, the members, to maintain secrecy, replied that they did not know.

The Party first appeared in Texas in 1854. Its appeal was evident when in that year it elected a complete slate of city officers for San Antonio and in the following year, the mayor of Galveston. The Party's Grand Council met at Washington on the Brazos in June, 1855, and backed by Sam Houston, it formed a state organization, made plans to organize in every community throughout the state, and secretly nominated candidates for state and congressional offices. For the first time in Texas, there was an active organized political opposition to the superiority of the hitherto unchallenged Democratic Party. It had surprising success that year in capturing a great many local offices, a number of places in the legislature, one seat in Congress, and in polling a close gubernatorial vote. This success inspired the party to hold an open state convention in 1856, at which time it adopted and published the following platform.

## RESOLUTIONS

The American party of the State of Texas, in convention assembled, declare as the cardinal principles of its organization:

1. The elevation to political office, executive, legislative, judicial, and diplomatic, of those only who are native Americans, or who being citizens of the Republic of Texas at the time of its annexation to the United States, made citizens thereof by the act of both governments.

2. The preservation and perpetuation of the Constitution and the Federal Union as the bulwark of our liberties in war, and a prime source of National greatness and individual happiness, and hence: first, opposition to all attempts to weaken or destroy it; second, opposition to the formation or encouragement of sectional or geographical parties—at this time the most threatening adversary to its stability.

3. A strict construction of the Constitution of the United States, and the preservation of all the rights of the States, secured or reserved in the Constitution; inculcating forbearance and a harmonizing spirit in settling apparent or real conflicts of jurisdiction; and repudiating the exercise of doubtful powers by the Federal government.

4. The extension of the period for the naturalization of foreigners to the term of twenty-one years, to be prospective in its operation, and the repeal by the legislatures of the States, in which they exist, of all laws conferring the right of suffrage on unnaturalized foreigners.

5. Liberty of conscience and liberty of the press. The right to worship God according to the dictates of conscience being secured by the Constitution and laws, any attempt to impair or abridge it would strike at the liberties of the people and should be resisted; but this inestimable privilege is never to be used as a pretext for violations of the Constitution or laws, or the practice of principles, creed, or system under the guise of religious belief, destructive of the principles of free republican government, or in conflict with the laws, and hence, opposition to all "higher law" doctrines which look to any power, foreign or domestic, civil, ecclesiastic or otherwise, for rule of civil or political action paramount to the Constitution and laws.

6. Congress possesses no power under the Constitution to legislate upon slavery in the States where it does or may exist, or to refuse the admission of a new State into the Union because its constitution does or does not recognize slavery as part of its social system; nor to legislate upon the subject of slavery in the Territories of the United States; and any interference by Congress with slavery in the District of Columbia would be a violation of the spirit and intention of the compact by which the State of Maryland ceded the district to the United States, and breach

of the National faith; nor should Congress repeal the Fugitive Slave Law. And while we disapprove that principle of the Kansas-Nebraska Act which confers the right of suffrage upon unnaturalized foreigners and that which recognizes the right of the territorial legislature to establish or exclude slavery, we cordially approve the principle of nonintervention by Congress, and are opposed to the repeal of the act, and oppose any further agitation of the subject of slavery in the Halls of Congress.

7. The enactment of laws to prevent the transmission to our shores of felons and paupers from foreign countries.

8. A constant and efficient protection of the frontier against the predatory incursions of the Indians, being an act of justice due to the citizens of the frontier settled thereon and a measure of policy necessary to the growth and prosperity of our State, it is the duty of the general government to provide such protection, and default thereof it is the duty of the State government to provide the same fully, effectually and promptly.

9. We adhere to the National organization of the American party upon the basis of the platform of principles adopted at the Philadelphia convention in June, 1855, rec-

ommending the next National convention to modify the eighth article of said platform by striking out the words "Resistance to the aggressive policy and corrupting tendencies of the Roman Catholic church in our country," for the reason that it has been so much misconstrued as to cast upon us the imputation of religious intolerance and a desire to abridge the liberty of conscience, which we utterly repudiate. But while we disclaim any intention to abridge or impair or interfere with the right of any citizen of whatever faith or denomination to worship God according to the dictates of his own conscience, we claim the right, indispensable to the security of free institutions, to resist and oppose, through the ballot box, every principle or policy, whether claimed or exercised as a right appertaining to any church government, or under pretext of any religious belief, hostile to liberty, or liberty of conscience, or liberty of the press, or liberty of suffrage, or to any other essential element of liberty, under the constitution and laws.

10. It is declared that all secrecy, obligations, pass words, and signs are abolished. . . .

## 82. THE CAMEL EXPERIMENT

### June 24—August 15, 1860

From Lieutenant William H. Echols, "Report," in United States, Thirty-sixth Congress, Second Session, *Senate Executive Document,* No. I (Washington, 1861), 37-50.

After his proposal to build a transcontinental railroad along the line of the thirty-second parallel had been blocked by sectional politics over slavery in the territories, Secretary of War Jefferson Davis, in an experiment to solve the need for transportation across the "Great American Desert" to the new state of California and to the intervening army posts, introduced in 1856 and 1857 seventy-five camels into Texas. Although many Congressmen considered the camel-plan unrealistic and fantastic, an appropriation of thirty thousand dollars had been made for the purpose. After all, were not camels the logical beasts of burden with which to cross a desert?

The first of two shipments was landed at Indianola on May 14, 1856, and then was moved to Camp Val Verde, the eastern terminus of the projected camel route, located just south of present-day Kerrville. Tests were begun immediately to determine whether the camels or the tried-and-true pack mules were superior modes of transportation in the Southwest. One test was the reconnaissance expedition of Lieutenant William H. Echols in the summer of 1860 into the perilous Big Bend Country. Echols' journal of the expedition appears below not only because of the interest in the camel experiment but because of its description of that part of Texas. There were also other trips, some extending as far as California; but with the outbreak of the Civil War the military personnel were recalled from the Texas frontier, and within a few years the abandoned camels had vanished.

. . . *June* 24, 1860.—I left San Antonio on the 11th instant, with orders to resume the reconnoisance commenced last year of that portion of northwestern Texas lying between the San Antonio or El Paso road, the Rio Grande and Pecos rivers, with twenty camels and twenty-

five pack mules, with an escort under the command of Lieutenant Holman, first infantry, of twenty infantry men, reinforced by eleven from Camp Hudson on my arrival at that post.

The camels are in fine condition; and with some improvements, which my experience with them last year taught me to suggest to be made, respecting the packing of them, such as iron loops on the water barrels to prevent them from shifting, and larger water barrels, which are the most important changes, I hope to be freed of a great deal of delay and vexation which I encountered the previous year. The male camels were all left, with the exception of one. Although much stouter and more serviceable than the females, they occasion a deal more trouble and attention from their belligerent propensities to one another. The command now consists of thirty-one men, exclusive of the herders and camel attendants, with the twenty camels and fifteen mules for packing, the remainder being left at Camp Hudson, with the exception of two mules that strayed on the road, and not recovered. We have capacity for carrying nearly 500 gallons of water, and are rationed from Camp Hudson for twenty days. Camped two miles from the wood at Bearn lake, near the head of Rio San Pedro, known more generally as Rio Diablo, or Devil's river; from which point I set out to-morrow directly to the Pecos, thence to Fort Davis, intending to cross the country in a more southerly direction than my last trail to that post. Another improvement in measuring distances I have succeeded in contriving, consisting of shafts, two light wheels on an axle three and a half feet long, a chest on a spring, answering for a seat for the driver, all very light, and attaching the odometer, and the machine is complete.

*June* 25.—Left camp this morning at six o'clock, being somewhat retarded in our preparations for departure by having to soak our water barrels in the lake till morning, and, being the first time they had been filled for transportation, to distribute and adjust the loading accordingly; but after setting out, I was much pleased with the manner in which the command was able to move, without the hindrance so frequently occuring before the improvements, mentioned yesterday as having been made, were made. I think not a pack has fallen to-day; and if such success attend our movements, even in this respect, how much trouble will we be relieved of.

After leaving our camp ground this morning, we reached the main road in about 1.5 mile, and in 2.8 miles left it in an attempt to approach the Pecos; but the cañon proved to be very short and rugged, and headed by precipices by which we were turned again to the road, and having marched 3.6 miles, in which short distance the odometer upset, breaking one of the shafts; which, however, was soon temporarily repaired by a rope. I followed the road, on a lookout for a prospect of leaving it on a new trail; but all were bad, till we reached the place upon which we are now dry camped, fifteen miles from the point at which we returned to the road, and within thirty miles of Howard's spring, and a few miles of Johnson's run, where, within a few months past, several trains have been attacked by Indians, and to-day saw their tracks in the cañon where we left the road. Our camp is well supplied with grass, but no water from Beaver lake to Howard's spring. The mail coach passed our camp this afternoon, and reported that twenty-eight mounted Indians made their appearance at the mail station at Howard's spring day before yesterday, and filled up the spring, which is a small hole below the surface, with rocks, and carried off one horse.

Watered our mules from the barrels this afternoon, giving each two and a half gallons.

*June* 26.—Left the road this morning at camp, taking about a northwesterly course; in about two miles entered the head of a cañon, in which we are now camped dry. Plenty good grass, wood, and indications of water, such as animals, birds, &c., but none yet found; country exceedingly rugged, and bad prospect for maintaining our course. Made a good deal of westering for about nine miles, when the cañon turned to the south; marched 16.1 miles.

A rain water hole was found by one of the camel herders about a quarter of a mile from camp late in the afternoon, containing a good supply of water. All the animals watered. Lieutenant Holman rode a short distance from camp, and reported on his return some Indian signs.

*June* 27.—Had four of the twenty gallon barrels filled at the water hole this morning, with which we will have an abundance of water for two more dry camps. About a mile passed another good rain water hole, and five miles further another very fine one. The animals were watered— at least it was offered them whenever found. The cañon in which we traveled yesterday appeared to take us to

Devil's river, and we left it at camp, taking up a side cañon bearing a little south of west about six miles. Then going out on a rolling land, crossed the heads of several cañons, marching a northwestern direction about 4.5 miles before taking the one we are in now, which carried us to the north of west about four miles, then turning southerly to our camp, struck one of my former trails. Country very rough. Grass not good for want of rain. No indications of water whatever.

The odometer machine has overturned several times— no harm done. Made 21.2 miles. Gave the mules two and a half gallons of water from barrels.

*June* 28.—Continued down the cañon this morning on my old trail about six miles. I have been almost forced to take this trail for want of an outlet from the cañon. Following the main cañon nearly south four miles, it then turned to the west to the Pecos about 3.5 miles.

One and a half miles from the river, we discovered in the cañon a large, fine, limpid, running stream of fresh water, which is named Piscas creek, abounding in fish of various kinds, which we could see running about in every direction. This afternoon we went fishing. I suppose the command has caught about a dozen fine ones, weighing from twelve to fifteen pounds each. Lieutenant Holman caught two of them. Command in fine order. Wood and grass plenty. Marched 13.5 miles. Cañon rough. The mountains here gradually grown larger, higher, rougher, and more rocky since entering the cañon, which is generally, I am sorry to say, characteristic of every one which you may descend, and of them this whole region is an interminable succession, all of them barren and bleak.

*June* 29.—Left camp and proceeded up the east bank of the Pecos, ascending the side of the mountains several hundred feet above the river, to avoid an immense jungle lying along the base. The camels performed well; also the mules. The odometer upset and turned a complete somersault, with the mule, down the side of a precipitous rocky slope, after which the machine was drawn by hand the remainder of the mountainous road, as a high bluff lay immediately under the trail. On this trail we saw a corn sack and Indian tracks. Three of the men crossed the jungle, and came across an Indian camp but two or three days old, composed of about a half dozen, the men on foot. A great deal of game on the river—bear, deer, antelope, and turkey. We passed three live oak mats in the mouths of cañons. At one had to cut through a jungle. At 7.4 miles from camp we passed Makin's spring, a very fine one, and 3.5 further we crossed the river and camped, and made preparations for a long and dry march toward Fort Davis. The camels succeeded remarkably well, better than usual in crossing without difficulty; but they are lightly laden, the water barrels being empty. We have had no delay by the falling of packs, as last year, all attributable to the improvements. I do not think a single one has dropped to-day. The mules are never turned out without hopples, nor picketed without them at night, to prevent a stampede, which is likely to occur at any moment. Made to-day 10.9 miles. Wood and tolerable grass.

*June* 30.—Left the Pecos at camp this morning with intention of making our way across the country to Fort Davis. Proceeded up a cañon which in two miles proved to be an unfavorable one for our purpose. Came to a head in a very few miles. Very rugged high bluffs on the sides, and may be classed among the innumerable impassable ones which abound in this region. We retraced our steps to the river, took up it about 1.5 miles, when we came to the mouth of another presenting more favorable features, which we took for our route, and arrived at its head this afternoon and dry camped on the table land ten miles from the Pecos. General course west six miles, northwest four. Grass very dry; brushwood. Whilst ascending to the Mera two camels fell and bursted two of the kegs and injured several others, wasting about forty gallons of our most appreciated loading. The animals I believe are not injured. One of them lost its foothold, fell, and pulled the others from the trail by the rope attaching the train. Others might have suffered the same fate but for the timely assistance of Lieutenant Holman, who cut the lead line. During the ascent they had to resort to their feat of walking on their knees, which they do when the inclination of the trail is very great and heavily laden, to throw the center of gravity equally over the four legs, or on a slipping trail when their feet slip from under them. Marched 15.4 miles.

*July* 1.—Did not get as early a start this morning as desired, and again delayed by vain endeavors to proceed on our march across cañons too huge to attempt, retraced our steps after a march of more than two miles, and took an Indian trail passing near our camp to the south, on which one of the men picked up a butcher knife, not long lost. Followed it 2.1 miles, then changed our course westwardly about four miles, northwest 3.5, west and southwest 3.2, being obliged to keep on the divide between the cañons where we set out. Country very rough, rocky, barren, dry, apparently no rain on the region over which we passed to-day for a year. Every blade of grass dry and dead, and not of this year's growth. Our mules will not fare well—no forage and a very limited supply of water. The camels have performed most admirably to-day. No such march as this could be made with any security without them. It is with difficulty that the mules can be kept from the water barrels, particularly when the water is being issued. I might say the same of men. Grass bad; brushwood about the size of a finger. Made 27.2 miles. Gave the mules two and a half gallons of water.

*July* 2.—Marched westwardly most of the day, and after a long march of 29.4 miles over a rough country, camped dry without any prospects of finding water, in about the poorest prospect of making progress I have ever been situated. We are all very uneasy, not to say a little frightened, for our welfare. The mules must go without water to-night, are broken down now, and some are expected to be abandoned on the march to-morrow. We have only water sufficient for the men thirty hours. The Pecos, Rio Grande, and Fort Stocton, are too distant to reach, and the water on the Camanche trail. San Francisco creek, or Willow Spring, which we expected to attain, we may be unable to reach from the impassibility of the region. Our march to-day has been rough, and too rough to-morrow, I fear, for many lives that are now with us to stem. The animals go to the barrels and draw the bungs with their teeth and knaw at the bung holes. The second time in my life I have seen a quart of water priceless, almost. We have sent a man to search for water, to be paid liberally if he succeeds; if not, all the mules we expect to lose.

A canteen of water was issued to the men with enough to make a cup of coffee. This is the fourth day since the camels drank, which was at the Pecos, brackish water, the same that we have, not only brackish, but when the bung is taken from a barrel a stench proceeds; it contains so much filth and impurity, and being barreled so long. The camels display quite a thirst.

*July* 3.—Continued our march over very rugged country, retaining our course a little south of west, marched all day with much hope at heart, but very little sign or prospect of success of our only object in life to-day, that of reaching water. The whole command is very uncomfortable with regard to its future prospects. The animals of burden are almost ceased to be talked of, and the topic has become one of self interest alone. Drought depresses the most buoyant spirit, and keeps the mind in full operation and anxiety. Some of the men are very weak, and have several times reported about to give up and no water to drink. All we can tell them is, if they stop, they must risk the consequences, that not a moment can be lost for any one. We have some apprehensions for the safety of the command, and to-morrow a dispersion must take place in small parties to look for water according to individual judgment, to seek one another, if successful; if not, never to meet again but by chance. The men have a quart of water issued to-night, and have enough for two drinks to-morrow, but they are so feeble and thirsty that it all would not last them an hour if they could get to it. The mules have stood it most admirably, much to the wonder of every one. All are in camp to-night, but cannot graze for their thirst. The camels are continually bellowing, which I suppose, as it is unusual, a sign of a want of water.

A part of our quartermaster and commissary stores were abandoned at camp this morning. The mules were too feeble to be laden; and, fearing it too much for our camels, marched thirty miles, good grass region bleak and dreary.

*July* 4.—Although the command was very weary last night, it did not rest as well as I have seen it; the whole conversation was of "something to drink." We had to use our canteens for pillows to secure our water, as none of the most thirsty show much reluctance in emptying any one they may come across at a draught. This morning brought forth many serious and despondent countenances in the command as they prepared to march with their two drinks of water, and not knowing when or where the next was to be had, if at all. After marching four miles one of these was given out, when serious thoughts of dispersion, every one to do the best he could for himself and comrade. When ascending a little rise, to my delight, I recognized looming up in the distance, about fifteen miles, Camel's Hump mountain, at whose base the head of San Francisco creek lies, and all pushed eagerly on to taste the sparkling treasure. No one can imagine the feelings of a thirsty man till he sees one. I would not describe it by a vain attempt, as vain almost as that would be which I might use in describing the region of country just passed over which made them so; a region in its original chaotic state, as if the progress of civilization was too rapid for the arrangement of chaos; a picture of barrenness and desolation, when the scathing fire of destruction has swept with its rabid flame mountains, cañons, ravines, precipices, cactus, soap weed, intense reflection from the limestone cliffs, and almost every barrier that one can conceive of to make an impossibility to progress.

Thus, and most joyfully, too, have we celebrated this memorable day; if it ever would have been, now, never will it escape having its anniversary remembered; the camp resounds with "hurrah for the 4th." The animals exhibited a remarkable knowledge of approaching water some time before reaching it, particularly the camels, which made a remarkable change in their speed ten miles from it. They had to be held back to keep them with the mules that before had been leading them.

This is the fifth day since leaving the Pecos; the men are on foot, with half allowance of water; marched 120 miles, thermometer about 100° in shade, intense reflection, no wood, over the most rugged country known, the last days made about thirty miles. The mules were watered only twice on half allowance, and on the sixth day from water. The camels stood it well. To-day, however, four mules gave out before reaching camp, two of which managed to reach camp after the command; the others abandoned. It was strange to see how eagerly they would seize a canteen whenever they were near it, and try to tear it to pieces. I saw one take a cork from one that was hanging up, and was drinking water from it by turning it about and catching the water as it was spilled. The men were cautioned about permitting them to drink too much at a time, as it sometimes proves fatal. After marching four miles, we encountered one of the highest, roughest, and most difficult descents we have met, which required a long while to overcome. One of the camels fell, notwithstanding great caution was taken with them, but not hurt. The odometer machine was abandoned, but will be sent for to-morrow; also the mules. Camped at a water-hole about a mile before reaching the creek, which stands in pools from ten to twenty-five feet deep, good water, we found fine grass in the Creek valley, which presents comparatively a refreshing appearance. Crossed my trail in 1859 going north from the Rio Grande about ten miles from camp. Marched 17.5 miles.

*July* 5.—Remained in camp to recruit; sent out to get the mules abandoned, but could not find them; water was carried for them on the camels; the machine was brought in. One of the mules in camp died last night; several of the men complaining of sickness.

*July* 6.—In camp still; the mules look badly; one of the men very sick last night, but a great deal better this morning, walking about camp.

*July* 7.—This morning packed up and went down San Francisco creek about a mile to a large fine water-hole to fill up our barrels, which occupied a good portion of the best traveling part of the day, but we only intended to make a short march and camp at water, not very good, nor a great deal of it, so we filled up before starting. After making our second start, marched toward "Camel Hump," about five miles from our camp, and accidentally crossed the Camanche trail without seeing it, perhaps when it had been almost washed away. Ascertaining the fact, we soon gained it and marched up it 10.3 miles to Willow spring, where we find a supply of water, also some rain water. We have no guide, and I have been guiding, but not being a very experienced one, after having crossed the Camanche trail unnoticed, lost it again after having found it; but,

knowing about the location of Willow spring in directing my course accordingly, soon recovered it. Camped at the spring; good grass, little wood; marched 16.4 miles. The camels perform admirably. I never hear the eternal "hold on, a pack is down" of last year. Our improvements are perfection. The mules are not doing so well. A good many of them are worthless to us, with sore backs, &c., and a perfect encumbrance, drinking our water. The odometer goes very well, but has broken *four* shafts. This spring is about one fourth of a mile west of the trail in a small ravine, among rushes, immediately above a large rock, strata inclined about 45°, crossing the bed—several such are passed before reaching the spring; willows growing.

*July* 8.—Set out early this morning, as usual, about sunrise, and left the Camanche trail at camp for Fort Davis; marched about W. 20° N. all day; pretty good trail, but large mountains on every side, and camped among them this evening. We are making more westing than we like, but it cannot be prevented. At Camel's Hump we first reached the primitive rocks, and have been on the line of demarkation since leaving that mountain; found large herds of antelope on our route to-day, killed one.

The mules have two and a half gallons of water this evening, some of them looking badly; command well. The herder, late yesterday afternoon, reported that he saw an Indian mounted, within a mile of camp, but we were not disturbed.

The mornings are very cool, indeed; overcoats and blankets come freely into use. The water in our canteens almost as cold as ice water, at noon the thermometer is generally not much over 100°. Pretty good grass at camp; wood scarce; marched 22.1 miles.

*July* 9.—Soon after leaving camp this morning, I endeavored in vain to cross the mountain range north of us, after expending a march of about four miles. Afterward returning to the valley, prolonged our trail, and in a few miles were fortunate in finding that the cañon made a turn N. 40° W., and then opened into a broken region of country to the west, several miles; and in the distance stood Mitre Peak, sixteen miles from Fort Davis. After marching twenty miles, found a rain-water hole; five miles further found another very large, where we camped, having marched twenty-five miles. About thirteen miles from last camp, passed a very large grove of cedars, about two miles long. Antelopes very numerous. Country passed over to-day, very dry. Very little grass at camp, and no wood at all.

*July* 10.—Less than half a mile from camp this morning, we crossed a new road to Presidio del Norte, from Fort Stockton, leaving the El Paso road at Leon Hales; proceeded on our course toward Mitre Peak, and after 8.8 miles, our nearest point to it, turned towards the north, and in about a half mile struck the trail on which I went to Fort Davis last year, which has been worked by Mexicans, and has become a traveled and passable road for Mexican carates, several have already passed over it to the post.

From the nearest point of the trail to Mitre Peak, to Fort Davis, is 15.7 miles, and from Musqueir ranch, to Fort Davis, is 7.4 miles. In the cañon where this ranch is located, and in which the trail runs, is a small creek, and water to be found from the ranch to Mitre Peak. About two miles from the post it began to rain and hail heavily, which continued till after we went into camp on the Limpia; good camping ground; marched 24.5 miles. Found Colonel Seawell preparing to move the headquarters of the eighth infantry to San Antonio, with Lieutenant Dye, quartermaster, and Lieutenant Jones, adjutant, and will leave to-morrow morning. Lieutenant Van Horn will also leave to-morrow morning, with about ten prisoners for El Paso, to be tried for a case of hanging, by the civil authorities, which occured here a few months since. Colonel Seawell also takes five with him to San Antonio, accomplices in the same. We will remain at Fort Davis several days to recruit; several men and mules will have to be left here, unable to proceed. Command generally pretty well. Camels doing finely, no indication of having undergone any severities.

*July* 14.—Remained at Fort Davis till this morning, spent a most pleasant visit. Colonel Bomford, from Fort Quitman, with a detachment of his company in command, set out for Presidio del Norte, with 160 gallons of water, expecting to find some water, about forty miles from the post, found a little rain water at nineteen miles. Left nine mules at the post, and one of the men lame; the others who were complaining of ophthalmia had sufficiently recovered to march; took in a supply of new shoes for the men, expecting to be out about thirty days before reaching another post, we have taken rations for that period. Made a march of twenty-five miles, all on foot; camped dry; no wood; grass not very good. We have not yet been able to obtain a guide to suit our wishes. Had some fine water melons, musk melons, and some small apples and pears at Fort Davis, usually brought from Mexico.

*July* 15.—Passed the San Estaban to-day, about ten miles from camp. It was off the road to the east a mile or two, and we did not go to it. One of the men went out to the water and reported it unfit for drinking. Eight miles from camp passed a spring in the bed of arroyo Rancherillo spring, made by digging, splendid water, and now camped on a fine permanent water called Pealagos, 18.9 miles from last camp; good grass; no wood; command in fine order. We have been traveling on the Fort Davis and Presidio del Norte road, and so far it is magnificent one. Country rather open. About 25 miles north and east of us there was a fine rain this morning, and we had a slight sprinkle. Very warm this morning, but a fine breeze this afternoon. At the lone cedar off the road, to the right, is frequently found rain water; seven or eight miles from San Estaban.

*July* 16.—Marched to-day 25.9 miles, and camped at _____. There were water holes in the bed of an arroyo; perhaps permanent water; found the greatest abundance of fine water along the road to-day in the bed of an arroyo, each place having its name; six miles reached the Penitas; about three miles another water; four and eight another; at eleven the Varras, very fine large holes an hundred feet long, very deep, and running stream; the last hole is called the "Punta del Agua;" country mountainous, but road fine; camels performing beautifully and heavily laden. In addition to their almost unlimited variety of food—bushes, briars, and grass—I can add the thistle and several species of the cactus—the prickly pear is one. Another circumstance has occurred to-day to make me mention the old song of "the falling of packs," which I had forgotten, being not reminded of it for some time till to-day, when we had to stop twice for their readjust-

ment, as unusual now as to have marched two hours without it last year; country very dry; wood, but little grass. A wagon load of watermelons passed us this afternoon for Fort Davis from Presidio del Norte.

*July* 17.—Came to the Alamo spring 4.1 miles from camp; fine running water in abundance in a cluster of a half dozen large alamos; crossed a steep range of mountains immediately after leaving camp; surface quite rolling and uneven till we came about eleven miles, where we found water in a cave, scarcely accessible by a man; from there to Fort Leaton surface very curiously broken; ravines in cañons and on table lands; hills in the bottom of cañons, isolated and dotted about; soil loose; road tolerably good, however, but rendered quite heavy by loose, deep sand for twelve miles before reaching Presidio del Norte; reached the Rio Grande at Fort Leaton 4.1 miles from the town—an old ranche established for a trading post, &c., on a grant from the Mexican government, made about twenty-five years ago; several fine ranches along the river before reaching the town owned by Americans; camped on the river bank in a coral, good camp; marched 24.9 miles.

*July* 20.—Remained camped at Presidio del Norte till this morning; made visits to the city on the 18th and 19th; called on the Alcalde; saw a good deal of the place, but found very little worth seeing. All the buildings are of adobe, and present much the appearance of a large dirt-dauber's nest. The population is 3,100, according to the Alcalde; but about half, or less, are a den of thieves. The few Americans settled around the place seem to be gentlemen, and treated us with much cordiality. The Alcalde came into camp and spent about an hour, admiring the camels. Visits from the Mexicans have been numerous; saw the Mexican women carrying ollas of water on their heads, weighing about seventy pounds. . . .

Leaving Presidio del Norte, we intend marching eastwardly, if possible, and it has always been reported an impossibility to reach the San Carlos trail, and made to-day 7.8 miles, camped on the Rio Grande; stopped to dine with Mr. Leaton, and had a magnificent dinner, and abundance of water melons; plenty of them and musk melons in the vicinity.

*July* 21.—Left the river at camp this morning, and took up a cañon, making a little northing, country very mountainous, or rather all mountains. At 13.5 miles, reached a fine spring in a narrow deep cañon, splendid running water in abundance; about a mile further up the cañon we came to the first water of the spring, which is about ten feet deep and large. Fine alamos grow along the water which is named Ternesa spring. Here we filled our barrels for camping; had a little rain about noon; marched 21.7 miles; camped; dry brush and grass.

*July* 22.—Had a rough road four miles and a half after leaving camp this morning; a better one for about ten miles, and then the most rugged, roughest, most tortuous and cragged one I have ever seen for about eight miles to camp, rougher than any I saw between the Pecos and the Camanche trail for the same distance. I never conceived that there could be such a country. The guide says he could have brought us a little nearer route, but that it would have been rougher. I cannot conceive it possible. I cheerfully concur with all who regard this region as impassable. At 10.4 miles from camp, we reached a beautiful spring, splendid water in abundance. A few very large alamos grow along the water. Here we found a large bear; wounded and chased it, but to no avail, the country was too rough; and I have called it Bear spring. The odometer had several severe falls, and broke both of the shafts which have been several times replaced by saplings, and damaged a little otherwise, but not seriously. We are to-night camped at the most delightful water I have ever seen in the State; very, very cold, flowing from the base of a precipice, projecting about 15°, and about 600 feet high, on the face of an immense mountain about twice the height of the precipice; the guide says it has no name, and I have called it Icy Branch. Marched 22.8 miles; wood and grass; had a shower to-day.

*July* 23.—We went into camp so late yesterday, after a hard day's march, that we remained about two hours later than usual at camp, and turned out the animals to graze; made a very short march, only 12.9 miles; the country exceedingly rugged. Marched 4.9 miles, and reached the Lates Lengua, and have continued down the arroyo since; found rain-water holes in its bed continually, brush and good grass. Saw another bear to-day. Some of the camels' backs are sore. The odometer requiring the services of three men to progress over this country.

*July* 24.—Continued our march down the arroyo Lates Lengua, and found the road rugged several miles. At 6.5 miles, reached the Camanche trail to the Lahita crossing, and to San Carlos; followed it about 6.5 miles, where it crossed a mountain unsurmountable for the camels—so Lieutenant Holman regarded it—and we retraced our steps to the base, and attempted to pass around by an arroyo to the east, but were again turned back by too great a dissention by offsets in the bed; passed by another a little further to the north, and by circuituous route, found a passable road to where we are camped, within a few miles of the river, on the Lates Lengua. In this arroyo we have found plenty water since we first reached it; bushes, but little grass. From where the trail came into the Lates Lengua to camp, a road can be made, but not to follow the trail over the mountain that turned us back. We hope to reach the crossing to-morrow, if we can gain the trail again. Marched, twenty-one miles. On the last twelve miles, great many hills of loose sliding earth, resembling sand hills very much in appearance, perfectly made, and a good deal of selenite on the surface of some.

*July* 25.—Went to the river this morning, 6.3 miles from camp, to see a wonderful curiosity, which the guide told us of; a place where the stream runs through a mountain precipice, about 1,500 feet high. The opening is just the width of the stream, perhaps a little narrower than usual, the precipice springing vertically from the water to its summit. Velocity, not as great as ordinarily at other points. From here, we took up the river at a distance from it, and reached the San Carlos Camanche trail at about seven miles, and found it tolerably good; the remainder of the route to the Rio Grande, by this and the circuit which I made, a road can be built. At 6.3 from the river is a watering place called the Lahita, but now dry. The camels are getting on pretty well. We have only sixteen mules in the command, for riding purposes only; one or two of them are very slow. The arroyo Lates Lengua empties into the river immediately at the pass through the mountains. I have called this pass, "The Grand Puerta;" found

a water hole seven miles from this pass. There is not a good site here for a post, there is nothing very attractive about the spot whatever; a few bushes and small willows grow on the bank of the stream; not more than a half dozen trees to be found in the flat which is not large, and confined up and down the river by bluffs, against which the water flows, the intermediate space between two and three miles, and back from the river about a mile. The surrounding mountains, large. There is no moderately elevated spot sufficiently large for a post. Very little wood. There is a great deal of dry grass, not good now, but indicates plenty, in a good season, in the cañon and in the little hills leading to the river. The place is not very prepossessing.

*July* 26.—Left the crossing of the San Carlos Camanche trail, by the Lachita, this morning, and followed our trail of yesterday to the Lates Lengua, which we crossed, and continued down the river in search of a location for a post. The alcalde of Presidio del Norte told us of a most beautiful one known as the Los Chiras crossing, where another branch of the great Camanche trail crosses the Rio Grande—Los Chiras is on some large mountains which terminate in a range on the river at this point. We were told by every one that no one had been or could go to it on this side of the river. Marched about four miles from the Grande Puerta down the river, and camped at a spot which attracted my attention very much for a post. Very pretty; plenty of timber; abundance of wood; grass plenty; building sites. Have found about what I was in search of; but will go further to-morrow, and see how the valley appears further down the stream.

*July* 27.—After marching a few miles down the river this morning, I turned back without going to Los Chiras, satisfied that there is no better place on the river for building a post of any dimensions than that I had found. The river has a fine valley on each side, about twenty-five miles down; more timber and wood than a post can use. I saw one or two good sites on moderately elevated gravel mesas, easily accessible from the river and bottom, elevated just sufficiently for the purpose; plenty grazing for animals; some small canebrakes in the bottom; in a word, the location is well adapted for the purpose of building a post. This location is about twenty miles below the Camanche crossing, and is within a few miles of where the road would have to run to reach that place, and is well situated for accomplishing the purpose of establishing a post at the crossing. There is sufficient valley land to cultivate on either side of the river to supply any post and settlements, both of Americans and Mexicans, would render it as economical as posts generally. The Mexican population are anxious about the establishment of this post. Fort Davis and others of our posts receive many of their supplies from Mexico. Presidio del Norte furnishes to Fort Davis corn, vegetables, &c.; and from San Carlos, a great fruit and vegetable country, many supplies could be obtained; and from Presidio del Norte there is a road to the crossing, and but little work from there to the site. Returning from the location, I took a different route from the one going down, both of which can be very easily rendered wagon roads, and struck the Lates Lengua several miles higher up; also made a cut-off of several miles by leaving the arroyo when I reached it, and marching due north to camp July 27, where we found rain water and most excellent grass. Marched twenty miles. Thus far a wagon road can be built readily at no great expense.

*July* 28.—After a march of two and one fifth miles, reached the trail, and four miles further it left the Lates Lengua, going more to the east; then, at five miles, encountered a bad hill; road a little rough for four miles further; remainder to camp a fine road; but little work, however, will make it all good. About six miles before reaching camp this afternoon we passed a pretty good rainwater hole, and about two miles nearer passed a spot in which rushes grow; perhaps water can be had by digging. We are camped dry in a large valley; brought a supply of water in expectation of it. Marched 19.5 miles.

*July* 29.—Continued up the trail, and found the road good until at twelve miles, when it ascended a mountain, not very large, however, nor very rugged, but requiring work; from there to within one and one half miles of camp, the road will also require some; and here we have unfortunately encountered a descent, very rugged and steep, which, I fear, may ruin the so far good prospects for a road. The trail is impracticable at this point without very much labor, and the vicinity appears no better. A further examination will be made. Just before descending this mountain, we discovered from the top, in a deep cañon, very narrow, with precipitous sides about a thousand feet high, a beautiful water, which we could not reach; we descended, went to the mouth of the cañon, which we could not enter, and encamped. From here none of the animals can be taken to the water by any assistance that men are able to give them; it is a severe trail to reach it on foot. The animals have been without water two days, as we would not provide it for them with so much labor as to make the men bring it for them in small quantities, nearly a mile, over the most cragged road. The water appeared from the mountain top about three feet in diameter, but we find it to be about thirty, and deep; another water, about fifty yards further up the cañon, was found; it is very fine and cold; the sun has never shone on it; I have called it the "Inaccessible Tank." Marched 18.9 miles.

*July* 30.—This morning I rode down the precipice, at whose base we were encamped, to look for a place to cross the precipitous mountain of yesterday. I went down four or five miles, from where I could see about six further, where it was smaller and more broken, but yet presented a formidable obstacle; but not so bad as at the trail. In going up the precipice, as far as I could examine, several miles, it appeared to increase in height. Proceeding up the trail six and a half miles we entered a rough cañon, but short and passable. One and one fifth miles further, we arrived opposite the Sierra Santiago, on whose side is reported a sulphur spring, upon which we had placed much dependence, but, to our sad disappointment, it was dry, which prevented making a halt to examine for another route around the mountain. We had only to push ahead and seek water, and found a nice spring or creek at 7.4 miles from Sierra Santiago. I have named it "Forked Branch." The camels were without water three days; the mules also, except a very limited supply last night; both are beginning to show exhaustion; the mules are lame and halt; the camels have several sore feet; their soles have actually been abraded off to the quick by the sharp cragged rocks, and others have very sore backs, indeed; holes in

the humps are large enough to thrust in both fists; these sores do not injure them so much, being in the fleshy part of the hump, so long as they can be kept from the bones. Camped at Forked branch. Marched 15.8 miles.

I would recommend to any one using the camels over rough country, in case of tender feet, to shoe them with a piece of (circular) raw hide, gather around the leg by a slipping cord; this will be found an absolute necessity in some instances. One of the men left the command a short distance yesterday, and has not been seen or heard of since.

*August* 1.—Remained camped at Forked Branch yesterday to rest the animals; fine water and good grass. After making a further examination of the water, we find many large water holes six feet deep up and down the arroyo; permanent water. To-day, having filled our kegs, proceeded up the trail, and 16.4 miles struck the Camanche trail a few miles north of "Camel's Hump," at a water hole which last year and also a month ago indicated permanency, but now dry. A few miles further passed another rain-hole with water. Camped at Willow Spring; dry but muddy; got water by digging a foot; a mile from camp in the same bed found water; route good; marched 25.5 miles; saw fresh mule track on the trail to-day, perhaps of one we abandoned.

*August* 2.—Marched 19.2 miles up the Camanche trail to-day and camped dry. No wood; grass very dry. Went about a mile down the arroyo this morning, to fill some kegs at the water, and 7.5 miles up the trail passed a water hole. At 3.6 miles another where Captain Brockett camped last year; several others with water, most of it not very good, and drying away very rapidly. The country very dry. Where we are camped is about the point at which I wished to leave the trail last year for the Pecos, but the condition of the animals was too bad to undertake it, and our water too scarce. Now the condition of the animals is even worse, nearly every mule barefooted and lame, or exhausted, several of the camels almost unable to march at all from tender feet. We have water in our barrels, but to attempt the trip would be at the expense of several, both mules and camels. We will have to go to Fort Stockton to leave those that cannot go and have the mules shod. One of the men has the opthalmia; another wounded himself in the hand this afternoon by the accidental discharge of his pistol; the one who was lost on the 29th ultimo has not appeared.

*August* 3.—Marched 19.7 miles on the trail; found no water; the grass little green. Camped dry, near where we left the camel last year; no tidings of him, nor of the lost man. Several camels have sore backs, but fit for use; three have tender feet, and march slowly; make about two miles an hour on good road; have to take them to Fort Stockton to save them; one has not browsed for two days; feet too sore to move about.

*August* 4.—Went into Fort Stockton. Marched 16.4 miles with some difficulty. Some of our rations are short also. Discharged our guide. Will remain here two days and fit up that portion of the command able to resume the reconnoissance.

*August* 15.—Came into Camp Hudson to-day, and regret to say that I had to lose that portion of the reconnoissance which I had all the while intended to make from

Fort Stockton across the country to this post, and came by the road. Lieutenant Holman stated that the escort was no longer capable of performing more work in the field. Very little water on the road; no grass. Left one man at Fort Lancaster, and one camel, with a man to attend to it, at Fort Stockton, and two mules. Have not yet heard of the man who was lost on the trail.

WILLIAM H. ECHOLS,
Brevet Second Lieut. Topographical Engineers.

## 83. TEXAS SECEDES FROM THE UNION

### February 1 and 2, 1861

The election of Lincoln in 1860 triggered the secession of South Carolina on December 20. Five other southern states quickly followed. In Texas, secessionist leaders were blocked temporarily in taking Texas out of the Union, largely because Governor Houston refused to call a special session of the legislature to authorize a convention. To circumvent Houston, the secessionists, on December 3, addressed the people of Texas requesting an election on January 8 to name delegates to a January 28 convention to meet in Austin. To give this extra-legal action an aura of legality, and also hoping to forestall drastic action, Houston issued a call for a special session of the legislature to convene on January 21. When it convened, the legislature validated the authority of the convention, but with the restriction that any decision made must be submitted to a referendum.

The convention met on the appointed day, and on February 1, amidst cheering and hissing from the excited crowds in the galleries, passed an ordinance repealing the ordinance of annexation of 1845 by a vote of 166 to 8. On the following day, the convention adopted a committee address setting forth the causes which induced the State of Texas to secede from the Federal Union. Both documents are reproduced below.

### 1. THE ORDINANCE OF SECESSION

#### February 1, 1861

From *Journal of the Secession Convention of Texas, 1861* (E. W. Winkler, ed.; Austin, 1912), 35-59; H. P. N. Gammel (comp.), *The Laws of Texas, 1822-1897* (10 vols.; Austin, 1898), IV, 1519-1520.

An Ordinance to dissolve the union between the State of Texas and the other States, united under the compact styled "The Constitution of the United States of America."

Whereas, the Federal Government has failed to accomplish the purposes of the compact of union between the States, in giving protection either to the persons of our people upon an exposed frontier, or to the property of our citizens; and, whereas, the action of the Northern States of the Union is violative of the compact between the States and the guarantees of the Federal Constitution, and, whereas, the recent developments in Federal affairs, make it evident that the power of the Federal Government is sought to be made a weapon with which to strike down the interest and prosperity of the people of Texas and her sister slaveholding States, instead of permitting it to be, as was intended our shield against outrage and aggression: Therefore,

Sec. 1. We, the People of the State of Texas, by delegates in Convention assembled, do declare and ordain, that the ordinance adopted by our convention of delegates, on the 4th day of July, A. D. 1845, and afterwards ratified by us, under which the Republic of Texas was admitted into union with other States and became a party to the compact styled "The Constitution of the United States of America" be, and is hereby repealed and annulled; that all the powers which by said compact were delegated by Texas to the Federal Government are revoked and resumed; that Texas is of right absolved from all restraints and obligations incurred by said compact, and is a separate sovereign State, and that her citizens and people are absolved from all allegiance to the United States, or the Government thereof.

Sec. 2. This ordinance shall be submitted to the people of Texas for their ratification or rejection by the qualified voters thereof, on the 23d day of February, 1861, and, unless rejected by a majority of the votes cast, shall take effect and be in force on and after the 2d day of March, A. D. 1861. Provided that in the representative district of El Paso said election may be held on the 18th day of February, A. D. 1861.

Done by the people of the State of Texas, in Convention assembled, at Austin, this 1st day of February, A. D. 1861.

### 2. A DECLARATION OF THE CAUSES WHICH IMPEL THE STATE OF TEXAS TO SECEDE FROM THE FEDERAL UNION

From *Journal of the Secession Convention of Texas, 1861* (E. W. Winkler, ed.; Austin, 1912), 61-65.

The government of the United States, by certain joint resolutions, bearing date the 1st day of March, in the year A. D. 1845, proposed to the Republic of Texas, then *a free, sovereign and independent nation,* the annexation of the latter to the former, as one of the co-equal States thereof,

The people of Texas, by deputies in convention assembled, on the fourth day of July of the same year, assented to and accepted said proposals and formed a constitution for the proposed State, upon which on the 29th day of December in the same year, said State was formally admitted into the Confederated Union.

Texas abandoned her separate national existence and consented to become one of the Confederated States to promote her welfare, insure domestic tranquility and secure more substantially the blessings of peace and liberty to her people. She was received into the confederacy with her own constitution, under the guarantee of the federal constitution and the compact of annexation, that she should enjoy these blessings. She was received as a commonwealth holding, maintaining and protecting the institution known as negro slavery—the servitude of the African to the white race within her limits—a relation that had existed from the first settlement of her wilderness by the white race, and which her people intended should exist in all future time. Her institutions and geographical position established the strongest ties between her and other slave-holding States of the confederacy. Those ties have been strengthened by association. But what has been the course of the government of the United States, since our connection with them?

The controlling majority of the Federal Government, under various pretences and disguises, has so administered the same as to exclude the citizens of the Southern States, unless under odious and unconstitutional restrictions, from all the immense territory owned in common by all the States on the Pacific Ocean, for the avowed purpose of acquiring sufficient power in the common government to use it as a means of destroying the institutions of Texas and her sister slave-holding States.

By the disloyalty of the Northern States and their citizens and the imbecility of the Federal Government, infamous combinations of incendiaries and outlaws have been permitted in those States and the common territory of Kansas to trample upon the federal laws, to war upon the lives and property of Southern citizens in that territory, and finally, by violence and mob law, to usurp the possession of the same as exclusively the property of the Northern States.

The Federal Government, while but partially under the control of these our unnatural and sectional enemies, has for years almost entirely failed to protect the lives and property of the people of Texas against the Indian savages on our border, and more recently against the murderous forays of banditti from the neighboring territory of Mexico; and when our State government has expended large amounts for such purpose, the Federal Government has refused reimbursement therefor, thus rendering our condition more insecure and harassing than it was during the existence of the Republic of Texas.

These and other wrongs we have patiently borne in the vain hope that a returning sense of justice and humanity would induce a different course of administration.

When we advert to the course of individual non-slave-holding States, and that a majority of their citizens, our grievances assume far greater magnitude.

The States of Maine, Vermont, New Hampshire, Connecticut, Rhode Island, Massachusetts, New York, Pennsylvania, Ohio, Wisconsin, Michigan and Iowa, by solemn legislative enactments, have deliberately, directly or indirectly violated the 3rd clause of the 2nd section of the 4th article of the federal constitution, and laws passed in pursuance thereof; thereby annulling a material provision of the compact, designed by its framers to perpetuate amity between the members of the confederacy and to secure the rights of the slave-holding States in their domestic institutions—a provision founded in justice and wisdom, and without the enforcement of which the compact fails to accomplish the object of its creation. Some of those States have imposed high fines and degrading penalties upon any of their citizens or officers who may carry out in good faith that provision of the compact, or the federal laws enacted in accordance therewith.

In all the non-slave-holding States, in violation of that good faith and comity which should exist between entirely distinct nations, the people have formed themselves into a great sectional party, now strong enough in numbers to control the affairs of each of those States, based upon the unnatural feeling of hostility to these Southern States and their beneficent and patriarchal system of African slavery, proclaiming the debasing doctrine of the equality of all men, irrespective of race or color—a doctrine at war with nature, in opposition to the experience of mankind, and in violation of the plainest revelations of the Divine Law. They demand the abolition of negro slavery throughout the confederacy, the recognition of political equality between the white and the negro races, and avow their determination to press on their crusade against us, so long as a negro slave remains in these States.

For years past, this abolition organization has been actively sowing the seeds of discord through the Union, and has rendered the congress the arena for spreading firebrands and hatred between the slave-holding and non-slave-holding States.

By consolidating their strength, they have placed the slave-holding States in a hopeless minority in the federal congress, and rendered representation of no avail in protecting Southern rights against their exactions and encroachments.

They have proclaimed, and at the ballot box sustained, the revolutionary doctrine that there is a "higher law" than the constitution and laws of our Federal Union, and virtually that they will disregard their oaths and trample upon our rights.

They have for years past encouraged and sustained lawless organizations to steal our slaves and prevent their recapture, and have repeatedly murdered Southern citizens while lawfully seeking their rendition.

They have invaded Southern soil and murdered unoffending citizens, and through the press their leading men and a fanatical pulpit have bestowed praise upon the actors and assassins in these crimes, while the governors of several of their States have refused to deliver parties implicated and indicted for participation in such offences, upon the legal demands of the States aggrieved.

They have, through the mails and hired emissaries, sent seditious pamphlets and papers among us to stir up servile insurrection and bring blood and carnage to our firesides.

They have sent hired emissaries among us to burn our towns and distribute arms and poison to our slaves for the same purpose.

They have impoverished the slave-holding States by unequal and partial legislation, thereby enriching themselves by draining our substance.

They have refused to vote appropriations for protecting Texas against ruthless savages, for the sole reason that she is a slave-holding State.

And, finally, by the combined sectional vote of the seventeen non-slave-holding States, they have elected as president and vice-president of the whole confederacy two men whose chief claims to such high positions are their approval of these long continued wrongs, and their pledges to continue them to the final consummation of these schemes for the ruin of the slave-holding States.

In view of these and many other facts, it is meet that our own views should be distinctly proclaimed.

We hold as undeniable truths that the governments of the various States, and of the confederacy itself, were established exclusively by the white race, for themselves and their posterity; that the African race had no agency in their establishment; that they were rightfully held and regarded as an inferior and dependent race, and in that condition only could their existence in this country be rendered beneficial or tolerable.

That in this free government *all white men are and of right ought to be entitled to equal civil and political rights;* that the servitude of the African race, as existing in these States, is mutually beneficial to both bond and free, and is abundantly authorized and justified by the experience of mankind, and the revealed will of the Almighty Creator, as recognized by all Christian nations; while the destruction of the existing relations between the two races, as advocated by our sectional enemies, would bring inevitable calamities upon both and desolation upon the fifteen slave-holding States.

By the secession of six of the slave-holding States, and the certainty that others will speedily do likewise, Texas has no alternative but to remain in an isolated connection with the North, or unite her destinies with the South. . . .

## 84. GOVERNOR HOUSTON DEPOSED

### March 16, 1861

From *The Ordinances and Resolutions of the Convention Held in the City of Austin, 1861* (Austin, 1861), 13-14.

The Secession Convention, after having recessed on February 5, reconvened on March 2 to canvass the popular vote on the secession ordinance. Finding that the ordinance carried (46,129 to 14,697), it proceeded over the opposition of Governor Houston to unite Texas with the Confederate States of America (March 5), and then to modify the state government to conform with that of the Confederacy, including an oath of allegiance for all state officials. When Houston refused to appear to take the oath, the Convention by a vote of 127 to 4 adopted the following ordinance.

Whereas, an ordinance was adopted by the people of the State of Texas, in Convention assembled, at the city of Austin, on Thursday, the 14th day of March, A. D. 1861, entitled "An Ordinance to provide for the continuance of the existing State Government," by the provisions of which it was made incumbent upon the Governor, Lieutenant-Governor, Secretary of State, Comptroller, Treasurer, Attorney General and Commissioner of the General Land Office, to take an official oath, prescribed by "An Ordinance to amend the 1st section of the 7th article (general provisions) of the Constitution of the State of Texas," adopted March 14, A. D. 1861, at such time as the President should appoint, within three days from the date of said Convention, in obedience to the provisions of said first named ordinance, did appoint the hour of 12 o'clock M., of Satur-day, the 16th day of March, 1861, as the hour at which said official oath should be taken, by said officers, and did cause to be given to said officers due and timely notice of the same; and, whereas, at the hour of 12 M., of Saturday, the 16th day of March, 1861, the Convention being in session and the president thereof having announced that the officer appointed therefor was prepared to administer the prescribed oath of office to said officers; and, whereas Sam Houston, Governor, and E. W. Cave, Secretary of State, failed and refused to appear and take the said oath, as Governor and Secretary of State; and, whereas, Edward Clark, Lieut.-Governor of the State of Texas, did at that hour take and subscribe the oath aforesaid, as Lieut.-Governor of the State; therefore,

Section 1. Be it ordained by the people of Texas, in Convention assembled, That the office of Governor of the State of Texas, by reason of the refusal of the late Governor, Sam Houston, to take the official oath, is vacant, and that the Lieut.-Governor, Edward Clark, is hereby required and authorized to exercise the powers and authority appertaining to the office of Governor, until another be chosen at the periodical election, and be duly qualified. . . .

Adopted in Convention, at Austin, the 16th day of March, A. D. 1861.

## 85. THE BATTLE OF SABINE PASS

### September 8, 1863

From United States, *War of the Rebellion: Official Records of the Union and Confederate Armies* (Washington, 1889) Series I, XXVI, Part I, 294-297, 311-312.

Texas remained free from occupation by Union troops during the entire period of the Civil War except for intermittent landings along the coast. Although its good fortune may be credited largely to its geographical location, determined resistance also played an important part. The most dramatic event occurred on September 8, 1863, when Lieutenant Richard ("Dick") W. Dowling and his small garrison turned back a major thrust at Sabine Pass by a Union force under Major General W. B. Franklin. The successful repulse of this invasion not only spared Texas a possibly lengthy military campaign and occupation, but acted also as an important boost for Confederate morale after the Gettysburg and Vicksburg campaigns.

### 1. GENERAL FRANKLIN'S REPORT

On board the Steamship Suffolk, September 11, 1863.

General: I have the honor to report that, . . . [on] Friday, [September 4,] at 5 p.m., Brigadier-General

Weitzel started from New Orleans with about 1,000 infantry, who were to land as soon as the Clifton began to of 20-pounder, of First Indiana Artillery, in the steamers Belvidere, Banks, Landis, and Saint Charles. The remainder of the force, with few exceptions, embarked during Friday night, and arrived at the mouth of the river during all of Saturday.

General Weitzel's instructions were to proceed as far as off Berwick Bay, in company with the gunboat Arizona, when he was to be joined by Lieutenant-Commander Crocker, U. S. Navy, with the gunboats Clifton and Sachem; thence they were to proceed in company to Sabine Pass, off which they expected to arrive during Sunday night. On Monday morning, at daylight, they were to enter the mouth of Sabine River. The gunboats were to engage and silence the rebel battery, and General Weitzel's troops were to co-operate, and were to hold a position on shore until the arrival of the other troops. Unfortunately the gunboat Granite City, which had been dispatched to the Pass several days before to carry Captain Crocker's pilot, who was well acquainted with the channel of the Pass, and who was to place a light to enable him to run in at daylight, did not arrive at the Pass until Monday afternoon; also, on Sunday night there were no blockaders off the Pass. The consequence was, that Captain Crocker missed Sabine Pass on Sunday night; imagined that he had run past it; ran back, and at daylight on Monday morning was off Calcasieu Pass, the next opening to the eastward, instead of being ready to run into Sabine Pass.

On Monday morning, about 11 o'clock, I arrived off Sabine Pass at the head of the fleet of transports, crossed the bar, and was about to run in, when, seeing nothing to indicate the presence of our people, I recrossed the bar. It was not until late in the afternoon that I ascertained definitely that nothing had yet been done. I then learned that Captain Crocker now intended to make the attack on Tuesday morning, and that he had dispatched a gunboat to warn me to keep back, in order that the enemy might not see the transport fleet, but the gunboat only stopped some of the rear vessels of the fleet, missing the leading vessels entirely.

By this series of misfortunes, the attack, which was intended to be a surprise, became an open one, the enemy having had two nights' warning that a fleet was off the harbor, and, during Monday, a full view of most of the vessels composing it; besides, twenty-four hours of valuable time and good weather were uselessly consumed.

After consultation with Captain Crocker on Monday night, it was determined that the Clifton should go into the harbor at daylight, and make a reconnaissance, and that further operations should be determined by the report received from Captain Crocker.

He went in, made his reconnaissance, and signaled for the other vessels to come in. I therefore sent all of the transports which it was supposed could cross the bar, and found the greatest difficulty in getting over any vessels drawing more than 6 feet. About 10 o'clock, 700 infantry, one battery of field artillery, and eight heavy guns were inside of the bar, and a transport, with 700 infantry, was hopelessly aground. A tug drawing 6 feet was sent to her assistance, but had to return, not being able to reach her.

In company with General Weitzel and Captain Crocker, I made a reconnaissance of the Texas shore; small boats grounded in mud about 125 feet from the shore.

The shore itself is a soft marsh, and parallel to it, and about 50 feet inside of it, is a narrow strip of sand, on which is a road. This road strikes the water and high ground about one-half mile below the fort, at which point there is an old fort. Sailors wading sank into the mud above their knees; soldiers loaded with muskets and rations would have sunk to their middle.

The fort completely commands the road and the channels of the entrance, and contains six guns, three of which are, in my opinion, 9-inch guns, one a 7 or 8 inch rifled gun, and two others on siege carriages.

The channel divides about 1,000 yards below the fort, and the two channels unite at a short distance above it.

As there were four gunboats available for the attack, the following plan was adopted in conjunction with Captain Crocker: Three of the gunboats were to move up the channel to the point of separation; there two of them, the Sachem and the Arizona, were to take the channel to the right, and were to pass the fort by that channel, drawing its fire. The Clifton was to take the left-hand channel, moving slowly up, and, when about half a mile distant, was to go at full speed, within grape and canister range, and engage the fort at close quarters. General Weitzel was to keep near the Clifton with a boat containing 500 infantry, who were to land as soon as the Clifton began to go at full speed at the old fort; from there they were to advance upon the fort as skirmishers, endeavoring to drive the enemy from his guns, while the Clifton engaged the fort at close quarters. The fourth gunboat, the Granite City, was to support this movement.

While the arrangements necessary to carry out this plan were being made, the troops that were in the transport aground on the bar were brought in, to be in readiness to assist General Weitzel's movement in case of necessity.

The movement of the gunboats commenced at 3 o'clock, and progressed according to the plan for about thirty minutes, when the fort opened on the Sachem and Arizona, and in a few minutes put a shot through the boilers of the Sachem, killing and wounding many of her officers and men. She soon afterward hoisted a white flag. The Arizona was during part of this time aground.

The Clifton steamed slowly up her channel, firing slowly, and finally lay with her broadside toward the fort, engaged at close quarters. A shot went through her steam-pipe shortly afterward, disabling her, but she fought gallantly for ten minutes more, when she, too, surrendered.

As soon as she hoisted the white flag, the Arizona and Granite City steamed over the bar; the Arizona grounded, but got off during the night. . . .

After the engagement, my situation was as follows: I was in the mouth of the Sabine Pass with seven transports. These contained 1,200 infantry, which could be landed; twelve guns and fifty wagons, which could not be landed. The enemy had a heavy battery of six guns, two gunboats, and a field battery within 6 miles, and was being rapidly re-enforced. We had nothing to protect us, except the fire from the guns on our transports, which would have been of little use against the enemy's gunboats.

The enemy's battery commanded the whole landing, and he could, with his battery and gunboats, have destroyed us at any time.

The remainder of my force was outside the bar in vessels, all of which had to be lightened, and at least three days would have been required to land it.

The stock of fresh water was nearly exhausted, and the animals were already on short allowance of water; the men were living on uncooked rations, and there was no fuel on shore for cooking.

No fresh water could be obtained unless the fort was in our possession, and the day's experience had taught me that no attack which I could make with the troops which I had been able to get across the bar could possibly succeed. It would have been absurd to have attempted to have passed the fort with the troops already inside of the bar, there being but one means of access to Sabine City, and this commanded for 1½ miles by six heavy guns and whatever field artillery the enemy might have. There was no time to send to New Orleans to get instructions, and I therefore concluded to recross the bar and return to the mouth of the Mississippi.

I arrived at the mouth of the Mississippi this morning, having left Sabine Pass on the 9th instant, and believe there have been no losses except those reported by General Weitzel, and 200,000 rations thrown overboard from the Crescent (the grounded transport), to get her off the bar, where she would have been taken by the enemy, and 200 mules thrown overboard from the Laurel Hill, a steamer which had lost her smoke-stacks on account of the heavy sea. . . .

W. B. FRANKLIN,
Major-General, Commanding.

Maj. Gen. N. P. Banks
Commanding Department of the Gulf, New Orleans, La.

## 2. LIEUTENANT DOWLING'S REPORT

Fort Griffin, Sabine Pass, September 9, 1863.

Captain: On Monday morning, about 2 o'clock, the sentinel informed me the enemy were signaling, and, fearing an attack, I ordered all the guns at the fort manned, and remained in that position until daylight, at which time there were two steamers evidently sounding for the channel on the bar; a large frigate outside. They remained all day at work, but during the evening were reenforced to the number of twenty-two vessels of different classes.

On the morning of the 8th, the U. S. gunboat Clifton anchored opposite the light-house, and fired twenty-six shells at the fort, most of which passed a little over or fell short; all, however, in excellent range, one shell being landed on the works and another striking the south angle of the fort, without doing any material damage. The firing commenced at 6.30 o'clock and finished at 7.30 o'clock by the gunboat hauling off. During this time we had not replied by a single shot. All was then quiet until 11 o'clock, at which time the gunboat Uncle Ben steamed down near the fort. The U. S. gunboat Sachem opened on her with a 30-pounder Parrott gun. She fired three shots, but without effect, the shots all passing over the fort and missing the Ben. The whole fleet then drew off, and remained out of range until 3.40 o'clock, when the Sachem and Arizona steamed into line up the Louisiana channel, the Clifton and one boat, name unknown, remaining at the junction of the two channels. I allowed the two former boats to approach within 1,200 yards, when I opened fire with the whole of my battery on the foremost boat (the Sachem), which, after the third or fourth round, hoisted the white flag, one of the shots passing through her steam-drum. The Clifton in the meantime had attempted to pass up through Texas channel, but receiving a shot which carried away her tiller rope, she became unmanageable, and grounded about 500 yards below the fort, which enabled me to concentrate all my guns on her, which were six in number—two 32-pounder smooth-bores; two 24-pounder smooth-bores; two 32-pounder howitzers. She withstood our fire some twenty-five or thirty-five minutes, when she also hoisted a white flag. During the time she was aground, she used grape, and her sharpshooters poured an incessant shower of Minie balls into the works. The fight lasted from the time I fired the first gun until the boats surrendered; that was about three-quarters of an hour. I immediately boarded the captured Clifton, and proceeded to inspect her magazines, accompanied by one of the ship's officers, and discovered it safe and well stocked with ordnance stores. I did not visit the magazine of the Sachem, in consequence of not having any small boats to board her with. The C. S. gunboat Uncle Ben steamed down to the Sachem and towed her into the wharf. Her magazine was destroyed by the enemy flooding it. . . .

Thus it will be seen we captured, with 47 men, two gunboats, mounting thirteen guns of the heaviest caliber, and about 350 prisoners. All my men behaved like heroes; not a man flinched from his post. Our motto was "victory or death."

I beg leave to make particular mention of Private Michael McKernan, who, from his well-known capacity as a gunner, I assigned as gunner to one of the guns, and nobly did he do his duty. It was his shot struck the Sachem in her steam-drum.

Too much praise cannot be awarded to Maj. [Col.] Leon Smith for his activity and energy in saving and bringing the vessels into port. . . .

R. W. DOWLING,
First Lieut., Comdg. Co. F, Cook's Art.,
Fort Griffin, Sabine Pass.

Capt. F. H. Odlum,
Commanding Post.

## 86. JOHNSON'S PLAN OF RECONSTRUCTION

### 1865

The painful process of "reconstructing" the southern states had already been started by President Lincoln when he was assassinated. Andrew Johnson, succeeding to the presidency, accepted as legal the four loyal governments already organized, and then in a proclamation on May 29, 1865, dealt with the reconstruction of the remaining seven, including Texas. A second proclamation on the same day established a provisional government for North Carolina. On June 17 an identical proclamation was issued for Texas. Below are two of Johnson's proclamations: the first, that of May 29, granted amnesty to all ex-Confederates who would take the oath of allegiance to the United States, with the exception of certain classes who must make individual application for a presidential pardon; the second provided for a reconstruction government in Texas.

### 1. JOHNSON'S AMNESTY PROCLAMATION

#### May 29, 1865

From United States *Statutes at Large*, Vol. XIII, 758-760.

Whereas the President of the United States, on the 8th day of December, A. D. eighteen hundred and sixty-four, did, with the object to suppress the existing rebellion, to induce all persons to return to their loyalty, and to restore the authority of the United States, issue proclamations offering amnesty and pardon to certain persons who had directly or by implication participated in the said rebellion; and whereas many persons who had so engaged in said rebellion have, since the issuance of said proclamations, failed or neglected to take the benefits offered thereby; and whereas many persons who have been justly deprived of all claim to amnesty and pardon thereunder, by reason of their participation, directly or by implication, in said rebellion, and continued hostility to the government of the United States since the date of said proclamations, now desire to apply for and obtain amnesty and pardon.

To the end, therefore, that the authority of the government of the United States may be restored, and that peace, order, and freedom may be established, I, ANDREW JOHNSON, President of the United States, do proclaim and declare that I hereby grant to all persons who have, directly or indirectly, participated in the existing rebellion, except as herein after excepted, amnesty and pardon, with restoration of all rights of property, except as to slaves, and except in cases where legal proceedings, under the laws of the United States providing for the confiscation of property of persons engaged in rebellion, have been instituted; but upon the condition, nevertheless, that every such person shall take and subscribe the following oath, (or affirmation,) and thenceforward keep and maintain said oath inviolate; and which oath shall be registered for permanent preservation, and shall be of the tenor and effect following, to wit:

"I, _____, do solemnly swear, (or affirm,) in presence of Almighty God, that I will henceforth faithfully support, protect, and defend the Constitution of the United States, and the union of the States thereunder; and that I will, in like manner, abide by, and faithfully support all laws, and proclamations which have been made during the existing rebellion with reference to the emancipation of slaves. So help me God."

The following classes of persons are excepted from the benefits of this Proclamation:

1st. All who are or shall have been pretended civil or diplomatic officers, or otherwise domestic or foreign agents, of the pretended confederation government;

2d. All who left judicial stations under the United States to aid the rebellion;

3d. All who shall have been military or naval officers of said pretended confederate government above the rank of colonel in the army or lieutenant in the navy;

4th. All who left seats in the Congress of the United States to aid the rebellion;

5th. All who resigned or tendered resignations of their commissions in the army or navy of the United States to evade duty in resisting the rebellion;

6th. All who have engaged in any way in treating otherwise than lawfully as prisoners of war persons found in the United States service, as officers, soldiers, seamen, or in other capacities;

7th. All persons who have been, or are, absentees from the United States for the purpose of aiding the rebellion;

8th. All military and naval officers in the rebel service, who were educated by the government in the Military Academy at West Point or the United States Naval Academy;

9th. All persons who held the pretended offices of governors of states in insurrection against the United States;

10th. All persons who left their homes within the protection of the United States, and passed beyond the federal military lines into the pretended confederate states for the purpose of aiding the rebellion;

11th. All persons who have been engaged in the destruction of the commerce of the United States upon the high seas, and all persons who have made raids into the United States from Canada, or been engaged in destroying the commerce of the United States upon the lakes and rivers that separate the British Provinces from the United States;

12th. All persons who, at the time when they seek to obtain the benefits hereof by taking the oath herein prescribed, are in military, naval, or civil confinement, or custody, or under bonds of the civil, military, or naval authorities, or agents of the United States as prisoners of war, or persons detained for offences of any kind, either before or after conviction;

13th. All persons who have voluntarily participated in said rebellion, and the estimated value of whose taxable property is over twenty thousand dollars;

14th. All persons who have taken the oath of amnesty as prescribed in the President's Proclamation of December 8th, A.D. 1863, or an oath of allegiance to the government of the United States since the date of said proclamation, and who have not thenceforward kept and maintained the same inviolate.

*Provided,* That special application may be made to the president for pardon by any person belonging to the excepted classes; and such clemency will be liberally extended as may be consistent with the facts of the case and the peace and dignity of the United States.

The Secretary of State will establish rules and regulations for administering and recording the said amnesty oath, so as to insure its benefit to the people, and guard the government against fraud.

In testimony whereof, I have hereunto set my hand, and caused the seal of the United States to be affixed.

Done at the city of Washington, the twenty-ninth day of May, in the year of our Lord one thousand eight hundred and sixty-five, and of the Independence of the United States the eighty-ninth.

ANDREW JOHNSON

## 2. JOHNSON'S PROCLAMATION OF THE RESTORATION OF CIVIL GOVERNMENT FOR TEXAS

### June 17, 1865

From United States *Statutes at Large,* Vol. XIII, 765-767.

Whereas the fourth section of the fourth article of the Constitution of the United States declares that the United States shall guarantee to every state in the Union a republican form of government, and shall protect each of them against invasion and domestic violence; and whereas the President of the United States is, by the constitution, made commander-in-chief of the army and navy, as well as chief civil executive officer of the United States, and is bound by solemn oath faithfully to execute the office of President of the United States, and to take care that the laws be faithfully executed; and whereas the rebellion, which has been waged by a portion of the people of the United States against the properly constituted authorities of the government thereof, in the most violent and revolting form, but whose organized and armed forces have now been almost entirely overcome, has, in its revolutionary progress, deprived the people of the State of Texas of all civil government; and whereas it becomes necessary and proper to carry out and enforce the obligations of the United States to the people of the State of Texas, in securing them in the enjoyment of a republican form of government:

Now, therefore, in obedience to the high and solemn duties imposed upon me by the Constitution of the United States, and for the purpose of enabling the loyal people of said state to organize a state government, whereby justice may be established, domestic tranquility insured, and loyal citizens protected in all their rights of life, liberty, and property, I, ANDREW JOHNSON, President of the United States, and commander-in-chief of the army and navy of the United States, do hereby appoint Andrew J. Hamilton, of Texas, provisional governor of the State of Texas, whose duty it shall be, at the earliest practicable period, to prescribe such rules and regulations as may be necessary and proper for convening a convention, composed of delegates to be chosen by that portion of the people of said state who are loyal to the United States, and no others, for the purpose of altering or amending the constitution thereof; and with authority to exercise, within the limits of said state, all the powers necessary and proper to enable such loyal people of the State of Texas to restore

said state to its constitutional relations to the federal government, and to present such a republican form of government as will entitle the state to the guarantee of the United States therefor, and its people to protection by the United States against invasion, insurrection, and domestic violence; *Provided* that in any election that may be hereafter held for choosing delegates to any state convention as aforesaid, no person shall be qualified as an elector, or shall be eligible as a member of such convention, unless he shall have previously taken and subscribed the oath of amnesty, as set forth in the President's Proclamation of May 29, A. D. 1865, and is a voter qualified as prescribed by the constitution and laws of the State of Texas in force immediately before the first [1st] day of February, A. D. 1861, the date of the so-called ordinance of secession; and the said convention, when convened, or the legislature that may be thereafter assembled, will prescribe the qualifications of electors, and the eligibility of persons to hold office under the constitution and laws of the state,—a power the people of the several states composing the Federal Union have rightfully exercised from the origin of the government to the present time.

And I do hereby direct,—

*First.* That the military commander of the department, and all officers and persons in the military and naval service, aid and assist the said provisional governor in carrying into effect this Proclamation, and they are enjoined to abstain from, in any way, hindering, impeding, or discouraging the loyal people from the organization of a state government as herein authorized.

*Second.* That the Secretary of State proceed to put in force all laws of the United States, the administration whereof belongs to the State Department, applicable to the geographical limits aforesaid.

*Third.* That the Secretary of the Treasury proceed to nominate for appointment assessors of taxes, and collectors of customs and internal revenue, and such other officers of the Treasury Department as are authorized by law, and put in execution the revenue laws of the United States within the geographical limits aforesaid. In making appointments, the preference shall be given to qualified loyal persons residing within the districts where their respective duties are to be performed. But if suitable residents of the districts shall not be found, then persons residing in other states or districts shall be appointed.

*Fourth.* That the Postmaster-General proceed to establish postoffices and post-routes, and put into execution the postal laws of the United States within the said state, giving to loyal residents the preference of appointment; but if suitable residents are not found, then to appoint agents, &c., from other states.

*Fifth.* That the district judge, for the judicial district in which Texas is included, proceed to hold courts within said state, in accordance with the provisions of the act of congress. The Attorney-General will instruct the proper officers to libel, and bring to judgment, confiscation, and sale, property subject to confiscation, and enforce the administration of justice within said state in all matters within the cognizance and jurisdiction of the federal courts.

*Sixth.* That the Secretary of the Navy take possession of all public property belonging to the Navy Department within said geographical limits, and put in operation all acts of congress in relation to naval affairs having application to the said state.

*Seventh.* That the Secretary of the Interior put in force the laws relating to the Interior Department applicable to the geographical limits aforesaid.

In testimony whereof, I have hereunto set my hand, and caused the seal of the United States to be affixed.

Done at the city of Washington this seventeenth day of June, in the year of our Lord one thousand eight hundred and sixty-five, and of the Independence of the United States the eighty-ninth.

ANDREW JOHNSON

## 87. GRANGER'S PROCLAMATION ABOLISHING SLAVERY IN TEXAS

### June 19, 1865

From *Houston Tri-weekly Telegraph*, June 23, 1865 (MS transcription of the proclamation, Texas State Library, Archives).

After the cessation of hostilities in April, 1865, Texas had no central government for more than two months. On May 29, General P. H. Sheridan was assigned to the command of the Military Division of the Southwest with headquarters at New Orleans, but because of the lack of troop transports it was three weeks before he was able to take possession of Texas. He ordered General Gordon Granger to proceed to Texas with eighteen hundred men on June 10. Granger arrived at Galveston on June 19, and on the same day issued a proclamation declaring that all slaves were free.

Headquarters, District of Texas.
Galveston, June 19, 1865.

### GENERAL ORDERS, No. 3.

The people of Texas are informed that in accordance with a Proclamation from the Executive of the United States, all slaves are free. This involves an absolute equality of rights and rights of property between former masters and slaves, and the connection heretofore existing between them becomes that between employer and free laborer. The freedmen are advised to remain at their present homes and work for wages. They are informed that they will not be allowed to collect at military posts, and that they will not be supported in idleness, either there or elsewhere. By order of

G. Granger
Major General Commanding

## 88. JOHN H. REAGAN'S FORT WARREN PRISON LETTER ON RECONSTRUCTION

### August 11, 1865

From John H. Reagan, *Memoirs* (Walter F. McCaleb, ed.; New York and Washington, 1906), 286-295.

As reconstruction in Texas got underway in the summer of 1865, there was an evident reluctance among many Texans to meet the requirements of the provisional government. One who saw clearly the implications of this reluctance was John H. Reagan, a prominent Texan who had served in the United States Congress before secession and in the Confederate cabinet during the life of that government. From his prison in Fort Warren, where he was held as a prisoner of war, Reagan composed the celebrated letter excerpted below, courageously urging compliance with the relatively mild reconstruction measures lest the Federal government instead impose military government and universal Negro suffrage. It understandably prejudiced his popularity for a time, since it seemingly ranged him on the side of the radicals; but later he was to emerge as an even stronger leader and to build a long record of solid service in both state and national affairs.

In Prison, Fort Warren,
Boston Harbor, August 11, 1865

To the People of Texas:

. . . As our condition forces unwelcome thoughts and actions on us, and as, in my judgment, your best interests require you to assent to facts and conclusions, and to adopt measures, conforming to the new order of things, which must be repugnant to your past experience and to your reason and prejudices, I take the liberty of suggesting to you . . . to accept the present condition of things, as the result of the war, and of inevitable necessity, and from this, as a starting point, to inquire what policy our people should adopt for the future.

You must, in the first place, recognize the necessity of making the most you can of your present condition, without the hope of doing all you might desire. This is required both by reason and necessity.

The State occupies the condition of a conquered nation. State government and State sovereignty are in abeyance, and will be so until you adopt a government and policy acceptable to the conquerors. A refusal to accede to these conditions would only result in a prolongation of the time during which you will be deprived of a civil government of your own choice.

And it would do more than this—it would keep questions of the gravest character open for discussion and agitation, and by degrees accustom the whole country to a sort of military government, which, if greatly protracted, must necessarily subvert the civil government, and result in the establishment of a military despotism, without bringing you any nearer to the attainment of your wishes than you are at present. In order to secure to yourselves again the blessings of local self-government, and to avoid military rule, and the danger of running into military despotism, you must agree:

First, to recognize the supreme authority of the Government of the United States, within the sphere of its powers, and its right to protect itself against disintegration by the secession of the States.

And, second, you must recognize the abolition of slavery, and the rights of those who have been slaves to the privileges and protection of the laws of the land.

From what I can see this much will be required as the least that would likely satisfy the Government, and secure to you the benefits of civil government, and the admission of your members into the Congress of the United States.

But even this may fail of the attainment of those ends, unless provision shall be made, by the new State government, for conferring the elective franchise on the former slaves. And present appearances indicate that this will be required by Northern public opinion and by Congress. And our people are in no condition to disregard that opinion or power with safety. . . . This is new language to employ in addressing you, and will be as unwelcome to you as it is sorrowful to me. . . .

While the Government offers its terms for the restoration of the State to the Union, it demands no other sacrifices than those already made by the result of the war, of renouncing the right of secession, and recognizing the abolition of slavery, with its necessary consequences. These demands being complied with, the civil governments will be organized, the military government withdrawn, your members will be admitted to their seats in Congress, and the State will be in the Union on an equality in all respects with the other States; with no further disabilities, save only such as may attach to individuals. While the Government prescribes the conditions of this return, it authorizes the people of the State, through representatives of their own choice, to execute them. It seems to be the object of the Government, in pursuing this course, to secure what it regards as the fruits of the victory it has won, and, at the same time, to preserve our form of government and the liberties of the people. I know that those who look to the past only, with its sacrifices and losses of principles believed to be true, of property possessed, of national independence sought, and of the heroic dead, may say why talk of liberty now, and of equality in the Union? The answer is, that having attempted to secure and preserve these by an appeal to the God of battles, we failed, and they now, so far as it relates to our political restoration, belong to the dead past, where it is the policy of the conquerors to leave them, and we are required to look to the living present and to the future. If it be thought hard to surrender so much, it must be remembered that such is the fate of war, and we must not forget that by the appeal to arms, whether willingly made or not, we staked

not only what the Government exacts, but all our rights and property on the result. That we are not required to surrender all is due, not to the laws of war, but to the enlightened and Christian age and country in which we live, to the liberality of the Government, and to the spirit and genius of our institutions. The questions as to which party to the contest was right or wrong, or as to whether both were partly right and partly wrong, and as to whether we did right or wrong in staking all on the fate of battle, were discussed before the war was commenced, and were decided by each party for itself, and, failing to agree, they made their appeal to the dread arbitrament of arms. It was precisely because the parties could not agree as to the issues between them that they went to war, to settle them in that way. Why should we now think of reopening the discussion of these questions? What good would come of doing so? Wisdom requires us to accept the decision of battle upon the issues involved, and to be thankful that no more has been demanded by the conquerors, and to unite frankly, and as cheerfully as we can, with the Government in carrying out the policy it has propounded. . . . The only wise and safe course for you to pursue is to accept promptly, unreservedly, and in good faith the terms and policy offered, and to go forward in the work of reorganization and restoration to the Union. This requires your assent to great pecuniary sacrifices, momentous changes in your social and industrial system and a surrender of your opinions and prejudices on most important questions. . . .

To the conferring of the elective franchise on your former slaves, I anticipate stubborn and sincere opposition, based upon the ignorance of the great mass of them, and their total want of information and experience in matters of legislation, administration, and everything which pertains to the science of government, and upon the pride of race. . . . I have no doubt that you can adopt a plan which will fully meet the demands of justice and fairness, and satisfy the Northern mind and the requirements of the Government, without endangering good government and repose of society. This can be done by:

First, extending the privileges and protection of the laws over the negroes as they are over the white, and allowing them to testify in the courts on the same conditions, leaving their testimony subject to the rules relating to its credibility, but not objecting to its admissibility. . . .

And, second, by fixing an intellectual and moral, and, if thought advisable, a property test, for the admission of all persons to the exercise of the elective franchise, without reference to race or color, which would secure its intelligent exercise. My own views would be . . . that no person now entitled to the privilege of voting should be deprived of it by any new test. I would recognize in this the difference between taking away a right heretofore enjoyed, and the conferring of a right not heretofore exercised. . . .

The adoption of these measures in addition to those before mentioned, would, in my judgment, meet the ends of justice and fairness, secure the reestablishment of the State government, the admission of her Senators and Representatives in Congress, the suspension of military rule, and the restoration of civil, constitutional, and local self-government. And it would do more. It would secure your protection against other great and pending evils, and is, I am persuaded, of the greatest consequence to your future peace, prosperity and happiness. And for these reasons:

First, it would remove all just grounds of antagonism between the white and black races. Unless this is done, endless strife and bitterness of feeling must characterize their relations, and, as all history and human experience teach us, must sooner or later result in a war of races. . . .

Second, this course would disarm and put an end to interstate, sectional, political agitation on this subject at least, which has been the special curse of our country for so many years, and which was the cause of the unnumbered woes we have recently experienced and still suffer, by depriving the agitators of a subject on which to keep up such agitation, and of the means of producing jealousy, animosity, and hatred between the different parts of the country, and between the different races. And this would do much toward a renewal of the ancient relations of na-

tional harmony and fraternal good will between all parts of the country. . . .

If the State will adopt this policy at once it will attain the great ends heretofore mentioned, and it will save its own people from years of painful strife and agitation on these questions, which would at last, probably after years of contention, be found to be the only means of bringing it to an end, even if we are driven to nothing worse. How infinitely better it will be for you, . . . if you will unhesitatingly recognize the existing unalterable facts as to your condition, . . . and hasten, as it is in your power to do, the return of the blessings of civil government and constitutional liberty; and avoid . . . the fearful perils which now lie before you. . . .

Very truly and respectfully,
John H. Reagan.

## 89. PRESIDENT JOHNSON'S PROCLAMATION RECOGNIZING THE RESTORATION OF CIVIL GOVERNMENT IN TEXAS

### August 20, 1866

From United States *Statutes at Large*, Vol. XIV, 814-817.

The convention which Governor A. J. Hamilton convened in February, 1866, took the following six steps: (1) agreed to the abolition of slavery by a vote of 56 to 26, (2) declared secession null and void by a vote of 55 to 21, (3) repudiated the debt incurred by the state in support of the war, (4) adopted limited civil rights for the benefit of the new freedmen, (5) revised the state constitution to conform to that of the nation, and (6) proposed several amendments to the state constitution for the consideration of the voters at an election to be held on the fourth Monday in June following. At the polls, the people accepted reconstruction under the President's plan by adopting the proposed changes in the constitution and by naming for governor James W. Throckmorton, a conservative, over E. M. Pease, an ex-governor and a radical, by a vote of 49,277 to 12,168. The newly elected legislature assembled on August 6; three days later Throckmorton was inaugurated, and Johnson on August 20 proclaimed the insurrection in Texas at an end and recognized the new civil government.

. . . And whereas, the laws can now be sustained and enforced in the said State of Texas, by the proper civil authority, State or Federal, and the people of the said State of Texas, like the people of the other States before named, are well and loyally disposed, and have conformed or will conform in their legislation to the condition of affairs growing out of the amendment of the Constitution of the United States, prohibiting slavery within the limits and jurisdiction of the United States; . . .

And whereas, adequate provision has been made by military orders, to enforce the execution of the acts of Congress, aid the civil authorities, and secure obedience to the Constitution and laws of the United States within the State of Texas, if a resort to military force for such purpose should at any time become necessary;

Now, therefore, I, ANDREW JOHNSON, President of the United States, do hereby proclaim and declare that the insurrection which heretofore existed in the State of Texas is at an end, and is to be henceforth so regarded in that State, as in the other States before named, in which the said insurrection was proclaimed to be at an end, by the aforesaid proclamation of the second day of April, one thousand eight hundred and sixty-six.

And I do further proclaim that the said insurrection is at an end, and that peace, order, tranquility, and civil authority now exist in and throughout the whole of the United States of America.

In testimony whereof, I have hereunto set my hand and caused the seal of the United States to be affixed.

Done at the city of Washington this twentieth day of August, in the year of our Lord one thousand eight hundred and sixty-six, and of the Independence of the United States of America the ninety-first.

Andrew Johnson

## 90. THE CONGRESSIONAL PLAN OF RECONSTRUCTION

### March 2, March 23, and July 19, 1867

From United States *Statutes at Large,* XIV, 428-429; XV, 2-4; XV, 14-16.

When radical Republicans won the off-year elections in 1866, for a variety of reasons ranging from the political fear of a Democratic resurgence to the genuine belief that the South had not been adequately punished, they were for the first time in a position to repudiate the leadership of President Johnson. When Congress met in December, the radicals constituted the Joint Committee on Reconstruction to make recommendations on reconstruction policy. Ignoring the progress made already by Lincoln and Johnson in this area, Congress in 1867 passed three acts which all together are called the Congressional Plan of Reconstruction. The following pertinent extracts from the three acts illustrate the basic points of the plan.

### 1. THE FIRST CONGRESSIONAL RECONSTRUCTION ACT

#### March 2, 1867

*An Act to provide for the more efficient Government of the Rebel States.*

Whereas no legal State governments or adequate protection for life or property now exists in the rebel States of Virginia, North Carolina, South Carolina, Georgia, Mississippi, Alabama, Louisiana, Florida, Texas, and Arkansas; and whereas it is necessary that peace and good order should be enforced in said States until loyal and republican State governments can be legally established: Therefore,

*Be it enacted by the Senate and House of Representatives of the United States of America in Congress assembled,* That said rebel States shall be divided into military districts and made subject to the military authority of the United States as hereinafter prescribed, and for that purpose Virginia shall constitute the first district; North Carolina and South Carolina the second district; Georgia, Alabama, and Florida the third district; Mississippi and Arkansas the fourth district; and Louisiana and Texas the fifth district.

Sec. 2. *And be it further enacted,* That it shall be the duty of the President to assign to the command of each of said districts an officer of the army, not below the rank of brigadier-general, and to detail a sufficient military force to enable such officer to perform his duties and enforce his authority within the district to which he is assigned.

Sec. 3. *And be it further enacted,* That it shall be the duty of each officer assigned as aforesaid, to suppress insurrection, disorder, and violence, and to punish, or cause to be punished, all disturbers of the public peace and criminals; and to this end he may allow local civil tribunals to take jurisdiction of and to try offenders, or, when in his judgment it may be necessary for the trial of offenders, he shall have power to organize military commissions or tribunals for that purpose, and all interference under color of State authority with the exercise of military authority under this act, shall be null and void.

Sec. 4. *And be it further enacted,* That all persons put under military arrest by virtue of this act shall be tried without unnecessary delay, and no cruel or unusual pun-ishment shall be inflicted, and no sentence of any military commission or tribunal hereby authorized, affecting the life or liberty of any person, shall be executed until it is approved by the officer in command of the district, and the laws and regulations for the government of the army shall not be affected by this act, except in so far as they conflict with its provisions: Provided, That no sentence of death under the provisions of this act shall be carried into effect without the approval of the President.

Sec. 5. *And be it further enacted,* That when the people of any one of said rebel States shall have formed a constitution of government in conformity with the Constitution of the United States in all respects, framed by a convention of delegates elected by the male citizens of said State, twenty-one years old and upward, of whatever race, color, or previous condition, who have been resident in said State for one year previous to the day of such election, except such as may be disfranchised for participation in the rebellion or for felony at common law, and when such constitution shall provide that the election franchise shall be enjoyed by all such persons as have the qualifications herein stated for electors of delegates, and when such constitution shall be ratified by a majority of the persons voting on the question of ratification who are qualified as electors for delegates, and when such constitution shall have been submitted to Congress for examination and approval, and Congress shall have approved the same, and when said State, by a vote of its legislature elected under said Constitution, shall have adopted the amendment to the Constitution of the United States, proposed by the Thirty-ninth Congress, and known as article fourteen, and when said article shall have become a part of the Constitution of the United States, said State shall be declared entitled to representation in Congress, and senators and representatives shall be admitted therefrom on their taking the oath prescribed by law, and then and thereafter the preceding sections of this act shall be inoperative in said State: *Provided,* That no person excluded from the privilege of holding office by said proposed amendment to the Constitution of the United States, shall be eligible to election as a member of the convention to frame a constitution for any of said rebel States, nor shall any such person vote for members of such convention.

Sec. 6. *And be it further enacted,* That until the people of said rebel States shall be by law admitted to representation in the Congress of the United States, any civil governments which may exist therein shall be deemed provisional only, and in all respects subject to the paramount authority of the United States at any time to abolish, modify, control, or supersede the same; and in all elections to any office under such provisional governments all persons shall be entitled to vote, and none others, who are entitled to vote, under the provisions of the fifth section of this act; and no person shall be eligible to any office under any such provisional governments who would be disqualified from holding office under the provisions of the third *article* of said constitutional amendment.

Schuyler Colfax, *Speaker of the House of Representatives.*
La Fayette S. Foster, *President of the Senate, pro tempore.*

## 2. THE SECOND RECONSTRUCTION ACT
### March 23, 1867

*An Act supplementary to an Act entitled "An Act to provide for the more efficient Government of the Rebel States," passed [March 2, 1867], and to facilitate Restoration.*

*Be it enacted by the Senate and House of Representatives of the United States of America in Congress assembled,* That before the first day of September, eighteen hundred and sixty-seven, the commanding general in each district . . . [as defined in the Act of March 2, 1867], shall cause a registration to be made of the male citizens of the United States, twenty-one years of age and upwards, resident in each county or parish in the State or States included in his district, which registration shall include only those persons who are qualified to vote for delegates by the act aforesaid, and who shall have taken and subscribed the following oath or affirmation: "I, _____, do solemnly swear (or affirm), in the presence of Almighty God, that I am a citizen of the State of _____, or the parish of _____, in said State (as the case may be); that I am twenty-one years old; that I have not been disfranchised for participation in any rebellion or civil war against the United States; nor for felony committed against the laws of any State or of the United States; that I have never been a member of any State legislature, nor held any executive or judicial office in any State and afterwards engaged in insurrection or rebellion against the United States, or given aid or comfort to the enemies thereof; that I have never taken an oath as a member of Congress of the United States, or as an officer of the United States, or as a member of any State legislature, or as an executive or judicial officer of any State, to support the Constitution of the United States, and afterwards engaged in insurrection or rebellion against the United States, or given aid or comfort to the enemies thereof; that I will faithfully support the Constitution and obey the laws of the United States, and will, to the best of my ability, encourage others so to do, so help me God"; which oath or affirmation may be administered by any registering officer. . . .

Sec. 6. *And be it further enacted,* . . . That if any person shall knowingly and falsely take and subscribe any oath in this act prescribed, such person so offending and being thereof duly convicted shall be subject to the pains, penalties, and disabilities which by law are provided for the punishment of the crime of wilful and corrupt perjury. . . .

## 3. THE THIRD RECONSTRUCTION ACT
### July 19, 1867

*An Act supplementary to an Act entitled "An Act to provide for the more efficient Government of the Rebel States," passed [March 2, 1867], and the Act supplementary thereto, passed [March 23, 1867].*

. . . Sec. 2. *And be it further enacted,* That the commander of any district named in said act [March 2, 1867] shall have power, subject to the disapproval of the General of the army of the United States, and to have effect till disapproved, whenever in the opinion of such commander the proper administration of said act shall require it, to suspend or remove from office, or from the performance of official duties and the exercise of official powers, any officer or person holding or exercising, or professing to hold or exercise, any civil or military office or duty in such district under any power, election, appointment or authority derived from, or granted by, or claimed under, any so-called State of the government thereof, or any municipal or other division thereof, and upon such suspension or removal such commander, subject to the disapproval of the General as aforesaid, shall have power to provide from time to time for the performance of the said duties of such officer or person so suspended or removed, by the detail of some competent officer or soldier of the army, or by the appointment of some other person, to perform the same, and to fill vacancies occasioned by death, resignation, or otherwise.

Sec. 3. *And be it further resolved,* That the General of the army of the United States shall be invested with all the powers of suspension, removal, appointment, and detail granted in the preceding section to district commanders. . . .

Sec. 6. *And be it further enacted,* That the true intent and meaning of the oath prescribed in said supplementary act [March 23, 1863], (among other things,) that no person who has been a member of the legislature of any State, or who has held any executive or judicial office in any State, whether he has taken an oath to support the Constitution of the United States or not, and whether he was holding such office at the commencement of the rebellion, or had held it before, and who has afterwards engaged in insurrection or rebellion against the United States, or given aid or comfort to the enemies thereof, is entitled to be registered or to vote; and the words "executive or judicial office in any State" in said oath mentioned shall be construed to include all civil offices created by law for the administration of justice.

Sec. 7. *And be it further enacted,* That the time for completing the original registration provided for in said act may, in the direction of the commander of any district be extended to the first day of October, eighteen hundred and sixty-seven; . . .

Sec. 8. *And be it further enacted,* That section four of said last-named act shall be construed to authorize the commanding general named therein, whenever he shall deem it needful, to remove any member of a board of registration and to appoint another in his stead, and to fill any vacancy in such board. . . .

Sec. 10. *And be it further enacted,* That no district commander or member of the board of registration, or any of the officers or appointees acting under them, shall be bound in his action by any opinion of any civil officer of the United States. . . .

## 91. CHIEF TEN BEARS' SPEECH SETTING FORTH THE CASE OF THE COMANCHES AT THE COUNCIL OF MEDICINE LODGE

October 20, 1867

From Ten Bears (Comanche chief), "Speech," October 20, 1867, "Record Copy of the Proceedings of the Indian Peace Commission Appointed under the Act of Congress Approved July 20, 1867" (MS, Office of Indian Affairs, National Archives, Washington, D. C.), I, 104.

The Federal government in 1865 made the unsatisfactory Treaty of the Little Arkansas with the Comanche and Kiowa Indians. By the summer of 1866 the Indians were violating it, as a government investigating commission later confirmed. Congress then in June, 1867, authorized a peace commission to correct the causes of the Indian complaints and to secure a lasting peace. The commissioners met the Indians at Medicine Lodge Creek, near the present site of Medicine Lodge, Barber County, Kansas, and on October 21, 1867, signed a treaty of peace with the southern tribes. It was the last ever made with the Comanches, Cheyennes, Arapahos, Kiowas, and Kiowa-Apaches, and was the occasion of one of the last old-fashioned Indian gatherings. When the council opened, the Indians were told that they had been violating the treaties and were urged to state their side of the case. Ten Bears of the Yep-eaters (the most northern Comanche band) spoke for the Comanches on October 20. Having seen the numbers of the white man, as well as his wealth and power, on his visit to Washington two years before, he realized that the proposals represented an alternative between refuge on the white man's terms or utter destruction, but he pleaded the Comanche case. His presentation is a masterpiece of logic and oratory.

My heart is filled with joy when I see you here, as the brooks fill with water when the snows melt in the spring; and I feel glad as the ponies do when the fresh grass starts in the beginning of the year. I heard of your coming when I was many sleeps away, and I made but few camps before I met you. I knew that you had come to do good to me and to my people. I looked for benefits which would last forever, and so my face shines with joy as I look upon you. My people have never first drawn a bow or fired a gun against the whites. There has been trouble on the line between us, and my young men have danced the war dance. But it was not begun by us. It was you who sent out the first soldier and we who sent out the second. Two years ago, I came upon this road, following the buffalo, that my wives and children might have their cheeks plump and their bodies warm. But the soldiers fired on us, and since that time there has been a noise like that of a thunderstorm, and we have not known which way to go. So it was upon the Canadian. Nor have we been made to cry once alone. The blue-dressed soldiers and the Utes came from out of the night when it was dark and still, and for camp-fires they lit our lodges. Instead of hunting game they killed my braves, and the warriors of the tribe cut short their hair for the dead.

So it was in Texas. They made sorrow come in our camps, and we went out like the buffalo bulls when the cows are attacked. When we found them we killed them, and their scalps hang in our lodges. The Comanches are not weak and blind, like the pups of a dog when seven sleeps old. They are strong and far-sighted, like grown horses. We took their road and we went on it. The white women cried and our women laughed.

But there are things which you have said to me which I do not like. They were not sweet like sugar, but bitter like gourds. You said that you wanted to put us upon a reservation, to build us houses and make us medicine lodges. I do not want them. I was born upon the prairie, where the wind blew free and there was nothing to break the light of the sun. I was born where there were no enclosures and everything drew a free breath. I want to die there and not within walls. I know every stream and every wood between the Rio Grande and the Arkansas. I have hunted and lived over that country. I live like my fathers before me and like them I lived happily.

When I was at Washington the Great Father told me that all the Comanche land was ours, and that no one should hinder us in living upon it. So, why do you ask us to leave the rivers, and the sun, and the wind, and live in houses? Do not speak of it more. I love to carry out the talk I get from the Great Father. When I get goods and presents, I and my people feel glad, since it shows that he holds us in his eye.

If the Texans had kept out of my country, there might have been peace. But that which you now say we must live in, is too small. The Texans have taken away the places where the grass grew the thickest and the timber was the best. Had we kept that, we might have done the things you ask. But it is too late. The whites have the country which we loved, and we only wish to wander on the prairie until we die. Any good thing you say to me shall not be forgotten. I shall carry it as near to my heart as my children, and it shall be as often on my tongue as the name of the Great Spirit. I want no blood upon my land to stain the grass. I want it all clear and pure, and I wish it so that all who go through among my people may find peace when they come in and leave it when they go out.

## 92. THE RITUAL OF A SECRET SOCIETY

### June 4, 1868

From "Ritual or Rules of Proceedings for the Initiation of Candidates and the Transaction of Business in the Order of the x$^x$x. x$^x$x. x$^x$x. [Knights of the Golden Circle]" (Adopted at a General Convention of the Order, June 4, 1868; New Orleans, 1868; transcript, Archives, University of Texas Library, Austin).

The radical program of reconstruction tried, to paraphrase Professor Rupert Norval Richardson, to stand the triangle of social organization on its apex by systematically disfranchising articulate, responsible leaders in the South and enfranchising men recently freed from slavery and not yet sensitive to the responsibilities of a democracy. In response several organizations sprang up in the South, including such well-known orders as the Ku Klux Klan and the Knights of the White Camelia.

The following document, the initiation ritual for the Knights of the Golden Circle, illustrates the intentions of one of these groups in Texas.

### FORM OF INITIATION

The candidate is introduced into the anteroom, where the Cr. shall administer to him the following

#### OATH.

I do solemnly swear that I will true and faithful make answers to all questions which may be propounded to me, and that if, in the course of the proceedings which are about to take place, anything contrary to my views, feelings and principles should induce me to forego the purpose of joining this Association, I will always be under the most sacred obligation never to reveal or cause to come to the knowledge of any one, either by word, writing, sign, inference, or in any other manner, what I may see, hear, understand, or suspect, within this building, or in any other place, concerning this Association. And, if I ever do violate this Oath, I consent to become an object of scorn to all men, and to deserve the lasting contempt of all the members of this Association.

The candidate is now blindfolded by the Cr. and led to the door of the Council Chamber. The Cr. shall give two raps at the door. The L. C. shall open the door and, standing on the threshold, the following dialogue shall take place between him and the Cr.:

L. C. — Who comes there?

Cr. — A son of your race.

L. C. — What does he wish?

Cr. — Peace and order: the observance of the Laws of God; the maintenance of the Laws and Constitution as established by the Patriots of 1776.

L. C. — To obtain this, what must be done?

Cr. — The cause of our race must triumph.

L. C. — And to secure its triumph what must we do?

Cr. — We must be united as are the flowers that grow on the same stem, and, under all circumstances, band ourselves together as brethren.

L. C. — Will he join us?

Cr. — He is prepared to answer for himself, and under oath.

L. C. — Let him enter.

The Cr. shall then take the candidate by the right hand and conduct him into the presence of the C., who shall propound the following questions, each of which shall be answered in a manner satisfactory to the Council.

Should the candidate fail to answer any of these questions satisfactorily, no further question will be put to him, and he shall immediately be made to retire blindfolded and dismissed by the Cr.

Previous to propounding the questions the C. shall address the candidate as follows:

L. C. — My friend, it becomes my duty to propound to you certain questions, which you are expected to answer truthfully; and your admission in the Order will depend on your replies.

#### QUESTIONS

(When several candidates are initiated together, the C. will take care to use the plural number wherever necessary. The answers shall be prompted by the Cr.)

1. — Do you belong to the White race?

Ans. — I do.

2. — Did you ever marry any woman who did not, or does not, belong to the White race?

Ans. — No.

3. — Do you promise never to marry any woman but one who belongs to the White race?

Ans. — I do.

4. — Do you believe in the superiority of your race?

Ans. — I do.

5. — Will you promise never to vote for any one, for any office of honor, profit or trust, who does not belong to your race?

Ans. — I do.

6. — Will you take a solemn oath never to abstain from casting your vote at any election in which a candidate of the negro race shall be opposed to a white man attached to our principles, unless prevented by severe illness or any other physical disability?

Ans. — I will.

7. — Are you opposed to allowing the control of the political affairs of this country to go, in whole or in part, into the hands of the negro or African race, and will you do everything in your power to prevent it?

Ans. — Yes.

8. — Will you devote your intelligence, energy and influence to the furtherance and propagation of the principles of our Order?

Ans. — I will.

9. — Will you, under all circumstances, defend and protect persons of the White race in their lives, rights and property, against all encroachments or invasions from any inferior race, and especially the African race?

Ans. — I will.

10. — Are you willing to take an oath forever to cherish these grand principles, and to unite yourself with others who, like you, believing in their truth, have firmly bound themselves to stand by and defend them against all?

Ans. — I am.

The C. shall then add:

If you consent to join our Association, raise your right hand and I will administer to you the oath which we have all taken:

### OATH

I do solemnly swear, in the presence of these witnesses, never to reveal, without authority, the existence of this Order, its objects, its acts, and its signs of recognition; never to reveal or publish, in any manner whatsoever, what I shall see or hear in this Council; never to divulge the names of the members of the Order, or their acts done in connection therewith; I swear to maintain and defend the social and political superiority of the White race on this Continent; always and in all places to observe a marked distinction between the White and African races; to vote for none but white men for any office of honor, profit or trust; to devote my intelligence, energy and influence to instil these principles in the minds and hearts of others; and to protect and defend persons of the White race, in their lives, rights and property, against the encroachments and aggressions of persons of an inferior race.

I swear, moreover, to unite myself in heart, soul and body with those who compose this Order; to aid, protect and defend them in all places; to obey the orders of those who, by our statutes, will have the right of giving those orders; to respond, at the peril of my life, to a call, a sign or a cry coming from any fellow-member whose rights are violated; and to do everything in my power to assist him through life. And to the faithful performance of this Oath, I pledge my life and sacred honor.

The oath having been taken by the candidate, the C. shall now say:

Brother, by virtue of the authority to me delegated, I now pronounce you a Knight of the x<sup>x</sup>x.

The blindfold is now removed from the new Brother, and the C. will instruct him in the principles of the Order; and after having concluded his charge, shall add:

Brother, I now consign you to the L. C. of this Council, who will instruct you as to the signs and other means of recognition of this Association, and other details of its organization and order.

The L. C. shall now instruct the new Brother as to the sign, cry, dialogue, rap, pass-word, &c., &c., taking care to charge him particularly as to the circumstances and occasion of their use. He shall also inform him of the mode of initiation and other details of order which he is required to know.

## 93. TEXAS v. WHITE: THE CONSTITUTIONALITY OF RECONSTRUCTION

### 1869

From John William Wallace (reporter), *Cases Argued and Adjudged in the Supreme Court of the United States,* December Term, 1868 (Washington, 1870), VII, 700-743.

Texas, at the time of secession, still had not disposed of all the bonds received as a result of the Compromise of 1850. These remaining bonds, after secession, were sold to White and Chiles to raise money for use in the defense of the state. After the War, the military government of Texas established by the congressional acts of 1867 brought suit to prevent payment of the bonds on the grounds that the secession legislature had not been a legal body.

Two essential questions faced the court in this case. The first had to do with the legality of secession; if it were legal, then the sale would be also, since the bonds were disposable in any way by the state government. The second question concerned the constitutionality of the reconstruction governments in the southern states. Since they were based on military power and were not republican in form as guaranteed in the Constitution, were they constitutional and therefore eligible to institute suit in the Federal courts?

In this case, the Supreme Court gave constitutional validity to the doctrine of the indissolubility of the Union and at the same time gave validity to the constitutionality of the radical congressional reconstruction program.

1. The word State describes sometimes a people or community of individuals united more or less closely in political relations, inhabiting temporarily or permanently the same country; often it denotes only the country, or territorial region, inhabited by such a community; not unfrequently it is applied to the government under which the people live; at other times it represents the combined idea of people, territory, and government.

2. In the Constitution the term State most frequently expresses the combined idea just noticed, of people, territory, and government. A State, in the ordinary sense of the Constitution, is a political community of free citizens, occupying a territory of defined boundaries, and organized under a government sanctioned and limited by a written constitution, and established by the consent of the governed.

3. But the term is also used to express the idea of a people or political community, as distinguished from the government. In this sense it is used in the clause which provides that the United States shall guarantee to every State in the Union a republican form of government and shall protect each of them against invasion.

4. The Union of the States never was a purely artificial and arbitrary relation. It began among the Colonies, and grew out of common origin, mutual sympathies, kindred principles, similar interests, and geographical relations. It was confirmed and strengthened by the necessities of war, and received definite form, and character, and sanction, from the Articles of Confederation. By these the Union was solemnly declared to "be perpetual." And, when these Articles were found to be inadequate to the exigencies of the country, the Constitution was ordained "to form a more perfect Union."

5. But the perpetuity and indissolubility of the Union by no means implies the loss of distinct and individual existence, or of the right of self-government by the States.

On the contrary, it may be not unreasonably said, that the preservation of the States, and the maintenance of their governments, are as much within the design and care of the Constitution, as the preservation of the Union and the maintenance of the National government. The Constitution, in all its provisions, looks to an indestructible Union, composed of indestructible States.

6. When Texas became one of the United States, she entered into an indissoluble relation. The union between Texas and the other States was as complete, as perpetual, and as indissoluble as the union between the original States. There was no place for reconsideration or revocation, except through revolution or through consent of the States.

7. Considered as transactions under the Constitution, the ordinance of secession, adopted by the convention, and ratified by a majority of the citizens of Texas, and all the acts of her legislature intended to give effect to that ordinance, were absolutely null. They were utterly without operation in law. The State did not cease to be a State, nor her citizens to be citizens of the Union.

8. But in order to the exercise, by a State, of the right to sue in this court, there needs to be a State government, competent to represent the State in its relations with the National government, so far at least as the institution and prosecution of a suit is concerned.

9. While Texas was controlled by a government hostile to the United States, and in affiliation with a hostile confederation, waging war upon the United States, no suit, instituted in her name, could be maintained in this court. It was necessary that the government and the people of the State should be restored to peaceful relations to the United States, under the Constitution, before such a suit could be prosecuted.

10. Authority to suppress rebellion is found in the power to suppress insurrection and carry on war; and authority to provide for the restoration of State governments, under the Constitution, when subverted and overthrown, is derived from the obligation of the United States to guarantee to every State in the Union a republican form of government. The latter, indeed, in the case of a rebellion which involves the government of a State, and, for the time, excludes the National authority from its limits, seems to be a necessary complement to the other.

11. When slavery was abolished, the new freemen necessarily became part of the people; and the people still constitute the State: for States, like individuals, retain their identity, though changed, to some extent, in their constituent elements. And it was the State, thus constituted, which was now entitled to the benefit of the constitutional guaranty.

12. In the exercise of the power conferred by the guaranty clause, as in the exercise of every other constitutional power, a discretion in the choice of means is necessarily allowed. It is essential only that the means must be necessary and proper for carrying into execution the power conferred, through the restoration of the State to its constitutional relations, under a republican form of government, and that no acts be done, and no authority exerted, which is either prohibited or unsanctioned by the Constitution.

13. So long as the war continued, it cannot be denied that the president might institute temporary government within insurgent districts, occupied by the National forces, or take provisional measures, in any State, for the restoration of State government faithful to the Union, employing, however, in such efforts, only such means and agents as were authorized by constitutional laws. But, the power to carry into effect the clause of guaranty is primarily a legislative power, and resides in Congress, though necessarily limited to cases where the rightful government is subverted by revolutionary violence, or in imminent danger of being overthrown by an opposing government, set up by force within the State.

14. The several executives of Texas, partially, at least, reorganized under the authority of the President and of Congress, having sanctioned this suit, the necessary conclusion is, that it was instituted and is prosecuted by competent authority.

15. Public property of a State, alienated during rebellion by an usurping State government for the purpose of carrying on war against the United States, may be reclaimed by a restored State government, organized in allegiance to the Union, for the benefit of the State.

16. Exact definitions, within which the acts of a State government, organized in hostility to the Constitution and government of the United States, must be treated as valid or invalid, can not be attempted. It may be said, however, that acts necessary to peace and good order among citizens, such, for example, as acts sanctioning and protecting marriage and the domestic relations, governing the course of descents, regulating the conveyance and transfer of property, real and personal, and providing remedies for injuries to person and estate, and other similar acts, which would be valid if emanating from a lawful government, must be regarded in general as valid when preceding from an actual, though unlawful government; and that acts in furtherance or support of rebellion against the United States, or intended to defeat the just rights of citizens, and other acts of like nature, must, in general, be regarded as invalid and void.

17. Purchasers of United States bonds issued payable to the State of Texas or bearer, alienated during rebellion by the insurgent government, and acquired after the date at which the bonds became redeemable, are affected with notice of defect of title in the seller. [That is, the title of the state was not divested by act of the rebellious Texas government in entering into this contract.]

# 94. THE CONSTITUTION OF THE STATE OF WEST TEXAS

## January, 1869

From *Constitution of the State of West Texas* (This thirty-five page document bears no signature, date, publication data, or explanation. The original manuscript copy cannot be located, but identical printed copies are in the Texas Technological College Library, Texas State Library, the Bancroft Library, and the Library of Congress.)

By virtue of its annexation agreement, Texas had the right to divide itself into four additional states. Several efforts seeking division were made after 1847, but the most serious occurred in the Constitutional Convention of 1868-1869, where the question of division became entangled with that of reconstruction. The question was bruited even in Congress by the radical leader, Thaddeus Stevens.

The Constitutional Convention devoted a large amount of its time to this end. Several proposals were made, and one, to erect a state west of the Colorado River, commanded much attention. Since the people of the western part of Texas had strongly opposed secession and many had remained hostile to the Civil War, some of their leaders now contended that their section should be re-admitted to the Union as a separate state. E. J. Davis, president of the Convention and the prime mover in behalf of the cause, announced on January 2, 1869, that he and six other delegates at the Convention had prepared a "Constitution for the State of West Texas." When the opponents of division, led by A. J. Hamilton, succeeded through obstructionist tactics, including several alternate proposals, in blocking the plan, Davis permitted the Convention to break up without completing a constitution for Texas, and hastened to Washington to seek the admission of West Texas as a state. Though a bill was introduced into Congress to this effect, and Davis worked diligently to secure its passage, it never emerged from the Committee on Reconstruction to which it was referred.

We, the people of West Texas, acknowledging with gratitude the grace of God in permitting us to make choice of our form of Government, do ordain and establish this Constitution:

## ARTICLE I.
### BILL OF RIGHTS.

That the general, great and essential principles of liberty and free government may be recognized and established, we declare:

Section 1. All political power is inherent in the people, and all free governments are founded on their authority, and instituted for their benefit; and the people of this State have at all times the unalienable right to alter or reform their form of government, in such manner as they may think expedient, subject to the Constitution and Laws of the United States.

Sec. 2. All freemen, when they form a social compact, have equal rights; and no man, or set of men, is entitled to exclusive separate public emoluments or privileges, but in consideration of public services. . . .

Sec. 15. No person shall ever be imprisoned for debt. . . .

Sec. 21. The equality of all persons before the law is herein recognized, and shall ever remain inviolate; nor shall any citizen ever be deprived of any right, privilege, or immunity, nor be exempted from any burden, or duty, on account of race, color, or previous condition.

Sec. 22. Importations of persons "under the name of coolies," or any other name or designation, or the adoption of any system of "peonage," whereby the helpless and unfortunate may be reduced to practical bondage, shall never be authorized, or tolerated by the laws of this State,

and neither slavery nor involuntary servitude, except as a punishment for crime whereof the party shall have been convicted, shall ever exist in this State.

Sec. 23. To guard against transgressions of the high powers herein delegated, we declare that every thing in this "Bill of Rights" is excepted out of the general powers of government, and shall forever remain inviolate, and all laws contrary thereto, or to the following provisions, shall be void; and we declare that the powers herein granted to the different departments of the government of this State are based upon the equality, in civil and political rights, of all human beings within the jurisdiction of this State; and should any department (either executive, legislative or judicial) attempt, in any manner, to deprive any person or persons of their herein guaranteed civil and political rights, such attempts shall be considered as a violation of the compact under which this State entered the Union.

## ARTICLE II.
### DIVISION OF THE POWERS OF GOVERNMENT.

Sec. 1. The powers of the Government of the State of West Texas shall be divided into three distinct departments, and each of them confided to a separate body of magistracy—to wit: those which are Legislative to one, those which are Executive to another, and those which are Judicial to another; and no person, or collection of persons, being of one of those departments, shall exercise any power, properly attached to either of the others, except in the instances herein expressly permitted.

## ARTICLE III.
### LEGISLATIVE DEPARTMENT.

Sec. 1. Every male person who shall have attained the age of twenty-one years, and who shall be (or who shall have declared his intention to become) a citizen of the United States, or who is, at the time of the acceptance of this Constitution by the Congress of the United States, a citizen of West Texas, and shall have resided in this State one year next preceding an election, and the last six months within the district or county, in which he offers to vote, and is duly registered, (Indians not taxed, excepted,) shall be deemed a qualified elector: . . .

Sec. 3. The Legislative powers of this State shall be vested in two distinct branches: the one to be styled the Senate, and the other the House of Representatives, and both together the "Legislature of the State of West Texas." . . .

Sec. 4. The members of the House of Representatives shall be chosen by the qualified electors, and their term of office shall be two years from the day of the general election; and the sessions of the Legislature shall be annual, at such times as shall be prescribed by law. . . .

Sec. 26. The Legislature shall cause an enumeration to be made every ten years, commencing on the sixth day of February, 1875, of all the inhabitants (including Indians taxed) of the State, designating particularly the number of registered voters, and the age, sex and color of all, (herein following the classification of the United States census,) and the whole number of Representatives shall, at the next session after the several periods of making such an enumeration, be fixed by the Legislature, and apportioned among the several counties, according to the number of population in each. The number of Representatives shall at present be fixed at twenty-six and when the population of the State may exceed the number of two hundred and sixty thousand persons, then one additional Representative for each ten thousand of such excess of population shall be added; Provided, that the whole number of Representatives shall never exceed forty-two. . . .

Sec. 28. The number of Senators shall at present be fixed at thirteen; and when the population of the State may exceed the number of two hundred and sixty thousand persons then one additional Senator for each twenty thousand of such excess of population shall be added; Provided that the whole number of Senators shall never exceed twenty-one.

Sec. 29. The first session of the Legislature, after the acceptance of this Constitution by the Congress of the United States, shall be held at the city of San Antonio, Bexar county, and thereafter until the year 1871, after which year the seat of government shall be permanently located by a vote of the people. . . .

## ARTICLE IV.
### JUDICIAL DEPARTMENT.

Section 1. The judicial power of this State shall be vested in one Supreme Court, in District Courts, and in such inferior courts as the Legislature may from time to time ordain and establish; and such jurisdiction may be vested in corporation courts as may be deemed necessary, and be directed by law.

Sec. 2. The Supreme Court shall consist of a Chief Justice and two Associates, any two of whom shall form a quorum. . . .

Sec. 5. The Judges of the Supreme Court shall hold their offices for the term of twelve years, and the Judges of the District Court for eight years. The terms of the Supreme Judges shall be arranged that the office of one shall become vacant at the end of every four years, and . . . Judges of the Supreme Court and District Courts, the Attorney General and District Attorneys, shall be appointed by the Governor, by and with the advice and consent of the Senate; Provided, that at the first general election after the year one thousand eight hundred and eighty (1880) the question shall be submitted to vote, whether these officers shall thereafter be elected by the people. . . .

Sec. 13. There shall be elected in each county by the qualified voters of the different precincts thereof as may be directed by law, at least five Justices of the Peace, one of whom shall reside, after the election, at the county seat, and not more than one of said Justices shall be a resident of the same Justice's precinct. . . .

Sec. 23. The Grand Jury system is hereby dispensed with in this State. The prosecution of offenses in this State shall be by information or presentment of the District Attorney or Attorney General. The filing before any competent officer of an affidavit charging an offense, shall be sufficient to authorize and require an information or presentment before the proper tribunal. To the District Attorney or Attorney General is given the same authority heretofore exercised by Grand Juries, and these officers are required to institute examinations in regard to any offenses that may be brought to their notice. For the institution of prosecutions for offenses less than felony, the Legislature may authorize some more simple proceeding. The Legislature shall provide all needful regulations for carrying out the spirit and intent of this and the last preceding section: provided, that if the dispensing with the Grand Jury system shall be found inconvenient, the Legislature may, after five years from the acceptance of this Constitution by the United States Congress, re-establish that system.

Sec. 24. In all trials by Jury, the agreement of three-fourths of the Jurymen shall be sufficient to find a verdict. . . .

## ARTICLE V.
### EXECUTIVE DEPARTMENT.

Sec. 1. The supreme executive power of this State shall be vested in the Chief Magistrate, who shall be styled the Governor of the State of West Texas. . . .

Sec. 4. The Governor shall hold his office for the term of four years . . . but shall not be eligible for more than eight years in any term of twelve years; and (after the first election) shall have resided in this State three years immediately preceding his election. . . .

## ARTICLE VII.
### GENERAL PROVISIONS.

Sec. 1. The boundaries of the State of West Texas are hereby defined as commencing at a point in the Gulf of Mexico, three miles from the shore opposite the middle of the main channel of Pass Caballo, thence up the middle of said channel and of Matagorda Bay to the mouth of Colorado River, thence up the middle of the main channel of said river, with its meanders to the point where said river is intersected by the thirty-second parallel of North latitude, thence along said parallel to a point [blank] miles west from said river, thence in a straight line to the junction of the Pecos river and Rio Grande, thence down the main channel of the Rio Grande, with its meanders, to the Gulf of Mexico, three miles from the land to the place of beginning.

Sec. 2. The Constitution and Laws of the United States of America, and the treaties and laws of the United States, made in pursuance of said Constitution, are the supreme law of this State. The laws enacted by the Legislature of the State of Texas, previous to the twenty-eighth day of January, eighteen hundred and sixty-one, where the same are not in conflict with the Constitution and laws of the United States and are not changed by this Constitution, shall remain the law of this State until repealed or amended by the Legislature of the same; Provided that all laws or parts of laws which were enacted for the purpose of protecting or sustaining the institution of slavery, or which recognize any distinction among human beings in regard to their civil or political privileges, rights, and duties, are to be considered as null and void, and of no binding force. . . .

Sec. 52. The people of this State, being largely engaged in the business of grazing, the Legislature is directed to provide for the protection and development of the stock raising interest. Provision shall be made for the inspection of animals and hides sold within the State. . . .

## ARTICLE VIII.
### REGISTRATION OF VOTERS.

Section 1. All male persons of the legal age, who have resided in this State for the length of time required by law, and who are citizens of the United States, or have declared their intention to become such, shall be entitled to register as voters, except those embraced under the following heads:

Head 1. All persons, who during the late rebellion against the United States Government, voluntarily aided or abetted the said rebellion in any manner, are prohibited from registry. Persons will not be considered as having voluntarily aided said rebellion, who throughout the rebellion disapproved of the same, but accepted office under the rebel government, or entered into the military force thereof, through compulsion, or for self-protection, or as a means of protecting their loyal friends. And all persons who abandoned the rebel service, and joined the United States forces at any time before the close of the rebellion, shall be authorized to register (if otherwise qualified) without regard to what may have been their motive in entering such rebel service. . . .

Head 3. All editors of newspapers, or ministers of the Gospel, who approved of, or aided the said rebellion, by writing, preaching, speaking or publishing their views in favor thereof, are prohibited from registry. . . .

Head 5. All persons who since the close of the said rebellion have continued as members of, or have become members of any secret organization designed in hostility to the United States, or the loyal people thereof, and known as "Sons of the South," or "Ku Klux Klan," or by any other name, are prohibited from registry; Provided, however, that all persons who are registered as voters under the reconstruction acts of Congress previous to voting on this Constitution, and who may vote for the adoption thereof, when the same is submitted to the people, shall be entitled to register (if otherwise qualified) though they may be excluded under the terms of any one of the foregoing heads. . . .

Sec. 3. The County Court of each county shall be the Board of Registry of the county, and shall sit for this purpose at such times as the Legislature may direct. The County Clerk shall keep a public registry of the voters, setting forth briefly the grounds of admission or rejection of the applicant for registry; and shall also keep a record of the oath (or affirmation) made by each registered voter. . . .

## ARTICLE IX.
### LAND OFFICE AND LANDS.

. . . Sec. 3. Immigrants to this State, from Europe and elsewhere, as well as residents of this State, who may settle on any part of the public lands of this State, shall be entitled to a portion of such land, as follows: Every head of a family, whether male or female, shall have one hundred and sixty acres; and every male person over the age of eighteen years, shall have eighty acres of the public lands. The only conditions attached to this donation, shall be, that each applicant for the same shall pay all expenses of survey thereof, and make such proof as the Legislature may require, that he or she has resided on the land to be donated, for three years preceding the issuance of the patent.

## ARTICLE X.
### IMMIGRATION.

Sec. 1. There shall be a Bureau, known as the "Bureau of Immigration," which shall have supervision and control of all matters connected with Immigration. . . .

Sec. 2. The Legislature shall have power to appropriate part of the ordinary revenue of the State, for the purpose of promoting and protecting Immigration. Such appropriation shall be devoted to defraying the expenses of this Bureau, to the support of agencies in foreign seaports, or seaports of the United States, and to the payment, in part, or in toto, of the passage of immigrants from Europe to this State, and their transportation within this State. . . .

## ARTICLE XII.
### PUBLIC SCHOOLS.

. . . Sec. 5. The Legislature, at its first session, (or as soon thereafter as may be possible,) shall pass such laws as will require the attendance on the Public Free Schools of the State, of all the Scholastic population thereof, for the period of at least four months of each and every year; Provided, that when any of the Scholastic inhabitants may be shown to have received regular instruction for said period of time in each and every year from any private teacher having a proper certificate of competency, this shall exempt them from the operation of the laws contemplated by this section.

Sec. 6. As a basis for the establishment and endowment of said Public Free Schools, all the funds, lands and other property heretofore set apart and appropriated, or that may hereafter be set apart and appropriated, for the support and maintenance of Public Schools, shall constitute the Public School Fund. And all sums of money that may come to this State, hereafter, from the sale of any portion of the public domain of the former State of Texas, shall also constitute a part of the Public School Fund. And said Fund, and the income derived therefrom shall be a perpetual fund, to be applied as needed, exclusively for the education of all the scholastic inhabitants of this State, and no law shall ever be made appropriating such fund, for any other use of purpose whatever. . . .

## 95. THE CONSTITUTION OF 1869

### February 8, 1869

From Francis Newton Thorpe (comp.), *The Federal and State Constitutions, Colonial Charters, and Other Organic Laws of the States, Territories, and Colonies* (7 vols.; Washington, 1909), VI, 3591-3620.

A convention assembled in Austin on June 1, 1868, to write a new constitution for Texas. This time the Constitution was to be written in conformity with the requirements imposed by Congress in the reconstruction acts. Of its ninety members, six had been in the Convention of 1866, twelve were conservatives, and nine were Negroes; all except the conservatives were Republicans, split between the moderates, headed by A. J. Hamilton, and the radicals, led by Edmund J. Davis and Morgan C. Hamilton. The Convention, having exhausted its appropriated funds, adjourned on August 31. It reassembled on the first Monday in December and resumed its wrangling over such questions as the illegality of secession, the division of the state, and the disfranchisement of the Ex-Confederates. Finally, after having spent over $200,000, the Convention broke up on February 8 without taking a formal vote on the Constitution. Forty-five of the ninety delegates signed the unfinished document. The military commander in the state appointed a committee to complete a draft from the confused records, and on November 30 and the three days following, the people of the state ratified the document by a vote of 72,395 to 4,924, hoping that its adoption would rid the state of military rule. This Republican Constitution was the fundamental law of the state until replaced in 1876 by another prepared by Democrats. Since it is too lengthy for full inclusion herein, a few parts have been selected to illustrate its character.

## CONSTITUTION OF TEXAS

We, the people of Texas, acknowledging with gratitude the grace of God in permitting us to make a choice of our form of government, do hereby ordain and establish this constitution:

### ARTICLE I

#### BILL OF RIGHTS

That the heresies of nullification and secession, which brought the country to grief, may be eliminated from future political discussion; that public order may be restored, private property and human life protected, and the great principles of liberty and equality secured to us and our posterity, we declare that—

Section 1. The Constitution of the United States, and the laws and treaties made and to be made in pursuance thereof, are acknowledged to be the supreme law; that this constitution is framed in harmony with and in subordination thereto; and that the fundamental principles embodied herein can only be changed subject to the national authority.

Sec. 2. All freemen, when they form a social compact, have equal rights; and no man or set of men is entitled to exclusive separate public emoluments or privileges. . . .

Sec. 21. The equality of all persons before the law is herein recognized, and shall ever remain inviolate; nor shall any citizen ever be deprived of any right, privilege, or immunity, nor be exempted from any burden or duty, on account of race, color, or previous condition.

Sec. 22. Importations of persons under the name of "coolies," or any other name or designation, or the adoption of any system of peonage, whereby the helpless and

unfortunate may be reduced to practical bondage, shall never be authorized or tolerated by the laws of this State; and neither slavery nor involuntary servitude, except as punishment for crime, whereof the party shall have been duly convicted, shall ever exist in this State. . . .

### ARTICLE II

#### DIVISIONS OF THE POWERS OF GOVERNMENT

The powers of the government of the State of Texas shall be divided into three distinct departments, and each of them be confided to a separate body of magistracy, to wit: those which are legislative to one, those which are executive to another, and those which are judicial to another; and no person, or collection of persons, being of one of those departments, shall exercise any power properly attached to either of the others, except in the instances herein expressly permitted.

### ARTICLE III

#### LEGISLATIVE DEPARTMENT

Section 1. Every male person who shall have attained the age of twenty-one years, and who shall be (or who shall have declared his intention to become) a citizen of the United States, or who is at the time of the acceptance of this constitution by the Congress of the United States a citizen of Texas, and shall have resided in this State one year next preceding an election, and the last six months within the district or county in which he offers to vote, and is duly registered, (Indians not taxed excepted,) shall be deemed a qualified elector; . . .

Sec. 3. The legislative power of the State shall be vested in two distinct branches; the one to be styled the senate and the other the house of representatives; and both together, the legislature of the State of Texas. . . .

Sec. 4. The members of the house of representatives shall be chosen by the qualified electors, and their term of office shall be two years from the day of general election; and the sessions of the legislature shall be annual, at such times as shall be prescribed by law. . . .

Sec. 6. All elections for State, district, and county officers shall be held at the county seats of the several counties until otherwise provided by law; and the polls shall be opened for four days, from 8 o'clock a.m. until 4 o'clock p.m. of each day.

Sec. 7. The house of representatives shall consist of ninety members, and no more.

Sec. 8. The senators shall be chosen by the qualified electors here after for the term of six years. . . .

Sec. 10. The senate shall consist of thirty senators, and no more. . . .

Sec. 24. Bills may originate in either house, and be amended, altered, or rejected by the other; . . .

Sec. 35. The members of the legislature shall, at their first session hereafter, receive from the treasury of the

State as their compensation eight dollars for each day they shall be in attendance, and eight dollars for each twenty-five miles in travelling to and from the seat of government. . . .

Sec. 36. The legislature . . . after the ratification of this constitution, . . . shall proceed to ratify the thirteenth and fourteenth articles of amendment to the Constitution of the United States of America. . . .

## ARTICLE IV
### EXECUTIVE DEPARTMENT

Section 1. The executive department of the State shall consist of a chief magistrate, who shall be styled the governor, a lieutenant-governor, secretary of state, comptroller of public accounts, treasurer, commissioner of the general land-office, attorney-general, and superintendent of public instruction. . . .

Sec. 4. The governor shall hold his office for the term of four years from the time of his instalment, and until his successor shall be duly qualified. . . .

Sec. 5. The governor shall, at stated times, receive a compensation for his services, which shall . . . be five thousand dollars, until otherwise provided by law, exclusive of the use and occupation of the governor's mansion, a lieutenant-governor possessing the same qualifications as fixtures and furniture.

Sec. 6. He shall be commander-in-chief of the militia of the State except when they are called into the actual service of the United States. . . .

Sec. 11. In all criminal cases, except treason and impeachment, he shall have power, after conviction, to grant reprieves and pardons; . . .

Sec. 15. At the time of the election of a governor, there shall also be elected by the qualified voters of the State the governor, and who shall continue in office for the same period of time. He shall, by virtue of his office, be president of the senate; . . .

## ARTICLE V
### JUDICIAL DEPARTMENT

Section 1. The judicial power of this State shall be vested in one supreme court, in district courts, and in such inferior courts and magistrates as may be created by this constitution, or by the legislature under its authority.

The legislature may establish criminal courts in the principal cities within the State with such criminal jurisdiction, coextensive with the limits of the county wherein such city may be situated, and under such regulations as may be prescribed by law; . . .

Sec. 2. The supreme court shall consist of three judges, any two of whom shall constitute a quorum. They shall be appointed by the governor, by and with the advice and consent of the senate, for a term of nine years. But the judges first appointed under this constitution shall be so classified by lot that the term of one of them shall expire at the end of every three years. . . .

Sec. 3. The supreme court shall have appellate jurisdiction only, which, in civil cases, shall be coextensive with the limits of the State. In criminal cases no appeal shall be allowed to the supreme court unless some judge thereof shall, upon inspecting a transcript of the record, believing

that some error of law has been committed by the judge before whom the cause was tried: . . .

Sec. 6. The State shall be divided into convenient judicial districts, for each of which one judge shall be appointed by the governor, by and with the advice and consent of the senate, for a term of eight years, who shall after his appointment reside within the district, and shall hold a court three times a year in each county thereof, at such time and place as may be prescribed by law: . . .

Sec. 8. In the trial of all criminal cases the jury trying the same shall find and assess the amount of punishment to be inflicted, or fine to be imposed, except in cases where the punishment or fine shall be specifically imposed by law: . . .

Sec. 13. The judges of the supreme court shall receive a salary of not less than four thousand five hundred dollars annually, and the judges of the district court a salary not less than three thousand five hundred dollars annually. . . .

Sec. 17. Every criminal offence that may by law be punished by death, or in discretion of the jury by imprisonment to hard labor for life, and every offence that may by law be punished by imprisonment in the State penitentiary, shall be deemed a felony, and shall only be tried upon an indictment found by a grand jury. . . .

Sec. 18. One sheriff for each county shall be elected by the qualified voters thereof, who shall hold his office for four years, . . .

Sec. 19. There shall be elected in each county, by the qualified voters thereof, as may be directed by law, five justices of the peace, one of whom shall reside after his election at the county-seat; and not more than one of said justices shall be a resident of the same justice's precinct. They shall hold their offices for four years; . . .

Sec. 20. Justices of the peace shall have such civil and criminal jurisdiction as shall be provided by law. And the justices of the peace in each county, or any three of them, shall constitute a court, having such jurisdiction, similar to that heretofore exercised by county commissioners and police courts, as may be prescribed by law. And, when sitting as such court, the justice who resides at the county-seat shall be the presiding justice. . . .

Sec. 21. Each county shall be divided into five justices' precincts. And the justices of the peace in each county, sitting as a county court, shall appoint one constable for each justice's precinct. . . .

## ARTICLE VI
### RIGHT OF SUFFRAGE

Every male citizen of the United States of the age of twenty-one years and upwards, not laboring under the disabilities named in this constitution, without distinction of race, color, or former condition, who shall be a resident of this State at the time of the adoption of this constitution, or who shall thereafter reside in this State one year, and in the county in which he offers to vote sixty days next preceding any election, shall be entitled to vote for all officers that are now or hereafter may be elected by the people, and upon all questions submitted to the electors at any election: *Provided,* That no person shall be allowed to vote or hold office who is now, or hereafter may be, disqualified therefor by the Constitution of the United States, until such disqualification shall be removed by the Congress of the United States: *Provided further,* That no person while kept in any asylum, or confined in prison, or who has been convicted of a felony, or who is of unsound mind, shall be allowed to vote or hold office.

## ARTICLE VII
### MILITIA

The governor shall have power to call forth the militia to execute the laws of the State, to suppress insurrection, and to repel invasions. . . .

## ARTICLE IX
### PUBLIC SCHOOLS

Section 1. It shall be the duty of the legislature of this State to make suitable provisions for the support and maintenance of a system of public free schools, for the gratuitous instruction of all the inhabitants of this State between the ages of six and eighteen years.

Sec. 2. There shall be a superintendent of public instruction, who . . . shall be elected by the people . . . for the term of four years. He shall receive an annual salary of two thousand five hundred dollars, until otherwise provided by law. . . .

Sec. 3. . . . The legislature may lay off the State into convenient school districts, and provide for the formation of a board of school directors in each district. It may give the district boards such legislative powers, in regard to the schools, schoolhouses, and school-fund of the district, as may be deemed necessary and proper. It shall be the duty of the superintendent of public instruction to recommend to the legislature such provisions of law as may be found necessary, in the progress of time, to the establishment and perfection of a complete system of education, adapted to the circumstances and wants of the people of this State. . . .

Sec. 4. The legislature shall establish a uniform system of public free schools throughout the State.

Sec. 5. The legislature, at its first session, (or as soon thereafter as may be possible,) shall pass such laws as will require the attendance on the public free schools of the State of all the scholastic population thereof, for the period of at least four months of each and every year: . . .

Sec. 6. As a basis for the establishment and endowment of said public free schools, all the funds, lands, and other property heretofore set apart and appropriated, or that may hereafter be set apart and appropriated, for the support and maintenance of public schools, shall constitute the public-school fund. And all sums of money that may come to this State hereafter from the sale of any portion of the public domain of the State of Texas shall also constitute a part of the public-school fund. And the legislature shall appropriate all the proceeds resulting from sales of public lands of this State to such public-school fund. The legislature shall set apart, for the benefit of public schools, one-fourth of the annual revenue derivable from general taxation; and shall also cause to be levied and collected an annual poll-tax of one dollar, on all male persons in this State, between the ages of twenty-one and sixty years, for the benefit of public schools. . . .

Sec. 7. The legislature shall, if necessary, in addition to the income derived from the public-school fund, and from the taxes for school purposes provided for in the foregoing section, provide for the raising of such amount by taxa-

tion, in the several school districts in the State, as will be necessary to provide the necessary school-houses in each district, and insure the education of all the scholastic inhabitants of the several districts. . . .

Sec. 9. . . . It is made the imperative duty of the legislature to see to it that all the children in the State, within the scholastic age, are, without delay, provided with ample means of education. . . .

## ARTICLE X
### LAND-OFFICE

. . . Sec. 5. All public lands heretofore reserved for the benefit of railroads or railway companies shall hereafter be subject to location and survey by any genuine land certificates.

Sec. 6. The legislature shall not hereafter grant lands to any person or persons, nor shall any certificates for land be sold at the land-office, except to actual settlers upon the same, and in lots not exceeding one hundred and sixty acres. . . .

Sec. 8. To every head of a family, who has not a homestead, there shall be donated one hundred and sixty acres of land, out of the public domain, upon the condition that he will select, locate, and occupy the same for three years, and pay the office fees on the same. To all single men, twenty-one years of age, there shall be donated eighty acres of land, out of the public domain, upon the same terms and conditions as are imposed upon the head of a family.

## ARTICLE XI
### IMMIGRATION

Section 1. There shall be a bureau, known as the "bureau of immigration," which shall have supervision and control of all matters connected with immigration. The head of this bureau shall be styled the "superintendent of immigration." He shall be appointed by the governor, by and with the advice and consent of the senate. He shall hold his office for four years, and, until otherwise fixed by law, shall receive an annual compensation of two thousand dollars. He shall have such further powers and duties, connected with immigration, as may be given by law.

Sec. 2. The legislature shall have power to appropriate part of the ordinary revenue of the State for the purpose of promoting and protecting immigration. Such appropriation shall be devoted to defraying the expenses of this bureau, to the support of agencies in foreign sea-ports, or sea-ports of the United States, and to the payment, in part or *in toto,* of the passage of immigrants from Europe to this State, and their transportation within this State.

## ARTICLE XII
### GENERAL PROVISIONS

Section 1. Members of the legislature, and all officers, before they enter the duties of their offices, shall take the following oath or affirmation: "I, A. B., do solemnly swear [or affirm] . . . that I am not disqualified from holding office under the fourteenth amendment to the Constitution of the United States, [or, as the case may be, my disability to hold office under the fourteenth amendment to the Constitution of the United States has been removed by act of Congress;]" . . .

Sec. 14. The rights of married women to their separate property, real and personal, and the increase of the same, shall be protected by law; . . .

Sec. 15. The legislature shall have power, and it shall be their duty, to protect by law from forced sale a certain portion of the property of all heads of families. . . .

Sec. 27. All persons who, at any time heretofore, lived together as husband and wife, and both of whom, by the law of bondage, were precluded from the rites of matrimony, and continued to live together until the death of one of the parties, shall be considered as having been legally married; and the issue of such cohabitation shall be deemed legitimate. And all such persons as may be now living together in such relation shall be considered as having been legally married; and the children heretofore or hereafter born of such cohabitation shall be deemed legitimate. . . .

Sec. 31. No minister of the gospel or priest of any denomination whatever, who accepts a seat in the legislature as representative, shall, after such acceptance, be allowed to claim exemption from military service, road duty, or serving on juries, by reason of his said profession.

Sec. 32. The inferior courts of the several counties in this State shall have the power, upon a vote of two-thirds of the qualified voters of the respective counties, to assess and provide for the construction of internal improvements: . . .

Sec. 33. The ordinance of the convention passed on the first day of February, A. D. 1861, commonly known as the ordinance of secession, was in contravention of the Constitution and laws of the United States, and therefore null and void from the beginning; and all laws and parts of laws founded upon said ordinance were also null and void from the date of their passage. The legislatures which sat in the State of Texas from the 18th day of March, A. D. 1861, until the 6th day of August, A. D. 1866, had no constitutional authority to make laws binding upon the people of the State of Texas: *Provided,* That this section shall not be construed to inhibit the authorities of this State from respecting and enforcing such rules and regulations as were prescribed by the said legislatures which were not in violation of the Constitution and laws of the United States, or in aid of the rebellion against the United States, or prejudicial to the citizens of this State who were loyal to the United States, and which have been actually in force or observed in Texas during the above period of time; nor to affect, prejudicially, private rights which may have grown up under such rules and regulations; nor to invalidate official acts not in aid of the rebellion against the United States during said period of time. The legislature which assembled in the city of Austin on the 6th day of August, A. D. 1866, was provisional only, and its acts are to be respected only so far as they were not in violation of the Constitution and laws of the United States, or were not intended to reward those who participated in the late rebellion; or to discriminate between the citizens on account of race or color; or to operate prejudicially to any class of citizens.

Sec. 34. All debts created by the so-called State of Texas, from and after the 28th day of January, 1861, and prior to the 5th day of August, 1865, were and are null and void; and the legislature is prohibited from making any provision for the acknowledgment or payment of such debts. . . .

## 96. THE TAX-PAYERS' CONVENTION

### September 22-25, 1871

From *Proceedings of the Tax-Payers' Convention of the State of Texas* (Galveston, 1871), 13-25.

The "obnoxious acts" of the radical Davis administration in Texas aroused resentment among thoughtful men irrespective of political preference. The Democratic State Convention in January, 1871, denounced the "unconstitutional and oppressive" acts of the radicals, and called for a non-partisan effort to release the people from "oppressive, ruinous, and unequal taxation." Sporadic agitation continued, but the most important and best organized opposition was the Tax-Payers' Convention, resulting from a call issued by a non-partisan group including some of Davis' former staunch supporters.

This Convention, composed of delegates from ninety-four counties, met in Austin on September 22, 1871, to consider the "exorbitant expenditure and enormous taxes" of the Davis government and to inquire into the constitutionality of many of its acts. Ex-Governor E. M. Pease was elected chairman of the Convention, and two committees were named to consider its grievances. Needless to say, Governor Davis spurned the Convention's invitation to cooperate. Excerpts from committee reports, which were adopted by the Convention on September 25, follow.

### 1. REPORT OF THE COMMITTEE OF TWENTY-ONE ON VIOLATIONS OF CONSTITUTION AND LAWS

The violations of Constitutions and disregard of law have been very frequent and are very numerous; but, frequent as they have been and numerous as they are, we have been unable to find a single one, of either class, based on an honest desire to accomplish good to the people of the State, or to secure prosperity to the country. On the contrary, their apparent cause seems uniformly to spring from one grand purpose, viz: to concentrate power in the hands of one man, and to emasculate the strength of the citizens of Texas as a free people.

However hopeless such a design might have appeared, and however little feared by the reasoning and intelligent mind eighteen months ago, yet at this day, we must confess, the scheme has far progressed toward consummation, and the people stand stripped of inalienable rights of freemen, while he who is now clothed with these lost rights of the people, gloats on their humiliation and congratulates himself on the possession of kingly power.

We may safely state that the practical effect of each of the acts we shall name has been, and is now, to abridge the rights of the citizen, and to enlarge, solidify and confirm the power of the Executive.

And, 1. Duly elected and qualified members of the Legislature, in both houses, have been expelled or denied seats, to give place to persons who were not elected by a majority of voters, and who were not in law entitled to seats. (Case of Alford in the Senate. Case of Plato in the House, *et al.*)

2. At a time when measures of grave importance of themselves, and of vital interest to all the people were under discussion in the Senate and not matured, the majority in the State Senate, arbitrarily and without authority of law, placed nearly all the minority under arrest and deprived them of a voice in behalf of the people, and so held them in arrest and silent until the Militia Law, the Police Bill, the Enabling Act, the Registration Act, and the Election Law were passed, and until nominations for judicial and other important officers were approved of; all of which measures go to the oppression of the people; and many of the officers confirmed were unqualified as to capacity, corrupt as to morals, and entirely unfit for high position in any State.

3. A multitude of new offices have been created, and officers appointed to fill them, without the consent and against the will of the people.

4. Important and useful legislation to the country has been postponed and delayed at great expense, until odious and oppressive laws were fastened upon the people.

5. Without authority of law, and in violation of the constitution, the term of office of the present members of the Legislature has been extended one year. They were elected on the 30th day of November and 1st, 2d and 3d days of December, 1869; and now, under an act passed and construed by themselves, claim to hold until a general election in the year 1872, notwithstanding Sec. 4, Art. 3 of the Constitution.

6. The Executive has omitted and failed to order elections to fill vacancies in the Legislature, caused by death or otherwise, within the time prescribed by law, and has thus, for many months, denied representation to large bodies of the people, although they were taxed, and have been forced to perform militia duty. (Sec. 19, Art. 3, Constitution; Sec. 11, p. 130, Laws of 1870.)

7. The present State administration bases its authority on the claimed results of the general election held on the 30th November and 1st, 2d and 3d days of December, 1869, and yet has omitted and refused to order and provide for a general election until the first Tuesday after the first Monday in November, 1872; thus throwing the second general election nearly three years from the first. (Sec. 4, Art. 3, Constitution; Laws of 1870, p. 129, Sec. 7.)

8. The State of Texas is practically left without a Legislature from December, 1871, until November, 1872, and that, too, while the Executive is clothed with despotic power.

9. Newspapers have been established in the several judicial districts of the State to bolster up the present despotism, and to familiarize the people with Executive usurpation, and, through forced patronage, to gain great profit, and thereby help to impoverish the citizens. (Laws of 1870, p. 74.)

10. The courts of the State are effectually closed against the approach of the citizen, and prohibited from extending relief for an existing wrong—in this, that though the judges of election may willfully and corruptly refuse to permit a qualified elector to vote, yet the courts are forbidden to compel such officers to do their duty, or refrain from the commission of a wrong by injunction, mandamus, or otherwise. (Laws of 1870, p. 132, Sec. 22; Constitution, Sec. 11, Art. 1.)

11. An election law has been passed, and is now enforced, which breaks down in practical effect all the safeguards of the ballot, and places in the hands of those who receive and count the votes, the unrestrained power to defeat the will of the electors, and to substitute their own instead; it authorizes those who have the handling of the votes, on one pretext and another, to cast out large proportions of the votes and to announce partial and untrue results; it, by the non-identification of tickets voted, prevents fair and full investigation in cases of contested elections; it requires electors to travel long distances, to undergo heavy expense, and to consume much time needlessly to exercise the right of suffrage, thus compelling the citizen to forego the exercise of the elective franchise, or else to submit to exactions, oppressions, and wrongs to person and property. (Laws of 1870, p. 130, *et seq.*)

12. The enabling act places great power in the hands of the Executive, in palpable violation of the Constitution, in that it authorizes him to appoint various important officers, who are charged with responsible duties, who under the Constitution are elective by the people, and to remove others, who are alone removable by due course of law. (Laws of 1870, pp. 17, 18; Constitution, Sec. 12, Art. 5.)

13. The terms of the Police Bill constitute of themselves an authorized violation of nearly every private right of the citizen. The police force is chosen by the Executive, and placed under his command without restriction or responsibility; it is always ready for action, with arms in hand, having for its duties the part of spies, informers and detectives, circulating through the whole community. The very vocation of such a force renders them odious to the people, and unprincipled of themselves; they are dangerous as hirelings to the reputation and lives of the people. The practical workings of this force, raised under the pretence of securing peace and quiet, and to arrest violators of the law, has demonstrated, beyond doubt, that it is a body of armed men, massed to overawe the citizen and to give an active arm to the Executive, to uphold and sustain him in his usurpations and exercise of the unlawful power concentrated in him. Its work has been a succession of wrongs, mingled with blood, its continuance is death to every private right, and, in innumerable instances, to life itself. (Laws of 1870, p. 19.)

14. Large amounts of money have been subjected and appropriated to the use of the Executive, obtainable on requisition, and on the sale of State bonds, to be held and used by him without any of the restrictions and safeguards

which the laws require of all others who handle public moneys. (Laws 1870.)

15. Under the authority of the Militia Law, now in force, and being daily executed, the Executive is vested with unlimited power. He may organize a standing army in a time of profound peace; in the face of heavy pains and penalties, the citizen is required to perform military duty, and to form part of such standing army. A State Guard is provided for, the men and officers of which are chosen and selected by the Executive, thus creating a special organization of great strength, composed of the pets, favorites and tools of the Governor, whose interest is to maintain him in his usurpations, and to enforce his orders, whatever they may be. This is an armed body of men, who may be thrown into any city or county of the State, and there, with rapidity and unscrupulousness, execute any order the Executive may give. He is clothed with the power, to declare martial law on the most paltry pretexts. He may, to all intents and purposes, suspend the writ of *habeas corpus* when there is no rebellion, no invasion, and when the public safety does not require it. With martial law declared, and the writ of *habeas corpus* practically suspended, the Executive becomes Dictator in Texas, and his will the sole guide to his action, he may take property or life, and be responsible to no tribunal of justice in the State, so long as he remains Governor under existing laws. (Laws 1870, p. 11; Constitution, Sec. X, XVII, Art 1.)

It might possibly be said, that though such unlimited power is with the Executive, yet that all the probabilities are that he will not call it into exercise; but already, under the arbitrary power conferred, he declared martial law in the county of Hill, and through machinery rapidly extemporized, gathered, by the hands of his Adjutant General, large sums of money from citizens, while under duress, and without a judgment of any court of competent jurisdiction; and under the same arbitrary power, martial law was declared in Walker county, and then, under like machinery, gathered large sums of money from the people, and, in addition thereto, incarcerated a freeman of the State of Texas in the penitentiary; and all this in a time of profound peace, when there was no rebellion, no invasion, when the public safety was not threatened, and when the civil officers in the respective counties were fully able to execute all process, and to arrest all violators of the law. And again in the county of Bastrop, martial law was time and again threatened, and held in terrorum over the people thereof, with intent to force the grand jury of said county to indict, by false indictments, the good people thereof, and thus forge a reputation for that people, of being a lawless and criminal people.

These things have grown into history, and are now recognized as authentic occurrences of the times.

16. The Executive is now enforcing the execution of a repealed law, and thereby greatly increasing the taxes demanded of the people, and gaining the possession and control of enormous sums of money, the distribution whereof is subject to his will, in connection with those about him, who hold position by his appointment, and whose terms of office depend on his pleasure. . . . [The reference is to two conflicting tax laws. On April 12, 1871, the legislature sent the Governor a bill authorizing each school district to levy a tax not exceeding one per cent for school purposes. According to the Constitution the bill became law on April 17 without the Governor's approval. On April 22 the Governor signed a bill providing for a tax of one-eighth of one per cent for school house purposes and for the repeal of all conflicting legislation. Then, two days later the Governor signed the first law. The Convention report charged that the Governor, by signing the first bill seven days after it became law, had attempted to give it precedence over the second, and that the higher tax had been collected illegally.]

17. The people have been disarmed throughout the State, notwithstanding their constitutional right "to keep and bear arms." (Constitution, Sec. 13, Art. 1. Laws 1871, p. 25.)

The Police and State Guards are armed, and lord it over the land, while the citizen dare not, under heavy pains and penalties, bear arms to defend himself, unless he has reasonable grounds for fearing an unlawful attack on his person, and that such grounds of attack shall be immediate and pressing. The citizen is at the mercy of the policeman and the men of the State Guard, and that too when these bodies of men embrace in them the most lawless and abandoned men in the State, many of whom are adventurers—strangers to the soil—discharged or pardoned criminals, forgetful of law—unrestrained by the customs of society, and without interest or ties to the State.

18. The Election Order, under the operation of which the near approaching election will be holden, is a monstrosity, and could only emanate from a mind deliberately determined to insult and humiliate the people to the last extreme, on the one hand, while on the other, it willfully orders the violation of the Constitution, by the agents who are to carry said order into execution. It forbids the assembling of the people on the days of election; it prohibits free speech; it forbids the free and lawful movement of the citizen in person; it forbids the citizen the right to advocate the election of the candidate of his choice; it authorizes the judges of election to close the polls on the merest pretexts; it subjects the citizen's motives and purposes to the judgment of policemen; it authorizes policemen to disperse bodies of citizens without warrant of law, and when they have been guilty of no violation of law; it subjects the citizen to arrest and detention while in attendance at an election, when he has not been guilty of treason, felony, or breach of the peace; it is ordered to be executed as a criminal law of the State when it has not a single feature of a law; it is the unlawful armed police upon an unarmed people; it is the will of a despot and the act of a tyrant overriding the supreme law of the land. (Sec. 2, Art. 3, Constitution.)

19. By orders executed through his armed bodies of police, the Executive has taken control of peaceable assemblies of the people, called together for peaceful and lawful purposes, and there suppressed free speech, under threats of arrest, and subjection to punishment as criminals. (Galveston case.)

20. The Executive has deliberately disregarded the solemn judgment of the District Court, and ordered his policemen to contemn the Court, and by force, with arms in their hands, to defy the Court, and to execute his will in a question of law where the Court had decided the case and entered its judgment of record. (Brownsville case.)

21. For the purpose and with the intent to retain the power they now hold, and to avoid having the free will

of the people expressed in the enactment of laws, the Executive and others in authority contemplate (and are now actively engaged to accomplish their object) so apportioning representation in the Legislature as that only the voice of a small proportion of the people shall be heard. It is proposed to give some localities much larger representation than the population thereof lawfully authorizes, and to take from other localities representation to which their population entitles them. It is purposed to ignore local representation and to make large areas of territory representative districts, to the end that the sentiment of the population of a few localities may control the voice of the State in the enactment of laws. (Bill in both Houses.) . . .

Without enlarging, we may say that the . . . people of this State no longer govern themselves, but are governed by E. J. Davis, as completely as if there were no Constitutions, State or Federal. While in form we have a Republican government, in substance and in fact we have a despotism, which constantly becomes more and more absolute, and will certainly end in unqualified enslavement of the people, unless some check is interposed.

## 2. REPORT OF THE COMMITTEE OF TWENTY-ONE ON TAXES AND STATISTICS

. . . We find from an examination of the laws that the Seventh Legislature appropriated to be paid from the State Treasury . . . for all purposes for the years 1858 and 1859, including . . . the old debt of the Republic, frontier defence, etc., amounted to only $809,592.49. We find from the same source that the . . . entire appropriations made by the Eleventh Legislature, that met in 1866, for all purposes for the expenses of the years 1867 and 1868, for the Legislature of 1866, and in addition thereto the expenses of the Government from the 13th of August to the 31st of December, 1866, amounted only to the sum of $956,-850.77.

We find from the same source that the appropriations made by the Legislature of 1870, . . . for the fiscal year, from the 1st of September, 1870 to the 1st of September, 1871, . . . for all purposes except the subsidy to the International Railroad, amounted to the sum of $1,632,270.50. The appropriations of the Legislature that met in the early part of this year (1871) . . . for the fiscal year, beginning on the 1st of September, 1871, and ending on the 31st of August, 1872 were [,] . . . exclusive of subsidies to railroads, $2,120,605.28.

It will be recollected that the Legislature of 1870 also voted a subsidy of $10,000 a mile to the International Railroad, which will impose upon our people a debt of at least $8,000,000, if the company complies with the terms of the law; and the Legislature of 1871 granted an additional subsidy of $6,000,000 to the Trans-Continental and Southern Pacific Railroads.

We find that the cost of the Legislature of 1857 was $159,760; that of 1866 was $167,000; that of 1870, $307,000, and that of 1871, $285,000, exclusive of the expenses of the adjourned session, which will probably be several hundred thousand dollars more, while the number of members, the per diem and mileage were the same for that of 1866 as for the Legislature of 1870 and 1871.

We find that the *ad valorem* tax upon property in the years 1858 and 1859 was for the State one-eighth of one per cent.; for the county one-half of that rate.

In 1866, the rate of taxation was increased, for the State to fifteen cents on each hundred dollars, and for county purposes, not exceeding one-half of that rate. The Legislature of 1871 increased the taxes as follows, viz:

*Ad valorem* State tax upon property, one-fourth of which is for schools, one-half of one per cent.; *ad valorem* county tax, one-quarter of one per cent.; *ad valorem* road and bridge tax, one-quarter of one per cent.; *ad valorem* tax for school-houses, one-eighth of one per cent.; tax for building school-houses and maintaining schools, one per cent.; a poll-tax of one dollar for schools; a poll-tax of one dollar for roads and bridges; besides the occupation and license taxes, and the tax for the frontier bonds, which is understood to have been fixed by the Comptroller at five cents on each hundred dollars, from which it will be seen that our present rate of taxation for State and county purposes is about two dollars and seventeen and a half cents ($2.17½) on each hundred dollars, besides the poll-tax and occupation and license taxes. . . .

In addition to the above, each tax-payer has to pay for the commission for assessing his *ad valorem* tax, which it is supposed will amount to about three per cent. on his *ad valorem* tax.

Your committee believe, from the best examination they have been able to give the subject, that the expenses of the Government and the present rate of taxation are excessive. They think the ordinary annual expenses of the Government should not exceed $695,000. They believe that an *ad valorem* tax of one-third of one per cent. for the State, and one-sixth of one per cent. for the counties, with the present poll-taxes and license and occupation taxes, will produce an amount of revenue ample to meet all necessary expenses, besides affording a liberal amount for public schools, and still leave a surplus in the Treasury. . . .

1. *Resolved,* That the present rates of taxation are greatly in excess of the legitimate and necessary wants of the Government.

2. *Resolved further,* That the Legislature now in session be, and they are hereby requested by this Convention, as the representatives of the tax-payers and citizens of the State, to revise and remodel the tax laws, so as to levy in lieu of all other direct *ad valorem* taxes, only one-third of one per cent. on all real and personal property, not exempt from taxation, for State purposes, and not exceeding one half that rate for county purposes. . . .

In view of the foregoing facts, showing the infractions of the Constitution and laws of the State, and in view of the extraordinary expenditures proposed by the authorities and Legislature of the State, and consequent burden of taxation levied upon the people to meet such expenditures, and in consequence of the violations of the rights and interests of the people, as are clearly shown to exist in the enactments of the Legislature, and in the exercise of unlawful and august powers assumed by the Governor of the State, therefore, be it . . .

1. *Resolved,* That while we are assembled here from every part of this great State, to protest to mankind against the grievous wrong under which the people are now laboring, we do at the same time solemnly and earnestly deprecate all violations of law and order, whether committed

by bodies of men calling themselves by one name or another, or called by others by any name whatever.

2. That we recognize the right of every person in the State, without regard to race or previous condition, to equal civil and political rights under the law, and to have protection for his life, liberty and property. That we are in favor of paying all lawful and reasonable taxes for the establishment of public free schools, and to carry on the government; but, at the same time, we recommend

to the people that they do not pay such portions of the tax now demanded as we here show to be illegal.

3. That we solemnly appeal to the deliberate judgment of the civilized world, and especially to that portion believing in the principles of Republican government, for their support and aid in our protest.

All of which is respectfully submitted.

A. J. HAMILTON, Chairman.

## 97. THE SEMI-COLON COURT: THE RODRIGUEZ CASE

### January 5, 1874

From 39 *Texas Reports* 706-776 (1882).

The Texas Democrats defeated the Republicans in the gubernatorial election in December, 1873, for the first time since reconstruction, by a two-to-one majority. But the Republicans did not accept the popular verdict, choosing rather to bring to the Supreme Court of Texas a case arising out of the election to establish that the election itself was unconstitutional. The court ruled in favor of the radicals.

Rodriguez' case was only indirectly related to the issue of constitutionality: the defendant had voted twice in the election in Harris County and presumably was guilty. The radicals entered suit for his innocence, not, however, on the grounds of the possibility of his having voted twice, but on the basis that the law establishing the election, signed by E. J. Davis himself, was unconstitutional. The following extract from the court's opinion, written by Judge Moses B. Walker, includes the court's explanation and argument.

. . . Having thus shown what we must regard as our duty in this case, we now come to the discussion of the point involved. Section 6 of article 3 of the constitution of 1869 reads thus: "All elections for state, district and county officers shall be held at the county seats of the several counties, until otherwise provided by law; and the polls shall be opened for four days, from 8 o'clock A.M. until 4 o'clock P.M. of each day."

The 12th section of the act of March 31, 1873, reads thus: "That all elections in this state shall be held for one day only at each election, and the polls shall be open on that day from 8 o'clock A.M. to 6 o'clock P.M."

The relator is charged under the 31st section of this act, with having voted more than once at the same election, which, if the election were valid, makes the offense a felony, punishable by imprisonment for not less than two nor more than five years.

In Dickey v. Hurlburt, 5 Cal. 343, the court held that time and place are of the substance of every election. This decision relates to a statute, and the provision was regarded as mandatory; but we are called on to construe a *constitutional* provision, and say whether an election, held in pursuance of an act which violates the constitution, as to the time for holding an election, is a valid election or not; and whether, if the relator did vote twice at such election, he is guilty of the felony denounced in the law.

In construing section 3 of article 5 of the constitution, in the matter of the International railroad, where the text of the clause reads thus, "The supreme court and the judges

thereof shall have power to issue the writ of *habeas corpus;* and, under such regulations as may be prescribed by law, may issue the writ of *mandamus* and such other writs as may be necessary to enforce its own jurisdiction," the different clauses here are separated by a *semicolon;* and this court held, that while the constitution gave us original jurisdiction in *habeas corpus,* the clause must be construed that our jurisdiction in *mandamus* was only appellate, and must be regulated by law.

In section 6 of article 3 we think we have a still plainer case of the separation of two clauses, one of which is subject to a limitation or condition, whilst the other is not. The legislature undoubtedly have the power to provide for holding the elections at places other than the county seats; but it is equally clear that the constitution is mandatory, and that the legislature have no power to limit the time within which the elections must be held; and section 12 of the act of March 31, 1873, is in open conflict with the constitution, and for that reason is null and void; and no valid election having been held at the city of Houston, in the county of Harris, on the second day of December, 1873, the relator is not guilty of a felony, and is therefore entitled to his enlargement. But the importance of making plain the true construction of section 6 of article 3 of the constitution demands some analysis of the section, and the application of well known canons of construction.

One principal object was in the mind of the convention when this section was framed and adopted, viz., the election. But two conditions were necessary to this object—place and time. It is very natural that the convention might deem it advisable to submit the regulation of one of these conditions to the legislature and withhold the power over the other; and thus the true sense of the section is this: the legislature may by law provide the places where the election shall be held, but the law governing the time given for the holding of an election shall never be changed by a legislature. The plain import of the words and the grammatical analysis of the sentences admit of no other construction, and there is no such doubt as would enable this court to follow the legislative construction. But able counsel have thought that section 33 of the 3d article of the constitution demands a different construction for section 6. The sections reads thus: "Elections for senators and representatives shall be general throughout the state, and shall be regulated by law." Undoubtedly this section is in harmony with section 6. The regulation by law must be the statute law touching the places of holding elections, and the time given for holding them by the constitution. Section 4 of article 3 of the constitution reads thus: "The members of the house of representatives shall be chosen by the qualified electors, and their term of office shall be two years from the day of general election; and the sessions of the legislature shall be annual at such times as shall be prescribed by law." Here the words "general election" are followed by a *semicolon,* and so far the clause is mandatory; but the remaining clause of the section, except that it provides that the sessions of the legislature shall be annual, leaves the legislature free to fix the time of its own meetings and adjournments. Here, then, in the same section, are different objects and conditions to those objects grouped together, but in different clauses. But one only of these conditions, and that found in the concluding part of the section, is left to legislative control. The members of the house of representatives must be chosen by the qualified electors; their term of office is two years; the legislature must meet annually; and over these conditions the legislature has no control; but they have control of the time of their meeting and adjournments.

Now, let us look again at section 6, and ask this question: if the convention had intended the words "until otherwise provided by law," to apply to both clauses of the section, why do not these words follow the second as well as the first clause, or why were they not inserted at the conclusion of the section where they could grammatically apply to both clauses? Neither will the rules of grammar nor of good composition admit of a proviso or condition, placed at the conclusion of an antecedent clause, applying to the subsequent clause of the sentence. . . .

Relator discharged.

## 98. PRESIDENT GRANT REFUSES TO SUPPORT DAVIS

### January 12 and 17, 1874

From *The Daily Herald* (San Antonio), January 19, 1874.

The decision of the Texas Supreme Court in the "semi-colon court" case was ignored by the public, and Richard Coke was inaugurated as governor on the night of January 15, 1874. Davis, supported by the Court's decision, appealed to President Grant to sustain him by use of the military. The replies of the President and his Attorney General follow.

Executive Mansion,
Washington, Jan. 12, 1874.

To Gov. Davis, Austin, Texas:

Your dispatch and letter regarding the action of the Supreme Court of Texas in declaring the late election unconstitutional, and asking for the use of troops to prevent apprehended violence are received. The call is not made in accordance with the Constitution of the United States and the acts of Congress under it and cannot therefore be granted. The act of the Legislature of Texas providing for the recent election having received your approval, and both political parties having made nominations and conducted a political campaign under its provisions, would it not be prudent as well as right to yield to the verdict of the people, as expressed by their ballots?

U. S. GRANT

Department of Justice,
Washington, Jan. 17, 1874.

To Gov. Davis, Austin, Texas:

Your telegram stating that according to the Constitution of Texas you were Governor until the 28th of April, and that Hon. Richard Coke has been inaugurated and will attempt to seize the Governor's office and building and calling upon the President for military assistance has been referred by him to me for answer and I am instructed to say that after considering the 14th section of article four of the Constitution of Texas providing that the Gov. shall hold his office for the term of 4 years from the time of his installation, under which you claim, and section 3 of the election declaration attached to said Constitution under which you were chosen and which provides that the State and other officers elected thereunder shall hold their respective offices for the term of years provided by the Constitution, beginning from the day of their election, under which the Governor elect claims the office, and more than four years having expired since your election, he is of the opinion that your right to the office of Governor at this time is at least so doubtful that he does not feel warranted in furnishing U. S. Troops to aid you in holding further possession of it, and he therefore declines to comply with your request.

GEO. H. WILLIAMS,
Attorney General

## 99. DECLARATION OF PURPOSES OF THE NATIONAL GRANGE

### February, 1874

From *Constitution and Declaration of Purposes of the National Grange, P. of H., Together with the Constitution of the Texas State Grange, By-laws for Pamona and Subordinate Granges, Relations to Subordinate Granges, General Provisions, and Rules for Trials* (Galveston, 1885), 10-13.

The National Grange of the Patrons of Husbandry, a private organization created in Washington, D. C., in December, 1867, had as its chief function improving the lot of the farmers. While other segments of the American society were enjoying increased prosperity, the farmers were suffering a depression occasioned by an oversupply of products caused by new lands being opened for cultivation, by improved machinery, and by the extension of railroad lines. The first local Grange in Texas was established at Salado, Bell County, in 1873; by 1874 the Order reached its peak strength with 45,000 members in chapters over the entire state. Though non-partisan in politics, the Grange was instrumental in obtaining a reduction in governmental expenditures, regulation of railroads, anti-trust legislation, anti-usury laws, the repeal of the farm produce tax, and a deep water harbor for the state. It was not so successful, however, in its efforts to aid farmers by creating cooperative stores, marketing agencies, credit facilities, and manufacturing concerns.

The "Declaration of Purposes" of the Grange as prepared at the annual session of the national organization in St. Louis in 1874 follows.

PREAMBLE. Profoundly impressed with the truth that the National Grange of the United States should definitely proclaim to the world its general objects, we hereby unanimously make this Declaration of Purposes of the Patrons of Husbandry.

GENERAL OBJECTS. 1. United by the strong and faithful tie of Agriculture, we mutually resolve to labor for the good of our Order, our country, and mankind.

2. We heartily endorse the motto, "In essentials, unity; in non-essentials, liberty; in all things, charity."

SPECIFIC OBJECTS. 3. We shall endeavor to advance our cause by laboring to accomplish the following objects:

To develop a better and higher manhood and womanhood among ourselves. To enhance the comforts and attractions of our homes, and strengthen our attachments to our pursuits. To foster mutual understanding and cooperation. To maintain inviolate our laws, and emulate each other in labor to hasten the good time coming. To diversify our crops, and crop no more than we can cultivate. To condense the weight of our exports, selling less in the bushel and more on hoof and in fleece; less in lint and more in warp and woof. To systematize our work, and calculate intelligently on probabilities. To discountenance the credit system, the mortgage system, the fashion system, and every other system tending to prodigality and bankruptcy. We propose meeting together, talking together, working together, buying together, selling together, and in general, acting together for our mutual protection and advancement, as occasion may require. We shall avoid litigation as much as possible by arbitration in the Grange. We shall constantly strive to secure entire harmony, good will, vital brotherhood among ourselves, and to make our Order perpetual. We shall earnestly endeavor to suppress personal, local, sectional, and national prejudices, all unhealthy rivalry, all selfish ambition. Faithful adherence to these principles will insure our mental, moral, social, and material advancement.

BUSINESS RELATIONS. 4. For our business interest, we desire to bring producers and consumers, farmers and manufacturers, into the most direct and friendly relations possible. Hence, we must dispense with a surplus of middlemen, not that we are unfriendly to them, but we do not need them. Their surplus and exactions diminish our profits. We wage no aggressive warfare against any other interest whatever. On the contrary, all our acts and all our efforts, so far as business is concerned, are not holy for the benefit of the producer and consumer, but also for all other interests that tend to bring these two parties into speedy and economical contact. Hence, we hold that transportation companies of every kind are necessary to our success; that their interests are intimately connected with our interests, and harmonious action is mutually advantageous, keeping in view the first sentence in our declaration of principles of action, that "Individual happiness depends upon general prosperity."

We shall therefore advocate for every State an increase in every practicable way of all facilities for transporting cheaply to the seaboard, or between home producers and consumers, all the productions of our country. We adopt it as our fixed purpose "to open out the channels in Nature's great arteries, that the life-blood of commerce may flow freely." We are not enemies of railroads, navigable or irrigating canals, nor of any laboring classes. In our noble Order there is no communism, no agrarianism. We are opposed to such spirit and management of any corporation or enterprise as tends to oppress the people and rob them of their just profits. We are not enemies to capital, but we oppose the tyranny of monopolies. We long to see the antagonism between capital and labor removed by common consent, and by an enlightened statesmanship worthy of the nineteenth century. We are opposed to excessive salaries, high rates of interest, and exorbitant per cent. profits on trade. They greatly increase our burdens, and do not bear a proper proportion to the profits of producers. We desire only self-protection and the protection of every true interest of our land by legitimate transactions, legitimate trade, and legitimate profits.

EDUCATION. We shall advance the cause of education among ourselves, and for our children, by all just means within our power. We especially advocate for our agricultural and industrial colleges, that practical agriculture, domestic science, and all the arts which adorn the home, be taught in their course of study.

THE GRANGE NOT PARTISAN. 5. We emphatically and sincerely assert the oft repeated truth taught in our organic law, that the Grange—National, State, or Subordinate—is not a political or party organization. No Grange, if true to its obligation, can discuss political or religious questions, nor call political conventions, nor nominate candidates, nor even discuss their merits in its meetings. Yet the principles we teach underlie all true politics, all true statesmanship, and if properly carried out will tend to purify the whole political atmosphere of our country, for we seek the greatest good to the greatest number. We must always bear in mind that no one, by becoming a Patron of Husbandry, gives up that inalienable right and duty which belongs to every American citizen, to take a proper interest in the politics of his country. On the contrary, it is right for every member to do all in his power legitimately, to influence for good, the action of any political party to which he belongs. It is his duty to do all he can in his own party to put down bribery, corruption and trickery; to see that none but competent, faithful and honest men, who will unflinchingly stand by our industrial interests, are nominated for all positions of trust; and to have carried out the principles which should always characterize every Patron, that THE OFFICE SHOULD SEEK THE MAN, AND NOT THE MAN THE OFFICE.

We acknowledge the broad principle that difference of opinion is no crime, and hold that "progress toward truth is made by differences of opinion," while "the fault lies in bitterness of controversy."

We desire a proper equality, equity, and fairness; protection for the weak, restraint upon the strong; in short, justly distributed burdens and justly distributed power. These are American ideas, the very essence of American independence, and to advocate the contrary is unworthy of the sons and daughters of the American republic.

We cherish the belief that sectionalism is, and of right should be, dead and buried with the past. Our work is for the present and future. In our agricultural brotherhood and its purposes we shall recognize no North, no South, no East, no West.

It is reserved by every Patron, as the right of a freeman, to affiliate with any party that will best carry out his principles.

OUTSIDE CO-OPERATION. 6. Our being peculiarly a farmers' institution, we cannot admit all to our ranks.

Many are excluded by the nature of our organization, not because they are professional men, or artisans, or laborers, but because they have not a sufficient direct interest in tilling the soil, or may have some interest in conflict with our purposes. But we appeal to all good citizens for their cordial co-operation to assist in our efforts toward reform, that we may eventually remove from our midst the last vestige of tyranny and corruption.

We hail the general desire for fraternal harmony, equitable compromises, and earnest co-operation, as an omen of our future success.

CONCLUSION. 7. It shall be an abiding principle with us to relieve any of our oppressed and suffering brotherhood by any means at our command.

Last, but not least, we proclaim it among our purposes to inculcate a proper appreciation of the abilities and sphere of woman, as is indicated by admitting her to membership and position in our Order.

Imploring the continued assistance of our Divine Master to guide us in our work, we here pledge ourselves to faithful and harmonious labor for all future time, to return by our united efforts to the wisdom, justice, fraternity, and political purity of our forefathers.

# 100. THE EXTERMINATION OF THE BUFFALO

## January-April, 1875

From John R. Cook, *The Border and the Buffalo* (Topeka, 1907), 110-150.

The extermination of millions of buffalo that grazed on the Great Plains was an event of major historical importance, for it forced the resolution of the Indian problem and permitted the cattle industry to expand across the area. The extermination occurred with amazing rapidity, once the value of buffalo hides in eastern markets was established upon the invention of new tanning processes. The slaughter began in earnest in 1870-1871 and ended generally in the southern region by 1878. This was a year in which 100,000 hides were taken in two months in Texas.

Hunters first swarmed into western Kansas, then southward into the Texas Panhandle. Their appearance there early in 1874 precipitated a renewal of the Indian wars; the Indians rightly perceived a mortal threat in the hunters. Five military forces converged on the area, however, and the natives were quickly forced onto reservations in western Oklahoma. The hunters then began their work. The activities of one group are described in the following passages written by one of the participants.

I reported to the famous hunter before alluded to. He was a six-footer, built like a greyhound, supple as a cat, a man of unusual vitality, long-winded in the chase, and an unerring shot at game. His name was Charles Hart. He was a Union ex-soldier, captured at the battle of Shiloh, and lived through the horrors of Andersonville prison. . . .

The man from northern Kansas was also a Union ex-soldier, named Warren Dockum. . . .

A man named Hadley was to accompany us with a freight team. He had six yoke of oxen and a heavy freight wagon.

Then there was Cyrus Reed, and his brother-in-law, Frank Williamson, a green, gawky boy, seventeen years old. These, with myself, completed the number in our outfit. We had two two-horse teams hitched to light wagons, on starting out. One of these teams hauled the provisions and camp outfit, which consisted of one medium and one large-sized Dutch oven, three large frying-pans, two coffee-pots, two camp-kettles, bread-pans, coffee-mill, tin cups, plates, knives, forks, spoons, pot-hooks, a meat-broiler, shovel, spades, axes, mess-box, etc. The other one hauled our bedding, ammunition, two extra guns, grindstone, war sacks, and what reading-matter we had and could get. . . .

We left the Sweet Water with enough provisions to last us three months. We had 250 pounds of St. Louis shot-tower lead in bars done up in 25-pound sacks; 4000 primers, three 25-pound cans of Dupont powder, and one 6-pound can. This description would be the basis for all hunting outfits complete, which would vary in the size of the crew, larger or smaller, and the length of time they expected to be away from supplies.

We left the Sweet Water a few days after New Year's Day, 1875, starting up Graham Creek; when at its head, we veered a little southwest until we crossed the north fork of Red River. Here we took and kept as near a due south course as we could get our wagons over. . . .

The sixth day we lay over in camp, to rest the stock; and the next we pulled up onto the Pease River Divide, and got a view of the rear of the great countless mass of buffaloes.

That night we camped on a tributary of Pease River, where there were five other hunting outfits, which had come from Sweet Water ahead of us, but had kept a few miles east of our route. These outfits can be named in this order, and like our own followed these animals to the last: Carr & Causey, Joe Freed, John Godey, Uncle Joe Horde, Hiram Bickerdyke. . . .

The next morning our outfit pulled out south, and that day we caught up with and passed through many strag-gling bands of these solemn-looking but doomed animals. And thus we traveled by easy stages four days more.

Arriving on the breaks of the Salt Fork of the Brazos River, we realized that we were in the midst of that vast sea of animals that caused us gladness and sorrow, joy, trouble and anxiety, but independence, for the succeeding years. . . .

About four miles to the west and south we found an ideal hunters' camp: plenty of fresh water, good grass, and wood in abundance. Here we made headquarters until April. . . . We were twenty-five miles west of the one-hundredth meridian, in plain view of the Kiowa Peak to our east and the Double Mountain to our south. We were in a veritable hunters' paradise. . . .

Too late to stop and moralize now. And sentiment must have no part in our thoughts from this time on. We must have these 3361 hides that this region is to furnish us inside of three months, within a radius of eight miles from this main camp. So at it we went. And Hart, whom we will hereafter call Charlie, started out, and in two hours had killed sixty-three bison.

Dockum and I for the first few days worked together. We two skinned thirty-three of this killing. Hadley and Cyrus worked together for a short time. It was now a busy time. Some days thirty and forty-odd hides, then a good day with eighty-five, and one day in February, one hundred and seventy-one; then again the same month, 203; and these 203 were killed on less than ten acres of ground. . . .

We fastened a forked stick to the center of the hind axle-tree of a wagon, letting the end drag on the ground on an incline to say 20 degrees; fastened a chain or rope to the same axle, then we would drive up quartering to the carcass and hook the loose end of the chain over a front leg. After skinning the upper side down, we would start the team up and pull the dead animal up a little, and stop. (The stick prevented the wagon from backing up.) Then we would skin the belly down mid-sides; start the team again, and pull the carcass over, having rolled the first side of the hide close to the backbone. Then we would skin down to the backbone, and the hide was separated from the carcass. We would then throw the hide in the wagon, and proceed as before until all the hides were skinned from the dead carcasses.

Many times we had in one killing more hides than the two ponies could pull to camp, in which case we spread the hide, flesh side down, by the carcass, in order to get them when there was a slack time in the work.

After the first ten days I went alone with the team, except on the occasion of a big day's killing. Each night Charlie got out his memorandum book and I got mine, and we put down the number of hides I had skinned that day. Isolated as we were, we kept track of the days of the week and the month of the year. This was Dockum's work. He was very methodical in everything he did.

He and Frank, the boy, attended to the reloading of the shells, pegged out the hides, and from three to five days after they were pegged out they turned them flesh side down, and every other day turned them back, until they were dried; after which they were stacked one on top of the other until the pile was eight feet high. Then they cut strings from a green hide and tied an end in a peghole at each corner of the bottom hide, ran it through the holes of the top one, and then drew them down as tight as they could and tie.

The pile was then ready for market. . . . We classified our hides as we piled them. All bulls to themselves, the cows the same way; the robe hides to themselves, and the younger animals into what was called the kip pile.

Charlie as a rule did the most of his killing from 8 A. M. until noon, but made some good killings in the evening, in which case the carcasses would lie all night before being skinned. These would bloat up and the hide would be tight and stiff, which made the work more tedious. We had to be more careful, too; for it was the pride of the skinner to bring in hides free from knife-gashes.

We had good hunting at this camp until the last of February, when all at once the buffaloes were not to be seen. . . .

We then had stacked up and drying 2003 hides; 902 of them I had skinned, and was so accredited. This was an average of 22 buffaloes a day for 41 days. At 25 cents per hide I had earned $225.50. . . .

The next morning Charlie got on his hunting-horse and rode south across the Brazos. He said on leaving us that he would ride until he found good hunting again. . . . He brought us good word for more hunting. It was under-stood that we were to move camp the next morning, cross the Brazos, and go to near the summit of the divide, be-tween it and Croton Creek, where he had found a spring of nearly fresh water, with several pools below it. . . .

This camp was nearly four miles from the first camp, and here we had fair hunting until the latter part of March. Then one morning on going to our lookout, not a buffalo could be seen. We were all satisfied, for we wanted a rest and change.

At this camp we got 906 hides, and I had skinned 407 of them, thereby earning $101.75.

We had run short of primers a few days previous to this lull in the hunt, and hearing big guns every day in different directions from us, Hadley was delegated to hunt up a camp, in the hope of getting enough primers to tide us over until Hadley could make a trip to Fort Griffin, where there was a supply store. The first camp he found was the Carr and Causey outfit, which had killed 3700 buffaloes. . . .

Dockum and I went with Hadley to our first camp and helped him to load 200 hides. He went to Fort Griffin, and did not get back for seven weeks. Our flour and coffee gave out, and we were three days without bread, when fortunately we heard of John Goff's camp to the southeast of us, and that he had nearly one thousand pounds of flour and would divide with us.

I took my hunting team and went to his camp, which I confess I found by accident more than by design. I had not gone five miles until I saw the great mass of moving creatures, on their annual northern swing. Looking to the east and south as far as the eye could reach, it seemed to me that I saw nothing but a solid mass of bison; and . . . to the southwest and west, I saw a moving sea of that one countless host. I decided that I was just as safe going ahead as turning back. . . .

From him [John Goff] I learned that a man named Hickey was at Griffin as agent for Loganstein & Company, of Leavenworth, Kansas, with instructions to buy all the buffalo-hides offered for sale; to pay for them on the range and haul them to Fort Worth, Texas, with freight teams. . . .

At 2 P. M. [next day] I was in our own camp, and not a soul there to greet me. Upon looking around I soon satisfied myself that all were busy skinning buffaloes. Charlie's hunting-horse was close hobbled near camp, his saddle lying by the tepee that we slept in, and a big pile of empty shells was lying by the ammunition-box. . . .

I was indeed fortunate both in going and coming through that apparently endless mass of buffaloes; for as I came back through them there seemed to be but little difference in the solidity of the herd from the day before; and within gunshot of camp as I drove in there were hundreds of them moving northward. Charlie had killed 197 the afternoon before, and took his knives and went early the next morning with the boys about one and one-half miles to help skin those buffaloes. . . .

All night long these ill-fated creatures passed our camp in silent tread, save the rattling of the dewclaws. We were all up early the next morning, and after breakfast Charlie went up over the slope toward Croton Creek. Soon the work of death began; and by the time I had hitched up and

driven on to the divide he had killed thirty-eight, mostly bulls.

I saw when I drove up on the ridge that the great mass of the buffaloes had passed by. . . . Charlie came to me, and said:

"John, it will soon be mighty poor hunting around here. The bulk of the buffaloes have passed; and I have been thinking, from what you told me last night about that man Hickey and his prices, that I would better sell this hunt to him, and let him receive them in camp. Now will you take my hunting horse to-morrow, go to Fort Griffin, and make a deal with him for me?" . . .

Here [at Quinn's Camp] I found Mr. Hickey, the hide-buyer, whom I had expected to find in Fort Griffin. There were 12,000 hides piled here, 2000 of them that the two Quinn Brothers had killed and traded for. . . .

Hickey . . . said all of Loganstein & Co.'s hides went to Europe; that the English army accoutrements of a leather kind were being replaced with buffalo leather, on account of its being more pliant and having more elasticity than cowhide; that buffalo leather was not fit for harness, shoes, or belting, but for leather buffers it could not be excelled. . . .

Mr. Hickey arrived at our camp late in the afternoon, and found everybody present. Not a buffalo had been seen that day.

The next morning Charlie and Hickey went to the first camp. Mr. Hickey made some little examination of the hides, and they returned. A satisfactory deal had been made between them. He gave Charlie a check for $2000, and agreed to pay the balance as soon as the hides reached Fort Griffin. . . . So it was arranged that they would all go to Fort Griffin, where Charlie could get his check cashed and settle up in full with all of them. . . .

The next morning they all pulled out for Griffin. I was left alone, in charge of 3363 hides, less the 200 Hadley had started with, in three different camps.

It was now the early part of April.

As Charlie bade me good-by, he being the last one to leave the camp, he said he would be back in six days. . . . To make a long story short, Charlie was twenty-one days getting back to camp. But he had had a glorious spree. He got his check cashed at the post sutler's; paid all the boys up, and deposited all that was coming to me with the sutler, taking his receipt for it. . . .

He said, "I never intended to get drunk; but what could a fellow do? There were about thirty outfits camped on the Clear Fork of the Brazos, under big pecan trees, and we all had a time. . . ."

## 101. GOVERNOR O. M. ROBERTS' LAND POLICY

### 1879

From Texas *House Journal*, Sixteenth Legislature, First Session (Austin, 1879), 106-115; H. P. N. Gammel (comp.), *The Laws of Texas, 1822-1897* (10 vols.; Austin, 1898), IX, 80-81.

When O. M. Roberts became governor in 1879, the state's indebtedness was at a rather high figure of approximately $5,500,000. In his first message to the legislature, Roberts, reflecting the conservative trend that followed radical reconstruction, proposed an economy program and an unlimited sale of the remainder of the public lands at a cheap price as a means of raising needed revenue. The legislative enactment of Roberts' recommendation regarding the public lands enabled a number of large domestic and foreign syndicates to acquire vast holdings in the western part of the state. East Texans, particularly the various farmers' organizations, insisted that the tillers had the best rights to the public lands, and demanded that the state sell such land in small tracts to only actual settlers. The land policy became a major political issue for several years.

Two documents follow. The first is an extract from Governor Roberts' recommendation to the legislature on the subject of the public lands; the second is the highly controversial law incorporating the Governor's proposal.

### 1. ROBERTS' RECOMMENDATION ON THE SALE OF PUBLIC LANDS

#### January 21, 1879

Fellow-Citizens, Senators and Representatives of the Legislature:

Called by the voice of the people to preside over the destinies of our large State at this important period of its history, I accept the position with a full appreciation of the responsibility resting upon me. . . . The State, emerging from the ruin of the civil war and from the consequent difficulties of its changed condition, has already advanced in the work of reforming its institutions and in resuscitating and husbanding its resources. Still, much remains to be done in that direction to establish permanently good and efficient government, economically administered. This is the impending necessity of the day; and whatever energy, influence and power I may have will be directed to that as the leading object. . . . The democratic party stands pledged to that policy, as announced in the late canvass, and their large majority at the late election for state officers fully endorse it. Nor did any opposing party dissent from it. It may, therefore, be taken to be in accordance with the common sentiment of the country. The democratic party, being now in full charge of all of the departments of the state government, is responsible for its being carried out as far as it is practicable under existing circumstances. . . .

Gradually, and much more in the last ten years, the State has been assuming other and extraneous burdens beyond the capacity of the productive wealth of the country to sustain, as is plainly evinced by the public debt. Some of these burdens are due to our frontier position in the Union and our extensive territory, and others of them are taken on to an extent not common in young and intrinsically feeble states. Reference is here made to the protection of our frontier and our police force; to the penitentiary and its enlargement; to our free common school system; to our schools for the blind and the deaf and dumb; to the establishment of an agricultural and mechanical college, so styled; to our lunatic asylum; to our quarantine establishment; to our pensions to Texas veterans and to our immigration bureau, formerly.

These are things which caused our public debt to be contracted, and which now cause a large amount of taxes to be assessed and collected annually. We are numerically a very poor people as compared with older states that have assumed these or similar burdens; much poorer, indeed, than the $300,000,000 worth of property appearing on the assessment rolls would, by its mere amount, indicate in reference to our capacity to support a government. Because an immense amount of that sum is made up by unimproved lands all over the State, which is dormant property, but is only estimated to be valuable because of its prospective value in the future. Its taxes have to be paid from the proceeds of productive property. The State in that regard is like a man who owns and pays taxes on a league of land and cultivates only one hundred acres of it. . . . The chief benefit yet derived from it has been the hastening the building of railroads in a portion of the State by the donation of portions of the public lands thus reserved. Another great benefit generally expected to be derived is from the donation of lands set apart to the permanent common school fund. This, however, will prove delusive if it is expected to raise a fund in a distant future under the present management that will relieve the people from the taxes which they now pay to support the free common schools. For under the present mode of disposing of these lands the scholastic population will increase faster than the fund. And the same thing applies to the lands set apart for the schools for the deaf and dumb, and blind, and for the lunatic asylum. And the same policy will postpone indefinitely the building of a university, which should be erected at the capital of the state for the education of Texas youths, instead of sending them out of the state to be educated, and to return home strangers to Texas. Another benefit counted on is giving pre-emption to settlers, by which the frontier is extended. While this is a great benefit to those now no longer occupying the frontier, the fact that it is extended increases the expense of the government in proportion to the population thereby increased, and such is our experience for the last twenty years, and will be for the next thirty or forty years, until the whole territory shall have been filled up with a self-sustaining and a locally self-governing population. For until that time arrives the frontier must be protected, and the sparse population on its border must occasionally be aided in the execution of the civil law,—under any line of policy that may be maintained. This necessarily follows from reserving territory to be governed by us. We have yet over thirty millions of public lands not appropriated that we are holding on to for the purpose of giving them away as we have done, while the people are struggling to pay nearly $400,000 annually in taxes on our bonded public debt, with a prospect of an indefinite increase of it, if there should be no change in the general management of the public affairs of the State. This debt is an obligation upon the State, the same as a mortgage upon all of the property and polls within it.

Now the question is, would it not be better as a business transaction to pay it with the property of the State not yet appropriated, by a sale of its land as soon as practicable, at a reasonable value, rather than from year to year to sell the lands of our citizens that they have worked for, and otherwise wrench from them taxes to pay the interest and ultimately the principal of the debt. There are other obligations imposed upon the government of the state by the constitution, of equally as high a nature, which are to devote one-half of all the public lands to the public school fund, and one million of acres to the university fund, and three millions of acres to the building of a capitol of the state. Under the present policy of procrastination these obligations will not be met, and the people will have to be taxed to perform them. I have reason to believe, from information that I have received, that the lands can be sold rapidly to persons both in and out of the State, for colonies of settlers and other purposes, if large tracts could be bought. . . .

The true policy of the State, in my opinion, under the present juncture of affairs, is to retrench expenses from top to bottom, wherever it can be done consistently with the efficiency of the public service, and inaugurate the policy now of disposing of the public lands at a fair value as soon as practicable to any purchaser that will buy them in any quantity, so as to meet the various obligations of the government, increase the school funds and asylum fund, and thereby if possible relieve the present generation from the onerous burden of taxation imposed upon them for the dim prospect of a future good which will never be realized. . . .

The Legislature is the controlling power of the State, and the responsibility rests with them to determine whether or not we shall continue to drag along, mending up an old policy, unadapted to the times and to our present condition, or to at once inaugurate a practical policy that directs us to a definite end, promising a relief to the present generation, and a fair chance for prosperity to the future.

It may be objected that this policy will stop immigration. Not so, for the railroad companies owning millions of acres are the best immigration agents we ever had, and those that buy the lands who are not settlers will help them.

It may be objected that a land monopoly will be created that will prevent poor men from buying lands. Not so, for poor men, white and black, are now buying cheap lands all over the State, except in a few localities, from private owners, at more advantage to themselves than if they were to take them up by pre-emption, or were they to buy school lands, where they can be obtained either at this time or in the future.

It may be objected that this policy will stop the progress of railroads by exhausting the donation lands, and leave large portions of the State unprovided with them. Not so: for this result will soon follow under the present policy. But if the obligations resting on the State are satisfied in a reasonable time, and the people are relieved from these extraordinary burdens of taxation, then we can well afford to devote a part of the taxes derived from the railroads then already constructed to the building of other roads, in the shape of a loan, the interest on which could be turned over to the available school fund, and thereby give all sections of the State indirectly the benefit of the land donations, that will have already been made for the building of railroads long after all of the lands may have been exhausted. In some such way as this alone can the effects of land grants to railroads be continued and perpetuated so as to give all sections of the State the benefit of them. . . .

O. M. ROBERTS

## 2. THE LAND LAW OF 1879
### July 14, 1879

Section 1. Be it enacted by the Legislature of the State of Texas, That all the vacant and unappropriated land situated in the following named counties, viz: Noland, Mitchell, Howard, Martin, Andrews, Gaines, Davidson [Dawson?], Borden, Scurry, Fisher, Stonewall, Kent, Garza, Lynn, Terry, Yoakum, Cockran, Hockley, Lubbock, Crosby, Dickens, King, Cottle, Motley, Floyd, Hale, Lamb, Bailey, Parmer, Castro, Swisher, Briscoe, Hall, Childress, Collingsworth, Donley, Armstrong, Randall, Deaf Smith, Oldham, Potter, Cordova, Gray, Wheeler, Hemphill, Roberts, Hutchinson, Moore, Hartley, Sherman, Hansford, Ochiltree and Lipscomb be and the same is hereby appropriated and set apart for sale, together with all the unappropriated lands situated and being within and included in the Pacific reservation, and together with such separate tracts of unappropriated public lands, situated in organized counties of the state, as contain not more than six hundred and forty acres; provided, that the three million and fifty thousand acres, heretofore appropriated for the building of a state capitol, shall have a preference right of location in the counties heretofore reserved for that purpose. The provisions of this act shall not be so construed as to prohibit the right of pre-empting within the bounds of the reservation here made; but any party shall have the same right of acquiring a homestead, within this reservation, under the pre-emption laws of this state, as he may have had prior to the passage of this act.

Sec. 2. That any person, firm or corporation, desiring to purchase any of the unappropriated lands herein set apart and reserved for sale, may do so by causing the tract or tracts which such person, firm or corporation desire to purchase to be surveyed by the authorized public surveyor of the county or district in which said land is situated.

Sec. 3. It shall be the duty of the surveyor, to whom application is made by responsible parties, to survey the lands designated in said application within three months from the date thereof, and within sixty days after said survey, to certify to, record and map the field-notes of said survey; and he shall also, within the said sixty days, return to and file the same in the general land office, as required by law in other cases. . . .

Sec. 5. Within sixty days after the return to and filing in the general land office of the surveyor's certificate, map and field-notes of the land desired to be purchased, it shall be the right of the person, firm or corporation who has had the same surveyed to pay or cause to be paid into the treasury of the state the purchase money therefor at the rate of fifty cents per acre, and upon the presentation to the commissioner of the general land office of the receipt of the state treasurer for such purchase money, said commissioner shall issue to said person, firm or corporation a patent for the tract or tracts of land so surveyed and paid for.

Sec. 6. No tract of land shall be sold under the provisions of this act that contains more than six hundred and forty acres, and no tract shall have a greater frontage on any running stream or permanent water, than one vara

per acre for each survey of three hundred and twenty acres, or less, and three-fourth of one vara per acre for all other surveys. . . .

Sec. 10. One-half of the net proceeds of sales under the provisions of this act, shall be and are hereby set apart for the benefit of the public free schools of this state, and the . . . balance of the net proceeds of sales under the provisions of this act shall be applied by the proper authorities to the payment and extinguishment of the bonded debt of the State of Texas as the same becomes due and payable. . . .

## 102.  THE FENCE-CUTTING WAR AND EFFORTS TO END IT

The great open-range cattle kingdom was of short duration. The introduction of barbed wire, and legislation favorable to the settler, were chief factors that brought it to an end. Barbed wire had been introduced into Texas in 1871, and by 1883 practically all the cattle country of South and Central Texas had been fenced. Ranchers fenced not only their own land, but often that over which they legally had no control. Their fences sometimes extended for fifty or more miles with no gates. Meanwhile, "nesters" pushed into the open range country, and the ensuing conflict between the two groups developed into frequent fence-cutting wars. Before the close of 1883 more than half of the 171 organized counties of Texas were directly affected. To meet the situation, Governor John Ireland, in 1883, called a special session of the legislature, which promptly made fence-cutting and grass-firing a felony, made it illegal to fence the land of another without authority, and provided for gates at three-mile intervals in long fences.

The legislative enactments, however, did not solve the problem. Four years later, in some areas not a fence was left uncut, and the Texas Rangers were kept busy in an effort to catch the guilty parties. Ranger Ira Aten in a series of letters to his captain dramatically indicated the situation at the time in the vicinity of Corsicana, describing his efforts to catch the fence-cutters and his plan to solve the problem permanently.

The first of the following documents is an excerpt from the legislature's famous fence-gate law of 1884; the second document contains two of Aten's informative and colorful letters.

### 1.  THE FENCE-GATE LAW

#### February 6, 1884

From H. P. N. Gammel (comp.), *The Laws of Texas, 1822-1897* (10 vols.; Austin, 1898), IX, 569.

Section 1. Be it enacted by the Legislature of the State of Texas: That it shall be unlawful for any person or persons by joining fences, or otherwise to build or maintain more than three miles lineal measure of fence, running in the same general direction, without a gateway in same, which gateway must be at least eight feet wide and shall not be locked; provided that all persons who have fences already constructed in violation of this section shall have six months within which to conform to the provisions hereof.

Sec. 2. If any person or persons shall build or maintain more than three miles lineal measure of fencing, running in the same general direction, without providing such gate-

way, he shall be deemed guilty of a misdemeanor, and upon conviction shall be fined in any sum not less than one nor more than two hundred dollars, and each day that such fence remains without such gateway shall constitute and be punished as a separate offence.

Sec. 3. The provisions of this bill shall only apply to pasture lands. . . .

### 2.  A TEXAS RANGER'S EFFORTS TO CATCH FENCE-CUTTERS

#### August-October, 1888

From Ira Aten, Co. D Ranger, to Captain L. P. Sieker, Austin, Texas (MSS; Adjutant General's Correspondence, Archives, Texas State Library, Austin).

Richland, Texas
Aug. 31st 1888

Capt. L. P. Sieker, Austin, Texas
Dear Sir:

We are among the fence-cutters in the best shape in the world. My plans have so far worked as I expected & we are here without the shadow of suspicion as far as we are able to tell. We came through Wortham & up to Richland & inquired the way to Kauffman Co. We saw everybody in Richland and they know we were going on to Kauffman Co. How-ever, our wagon tyre run off about a mile on the other side of Richland & in a little rough place our wagon wheel broke down & of course we dident have money enough to get it fixt, besides the blacksmith (as luck would have it,) had went to Corsicana on a "spree" & never came back for a week & of course we could not have got our wagon wheel fixt if we had wanted to but we dident want to very bad. After our wagon broke down, soon came along another wagon & the man helped us to move our wagon out of the road, & sympathize with us very much, owing to it looking so reasonable of breaking it's self down. However, I had a hard time pounding off the tyre & then had to break the wheel with an ax. This was about 4 o'clock in the evening 22nd inst. I came on back to Richland then on the mule & made a pitifull talk

& all seemed to sympathiz with us in our break down. Work was so awful scarce & people a leaving on that account. Nothing in the world to do as all of the cotton was so very late & very poor at that. I went back to where I left Jim King & the wagon & fell in with a noted fence-cutter & he told me where he thought we could get work making hay. He went by our wagon & took a good look at things &c. We camped at our wagon that night & the next morning drug it back to Richland on a pole & a large crowd of the fence-cutters was there shiping cattle. They all seen us & I dont think any of them suspicioned us being detectives for a moment. We stayed around Richland all day & established camp under some trees close by. We had most the names of the fence-cutters & we would know them when-ever one was called & we would locate him right then & there, & by that way we have about all of them located & know them when we see them. They would talk very freely about fence-cutting & didi'nt seem to care who was around, but I guess they thought we were all fence-cutters. That night they had a meeting of indignation in regards to the fence-cutter's that was caught cutting the fence by the sheriff & posse that I wrote you about in my other letter. The meeting was about six miles from Richland to the little station called Angus. Lot's of these fence-cutters went, & they made big *war talk* against the pasture-men, Sh'ff & every body that would try to stop fence-cutting, &c. Didi'nt either one of us go simply because we did-not have any reason for going & under these circumstances we were afraid it would cause suspicion besides I knew nothing could be learnt as it was a very public meeting & we would hear it all any way from those that did go. The next day I went over to see if I could get work making hay where the noted fence-cutter told me he thought we could. However, they had already got a supply of hands & dident need any more. We still staid at Richland with our broken wagon & seen every body that came to the little village. The next day I went over to see the gin man that run the gin right in Richland. Well, I got Jim King a Job a baling cotton for the season & I took a Job a picking 35 acres of cotton out for the son of the man that runs the gin & he is under bond now for fence-cutting. So you see we are slowly getting acquainted & prospects of getting better acquainted in the future. Cotton ginning will not commence for two weeks yet neither will cotton picking. We have been working all this week building a rock furnace around the gin boiler. It has been awfull hard work handling the rought and large rocks but we never grumbled in the least, but went at it like we were raised to it. Jim King says he would not work at it for less than $5.00 per day only under these circumstances. We got our furnace Job done yesterday & wont have anything else to do but odd Jobs until cotton picking & ginning. We get to see lot's of the fence-cutters every day as they come to Richland & often come down to the gin. We are slowly getting acquainted with the villians but it will take a *long time* to get their confidence sufficient to cut fence with them as I have heard them say often that *their* crowd dide'nt need any help to cut fence & an out-fit was a fool to take in any out sider's to help them. Lots of such talk I have heard them make. These fence-cutters are very near as bad as my Brown Co. fence-cutter's & when they once suspicion us they will no doubt try & murder us, but we will be at

the Killing &c. I dont feel any uneasyness as long as we are not given away by our friends unintentionally. Should they give us away, I will leave the Co. in disgust & say they dont need any assistance for they cant keep their mouths shut long enough for it to be given to them. The fence-cutters here are what I would call cow-boys or small cow men that own cattle from 15 head all the way up to perhaps 200 head of cattle & a few cow ponies &c. Some have a hundred acres of land & some more & some not so much & perhaps a little field in cultivation &c. They hate the granger as they call them for it is the granger (or farmers) that have the pasture with the exception of Frost & Barry & a very few others. In fact they hate any body that will fence land either for farming or pasture. . . . They had another indignation meeting over at Angus night before last in regards to the way those fence-cutters was caught over there &c. We didi'nt go as no opportunity offered itself & to go without a cause would create suspicion among the villians. Our gin man & son went & they told us all that occurred. The meeting was made public & about a hundred men was there. Among them was the Sh'ff but he came because they sent him word to come & explain how he caught the fence-cutters. . . . The most of these men that are holding these meeting &c. are villians of the deepest dye & death would be to good for them, but at the same time their are a few & very few at that, that are miss lead in to these meetings and are taking part for the fence-cutters &c. Now for the good citizens what do they deserve. I will simply state this, that a great many good citizens that dont own one-half as much as the parties that has been the instigator of all this fence-cutting in this sections have had their fence-cut from around their little horse pasture & even in several instance have had it cut from around their cultivated lands where corn & cotton was planted. They have quit cutting from around fields now but their are not a pasture of no kind up the west side of the Houston & Texas Central Railway in this section where these wild & wooly wire cutters oparate. I dont, write all from here say but from what I have seen myself. Small pastures that would not support but milk cow's & work horses for a very small farm have been cut time & again until the owner have not the mean to put up the wire any more & now all pastures are down & this is called the free range country. Many have took down their wire & rolled it up to save it from being cut &c. The fence-cutters them-selves have told me that while a man was putting up his fence one day in a hollow, a crowd of wire cutters was cutting it back behind him in another hollow back over the hill. They delight in telling all such things & most of it is true also. The good citizens hold the wire cutters in dread for they know they would not hesitate a moment to murder them. The Sh'ff is powerless to render them any assistance only what he has already done. He is a good man my friends tell me but the best evidence I have for that is that these fence-cutters hate him & cant say too many mean thing about him. I have dropped on a-nother plan to catch the villians much sooner I think than working in with them, that is this; to have two or three of these good citizens to put up their fence & I with one of the pasture men lay there two weeks if necessary & watch the fence ever night with double barrels shot guns & if they cut the fence, arrest them if possible & if we can't do that take them the best way we can &c. I have studied this plan over & over & I think it is the best now as their are no fence up that these wire-cutters want cut down. Unless the good citizens put up their fence again their will be no more fence-cutting in this section for their are no fence to cut. I am going to Corsicana this evening to see C. S. West (not Sh'ff West for he is no relation to him) & have him to have a-bout three good men to put up their fence about the middle of next week & by that time I can have a good excuse to leave here & will slip around to way-lay the fence. I will leave Jim King here & he can work all the points the same as both of us for a while yet. If I fail to catch any cutting-fence after laying on the fence for two week's I will come on back to Jim & see what we can do here yet, & if they dont cut any more fence at all, it is of no use for us to stay here after we find out such is the fact. These are my last fence-cutters whether I catch them or not. I don't want to make a failure in this but when I see that nothing can be done, rest assured I will report such to the Adjutant Gen. office for I would rather be in h--l than here. . . . Here-after it will take more than $50.00 per month to get me to go out to see how many lies I can tell, or to be placed in a possition so that I will have to tell them to keep from being murdered. I will do my best this time for these good citizens deserve assistance from course & if I can render it to them I will do it if my life pays the forfeit. Nothing will do any good here but a first class Killing & I am the little boy that will give it to them if they dont let the fence alone. I wish I had Hughes here to lay with me on the fence for it is awfull risky business as these villians are hard men & go well armed. How-ever I may ask for him yet & if I do I want him sent for you know I am not agoing to ask for anything I dont need. . . . Jim King fiddle comes in very handy. He draws large crowds very near every night & we make lot's new acquaintances by it.

Will close
Your's Very Respt.
Ira Aten

Corsicana Texas
Oct. 8th 1888

Capt. L. P. Sieker
    Quarter Master Front. Bat.
Dear Sir:
    . . . I have only one more chance with any hopes of stopping fence-cutting in this section & that is with my *dynamite boom* as I call it. I have had the law examined & it dont say any-thing about a man having the right to protect his property by the use of dynamite or by the use of a shot-gun either. So I have come to the conclusion if it was not against the law to guard a fence with a shot-gun to protect the property, it certainly would not be against the law to use dynamite for the same purpose. There-fore I have *invested some money* in *dynamite* & will in a few day's set my dynamite boom's upon the *few* fences that have been put up recently to protect them. Should the Gov. or the Genl. disapprove of this, all they have got to do is to notify me to that effect &c. They sent me here to stop fence-cutting any way I could, & to use my

own Judgement &c. how to do it. And that is what I am doing & if they will let me alone the balance of this month I will have my boom's set & when the fence is cut, why they will hear of it at Austin. The dynamite boom is entirely safe unless the wire is cut, or fence is torn entirely down. Stock in rubing against the post or wire *will not* explode the boom, but should they break all the wires where the boom is, then of course, it will explode. I cannot explain the working of my boom thoroughly but can give you an idea how it work's &c. It is simply taking an old shot-gun or musket, put some powder in it as if for shooting, then slide down a *dynamite cap* on the powder & then the dynamite on top of cap until you think you have enough, put cap on gun ready for shooting, fasten wire to triger & then to the bottom of a post that is not in the ground, place gun in a box made for the special purpose & place the box just under the ground & cover up so it can't be seen. Of course cock the gun when you put it in the box & a fellow will have to handle it carefully &c. So you see by this post being very crooked & not in the ground and only supported by the wires, & when wires are cut or torn down the post will fall & the end will fly up giving the wire at the bottom end of the post a jerk sufficient to shoot the gun off. The powder explodes the dynamite cap & the cap explodes the dynamite & then small pieces of that gun will *be found all over Navarro Co.* Well: if it dont kill the parties that cuts the fence, it will scare them so bad that they will never cut another fence, thinking it was a mere scratch that they never got killed, (and it will be a mere scratch if it dont kill them or cripple them.) When one of my boom's once explodes all fence-cutters will hear of it most likely & then all a pasture man has got to say to secure the safety of his fence against these midnight depredaton, (*I have dynamite boom upon my fence*) Why: if the talking of this is not sufficient, he can have them put there at a small expense & his fence will never be cut but once after-wards. But all pasture-men that I have ever struck are not willing to spend a cent in the world, only in paper & stamp's to write the Gov. & Adj. Gen. long winded & scarey tales how they are imposed upon &c. Well: it is true as I have written you before, they have been imposed upon by a lot of thieving villians, & deserve assistance but they are supposed to help them-selves a little when assistance comes. But when a detective is sent by the Gov. or the Adj. Gen. to their assistance, they think he has full sway to the State treasure & it makes no difference what their is to buy he is supposed to buy it &c. I have had a very hard time in getting these fellows to put up their fence & so far only about two have put them up yet. I believe they think the state ought to have them put up by the slowness they are putting them up. Some are cramped very badly for money, & others it is just their slowness.

Their has not been a fence cut since we have been in the co. mostly because there has been so few up where they cut fence at all. The fence-cutter's are badly scared & when they cut again it will be when it is least expected. . . . We have quit guarding the fence & now I am going to put on my boom & watch them very closely to see what success I can have in that way. This is our only showing to do any thing. Men who own the fence will know where the boom's are at &c.

I wrote you I would not work after fence-cutters after this time. Well: I take that back if you let me work my boom racket at the start. I would just as soon set dynamite booms the balance of my ranging days (which are numbered) as to do any thing else. So if you have any more long winded letters from pasture-men who are being imposed upon by fence-cutters, just turn them over to me & I will soon put a quietus on fence-cutting that it will soon enter into history. . . .

Keep your ear's pricked, you may hear my dynamite boom clear down there. Dont be uneasy about my actions for I will use the greatest precaution with my boom's & see that no innocent men get's hurt with them. They are dangers in setting them unless a man is awfull carefull. How-ever, if I get blowed up, you will know I was doing a good cause. . . .

> Your Very Resp't'ly
> Ira Aten
> Co. "D" Ranger

## 103. THE CATTLE KINGDOM

Within a period of fifteen years, after the close of the Civil War, the range-cattle industry spread over the entire Great Plains area. It originated between the Rio Grande and the Nueces River valleys, where abandoned stock from the days of the Spanish ranchers on the Rio Grande had gone back to a natural state. Then Anglo-American stockmen entered the area, adapted the Mexican techniques of handling cattle to their own needs, and proceeded to spread the cattle northward and westward wherever the free range existed.

The four descriptions that follow vividly illustrate many aspects of this dramatic period of American history.

### 1. THE WILD LONGHORN CATTLE

#### 1850's

From Richard Irving Dodge, *The Hunting Grounds of the Great West* (2d ed.; London, 1878), 148-152.

Colonel Richard I. Dodge, for many years an army officer on the southern Great Plains, described the longhorn cattle as he remembered them in the early 1850's.

I should be doing injustice to a cousin-german of the buffalo, did I fail to mention as game the wild cattle of Texas. It is the domestic animal run wild, changed in some of his habits and characteristics by many generations of freedom and self-care. I have already spoken of the ferocious disposition of some of the so-called tame cattle of Texas. A footman is never safe when a herd is in his vicinity; and every sportsman who has hunted quail in Texas will have experienced the uneasiness natural to any man around whom a crowd of longhorned beasts are pawing the earth and tossing their heads in anger at his appearance.

I admit some very decided frights, and on more than one occasion have felt exceedingly relieved when an aggressive young bull has gone off bellowing and shaking his head, his face and eyes full of No. 8 shot, and taking the herd with him. I speak, I am sorry to say, of an experience now more than twenty years old. Texas was a new country then, and certainly an aggressive country. Every bush had its thorn; every animal, reptile, or insect had its horn, tooth, or sting; every male human his revolver; and each was ready to use his weapon of offence on any unfortunate sojourner, on the smallest, or even without the smallest, provocation. . . .

The tame cow is nearly as dangerous as the bull; while in its wild state, the cow, except in defence of her calf, is as timid as a deer. The wild bull is 'on his muscle' at all times; and though he will generally get out of the way if unmolested, the slightest provocation will convert him into a most aggressive and dangerous enemy.

The wild cattle are not found in herds. A few cows and their calves may associate together for mutual protection, but the bulls are almost always found alone. Should two meet, a most desperate combat determines the mastery then and there, very frequently with the life of one of the combatants.

He who would enjoy the favours of a cow must win his way to them by a series of victories. The result of this is that the number of bulls is greatly disproportioned to the number of cows; and this disproportion is increased by the fact that it seems impossible for the bull to keep his mouth shut, and when not actually eating he is bellowing, or moaning, or making some hideous noise which indicates his whereabouts to the hunter. . . .

The wild cow takes the most anxious care of her calf, and is transformed by maternal affection from one of the most timid of animals to a most daring and desperate combatant, attacking the cougar, leopard, or even her own lord and master, should they come too near its hiding place. . . .

The wild cattle bury themselves in the closest recesses of the most dense chapparal, and rarely stray even in a lifetime beyond a few miles from their chosen haunts.

Wild cattle hunting is a sport either too exciting or not sufficiently so. There is no mean. The Mexicans ordinarily kill them by lying in wait, hidden in the thick branches of a tree at a water hole to which they resort. This is a slow, unsatisfactory, and cowardly way of taking game, but it is the only method by which these animals can be successfully and safely got at.

As I have said, the whereabouts of a bull can be readily discovered by his bellowing.

This would seem to give the hunter an easy success. Not always so, however. He is probably at that moment ensconced in the darkest recesses of a dense thicket of 'wait-a-bit' thorns. This bush generally puts a prompt quietus on the most sanguine temperament. It stands 'thick as hair on a dog's back,' about twelve feet high, the straight stems from the size of a pipe-stem to two inches in diameter. Lateral branches spring out from every stem so thickly as to make a jungle almost impenetrable even of themselves; and when each is armed with innumerable thorns bent like fish-hooks, sharp as needles, and strong and tough as steel, it will readily be seen that hunting in such a thicket is no sport. His broad horns, thick hide, and immense strength enable the bull to make his way through such a thicket with ease and immunity.

Suppose that, under cover of the noise made by the bull, a hunter has overcome the natural difficulties of the approach. Moving with the greatest care he finds himself within twenty feet of the unconscious animal. He plainly sees the outline of his quarry; but when he raises his rifle he finds a thousand tough twigs and branches between him and his aim, either of which is sufficient to deflect the bullet from a vital part. Suppose, however, that an accidental opening gives him a good shot. He knows that the chances are a thousand to one against his bringing the animal down with one shot, and that the explosion of the gun will bring the bull upon him in full charge; and this in a thicket through which the bull moves easily and quickly, while he can scarcely move at all, and where there is not a tree behind which he can take cover, or in the branches of which he may find refuge. A man must be endowed with more than the ordinary disposition for getting into scrapes who would attack under such circumstances.

Some times a bull may be caught feeding in an opening of the chaparral. In such case, as he will not run away, he becomes an easy prey, provided the hunter has the wind, keeps perfectly quiet after his shots, and is so covered by the thicket that the bull can see neither him nor the smoke of his piece. The bull seems to have little faculty of judging the position of an enemy by sound, unless the sound is very close.

The cows are extremely difficult to bay, being excessively timid, and hiding in the densest thicket at the first symptom of danger. If caught feeding and mortally wounded, a cow will generally manage to get into the thicket and elude her pursuer. Nothing but his approach to the hiding place of her very young calf will cause the mother to stand and show fight to her arch enemy—man.

There is an old army story to the effect that, when General Taylor's little army was on the march from Corpus Christi to Matamoras, a soldier on the flank of the column came upon and fired at a bull. The bull immediately charged, and the soldier, taking to his heels, ran into the column. The bull, undaunted by the numbers of enemies, charged headlong, scattering several regiments like chaff, and finally escaped unhurt, having demoralised and put to flight an army which a few days after covered itself with glory by victoriously encountering five times its numbers of human enemies. . . .

## 2. MANAGING A TRAIL HERD

### 1865-1888

From Charles Goodnight, "Managing a Trail Herd" (MS, J. Evetts Haley Library, Canyon, Texas); H. T. Burton, "A History of the JA Ranch," *The Southwestern Historical Quarterly*, XXXI (April, 1928), 330-355.

In the Cattle Kingdom marketing the cattle was imperative. In Texas there was an abundance of cattle and little cash, while in the north there was more money and a growing taste for meat. Enterprising men in an effort to get the legal tender and the cattle together began driving the cattle to the railroads. The railroads, however, were east of the Great Plains toward the Mississippi River and difficult to reach. Then it was discovered that cattle could be fattened after the long drive on grass on the western prairies; and when the railroads were prevailed upon to build out to the Kansas country, the future of the cattle business was assured. During the next few years cattle were driven north from Texas in such numbers that it is estimated that by 1890 ten million animals had gone up the trails, at the rate of 150 to 200 herds a year.

Charles Goodnight, owner of the JA Ranch in Palo Duro Canyon and one of the best known ranchers of the time, left a classic description of his trail drives.

So much has been said and written about the old trails that anything else may seem superfluous. But my trail experience was so long and varied that perhaps what I have to say may be of interest to someone.

The first thing that I did was to make up my mind that I was going to drive and then where to. When this was done I set about collecting the outfit. My first step towards this was to round up fifty or sixty good horses. Then the mess wagon was made ready with provisions to last the time it would take to make the drive. For instance, when the Goodnight Trail was laid off I had to prepare for a six hundred-mile stretch; that being the distance from Young County, Texas, my starting place, to Fort Sumner, New Mexico, where I expected to sell my cattle. In the meantime, of course, I had informed my neighbor stockmen that I was to drive to a northern market and would receive any cattle they wanted to go with the herd. I could always count on the cattle reaching me at a certain time, and was never over three days in putting a herd of three thousand together.

Owing to the danger of the Indians and the stampedes I always got out of the settlements as soon as possible, for cattle that were scattered were much easier traced on the trail than in the settlements, owing to the fact that mine would be the only cattle on the trail. In my drive of 1866, I had to lay out my own trail, as no trail had been made since 1859, and that one not in my direction, when Oliver Loving drove a herd out of Texas. I laid out my course by the aid of maps and my experience in exploring the frontier when I was a ranger, on the frontier during the war. My course led through a trackless wilderness, where fierce nomadic tribes of Indians prowled at will.

I started the herd with eighteen men to drive them. These men were thoroughly drilled regarding their places and duties. I always, of course, selected two of my most skillful men to be my "pointers." These men were to handle the front of the herd and keep them in line on the course given out by the foreman. These pointers were never changed from their positions at the head of the herd. However, they would exchange sides each morning to get some relief from the stifling dust from the herd.

Of course the side men were changed each morning, except the corner men, as it is a fact that the further up the herd, the lighter the work. This divides the horse labor. Besides 300 miles of the Pecos River is terrific in alkali dust. If you were second coming behind to the right today, you would be third left tomorrow. You would keep going up each day, and changing sides, until you reached the pointers. You then dropped back to first on the right. This is kept up during the whole drive. Each man knows his place and takes it each morning. The rest of the men were divided along the sides in proportion to the length of the herd. I always selected three steady men for the rear. These men were called "drag hands" for the reason that they were to look out for the weaker cattle. Since the speed of the herd was determined by the rear it was the duty of the rear men to see that the stronger cattle were kept forward and out of the way, so that the weaker cattle would not be impeded. This is what we called "keeping the corners." It was necessary to see that the rear of the herd was no wider than the "swing," which was that part between the front and rear. Should this not be done, great loss would be occasioned from overheating; for the heat from so many moving cattle was terrific. If the pointers found that the swing was too long, they simply checked up until the herd was the correct length—one-half mile.

Trail hands were well disciplined and were governed entirely by signals. They were too far from the leader to receive orders any other way. My guards were standing guards, that is to say, that the man who had the first watch the first night would have it all the way through the drive. If you left the choice to the old hands they invariably chose the standing guard.

I had system on my drives. My friends often laughed about it, but the most successful drives were always systematically ordered. We ate breakfast just as day broke. The pointers and two other men who were to relieve the last night guard, ate as soon as possible. If there were signs of Indians the herd was started from its bedding grounds and put to grazing as soon as they could see clear enough to take care of them and provided there were no Indians about; but when there was danger of an attack the herd was kept on the bed ground until all hands were mounted and around them, which was done in a very few minutes. The cattle were always headed toward the course we were taking. The men ate, saddled and fell into place as soon as possible. It is remarkable that during my ten years on the trail I rarely ever had a man who would shirk his duty; had he been so inclined, he would have been ridiculed out of it. It is certain that no deadheads ever stayed in a cow camp any length of time.

As soon as the cattle had grazed sufficiently, they were put in moving order without delay. A column of cattle would march either slowly or faster according to the distance the side men rode from the line. Therefore, when we had a long drive to make between watering places and it was necessary to move faster, the men rode closer to the line. Under normal conditions, the herd was fifty to sixty feet across, the thickness being governed by the distance we had to go before resting. When the signal was given to start the herd, the foreman would tell the men what width to make the herd. Therefore, the order might be ten feet or twenty feet. Narrowing the string was called "squeezing them down." Ten feet was the lowest limit, for when the line was this width, gaps came and the cattle began trotting to fill in the spaces. Then the pointers would check them in front. The fastest steppers would naturally go up a little; but they were never allowed to trot. After a herd was handled a month or two they became gentler and it was necessary to ride a little closer to obtain the same results.

In laying off a trail the foreman or the owner of the cattle would ride ahead twenty or thirty miles—that is, if he does not find water sooner. He always rode a good horse and explored both sides of the way, in his search for water holes. He preferred to find water holes twelve or fifteen miles apart, but he kept going until he did find it—with this exception, if he found that he was striking a desert, he would return to the herd and inform the men what they should expect. Then they knew that the cattle were to be moved with all possible speed without actually crowding them. The owner then changed horses and rode on ahead once more until he found water; then he would go back and signal to the men. This was kept up until our destination was reached. Our trail was now established and two or three more drives would plainly mark it. This is the way I laid off the Goodnight Trail.

On my first drive across the ninety-six-mile desert that lies between the Pecos and the Concho Rivers, I lost three hundred head of cattle. We were three days and nights crossing this desert, and during this time we had no sleep or rest, as we had to keep the cattle moving all the time in order to get them to the river before they died of thirst. I rode the same horse for the three days and nights, and what sleep I got was on his back. As the cattle got closer to the water, they had no sense at all and we had to hold them back as well as we could. When they reached the stream they swam right across and then doubled back before stopping to drink. During this trip those steers got as gentle as dogs.

After this trip across the desert we made it systematically and there was practically no more loss. And the time consumed in making the drives would not vary two hours. We would leave the Concho at noon and drive that afternoon and all night, the next day and the next night. About ten o'clock the next morning we would reach the Pecos. The mess wagon was always sent on ahead in making these drives and the men would eat and drink as they passed it with the suffering cattle.

But to return to the regular routine of the trail: A herd under ordinary conditions was ready for grazing in the morning at eleven o'clock. At this time the men stopped for dinner, which had been prepared while breakfast was cooking. It was always best to select a grazing ground where the ground met to straddle the trail; so that the cattle could be thrown to each side. If this was done, the foreman or one of the pointers would give the signal to split the herd, by waving his hand each way. The swing hands would fall into the center, turning the cattle both ways. It was a little troublesome the first few days, but the cattle soon learned it. This method brought the herd back into form in half the time it would take if the cattle were all on one side.

After this grazing at noon, the cattle would not eat any more until they got to water, which we always tried to reach before sundown. This gave us ample time to have the cattle filled and everything arranged for a pleasant night. After they had grazed they were bedded for the night. The herd was put in a circle, the cattle being a comfortable distance apart. When the drive was first started and the cattle were fresh, I used a double guard. That is, half the men guarded the first part of the night; the other half the latter part. In storms and stampedes we were all on duty. After the herd had been out fifteen days, it was "trail broke" and four men were sufficient to guard three thousand cattle. If we were out two or three months, the last month two men on duty at a time were sufficient. Each guard slept two hours at a time and a little over, for each guard always stayed up a little over time. It is a fact that the last guard had the shortest hours. After we had been out a month the men could easily stay awake their two hours, and when in camp would not sleep those two hours. We never had a watch to go by, but divided the time by the dipper; it was accurately measured in this way. The guards rode around the herd facing each other; in this way they passed each other twice as they went around. If a rattlesnake was heard in the guard line, the men hearing it informed his companions of its whereabouts and the next morning someone would go and kill it—rattlesnakes do not move at night. Cattle feared a rattler and always gave him a wide berth.

When cattle are first started, the risk of stampede is great. They are nervous and easily frightened, the slightest noise may startle them into running. Some cattle are stampeders by nature. The greatest losses occurred in the night when all was utter confusion. A herd was more likely to run on a dark night than on a moonlight night. The remarkable thing about it was that the whole herd started instantly, jarring the earth like an earthquake. We could not divide the course they were taking until they had gone far enough for the sound to guide us— unless they were coming toward us. In that case I led the herd, holding them back as much as possible. As soon as the herd was strung out, we would turn the leaders back. They would circle and go into what was called a "mill," invariably moving to the right (if any old trailman ever heard of a herd moving to the left, I would like to hear from him).

The cattle would run until they were tired and we gradually spread them and they would settle down. We never took the cattle back to the same bed ground, for we knew that they would run again. We always tried to find the highest ground. Once settled they would generally be quiet. As a rule it took several days to rid the cattle of the effects of a stampede. The most successful way I found was to drive them all night. This way had them under control with the men all around them. I placed two of my most skillful men behind at what we called the corners and four more in front. If it was dark and the cattle had been badly stampeded they would not go far until they began to run again; not all of them would be running, however. Strange to say, there would be about one-half the herd that were marching along as though nothing had happened, while the rest of the herd would be going at a mad rate. The stampeders would come up one side at full speed, but when they reached the front the men in the lead would catch them and turn them back on the other side; then the men on the corners would drive them back again. These cattle would run until they were in great distress. We followed this method again the next night and the cattle were cured. They never stampeded again.

On nights when an electric storm was in progress, we could see the lightning playing on the horns of the cattle and on the horses' ears, resembling lightning bugs.

I was the only trailman that I know of who used steer leaders. I conceived this idea after the first trip and found it to be of great advantage. I used two steers. The bells I put on them were of the very best type—ox bells. They were arranged with a strap which would easily stop the clapper. When the signal to graze was given the man in charge of the steers would fasten down the clappers, and turn the steers off the trail. After we had been out for a month, should the clapper come loose at night, the whole herd would be on its feet in no time. The lead steers were of great advantage in swimming the rivers and in penning, for the cattle soon learned to go where the bell called them. Before starting on a trail drive, I made it a rule to draw up an article of agreement, setting forth what each man was to do. The main clause was that if one man shot another he was to be tried by the outfit and hanged on the spot—if found guilty. I never had a man shot on the trail. When I passed through the ninety-six-mile desert, I used to see two lonely graves. At Horsehead crossing where we struck the Pecos, there were thirteen graves. All the result of pistol shots but one. I thought then, as I think now, that all foremen and owners should have been responsible for the lives of their men, not only against the Indians but against each other. I shall never forget the impression made upon me when I would see those lonely graves. The life of some dear brother or father had been snuffed out as a result of a trifle.

Taking all in all, my life on the trail was the happiest part of it. I wish I could find words to describe the companionship and loyalty of the men towards each other. It is beyond imagination. The cowboy of the old days is the most misunderstood man on earth. Few young people of the younger generation realize that the western men— the cowboys—were as brave and chivalrous as it is possible to be. Bullies and tyrants were unknown among them. They kept their places around a herd and under all circumstances; and if they had to fight they were always ready. Timid men were not known among them—the life did not fit them. Today many of the richest and greatest men of Texas were cowboys. Of the hands I employed there are now at least three millionaires. Fewer cowboys have been tried for crimes than any other class of men.

### 3.   A "GLIMPSE" OF RANCH LIFE

#### Circa 1902

From Frank S. Hastings, "Some Glimpses of Ranch Life," *The Story of the S.M.S. Ranch* (S.M.S. booklet consisting for the most part of pictures taken on the ranch, 106 pp., 1919), 86-91. By permission of W. G. Swenson.

The author of the following extract, who managed the vast Swenson Ranch (SMS) from 1902 until his death in 1922, was in an excellent position to describe ranch life as he found it, as well as to explain some of the "lingo" of the ranching profession. In so doing he implies the mixture of the Anglo-American and the Mexican culture in this industry.

. . . A Ranch in its entirety is known as an "Outfit," and yet in a general way the word "Outfit" suggests the wagon outfit, which does the cowwork and lives in the open from April 15th, when work begins, to December 1st, when it ends.

The wagon outfit consists of the "Chuck Wagon" which carries the food, bedding and tents, and from the back of which the food is prepared over an open fire. The "Hoodlum Wagon," which carries the water barrel, wood and branding irons, furnishes the chuck wagon with water and wood, the branding crew with wood and attends all round-ups or branding pens with supply of drinking water.

The Remuda (cow ponies) and Horse Wrangler always travel with the "Wagon." Remuda is the Spanish word for Saddle Horses.

The wagon crew consists of the Wagon Boss, usually foreman of the ranch, Cook, Hoodlum Driver, Horse Wrangler, Straw Boss, next in authority to Wagon Boss, and eight to twelve men as the work may demand. In winter the outfit is reduced to the regular year-around men who are scattered over the different ranch camps. . . .

Every cowboy has a mount of from eight to fourteen horses regulated by his work, and the class of horses. A line rider can get along with fewer horses than a "wagon" man, and the man with a good many young horses needs more than the man with an older or steadier mount. Every one of these men will claim they are "afoot" and that "There ain't no more good cow ponies," but woe to the "outfit" that tries to take one of the no-accounts away, or as the saying is "Monkey with a man's mount."

Horses are assigned and then to all intents and purposes they become the property of the man. Some foremen do not let their men trade horses among themselves, but it is quite generally permitted under supervision that avoids "sharking."

Every horse has a name and every man on the ranch knows every horse by name, . . . and what horses are in each man's mount. A man who does not love his mount does not last long in the cow business. Very few men are cruel to their horses, and a man who does not treat his mount well is only a "bird of passage" on most ranches, and always on the S. M. S. Ranch. There is an old ranch saying that between the shoulder and the hip belongs to the rider, and the rest to the company. Beating over the head or spurring in the shoulder means "time check." Cowboys' principal topic is their horses or of men who ride, and every night about the camp fire they trade horses, run imaginary horse races, or romance about their pet ponies. . . .

All the saddle horses of an outfit thrown together are called the Remuda—pronounced in Texas "Remoother"—slurring the "ther." The Remuda is in charge of a man, usually a half-grown boy known as the "Horse Wrangler," whose duty it is to have them in a band when wanted to change mounts, and to see that they are watered and grazed and kept from straying. They are always assembled early morning, at noon and at night, and at such other times as the work may demand a change, as, for instance, in making a round the boys use their wildest and swiftest horses—usually their youngest, to tame them down. When the round-up is together they use their "cutting" horses, which are as a rule their oldest and best horses.

The Remuda for an ordinary outfit will number from 125 to 150 horses. The Wrangler must know every horse by sight and name, and tell at a glance if one is missing. The Remuda always trails with the wagon, but is often sent to some round-up place without the wagon. A horse is a "Hoss" always in a cow camp. Horses ridden on grass may be called upon to be ridden until down and out, but are not hurt as a grain fed horse would be, and when

his turn comes again in a few days is chipper as ever. . . . The horse breaker or "Bronc Buster" usually names horses as he breaks them; and if the horse has any flesh marks or distinct characteristics, it is apt to come out in the name, and any person familiar with the practical can often glance at a horse and guess his name. For instance, if he has peculiar black stripes toward the tail with a little white in the tail you are pretty safe to guess "Pole Cat." If his feet are big and look clumsy, "Puddin Foot" is a good first chance. The following names occur in three mounts, and to get the full list I had to dig hard, and both men left out several horses until I asked about them, because always the suspicion that something was going to be done that would take a horse: Red Hell, Tar Baby, Sail Away Brown, Big Henry, Streak, Brown Lina, Hammer Head, Lightning, Apron Face, Feathers, Panther, Chub, Dumbbell, Rambler, Powder, Straight Edge, Scissors, Gold Dollar, Silver City, Julius Caesar, Pop Corn, Talameslie, Louse Cage, Trinidad, Tater Slip, Cannon Ball, Big Enough, Lone Oak, Stocking, Pain, Grey Wonder, Rattler, Whiteman, Monkey Face, Snakey, Slippers, Jesse James, Buttermilk, Hop Ale, Barefoot, Tetoler, Lift Up, Pancho, Boll Weevil, Crawfish, Clabber, Few Brains, Showboy, Rat Hash, Butterbeans, Cigarette, Bull Pup. Feminine names are often used, such as Sweetheart, Baby Mine, or some girl's name. . . .

Only geldings are used in outfits; stallions are worked or ridden in winter, but no mares are used except as the property of some individual, then never in the Remuda. . . .

A "Bronc" is a horse recently broken or about to be broken. . . . Every cowboy must, of course, be able to handle a mean horse if necessary.

An "Outlaw" is a horse which no amount of riding or handling will subdue. He is "turned in" and sold in the "Scalawag" bunch which goes out every year, and includes the horses no longer fit for cow use. They are bought by traders who take them into some of the older Southern States and sell them to the negro tenants for cotton horses.

A "Sunday Hoss" is one with an easy saddle gait—usually a single footer with some style. The boys go "Gallin" Sundays and in every mount of the younger men there is apt to be such a horse, but not in any sense saved from the regular work for Sunday.

"An Individual" is the private property of a cowboy and not very much encouraged, as it is only natural that he does not get much work, and is an encouragement to go "Gallin" when the foreman holds the boys down on ranch horses more on the boys' account because it is often a long night ride and impairs the boys' capacity for a hard day's work in busy times. . . .

A cow horse is trained so that he is tied when the reins are down. He can, of course, drift off and, when frightened, run, but stepping on the reins seems to intimidate him into standing still as a rule. There are two reasons for this: first, the cowboy frequently has work where it is vital to leap from his horse and do something quick; second, that there is rarely anything to tie him to; though even when tying a horse a fairly even pull will loosen the reins. Cow horses are easily startled and apt to pull back and break the reins.

The regular cowboy gait for pasture riding or line work of ordinary cross country riding is a "Jiggle"—a sort of fox trot that will make five miles per hour. For the round-up hard running is necessary part of the time and usually a stiff gallop the balance.

Cowboy life is very different from the ideas given by a Wild West Show or the "Movies." It is against Texas law to carry a pistol and the sale is unlawful. This, however, is evaded by leasing for 99 years. Occasionally a rider will carry a Winchester on his saddle for coyotes or Lobo wolves, but in the seventeen years the writer has been intimate with range life he has never seen a cowboy carry a pistol hung about him, and very few instances where one was carried concealed. There is always a gun of some sort with the outfit carried in the wagon. . . .

Nicknames are the rule. Anyone is comparatively safe to say "Hello, Red" to a man with red hair, or, as the range word has it, "Red Pointed." Every outfit has its "Slim" and "Shorty," which may fit or be the opposite. "Big Boy" or "Big Un" is apt to be in evidence. Then comes names which require special explanation. "Paint" came from the fact that his first job on the ranch was painting a wagon; "Doc" from having doctored a horse. A remarkable case occurred in Stamford, where a man came looking for a brother by the name of Dave Taylor, whom no one could locate. The man went away and came back saying that his brother must live here. Then someone said wonder if it would be "Queenie" Taylor, and sure enough it was. The nickname had come from the old open range days—had been adopted to the extent of signing checks, etc. While, of course, we have every man's name right on our pay roll, we are often unable to call men by their real names on sight, because so thoroughly established is his nickname. . . .

Every cowboy furnishes his own saddle, bridle, saddle blanket and spurs; also his bedding, known as "Hot Roll," a 16 to 20-oz. canvas "Tarp" about 18 feet long double and bedding in between, usually composed of several quilts known as "suggans" and blankets—rarely a mattress, the extra quilts serving for mattress. The top "Tarp" serves as extra covering and protects against rain. . . .

Working outfits are composed as far as possible of unmarried men, with the exception of the Wagon Boss, who is usually the Ranch foreman. They rarely leave the wagon at night, and as the result of close association an interchange of wit, or "josh," as it is called, has sprung up. There is nothing like the chuck wagon josh in any other phase of life, and it is almost impossible to describe, because so much of it revolves about or applies to the technical part of ranching. It is very funny, very keen and very direct, and while the most of it is understood by an outsider, he cannot carry it away with him.

At headquarters a bunk house is always provided, which usually is known as "The Dog House" or "The Dive." No gambling is permitted on the ranches, but the cowboys' great game, "Auction Pitch," or dominoes or stag dances or music fill the hours of recreation, divided with the great cowboy occupation of "Quirt" making, in which they are masters. . . .

## 4. THE MAKING OF A COWBOY
### 1902-1921

From Frank S. Hastings, *A Ranchman's Recollections* (Chicago, 1921), 227-235. By permission of the publisher, Breeder's Gazette.

Frank S. Hastings also narrated his experiences in a highly interesting book entitled *A Ranchman's Recollections.* Under the heading of "The Speckled Yearlin'" he described how an ambitious lad succeeded in becoming a cowboy. Hastings was unusually successful in capturing the local color of life in the cattle country.

April and May rains, followed by good growing weather, had made everything beautiful in the S. M. S. pastures. The turf of curly mesquite grass was like a beautiful rug, painted here and there with wild verbena, star daisies, white and yellow primroses, and the myriad coloring of west Texas flora. Branding time was on, and the S. M. S. Flat Top Mountain outfit had gone into camp at Coon Creek Tank, to begin work the next day.

"Scandalous John," the foreman and wagon boss, had been through the aggravating experience of getting an outfit together. It had been no trouble to find riders—cowboys who knew the game from start to finish—but to secure a cook, a "hoss wrangler" and a hoodlum wagon driver was a problem. No one wants to drive the hoodlum wagon, with the duties of supplying wood and water for camp and branding, helping the cook with his dishes or other odd jobs, unprofessional, from a cowboy standpoint, except so far as they lead to a "riding job," meaning regular cowboy work. The "hoss wrangler" was not hard to find, but whoever takes the job aches all the time to be promoted to a riding job, and is therefore dissatisfied. The hoodlum driver had worked one day, and quit. Scandalous was racking his brain to know where to look for another, and was saddling his horse to hunt for one when Four-Six, one of the cowboys, exclaimed, "Look what's comin'!"

Along the dim pasture road, miles from any dwelling, a figure on foot was approaching—a sight which always attracts attention in the big pasture country, since it is associated in the public mind with suspicion, if the footman is unknown. It often occurs that someone's horse will get away or give out. The rider then makes for the nearest cow camp to borrow a horse; but a man walking needs some explanation, although he is always fed without question. The boys were all quiet and indifferent, as they commonly are in a cow camp when a stranger approaches.

A lad of sixteen, rather the worse for wear, clad in a shirt and ducking trousers, badly frayed, a soft felt hat, full of holes, shoes badly run-down at the heels, and bare toes showing through the uppers, stopped within ten feet of the wagon. Scandalous paused in his saddling to say, "Well, son, in trouble?"

The lad's face, lit up by a broad grin, made an appeal to the whole outfit, and all were at attention for his answer. "No, I'm looking for the S. M. S. boss. They told me at the ranch house that he was here, and I'm looking for a job."

"You look hungry, son; come eat, an' then tell us all about it," said Scandalous.

As the lad ate, and refilled his plate and cup, the cook ventured, "Son, you're plumb welcome, but when did you eat last?"

"Night before last," the boy replied. "The brakies give me some bread and meat, but I sure was gittin ready to eat when I smelt your grub cooking down the road."

"Where be you from, son?"

"I'm from Virginia," came the reply, "and I'm sure glad to get here, and get a job."

"Virginia! A job?" exclaimed Scandalous. "How did you get here, an' how do you know you kin get a job?"

Again that good-natured grin appeared as the lad told his story.

"I walked some, and rode with the brakies some; they was mighty good to me, and give me a card to other brakies; sometimes they'd give me food they cooked in the caboose, and sometimes they took me home. I told them I was coming to the big S. M. S. Ranch to work. I worked on farms some, but hurried as much as I could, to be here branding time. Am I in time?"

The quiet assurance of the boy staggered Scandalous, but he recovered to ask, "How did you know about the S. M. S. Ranch? What made you think you could git a job? Ever done any cow work?"

The lad's grin broadened as he answered: "Well, a feller I worked for down in Virginia had one of them picture books about the S. M. S. Ranch, and I read where it said, 'No use to write for a job,' so I just cum. I kin do anything I start out to do; I wanted to work on a ranch ever since I was a little feller; I can learn to do anything you want done, and I sure am going to work for you."

Scandalous blinked again, and said, "Why, son, we would hev' to hev' permission from your pa and ma, even if we had a job, 'cause you might git hurt."

A shade of sadness swept for a moment over the young face; then it shone again with a new light of conviction.

"I ain't got no pa or ma, I been in the orphan asylum until two years ago, when a fine man, the one with the book, took me on his farm to do chores. I didn't run away from him, neither; he said I was so crazy about comin' I'd better start. I been on the road so long the things he give me wore out. I guess I walked about a month. They told me in town to go to the office, but I was afraid they'd turn me down, so I cum to camp, and I'm a-going to stay and work for nothing."

There is a straight path to the hearts of cowboys, if one knows the way, and Scandalous was glad to hear the chorus from the whole outfit, "Let him stay, Scandalous. We'll help him. Give the little boy a job."

"Reckon you kin drive the hoodlum wagon, 'Little Boy'," said John, and, like a flash, came this response: "I don't know what a hoodlum wagon is, but I kin drive it."

It was settled. "Little Boy" was hired, and "made good." Every moment that he could get from his work found him in the branding pen, and, as is the custom with cowboys in their work, he often rode big calves. The boys, watching his skill, would get him to pull off "stunts" for visiting cowmen, until it began to be noised about the "Little Boy" in the S. M. S. outfit "was sum calf-rider." Then came the proud day of his life, when an older man was found for the hoodlum wagon. The horse wrangler was promoted to a riding job, and "Little Boy" to horse wrangler.

The boys had from the outset contributed shirts and socks; ducking trousers had been cut off for a makeshift. The first month's wages had provided a fair outfit, including the much-coveted white shirts that cowboys love to have in their "war bags" for special occasions. Succeeding months brought saddle, bridle, spurs, horse blanket and a "hot roll." "Little Boy" was coming on, but had to content himself with shoes until he had all the major

necessities, and could acquire the two grand luxuries: a $15 John B. hat and $35 hand-made stitched top boots.

All through the summer "Little Boy" progressed, first from calves to yearlings in his play time, and then to outlaw broncs, until the boys in the outfit would say, "Thet kid sure kin ride; I'll bet he gets inside the money this fall at the Stamford rodeo."

Anything pertaining to an outlaw horse or steer becomes current gossip in the big pasture country, where horses and cattle form the basis of conversation about the wagon after working hours. Strange stories drifted in about a certain outlaw speckled yearling on the Lazy 7 Ranch—he had thrown every boy with rodeo aspirations who had tried to ride him, and seemed to be getting better all the time. The "Speckled Yearling" was tall, gaunt and quick as a cat. He had a mixed jump and weave that got his men about the third jump, but the boys on the Lazy 7 were keeping him to themselves, with a view to pulling off a prize "stunt" at the Stamford rodeo in September. All the little country towns held rodeos during the summer, with calf and goat roping, bronc-busting and steer riding, but the big event was to come, and the boys were getting ready for it. "Little Boy" had a heart-to-heart talk with his boss, and received permission to ride steers, and tackle the "Speckled Yearlin'," if opportunity permitted.

At last the time for the great event came. Cowboys from 100 miles around were on hand. Professionals were barred. It was to be an event for boys who were in actual service on ranches. The S. M. S. headquarters office was thrown open for all, and the Stamford Inn pulled off an old-time cowboy dance, with old-fashioned "squares" called by old-time punchers, with old-time fiddlers doing the music. The weatherman had done his best; some 2,000 people filled the grandstand, cheering the events of the first day, with now and then a call for the "Speckled Yearlin'," which was not mentioned in the programme.

Anyone who has not seen an unprofessional rodeo knows little of real cowboy sport, since it differs in its wild abandon, grace and skill from the staged events. As each favored son came on for his "stunt," he was cheered to the echo, and usually he pulled some original antic which sent the crowd wild.

The announcer, riding before the grandstand, waved for silence. "Listen, people: I want you to hear this; it's a surprise, and the big event. No one has ever been able to stay ten jumps on the 'Speckled Yearlin',' from the Lazy 7 Ranch. Nig Clary will now 'ride at' the 'Speckled Yearlin' on his own risk: A $50 prize if he stays on; a $25 forfeit if he gets throwed. If he rides him down, a hat collection will be took. If Nig can't ride him some other feller gets a chance tomorrow."

"If Nig can't nobody kin," shouted the grandstand. "Turn him a-loose." A wave from the judges' hands, and, like the cutting off of an electric current, all was still and tense. Then from the mounting chute shot the "Speckled Yearlin'," with Nig Clary up, clinging by two hand-holds to a surcingle and riding bare-back. The yearling was dead-red, with distinct white speckles about the size of one's thumb distributed well over his body. He carried long, sharp horns; his back was on the order of an Arkansas razorback hog. When it came to jumping and weaving his body at the same time, the "Speckled Yearlin' " was the limit.

Nig sat straight for three jumps, began to wabble in the fourth, and was on the ground at the fifth. Still jumping, the yearlin' turned and made for him, giving Nig only time by a scratch to climb up behind one of the judges.

The second day found "Little Boy" and Scandalous with their heads together. "I know I kin ride him, John, an' I sure want that prize money for my boots an' my John B. They's all I'm needin' to be a real cowboy."

"Yes, I know," said John, "but we're needin' live cowboys, an' I ain't feelin' right 'bout your tryin' that yearlin'. I'll hev to ask you to waive all blame fer the company, an' if you do git hurt they'll be blamin' me; but if you be bound to ride, us boys will pay the forfeit, if you get throwed."

Again on the second day the announcer waved his hand for silence. "Folks, yesterday the best rider and cowpuncher in Texas rode at that speckled yearlin'. Today 'Little Boy' from Flat Top Mountain Ranch says he's goin' to ride him. We hates to let a little orphan boy go agin this here steer, but he sez he ain't a-goin' to git hurt, an' if he does there ain't anybody but him. The management hopes he wins. If he does, git your change ready for a hat prize, an' I am a-goin' to start it with a five."

As boy and steer came out of the chute, the stillness fairly hurt. Every heart in that great crowd seemed to stop for the first three jumps, but "Little Boy" was sitting tight. From the crowd there came a mighty roar: "Stay with him, 'Little Boy'! He's got a booger on him. Ride him, 'Little Boy'!"

At the tenth jump "Little Boy" was still up, his grin growing broader and his seat getting steadier, while the yearling, maddened by his clinging burden, pitched and weaved, but, like Sinbad's "Old Man of the Sea," "Little Boy" kept "a-ridin'."

The crowd went daft. Every one was standing and shouting. The noise seemed to infuriate the yearling, and, turning from the end of the enclosure, he made straight for the grandstand, struck his head against the protecting wire, stood stock still, and glared, while "Little Boy" sat and grinned. Some one cried "Speech!" and, as stillness came, "Little Boy," still sitting on the dazed steer, broadened his grin and said, "I jest had to ride him. I needed them boots and thet John B., so's I could be a real cowboy, an' this yere speckled yearlin's done done it."

## 104. THE FARMERS' ALLIANCE: THE CLEBURNE PLATFORM

### August 7, 1886

From *The Dallas Morning News,* August 8, 1886; see also, August 4, 1886, and August 19, 1896.

The agricultural depression that began after the Civil War continued with increasing seriousness for three decades. After non-political approaches to the problem proved ineffective, farmers began to form other organizations with an intent to influence politics. Two of the most important of these were the Farmers' Alliance in the Northwest and the National Farmers' Alliance in the South. The latter, originated at Lampasas in 1874 or 1875, spread to several counties as the Grand State Alliance, but in 1878 went down with the Greenback Party. It was revived the next year in Parker County, later incorporated as a "secret benevolent association," and by 1885 claimed a membership of fifty thousand. Turning to politics to achieve their goal, the delegates to the state convention at Cleburne in August, 1886, drew up a series of demands which constituted a political program. The Texas organization, armed with an appealing program, then proceeded to absorb local farm groups throughout the South. These mergers having been completed, the newly formed Southern Farmers' Alliance confederated with the Knights of Labor, and in 1890 adopted the Cleburne platform. After casting its lot unsuccessfully with the Populists in 1892, the Southern Alliance returned to its earlier plan to gain control of the Democratic Party, and by 1896 the president of the Texas State Alliance was able to report that the Cleburne platform, with some modifications, had "in a great measure been indorsed by and recommended in the platform of the Democratic Party."

We, the delegates of the Grand State Alliance in convention assembled at Cleburne, Texas, August, 1886, do hereby recommend and demand of our State and national governments, according as the same shall come under the jurisdiction of the one or the other, or both, such legislation as shall secure to our people freedom from the onerous and shameful abuses that the industrial classes are now suffering at the hands of arrogant capitalists and powerful corporations.

We demand, first, the recognition by incoporation of trade unions, co-operative stores and such other associations as may be organized by the industrial classes to improve their financial condition or promote their general welfare.

2. We demand that all public school lands be sold in small bodies, not exceeding three hundred and twenty acres to each purchaser, for actual settlers on easy terms of payment.

3. That large bodies of land held by private individuals or corporations for speculative purposes shall be assessed for taxation at such rates as they are offered to purchasers on credit of one, two or three years in bodies of one hundred and sixty acres or less.

4. We demand that measures be taken to prevent aliens[1] from acquiring titles to land in the United States of America and to force titles already acquired by aliens to be relinquished by sale to actual settlers and citizens of the United States.

5. That the law making powers take early action upon such measures as shall effectually prevent the dealing in futures of all agricultural products, prescribing such procedure in trial as shall secure prompt conviction, and imposing such penalty as shall secure the most perfect compliance with the law.

---

[1]The confiscation of lands owned by alien corporations, where they had attained them by lawful means, was contemplated, but it was proposed to bring these lands on the market to settlers at fair practice by imposing a tax rate equivalent to that paid by small farmers.

6. That all lands forfeited by railroads or other corporation immediately revert to the government and be declared open for purchase by actual settlers on the same terms as other public or school lands.

7. We demand that all fences be removed, by force if necessary, from public or school lands unlawfully fenced by cattle companies, syndicates or any other form or name of monopoly.

8. We demand that the statute of the State of Texas be rightfully enforced by the Attorney General of the State to compel corporations to pay the taxes due the State and county.

9. That railroad property shall be assessed to the full nominal value of the stock on which the railroad seeks to declare dividends.

10. We demand the rapid extinguishment of the public debt of the United States by operating the mints to their fullest capacity in coining silver and gold, and the tendering the same without discrimination to the public creditors of the nation according to contract.

11. We demand the substitution of legal tender treasury notes for the issues of national banks; that the Congress of the United States shall regulate the amount of such issue by giving to the country a per capita circulation that shall increase as the population and business interest of the country expand.

12. We demand the establishment of a national bureau of labor statistics, that we may arrive at a correct knowledge of the moral, intellectual, and financial condition of the laboring masses of our citizens, and further, that the commissioner of this bureau be a Cabinet officer of the United States government.

13. We demand the enactment of laws to compel corporations to pay their employees according to contract in lawful money for their services, and the giving to mechanics and laborers a first lien upon the products of their labor to the extent of their full wages.

14. We demand the passage of an interstate commercial law that shall secure the same rates of freight to all persons for the same class of merchandise, according to the distance of haul, without regard to amount of shipment; to prevent the granting of rebates; to prevent pooling freights to shut off competition, and to secure to the people the benefits of railroad transportation at reasonable cost.

15. We demand that all convicts be confined in prison walls, and the contract system abolished.

16. We recommend a call for a national conference, to which all labor organizations shall be invited to send representative men to discuss such measures as may be of interest to the laboring classes. . . .

# 105. SOME EXPERIENCES OF AN EARLY SURVEYOR IN THE TEXAS PANHANDLE

## 1887

From J. C. Tolman, "Christmas 1887 in Palo Duro Canyon," West Texas Historical Association *Year Book,* XXXII (1956), 75-84 (reprinted from *The Texaco Star,* December, 1925). By permission of the Texas Company.

Surveyors have been in the vanguard of pioneers on every American frontier, but very few of them have left written records of their unusual way of life. The following account of the experiences of a surveying party in the Texas Panhandle in 1887 is a rare and an illuminating document. Some ten pictures, mostly showing the country at that time, accompanied the original article. Under one of the pictures the names of the party were listed as follows: Barrington Poynton, J. C. Tolman, P. G. Omohundro, Charley Howard, Ashur McCulloch, and Watt Morris.

Said Watt: "Bill, I done gathered all the buffeler chips offen four sections around this here camp and I ain't goin no further. If you cain't make out to cook two meals with this here cord of 'em, I guess we-all will go hungry."

"Umph," said Bill.

"Yeah," remarked Watt, "I know this here gol-darned drizzle drazzle done made the sap rise in the chips an' it's hard to get a het on the ovens; but it's forty miles to the nearest brush an' God knows how far to a tree, and my back is done give out toting chips."

"Bosh!" said Bill, as he lifted the top of a dutch-oven to take a look at the biscuits in which he took so much pride and which were always light and delectable when he could get a proper "het" on his ovens.

"Lordy, Bill!" exclaimed Watt, "I never seen you make

such biscuit. Them looks to me as though they had squat to rise and baked on the squat."

Bill threw a poker at him which he neatly dodged and it nearly hit Bill's pet wild-cat. Kitty spat irritably and lit on the top of the chuck-wagon, his perch in time of trouble.

Presently Watt said: "I hear the line-wagon about a mile off, comin' fast."

Presently Dave and Martin rode up and unsaddled and fed their ponies. By that time the line-wagon reached camp and both of the chainmen helped Sebe unharness and feed.

Presently the Major ambled up on "Old Sideways," the hip-shot cayuse provided by a rich corporation for this particular topographer. The surveying party was complete and present and hungry, as usual.

Bill pounded a three-foot iron pipe with a poker and eight members of a pioneer surveying party gathered around a table made of two boards and situated near the N. W. corner of Block No. 7, I. & G. N. R. R. Co. Survey, in the Panhandle of Texas, the time being late in the year 1887.

That was only thirty-eight years ago. Not very long in the life of a young man. Hardly to be considered in the life of a nation. But consider:

In 1887, between No-Man's Land on the north, the Palo

Duro on the south, the Indian Territory on the east, and New Mexico on the west, there were just thirty-six houses outside the town of Mobeetie, Fort Elliott's, and a little settlement at Tascosa. Mobeetie was the metropolis and boasted a population of three hundred and fifty humans.

There was no railroad; no graded road; no fence, except small horse pastures near headquarter ranch houses.

In the "breaks" and canyons one could find objects by which to guide oneself; but on the Llano Estacado there was only a grass-covered plain extending beyond the range of sight. This plain had been the home of the buffalo and their bones, skulls, and horns could be seen in any direction. Within the next few years the "bone-hunters" were to gather these and haul them many miles to be shipped by rail and made into fertilizer. The "buffalo-chip," or dried dung was the only fuel of the plains as long as it could be found.

At the time of this sketch there were thousands of antelope and many hundreds of mustangs on the plains.

"Prince Charlie" Goodnight had preserved a few buffalo on the J A ranch on the lower Palo Duro, and a few wild herds were reported on the North Plains; but all of the rest of the mighty herds were dead. It would have been so very easy to have preserved some of them. Our trees and birds and——But we are democratic, and——

At night the men slept on "blanket-rolls" on the ground. There is no finer bed for the tired outdoor man. Tents were pitched whenever the weather was unpleasant, but most of the time sleep was in the open. It was a hard but healthy life.

The drizzle ceased some time in the night and Bill had breakfast by daylight. He pounded on his loud pipe with his accursed iron poker and yelled his matin-song in a hideous voice: "Wake up, snakes! Day's a breakin'!"

Blessed sleep! Blessings brighten as they take their flight. For thirty-eight years one of that outfit has thought that old Bill might have developed a gentler method by which to dispel slumber. Well, anyhow, the outfit ceased to sleep and presently was washed and "grubbed," and the stock was fed and watered and saddled or hitched; the surveying outfit loaded in the light "line-wagon," and the tents and bedrolls piled near the camp wagons—so that the camp-rustler could load them with the least trouble.

Then the line party started for the point where they had quit work the night before. This was a small mound of sod and was visible for three miles. They reached it betimes and P. G., The Chief, had his transit set and took his first sight almost before the refraction of the sun's early rays ceased to interfere.

Dave, the front flagman, could lope his pony a half mile and take a sight and not miss the distance more than a few feet. P. G. had Sebe drive him up to the hub and dig up a chunk of sod to mark the spot. By that time P. G. would be ready for a back-sight on Martin's flag and Dave would be ready a half mile ahead. P. G. would set Dave and proceed. Martin would lope gaily up to the piece of sod—which could be seen half a mile—and find his tack-point in time for another sight.

It was lovely and easy for everybody—that is to say everybody who had an easy job. The chain-carriers, of course, had to walk every foot of the line and measure it carefully. If one of them made an error things would blow up. Somehow the poor devils averaged over seven miles

of measured line for each and every day for seven years, and didn't seem to make any appreciable error. Of course they were dull creatures, not temperamental nor given to flights of fancy.

Lines were run and marked to the north as far as the head of McClellan Creek. From a corner on this line another line was traced to the west, and corners established on the area where the town of Amarillo was afterwards started.

Lines were run to the east as far as to the line of the J A ranch. These lines were over the plains. As far as the eye could see, the corners of sections and blocks could be observed when the atmosphere was not disturbed.

Frequently the mirage played strange tricks on the Llano Estacado. One day near the head of North Fork, we suddenly saw Al Holland driving Beck and Sue—a team of mules—apparently about half a mile away. We thought he would reach us in a few minutes; but they jogged along for half an hour and then faded away. Afterwards it was found that at the time he was nearly twenty miles away.

A few days later P. G. took the outfit to the west line of the X range to meet Mr. Gray, who was to show some corners. When we arrived at the rendezvous we saw the two black ponies he drove, trotting along with his white canvas-topped buckboard, which we easily recognized. We waited an hour and he seemed no nearer, so we drove to meet him. At about a mile from the rendezvous his outfit very suddenly changed into a white buffalo skull with two black horns. While we stared at it Mr. Gray suddenly appeared from nowhere in another direction and reached us in a few minutes.

One day we started to run a line south. It was a clear still day and it seemed that visibility was infinite. We could see cattle ahead for miles and there were several herds of antelope and mustangs in sight. The Major, mounted on Old Sideways, was ambling on ahead. A topographer had mighty little to map on the plains; he drew a square for a section and lettered "L. P." neatly in a corner. Suddenly the Major and Old Sideways began to sink beneath the surface. We yelled and he turned and waved his hat as though cheering on his men at Kennesaw Mountain fight. Then he disappeared beneath the plain.

The cattle, antelope, and mustangs were in plain view for miles ahead beyond where he disappeared. A calm buzzard floated on motionless wings about a mile above us. We wondered if that meant anything. They are wise birds.

Dave loped ahead; started to sink; stopped and called for a point at short range.

We hurried on; reached and passed Dave; started down a gentle slope and stopped on the brink of the Palo Duro Canyon.

To see the sight in front of us was enough to make the heart miss a beat. It could not be looked upon without causing the beholder to thrill with appreciation of the wonderful works of the Great Architect of the universe.

Here, the result of the slow erosive action of waters through hundreds of thousands—perhaps millions—of years, was a gash cut through the plains for fifty miles. In places over a thousand feet deep and five miles in width, it is one of the wonder spots of America. Along the rim we saw a band of yellow, where the plains grass dipped to the rim rock. This rim rock, a heavy band of gray, capped the canyon as far as the eye could reach. Below it the exposed strata showed as though some giant hand had drawn brushes, dipped in many colors, along the miles of the canyon walls. Pink, blue, red, gray, green, yellow, purple, brown, blending in the distance into a lovely purple shade. At intervals were ledges clothed with the deep green of tall cedars. Diamond-like points of light were reflected from springs gushing out of the rocks to fall in terraced cascades and to be lost in the sand and gravel at the bottom of the gorge.

We gazed in silence for a long, long time. The air was like crystal in the canyon that crisp winter day.

Movements along a great cedar covered ledge, a half mile across the gash and five hundred feet down, caught Dave's huntsman's eyes. He pointed. "Look," he almost whispered, "two bears! And over there, turkeys—more than twenty!"

The Major sat on a rock feverishly doing topography. He had plenty to do. He was happy with the slopes of all degrees and directions with precipices every now and then.

To the south the same mustangs, antelope, and cattle contentedly grazed. We camped where we found some rain water caught in large potholes in the cap-rock.

Next day it took Dave half a day of hard climbing to reach the south side, where he established line points which we triangulated. We could not hope to measure accurately across that gorge.

The wagons had to go to the junction of the Palo Duro and Terra Blanca canyons to effect a crossing to the south side.

We ran many survey lines over the plains and in the canyons. Much of the work was by triangulation and was very interesting indeed.

We camped one Saturday night at a waterhole on a nameless creek which ran into the Palo Duro. Sunday morning all the men were in the tents resting, when P. G. went outside and at once called in an awe struck voice: "Great Caesar's Ghost! Boys, look here!"

The wonder working mirage was busy. The Palo Duro lay extended beneath us and up in the heavens was another Palo Duro Canyon—upside down! Every stratum of rock —every clump of trees—the gleaming surfaces of water— all, to the minutest detail, were plainly to be seen reversed in the sky above. The phenomenon lasted for nearly an hour. Seldom is such a wonderful sight beheld by man.

P. G. named the creek near our camp "Sunday Creek." It may be on the map now.

The work on the south side was completed, and we moved back to the north side of the canyon and worked until the latter part of December.

There had been no very severe weather. Rather warm days and cool delightful nights. The air was like fine wine. Work was a vast delight. Sleep under the stars was a dip into the fountain of perpetual youth.

One of the wagons had gone to town for supplies and returned two days before Christmas. On the morning of the twenty-fourth we broke camp and the heavy wagons started for a new camp site several miles to the east of where our first line had crossed the canyon. The line crew went several miles to the north and started to run a line south toward the new camp. All went well until about the middle of the afternoon.

Dave had just taken a front-sight and given the "O.K."

signal to come ahead, when we saw him wave his arms in a signal that meant "Look." He seemed to point to the north. We looked, but could see nothing unusual. When we reached Dave and asked what was the matter, he answered, "Norther coming," and loped off for another sight. There did seem to be a slight haze in the north— low down on the surface of the plains.

When we reached the next hub and looked back, there was a dun colored arch distinct above the plain, far to the north. At the next stop we established a corner and dug four pits and built an earth mound. I remember we were quite warm from the work. By the time we were through this—hardly three quarters of an hour from the time Dave's sharp eyes had seen the approaching norther—the dun colored arch extended to the horizon from east to west and was almost upon us from the north. It did not extend very far above the plains. P. G. gave the order to quit work and make for camp.

The outfit moved with celerity. The Major and Old Sideways had gone south some time before. Dave and Martin let their ponies lope. Sebe shook the reins at his long legged light-wagon team and they galloped madly from the storm. But it caught us in a few minutes. With a rush of ice cold wind, a snarl like an angry beast, an awful roar, changing into a long drawn out wail which continued to rise and fall—the yellow norther of the plains struck and enveloped us.

The air was full of ice needles that drove into the exposed flesh and stuck, but did not seem to melt. The snow seemed to parallel the ground in its flight; yet the plains grass was covered by it in a few minutes and it rolled along the ground with the wind. That wind didn't turn aside. When it hit you it just kept right on through your body, as though your flesh offered no obstruction to it. There wasn't a hill between us and the North Pole and that wind must have come all the way—and gathering power at every jump.

We had been sweating ten minutes before. Now we pulled the wagon sheet over us huddling under it. But the wind and cold were pitiless and cut and stung despite the cover.

Sebe let his mules run for several miles. They ran straight south and made no effort to turn. The norther attended to that.

We couldn't see ten feet ahead of the team, but we knew that somewhere ahead of us was a thousand foot canyon with sides nearly straight down for several hundred feet. We knew we had gone a long way and we thought we were within a mile of the cap-rock when those two Missouri mules suddenly stopped. Fortunately nothing broke and we managed to stay in the wagon.

Sebe pulled to the left and urged the team. They didn't want to turn sideways to the wind and sleet, but Sebe managed to make them move. Almost immediately we started down grade and in less than half a minute were below the plains level.

Sebe turned the team to the right, and we scrambled down on to a bench, high above the bottom of the canyon, but two hundred feet below the top of a precipice of solid rock.

The wind roared far above us but there was no gust that reached to our level. The snow fell in sheets about us, but dropped calmly straight down. And there, by our good luck, was the camp. The teamsters had pitched the tents—a courtesy extended only in times of stress—and Old Bill had a fire going and supper well on the way.

After we had thawed out and moved around a bit, one of the boys noticed a cleft in the face of the precipice about thirty feet above its base and in the cleft were three or four dead cedars. He threw a blazing piece of wood into the dry limbs and it hung there and set fire to one of the trees. In a short time we had a roaring torch fifty or sixty feet tall. We ate supper by its light and shortly thereafter the trees burnt off from the stumps and a wonderful avalanche of flaming wood and coals piled itself at the base of the rock. It burnt for hours and warmed quite a large space around camp.

When we had finished "first smoke," P. G. announced that he had a new novel by "The Duchess" and would read some to us. We helped Old Bill wash the dishes so that he could hear the story, he being naturally romantic and a great admirer of The Duchess.

The light from the great fire was sufficient and we gathered around P. G. and listened as he read of real high-toned society folk—even an occasional nobleman and titled lady—who entered the scenes with perfect grace and beauty and who made love in a most delicate and refined way. It was all so different from what we knew!

Late at night, while P. G. was reading a very tender passage, he was interrupted by a maniacal chorus of shrieks and howls—deep-throated, menacing, and terrifying. The reading ceased until the pack had yelled their way a long distance from our sheltering bank over the snow covered plain. The lobo wolves were hungry and were hunting.

Again P. G.'s voice took us back to the tenderness and beauty of the Irish land and we thrilled with the hero and laughed with "Dickey Browne."

The light from the fire died down; but the glowing coals still melted the snow around us. Old Bill lit a lantern and placed it on a tomato box by P. G.'s shoulder.

The Duchess was no mean writer, and her descriptions of garden fetes, picnics, balls, and love making gripped and held us. We were all young, in years at least, and each one saw himself the hero of the tale, and each made the delicate remarks at the proper time, and, at the end, each of us thrilled to the kiss of promise of the lovely heroine.

P. G. finished the tale and we sat awhile in blissful silence. Then Dave murmured:

"That's a hum dinger of a love story!"

"Let's go to Ireland on a cattle boat," suggested Martin. "Sure! Let's!"

P. G. looked at his watch. "Good gracious! It's past one o'clock! Merry Christmas!"

We all shook hands all around. Old Bill sighed very deeply:

"It sure started fine, Chief. I looked at my watch, just at twelve, an that cus was putting his arm around the lady for the first time; and it was a Christmas eve and she wished him, 'Mery Christmas.' Dogon the luck! G'night."

## 106. THE TEXAS ANTI-TRUST LAW

### March 30, 1889

From H. P. N. Gammel (comp.), *The Laws of Texas*, 1822-1897 (10 vols.; Austin, 1898), IX, 1169-1170.

The rural element in Texas, seeking reforms through political action, was successful in gaining control of the legislature in 1886 through the Farmers' Alliance. Among the problems attacked was that of the growth of large corporations, both in size and in number; that growth had been phenomenal during the 1870's and 1880's. The farmers blamed the corporations, particularly the railroads, for their ills, and set about to control them through legislation. Encouraged by similar movements in other states and by the support of Attorney General James S. Hogg, Texas in March, 1889, passed an anti-trust law, the second such in the nation and prior to any anti-trust legislation by the national government.

Section 1. Be it enacted by the Legislature of the State of Texas: That a trust is a combination of capital, skill, or acts by two or more persons, firms, corporations, or associations of persons, or of either two or more of them for either, any, or all of the following purposes: First—To create or carry out restrictions in trade. Second—To limit or reduce the production, or increase or reduce the price of merchandise or commodities. Third—To prevent competition in manufacture, making, transportation, sale, or purchase of merchandise, produce or commodities. Fourth—To fix at any standard or figure, whereby its price to the public shall be in any manner controlled or established, any article or commodity of merchandise, produce, or commerce intended for sale, use, or consumption in this state. Fifth—To make or enter into, or execute or carry out any contract, obligation, or agreement of any kind or description by which they shall bind or have bound themselves not to sell, dispose of, or transport any article or commodity, or article of trade, use, merchandise, commerce, or consumption below a common standard figure, or by which they shall agree in any manner to keep the price of such article, commodity, or transportation at a fixed or graduated figure, or by which they shall in any manner establish or settle the price of any article or commodity or transportation between them or themselves and others to preclude a free and unrestricted competition among themselves or others in the sale or transportation of any such article or commodity, or by which they shall agree to pool, combine, or unite any interest they may have in connection with the sale or transportation of any such article or commodity that its price might in any manner be affected.

Sec. 2. That any corporation holding a charter under the laws of the State of Texas which shall violate any of the provisions of this act shall thereby forfeit its charter and franchise, and its corporate existence shall cease and determine.

Sec. 3. For a violation of any of the provisions of this act by any corporation mentioned herein it shall be the duty of the attorney-general or district or county attorney, or either of them, upon his own motion, and without leave or order of any court or judge, to institute suit or quo warranto proceedings . . . for the forfeiture of its charter rights and franchise, and the dissolution of its corporate existence.

Sec. 4. Every foreign corporation violating any of the provisions of this act is hereby denied the right and prohibited from doing any business within this state, . . .

Sec. 6. Any violation of either or all the provisions of this act shall be and is hereby declared a conspiracy against trade, and any person who may be or may become engaged in any such conspiracy or take part therein, or aid or advise in its commission, or who shall, as principal, manager, director, agent, servant, or employe, or in any other capacity, knowingly carry out any of the stipulations, purposes, prices, rates, or orders thereunder or in pursuance thereof, shall be punished by fine not less than fifty dollars nor more than five thousand dollars, and by imprisonment in the penitentiary not less than one nor more than ten years or by either such fine or imprisonment. Each day during a violation of this provision shall constitute a separate offense. . . .

Sec. 11. That any contract or agreement in violation of the provisions of this act shall be absolutely void and not enforcable either in law or equity. . . .

Sec. 13. The provisions of this act shall not apply to agricultural products or live stock while in the hands of the producer or raiser. . . .

## 107. DEMANDS OF THE TEXAS FEDERATION OF LABOR

### July 3, 1889

From *Appleton's Annual Cyclopedia and Register of Important Events of the Year 1889* (42 vols.; New York, 1862-1903), XXIX (XIV, New Series; 1890), 791.

Representatives of labor held a convention at Dallas on July 3, 1889, "for the purpose of perfecting a State organization to further the eight-hour movement, and to do whatever else the convention may in its wisdom deem to be for the best interest of the wage-workers of Texas." They completed their organization, adopted the name "Texas Federation of Labor," and prepared the following platform.

We favor eight hours as a working day, and demand the passage of a law so declaring.

We favor a single tax, or a tax upon land values, and the repeal of all other taxes whatsoever.

We favor the repeal of the national bank law, and all other class laws.

The only equitable solution of the transportation question is in the Government ownership of the railways, telegraphs, and telephones.

We favor the abolition of the United States Senate and all State senators, because of the corruption practiced; the abolition of the grand jury system, because it is used by designing men to crush, ostracize, and persecute in some instances those who oppose existing systems, and the supremacy of either the Democratic or Republican factions, and to the end that our votes may be counted when cast and all corruption and the damnable boodle system be obliterated.

We favor the Australian system of holding elections; the election of all officers by the direct vote of the people.

We favor all that will secure a lien on the products of labor.

## 108. GOVERNOR JAMES S. HOGG ON RAILROAD REGULATION

### January 21, 1891

From James S. Hogg, "Message to the Legislature," January 21, 1891, Texas *Senate Journal,* Twenty-second Legislature, Regular Session (Austin, 1891), 55-58.

In response to the great agricultural depression that lasted for more than three decades after the Civil War, western farmers increasingly demanded government regulation of monopolies and trusts, particularly of railroads. Railroads were the symbol of control by eastern magnates of the economic forces of the country. Furthermore, they were the lifeline upon which the very existence of most farmers in the west depended, and it was felt that their rates for hauling farm products were exorbitant and unfair. The reluctance of the Democrats in Texas to attack big business led to a number of protest movements. The Farmers' Alliance, the strongest of these groups, in 1886 adopted a political program demanding strict regulation of railroads. This mandate, and the growing public demand for such control, influenced the Democratic Party in 1888 to adopt a similar plank; a bill (inspired by Attorney General James S. Hogg), however, providing for the creation of a commission to supervise the operations of the railroads was defeated in 1889 by the Senate, on the grounds of its allegedly questionable constitutionality. Using this as his major campaign issue, Hogg with the endorsement of the Farmers' Alliance won the governorship in 1890 and at the same time persuaded the voters to adopt a constitutional amendment granting the legislature power to create such a body. In his first message to the legislature, Governor Hogg made the following significant recommendations for the regulation of railroads in the state.

. . . Whatever the constitution requires is made the highest obligation upon the law maker, for that is the people's command. Obedience to it is pledged by the oath he takes. Next to this are the pledges adopted by the ascendant political party in its platform—one of the most solemn means used by a majority of the people in uniting to declare their will to the law making powers. If such demands and pledges are consistent with the constitution, then it comports with duty and propriety for all those who have been elected on that platform to heed and redeem them. In all particulars the constitution should be strictly adhered to and obeyed. In no respect should party pledges be slighted by its members when no fundamental law may be violated by giving them effect.

Thus obligated, most of the members of the present legislature and the executive are committed to the enactment of laws in the order named as follows:

1. Creating and providing for the successful operation of a railway commission.

2. Prohibiting corporate monopolies and perpetuities as to land and titles thereto.

3. To provide for the support and maintenance of public free schools for six months of each year.

4. For the proper endowment and maintenance of the university and its branches and other educational institutions.

5. Establishing and supporting a home for the disabled Confederate soldiers.

6. Requiring railways in the State to provide separate coaches for their white and black passengers. . . .

Neither of them is repugnant to the fundamental law, but they are all within legislative powers that can be safely exercised under the limitations of wisdom and caution. Consecutively they should be taken into account, and given that careful thought and faithful attention due to the source from which they spring, and the important relations they bear to public interests.

### RAILWAY COMMISSION.

For fourteen years the State constitution has provided that "the Legislature shall pass laws to correct abuses and to prevent unjust discrimination and extortion in the rates of freight and passenger fares on the different railroads in this State, and shall from time to time pass laws establishing reasonable maximum rates of charges for the transportation of passengers and freight on said railroads, and enforce all such laws by adequate penalties."

At no time has this mandate been obeyed, though at each recurring session of the Legislature since its promulgation futile efforts have been made to do so. Nothing contributed to that failure so much as the impracticability of the Legislature, as a body, performing such services. Establishment by it of "reasonable maximum rates of charges" for traffic carried over the railroads in Texas could not have been done unless the legislature had remained in almost perpetual session, which the constitution, by another section, prohibited. "Maximum" rates could have been adopted, it is true, but "reasonable" ones could not. . . . Confronted by such difficulties, the legislature wisely submitted, and the people with decided emphasis have adopted, an amendment to that section of the constitution, completely removing all real and imaginary impediments to the free exercise of their long known wishes on the subject. By that amendment the legislature is expressly required to "pass laws regulating railroad freight and passenger tariffs;" but it is also given the right, in the performance of the duty, to "provide and establish all requisite means and agencies with such powers as may be deemed adequate and advisable."

From the well known circumstances attending its submission by the legislature, added to the emphatic expression in the platform on the subject, the adoption of this amendment was tantamount to a sovereign command that a railway commission should be created. . . . [The Executive, therefore,] begs to suggest that the commission to be created should be composed of three members, to be appointed by the Governor, with the advice and consent of the Senate, and to be clothed with all the power necessary to make, establish and maintain, for government of railway companies, reasonable rates of charges and rules for the handling and transportation of passengers and freight by them having origin and destination within this State. The act should fully provide for the commission's organization and support, prescribe its powers and duties in making and publishing necessary rules and regulations to govern transportation; define the kind of common carrier to be regulated, which should by all means include express companies; require detailed reports from railway companies of their property, liabilities and business, and of their contracts and dealings in general with persons and corporations, according to the plan of account directed by the commission; authorize investigations of their affairs by inspections of the corporate books and on the testimony of witnesses; have them furnish duplicate freight receipts to shippers when demanded; prohibit and punish rebates, extortion and discrimination by them; make certain the amount of damage to become due to and subject to recovery in a court by any person whose freight the company shall refuse or neglect to carry at the rate so established; prescribe a penalty to be recovered in court by the State for the violation or disobedience by them of any rate or rule adopted by the commission, and in all respects vest it with power to fully accomplish its laudable purpose—to give freedom to commerce, security to the railroads and protection to the public. . . .

In the general arrangement and construction of the act judicious care should be exercised. Doubtless it would be wise to so frame it that each particular branch or topic treated will be confined to an independent section. Exceptions, provisos and qualifying clauses to any section should be avoided. If either of the like is proposed and possesses merit, let it stand alone. By this method any provision of the act that may be held invalid can be removed and yet leave the main object and effect of the law unimpaired. . . . Possessed of unlimited resources, the creatures upon whom the law must place reasonable restraints are amply able and may attempt to impede its efficacy by perverse litigation. If great care is not taken in its drafting and enactment, they may not only challenge in the State and Federal courts the authority of the commission to perform the duties in obedience to the act, but they may resort to perplexing contests with every citizen who seeks protection under the rules and regulations prescribed by it. No rights or remedies consistent with propriety or fair dealing ought to be denied the common carriers. On the other hand, a multiplicity of actions and expensive litigation should be avoided if possible, out of regard to the shipper's rights. To compass this it is well to provide that within a named period after the adoption of any rule or rate by the commission the company to be affected by or that objects to it shall file a protest with the commission, or proceed to enjoin its enforcement in a court of competent jurisdiction, or all privilege to do so elsewhere will be thereby waived; and further, that no defense impeaching the validity of a regulation or the reasonableness of or authority for a rate should be permitted to an action brought by a citizen to recover the damages prescribed by law for a failure of the company to respect his rights arising under it. In other words, the law can and ought to be so framed as to relieve the citizen from any contest with the common carriers involving the validity of any rate or rule prescribed by the commissioners, but all such questions should, if at all, be brought to an issue between the commission on the one side and the railway company on the other. Let it be made possible for every shipper to have a classification of the freights and a schedule of rates by which he can be guided as to his rights in dealing with them. He should know that when he tenders his commodities to the agent of the carrier for shipment, together with the money due therefor according to the rate prescribed in the schedule, he has

discharged all his obligations in the premises, and that on the company's failure or refusal to perform its duties in carrying the freight, he can go into the courts of his county and, on proof of these facts recover the penalty prescribed by the law. At once will be perceived the potency of such safeguards.

Rates fixed by the commission in most instances will be general. The question as to whether they are fair and reasonable can best be settled by the commission or between the railways and the commission in the courts of the country. Having the means and power necessary to procure full information on the subject, an intelligent commission, supported by the state government, could with more equality and assurance cope with the combined resistance of the railway companies in the adjustment of all important issues resulting from the enactment of this law than any citizen.

In the prolonged contest that may follow, all known technicalities, and delays naturally would be resorted to by the interested companies to avert the wholesome effect of the commission's work. To avoid the injury that may be caused the public by such a course on the part of the companies, it is respectfully suggested that your honorable bodies pass suitable laws in addition to the one under discussion, to continue in force until all litigation impeaching the authority of the commission shall have ceased. Properly guarded and carefully framed, with justice alone in view, such a measure would be constitutional, effectual, and of great general relief.

Before dismissing this important subject it is perhaps well to draw your attention to a few other important features valuable to incorporate in the law establishing the commission, which are: That all temptations to engage in business or to use the great powers reposed in the commissioners to subserve political ends be removed. This can be done by providing that no member of the commission during his term of office, shall engage in any commercial, agricultural, mining, or other avocation, or be holder or owner of any stock or bonds, or have an interest in or be employed by any railroad company or other common carrier during his term of office, or be eligible to any other public position of emolument or trust for the period of two years after the expiration of his term as commissioner. The wholesome purpose of these two suggestions is manifest. The salary ought to be sufficient to command the best talent and to relieve the commissioners of any necessity or inducement to engage in any other pursuit for the support of themselves and families during their public service. They should be paid well, and in return be expected to devote their entire time and talents to the grave and responsible duties demanded of them by the public. . . .

One of the great achievements by the commission, desirable by all classes, should be the removal of the railway from politics. With the feature of disqualification as suggested it is not impossible for this result to be fully attained. In many other respects a plain, circumspect law, administered by honorable, painstaking commissioners, will conduce much to the peace and prosperity of the railways and the public. The constant friction resulting in so many antagonisms between the citizens and the carriers will be abated. The biennial political agitations and corrupting influence of corporate power in the elections, always productive of discontent, jealousy and unhappiness among the just people, will be at an end; local commerce will become unfettered and free, and the wholesome influence and stimulus of reasonable, business like rates that the commission will doubtless prescribe cannot fail of general good. Instead of foreign traffic managers levying the highest rate that our local commerce can possibly bear—not for corporate purposes, but to support speculative schemes, unjust and hurtful alike of the railways and the people—we will have commissioners who will fix fair rates with the view of stimulating productions, swelling the volume of trade and developing the interests of both the public and the railways. As it is now, a large proportion of the products of the different sections of this state are denied transportation in exchange one for the other by reason of the arbitrary and high rates fixed by managers wholly unacquainted with, not to say indifferent to, our resources, necessities, and rights. A capable commission will not do violence to the interests of the common carriers or to their creditors; neither will it permit them to oppress commerce by high and unreasonable tolls. Under its wise

management the railways may certainly expect the people to be more congenial and friendly with them.

Influenced by equitable rates, it is confidently hoped and believed that the varied products of the State will become common articles of exchange; that factories and mills will spring up in every section to consume the raw material at hand and supply local demands for their finished goods; that the volume of business upon and net earnings of the railways will be greatly increased; that our commerce will seek its natural and cheapest route over the Gulf way to the markets of the world; that our domestic railways will be relieved from oppressing a people who have ever freely welcomed, paid and fostered them; that their builders and honest bondholders will be protected from the rapacity of speculators and stock-jobbers; that short roads will become plentiful and profitable under local ownership, control and management, as feeders to and having outlets over the trunk and waterways; and that general confidence in the ability of the government to judiciously control its corporate creatures will be restored to the sovereign people, whose will is the incorruptible fountain from whence flows freely the purest essence of justice. . . .

## 109. THE POPULIST PARTY: ITS FIRST STATE PLATFORM

### August 17-18, 1891

From *The Dallas Morning News,* August 18, 1891.

The Populist Party (officially titled The People's Party) was launched as a national organization at Cincinnati in May, 1891, in a convention composed mostly of delegates of the Northwest Farmers' Alliance. This move was the culmination of years of political protest against the major parties for their failure to espouse programs designed to alleviate the distressful condition of the farmer. But the Southern Farmers' Alliance, still hoping to capture control of the Democratic Party, was reluctant to join in the formation of a national party. However, it had already enunciated a set of demands that presaged its break with the Democrats, and in August about fifty delegates from Texas met in Dallas and drew up a platform and plans for the elections of the next year. The platform, which follows, repudiated both major parties and added eleven planks to those adopted at Cincinnati.

. . . . Profoundly impressed that we, the people's party of Texas, should declare to the world our position on vital issues and pledge ourselves to enact radical reforms of the abuses and usurpations of power by those who have been elevated to positions by the democratic and republican parties in the national and state governments, and trusting in the guidance of divine Providence, we do hereby charge that these parties have fastened a system of finance on the nation which is sapping the vitals of our institutions and enslaving our people. That they have extended every aid and fostering care to corporate enterprises, organized to oppress and enslave the people, and subvert the principles of Jefferson, Jackson, and Lincoln, and at the same time have, and do now, refuse to aid or assist the laborers, producers, and business men, by just and wholesome laws, to maintain their rights and interests and reap the full rewards of their own efforts, but do still assist the banks and sharks of Wall Street and Lombard Street in controlling the volume of money, bringing down prices, and bringing panics in business and stagnation to industry to

fill their coffers by using foreclosure and speculation. They have loaned money to banks, expositions, and railroads but refuse such relief to the producer. They have built warehouses for the importer's merchandise and the whiskey man's spirits, national parks for the pleasure seeking usurer and speculator, costly federal building to enhance real estate values in many cities, but refuse to accommodate the producer with a warehouse, by which he can paralyze the damning influences of speculators and shylocks. They have loaned money for various purposes and now find it wrong to assist the debt, mortgage, and usury ridden people of this country, who, under the guise of free men, are shivering in the wintry blasts of poverty and fast approaching the crisis which all free nations before us have come to—national decay and loss of national manhood.

They have denied us the free coinage of silver for eighteen years, although the millions of servile voters of both parties have demanded it earnestly. They have fastened unequal burdens on men, "grievous to be borne, but have not touched them with the tips of their fingers." They have snatched our government from the hands of economy and now a billion dollars is spent by a single Congress; both parties vieing with each other in making big appropriations for rivers, harbors, public buildings, extravagances of officials, congressmen, the pensioning of rich widows, burying dead congressmen, etc. They have denied the country an income tax law, while the taxes of the country should be collected from each man in proportion to his ability to support the government. They have suffered abuses in railway transportation and telegraph corporations to continue and to grow more aggravated and intense until these corporations are wielding dreaded influences in national and state politics and have become the able allies to produce speculators in controlling prices and enslaving the people. They have refused to amend our organic law so as to make United States senators and the president elective by direct vote of the people. While fraud and misrepresentation has run rampant in the selection of our chief executives, the United States senate has become a den of millionaires, who are infinitely a more terrible menace to free government than the dreaded house of lords of Great Britain. Stealing the guise of heaven in which to serve the purposes of hades, they have, in the name of democracy, here in Texas, squandered almost all the available public domain, the heritage of the people of this and future generations—an act which the much despised E. J. Davis administration would not dare to do. They have, at various times, at the different sittings of the legislature, passed laws granting an extension of the time in which railroads and other corporations could comply with the terms of their oft violated charters, which were first acquired unjustly, and many of which have long since been rendered null and void save for the acts above referred to. They have placed unequal burdens of taxation on the people, taxing the improved land of the farmer usually at from double to quadruple the price of the adjoining unimproved land of the speculator. They have failed to provide for the term of free schools as contemplated by our laws. They have failed to provide a uniform system of textbooks at the state's expense. They have hoarded the school fund in the state treasury while Texas home owners were sending out $5,000,000 per annum on $50,000,000 of foreign mortgages, when this money could have been loaned to our citizen landowners at a low rate of interest, which would have solved the school fund surplus question, lowered interest, and have stopped some of this big foreign drain on our finances. They have granted an eight hour law for the benefit of school-teachers, road workers, and all clerks and state officials, but refused it to the public employees who do hard labor for the state and municipal governments. They have failed to give the state an effective and just lien law to protect the mechanic, laborer, and material man. They have given the state a faulty, vicious, and corrupt convict system, which is a reproach to humanity and intelligence. They have refused a fair election law, similar to the Australian system, although the people have long felt the corrupting influence of the ward politician, bummer, and striker, as well as the more baleful effects of bribery and intimidation. Without recounting more of the evils of our body politic, we appeal to the people of Texas to forsake the ties which have so long deceivingly held them to this unreciprocated allegiance and come out in favor of a party pledged to the following principles, which are the platform of the people's party of Texas:

*Resolved,* That we reaffirm the principles enunciated in the national platform adopted at Cincinnati, Ohio, May 19, 20, and 21, 1891, as follows, to-wit:

1. In view of the great social, industrial, and economic revolution now dawning upon the civilized world, and the new and living issues confronting the American people, we believe that the time has now arrived for the crystallization of the political reform forces of our country and the formation of what should be known as the people's party of the United States of America.

2. That we most heartily indorse the demands of the platforms as adopted at St. Louis, Mo., in 1889, Ocala, Fla., in 1890, and Omaha, Neb., in 1891, and industrial organizations there represented, summarized as follows:

(1) The right to make and issue money is a sovereign power to be maintained by the people for the common benefit, hence we demand the abolition of national banks as banks of issue, and, as a substitute for national bank notes, we demand that legal tender treasury notes be issued in sufficient volume to transact the business of the country on a cash basis, without damage or especial advantage to any class or calling, such notes to be legal tender in payment of all debts, public and private, and such notes when demanded by the people shall be loaned to them at not more than 2 per cent per annum upon nonperishable products as indicated in the sub-treasury plan, and also upon real estate, with proper limitation upon the quantity of land and amount of money.

(2) We demand the free and unlimited coinage of silver.

(3) We demand the passage of laws prohibiting alien ownership of land, and that congress take prompt action to devise some plan to obtain all lands now owned by alien and foreign syndicates, and that all land held by railroads and other corporations in excess of such as is actually used and needed by them be reclaimed by the government and held for actual settlers only.

(4) Believing the doctrine of equal rights to all and special privileges to none, we demand that taxation—national, state, or municipal—shall not be used to build up one interest or class at the expense of another.

(5) We demand that all revenues—national, state, or county—shall be limited to the necessary expenses of the government, economically and honestly administered.

(6) We demand a just and equitable system of graduated tax on income.

(7) We demand the most rigid, honest, and just national control and supervision of the means of public communication and transportation, and if this control and supervision does not remove the abuses now existing, we demand the government ownership of such means of communication and transportation.

(8) We demand the election of president, vice-president and United States senators by a direct vote of the people.

We also recommend the following platform:

1. All the public lands of Texas remaining, and all that can be recovered, should be reserved as homesteads for actual settlers. All lands heretofore granted to individuals or corporations, in which the grantees have not complied with the conditions of the grant, should be forfeited to the State for homestead purposes; that no alien ownership of lands should be allowed in Texas; that the present alien land law should not be repealed; that domestic corporations shall not be allowed to own more land than they actually use in the prosecution of their business.

2. We demand and pledge ourselves to support a law requiring that wild or uncultivated lands, belonging to private individuals or corporations, in large or small bodies, be rendered for taxation at the same valuation per acre as improved lands of the same quality in the same county or district.

3. We favor an effective system of public free schools for six months in each year, in which the nature and effects of alcohol on the human system be taught.

4. We demand the adoption of a uniform series of text-books for the public schools of this state, and that they be published at the expense of the State, the use of which shall be furnished to the children in the schools free.

5. We favor an amendment to our state constitution authorizing the loaning of our permanent school fund not otherwise invested upon lands of the people of this state at a low rate of interest, with proper limitations upon the quantity of land and the amount of money.

6. We favor eight hours as a working day upon state and municipal work, and demand of the legislative power of this state the passage of a law so declaring; we pledge ourselves to do all in our power to establish and perpetuate the eight-hour system.

7. We are in favor of a more equitable and just lien law to protect laborers, mechanics, and material men.

8. We demand a reformation in the punishment of convicts; that convict labor be taken out of competition with citizen labor; that convicts be given intellectual and moral instructions, and that the earnings of the convict, above the expense of his keeping, shall go to his family.

9. Believing in the rule of the majority, we are in favor of a strict enforcement of the local-option law in all counties where the same is or may be legally adopted.

10. We demand that railroads be compelled to pay their employes monthly in the lawful money of the country, and in case of discharge that they be paid at the nearest station immediately upon their discharge.

11. We demand fair elections and an honest count of the votes, under either the Australian or some similar system of voting.

## 110. THE GREER COUNTY DISPUTE

### March 16, 1896

From 162 U.S. 1-91, 40 L. ed. 867-903 (1895).

The Adams-Onís Treaty in 1819 had placed the eastern boundary of what is now the Panhandle of Texas at the 100th meridian, as projected on the Melish map (Philadelphia) of 1818, a line subsequently accepted by both Texas and the United States. The true location of the line came under question, and surveys in 1859 and 1860 located it more accurately almost sixty miles west of the confluence of the two main forks of Red River rather than forty miles east of that point as shown on the Melish map. This posed the problem of whether the boundary was actually the true meridian or the line drawn on the Melish map; and the subsequent question, if the former, of which fork of Red River constituted its main course. The Texas legislature seemed willing to accept the true meridian, but claimed the north fork of the river as the main stream (*i. e.*, the boundary), creating in February, 1860, Greer County out of the territory between the two forks of the river east of the 100th meridian. The United States in 1879 incorporated this region in the Northern Judicial District of Texas.

Further difficulties arose when the United States Commissioner of Indian Affairs claimed the land as part of the Indian Territory. After a United States-Texas commission in 1886 failed to resolve the controversy, settlers, who had continued to move into the disputed area in disregard of a presidential proclamation suspending occupancy until an agreement had been reached, organized a county government. When the Post Office Department responded by changing its designations in the region to "Indian Territory," Texas retaliated by ordering the survey and sale of the public lands therein.

Finally, the United States instituted a suit in the United States Supreme Court to determine ownership of Greer County. The following document is the official summation of the Court's decision.

1. In fixing the boundary between the territory of the United States and Texas, the treaty of 1819 between the United States and Spain controls; and the entire instrument must be examined in order to ascertain the real intention of the contracting parties, and the Melish map referred to therein is to be given the same effect as if it had been expressly made a part of the treaty.

2. The Melish map of 1818, referred to in the treaty of 1819 between the United States and Spain as showing the 100th meridian, with other lines named in describing the boundary fixed by the treaty, was taken as a general basis for fixing the boundary, but was not intended to control the location of that meridian as against its true position astronomically located and differing from that on the map, but the treaty itself provided for fixing the boundary line with more precision by surveying and marking it.

3. The convention or contract between the United States and Texas, as embraced in their respective enactments of 1850, together with the subsequent acts of the two governments, adopts the true or actual 100th meridian, and not its false position on the Melish map, as the true boundary of Texas.

4. The Red river, or Rio Roxo, which by the treaty of 1819 between the United States and Spain was to be followed westward to the 100th meridian of longitude, must be taken to be the south or Prairie Dog Town fork, which most nearly answers to the description of the Red river as shown on the early maps, including that of Melish referred to in the treaty, instead of the north fork, the course of which would make the line run north and northwestwardly.

5. The inclusion of Greer county, Texas, among the counties named in the act of Congress of 1879 as constituting the northern judicial district in Texas, merely placed the territory claimed to constitute that county, but which the United States had claimed as part of the Indian territory, in that district for judicial purposes such as were competent to the United States courts, and was not intended to express the purpose of the United States to surrender its jurisdiction, and does not admit the right of Texas to that territory.

6. The designation for a short time of a postoffice as in Greer county, Texas, on petition of persons describing themselves as residents of such county, before the authorities of the Postoffice Department discovered that it was

located in the territory which was in dispute between the United States and Texas,—does not strengthen the claim of Texas to such territory.

7. The location of the line established by the treaty is to be determined by the course of rivers and degrees of latitude and longitude, rather than by routes, trails, or roads, the extent and character of which cannot be certainly known at this day, and over which, at the date of the treaty and prior thereto, travel by traders and trappers could have been only occasional and limited.

8. The territory east of the 100th meridian of longitude, west and south of the north fork of Red river, and north of a line following westward, as prescribed by the treaty of 1819 between the United States and Spain, along the south bank both of Red river and of the Prairie Dog Town fork or south fork of Red river until such line meets the 100th meridian of longitude, which territory is sometimes called Greer county,—constitutes no part of Texas, but is subject to the exclusive jurisdiction of the United States.

# 111. THE GREAT GALVESTON HURRICANE

## September 8, 1900

One of the most destructive storms in the nation's history struck Galveston on September 8, 1900, resulting in great loss of life and almost inestimable property damage. From this disaster two significant developments occurred. Measures were taken to avoid repetition of the tragedy, including the building of a sea wall to protect the island from high seas in the future. Secondly, and of broader importance, since business men had to assume the responsibility for the regeneration of the city upon the collapse of the older form of government, the commission form of city government evolved. The new form was recognized in a charter enacted by the legislature in 1901.

Two descriptions of the storm follow. The first, an official report presented from the point of view of a resident who underwent a most harrowing experience, was prepared by Dr. I. M. Cline, the official in charge of the Weather Bureau office at Galveston. The second selection was written by a representative of the Houston *Post*, James H. Quarles, who was among the first from the mainland to reach the island after the storm.

### 1. SPECIAL REPORT BY THE WEATHER BUREAU

#### September, 1900

From United States, Department of Agriculture, Weather Bureau, *Monthly Weather Review* (Washington, 1900), XXVIII, No. 9 (September, 1900), 371-376.

The hurricane which visited Galveston Island on Saturday, September 8, 1900, was no doubt one of the most important meteorological events in the world's history. The ruin which it wrought beggars description, and conservative estimates places the loss of life at the appalling figure, 6,000. . . .

The usual signs which herald the approach of hurricanes were not present in this case. The brick-dust sky was not in evidence in the smallest degree. This feature, which has been distinctly observed in other storms that have occurred in this section, was carefully watched for, both on the evening of the 7th and the morning of the 8th. There were cirrus clouds moving from the southeast during the forenoon of the 7th, but by noon only alto-stratus clouds from the northeast were observed. About the middle of the afternoon, the clouds were divided between cirrus, alto-stratus, and cumulus, moving from the northeast. During the remainder of the 7th, strato-cumulus clouds prevailed, with a steady movement from the northeast. A heavy swell from the southeast made its appearance in the Gulf of Mexico during the afternoon of the 7th. The swell continued during the night without diminishing, and the tide rose to an unusual height when it is considered that the wind was from the north and northwest. About 5 a.m. of the 8th Mr. J. L. Cline, Observer, called me and stated that the tide was well up in the low parts of the city, and that we might be able to telegraph important information to Washington. He having been on duty until nearly midnight, was told to retire and I would look into the conditions. I drove to the Gulf, where I timed the swells, and then proceeded to the office and found that the barometer was only one-tenth of an inch lower than it was at the 8 p.m. observation of the 7th. I then returned to the Gulf, made more detailed observations of the tide and swells, and filed the following telegram addressed to the Central Office at Washington:

Unusually heavy swells from the southeast, intervals one to five minutes, overflowing low places south portion of city three to four blocks from beach. Such high water with opposing winds never observed previously.

Broken stratus and strato-cumulus clouds predominated during the early forenoon of the 8th, with the blue sky visible here and there. Showery weather commenced at 8:45 a.m., but dense clouds and heavy rain were not in evidence until about noon, after which dense clouds with rain prevailed.

The wind during the forenoon of the 8th was generally north, but oscillated, at intervals of from five to ten minutes, between northwest and northeast, and continued so up to 1 p.m. After 1 p.m. the wind was mostly northeast, although as late as 6:30 p.m. it would occasionally back to the northwest for one or two minutes at a time. . . . A storm velocity was not attained until about 1 p.m., after which the wind increased steadily and reached a hurricane velocity about 5 p.m. The greatest velocity for five minutes was 84 miles per hour at 6:15 p.m., with two gusts at the rate of 100 miles per hour. The anemometer blew away at this time, and it is estimated that prior to 8 p.m. the wind attained a velocity of at least 120 miles per hour. For a short time, about 8 p.m., just before the wind shifted to the east, there was a distinct lull, but when it came out from the east and southeast it appeared to come with greater fury than before. After shifting to the south at about 11 p.m. the wind steadily diminished in velocity, and at 8 a.m. on the morning of the 9th was blowing at the rate of 26 miles per hour from the south.

The barometer commenced falling during the afternoon of the 6th and continued falling steadily but slowly up to noon of the 8th, when it read 29.42 inches. The barometer fell rapidly from noon until 8:30 p.m. of the 8th, when it registered 28.48 inches, a fall of pressure of about one inch in eight and one-half hours. After 8:30 p.m. the barometer rose at the same rapid rate that had characterized the fall. . . .

Storm warnings were timely and received a wide distribution not only in Galveston but throughout the coast region. Warning messages were received from the Central Office at Washington on September 4, 5, 6, 7, and 8. The high tide on the morning of the 8th, with storm warnings flying, made it necessary to keep one man constantly at the telephone giving out information. Hundreds of people who could not reach us by telephone came to the Weather Bureau office seeking advice. I went down on Strand street and advised some wholesale commission merchants who had perishable goods on their floors to place them 3 feet above the floor. One gentleman has informed me that he carried out my instructions, but the wind blew his goods down. The public was warned, over the telephone and verbally, that the wind would go by the east to the south and that the worst was yet to come. People were advised to seek secure places for the night. As a result thousands of people who lived near the beach or in small houses moved their families into the center of the city and were thus saved. Those who lived in large strong buildings, a few blocks from the beach, one of whom was the writer of this report, thought that they could weather the wind and tide. Soon after 3 p.m. of the 8th conditions became so threatening that it was deemed essential that a special report be sent at once to Washington. Mr. J. L. Cline, Observer, took the instrumental readings while I drove first to the bay and then to the Gulf, and finding that half the streets of the city were under water added the following to the special observation at 3:30 p.m.: "Gulf rising, water covers streets of about half city." Having been on duty since 5 a.m., after giving this message to the observer, I went home to lunch. Mr. J. L. Cline went to the telegraph offices through water from two to four feet deep, and found that the telegraph wires had all gone down; he then returned to the office, and by inquiry learned that the long distance telephone had one wire still working to Houston, over which he gave the message to the Western Union telegraph office at Houston to be forwarded to the Central Office at Washington.

I reached home and found the water around my residence waist deep. I at once went to work assisting people, who were not securely located, into my residence, until forty or fifty persons were housed therein. About 6:30 p.m. Mr. J. L. Cline, who had left Mr. Blagden at the office to look after the instruments, reached my residence, where he found the water neck deep. He informed me that . . . no further messages could be gotten off on account of all wires being down, and that he had advised everyone he could see to go to the center of the city; also, that he thought we had better make an attempt in that direction.

At this time, however, the roofs of houses and timbers were flying through the streets as though they were paper, and it appeared suicidal to attempt a journey through the flying timbers. Many people were killed by flying timbers about this time while endeavoring to escape the town.

The water rose at a steady rate from 3 p.m. until about 7:30 p.m., when there was a sudden rise of about four feet in as many seconds. I was standing at my front door, which was partly open, watching the water, which was flowing with great rapidity from east to west. The water at this time was about eight inches deep in my residence, and the sudden rise of 4 feet brought it above my waist before I could change my position. The water had now reached a stage 10 feet above the ground at Rosenburg avenue (Twenty-fifth street) and Q street, where my residence stood. The ground was 5.2 feet elevation, which made the tide 15.2 feet. The tide rose the next hour, between 7:30 and 8:30 p.m., nearly five feet additional, making a total tide in that locality of about twenty feet. . . . It is possible that there was 5 feet of backwater on the Gulf side as a result of debris accumulating four to six blocks inland. The debris is piled eight to fifteen feet in height. By 8 p.m. a number of houses had drifted up and lodged to the east and southeast of my residence, and these with the force of the waves acted as a battering ram against which it was impossible for any building to stand for any length of time, and at 8:30 p.m. my residence went down with about fifty persons who had sought it for safety, and all but eighteen were hurled into eternity. Among the lost was my wife, who never rose above the water after the wreck of the building. I was nearly drowned and became unconscious, but recovered through being crushed by timbers and found myself clinging to my youngest child, who had gone down with myself and wife. Mr. J. L. Cline joined me five minutes later with my other two children, and with them and a woman and child we picked up from the raging waters, we drifted for three hours, landing 300 yards from where we started. There were two hours that we did not see a house nor any person, and from the swell we inferred that we were drifting to sea, which, in view of the northeast wind then blowing, was more than probable. During the last hour that we were drifting, which was with southeast and south winds, the wreckage on which we were floating knocked several residences to pieces. When we landed about 11:30 p.m., by climbing over floating debris to a residence on Twenty-eighth street and Avenue P, the water had fallen 4 feet. It continued falling, and on the following morning the Gulf was nearly normal. While we were drifting we had to protect ourselves from the flying timbers by holding planks between us and the wind, and with this protection we were frequently knocked great distances. Many persons were killed on top of the drifting debris by flying timbers after they had escaped from their wrecked homes. In order to keep on the top of the floating masses of wrecked buildings one had to be constantly on the lookout and continually climbing from drift to drift. Hundreds of people had similar experiences.

Sunday, September 9, 1900, revealed one of the most horrible sights that ever a civilized people looked upon. About three thousand homes, nearly half the residence portion of Galveston, had been completely swept out of existence, and probably more than six thousand persons had passed from life to death during that dreadful night. The correct number of those who perished will probably never be known, for many entire families are missing. Where 20,000 people lived on the 8th not a house remained on the 9th, and who occupied the houses may, in many instances, never be known. On account of the pleasant Gulf breezes many strangers were residing temporarily near the beach, and the number of these that were lost can not yet be estimated. . . . That portion of the city west of Forty-fifth street was sparsely settled, but there were several splendid residences in the southern part of it. Many truck farmers and dairy men resided on the west end of the island, and it is estimated that half of these were lost, as but very few residences remain standing down the island. For two blocks, inside the shaded area, the damage amounts to at least fifty per cent of the property. There is not a house in Galveston that escaped injury, and there are houses totally wrecked in all parts of the city. All goods and supplies not over eight feet above floor were badly injured, and much was totally lost. The damage to buildings, personal, and other property in Galveston County is estimated at about thirty million dollars. The insurance inspector for Galveston states that there were 2,636 residences located prior to the hurricane in the area of total destruction, and he estimates 1,000 houses totally destroyed in other portions of the city, making a total of 3,636 houses totally destroyed. The value of these buildings alone is estimated at $5,500,000.

. . . The railroad bridges across the bay were washed away, but one of these has been repaired and direct rail communication was established with the outside world within eleven days after the disaster. Repairs and extensions of wharfs are now being pushed forward with great rapidity. Notwithstanding the fact that the streets are not yet clean and dead bodies are being discovered daily among the drifted debris, the people appear to have confidence in the place and are determined to rebuild and reestablish themselves here. Galveston being one of the richest cities of its size in the United States, there is no question but that business will soon regain its normal condition and the city will grow and prosper as she did before the disaster. . . . Improvements will be made stronger and more judiciously; for the past twenty-five years they have been made with the hurricane of 1875 in mind, but no one ever dreamed that the water would reach the height observed in the present case. The railroad bridges are to be built ten feet higher than they were before. The engineer of the Southern Pacific Company has informed me that they will construct their wharfs so that they will withstand even such a hurricane as the one we have just experienced.

I believe that a sea wall, which would have broken the swells, would have saved much loss of both life and property. . . .

From the officers of the U. S. Engineer tug *Anna,* I learn that the wind at the mouth of the Brazos River went from north to southwest by way of west. This shows that the center of the hurricane was near Galveston, probably not more than 30 miles to the westward. The following towns have suffered great damage, both in the loss of life and property: Texas City, Dickinson, Lamarque, Hitchcock, Arcadia, Alvin, Manvel, Brazoria, Columbia, and Wharton. Other towns further inland have suffered, but

not so seriously. The exact damage at these places can not be ascertained.

A list of those lost in Galveston, whose names have been ascertained up to the present time, contains 3,536 names.

## 2. A REPORTER'S DESCRIPTION OF GALVESTON AFTER THE STORM

### September 10-11, 1900

From the *Houston Daily Post,* September 12, 1900.

Martial law was proclaimed in Galveston on Monday and every soldier was called to duty. Mayor [Walter C.] Jones was appointed special policeman. When I found him on Tremont street, the orders were to protect the property of every citizen and to protect the dead. The military authorities gave orders that where a person was caught looting the dead that he was to be shot, and before I left the city at 4 p.m. the report was that four persons had been executed by the soldiers.

The citizens' committee established a number of morgues about the city and during the morning of Monday bodies were carried to these places. No effort was made Sunday to recover the dead, as the water was still high. A large number were collected before noon, and the burial of the dead began, but it was found impossible to dig graves on the island for this purpose. Messrs. McMaster and Morrisay then took charge of the duty, and engaging a tugboat and barge, they began arrangements to send the bodies to sea. Center street wharf was used for the loading, and every wagon, dray, boat, or cart to be found was impressed into service, and the bodies were carried to the wharf. There was no time to stop for identification. Decomposition had set in, the town was full of stench, and at once every one began to think of the pestilence which would follow unless the dead were at once disposed of. Volunteers were called for and a few responded. Others were impressed, and Father Kerwin of the Catholic church went through the city calling for volunteers to load the barge. I saw boatload after boatload, fifteen and twenty bodies at a time, brought to the wharf and put upon the barge. The endurance of men was not for a long time, however. They could not stand the stench and others were called for, but the curious crowd which gathered at the wharf would disperse whenever it was said that more men were needed. . . . The day I was there the barge was loaded with 1000 bodies and was towed out to sea. Weights were attached to each and they were buried in the gulf. The captain of the steamship Pensacola, which was in the harbor at the time, volunteered his ship for burial purposes and as I left the island arrangements were being made to load his vessel.

The estimates as to the loss of life are varied. . . . From what I could learn I consider that more than 5000 persons were lost. . . . The complete list will never be known. Families have been wiped out of existence and the condition of the minds of the people is such that they can not remember who were their friends and neighbors. It was almost insanity. They know not which way to turn for succor.

Up to Monday afternoon [drinking] water was a very scarce article. The water works plant was not in working condition and what water was on hand was used judiciously. . . .

There is no difference in any part of the city as regards the death rate. . . . They are found everywhere. They have been buried beneath the ruins of former homes, and they have been washed miles from the places where they once lived. . . .

The loss of animal life on the island was something terrible. Thousands of cattle and horses were drowned, and lay about the streets of the city. The committee decided that the best thing to do, would be to dump all of these bodies into the bay, and let them float out with the tide, and if caught in the gulf flow they would be taken far away. This was being done Monday. . . .

I came away from Galveston in a rowboat. We started from Twenty-first street bridge. I counted as many as

100 bodies floating near the wharfs. No effort was being made to handle them at that time, as it was deemed advisable with the limited force available to dispose of those on the island. . . .

It has been asked why the bodies are being hurried away, and no identification being made. Were one to see the dead, the question would be answered by a look at one body and one alone. The faces are swollen and blue. Timbers have bruised them, and to attempt to identify them would cause a delay which could not be allowed, and the effort would be without result in 99 cases out of a 100. The only possible way to ascertain a list of the dead, is for each family to call a roll when the present condition has been relieved and then the list would be far from complete.

# 112. SPINDLETOP AND THE BEGINNING OF THE MODERN OIL INDUSTRY

## 1901-1903

Since the first visits by Spaniards, petroleum had been known to exist in Texas, but paying quantities were first found in 1867 near Nacogdoches. The first field of commercial importance was accidentally discovered near Corsicana in 1896 by drillers of an artesian water well. But all these beginnings paled in significance when Anthony F. Lucas penetrated the salt dome structure near Beaumont and on January 10, 1901, brought in the spectacular gusher known as Spindletop. Within ten years, the well had produced 42,773,650 barrels of oil. The discovery marks the beginning of the modern petroleum industry and focused the industry's attention on Texas. Other drillers, inspired by Lucas' success, soon found vast underground reservoirs of oil. Boom towns sprang up over night in newly discovered fields, and nearby quiet villages took on boom town characteristics.

In the first of the following documents, Lucas recounts the details of bringing in Spindletop; in the second, a newly recruited oil field "hand" describes life as he witnessed it in Sour Lake, an oil boom town.

### 1. THE SPINDLETOP DISCOVERY

#### January 10, 1901

From Anthony F. Lucas, "The Great Oil Well near Beaumont, Texas" (paper read at the annual meeting, Richmond, February, 1901), American Institute of Mining Engineers, *Transactions* (New York: Published by the Institute, 1902), XXXI, 362-374. By permission of the American Institute of Mining, Metallurgical, and Petroleum Engineers, Inc.

Certain geological indications at Glady's station, four miles south of Beaumont, on the Sabine and East Texas railway (a branch of the Southern Pacific) induced me to undertake a thorough test of that locality by means of a well. I had been making reconnoissances for nearly two years in that part of Texas, before deciding upon this supreme effort.

Three previous attempts had been made in the same place: one in 1894 by Messrs. Sharp & Co.; one in 1896 by Mr. J. Looney; and one in 1898 by Messrs. Savage Bros. They had all failed to pass though the immense thickness

(500 ft.) of quicksand which underlies the surface soil, clay, etc. At first, I employed the system of boring which I had previously used in the Louisiana salt-deposits. But I soon found that this method was inadequate, without modification, to deal with the quicksand. Accordingly, I adopted the use of large and heavy castings, and pipes of 12, 10, 8, 6 and 4 in. diameter, successively telescoped one into the other. Boring was begun by Messrs. Hamill Bros., of Corsicana, contractors, about the middle of October, 1900; and on January 10, 1901, after many difficulties, a layer of rock containing marine shells was reached, at the depth of 1160 ft. For 150 ft. immediately above, the drill had passed through layers of sandstone and concretions of limestone. At this time there was about 600 ft. of 4-in. pipe, weighing at least 6 tons, in the well; and this, together with the next (6-in.) casing above, was filled with water. When the rock was penetrated the well "blew out," lifting the whole of the 4-in. pipe. Mr. Hamill was on the top of the 60-ft. derrick when the pipe began to move; but the beginning was so gradual that, warned by the outflow of the water, he had ample time to climb down and retire to a safe distance before the pipe was shot into the air. It went to a height of 300 ft. above the derrick, the upper works and heavy tackle of which it carried away; then, twisted and bent by the strong wind which was blowing at the time, it broke off with a crash and fell to the ground, fortunately injuring no one. The remaining 4-in. pipe, freed from the weight of the upper portion, followed with greater rapidity, and was shot through the top of the derrick. Simultaneously, the water which filled the well (being used to keep the pipe-lining clear by removing upward the *débris* of drilling) was expelled to a great height; and a column of gas, rock-fragments and oil followed it, at first at the rate of about 250 barrels per hour, rapidly increased to 500, 1000 barrels, etc., until on the third day the discharge (by that time carrying no solid matter and a diminished quantity of gas) was estimated by officials and engineers of the Standard Oil Co., who were naturally the most experienced judges, to be at

least 3000 42-gallon barrels of oil per hour, or about 75,000 barrels in 24 hours. Probably I had been too conservative in my previous estimates.

Since this unprecedented outbreak took us by surprise, it was necessary to improvise some means of preventing the total waste of the oil ejected, and at the same time to devise a method for getting the stream under control. To attain the first object, we hastily constructed dams or levees to surround the oil. The first one, about 2.5 ft. high, was overflowed in 24 hours; a second and a third, embracing larger and larger areas, the latter covering about 50 acres, were likewise overflowed. The clay soil seemed to hold the oil fairly well, but the constant danger of fire was a source of great anxiety, by reason not only of the direct loss of oil, but also of the incidental damage which it might occasion; and, above all, because the ignition of the spouting column itself would make it difficult or impossible to recover and control the well. Even more important, therefore, than the immediate saving of the oil was the shutting of the well. Operations for both purposes were carried on simultaneously.

I was flooded with telegrams, letters and personal applications by the hundred from parties proposing to undertake the closing of the well—for large rewards. Some of them required cash down (ranging from $30,000 to $100,-000); some would not divulge their proposed methods until paid; others submitted their plans; most of them were cranks, but a few had very sensible ideas. I decided to give the first opportunity to my contractors, Messrs. Hamill Bros., subject to my approval of their plan, which I gave, after suggesting certain modifications.

The apparatus used consisted of a carriage, anchoring an 8-in. gate-valve against upward movement; below the valve a short nipple, with an 8-in. tee attached. The whole apparatus was to be launched against the column of solid oil. This constituted the critical part of the operation. But, since the oil was spouting through a 6-in. pipe, and my main outside casing was 8 in. in diameter, the new 8-in. valve, if successfully placed over and connected with the 8-in. well-casing, would permit the stream to go on flowing, with an enlarged diameter (or, in other words, with one-inch "play" all round it), so that the flow would not be checked by this part of the operation. The result answered our hopes. Notwithstanding the violent impact of the oil-column, the carriage was successfully placed over the well, and the valve, etc., were drawn down with the aid of bolts until the tee could be screwed into the 8-in. casing.

When this had been accomplished the oil was freely flowing through the open 8-in. gate-valve. We then inserted into the tee outlet a piece of 6-in. horizontal pipe, with a 6-in. gate at the end; and after bracing the 8-in. valve as firmly as possible, we gradually closed it, diverting the stream into a horizontal direction, and carrying it out of our way. This gave us opportunity to dig around the well, beneath the derrick, and place foundations for an anchorage, which would effectively hold down not only the valves, etc., but also the casings.

After this we packed oakum tightly between the 8-in. and the 6-in. casing; placed a heavy wrought-iron clamp around the former, and by means of strong set-screws secured the 6-in. pipe against any possible upward movement. Finally, by closing the 6-in. gate-valve on the hori-

zontal pipe, the flow of oil was entirely cut off. This was done January 19th, at 11.10 A.M., nearly nine days after the well began to flow. The pressure after shutting-down, as determined by a gauge connected with the tee, was 104 lbs. per sq. in.—considerably less than had been inferred from the violence of the stream.

For further protection against fire, a large iron cylinder was constructed to contain the valves, tee, etc., above ground, with a surrounding packing of sand, so that a conflagration in the oil-pools may not be communicated to the well.

There was naturally some doubt whether the well would respond promptly when reopened after a period of complete closure. To test this point, the well was reopened about six weeks after the operation above described. Some gas was discharged at first; but the solid stream of oil was immediately restored.

The fragments of the rock, thrown violently out through the iron-casing from the depth of 1160 ft. were naturally much broken and abraded. Only one piece was two or three inches in diameter; the rest were much smaller. A handful of the latter, together with the larger one referred to, were submitted to Prof. Gilbert Van Ingen, of Columbia University, New York, who kindly consented to examine the rock and the shells therein contained. He reports that the rock is a compact quartz sandstone, with grains of pellucid quartz, varying from round to crystalline. The fossils are in layers, the oyster-shells having been apparently washed into their present position by wave-action. The interspaces between the oyster-shells are occupied by less compact sand, full of small lamellibranch shells. These are seldom perfect; and, on the whole, the material is so fragmentary that identification of the species is very difficult or impossible. They are clearly Tertiary, but whether Eocene or Miocene, does not clearly appear.

Nothing has been said in the foregoing paper concerning the commercial value of this oil, the pipe-line, tanks, etc., which have been established for its transport and export; the rapid development of the neighborhood, the numerous new enterprises in progress, etc., etc. Oil was struck in the Lucas well on January 10; and on February 20, when this paper was read at the Richmond meeting of the Institute, matters were still in the early stages of excited and incomplete development, and of many features a new description would have been required every day, so rapid were their changes. It is scarcely desirable to include in the present paper facts of later date; and a general discussion of the oil-resources of this region and their technical and commercial utilization may be with advantage postponed to a future occasion.

One exception, however, seems to be specially warranted, namely, a record of the fact that on March 3, the disaster so long and anxiously feared came upon us in a conflagration which destroyed all our workmen's boarding-houses, a considerable number of derricks and "rigs," which had been located near the Lucas well, and probably about 300,000 barrels of oil, the overflow of the first nine days after the well began to spout, and during which it was uncontrolled. We had this oil dammed against the railroad embankment about half a mile west of the well; and as the dam gave out on the third day, we had lost about 300 000 barrels before we finished a better dam. In the meantime this oil had ramified into all the drains and bayous in the vicinity of the well, and was slowly traveling towards the ports of Port Arthur and Sabine Pass. The new oil-lake itself contained the remainder of the outflow, estimated at 300,000 barrels, which was burned. The fire afforded a spectacle of unparalleled grandeur. Fortunately the wind was blowing in a direction which favored our efforts to limit the destruction somewhat. When we found that there was no possible hope of saving the oil, we started a counterfire about a mile below the oil-lake; and when the two conflagrations met, there was a heavy explosion, which threw the blazing oil high into the air, while the earth trembled as if shaken by an earthquake. We were glad to know that our great well was perfectly safe, having been covered with sand, in view of this very contingency....

## 2. LIFE IN AN OIL FIELD BOOM TOWN

### October, 1903

From Charlie Jeffries, "Reminiscences of Sour Lake," *The Southwestern Historical Quarterly*, L (July 1946), 25-35. By permission of the author.

During the first week of October, 1903, I went to Sour Lake. Boll weevils had ruined the cotton in my part of the country, and, like thousands of others, I went to the oil field to tide over a hard time. By pawning my fiddle and six-shooter and borrowing fifty cents from a friend, I scraped up enough money to buy a ticket; I got there without a cent....

I landed at the town in the afternoon. I had had no dinner but was not particularly hungry. I had nowhere to go, no definite plan for the immediate future. I had simply come to the place to get work and was blandly meeting difficulties as they arose. Several young men whom I knew worked around the oil fields, and one of these, Will Collins, I particularly hoped to find with the purpose of getting him to help me until I could get a start. I had not counted on the difficulty of finding a man in a seething mass of humanity, ten thousand souls perhaps, scattered over several miles of territory; but I set out, confidently hunting the needle in the haystack.

By chance, toward night, I did meet Ben Roberts, another boy whom I knew. The ties of acquaintance between Ben and me were strong enough to justify my applying to him for assistance. By way of reply, he said he was broke too. He said he had been sick, and I could see that he was not in a cheerful mood. We strolled along together on the edge of the oil field and after a while we met a man whom Ben knew. After a few words with the man, Ben asked him how much money he had. The man told him thirty cents. Ben told him to give it to him. The man did so, and Ben gave the money to me.

By late evening I was beginning to feel a little weak. I had had an attack of malaria a short time before, and the hardship of riding all night without sleep and doing without meals was no doubt telling on me. I went on to the business part of town that night and ate a five-cent supper; then I spent the other twenty-five cents for a bed. Next morning the proprietor of the sleeping place kindly gave me a cup of coffee and some tea cakes for breakfast.

That morning I began hunting in earnest for some one I knew, particularly Will Collins. What I did throughout the morning I can not now remember in a detailed way, but the events of the evening are more clear. I recall having a fever and lying down on a pine log by the roadside and sweating it off. The fever was not severe, and after it left me, I got up and went on my way, not a great deal the worse. The day was Saturday, and an unusual number of people were on the streets; I continued walking around, looking through them, hunting for someone I knew. I was becoming bothered by this time. Two days without anything like a square meal and with little prospect of a place to stay that night were making an impression on a young fellow not too well acquainted with hoboing.

Tired and feeling bad, I gave up walking after a time. Reasoning that I could look people over as well sitting down as moving around, I took a seat on a syrup barrel out in front of a store. There I watched the people go by. They went by in a stream, hundreds and hundreds of them; I scanned every face that came in view....

Finally, about sundown, my attention was attracted to a man ambling along down the sidewalk. I had probably become somewhat weary from glancing at so many faces, and the first thing I noticed about this man was that his hand was in a sling. In a subconscious sort of way, at the same time, I noticed that the ambling gait was familiar. These little acts of perception, of course, took the briefest amount of time; and when I took a square look at the man's face, I saw that he was George Wentz, another one of the boys from home. In my whole life, I do not remember having been so glad to see a person as I was that evening to see George Wentz.

George was really glad to see me too. He and his brother John owned a tent and a complete batching outfit, and they took me in.

For surging energy, unrestrained openness, and diabolical conditions otherwise, Sour Lake was head and shoulders above anything Texas had seen up until that time or perhaps has seen since. The site is on low ground. At that time little effort was made at drainage; and a short while after operations began, a large part of the field was worked up into such a mess of mud as can hardly be imagined.

One thing that made the mud so bad and rendered the place such an inferno in other ways was the crowded condition. There were few, if any, laws governing oil field operations; no such thing as restrictions on drilling existed. Landowners sold their land to anyone who came to buy it and in as small amounts as the buyer's purse spoke for. Aided by the ignorance of the people and the get-rich craze that swept the country, many men of small means came into the field and bought acreage. In many instances land in as small amounts as one-sixteenth, or even one thirty-second, of an acre was sold. The result was that the greater part of the field was soon a forest of derricks. As quantities of water are required to run a rotary drill, the slush which spread from these hundreds of wells and which was stirred up by the men working in it made the place a sight to behold.

As the oil field was the important feature of the Sour Lake scene as a whole, so was Shoestring the center of interest of the oil field. Shoestring was a long narrow strip of land in the middle of the oil-bearing district, where development was most intensified. In many ways it was the pulsing life center of the oil field. Here the wells were thickest; here the mud was deepest; here the gas was strongest; here the boilers roared the loudest; here the efforts of men had the fullest play. . . . This was the place with which men with pride of action liked to identify themselves. As the elect viewed, no one was deemed worthy of being connected with Sour Lake unless he had undergone his period of seasoning in Shoestring.

Not all the men in the field were in the mud wading around like turtles; not many of them, to be accurate, were reduced to that. Most of them were up out of it, or at least trying to stay out of it. The constant effort to stay clear of the mud added no little to the interest of the scene. The derrick floors were high, if not always dry; and other places absolutely essential to the drilling, like the ground around the boiler and engine were by a never-ending effort kept comparatively clear. But always near by, even on the holdings of the larger companies, was the waste from the overflowed slush pits, giving the place the appearance of a freshly drained pond.

The struggle between mud and men was close-locked. There were no roads, that is high, dry roads in Shoestring. The only way of getting around in that part of the field was by whatever means one could devise. A network of large pipes, not unlike a badly constructed spider web, ran about over the field. They had been laid without any regard to system, but they were usually up out of the mud, and these, to some extent, served as causeways. The pipes, together with the derrick floors and the little islands about the boilers, served as foundations for more bridging; the bridges usually consisted of two by twelve planks thrown down wherever the crying need of some little piece of work had demanded. On these frail structures the traffic of the field was conducted. . . .

Whenever anything heavy was needed to be brought in, it was hauled by wagon as close . . . as possible; then a gang of men would take it and carry it on to its destination. Packing along the road was fairly easy, but when it became necessary to turn out into the mud, that was another matter. The packers often had to lay down more planks; they had to twist like snakes around obstacles. Sometimes they had to lay the load down on a friendly derrick floor, skid it across to the other side, and then take it up again.

One hard day's work that I remember was helping pack a lot of eight-inch pipe. There was a good sized crew of us, and we would line up on each side of a joint and lift it up with a handstick; then with measured step we moved along the road to where we had to turn off into the tangle of Shoestring. Then the cautious creeping commenced. Slow and easy was the word as we felt our way along the insecure footage. All day we went thus, back and forth, back and forth, taking plenty of time, but the work was hard, and glad we were when quitting time came.

Sometimes when an object was too heavy to be carried bodily, it was put on rollers and pushed along. I remember one day coming upon an old acquaintance whom I had not seen in many years, who with a gang of five or six men was moving a large pump in this manner. They had it on a wobbly track slowly pinching it along. "Hello there, Ed, what you doing there," I said, by way of saluta-tion, thinking at least he would stop and have a word or two of confab.

"Working like a ———," he said; and never raising up and with the sweat dripping from his face, he kept urging the men "scoot," "scoot." . . .

Another highly noticeable feature of the field was the gas. The region is sulphurous, and the gas that comes out of the wells is highly impregnated with the mineral. As the pressure was enormous, forcing out millions of cubic feet of the poisonous fumes daily, it rendered the place highly dangerous. In the early days little effort was made to dispose of the gas; generally it was allowed to escape at the mouth of the wells, spread, and do such mischief as it would. On damp, still days it could be smelled a mile or more from the field. It had a scent something like rotten eggs and at first was quite offensive; but, strange to say, when a person got used to it, he rather liked it. This particular kind of gas was what the people about the oil field called "rotten" gas. While it was disagreeable to be in, it was not the kind that was dangerous.

It was the gas fresh from the wells, less diffused and more highly impregnated with sulphur that the workers dreaded. This kind had hardly any scent, but it was as deadly as a murderer. Its effect when breathed was much like that of chloroform. If a person, or any other living animal, inhaled a few strong breaths of it, he would fall over unconscious; and if he lay in it and continued to breathe it, he would die as surely as if chloroformed.

As results actually went, however, the gas did not cause a great number of fatalities. A person had to get an extremely strong dose and keep breathing it for some time for it actually to kill him; experienced workers in the field understood its ways and were constantly on guard against it. They knew when they were breathing gas, and they knew about how much they could stand. When one felt that he was getting too much, he would go away a short distance and breathe fresh air till refreshed. Still sometimes, in spite of every precaution, one would be overcome, and if help were not at hand, his life would be the forfeit.

One evening we were working at a bad well. We were, I think, pulling pipe, and the gas was coming out of the hole, not in the strong pressure of a newly-made well, but plainly visible, looking like hot air rising from a boiler. We would work awhile, bucking the chain tongs till we got as much of the poison as we could stand, then go away a few yards and breathe good air awhile, and then come back and go to work again. I had done this many times during the evening, and after awhile, on getting an extra strong dose, I started for air again. It happened that as I walked away, a little breeze blew the gas straight after me, and I drew in another breath or two. That proved too much. I got to the edge of the derrick floor, and I remember putting out my hand, trying to reach a post for support, but I could not reach it. Consciousness left me, and over into the mud I went. When I came to, the well crew was carrying me out to safety.

Another bad effect of the gas, while not so dangerous but much more painful, occurred when a person got it in his eyes. This affliction did not give much warning of approach. A man might be working along in a gassy place, thinking he was doing well; then perhaps late in the evening, his eyes would begin to itch a little and feel as if they had dust in them. That would be a signal that he had better quit and get away from that place. If he did not quit immediately, the chances were that he was in for some days of near blindness and about as keen pain as he ever felt.

We had been working on a well two or three days. The gas had been rather bad, but we had managed to keep clear of it. Then on the third day, awhile before quitting time, my eyes began to bother me a little. I did not know much about gas at the time and paid little attention to this warning. The work was dirty; my hands were covered with black oil, and fortunately I could not rub my eyes, but kept working like one in a smoky room, till the end of the day. When I reached the boarding tent, I washed my face and hands and gave my eyes a good rubbing. They had given me hardly any pain until then, but that rubbing seemed to set them on fire. It must have irritated them slightly so that the sulphur could get at them better. At any rate, they grew rapidly worse. . . .

When morning came, the men of the place looked at me, and they said that I had as bad a case of gassed eyes as they had ever seen. Indeed, they must have been a sight, swollen and red and strutted like those of a crawfish, and with tears running out of them like rain.

I lay in bed all day. If from necessity I had to open my eyes for something, it would be only for the fraction of a second, so painful was the light. I continued to lie there another day, practically as blind as a bat. Then, toward morning of the third day, the affliction left me. Not a great deal the worse from the experience, I was able to get up and go about my business.

That much for the struggle of men against natural forces. Other things went on there of a more personal kind and of fully as much interest. One of the most prominent of these was work: the strenuous work, the work in the gas, the work in the heat, the work in the danger, this last especially. How many men in the hurry, scurry, and irresponsible management in the field were taken out maimed, mashed, struck dead, will never be known. To get the oil out of the earth and get it converted into money was the sole thought of acreage owners; and those engaged in other forms of business were moved by like motives. They halted at no obstacles. Employers paid good wages for what they had done, and slam, bang, clang, they had to have results. Hence firemen with eyes so badly gassed they could hardly see the steam gauges worked around boilers; hence well crews worked with old rattletrap outfits that were liable any minute to fly to pieces and knock them to kingdom come; hence men worked in the top of derricks, hanging on with one hand, straining with the other to the limit of their muscles to adjust something that had gone wrong. After forty years of sobering absence, it still seems to me that there was more high-pressure work going on in Sour Lake than in any other place I have ever seen.

Amid this orgy of work, there was plenty of idleness, be not mistaken in that. Probably in the previous months, during the high tide of development, there had been work for all applicants, but when I got there, there were not a few men hunting jobs. I was not acquainted with anyone of importance in the place, belonged to no fraternal order, and perhaps had little aptitude for approaching employers.

Those who did hire me, I imagine, had happened to be needing hands badly at the time, as during the first few months the jobs I did get lasted only a few days. Consequently much of the time I was without work. Being without work meant being without money, and being without money, in that place, meant being without food.

Some of the other boys of my acquaintance were in my situation. We lived in various ways. Sometimes we boarded at regular boarding places; sometimes we slept in sleeping tents and took our meals at restaurants; more often we batched straight. But anyway we lived; we were on our own resources; and our experience in keeping the wolf from the door would fill a thin volume.

One morning, Will Collins and I awoke to the fact that we were dead broke and without a bite to eat. We separated and went different paths to try to make a raise. I had no success whatever, but when I came back that night, Will displayed a bright silver dollar. He had hit some doctor, or somebody that he knew, and struck it lucky. Hungry as he must have been around dinner time, he had not broken the dollar, but had faithfully waited to share it with me.

Another night I was hungry with long developed hunger. I was working hard at the time, and had money coming but had none in my pocket. For several days my provisions had been running low. The day before I had not had half enough to eat, not a third enough. That morning for breakfast, I had a few fried Irish potatoes; for dinner potatoes again, but in a still smaller quantity. I remember well that when we went to eat, I slipped off to one side so the others of the crew could not see how scant my dinner was and how I gobbled it down. That night, my cupboard was completely bare.

Standing around a little fire in front of my tent, I wondered what to do. I had a pair of old overalls that I had not worn in some time hanging out in front of the tent on a pine tree. My mind groping, I thought I would feel in the pockets to see what I could find. I found a nickel. There was a baker shop a half mile or so away, and for this I headed. When I came in smelling distance of the shop, the odor of bread baking drove me a bit wild. I walked in and called for a loaf. The man wrapped it up and gave it to me; and I could hardly wait till I got out of the door before I bit into it. All the way back to the tent, without water, I continued to tear off the bread and swallow it, a highly relished meal.

One more string of these pronouns, first person, singular number. The boarding tent that I went to the time my eyes were gassed was a new place to me. I had never seen the proprietor before and had gone there at the suggestion of some of the well crew and on the strength of paying my board when I collected my wages. When I went in that night, I knew that my top shirt was badly soiled with oil but did not know that the oil had gone through all my clothes. When I stripped to go to bed, I could not see and still did not know that my underclothes were greasy too. Nor did I know it till the morning I got up, and then I saw I had ruined the bed.

After breakfast, I told the proprietor that I had no money and asked him if he would mind waiting for a settlement until I could go to collect my wages. He agreed readily. I then went further with my assurance. The man had happened to mention that he was going to town on some errand, and I asked him if he would buy and bring me back a clean undershirt. He said he would do this too. True to his promise, when he returned, in an hour or two, he brought a new shirt, for which he had paid fifty cents out of his own pocket. I washed and put on the shirt and left. As I went away, I wondered if he thought he would ever see me again. He saw me. It would have taken chains around my neck to prevent his seeing me again. . . .

In saloons, Sour Lake ranked high. These were of all sizes and quality; they had appropriate names. There was the House of Lords, a place where the big boys gathered and played pool and rowdied around. There was the Derrick Saloon, and there was the Big Thicket Saloon, and there was Dad's Saloon; this last was a noted hangout for blacklegs and cutthroats. Considering the character of the town, it is almost a waste of words to say that the saloons were well patronized; but the extent to which the patronage sometimes went was an eye opener to even an old denizen. After payday, when a gang of pipe-liners came to town, especially if it happened to be a chilly, drizzly evening, the sidewalk for a block or more would be filled with jabbering, reeling men.

As for other evidences of heavy drinking, there were plenty of these too, such as empty flasks by the wayside. It was a sight I never did quite become indifferent to, the number and variety of whiskey bottles lying in the weeds along the paths through the oil field.

The saloons served other purposes than mere drinking places. They were recreation centers, of a sort. Here often men met and talked and played dominoes and transacted business without drinking much, if any. Also, when a man was cold, he could go in one and warm. They were convenient places too in which to get checks cashed. Dad's Saloon had the reputation of cashing a check when no other place in town would.

In the back end of nearly every saloon was a gambling house. They were all wide open and, like the saloons, did a land-office business. My experience with these was limited, but what experience I did have was to the effect of putting my money back into circulation.

Of skin game places and other tough joints, they were likewise there in plenty. Judging from general appearances, they too were there for something besides their health.

Apology may be due for so little being said of the gentler side of the picture; for a gentler side there indubitably was. Friendships were strong; generosity flourished; and deeds of noble conduct in many ways were to be seen constantly. But it is not these softer things that the old-timer usually recalls when his mind runs back on the past in this place. The rip-roaring side of life was typical of Sour Lake in the boom days.

## 113. THE HIGH PLAINS: A GEOLOGICAL DESCRIPTION

### 1901

From Willard D. Johnson, "The High Plains and Their Utilization," *Twenty-first Annual Report of the United States Geological Survey* (Washington, 1901), Part IV, 612-627, 733-736.

Texas is divided approximately along the 98th meridian into two distinct geographical regions, the eastern being attached to the Gulf Coastal region and the western comprising a segment of the southern portion of the Great Plains. The differences between the two had a profound effect on the history, economy, and culture of Texas, causing the pioneers to make sweeping changes in their way of living when they entered the western or Great Plains region.

The pioneer, classic geological description of the High Plains was published by Willard D. Johnson in 1901. The following extracts from that work explain how the High Plains were formed and the nature of their underground water.

. . . The Great Plains are of such vast dimensions, it is only in imagination that they can be regarded as a foot slope of the Rocky Mountains. However, in the sense that, superficially, ranging down to several hundred feet in depth, they have been built to a smooth surface by mountain waste, stream-spread to great distances, they have this character. At the base of the mountains the Plains mass has a thickness, to sea level, of several thousand feet. It is made up in the main of marine-rock sheets with a general inclination eastward, due to broad regional tilting, in which plains and mountain have shared together.

But the present surface grade of the Plains is not that of the original tilting. The surface has undergone a series of transformations. These have all been accomplished by the eastward-flowing streams from the mountains. In a first stage the mountain streams, traversing the Plains, cut into their smooth structural slope and produced a topography of parallel broad valleys and ridges. In a second stage they ceased to cut, depositing instead, and refilling the valleys they had excavated, even burying the intervening ridges, to a smooth upper surface. The original surface was a product of deformation, the second of a destructive process of stream erosion, the third a product of stream deposit and construction, involving the spreading of a waste sheet to great distances and a uniform level, and to a depth over the greater valleys often of several hundred feet. In the final and present stage, virtually the same streams have returned to the earlier destructive habit, and erosion has in a large part carried away the high-level plain of stream construction. About midway of the long slope, in a north-south irregular belt, large uneroded fragments of the smooth constructional plain remain. . . .

A mountainous tract in an arid region is, relatively, a humid tract. Its streams may not have the perennial character of streams in a humid climate, but they run strong, and they carry through—i. e., they do not fail appreciably in volume and deposit their load. But beyond the mountain boundaries they deposit, because the climate there is dry. They sustain losses only and are not replenished.

The stream upon the desert proper is dwindled, and finally brought to an end, depositing the whole of the load which it carries in suspension, and a part of that in solution, because of excessive evaporation into the dry air on the one hand, and because, on the other, of absorption into the dry ground. The stream in humid lands runs upon ground already saturated by the local rainfall; it runs also, normally, below the general level, cutting into it and receiving contribution from the ground water. The desert stream, on the contrary, normally runs and spreads upon the surface, which either it has itself built up or is engaged in building up; and by seepage loss it contributes to the ground water.

All streams are variable in flow, and with respect to their really effective work in erosion, they are periodic. Effective work is done during flood periods only. During the period of light flow, comparatively of long duration, there would be accomplished a considerable measure of work except for the fact that flood flow leaves the stream bed paved with large material, too heavy for the stream in its feeble stages to handle. The stream upon the desert differs from that of humid lands in that commonly its periods of strong flow alternate with periods of no flow at all. . . .

The perennial stream maintains the ground over which it runs in a condition of saturation. In arid lands the ground water of saturation sinks, between the periods of flow of the intermittent stream, and has first to be replenished. The ground water thus robs the desert stream. In transportation of load, stream velocity is the prime factor, but stream volume is a secondary factor and may at times assume primary importance. The delta is built at standing-water level because velocity is brought to an end there on a bed without grade, but on the comparatively steep grade of the desert alluvial fan the load in transportation—relatively heavy because desert degradation is easy—becomes an overload, not because, primarily, velocity is diminished, but because volume is diminished. The intermittent stream finds its end, not at base-level, in the sea, but at an early stage on the way to it in the ground. . . .

In spite of the fact that the stream early loses the symmetrical fan form of extension, it nevertheless spreads symmetrically its fan of débris, to the farthest reach of its divergent, wandering threads. During any single period of flow of the intermittent stream, these threaded currents wander over a fraction merely of the total surface. They do not distribute uniformly their addition to it. In successive periods, however, successive sets of stream threads wander repeatedly over the whole, and as each patchwork addition is in fact but slight, construction is carried forward with substantial uniformity. In effect, also, considering the successive different courses together, laced flow may be regarded as coextensive with the débris fan.

Recognition of this process of building is important as bearing upon questions of ground structure, in their relation to well making and to the delivery or "flow" of wells. For every stream has a line of swiftest motion, relatively quite narrow, along which its coarsest material is deposited,

and broadly bordering which, on either hand, it deposits finer material, so that a débris slope, built up by a virtual net of shifting streams, will have a structure reflecting such a process. It will be a structure, not of bedded sheets, as the alternate occurrence of coarse and fine material in well sections would seem locally to indicate, but of interlaced gravel courses penetrating a mass of fine material. . . .

The degrading stream persists upon a line once taken; but the aggrading stream shifts from course to course, abandoning considerable lengths at a time. And fan building is accomplished not by a net of streams working simultaneously over the whole area, but by a few threads of stream continual shifting, producing a net of stream courses in final plan. . . .

The High Plains in several respects are notable topographic forms. They are gravel plains unscored by drainage, yet standing in relief. The Arid Region affords many examples of gravel-plain plateaus, but on a small scale. These of the Great Plains slope are remarkable by reason of their extraordinary dimensions. The common understanding of a plateau is that, structurally, it is a rock-sheet platform, owing its form and its survival to this horizontal structure and the resistant character of its material. The High Plains, on the contrary, are of soft material, unconsolidated, or but very partially and lightly consolidated. There are such plains, built under water and subsequently uplifted, which have a structure representing the extreme of evenness in the grading of material. Also there are soft plains of glacial origin, representing in their mass the other extreme of no orderly structure whatever. But the High Plains exhibit, in the main, in their sections, both artificial and natural, unmistakable evidence that they were built upon dry land by streams. They are remnants of an old débris apron. Their surfaces are residual patches of a former vastly extended gradation plane. That this is so—that the deep silt, sand, and gravel accumulation is of fluvial origin—unmistakably appears upon detailed examination of its composition and structure.

The gravel is disposed in courses, always, so far as they are traceable, closely following the direction of slope of the Plains. It is far traveled—i. e., is well rounded, and of material which, in long transportation, would most successfully resist both mechanical wear and chemical decomposition. In this respect the gravel of plain-building streams, well away from the source of derivation, differs from shore gravel. The latter, while made up largely of resistant material, well rounded, is nevertheless to some extent graded, including always fragments of freshly derived. Again, in the mid-slope region as well as close to the mountains, the Plains gravel is seemingly identical in composition with the harder crystalline rocks of the eastern Rocky Mountain front. It contains pebbles of volcanic rocks eastward of the range foot, in southern Colorado. Pebbles of basalt occur at all levels in canyon sections across the High Plains to the eastward of the basalt areas in northeastern New Mexico. In short, the source of the material was the Rocky Mountains; the agency in its transportation running water —i. e., streams from the mountains—and these, extending into a desert climate, had the desert habit of branching and lacing flow, and built up the desert surface with their burden of débris from the mountains to a delicately adjusted slope of equilibrium.

But the Great Plains, as we have seen, are only superficially a débris slope. . . . Except superficially, they are a structural slope of marine-rock sheets uplifted, with generally uniform eastward inclination. They are merely mantled by débris. The traversing streams from the mountains, as the alluvial covering attests, have found the structural surface, however, below "grade," and have at some time brought it up to grade, or have striven to do so, by building upon it. But while the buried rock sheets are virtually uniform in their eastward inclination, wherever the bed-rock surface is exposed by degradation it is apparent that previous to burial they had been eroded. The covered surface had a topography of considerable diversity and relief.

While, then, the Great Plains are to be regarded as in the main a structural slope merely modified by streams, they are yet superficially, and to the depth of their alluvial veneer, a débris apron of the Rocky Mountains. Absolutely, from the point of view of the well maker, the depth of the veneer is often very considerable. It is least close to the mountains, but midway, upon the High Plains flats, it sometimes reaches a thickness above the old valleys of the bed-rock topography of 500 feet. . . .

Streams in their flood flow represent the run-off from precipitation direct; but essentially it is from the ground water seeking to adjust diverse grades to a mean grade of equilibrium that streams in their normal perennial flow are sustained. Perennial streams, strictly so called, lie below the water plane; intermittent streams, above. Even in humid lands the branchings of a system of drainage at relatively high grades are intermittent—have flood flow only. In this zone above the plane of ground-water equilibrium the whole surface may be regarded as covered with them. Below is the zone of ground-water escape. But as the permeability of ground materials is very widely variable, escape will take the form of springs, heading streams, or contributing to their flow from beneath; and as clear running water cuts channels, the slowly permeable interstream areas will be drained down approximately to stream level, as a marsh is drained by ditching. Thus there is an upper zone in which normally dry stream beds everywhere lie above the ground water, though in flood they in a measure contribute to it, and another in which the ground water extends its surface sensibly above the streams, maintaining them in perennial flow after the surface contribution has passed. Toward the close of a protracted period of drought the spring sources of perennial flow become largely revealed. The perennial streams, then, in their upper reaches at least, are the measure and indicate the importance of the ground-water contribution to run-off.

But while the regions of higher elevation everywhere are the zones of intermittent flow, in arid lands the saturation surface underlies usually at a considerable depth the areas of low elevation as well. There are normally no perennial streams. Spring flow may for short distances occur in canyons at the sharp change of slope at the foot of a desert range. Or, under exceptional conditions, such as obtain at present upon the Plains, the intermittent drainage from a range may be reversed from the aggrading to the degrading habit, and, sunk in valleys to the desert ground

water, be sustained thereby between the infrequent rains. But normally in arid lands the water plane everywhere underruns the ground surface, and after floods drainage lines quickly resume their characteristic aspect of dry stream beds—not because the flood water has passed on to the sea as in humid lands, but because it has been extended upon unsaturated ground and become absorbed.

The fact that under normal conditions the water plane in desert lowland regions of seaward inclination nowhere intersects the surface, but, on the contrary, is almost universally low lying, is not to be attributed to the relatively light precipitation. The explanation is to be looked for in the deep burial of bed rock under open-textured material, which affords opportunity for relatively rapid drainage. At the same time in deserts, as regions of aggradation, the tendency is away from topographic diversity toward uniformity of grade. Thus the ground-water surface has the impressive character of a vastly extended plane. . . .

On the desert plains, built and spread out by these accumulations, the depth of burial of the bed-rock floor is comparatively great. It is variable; for, while the ground surface does not have the diversified relief characteristic of humid lands, the buried bed-rock surface will usually be uneven; nevertheless, in deserts this covering of loose material is relatively continuous and deep. At the same time, it is true, the depth to the water plane is notably greater than in humid lands. As a rule, however, the depths to water is but a small part of the total depth in water to the floor.

Commonly it is in loose material only that ground water delivers to wells freely. The fact of its occurrence in sound, unfissured rock (below the universal water plane) is not appreciable to the well user. The "voids" which are present even in fine-grained rock may be completely filled—that is, the rock may be saturated—and yet the rate of escape into a well opening under the head created by the depth of well excavation below the water plane will be inappreciably slow. A block of building stone, for example, removed to the open air from below the water plane, or "water table" as it is styled in quarries, may take days or months to dry out. On the other hand, and at the other extreme, open-textured sandstone may have about equal permeability to that of clay beds in unconsolidated material. But while, generally speaking, the actual saturation content per unit of mass of consolidated and unconsolidated material does not greatly differ, there is such very marked difference in their rates of delivery that in matters of water supply, as a rule, it is only loose ground that may be said to be "water-bearing" at all. Since all materials of the earth's crust have this nearly equal capacity for water, the more accurate expression would be "water yielding;" yet as the rates of permeability, or, what is the same thing, the rates of delivery under pressure, diminish at a rapidly increasing ratio with diminution of the openings between grains, a well in bed rock if the rock be unfissured is virtually non-yielding. Ground water seemingly ends where loose ground comes to a bottom on solid rock. Within such limits it is the water of the common well. . . .

## 114. THE TERRELL ELECTION LAW

### May 14, 1905

From Texas, *General Laws of the State of Texas,* Twenty-ninth Legislature, First Called Session (Austin, 1905), 520-565.

Interest in electoral reform, a product of the Progressive movement, was aroused by the unsatisfactory operation of the nominating system and the political abuses associated with it. This concern reached the point of official action in 1891, when a constitutional amendment required the registration of voters in cities of over ten thousand population. Then, beginning in 1895, each successive legislature gave some attention to the methods by which political parties nominated their candidates for office. A constitutional amendment of 1902 making a poll tax a prerequisite for voting provided a system for registering voters, making it possible to eliminate some abuses. Legislation in 1903 allowed a political party the option of nominating its candidates by either a primary or a convention. The culmination of legislative action came in 1905 with the enactment of the A. W. Terrell Election Law, which is the basis of today's electoral procedures. The following extracts from the law show its general nature and include its salient features.

SECTION 1. The following classes of persons shall not be allowed to vote in this State: First, persons under twenty-one years of age; second, idiots and lunatics; third, all paupers supported by the county; fourth, all persons convicted of any felony, except those restored to full citizenship and right of suffrage, or pardoned; fifth, all soldiers, marines and seamen employed in the service of the army or navy of the United States.

SEC. 2. Every male person subject to none of the foregoing disqualifications who shall have attained the age of twenty-one years, and who shall be a citizen of the United States, and who shall have resided in this State one year next preceding an election and the last six months within the district or county in which he offers to vote, shall be deemed a qualified elector; and every male person of foreign birth, subject to none of the foregoing disqualifications, who has not less than six months before an election in which he offers to vote declared his intention to become a citizen of the United States, in accordance with the Federal naturalization laws, and shall have resided in this State one year next preceding such election and the last six months in the county in which he offers to vote shall also be deemed a qualified voter; and all electors shall vote in the voting precinct of their residence; provided, that the electors living in an unorganized county may vote at an election precinct in the county to which such county is attached for judicial purposes; and provided further, that any voter who is subject to pay his poll tax under the laws of the State of Texas or ordinances of any city or town in this State shall have paid said tax before he offers to vote at any election in this State, and hold a receipt showing the payment of his poll tax before the first day of February next preceding such election; if he is exempt from paying a poll tax and resides in a city of ten thousand inhabitants or more he must procure a certificate showing his exemption, as required by this act. Or if such voter shall have lost or misplaced said tax receipt he shall be entitled to vote upon making affidavit before any officer authorized to administer oaths that such tax was actually paid by him before said first day of February next preceding such election at which he offers to vote and that said receipt has been lost. Such affidavit shall be made in writing and left with the judge of the election. . . .

SEC. 6. Every male person who is more than sixty years old or who is blind or deaf and dumb, or is permanently disabled, or has lost one hand or foot, shall be entitled to vote without being required to pay a poll tax, if he has obtained his certificate of exemption from the county collector when the same is required by the provisions of this act. . . .

SEC. 12. The poll tax required by the Constitution and laws in force shall be collected from every male person between the ages of twenty-one and sixty, who resided in this State on the first day of January preceding its levy; Indians not taxed; persons insane, blind, deaf or dumb and those who have lost a hand or foot or permanently disabled excepted; which tax shall be collected and accounted for by the tax collector each year and appropriated as required by law. It shall be paid at any time between the first day of October and the first day of February following, and the person when he pays it shall be entitled to his poll tax receipt, even if his other taxes are unpaid. . . .

SEC. 23. Every male person who will be twenty-one years old on or before the day of an election and was not subject to a poll tax preceding the election at which he desires to vote, and who by reason of minority has not theretofore been subject to a poll tax but has or will become twenty-one years old on or before the date of any election, and who possesses all the other qualifications of a voter, shall be entitled to vote at such election, if he has obtained a certificate of exemption from the county collector before the first day of February, which shall specify the day when he will be twenty-one years old, and contain all the other requisites of a certificate of exemption. . . .

SEC. 38. . . . Each polling place, whether provided with voting booths or not, shall be provided with a guard rail, so constructed and placed that only such persons as are inside of such guard rail can approach the ballot boxes or compartments, places or booths at which the voters are to prepare their votes, and that no person outside of the guard rail can approach nearer than six feet of the place where the voter prepares his ballot. The arrangement shall be such that neither the ballot boxes nor voting booths nor the voters while preparing their ballots shall be hidden from view of those outside the guard rail, or from the judges, and yet the same shall be far enough removed and so arranged that the voter may conveniently prepare his ballot for voting in secrecy. There shall be provided in each voting place voting booths where voting booths are required, with three sides closed and the front side open. . . .

SEC. 52. The name of no candidate of any political party that cast one hundred thousand votes or more at the last preceding general election shall be printed on any official ballot for a general election unless nominated by primary election, on primary election day, except as herein otherwise provided.

SEC. 53. All ballots shall be printed with black ink on clear white paper of sufficient thickness to prevent the marks thereon to be seen through the paper, and of uniform style. The tickets of each political party shall be placed or printed on one ballot, arranged side by side in columns separated by parallel rule. The space which shall contain the title of the office and the name of the candidate or candidates, if more than one is to be voted for for the same office, shall be of uniform style and type in said tickets. At the head of each ticket shall be printed the name of the party. When a party has not nominated a full ticket the names of those nominated shall be in position opposite the same office in a full ticket and title of the offices shall be printed in the corresponding position in spaces where no nominations have been made. In the blank columns and independent columns, the titles of the offices shall be printed in all blank spaces to correspond with a full ticket. . . .

SEC. 55. . . . The judges shall cause to be placed at the distance of one hundred feet from the entrance of the room at which the election is held, visible distance markers in each direction of approaches to the polls on each of which shall be printed in large letters the words, "distance markers." "No electioneering or loitering between this point and the entrance to the polls." The judges shall examine the ballot boxes and then relock them, after all present can see they are empty. The instruction card and distance markers shall be posted up and shall not be defaced or removed during the progress of the election. . . .

SEC. 56. Before opening the polls the presiding judge of election shall, in an audible voice, take the following oath of affirmation, which shall be uttered slowly and distinctly and each of the other judges and clerks shall repeat the same after him: "I solemnly swear (or affirm) that I will not in any manner request or seek to persuade or induce any voter to vote for or against any particular candidate or candidates, or for or against any proposition to be voted on; that I will not keep or make any memoranda or entry of anything occurring within the booths or polling places, as the case may be, nor disclose how any one whom I am permitted to assist in voting has voted, except I be called on to testify in a judicial proceeding; and that I will faithfully perform this day my duty as officer of the election, and guard as far as I am able the purity of the ballot box, so help me God." . . .

SEC. 61. A general election shall be held on the first Tuesday after the first Monday in November, A. D. 1906, and every two years thereafter, at such place as may be prescribed by law, after notice given as prescribed by law. . . .

SEC. 63. In all cases, except treason, felony or breach of peace, voters shall be privileged from arrest during their attendance at elections, and in going to and returning therefrom. . . .

SEC. 67. Judges of elections are authorized to administer oaths to ascertain all facts necessary to a fair and impartial election. The presiding judge of election, while in the discharge of his duties as such shall have the power of the district judge to enforce order and keep the peace. . . .

SEC. 77. No officer of election shall unfold or examine the face of a ballot when received from an elector, nor the indorsement on the ballot, except the signature of the judge, or the words stamped thereon, nor compare it with the clerk's list of voters, when the ballots are counted, nor shall he permit the same to be done, nor shall he examine nor permit to be examined the ballots after they are deposited in a ballot box, except as herein provided for in canvassing the votes, or in cases specially provided by law. . . .

SEC. 82. Not more than one person at the same time shall be permitted to occupy any one compartment, voting booth or place prepared for a voter, except when a voter is unable to prepare his ballot from inability to read or write, or physical disability, two judges or an interpreter, if he can not both read and speak the English language, shall assist him, they having been first sworn that they will not suggest by word or sign or gesture how the voter shall vote; that they shall confine their assistance to answering his questions, to naming candidates, and the political parties to which they belong, and that they will prepare his ballot as the voter himself shall direct. The judges who assist the voter in preparing his ballot shall be of different political parties, if there be such judges present, and an election supervisor or supervisors may be present, but must remain silent, except in case of irregularity or violation of the law. . . .

SEC. 84. The election judges shall prevent loitering and electioneering while the polls are open within one hundred feet of the door through which voters enter to vote, and within one hundred feet of the place where the voter is required to prepare his ballot, and for this purpose they shall appoint a special constable to enforce this authority. . . .

SEC. 90. Within ten days after a primary and also after a final election all candidates for office at such election shall file a written itemized statement under oath with the county judge of the county of their residence of all the expenses incurred during the canvass for the office, and for the nomination, including amounts paid to newspapers, hotel and traveling expenses, and such statement shall be sworn to and filed, whether the candidate was elected or defeated, which shall at all times be subject to inspection of the public. . . .

SEC. 99. Each political party whose nominee for Governor in the last preceding general election received as many as ten thousand (10,000) and less than one hundred thousand (100,000) votes [later raised to 200,000], may nominate candidates for State, district and county officers under the provisions of this law by primary election and they may nominate candidates for State offices at a State convention, which shall be held the second Tuesday in August and which shall be composed of delegates elected in the various counties and county conventions held on the first Saturday after primary election day which shall be composed of delegates from the general election precinct in such counties elected therein at primary conventions held in such precincts on the fourth Saturday in July.

The State committee of all such parties shall meet at some place in the State to be designated by the chairman thereof on the second Tuesday in May and shall decide and by resolution declare whether they will nominate State, district and county officers by convention or by primary elections, and shall certify their decision to the Secretary of State.

Nominations for district offices made by such parties shall be made by conventions held on the same day as herein prescribed for district conventions of other parties composed of delegates elected thereto at county conventions held on the same day herein prescribed for such county conventions of other parties, all of which county conventions shall nominate candidates for county offices of such party of such county. All nominations so made by a State or district convention shall be certified by the chairman of the State or district committees of such parties to the Secretary of State, and nominations made by county conventions by the chairman of the county committee. No person shall be allowed to vote or participate in any such primary convention unless he shall have first produced evidence that he has paid his poll tax or is exempt, and no person shall be allowed to participate in any such convention who has participated in the convention or primary of any other party held on the same day.

SEC. 100.  Any political party not having a State organization but desiring to nominate candidates for county and precinct offices only, may nominate such candidates therefor under the provisions of this act by primary elections or by a county convention held on the legal primary election day, . . .

SEC. 101.  No new political party shall assume the name of any pre-existing party, and the party name printed on the official ballot shall not consist of more than three words.

SEC. 102.  The term "Primary Election" as used in this act, means an election held by the members of an organized political party for the purpose of nominating the candidates of such party to be voted for at a general or special election, or to nominate the county executive officers of a party.

SEC. 103.  No one shall vote in any primary election unless he has paid his poll tax or obtained his certificate of exemption from its payment, in cases where such certificate is required, before the first of February next preceding, which fact must be ascertained by the officers conducting the primary election by an inspection of the certified lists of qualified voters of the precinct and of the poll tax receipts or certificate of exemption; nor shall he vote in any primary election except in the voting precinct of his residence; provided, that if this receipt or certificate be lost or misplaced, or inadvertently left at home, that fact must be sworn to by the party offering to vote; . . .

SEC. 104.  To guard against fraud, a certified list and supplemental list of the qualified voters of the voting precinct furnished by the collector of taxes shall be in the possession of the officers conducting the primary election for reference and comparison, and opposite the name of every voter on said list shall be stamped when his vote is cast with a rubber or wooden stamp, or written with pen and ink the words, "primary—voted," with the date of such primary under the same; . . .

SEC. 105.  The fourth Saturday in July in the year 1906 and every two years thereafter shall be legal "primary election day" and primary elections to nominate candidates for a general election shall be held on no other day except when specially authorized. Any political party may hold a second primary election on the second Saturday in August to nominate candidates for a county or precinct office where a majority vote is required to make a nomination; but at such second primary only the two candidates who received the two highest votes at the first primary for the same office shall be voted for. . . .

SEC. 112.  All county executive committees of organized political parties shall meet the first Saturday after each primary election to canvass the result of such election.

SEC. 113.  It shall be the duty of the various county committees of any political party on the day and date set apart by this act for arranging for primary elections to determine the order in which the name of the various candidates for State or district or county and precinct offices shall appear on the ticket and said order shall be determined by lot so no preference shall be given to any candidate. . . .

SEC. 115.  On the first Saturday after primary election day for 1906, and each two years thereafter, there shall be held in each county a county convention of each party, to be composed of one delegate from each precinct in such county or each twenty-five votes or a major fraction thereof cast for the party's candidate for governor at the last preceding election, which delegates shall be elected by the voters of each precinct on primary election day in such manner as may be prescribed by the county executive committee at their meeting on the second Monday in June, which convention shall elect one delegate to the State and several district conventions for each three hundred votes or a major fraction thereof, cast for the party's candidate for governor in such county at the last preceding general election, and the delegates to the said convention, so elected, or such of them as may attend the said convention, shall cast the vote of the county in such conventions. . . .

SEC. 116.  All party State conventions to announce a platform of principles and announce nominations for Governor and State offices shall, except as otherwise provided, meet at such places as may be determined by the parties respectively on the second Tuesday in August, A. D. 1906, and every two years thereafter, and they shall remain in session from day to day until all nominations are announced and the work of the convention is finished. . . .

SEC. 117.  On primary election day in 1906 and every two years thereafter, candidates for Governor and for all other State offices to be chosen by a vote of the entire State, and candidates for Congress and all district offices to be chosen by the vote of any district comprising more than one county, to be nominated by each organized political party that cast one hundred thousand votes or more at the last general election shall together with all candidates for offices to be filled by the voters of a county or of a portion of a county, be nominated in primary elections by the qualified voters of such party. . . .

SEC. 139.  Any political party desiring to elect delegates to a national convention shall hold a State convention at such place as may be designated by the State executive committee of said party on the fourth Tuesday of May, 1908, and every four years thereafter. Said convention shall be composed of delegates duly elected by the voters of said political party in the several counties of the State at primary conventions to be held on the first Saturday in May, 1908, and every four years thereafter.

Said primary convention shall be held between the hours of 10 o'clock a. m. and 8 o'clock p. m. These primary conventions shall elect delegates to the county convention of the several counties, which shall be held on the first Tuesday after the first Saturday in May, 1908, and every four years thereafter.

The qualified voters of each voting precinct of the county shall assemble on the date named and shall be presided over by a chairman who shall have been previously appointed by the county executive committee of the party and shall be a qualified voter in said election precinct and said convention may elect from among their number a secretary and such other officers as may be necessary to conduct the business of the convention.

The chairman of said convention shall possess all the power and authority that is given to election judges under the provisions of this Act. Before transacting any business the chairman shall make or cause to be made a list of all qualified voters present and the name of no person shall be entered upon said list nor shall he be permitted to vote or to participate in the business of such convention until it is made to appear that he is a qualified voter in said precinct from a certified list of qualified voters the same as is required in conducting a general election.

After the convention is organized as above provided it shall elect its delegates to the county convention and transact such other business as may properly come before it.

The officers of said convention shall keep a written record of its proceedings, including a list of the delegates elected to the county convention, which record shall constitute the returns from said convention. The same shall be signed officially, sealed up and safely transmitted by the officers thereof to the chairman of the county executive committee of the party and to be used by the executive committee in making up a roll of the delegates to the county convention.

SEC. 140. Whenever delegates are to be selected by any political party to any State or county convention by primary election or primary convention or candidates are instructed for or nominated it shall be the duty of the chairman of the county or precinct executive committee of said political party, upon the application of ten per cent of the members of said party, (who are legally qualified voters in said county or precinct) to submit at the time and place of selecting said delegates any proposition, desired to be voted upon by said voters, and the delegates selected at that time shall be considered instructed for whichever proposition for which a majority of the votes are cast; provided, that the number of voters belonging to said political party shall be determined by the votes cast for the party nominee for governor at the preceding election; and provided further, that said application is filed with the county or precinct chairman at least five days before the tickets are to be printed, and the chairman may require a sworn statement that the names of said applicants are genuine. . . .

SEC. 148. Any person who is found guilty of a misdemeanor under this act shall be subject to a fine of not less than two hundred dollars nor more than five hundred dollars, or to hard labor on the public roads of the county in which the offense was committed for any period of time not less than sixty days nor more than one year, or to both such penalties.

SEC. 149. Any person who at a general, special or primary election willfully votes or attempts to vote in any other name than his own, or who votes or attempts to vote more than once is guilty of a misdemeanor. . . .

SEC. 153. Any judge or clerk of an election, chairman or member of a party executive committee, or officer of a primary, special or general election, who willfully makes any false canvass of the votes cast at such election, or a false statement of the result of a canvass of the ballots cast, is guilty of a felony, and upon conviction shall be punished by confinement in the penitentiary not less than two years nor more than five years.

SEC. 155. Any judge of an election or primary who willfully or knowingly permits a person to vote, whose name does not appear on the list of qualified voters of the precinct, and who fails to present his poll tax receipt or certificate of exemption, or makes affidavit of its loss or that it was misplaced, or inadvertently left at home, except in cases where no certificate of exemption or tax receipt is required, is guilty of a misdemeanor.

SEC. 156. Any judge, clerk, supervisor or other person who may be in the room where an election, either primary, special or general, is being held, who there indicates by a word, writing, sign or token how he desires a citizen to vote or not to vote, shall be fined not less than two hundred nor more than five hundred dollars, and shall in addition be confined in jail or worked as a convict on the public road not less than ten nor more than thirty days.

SEC. 157. Any person who knowingly becomes agent to obtain a poll tax receipt or certificate of exemption, except as provided by this act, or any one who gives money to another to induce him to pay his poll tax is guilty of a misdemeanor. . . .

SEC. 160. Any person who lends or contributes or offers or promises to lend or contribute or pay any money or other valuable thing to any voter, to influence the vote of any other person, whether under the guise of a wager or otherwise, or to induce any voter to vote or refrain from voting at an election for or against any person or persons, or for or against any particular proposition submitted at an election, or to induce such voter to go to the polls or to remain away from the polls at an election, or to induce such voter or other person to place or cause to be placed his name unlawfully on the certified list of qualified voters that is required to be furnished by the county tax collector, is guilty of a felony, . . .

SEC. 161. Any person who gives or offers to give any office, employment or thing of value, or promises to secure any office, thing of value or employment to or for any voter or to or for any other person to vote or refrain from voting at an election for or against any person, or for or against any proposition submitted at an election, or to obtain his certificate of exemption, is guilty of a felony. . . .

SEC. 163. Any candidate for any public office who fails to file with the county judge of his county within ten days after the date of a primary or general election an itemized statement of all money or things of value paid or promised by him before or during his candidacy for such office, including his traveling expenses, hotel bills and money paid to newspapers, and make affidavit to the correctness of such account, showing to whom paid or promised, whether he was elected or not, is guilty of a misdemeanor, and on conviction shall be fined not less than two hundred nor more than five hundred dollars, and may be sentenced to work on the county roads not less than thirty days nor more than twelve months.

SEC. 164. Any candidate for office or other person who

pays or procures another to pay the poll tax of a citizen, except as is permitted by law, is guilty of a felony, and shall be punished by confinement in the penitentiary not less than two nor more than five years. . . .

SEC. 168. If any editor or manager of a newspaper or printed journal, or if any person or persons having control thereof, shall demand or receive any money, thing of value, reward or promise of future benefit for publishing anything as editorial matter in advocacy of or opposition to any candidate, or for or against any proposition submitted to a vote of the people, he or they, and also the individual or parties offering such reward shall be punished. . . .

SEC. 170. Any person who loans or advances money to another knowingly to be used for paying the poll tax of such other person, is guilty of a misdemeanor.

SEC. 171. Any person who votes or offers to vote at a primary election or convention of a political party, having voted at a primary election or convention of any other party on the same day, is guilty of a misdemeanor. . . .

SEC. 175. Any person or corporation who refuses to an employe entitled to vote the privilege of attending the polls, or subjects such employe to a penalty or deduction of wages because of the exercise of such privilege is guilty of a misdemeanor. . . .

SEC. 177. Any person who attempts to falsely personate at an election another person, and vote or attempt to vote on the authority of a poll tax receipt or certificate of exemption not issued to him by the county tax collector, is guilty of a felony, and shall be punished by hard labor within the walls of a penitentiary not less than three nor more than five years.

SEC. 178. If any person shall make a false affidavit that his poll tax receipt or certificate of exemption has been lost or mislead, or willfully and corruptly induce another to make such affidavit, he shall be punished by imprisonment in the penitentiary not less than three nor more than five years.

SEC. 179. If any person shall willfully alter or obliterate, suppress or destroy any ballots, election returns or certificates of election, he shall be deemed guilty of a felony and shall be punished by imprisonment in the State penitentiary not less than three nor more than five years.

SEC. 180. Any collector of taxes who shall knowingly or willfully issue and deliver a poll tax receipt or certificate of exemption to a fictitious person shall be punished by confinement in the State penitentiary not less than three nor more than five years. . . .

SEC. 190. Any officer or employe of the State, or of a political subdivision thereof, who directly or indirectly uses his authority or official influence to compel or induce any officer, clerk or employe of the State, or any political subdivision thereof, to subscribe, pay or promise to pay, any political assessment, shall be guilty of a misdemeanor.

SEC. 191. Any person who, while holding a public office, or seeking a nomination or appointment thereof, corruptly uses or promises to use, directly or indirectly, any official authority, or influence possessed or anticipated, in any way to aid any person in securing an office or public employment, or any nomination, confirmation, promotion, appointment or increase of salary, upon consideration that the vote or political influence or action of the person so to be benefited, or any other person, shall be given or used in behalf of any candidate, officer or party, or upon any other corrupt consideration, is guilty of a misdemeanor.

SEC. 192. Any head of any of the departments of State, or other public officer, who shall demand or receive any money or thing of value from any clerk or other person in his office, for his election expenses, or to reimburse him for money already expended, or who shall remove from any office any competent clerk who declines to make such contribution, shall be deemed guilty of a misdemeanor. . . .

Sent to Governor May 15, 1905. Not signed nor returned. Took effect 90 days after legislature adjourned.

# 115. JOSEPH WELDON BAILEY AND "BAILEYISM"

## January 23, 1907

From Joseph Weldon Bailey, "Address to a Joint Session of the Texas Legislature," January 23, 1907, Texas *House Journal,* Thirtieth Legislature, Regular Session (Austin, 1907), 242-250.

The foremost political issue in Texas immediately following the turn of the century was "Baileyism." Joseph Weldon Bailey, after serving five terms in Congress, was elected to the United States Senate in 1900. Shortly thereafter, he accepted retainers from several large corporations, notably from Standard Oil Company and its subsidiary, the Waters-Pierce Oil Company. Since all trusts were regarded as enemies of the common people, Bailey's opponents began using his association with these corporations to their political advantage; nonetheless, in the Democratic primary in July, 1906, a majority of the voters favored the re-election of Senator Bailey.

Before the legislature convened, however, the publicity given to Bailey's connections with the corporations, particularly with Waters-Pierce, then operating illegally in Texas, aroused a storm of protest. Many voters now came to consider Bailey a sort of "political saint;" others regarded him merely as a representative of "predatory wealth," who used his high office for personal gain. After several counties had called referendum elections to reinstruct their legislators on the election

of a senator, Bailey returned to Texas to "drive into the Gulf of Mexico . . . the peanut politicians" who opposed his re-election. When the legislature met in January, 1907, it re-elected Bailey by a sizeable majority even before a legislative committee had completed its investigation of his case. On the next day Bailey addressed a joint session of the legislature, most of his remarks being devoted to a defense of his record. An abridgement of his speech, which reveals some of the political attractiveness of the speaker, appears below.

It is customary on occasions like this for a man to thank his friends and forgive his enemies. I shall conform to that custom far enough to say that the men who stood by me so loyally in this long and bitter contest can command me to the last drop of my heart's best blood; but I will not play the hypocrite by pretending to forgive my enemies.

For four months we have witnessed the most desperate efforts to defeat the clearly expressed will of the people, and among the many remarkable circumstances connected with it, perhaps no circumstance is more remarkable than that this effort was inspired and inaugurated by a man who was never a citizen of Texas, and who feels no interest in the honor of the State nor in the welfare of its people. William R. Hearst inaugurated this campaign against me last June with an article in his Cosmopolitan Magazine, and he closed this campaign with a three-page libel published in his Chicago newspaper on the 21st day of January. . . .

Mark my words—the people of this State will soon learn that this is but the initial battle for the control of the Democratic party in Texas. It may surprise you—I know it will surprise the Democrats in Texas—when I declare that this fight, even as led in the Legislature, was led by the friends and supporters of William R. Hearst. And if when the next Democratic National Convention is to assemble, they dare to make a trial of their strength, you will find this same force reaching for the throat of William J. Bryan, just as they are reaching for my throat today.

Hearst is a man whose ambition is as boundless as his ability is limited. . . . All his millions and all of his newspapers could not attract me to the support of such a man, and when, with a recklessness never before witnessed in American politics, he set to work to destroy me as he had others before me, but he did not know the people with whom he had to deal. He did not know that Texans are always faithful to men who have always been faithful to them. . . . Like many other people he says things about me that they would not for their lives say to me. . . .

If there was ever any doubt about the wisdom of permitting the Democrats of this State to nominate by direct and primary vote their candidate for the Senate of the United States the experience of the last four months has removed that doubt. This is a government of the people and for the people and by the people.

You gentlemen of the Legislature are not sent here to represent yourselves. You are sent here to represent your constituents. And whenever you reach the point that you can not conscientiously do what your people have told you to do, as honest men you ought to surrender back to the people the office which they gave you. . . . My judgment is that there is no principle underlying free government which is more sacred than obedience to the will of the people. . . .

I did not know, I had no idea that when the contest amongst the people and before the people was over that there would be any contest in the Legislature. If I had—no, I will not phrase it that way. If the people had known that, some of the men who are here would not be here. . . .

I appeal to you, when the heat and bitterness of this conflict has died out in your minds, I appeal to you whether there will be one amongst you willing to stand up and say that any man ought to hold the people's office and disregard the people's will. That's fundamental; that's axiomatic; that is essential to the security and the perpetuity of these free institutions. . . .

Who will affirm that 163, taken by honorable distinction from the body of their fellow citizens, can make a wiser choice than the 300,000 Democrats who participated in the primary? . . .

Now fellow citizens, I have had some delightful experiences in this ordeal. I have walked through the fire and, thank God, like the Hebrew children, a spirit walked with me, preserving my garments from even the smell of the flame. One of the most delightful recollections that I shall always cherish of this contest is the fidelity of the Democratic farmers of this State. When they inaugurated this campaign and described me as an attorney for corporations, as a rich and prosperous lawyer, they thought they would inflame the minds of the farmers in this State to a point of incomparable indignation; and yet, so far from that expectation having been fulfilled, 80 per cent of the Democratic farmers of Texas are with me today as they were with me before this crusade began. . . .

The whole war on me has been based upon some moral or ethical principle. It has not been charged that in all my practice of the law I ever took a lawsuit that related in the remotest degree to the legislation in Congress. I know it has sometimes been said, as a matter accepted for the truth, that I have been practicing law for public service corporations subject to the jurisdiction of Congress. There is no truth in it so far as it relates to me. I will not say that a man can not be honest and do it, because I do know some honest Senators and Representatives in Congress who are doing it, but I have never done it, because it did not appeal to me as exactly the suitable thing to do. No pretense that I ever had a lawsuit that affected any department of the Government, State, Federal, country or municipal, but the whole thing has been a moral and an ethical question they say; but if it is a moral and ethical question, I would rather allow the ministers to settle that than the politicians. I think they are better judges of a question like that than some politicians that I know. . . .

Sixteen years ago I entered the House of Representatives, the youngest member of that body. I bore myself in a manner and with a diligence that I won my way to the first place in my party there. In six years after I had entered there, the youngest member, I had the honor to be nominated by my party as its candidate for Speaker of that great assembly, a distinction which never before then or since has been conferred upon a Representative from Texas. I served in that high capacity. While I do not claim to have served with a wisdom that I could have wished, yet I so led my party that at the next election, though it was held amidst the clash and resounding of victorious arms following the conclusion of the Spanish War, I so led it that a change in seven Congressional Districts in the United States would have reduced our Republican adversaries to a minority in the House of Representatives. The margin has never been so narrow since then. After I had served in the House ten years, I was called by the people of Texas to a broader and a higher field of usefulness. I was transferred to the Senate, and before I had completed my first term there, by the unanimous and common consent of my Democratic associates, there was imposed upon me the responsibility of its leadership in the mightiest conflict that has been witnessed in that great hall since the close of the Civil War. [The reference was to a proposal in Congress to regulate railroad rates and fares.—Eds.]

## 116. PROHIBITION VERSUS LOCAL OPTION

### 1908-1910

The major political issue in Texas between 1907 and 1914 was statewide prohibition versus local option. Unlike the farmers' demand for reform, the prohibition movement was primarily moral rather than economic, and its development must be credited largely to the churches and allied organizations. An attempt to substitute statewide prohibition for local option by constitutional amendment failed in 1887, but the prohibitionists refused to concede failure, and shortly renewed their fight. Their growing strength and success, both in local option elections and in the legislature, inspired their opponents to organize the Texas Local Option Association, the Texas Brewers' Association, and the Retail Liquor Dealers' Association. When the electorate in the 1908 Democratic Party primary requested that the legislature submit a constitutional amendment on prohibition, the anti-prohibitionists, in a strategy meeting at Houston, led by C. K. Bell and Jacob W. Wolters, on October 12 adopted the platform and resolutions which appear in the first document below.

The prohibitionists were unable to muster the necessary two-thirds of the legislature to have the amendment submitted, but the voters in the Democratic Party primary in 1910 again favored submission, this time by a substantial majority. Thus encouraged, the prohibitionists, led by Thomas H. Ball of Houston, held a mass meeting in Fort Worth and on December 8 adopted the platform and resolutions that appear in the second document below. Notwithstanding such intense activity, the proposed amendment was defeated by a small majority in 1911 after an unusually bitter contest, the active opposition of Governor O. B. Colquitt being, possibly, the determining factor.

### 1. THE ANTI-PROHIBITIONISTS' PLATFORM

#### October 12, 1908

From *The Dallas Morning News,* October 13, 1908.

Whereas, there exists in the State of Texas an organized movement having for its purpose by means of a constitutional amendment, to be followed by harsh and oppressive laws, the prohibition of the manufacture, gift, sale, exchange or transportation of spirituous liquors, except for medicinal and sacramental purposes; and

Whereas, we regard the object . . . as inimical to the prosperity of this State and subversive of those principles by which a free people should be governed; therefore be it, by this convention

Resolved, that we are unalterably opposed to State wide prohibition for the following reasons:

It . . . involves an unwarranted interference with the personal happiness and liberties of the people and violates the well-established principles of government set forth in the great Declaration of Independence.

It . . . inevitably leads to a union of Church and State.

It announces the heresy that those who are governed best are governed most, in direct conflict with the vows of the founder of the Republic.

We further contend that whatever evils result from the liquor can be better cured by proper regulation and by local laws for the obvious reason that the unit of law enforcement under our form of State government is the county and the precinct. . . .

Its adoption would practically destroy the value of a vast amount of property invested in by our citizens with the sanction of our laws; would throw many wage-earners out of employment and greatly decrease our business in all lines, decrease our revenue and increase our property taxation.

Our State, by reason of our vast geographical extent and the distinct interests of our different sections, demands for her successful development the largest measure of local self-government. This necessity is recognized and provided for by our present Constitution. We denounce the threatened assault upon that Constitution by the Prohibitionists as an attempt by tyranny of a numerical majority in one section to impose upon the citizens of other and different communities, a system of laws foreign to their tastes, inclinations and traditions, as subversive of local rights and Constitutional form, and promotive of that sectional bitterness which is unfortunately calculated to foster a sentiment favorable to the division of the State.

The experience of various states that have adopted and subsequently repealed State prohibition abundantly proves that it is a failure, and that it promotes intemperance and crime rather than decreases it. . . .

We therefore earnestly call upon the sovereign voters of Texas, irrespective of their political affiliation, regardless of their vocations, callings, or professions, and whatever may be their religious beliefs to assist our efforts to defeat all such proposed legislation. . . .

### 2. THE PROHIBITIONISTS' PLATFORM AND RESOLUTIONS

#### December 8, 1910

From *The Dallas Morning News,* December 9, 1910.

As State-wide prohibitionists, from every section of Texas, assembled in mass convention, without regard to personal, political, or party differences upon other questions or issues, having one purpose in common, and that to make "Texas Dry," we arraign the liquor traffic before the bar of public opinion upon the specific charges which follow, and submit them to the people of Texas as ample warrant for dissolving the alliance now existing between King Alcohol and our great commonwealth.

The history of the liquor traffic is a history of crime, degradation, sorrow, suffering, poverty, pauperism, insanity and woeful economic waste, without a single virtue to its credit, or a sane reason for its license, toleration or existence.

Its continuance is so indefensible from an economic standpoint as to challenge the thoughtful attention of the business world and demand its abatement. It stands for absolute waste of at least sixty million dollars annually expended by the people of Texas for alcoholic beverages, hurtful and not helpful to their consumers. It calls for burdensome taxes to meet the cost of State and local judicial and constabulary expenditures, and maintenance of prisoners, paupers and lunatics chargeable to its agency.

Its cost for consumption of its products and . . . taxes due to its existence is overshadowed by the fearful results of its daily work of sapping the moral, mental and physical productive force and energy of its victims. Minds, weakened or lost; characters, undermined or destroyed; bodies, diseased or killed, bear constant witness to these facts. . . .

It is the prolific source of more crime than any other agency, if not more than all other agencies combined, and its unfortunate patrons constitute a large majority of those who fill our jails and penitentiaries. It kills more men every year than all the people of Texas kill. . . .

It is provable by the highest scientific authority to be without a rival in its contribution to our insane asylum. . . .

It is the brutal parent of a larger family of paupers than any other author can claim to its discredit, and refuses to claim or provide for its own.

It brings shame, woe and poverty to countless homes, and an army of helpless women and children. It absorbs the earnings of labor, . . . and is an ever-present snare for men and boys weak in will power or cursed with a diseased appetite. . . .

It is the greatest menace of the twentieth century to civic righteousness, clean politics, pure elections and the sanctity of the ballot box, upon which depends the value and success of popular government.

It is an enemy to the great cause of universal education, . . . and a foe to all institutions of learning. . . .

It is the lion in the pathway of the onward march of the Christian religion in its supreme struggle to uplift humanity, save men and women from sin and evangelize the world.

. . . In Texas it is the only business authorized or permitted by law which, by express Constitutional provisions, may be outlawed by popular vote of any local community in the State.

In Texas, it is the only business authorized or permitted by law to live which in effect is declared by various statutes to be dangerous to the morals of our youth, inimical to the cause of education, repugnant to the Christian religion, subversive of the Sabbath and workmen's rest day, menacing to our homes and firesides, a foe to the wives and female relatives of its patrons, and so destructive of the purity of elections and the sanctity of the ballot box that it must hide its head from twelve hours before until twelve hours after the touch of a ballot by a freeman's hand.

. . . [T]he decisions of . . . courts, . . . and the statutes of Texas . . . for the prohibition, regulation and suspension of the liquor business . . . occupy more pages in our civil and criminal statutes than do all capital felonies combined, and liquor sellers break them all.

. . . Before local, prohibitory laws, when voted, become effective, brewers, distillers, saloons and their allied bootleggers and hirelings begin the work of preparing for the introduction of their vile decoctions of liquor . . . into dry territory. They overthrow and violate the law, until they are a stench in the nostrils of law-abiding citizens and then, with brazen effrontery, point to their work as evidence that prohibition does not prohibit and that the use of liquor is greater under prohibition than under license, a claim which, if true, would make every brewer and distiller a prohibitionist.

To the misleading cry of local self-government, as applied to the whisky business, we answer that the State is sovereign, and is the unit which should deal with a State-wide evil, which no local community can confine within its borders . . . ; that the principle of local self-government no more applies to the liquor business than it does to pistol toting, horse-racing, gambling, bucket-shops, or any other crime against the peace and dignity of the State.

To the charge that State-wide prohibition will not prohibit in communities opposed to its passage, we reply: Not we, but you, insult such communities in assuming that because a majority therein may oppose the passage of a law such majority are ready to join the criminal class by nullifying it, although it is, by popular vote, engrafted in our organic law. Once a part of our Constitution, law-abiding, patriotic anti-prohibitionists, with no masters to serve and no liquors to sell, will join law-abiding prohibitionists and constitute a majority for the majesty of the law, to disprove this anarchistic cry.

The liquor interests, fearful that . . . the people of Texas will overthrow their business by popular vote when the constitutional amendment is submitted, . . . now boldly undertake to turn loose their ill-gotten gains in perfecting an organization . . . [to] protect their business by controlling the politics of Texas and shaping her future policies and destinies. To prevent this unspeakable calamity, we have gathered to call the people of Texas—not to arms—but to a battle of ballots, for the sole purpose of applying the only effective remedy to meet existing conditions, that of State-wide prohibition.

Upon the foregoing declaration of self-evident truths, we call upon the Texas Legislature to submit to the qualified voters of Texas, upon the regular primary day, in July, 1911, an amendment to our Constitution prohibiting the manufacture and sale of intoxicating liquors in our State, and for its adoption, when submitted, we pledge our faith and service and invoke the all of every Texan, without regard to race or color, age or sex, faith or creed, profession or occupation, personal or political affiliations, who honors God or loves his fellow man.

## 117. JAMES E. FERGUSON: HIS PLATFORM AND HIS IMPEACHMENT

James E. Ferguson, a banker and a merchant from Temple who made his political debut in 1914 as a successful candidate for governor of Texas, was to control the administration of the state longer than any other man, wielding a powerful influence in its affairs for a quarter of a century. During his first campaign and term in office, he won the unwavering loyalty of large segments of the electorate, particularly the tenant farmers who in 1910 operated 52.6 per cent of the farms in the state as compared with only 37 per cent in 1880, and who constituted the largest economic and social bloc in the Texas electorate.

During the election campaign of 1916, some irregularities on the part of the Governor were rumored. No further attention probably would have been given them had the Governor not antagonized the supporters of The University of Texas by refusing in 1917 to sign the appropriation bill for its operation, presumably because certain faculty members objectionable to him had not been removed as he had requested. Other charges were now made against him. As a result, he appeared voluntarily before the Travis County grand jury on July 21, and was indicted on nine counts.

Immediately, the Speaker of the House of Representatives, without constitutional authority, called a special session of the legislature to consider the charges. Ferguson supported this action, however, by issuing a call himself, probably because he preferred impeachment proceedings to court action. The House on August 24 impeached the Governor on twenty-one counts; the Senate on September 24 found him guilty on ten of the charges. He was thereupon removed from office and declared ineligible to hold any office of public trust in Texas.

Nevertheless, Ferguson became a candidate for governor in 1918, for president of the United States in 1920, and for the United States Senate in 1922; and it is generally conceded that he exercised great influence in state affairs from 1925 to 1927 and from 1933 to 1935 when his wife, Mrs. Miriam A. Ferguson, was governor. In all of Mrs. Ferguson's races for governor, including unsuccessful attempts in 1926, 1930, and 1940, her husband did most of the campaigning.

The first of the following documents is Ferguson's platform, issued when he announced his first candidacy; the second is the Senate's report of his trial and conviction.

### 1. FERGUSON'S FIRST GUBERNATORIAL PLATFORM

November 15, 1913

From *The Dallas Morning News*, November 16, 1913.

To the Democrats of Texas: In announcing myself as a candidate for the high office of Governor of Texas, I am not unmindful of the discussion which I may arouse, or perhaps the criticism which I may bring forth.

For years and years it has been quite the custom to elect our Governors under a rule which we might term political succession. . . . So, I realize that when I, a country lawyer, a country banker and a good country farmer, if you please, try to land myself in the Governor's chair at one fell swoop, I imagine I can already hear the thundering tones of "Nay, verily, we were here first." And here the issue is raised. If it can be shown that State affairs have been under the old rule administered in an economical and business way, then I am frank to agree that there is no particular demand for my candidacy, and I will have no one to blame should I be disappointed in my ambition. But the burden of proof is upon those who would thus criticise my announcement, and should the proof not be sustained, then the propriety of my candidacy is established, and upon my merits of my platform I shall indulge

in the hope that the great mass of Texas Democrats will give me their favorable consideration.

I am a native Texan. Was raised on a farm in Bell County. Am 42 years old. Seven years of my life were given to the practice of law. For the past eight years I have been engaged in banking, farming and stock raising. I believe I can show as fine a herd of Durham cattle as there is in Texas. I have never sought a public office, but have always taken interest and part in public affairs. I believe my training will in some measure qualify me for the office of Governor.

It is my intention to make an active campaign and discuss my platform which is:

1. Until such time as all State institutions and State finances are put on a sound basis, all other matters of legislation should be put aside. Realizing the imperative need of this policy and recognizing the attempt of certain candidates to ride into office on the prohibition issue, to the exclusion and detriment of the pressing business demands of the State, and in order that the issue may be clearly made, I hereby pledge myself, if elected Governor, to promptly and surely veto to the extent of my power any legislation which may be passed, through pro or anti influence, pertaining to or dealing with the liquor question in any manner or form.

Present laws are sufficient. I ask no man to surrender his views on prohibition, but the deplorable condition of our State institutions and finances makes a grave condition. It can only be met by ceasing for a time at least the factional strife which is destroying the State. Let us have more business and less talk. Instead of wrangling over the question of whether man shall drink, let us consider for a time how he and his loved ones may get something to eat and something to wear. Three years ago I voted for submission of the prohibition question to the people. An election was held and by a clear majority the issue was decided against prohibition. Frequent elections on this question will only bring renewed agitation and strife. I therefore am opposed to any resubmission of the question at this time.

2. I am heartily in favor of any legislation looking to the improvement and advancement of our public schools, the A. & M. College and our State University. In the matter of appropriations for such purposes I would only be restricted by the ability of the State to pay and an economical expenditure of public money. If we get our money's worth, let us buy all the education we can pay for. And let us begin with the little school house on the country road.

3. . . . If elected Governor, I pledge my best efforts as a business man to put all State prisons on a self-sustaining basis. If it would not involve the State in loss, I am in favor of using our convict labor to build permanent roads.

4. I am opposed to any reduction in rates charged by railroads. Railroads are entitled to earn a fair return on their investment. If railroad investment is not assured of a fair return on the investment, Texas will wait long in the future before other railroads are built.

Again, if rates are reduced the railroads will use such

action as a pretext to decrease the wages of organized labor and will use it as an excuse for their failure to furnish proper service to the patient public. I favor such firm and prompt regulation of the railroads by legislation and by our Railroad Commission as will relieve the people from the discomfort of bad crossings, late trains, delayed shipments and discourteous employees. The passenger who pays 3¢ a mile is entitled to a seat. The shipper who is forced to pay extra because he does not unload the car is certainly entitled to reimbursement when no car is furnished for him to load. . . .

5. I favor the establishment of a system of bonded warehouses with power to issue negotiable receipts, all under the sanction and supervision of the State. The demand for this legislation is apparent to every one. A gradual marketing of farm products can never be brought about unless some general plan of storage is available. Not one farmer in fifty has or is able to purchase facilities to store and house through the winter months all of the cotton or grain which he can raise. Yet unless they have this facility our entire crops must go to the markets at one time to prevent destruction or damage from wind and storm. The bad effect of enforced marketing on the price of farm products in Texas and in the South causes the loss of more money every year than any other one thing.

6. Perhaps of greater moment than all other questions is the question of land tenure and land rents. History reveals that the fall of all Nations was closely connected with, if not directly caused by the failure to promptly meet and equitably adjust the division of land production between landlord and tenant. Let us not be deceived into thinking that Texas is not confronted with this question right now. Until a short time ago a fourth of the cotton and a third of the grain crops was considered for fifty years in Texas as the equitable rent which the tenant should pay for the use of the land rented. Under this rule Texas has prospered and grown from one financial triumph to another.

But lately with the appearance of high-priced lands, the argument has become quite popular that rents should go higher to keep pace with the earning power of money. As a result it is becoming a custom to demand and collect of the tenants a bonus in addition to the usual rents or to demand a cash rent exceeding the customary rent. It is true that for a few years we have had an era of high prices and so far the tenant has been able to pay the increased rent and live without any great inconvenience. But it must be borne in mind that an acre of land that now sells for $100 does not produce any more cotton or corn than it did when it sold for $30 per acre.

As perhaps a majority of our rural citizenship are tenants, it is folly to argue that the good of society is not involved in the matter of a material increase in rents. An increase in rents necessarily impairs the ability of the tenant to raise and educate his family. Therefore, it must follow that in such proportion as rents go up, comfort and education, so far as the tenant is concerned, must go down.

Therefore, as a solution to this vexing question, . . . I, if elected Governor, will urge upon the Legislature to bring about, by statute or constitutional amendment, as may be proper, the passage of a law that will make the collection of rent in amount in excess of one-fourth of the value of the cotton or one-third of the value of grain

crops, usury, the penalty for which shall be a forfeiture of double the amount of rent collected, to be recovered in any court of competent jurisdiction; provided, that the landlord may collect rent in any amount equal to one-half the value of all crops where the landlord furnishes all the tools, implements, feed and teams with which the tenant makes the crop. Such a law is not only essentially progressive, but necessary. It involves not only the good of society, but the life of the government itself. . . .

JAMES E. FERGUSON.

Temple, Tex.
Nov. 15, 1913

## 2. THE IMPEACHMENT OF GOVERNOR FERGUSON

### September 24, 1917

From *Record Proceedings of the High Court of Impeachment on the Trial of Hon. James E. Ferguson, Governor* (Published by Authority of the Legislature; Austin, 1917), 862-865.

State of Texas vs. Jas. E. Ferguson.

Whereas, the House of Representatives of the State of Texas did, on the 24th day of August, 1917, exhibit to the Senate of the State of Texas articles of impeachment against James E. Ferguson, Governor of the State of Texas, and the said Senate, after a full hearing and an impartial trial, has by the votes of two-thirds of the members present this day determined that the said James E. Ferguson is guilty as charged in the first, second, sixth, seventh, eleventh, twelfth, fourteenth, sixteenth, seventeenth, and nineteenth of said articles of impeachment.

Said articles and the votes thereon being as follows, to wit:

Article 1. That there was paid from the funds of the Canyon City Normal School deposited with the Temple State Bank on August 23, 1915, a note of $5,000, together with $600 interest, due by James E. Ferguson to the First National Bank at Temple, Texas. That said amount has never been refunded to the State of Texas. That in part payment of the total due for the building of the Canyon City Normal College he used other funds, a portion of which belonged to the State, and the balance being in his hands as Governor, and deposited to his credit as Governor in the American National Bank of Austin, which acts constitute a violation of law. The vote for sustaining this article being 27 for and 4 against.

Art. 2. That James E. Ferguson received from former Governor O. B. Colquitt more than $101,000, the proceeds from insurance policies on the Canyon City Normal School. That at the time said moneys were turned over to him they were on deposit in banks bearing interest at from 4½ to 5 per cent and which remained there for approximately one year, and that he deposited the other amounts in banks in which he was interested as a stockholder, and in the American National Bank, to which he shortly afterwards became indebted. That he received direct and personal profit as a stockholder of the Temple State Bank from the deposit placed with it; thus using and misapplying State funds for his individual benefit and profit. The vote for sustaining this article being 26 for and 5 against.

Art. 6. That there was deposited by James E. Ferguson in the Temple State Bank on or about the month of January, 1917, the sum of $60,000 belonging to the State of Texas and in the possession of the Secretary of State by virtue of his office, said amount being represented by a check of the Secretary of State, although the State Treasury was open for the purpose of receiving same. That James E. Ferguson was a stockholder in said bank, owning more than one-fourth of the stock, and that the said Temple State Bank and James E. Ferguson used said funds and received the profit and benefit, the said James E. Ferguson receiving more than one-fourth of the profits and of the benefits. The vote for sustaining this article being 24 for and 7 against.

Art. 7. That on or about May 29, 1917, James E. Ferguson accompanied T. H. Heard, president of the Temple State Bank, to the American National Bank at Austin, and the said T. H. Heard deposited to the credit of the Temple State Bank with the knowledge and consent of the said James E. Ferguson the sum of $250,000 of the funds belonging to the State of Texas and in the possession of the Secretary of State, said funds being represented by five checks drawn by the Secretary of State in the sum of $50,000 each, although the State Treasury was then and there open for the purpose of receiving same. That the said James E. Ferguson owned more than one-fourth of the stock of the Temple State Bank and that said amount was used by the Temple State Bank for its own profit and benefit, more than one-fourth of which profit and benefit belonged to James E. Ferguson. The vote for sustaining this article being 26 for and 5 against.

Art. 11. That in this investigation of James E. Ferguson by the Committee of the Whole House of Representatives said James E. Ferguson testified that during the Regular Session of the Thirty-fifth Legislature and shortly thereafter he received from parties certain currency in varying amounts, the total of which was about $156,500. That said transaction is unusual and questionable, and that the said James E. Ferguson, when questioned as to who loaned him this money, declined to answer, although the officer of the Committee of the Whole appointed to pass on the admissibility of testimony ruled that he should answer, and the Committee sustained said ruling. That he is thus not only in contempt of the House and its Committee, but he insists that he is not required to give before the Representatives of the people of Texas an accounting of said $156,500 in currency which he received during sessions of the Legislature or shortly thereafter, and the receipt of such sums in currency, and the failure to account for same, constitutes official misconduct. The vote for sustaining this article being 27 for and 4 against.

Art. 12. That James E. Ferguson had on deposit during the year of 1916 in the American National Bank to his account as Governor certain sums of money belonging to the Adjutant General's Department of Texas aggregating more than $3,000, said funds being the property of the State of Texas but set aside for that department. That in violation of the statutes of Texas he diverted these funds from their lawful purpose and paid same as a portion of the amount for the construction of buildings of the Normal College located at Canyon City. The vote for sustaining this article being 27 for and 4 against.

Art. 14. That by an express provision of the Constitu-

tion and his oath of office the Governor is bound to enforce all laws of the State of Texas. The laws of Texas during the period of his administration expressly forbade State banks to lend money in excess of 30 per cent of its capital stock. This was known to the Governor, yet in violation of this provision of the law he induced the officers of the Temple State Bank to lend to him, James E. Ferguson, an amount far in excess of that authorized by law, which loans were made during the years 1916 and 1917. The vote for sustaining this article being 26 for and 5 against.

Art. 16. Section 30a of Article 16 of the Constitution of Texas provides for the Board of Regents for the University of Texas, who shall hold office for six years, their terms expiring one-third every two years. The purpose of the people of Texas in the adoption of this provision was to take the University of Texas and all other such State institutions from the control of politics, and to keep the different boards from being under the control and domination of whoever might happen to be Governor. By Articles 2639 and 2640 of the Revised Civil Statutes of 1911 the Board of Regents are given the management of the affairs of the University of Texas with the discretion to remove members of the faculty when in their judgment it is deemed best. That it is the duty of the Governor, or any private citizen, to call attention of the Board of Regents to any mismanagement or improper practices at the University or any other State institution is readily conceded. The people themselves have given to the Board of Regents by constitutional enactment, which has been confirmed by statutory law, the sole right to judge of the truth of the charges and the punishment to be inflicted against members of the faculty. The Board of Regents in their sphere are just as supreme as the Governor is in his, each having both constitutional and statutory duties to perform, and each being answerable to the people of Texas. The Governor of Texas not only filed charges against certain members of the faculty, as he had a right to do, but after the members were exonerated by the Board of Regents he has sought to have the members of the faculty expelled from that institution because he desired it. He has thus sought to set aside the Constitution and law giving to the Board of Regents the discretion in matters of this kind and assert instead of their legal judgment his own autocratic will. The vote for sustaining this article being 22 for and 9 against.

Art. 17. Article 6027 of the Revised Civil Statutes of 1911 provides for the removal of members of the Board of Regents (among other officials) for "good and sufficient cause." The Governor has sought to remove members of the Board of Regents without such cause, has demanded resignations of others without reason simply and only because he could not dictate to them as to how they should cast their votes in reference to matters arising before them. Such conduct was a clear violation of the law, and would serve to make inoperative the provision of the Constitution providing for six-year terms of office. The vote for sustaining this Article being 22 for and 8 against (1 present and not voting.)

Art. 19. The governor of Texas has sought to use the power of his office to control members of the Board of Regents. The Chairman of the Board of Regents had become surety on a bail bond, the case pending in Jones

County, Texas. The defendant escaped and judgment was secured on the said bond in the sum of $5000.00 against the principal and sureties, one of the sureties being Wilbur P. Allen, chairman of the Board of Regents of the University of Texas. He applied to the Governor of Texas for the remission of the judgment, which he would have had to pay and without good reason but only to influence his action as a member of the Board of Regents, Jas. E. Ferguson as Governor remitted the forfeiture of $5000,

which except for such action of Jas. E. Ferguson, would have belonged to the people of Texas. The vote for sustaining this Article being 21 for and 10 against.

Now, therefore, it is adjudged by the Senate of the State of Texas sitting as a Court of Impeachment, at their Chamber, in the city of Austin, that the said James E. Ferguson be and he is hereby removed from the office of Governor and be disqualified to hold any office of honor, trust or profit under the State of Texas. . . .

## 118. THE KU KLUX KLAN CREED

### July, 1923

From "The Ku Klux Klan Kreed," *Papers Read at the Meeting of Grand Dragons Knights of the Ku Klux Klan* (Asheville, N. C., July, 1923), 133-134.

The State of Georgia on July 1, 1916, chartered a fraternal order under the name of the "Knights of the Ku Klux Klan" as a "patriotic, secret, social, and benevolent order." The Klan made very little progress until after World War I, when a large influx of foreigners and other circumstances combined to promote its amazing growth, particularly in the South. The new order was nativist, anti-catholic, and anti-Jewish; it strongly advocated the doctrine of white supremacy, and declared war on crime. This last aspect appealed to many Americans who had no sympathy with its other principles but who were unhappy with the postwar relaxation in morals, both public and private. In Texas the Klan attained its maximum strength in the early 1920's during a crime wave when, according to Governor Pat M. Neff, "not ten per cent of those who violated the law are arrested, and not half of those who are arrested are convicted." The Klan became strong in almost every community, and a potent political force, particularly in the elections of 1922 and 1924.

WE, THE ORDER of the Knights of the Ku Klux Klan, reverentially acknowledge the majesty and supremacy

of the Divine Being, and recognize the goodness and Providence of the same.

WE RECOGNIZE our relation to the Government of the United States of America, the Supremacy of its Constitution, the Union of the States thereunder, and the Constitutional Laws thereof, and we shall be ever devoted to the sublime principles of a pure Americanism and valiant in the defense of its ideals and institutions.

WE AVOW THE distinction between the races of mankind as same has been decreed by the Creator, and shall ever be true in the faithful maintenance of White Supremacy and will strenuously oppose any compromise thereof in any and all things.

WE APPRECIATE the intrinsic value of a real practical fraternal relationship among men of kindred thought, purpose and ideals and the infinite benefits accruable therefrom, and shall faithfully devote ourselves to the practice of an honorable Klanishness that the life and living of each may be a constant blessing to others.

## 119. NIXON v. HERNDON: THE TEXAS "WHITE PRIMARY" LAW INVALIDATED

### March 7, 1927

From 237 U. S. 536-541, 71 L. ed. 759-761.

The Texas so-called "White Primary" statute of 1923 excluded Negroes from participation in the primary elections of the Democratic Party in the state. The law was declared unconstitutional in 1927 by the Supreme Court of the United States upon the ground that it was contrary to the "equal protection" guaranteed in the Fourteenth Amendment. The opinion of the Court, which includes a resume of the facts of the case, delivered by Justice Wendell Holmes, follows.

This is an action against the judges of elections for refusing to permit the plaintiff to vote at a primary election in Texas. It lays the damages at $5,000. The petition alleges that the plaintiff is a negro, a citizen of the United

States and of Texas and a resident of El Paso, and in every way qualified to vote, as set forth in detail, except that the statute to be mentioned interferes with his right; that on July 26, 1924, a primary election was held at El Paso for the nomination of candidates for a senator and representatives in Congress and state and other officers, upon the Democratic ticket; that the plaintiff, being a member of the Democratic party, sought to vote, but was denied the right by defendants; that the denial was based upon a statute of Texas enacted in May, 1923, and designated article 3093a, by the words of which "in no event shall a negro be eligible to participate in a Democratic party primary election held in the state of Texas," etc., and that this statute is contrary to the 14th and 15th Amendments to the Constitution of the United States. The defendants moved to dismiss upon the ground that the subject-matter of the suit was political and not within the jurisdiction of the court and that no violation of the Amendments was shown. The suit was dismissed and a writ of error was taken directly to this court. Here no argument was made on behalf of the defendants but a brief was allowed to be filed by the attorney general of the state.

The objection that the subject-matter of the suit is political is little more than a play upon words. Of course, the petition concerns political action, but it alleges and seeks to recover for private damage. That private damage may be caused by such political action, and may be recovered for in a suit at law, hardly has been doubted for over two hundred years, . . . If the defendants' conduct was a wrong to the plaintiff the same reasons that allow a recovery for denying the plaintiff a vote at a final election allow it for denying a vote at the primary election that may determine the final result.

The important question is whether the statute can be sustained. But although we state it as a question the answer does not seem to us open to doubt. We find it unnecessary to consider the 15th Amendment, because it seems to us hard to imagine a more direct and obvious infringement of the 14th. That Amendment, while it applies to all, was passed, as we know, with a special intent to protect the blacks from discrimination against them. . . . That Amendment "not only gave citizenship and the privileges of citizenship to persons of color, but it denied to any state the power to withhold from them the equal protection of the laws. . . . What is this but declaring that the law in the states shall be the same for the black as for the white; that all persons, whether colored or white, shall stand equal before the laws of the states, and, in regard to the colored race, for whose protection the Amendment was primarily designed, that no discrimination shall be made against them by law because of their color?" . . . The statute of Texas, in the teeth of the prohibitions referred to, assumes to forbid negroes to take part in a primary election the importance of which we have indicated, discriminating against them by the distinction of color alone. States may do a good deal of classifying that it is difficult to believe rational, but there are limits, and it is too clear for extended argument that color cannot be made the basis of a statutory classification affecting the right set up in this case.

Judgment reversed.

## 120. THE TRANSACTION TAX: GOVERNOR W. LEE O'DANIEL'S REVENUE PROPOSAL

### January 18, 1939

From Governor W. Lee O'Daniel, "Address to the Forty-sixth Legislature," January 18, 1939, Texas *Senate Journal,* Forty-sixth Legislature, Regular Session (Austin, 1939), 85-95.

The most urgent legislative problem after the Great Depression was the financing of the state's growing program of social welfare. The question became the principal issue in the gubernatorial campaign of 1936, all candidates proposing to solve the problem by new or additional taxes on incomes, natural resources, gross receipts, or by various combinations of these. Governor James V. Allred was re-elected on his contention that only a small increase in natural resource taxes was sufficient; but the voters in November by constitutional amendments broadened the social welfare program considerably, thereby imposing further demands on the treasury.

The question was again the great issue in the primary election of 1938. W. Lee O'Daniel, in an exciting and unorthodox campaign, won in the first primary over a field of thirteen aspirants by promising old age pensions and other social programs and a new scheme for raising revenue that was neither a sales tax nor an ad valorem tax. His anxiously-awaited proposal, made public in his message to the legislature in January, 1939, called for a "transaction" tax. The proposed tax met a storm of public opposition and was finally defeated by a highly tense House of Representatives, although an even more liberal old age pension plan was enacted at the same time. Pertinent excerpts from Governor O'Daniel's speech follow.

During my campaign for the office of Governor, I advocated a liberal policy in meeting the obligations of the State of Texas for the aged of this State. I said then and I believe now that when the State of Texas adopted the amendment authorizing the payment of old age pensions, that the citizens thereby assumed an obligation to pay these pensions and in my judgment I believe that the most important problem now facing the Texas Legislature is the discharge in full of the obligation which the voters of this State assumed at that time. . . . And I assure you . . . that I am submitting to you . . . [a proposed constitutional amendment] which I believe is the best plan that the Legislature can adopt to solve this important problem, because in dealing with this problem the State faces three definite limitations: first, the State Constitution provides that in no case shall payment to an individual pensioner exceed $15.00 per month; the second limitation lies in the fact that the payment of old age pensions in Texas is a part of the National Plan set up under the provisions of the National Social Security Act; therefore, if we are to retain the support of the Federal Government, the Texas law must conform to the broad fundamental principles laid down in the Federal law. The third limitation which we must consider is the ability of the taxpayers of Texas to pay more taxes. . . .

If the constitutional amendment which I recommend is adopted, we shall then have in the Constitution of this State a guarantee of an income of $30.00 per month to every person sixty-five years of age and over, who meets the other requirements of the Act as to residence, etc., and a guarantee that the money will be raised each year to pay these pensions. . . .

I do not believe that the ownership of property should prevent an old person, otherwise qualified, from receiving an old age pension. . . . I am persuaded that there are many cases in Texas where old people have property of a potential value of several thousand dollars but who are possibly in actual want. I do not believe that such persons should be forced to sacrifice their property at a forced sale; and for that reason the bill which I am submitting to you does not prevent a man from receiving a pension simply because he owns property.

Based on the studies which I have made, I am convinced that it is unsound public policy to refuse to grant old persons a pension simply because perchance they may have a son or daughter able to care for them. . . .

. . . [T]he Federal Government has set up $15.00 per month as the limit it will pay in a cooperative plan of carrying one-half of the cost of old age pensions in the various States. I have been impressed with the fact that in a great majority of cases the States likewise have set up a limit of $15.00. I have examined much information issued by the Federal Government on costs of living and I have reached the conclusion that it was in the minds of those who made the original study that $30.00 per month was a reasonable income to enable an old person to live in comfort and decency. . . .

You will note the plan which I am submitting to you proposes that out of the funds raised, there shall be set aside annually an adequate amount of money to meet the obligation of the State for dependent children, to pay Confederate pensions, and to meet the obligation of the State for teacher retirement. . . .

Now with reference to the tax provisions of this bill. . . . I have made a diligent study of many suggested means of raising the necessary revenue to pay old age pensions and I recommend that the money be raised by the levying of a 1.6% transaction tax, because I believe that this will give the broadest possible base from which to secure this revenue. A transaction tax, such as I recommend, is applied alike to every line of business and industry. It does not pick out manufacturing and levy a tax on that to the exclusion of wholesaling and retailing. It does not exempt the producing industries which are largely our natural resource industries. It does not centralize all of the tax raising within the retail industry, as would be done by a retail sales tax. It is my opinion that the best interests of the State generally would be served if our producing or natural resource industries, our manufacturing, our wholesaling, our retailing, and our service industries all bear a part of this tax burden.

The revenue could be raised by a three or four per cent retail sales tax. But I am definitely opposed to a retail sales tax for the following reasons: . . . I do not believe that it is fair to single out the retail industry and make that industry alone responsible for collecting all this revenue and place this tax exclusively on the purchases of consumable goods and at the same time exempt many business transactions which are far more profitable than retailing. . . .

There are, of course, a number of methods whereby the necessary amount of revenue could be raised. It has been suggested that this money be raised exclusively by

a tax on oil. . . . I have not recommended this tax to the Legislature for the reason that I believe it would be unwise to attempt to raise this amount of money for this purpose from our natural resource industries.

I considered carefully the proposal to levy a flat gross receipts tax on oil, sulphur, insurance companies, public utilities, and other major lines of business and I reached the conclusion that if this character of tax were levied, it would preclude writing the tax into the Constitution because of the numerous exceptions and variations which it would be necessary to have if such a plan of raising the revenue was to be made workable. This plan possesses the further disadvantage, I think, of not providing a sufficiently broad tax base.

If a net income tax at approximately double the Federal rate should be levied in Texas and the exemptions placed at a lower rate, this would provide sufficient revenue to pay old age pensions. But as I see it, this plan is subject to two criticisms: one is that the Federal Government is now occupying the income tax field and has increased rather drastically income taxes during the last few years. A State income tax levied at a rate high enough to meet the needs for the purpose under consideration would, in my judgment, serve as a brake against bringing new industries to our State and developing new sources of employment for our citizens.

It has been suggested that the money be raised by a low rate gross income tax. A gross income tax of one and one-half per cent would probably produce the amount of revenue needed to pay the old age pensions and I think a gross income tax levied at a low rate has many things to recommend it. But if the tax is studied in all its details, it reveals some very definite disadvantages. Of one thing I am certain. If the Legislature elects to utilize the gross income tax as a means of raising revenue to pay old age pensions, then the tax should be levied on the gross income of every line of business and industry alike. . . .

It is my deliberate judgment that the transaction tax is the best means of raising the money. But I have no desire to even attempt to dictate to the Legislature how this task should be accomplished. . . .

I am definitely of the opinion that we should write into the Constitution of this State a provision abolishing all State ad valorem taxes. . . . In light of the fact that this proposed plan to abolish the State ad valorem tax is dependent upon the new plan to finance the pension fund, the teacher retirement fund and the aid for destitute children, it becomes proper, in my judgment, that these propositions be submitted to the people in one constitutional amendment because each proposition is dependent upon the other. . . .

There is another phase of this question which I think should be considered. Local units of government are clamoring for aid from the State. It seems to me that one of the best methods that the State could adopt to aid local units of government, would be to get out of the field of ad valorem taxes. I am opposed in principle to the general idea of the State appropriating money and turning it over to local units of government to spend. I think it encourages extravagance. I think it causes people to measure the value of our public servants by the amount of money they can get out of the State rather than by some sound standard. But here is one way we can release to the local units of government a source of revenue, but at the same time leave on these local units of government full responsibility for raising their own taxes and paying their own bills. . . .

In my opinion in levying the tax to meet these obligations [imposed by constitutional amendments upon the state] it is essential that the tax be most widely distributed, to the end that all citizens of Texas will be required to pay a part of this tax and that they will know they are paying it. Such a tax will then serve as a brake against fantastic schemes which may be advanced in the future, and it is for this reason that I deem it especially important that this question of old age pensions now be solved; first, by writing a definite plan in the Constitution; and second, that it be supported by a tax with a wide base that will be paid and felt by every citizen of this State. . . .

May I call the attention of the Legislature to the exemptions which I have recommended in the plan to raise State revenue. I have recommended that educational and charitable institutions be exempt and have, of course, included other exemptions necessary so as to not have the tax apply to transactions which the State by virtue of the Federal Constitution is prevented from taxing; aside from these, the only exemptions which I recommend are as follows: . . .

(a) Salaries and wages and professional fees. . . .

(b) I have recommended that the first sale by the producer of all agricultural and livestock products be exempt. . . .

(c) I have recommended that street car passenger fares up to ten cents and street sales of newspapers be exempt. . . .

May I conclude this message by urging the special importance of some of the things which I have already mentioned. When you are paying money out of the Treasury of the State to citizens of the State, no matter how meritorious your cause may be, there are always those who seek to abuse it; there are always those who seek to make a political racket out of it. . . .

I, therefore, believe it is tremendously important that in the passage of this bill, two things be kept in mind: One, the importance of writing what we decide to do into the Constitution of this State so that it will not be subject to the changing fancies of Governors and members of the Legislature; the other is levying a tax with a base broad enough that all the people will pay and will know they are paying. As I see it, these two fundamental things are

essential both for the protection of the taxpayer and for the protection of the old people of this State. . . .

Based on the best information I have been able to obtain, it is my judgment that the transaction tax herein levied will produce in excess of $45,000,000 (millions). But in this connection I would especially invite the attention of the Legislature to the fact that I am endeavoring in this legislation to definitely fix in the Constitution the tax rate and to fix it in a manner that it cannot be changed except by a vote of the people. . . .

Therefore, while I believe a transaction tax slightly in excess of 1% would be adequate during a good business year, it probably would not be adequate during a year of substantial business recession. I have, therefore, recommended that the tax rate be fixed at 1.6% and have placed two safeguards in the constitutional amendment as follows:

(a) The amount of old age pensions which can be paid is definitely fixed in the amendment by stating specifically who shall be entitled to receive pensions. In other words, a surplus of money in this fund could not increase the amount which those eligible to receive pensions would receive.

(b) I have included a second safety clause providing that whenever the excess in this fund reaches 25% of the cost for the previous biennium, that such excess shall be automatically transferred to the General Fund.

I recommend, therefore, that this rate of transaction tax be included in the amendment as a safety measure. I do this for the reason stated and for the further reason that we are in this amendment doing away with $20,000,000 (millions) ad valorem tax. Therefore, the net increase which a 1.6% transaction tax will make in the sum total tax bill is substantially less than the total amount which the new tax actually raises, in fact, we will only be collecting, in round figures, in the neighborhood of $25,000,000 (millions) in new taxes and out of that we will be caring for old age pensions, teacher retirement, aid for dependent children, and Confederate pensions. . . .

. . . I most respectfully urge that action on these matters be expedited to the end that these pressing obligations of the State be met not in a temporary manner, but in a permanent manner.

Respectfully,
W. LEE O'DANIEL,
Governor

## 121. SMITH v. TEXAS: NEGROES AND GRAND JURY SERVICE

### November 25, 1940

From 331 U. S. 128-132, 85 L. ed. 84-87.

In Smith v. Texas, an important case in civil rights in Texas, the United States Supreme Court held that discrimination against Negroes in the selection of persons for grand jury service is unconstitutional.

. . . In Harris County, Texas, where petitioner, a negro, was indicted and convicted of rape, negroes constitute over 20% of the population, and almost 10% of the poll-tax payers; a minimum of from three to six thousand of them measure up to the qualifications prescribed by Texas statutes for grand jury service. The court clerk, called as a state witness and testifying from court records covering the years 1931 through 1938, showed that only 5 of the

384 grand jurors who served during that period were negroes; that of 512 persons summoned for grand jury duty, only 18 were negroes; that of these 18, the names of 13 appeared as the last name on the 16 man jury list, the custom being to select the 12 man grand jury in the order that the names appeared on the list; that of the 5 negroes summoned for grand jury service who were not given the number 16, 4 were given numbers between 13 and 16, and 1 was number 6; that the result of this numbering was that of the 18 negroes summoned, only 5 ever served, whereas 379 of the 494 white men summoned actually served; that of 32 grand juries empanelled, only 5 had negro members, while 27 had none; that of these 5, the same individual served 3 times, so that only 3 individual negroes served at all; that there had been no negroes on any of the grand juries in 1938, the year petitioner was indicted; that there had been none on any of the grand juries in 1937, that the service of negroes by years had been: 1931, 1; 1932, 2; 1933, 1; 1934, 1; 1935, none; 1936, 1; 1937, none; 1938, none.

It is petitioner's contention that his conviction was based on an indictment obtained in violation of the provision of the Fourteenth Amendment that "No state shall . . . deny to any person within its jurisdiction the equal protection of the laws." And the contention that equal protection was denied him rests on a charge that negroes were in 1938 and long prior thereto intentionally and systematically excluded from grand jury service solely on account of their race and color. That a conviction based upon an indictment returned by a jury so selected is a denial of equal protection is well settled, and is not challenged by the state. But both the trial court and the Texas Criminal Court of Appeals were of opinion that the evidence failed to support the charge of racial discrimination. . . . But the question decided rested upon a charge of denial of equal protection, a basic right protected by the Federal Constitution. And it is therefore our responsibility to appraise the evidence as it related to this constitutional right.

It is part of the established tradition in the use of juries as instruments of public justice that the jury be a body truly representative of the community. For racial discrimination to result in the exclusion from jury service of otherwise qualified groups not only violates our Constitution and the laws enacted under it but is at war with our basic concepts of a democratic society and a representative government. We must consider this record in the light of these important principles. The fact that the written words of a state's laws hold out a promise that no such discrimination will be practiced is not enough. The Fourteenth Amendment requires that equal protection to all must be given—not merely promised.

Here, the Texas statutory scheme is not in itself unfair; it is capable of being carried out with no racial discrimination whatsoever. But by reason of the wide discretion permissible in the various steps of the plan, it is equally capable of being applied in such a manner as practically to proscribe any group thought by the law's administrators to be undesirable. And from the record before us the conclusion is inescapable that it is the latter application that has prevailed in Harris County. Chance and accident alone could hardly have brought about the listing for grand jury service of so few negroes from among the thousands shown by the undisputed evidence to possess the legal qualifications for jury service. Nor could chance and accident have been responsible for the combination of circumstances under which a negro's name, when listed at all, almost invariably appeared as number 16, and under which number 16 was never called for service unless it proved impossible to obtain the required jurors from the first 15 names on the list.

The state argues that the testimony of the commissioners themselves shows that there was no arbitrary or systematic exclusion. And it is true that two of the three commissioners who drew the September, 1938, panel testified to that effect. Both of them admitted that they did not select any negroes, although the subject was discussed, but both categorically denied that they intentionally, arbitrarily or systematically discriminated against negro jurors as such. One said that their failure to select negroes was because they did not know the names of any who were qualified and the other said that he was not personally acquainted with any member of the negro race. This is, at best, the testimony of two individuals who participated in drawing 1 out of the 32 jury panels discussed in the record. But even if their testimony were given the greatest possible effect, and their situation considered typical of that of the 94 commissioners who did not testify, we would still feel compelled to reverse the decision below. What the Fourteenth Amendment prohibits is racial discrimination in the selection of grand juries. Where jury commissioners limit those from whom grand juries are selected to their own personal acquaintance, discrimination can arise from commissioners who know no negroes as well as from commissioners who know but eliminate them. If there has been discrimination, whether accomplished ingeniously or ingenuously, the conviction cannot stand.

Reversed.

## 122. SMITH v. ALLWRIGHT: THE "WHITE PRIMARY" CASE

### April 3, 1944

From 321 U. S. 649, 88 L. ed. 990-998.

Lonnie E. Smith, a Negro citizen of Harris County, brought suit in the United States District Court. He contended that he was denied a ballot in the Democratic primaries in Texas solely on the grounds of his race. His petition was denied; but the United States Supreme Court, in a decision of historical importance, overruled the lower courts and reversed its own doctrine with regard to the right of a political party to determine its own membership and, consequently, to vote in its primaries. The essential facts in the case are covered in the following excerpt from the Court's opinion.

. . . The State of Texas by its Constitution and statutes provides that every person, if certain other requirements are met which are not here in issue, qualified by residence in the district or county "shall be deemed a qualified elector." Primary elections for United States Senators, Congressmen and state officers are provided for by Chapters Twelve and Thirteen of the statutes. Under these chapters, the Democratic Party was required to hold the primary which was the occasion of the alleged wrong to petitioner. . . . These nominations are to be made by the qualified voters of the party.

The Democratic party of Texas is held by the Supreme Court of that state to be a "voluntary association," protected by Section 27 of the Bill of Rights, Art. 1, Constitution of Texas, from interference by the state except that:

"In the interest of fair methods and a fair expression by their members of their preferences in the selection of their nominees, the State may regulate such elections by proper laws." . . .

The Democratic party on May 24, 1932, in a State Convention adopted the following resolution, which has not since been "amended, abrogated, annulled or avoided":

"Be it resolved that all white citizens of the State of Texas who are qualified to vote under the Constitution and laws of the State shall be eligible to membership in the Democratic party and, as such, entitled to participate in its deliberations."

It was by virtue of this resolution that the respondents refused to permit the petitioner to vote.

Texas is free to conduct her elections and limit her electorate as she may deem wise, save only as her action may be affected by the prohibitions of the United States Constitution or in conflict with powers delegated to and exercised by the National Government. The Fourteenth Amendment forbids a state from making or enforcing any law which abridges the privileges or immunities of citizens of the United States and the Fifteenth Amendment specifically interdicts any denial or abridgment by a state of the right of citizens to vote on account of color. Respondents appears in the District Court and the Circuit Court of Appeals and defended on the ground that the Democratic party of Texas is a voluntary organization with members banded together for the purpose of selecting individuals of the group representing the common political beliefs as candidates in the general election. As such

a voluntary organization, it was claimed, the Democratic party is free to select its own membership and limit to whites participation in the party primary. Such action, the answer asserted, does not violate the Fourteenth, Fifteenth or Seventeenth Amendments as officers of government cannot be chosen at primaries and the Amendments are applicable only to general elections where governmental officers are actually elected. Primaries, it is said, are political party affairs, handled by party not governmental officers. . . .

When Grovey v. Townsend [295 U. S. 45] was written, the Court looked upon the denial of a vote in a primary as a mere refusal by a party of party membership. As the Louisiana statutes for holding primaries are similar to those of Texas, our ruling in Classic as to the unitary character of the electoral process calls for a reexamination as to whether or not the exclusion of Negroes from a Texas party primary was state action. . . .

It may now be taken as a postulate that the right to vote in such a primary for the nomination of candidates without discrimination by the State, like the right to vote in a general election, is a right secured by the Constitution. . . .

We are thus brought to an examination of the qualifications for Democratic primary electors in Texas, to determine whether state action or private action has excluded Negroes from participation. . . .

We think that this statutory system for the selection of party nominees for inclusion on the general election ballot makes the party which is required to follow these legislative directions an agency of the state in so far as it determines the participants in a primary election. The party takes its character as a state agency from the duties imposed upon it by state statutes; the duties do not become matters of private law because they are performed by a political party. The plan of the Texas primary follows substantially that of Louisiana, with the exception that in Louisiana the state pays the cost of the primary while Texas assesses the cost against candidates. In numerous instances, the Texas statutes fix or limit the fees to be charged. Whether paid directly by the state or through state requirements, it is state action which compels. When primaries become a part of the machinery for choosing officials, state and national, as they have here, the same tests to determine the character of discrimination or abridgment should be applied to the primary as are applied to the general election. If the state requires a certain electoral procedure, prescribes a general election ballot made up of party nominees so chosen and limits the choice of the electorate in general elections for state offices, practically speaking, to those whose names appear on such a ballot, it endorses, adopts and enforces the discrimination against Negroes, practiced by a party entrusted by Texas law with the determination of the qualifications of participants in the primary. This is state action within the meaning of the Fifteenth Amendment.

The United States is a constitutional democracy. Its organic law grants to all citizens a right to participate in the choice of elected officials without restriction by any state because of race. This grant to the people of the opportunity for choice is not to be nullified by a state through casting its electoral process in a form which permits a private organization to practice racial discrimination in the election. Constitutional rights would be of little value if they could be thus indirectly denied.

The privilege of membership in a party may be, as this Court said in Grovey v. Townsend, no concern of a state. But when, as here, that privilege is also the essential qualification for voting in a primary to select nominees for a general election, the state makes the action of the party the action of the state. In reaching this conclusion we are not unmindful of the desirability of continuity of decision in constitutional questions. However, when convinced of former error, this Court has never felt constrained to follow precedent. In constitutional questions, where correction depends upon amendment and not upon legislative action this Court throughout its history has freely exercised its power to reexamine the basis of its constitutional decisions. This has long been accepted practice, and this practice has continued to this day. This is particularly true when the decision believed erroneous is the application of a constitutional principle rather than an interpretation of the Constitution to extract the principle itself. Here we are applying, contrary to the recent decision in Grovey v. Townsend, the well established principle of the Fifteenth Amendment, forbidding the abridgment by a state of a citizen's right to vote. Grovey v. Townsend is overruled.

Judgment reversed.

# 123. THE GILMER-AIKIN SCHOOL LAWS

## June 1 and 8, 1949

From Vernon's Texas *Civil Statutes,* 1950 Supplement, Articles 2654—1-6, 2922—11-16, 214-222, 298-312.

The Gilmer-Aikin acts of 1949 constitute one of the most significant developments in the history of education in Texas. From the beginning, the public school system of Texas had been principally under local control; the Gilmer-Aikin acts set up a new system under which state control was greatly increased. The improvement of the public road system, which permitted the transportation of children over long distances, and the demand for better educational facilities and programs, including supplemental support for the poorer districts, were factors that promoted reorganization. Since the laws are minutely detailed and extraordinarily lengthy, only extracts have been included here, but these are sufficient to show their general nature.

ARTICLE 2654-1. CENTRAL EDUCATION AGENCY

Section 1. There is hereby established a Central Education Agency composed of the State Board of Education, the State Board for Vocational Education, the State Commissioner of Education, and the State Department of Education. It shall carry out such educational functions as may be assigned to it by the Legislature, but all educational functions not specifically delegated to the Central Education Agency shall be performed by County Boards of Education or District Boards of Trustees. . . .

Sec. 3. The Central Education Agency shall be the sole agency of the State of Texas empowered to enter into agreements respecting educational undertakings, including the providing of school lunches and the construction of school buildings, with an agency of the Federal Government, except such agreements as may be entered into by the Governing Board of a State university or college. No County Board of Education or Board of Trustees of a school district shall enter into contracts with, or accept moneys from, an agency of the Federal Government except under rules and regulations prescribed by the Central Education Agency.

ART. 2654-2. STATE BOARD OF EDUCATION

Section 1. There is hereby created the State Board of Education, to consist of twenty-one (21) members. One (1) member of the State Board of Education shall be elected from each of the twenty-one (21) Congressional Districts of the State of Texas. . . .

Sec. 5. . . . At the general election in 1952 and at each general election thereafter, members shall be elected, in conformity with the general election laws of this State, to the Board of offices which will become vacant on December 31 of that year [one-third the total number]. The members thus elected shall hold office for a term of six (6) years, beginning January 1 immediately following such election. . . .

Sec. 8. A meeting of the Board members elected at the election on the second Tuesday in November, 1949, shall be called by the Secretary of State . . . , and at such meeting, or as soon as practicable thereafter, said Board shall elect a State Commissioner of Education whose term shall begin immediately upon election by said Board and shall run until May 31, 1953, . . .

ARTICLE 2654-3. POWERS AND DUTIES OF BOARD

Section 1. The State Board of Education is hereby declared to be the policy forming and planning body for the Public School System of the State. It shall also be the State Board for Vocational Education, and as such, said Board shall have all the powers and duties conferred upon it by the various existing statutes now in effect relating to the State Board for Vocational Education. . . .

ART. 2654-4. STATE TEXTBOOK COMMITTEE

. . . Sec. 5. It shall be the duty of the Textbook Committee to recommend to the Commissioner a complete list of textbooks which it approves for adoption at the various grade levels and in the various school subjects. . . .

ART. 2654-5. STATE COMMISSIONER OF EDUCATION

Section 1. There is hereby established the position of

State Commissioner of Education. All powers and duties heretofore vested in the State Superintendent of Public Instruction shall be discharged by this Commissioner, provided said powers and duties are not in conflict with the provisions of this Act. The State Board of Education shall elect, by and with the consent of the Senate, the State Commissioner of Education to serve for a period of four (4) years, his term beginning on June 1st and ending May 31st; and may re-appoint him for successive terms of four (4) years, at a salary to be set up by the Board. . . .

Sec. 3. The Commissioner of Education shall serve as the executive officer of the Board of Education, and shall be its Executive Secretary.

Sec. 4. It shall be the duty of the State Commissioner of Education to issue teaching certificates to public school teachers and administrators and to voucher the expenses of the central educational agencies according to the rules and regulations prescribed by the State Board of Education. The decisions of the State Commissioner of Education shall be subject to review by the State Board of Education. . . .

Art. 2654-6. State Department of Education

Section 1. There is hereby established the State Department of Education, which shall be the professional, technical, and clerical staff of the Central Education Agency. . . .

FOUNDATION SCHOOL PROGRAM [NEW]

Art. 2922-11. Title of Act and Purpose

This Act shall be known as the Foundation School Program Act. It is the purpose of this Act to guarantee to each child of school age in Texas the availability of a minimum Foundation School Program for nine (9) full months of the year, and to establish the eligibility requirements applicable to Texas public school districts in connection therewith. . . .

Sec. 2. To effectuate the Foundation School Program proposed and guaranteed herein, school districts are authorized to utilize the following professional positions and services: . . .

Provided that the total number of professional units allotted to each district shall be the sum of the professional units, hereinafter prescribed, for classroom teachers, vocational teachers, special service teachers, teachers of exceptional children, supervisors and/or counsellors, full-time principals and superintendents. Such professional unit allotments shall be contingent upon the employment of qualified personnel and upon the payment of not less than the minimum salary as hereinafter prescribed.

No district will be required to employ professional personnel for the full number of professional units for which it is eligible, but where a fewer number are employed, grants shall be based upon the number actually employed during the current school year.

Art. 2922-13. Units

Section 1. The number of professional units allotted for the purpose of this Act to each school district, except as otherwise provided herein, shall be based upon and determined by the average daily attendance for the district for the next preceding school year, separate for whites and separate for negroes. Such allotments based upon white attendance shall be utilized in white schools, and allotments based upon negro attendance shall be utilized in negro schools. Provided, that where . . . there is a marked

increase or decrease in the attendance of any school district, adjustments in professional allotments shall be made by the State Commissioner of Education, . . .

*(1) Classroom Teacher Units.* . . .

a. School districts having fewer than fifteen (15) pupils in average daily attendance shall not be eligible for any classroom teacher units, except that in cases of extreme hardship, . . .

b. School districts having from fifteen (15) to twenty-five (25) pupils, inclusive, in average daily attendance, one (1) classroom teacher unit:

c. School districts having from twenty-six (26) to one hundred nine (109) pupils, inclusive, in average daily attendance, two (2) classroom teacher units for the first twenty-six (26) pupils and one (1) classroom teacher unit for each additional twenty-one (21) pupils (No credit for fractions);

d. School districts having from one hundred ten (110) to one hundred fifty-six (156) pupils, inclusive, in average daily attendance, six (6) classroom teacher units;

e. School districts having from one hundred fifty-seven (157) to four hundred forty-four (444) pupils, inclusive, in average daily attendance, one (1) classroom teacher unit for each twenty-four (24) pupils, or a fractional part thereof in excess of one-half (½);

f. School districts having from four hundred forty-five (445) pupils to four hundred eighty-seven (487) pupils, inclusive, in average daily attendance, one (1) classroom teacher unit for each twenty-five (25) pupils, or a fractional part thereof in excess of one-half (½);

g. School districts having from four hundred eighty-eight (488) to one thousand, five hundred twelve (1,512) pupils, inclusive, in average daily attendance, one (1) classroom teacher unit for each twenty-five (25) pupils, or a fractional part thereof in excess of one-half (½);

h. School districts having from one thousand, five hundred thirteen (1,513) to one thousand, five hundred ninety-nine (1,599) pupils, inclusive, in average daily attendance, sixty-one (61) classroom teacher units;

i. School districts having one thousand, six hundred (1,600) or more pupils in average daily attendance, one (1) classroom teacher unit for each twenty-six (26) pupils, or a fractional part thereof in excess of one-half (½);

*(2) Vocational Teacher Units.* . . .

a. Each four-year accredited high school shall be eligible, subject to the provisions of the State Plan for Vocational Education as approved by the State Board for Vocational Education, for two (2) vocational teacher units to teach one or more vocational programs in agriculture, home economics, trades and industries, or distributive education, provided there is a need thereof, and provided the programs shall have been approved by the State Commissioner of Education. . . .

c. Each unaccredited high school and each high school classified lower than a four-year high school may be eligible, according to the provisions of said State Plan for Vocational Education, for vocational teacher units to teach one or more vocational programs in agriculture, home economics, trades and industries, and distributive education in the number to be determined by the State Commissioner of Education. . . .

*(3) Special Service Teacher Units. . . .*

a. Such allotments shall be based upon the number of approved classroom teacher units, separate for whites and separate for negroes.

b. Districts which have twenty (20) or more approved classroom teacher units shall be eligible for one (1) special service teacher unit for each twenty (20) classroom teacher units. (No credit for fractions). . . .

*(4) Exceptional Children Teacher Units. . . .*

a. It is the purpose of this allotment of exceptional children teacher units to provide competent educational services for the exceptional children in Texas between and including the ages of six (6) and seventeen (17), for whom the regular school facilities are inadequate or not available. . . .

*(5) Supervisor and/or Counsellor Units. . . .*

a. One (1) supervisor or counsellor unit for the first forty (40) classroom teacher units and one (1) supervisor or counsellor unit for each additional fifty (50) classroom teacher units, or major fractional part thereof. If a district is eligible for one such unit, the district may employ for such unit either a supervisor or a counsellor, but not both. If a district is eligible for two or more such units, the district may employ supervisors only, counsellors only, or a combination of the two to the extent of total eligibility. . . .

b. Districts having fewer than forty (40) classroom teacher units may enter, by vote of their respective Boards of Trustees, into one cooperative agreement to provide supervisors and/or counsellors to be recommended and supervised by the County School Superintendent and employed by the County School Board. . . .

2922—14. SALARIES

Section 1. Beginning with the school year of 1949-50, the Board of Trustees of each and every school district in the State of Texas shall pay their teachers, both whites and negroes, upon a salary schedule providing a minimum beginning base salary plus increments above the minimum for additional experience in teaching as hereinafter prescribed. The salaries fixed herein shall be regarded as minimum salaries only and each district may supplement such salaries.

All teachers and administrators shall have a valid Texas certificate. Salary increments for college training shall be based upon training received at a college recognized by the State Commissioner of Education for the preparation of teachers. . . .

Provided that payment of at least the minimum salary schedule provided herein shall be a condition precedent: (1) to a school's participation in the Foundation School Fund; and (2) to its name being placed or continued upon the official list of affiliated or accredited schools. The annual salaries as provided herein may be paid in twelve (12) payments at the discretion of the local school boards.

The salary of each professional position listed in Section 2 of Article II of this Act shall be determined as follows:

1. Classroom teachers. The annual salary of classroom teachers shall be the monthly base salary, plus increments, multiplied by nine (9); provided that if the length of the school term is less than nine (9) months, the annual salary shall be such base salary and increments multiplied by the number of months in the term.

a. The minimum base pay for a classroom teacher who holds a Bachelor's Degree and no higher degree, shall be Two Hundred Sixty-seven ($267.00) Dollars per month. Six ($6.00) Dollars per month shall be added for each year of teaching experience not to exceed Seventy-two ($72.00) Dollars per month. . . .

ART. 2922—15. SERVICES AND OPERATING COSTS

Section 1. The total current operating cost for each school district, other than professional salaries and transportation, shall be based upon the number of approved classroom teacher units and such exceptional children teacher units as are utilized for convalescent classes, separate for whites and separate for negroes, and grants therefor shall be allotted and determined in the following manner:

a. Districts having from one (1) to seventy-four (74) such units shall be allotted the sum of Four Hundred ($400.00) Dollars for each of said units.

b. Districts having from seventy-five (75) to eighty-four (84) such units shall be allotted the sum of Twenty-nine Thousand, Seven Hundred ($29,700.00) Dollars.

c. Districts having eighty-five (85) or more such units shall be allotted the sum of Three Hundred Fifty ($350.00) Dollars for each of said units.

Sec. 2. The County Superintendents and County School Boards of the several counties of this State, subject to the approval of the State Commissioner of Education, are hereby authorized to annually set up the most economical system of transportation possible for the purpose of transporting pupils from their districts, and within their districts. The county shall be regarded as the unit and state warrants for transportation shall be made payable to a County School Transportation Fund in each county for the total transportation earned within the county to the extent allowed under the provisions of this Act and which shall not exceed the total actual approved cost thereof. . . .

ART. 2922—16. FINANCES

Section 1. The Foundation School Program established in this Act shall be financed by:

a. An equalized local school district effort to the extent hereinafter provided toward the support of this program;

b. Distribution of the State and County Available School Funds on the basis of the number of scholastics; and

c. Allocation to each local district a sum of State money appropriated for the purposes of this Act sufficient to finance the remaining costs of the Foundation School Program in that district computed and determined in accordance with the provisions of this Act.

Sec. 2. The sum of the amounts to be charged annually against the local school districts of the State toward such Foundation School Program shall be Forty-five Million ($45,000,000.00) Dollars. The State Commissioner of Education, subject to the approval of the State Board of Education, shall assign each school district according to its taxpaying ability its proportionate part of such Forty-five Million ($45,000,000.00) Dollars to be raised locally and applied towards the financing of its minimum foundation school program.

Sec. 3. In determining the taxpaying ability of each school district, the State Commissioner of Education, subject to the approval of the State Board of Education, shall calculate an economic index of the financial ability of each county to support the Foundation School Program. The economic index of a county shall be calculated to approximate the percent of the total taxpaying ability in the State which is in a given county, and shall constitute for the purpose of this Act a measure of one county's ability to support schools in relation to the ability of other counties in the State. The economic index for each county shall be based upon and determined by the following weighted factors:

a. Assessed valuation of the county—weighted by twenty (20);

b. Scholastic population of the county—weighted by eight (8);

c. Income for the county as measured by: Value added by manufacture, value of minerals produced, value of agricultural products, payrolls for retail establishments, payrolls for wholesale establishments, payrolls for service establishments weighted collectively by seventy-two (72). . . .

Sec. 4. The State Commissioner of Education shall calculate and determine the total sum of local funds that the school districts of a county shall be assigned to contribute toward the total cost of this Foundation School Program by multiplying Forty-five Million ($45,000,-

000.00) Dollars by the economic index determined for each county. The product shall be regarded as the local funds available in each respective county toward the support of the Foundation School Program, and shall be used in calculating the portion of said amount which shall be assigned to each school district in the county.

Sec. 5. The State Commissioner of Education shall determine the amount of local funds to be charged to each school district and used therein toward the support of the Foundation School Program, which amount shall be calculated as follows:

Divide the State and county assessed valuation of all property in the county subject to school district taxation for the next preceding school year into the State and county assessed valuation of the district for the next preceding school year, finding the district's percentage of the county valuation. Multiply the district's percentage of the county valuation by the amount of funds assigned to all of the districts in the county. The product shall be the amount of local funds that the district shall be assigned to raise toward the financing of its Foundation School Program. . . .

## 124. SWEATT v. PAINTER: DESEGREGATION OF INSTITUTIONS OF HIGHER LEARNING

### June 5, 1950

From 339 U.S. 629-636, 94 L. ed. 1114-1120 (1950).

Heman Marion Sweatt, a Negro, was denied admission to The University of Texas Law School in 1946 under the law providing for separate educational facilities for Negroes and whites. He thereupon brought suit in Texas courts to gain admittance, with the argument that facilities elsewhere in the state were not equal in quality to those at The University. The lower courts found against him, but the United States Supreme Court reversed the ruling. The case is significant because it established a precedent for desegregation of institutions of higher learning in Texas prior to the more sweeping decision of the Supreme Court in 1954.

. . . In the instant case, petitioner filed an application for admission to the University of Texas Law School for the February, 1946 term. His application was rejected solely because he is a Negro. Petitioner thereupon brought this suit for mandamus against the appropriate school officials, respondents here, to compel his admission. At that time, there was no law school in Texas which admitted Negroes.

The State trial court recognized that the action of the State in denying petitioner the opportunity to gain a legal education while granting it to others deprived him of the equal protection of the laws guaranteed by the Fourteenth Amendment. The court did not grant the relief requested, however, but continued the case for six months to allow the State to supply substantially equal facilities. At the expiration of the six months, in December, 1946, the court denied the writ on the showing that the authorized university officials had adopted an order calling for the open-

ing of a law school for Negroes the following February. While petitioner's appeal was pending, such a school was made available, but petitioner refused to register therein. The Texas Court of Civil Appeals set aside the trial court's judgment and ordered the cause "remanded generally to the trial court for further proceedings without prejudice to the rights of any party to this suit."

On remand, a hearing was held on the issue of the equality of the educational facilities at the newly established school as compared with the University of Texas Law School. Finding that the new school offered petitioner "privileges, advantages, and opportunities for the study of law substantially equivalent to those offered by the State to white students at the University of Texas," the trial court denied mandamus. The Court of Civil Appeals affirmed. Petitioner's application for a writ of error was denied by the Texas Supreme Court. We granted certiorari because of the manifest importance of the constitutional issues involved.

The University of Texas Law School, from which petitioner was excluded, was staffed by a faculty of sixteen full-time and three part-time professors, some of whom are nationally recognized authorities in their field. Its student body numbered 850. The library contained over 65,000 volumes. Among the other facilities available to the students were a law review, moot court facilities, scholarship funds, and Order of the Coif affiliation. The school's alumni occupy the most distinguished positions in the private practice of the law and in the public life of the

State. It may properly be considered one of the nation's ranking law schools.

The law school for Negroes which was to have opened in February, 1947, would have had no independent faculty or library. The teaching was to be carried on by four members of the University of Texas Law School faculty, who were to maintain their offices at the University of Texas while teaching at both institutions. Few of the 10,000 volumes ordered for the library had arrived, nor was there any full-time librarian. (Students of the interim School of Law of the Texas State University for Negroes had use of the State Law Library in the Capitol Building.) The school lacked accreditation.

Since the trial of this case, respondents report the opening of a law school at the Texas State University for Negroes. It is apparently on the road to full accreditation. It has a faculty of five full-time professors; a student body of 23; a library of some 16,500 volumes serviced by a full-time staff; a practice court and legal aid association; and one alumnus who has become a member of the Texas Bar.

Whether the University of Texas Law School is compared with the original or the new law school for Negroes, we cannot find substantial equality in the educational opportunities offered white and Negro law students by the State. In terms of number of the faculty, variety of courses and opportunity for specialization, size of the student body, scope of the library, availability of law review and similar activities, the University of Texas Law School is superior. What is more important, the University of Texas Law School possesses to a far greater degree those qualities which are incapable of objective measurement but which make for greatness in a law school. Such qualities, to name but a few, include reputation of the faculty, experience of the administration, position and influence of the alumni, standing in the community, traditions and prestige. It is difficult to believe that one who had a free choice between these law schools would consider the question close.

Moreover, although the law is a highly learned profession, we are well aware that it is an intensely practical one. The law school, the proving ground for legal learning and practice, cannot be effective in isolation from the individuals and institutions with which the law interacts. Few students and no one who has practiced law would choose to study in an academic vacuum, removed from the interplay of ideas and exchange of views with which the law is concerned. The law school to which Texas is willing to admit petitioner excludes from its student body members of the racial groups which number 85% of the population of the State and include most of the lawyers, witnesses, jurors, judges and other officials with whom petitioner will

inevitably be dealing when he becomes a member of the Texas Bar. With such a substantial and significant segment of society excluded, we cannot conclude that the education offered petitioner is substantially equal to that which he would receive if admitted to the University of Texas Law School.

It may be argued that excluding petitioner from that school is no different from excluding white students from the new law school. This contention overlooks realities. It is unlikely that a member of a group so decisively in the majority, attending a school with rich traditions and prestige which only a history of consistently maintained excellence could command, would claim that the opportunities afforded him for legal education were unequal to those held open to petitioner. That such a claim, if made, would be dishonored by the State, is no answer. "Equal protection of the laws is not achieved through indiscriminate imposition of inequalities."

It is fundamental that these cases concern rights which are personal and present. This Court has stated unanimously that "The State must provide [legal education] for [petitioner] in conformity with the equal protection clause of the Fourteenth Amendment and provide it as soon as it does for applicants of any other group." That case "did not present the issue whether a state might not satisfy the equal protection clause of the Fourteenth Amendment by establishing a separate law school for Negroes." Fisher v. Hurst, 333 US 147, 150, 92 L ed 604, 606, 68 S Ct 389 (1948). In Missouri ex rel. Gaines v. Canada, 305 US 337 351, 83 L ed 208, 214, 59 S Ct 232 (1938), the Court, speaking through Chief Justice Hughes, declared that "petitioner's right was a personal one. It was as an individual that he was entitled to the equal protection of the laws, and the State was bound to furnish him within its borders facilities for legal education substantially equal to those which the State there afforded for persons of the white race, whether or not other Negroes sought the same opportunity." . . .

In accordance with these cases, petitioner may claim his full constitutional right: legal education equivalent to that offered by the State to students of other races. Such education is not available to him in a separate law school as offered by the State. . . .

We hold that the Equal Protection Clause of the Fourteenth Amendment requires that petitioner be admitted to the University of Texas Law School. The judgment is reversed and the cause is remanded for proceedings not inconsistent with this opinion.

Reversed.

## 125. THE TIDELANDS CASE

### June 5, 1950

From 339 U. S. 707-724, 94 L. ed. 1221-1230.

The United States brought suit against the State of Texas asserting ownership of the "tidelands" in the Gulf of Mexico, that are lying between the ordinary low-water mark outside the inland waters and the outer edge of the continental shelf. It also required Texas to account for all the income she had derived from it. In its defense Texas claimed that by the Resolution of Annexation it had retained all its lands and minerals, and that the United States had officially recognized, and acquiesced in, this claim. But the Court regarded the earlier decisions in *United States* v. *California* and *United States* v. *Louisiana*—that the United States has paramount rights in submerged lands lying off the coast of these states—as controlling in this case, although two justices dissented and a third, without dissenting, stated that it remained a puzzle to him how any shift of the rights of Texas to the United States took place upon its admission to the Union.

The tidelands became an important issue in the presidential campaign of 1952, when the Republican candidate, Dwight D. Eisenhower, promised, if elected, to work for their restoration to Texas. This was done by law in 1953.

Pertinent excerpts from the majority decision of the Court appear below.

. . . The complaint alleges that the United States was and is "the Owner in fee simple of, or possessed of paramount rights in, and full dominion and power over, the lands, minerals and other things underlying the Gulf of Mexico, lying seaward of the ordinary low-water mark on the coast of Texas and outside of the inland waters, extending seaward to the outer edge of the continental shelf and bounded on the east and southwest, respectively, by the eastern boundary of the State of Texas and the boundary between the United States and Mexico.

The complaint is in other material respects identical with that filed against Louisiana. The prayer is for a decree adjudging and declaring the rights of the United States as against Texas in the above-described area, enjoining Texas and all persons claiming under it from continuing to trespass upon the area in violation of the rights of the United States, and requiring Texas to account to the United States for all money derived by it from the area subsequent to June 23, 1947. . . .

Texas in her answer, as later amended, renews her objection that this case is not one of which the Court has original jurisdiction; denies that the United States is or ever has been the owner of the lands, minerals, etc., underlying the Gulf of Mexico within the disputed area; denies that the United States is or ever has been possessed of paramount rights in or full dominion over the lands, minerals, etc., underlying the Gulf of Mexico within said area except the paramount power to control, improve, and regulate navigation which under the Commerce Clause the United States has over lands beneath all navigable waters and except the same dominion and paramount power which the United States has over uplands within the United States, whether privately or state owned; denies that these or any other paramount powers or rights of the United States include ownership or the right to take or develop or authorize the taking or developing of oil or other minerals in the area in dispute without compensation to Texas; denies that any

paramount powers or rights of the United States include the right to control or to prevent the taking or developing of these minerals by Texas or her lessees except when necessary in the exercise of the paramount federal powers, as recognized by Texas, and when duly authorized by appropriate action of the Congress; admits that she claims rights, title, and interests in said lands, minerals, etc., and says that her rights include ownership and the right to take, use, lease, and develop these properties; admits that she has leased some of the lands in the area and received royalties from the lessees but denies that the United States is entitled to any of them; and denies that she has no title to or interest in any of the lands in the disputed area.

As an affirmative defense Texas asserts that as an independent nation, the Republic of Texas had open, adverse, and exclusive possession and exercised jurisdiction and control over the land, minerals, etc., underlying that part of the Gulf of Mexico within her boundaries established at three marine leagues from shore by her First Congress and acquiesced in by the United States and other major nations; that when Texas was annexed to the United States the claim and rights of Texas to this land, minerals, etc., were recognized and preserved in Texas; that Texas continued as a State, to hold open, adverse and exclusive possession, jurisdiction and control of these lands, minerals, etc., without dispute, challenge or objection by the United States; that the United States has recognized and acquiesced in this claim and these rights; that Texas under the doctrine of prescription has established such title, ownership and sovereign rights in the area as preclude the granting of the relief prayed.

As a second affirmative defense Texas alleges that there was an agreement between the United States and the Republic of Texas that upon annexation Texas would not cede to the United States but would retain all of the lands, minerals, etc., underlying that part of the Gulf of Mexico within the original boundaries of the Republic.

As a third affirmative defense Texas asserts that the United States acknowledged and confirmed the three-league boundary of Texas in the Gulf of Mexico as declared, established, and maintained by the Republic of Texas and as retained by Texas under the annexation agreement. . . .

We are told that the considerations which give the Federal Government paramount rights in the marginal sea off the shores of California and Louisiana should be equally controlling when we come to the marginal sea off the shores of Texas. It is argued that the national interests, national responsibilities, and national concerns which are the basis of the paramount rights of the National Government in one case would seem to be equally applicable in the other.

But there is a difference in this case which, Texas says, requires a different result. That difference is largely in the preadmission history of Texas.

The sum of the argument is that prior to annexation Texas had both *dominium* (ownership or proprietary rights) and *imperium* (governmental powers of regulation and control) as respects the lands, minerals and other products underlying the marginal sea. In the case of California we found that she, like the original thirteen colonies, never had *dominium* over that area. The first claim to the marginal sea was asserted by the National Government. We held that protection and control of it were indeed a function of national external sovereignty. The status of Texas, it is said, is different: Texas, when she came into the Union, retained the *dominium* over the marginal sea which she had previously acquired and transferred to the National Government only her powers of sovereignty—her *imperium*—over the marginal sea.

This argument leads into several chapters of Texas history.

The Republic of Texas was proclaimed by a convention on March 2, 1836. The United States and other nations formally recognized it. The Congress of Texas on December 19, 1836, passed an act defining the boundaries of the Republic. The southern boundary was described as follows: "beginning at the mouth of the Sabine river, and running west along the Gulf of Mexico three leagues from land, to the mouth of the Rio Grande." (The traditional three-mile maritime belt is one marine league or three marine miles in width. One marine league is 3.45 English statute miles.) Texas was admitted to the Union in 1845 "on an equal footing with the original States in all respects whatever." Texas claims that during the period from 1836 to 1845 she had brought this marginal belt into her territory and subjected it to her domestic law which recognized ownership in minerals under coastal waters. This the United States contests. Texas also claims that under international law, as it had evolved by the 1840's, the Republic of Texas as a sovereign nation became the owner of the bed and sub-soil of the marginal sea vis-a-vis other nations. Texas claims that the Republic of Texas acquired during that period the same interest in its marginal sea as the United States acquired in the marginal sea off California when it purchased from Mexico in 1848 the territory from which California was later formed. This the United States contests.

The Joint Resolution annexing Texas provided in part: "Said State, when admitted into the Union, after ceding to the United States, *all public edifices, fortifications, barracks, ports and harbors, navy and navy-yards, docks, magazines, arms, armaments, and all other property and means pertaining to the public defence* belonging to said Republic of Texas, shall retain all the public funds, debts, taxes, and dues of every kind, which may belong to or be due and owing said republic; and shall also retain *all the vacant and unappropriated lands lying within its limits,* to be applied to the payment of the debts and liabilities of said Republic of Texas, and the residue of said lands, after discharging said debts and liabilities, to be disposed of as said State may direct; but in no event are said debts and liabilities to become a charge upon the Government of the United States." (Italics added.)

The United States contends that the inclusion of fortifications, barracks, ports and harbors, navy and navy-yards, and docks in the cession clause of the Resolution demonstrates an intent to convey all interests of the Republic in the marginal sea, since most of these properties lie side by side with, and shade into, the marginal sea. It stresses the phrase in the Resolution "other property and means pertaining to the public defence." It argues that possession by the United States in the lands underlying the marginal sea is a defense necessity. Texas maintains that the construction of the Resolution both by the United States and Texas has been restricted to properties which the Republic actually used at the time in the public defense.

The United States contends that the "vacant and unappropriated lands" which by the Resolution were retained by Texas do not include the marginal belt. It argues that the purpose of the clause, the circumstances of its inclusion, and the meaning of the words in Texas and federal usage give them a more restricted meaning. Texas replies that since the United States refused to assume the liabilities of the Republic, it was to have no claim to the assets of the Republic except the defense properties expressly ceded.

In the California Case, neither party suggested the necessity for the introduction of evidence. But Texas makes an earnest plea to be heard on the facts as they bear on the circumstances of her history, which, she says, sets her apart from the other States on this issue. . . .

We conclude, however, that no such hearing is required in this case. We are of the view that the "equal footing" clause of the Joint Resolution admitting Texas to the Union disposes of the present phase of the controversy.

The "equal footing" clause has long been held to refer to political rights and to sovereignty. It does not, of course, include economic stature or standing. There has never been equality among the States in that sense. Some States when they entered the Union had within their boundaries tracts of land belonging to the Federal Government; others were sovereigns of their soil. Some had special agreements with the Federal Government governing property within their borders. Area, location, geology, and latitude have created great diversity in the economic aspects of the several States. The requirement of equal footing was designed not to wipe out those diversities but to create parity as respects political standing and sovereignty.

Yet the "equal footing" clause has long been held to have a direct effect on certain property rights. Thus the question early arose in controversies between the Federal Government and the States as to the ownership of the shores of navigable waters and the soils under them. It was consistently held that to deny to the States, admitted subsequent to the formation of the Union, ownership of this property would deny them admission on an equal footing with the original States, since the original States did not grant these properties to the United States but reserved them to themselves. The theory of these decisions was aptly summarized by Mr. Justice Stone speaking for the United States v. Oregon, as follows:

"Dominion over navigable waters and property in the soil under them are so identified with the sovereign power of government that a presumption against their separation from sovereignty must be indulged, in construing either grants by the sovereign of the lands to be held in private ownership or transfer of sovereignty itself. For that reason, upon the admission of a State to the Union, the title of the United States to lands underlying navigable waters within the States passes to it, as incident to the transfer to the State of local sovereignty, and is subject only to the paramount power of the United States to control such waters for purposes of navigation in interstate and foreign commerce."

The "equal footing" clause, we hold, works the same way in the converse situation presented by this case. It negatives any implied, special limitation of any of the paramount powers of the United States in favor of a State. Texas prior to her admission was a Republic. We assume that as a Republic she had not only full sovereignty over the marginal sea but ownership of it, of the land underlying it, and of all the riches which it held. In other words we assume that it then had the dominium and imperium in and over this belt which the United States now claims. When Texas came into the Union, she ceased to be an independent nation. She then became a sister State on an "equal footing" with all the other States. That act concededly entailed a relinquishment of some of her sovereignty. The United States then took her place as respects foreign commerce, the waging of war, the making of treaties, defense of the shores, and the like. In external affairs the United States became the sole and exclusive spoksman for the Nation. We hold that as an incident to the transfer of that sovereignty any claim that Texas may have had to the marginal sea was relinquished to the United States.

We stated the reasons for this in United States v. California, as follows:

"The three-mile rule is but a recognition of the necessity that a government next to the sea must be able to protect itself from dangers incident to its location. It must have powers of dominion and regulation in the interest of its revenues, its health, and the security of its people from wars waged on or too near its coasts. And insofar as the nation asserts its right under international law, whatever of value may be discovered in the seas next to its shores and within its protective belt, will most naturally be appropriated for its use. But whatever any nation does in the open sea, which detracts from its common usefulness to nations, or which another nation may charge detracts from it, is a question for consideration among nations as such, and not their separate governmental units. What this Government does, or even what the states do, anywhere in the ocean, is a subject upon which the nation may enter into and assume treaty or similar international obligations. The very oil about which the state and nation here contend might well become the subject of international dispute and settlement."

And so although dominium and imperium are normally separable and separate, this is an instance where property interests are so subordinated to the rights of sovereignty as to follow sovereignty.

It is said that there is no necessity for it—that the sovereignty of the sea can be complete and unimpaired no matter if Texas owns the oil underlying it. Yet, as pointed out in the United States v. California, once low-water mark is passed the international domain is reached. Property rights must then be so subordinated to political rights as in substance to coalesce and unite in the national sovereign. Today the controversy is over oil. Tomorrow it may be over some other substance or mineral or perhaps the bed of the ocean itself. If the property, whatever it may be, lies seaward of low-water mark, its use, disposition, management, and control involve national interests and national responsibilities. That is the source of national rights in it. Such is the rationale of the California Decision which we have applied to Louisiana's Case. The same result must be reached here if "equal footing" with the various States is to be achieved. Unless any claim or title which the Republic of Texas had to the marginal sea is subordinated to this full paramount power of the United States on admission, there is or may be in practical effect a subtraction in favor of Texas from the national sovereignty of the United States. Yet neither the original thirteen States nor California nor Louisiana enjoys such an advantage. The "equal footing" clause prevents extension of the sovereignty of a State into a domain of political and sovereign power of the United States from which the other States have been excluded, just as it prevents a contraction of sovereignty which would produce inequality among the States. For equality of States means that they are not "less or greater, or different in dignity or power."

Texas in 1941 sought to extend its boundary to a line in the Gulf of Mexico twenty-four marine miles beyond the three-mile limit and asserted ownership of the bed within that area. And in 1947 she put the extended boundary to the outer edge of the continental shelf. The irrelevancy of these acts to the issue before us has been adequately answered in United States v. Louisiana. The other contentions of Texas need not be detailed. They have been foreclosed by United States v. California and United States v. Louisiana.

The motions of Texas for an order to take depositions and for the appointment of a Special Master are denied. The motion of the United States for judgment is granted. . . .

So ordered.

## 126. HURRICANE CARLA

### September 3-15, 1961

From United States, Department of Commerce, Weather Bureau, *Climatological Data, National Summary,* 1961 (Asheville, 1962), XII, No. 13, 59-63.

Hurricane Carla, second in viciousness only to the great hurricane of 1900, hit the Texas coast at Port O'Connor on Lavaca Bay on September 11, 1961, leaving a path of destruction extending from Corpus Christi to Louisiana. Yet in contrast to the earlier disaster loss of both lives and property was remarkably light, owing particularly to early warnings and to the mass, orderly exodus of the population. Estimates placed the number of evacuees as high as 500,000, and *The Dallas Morning News* reported that of the population of Port Arthur (135,000), Galveston (75,000), and Port Lavaca (10,000) respectively 100,000, 60,000, and 9,200 moved inland to escape the storm.

The United States Weather Bureau made the following official report on Hurricane Carla.

One of the most severe, destructive, and extensive Gulf hurricanes of this century developed in an area of squalls which was first noted in the intertropical convergence zone north of Panama and northwestern Colombia on September 3. The disturbed area moved northwestward; a depression formed on the 4th; and tropical storm force winds appeared by the morning of the 5th. Steady intensification resulted in hurricane force winds on the 6th as the storm, rapidly increasing in size, moved north-northwestward into the Yucatan Channel. By the next day the maximum winds had increased to 110 m.p.h. and gales extended outward from the center for several hundred miles, affecting the Yucatan Peninsula, western Cuba, and the southern Gulf of Mexico. During September 8 and 9 the center of the hurricane moved between west-northwest and northwest toward the Texas coast at a rate of about 9 m.p.h. On the 9th the circulation extended over the entire Gulf of Mexico with fringe effects being felt in all the Gulf Coast States, and the maximum winds near the center estimated by reconnaissance at 135 m.p.h. . . .

As the center of the hurricane closed on the middle Texas coast on the 10th, reconnaissance estimates of maximum winds near the center were 150 m.p.h. Late on the 10th when the "eye" was about 80 miles southeast of Matagorda Island the average forward speed decreased to about 6 m.p.h. and the center, approximately 30 miles in diameter, remained almost stationary at times, finally moving over the northeastern tip of Matagorda Island and inland over the Port Lavaca-Port O'Connor section. The leading edge of the center reached Port O'Connor about 1400 c.s.t. on September 11 and Port Lavaca at 1545. The highest wind on the coast, an estimated peak gust of 175 m.p.h., and the lowest pressure, 935 mb., were reported at the Bauer Dredging Company Office in Port Lavaca. A wind gust of 153 m.p.h. was observed at this place at 1414 c.s.t. before the anemometer failed, and the maximum sustained wind was estimated at 145 m.p.h. . . .

The center of the storm followed a northwesterly course from the coastal area, passing over the towns of Inez, Yoakum, and Waelder. No "eye" was apparent after the center left the Waelder area about 0100 c.s.t. on the 12th. The gradually weakening storm center moved to just east of Austin by 0600 c.s.t., then curved slightly east of north, passed just west of Waco at noon and between Dallas and Ft. Worth about 1800. After moving into east-central Oklahoma during the night the circulation acquired the features of an extratropical low. It moved with increasing forward speed northeastward through the Mississippi Valley, and reached the Lake Huron area on the 14th. . . .

Carla's great size is indicated by the broad coastal area covered by the strong winds. Hurricane force gusts were reported all along the Texas coast from a short distance north of Brownsville to the Port Arthur area—a distance of over 300 miles. Hurricane gusts also reached far inland near the center of the storm, extended almost to Austin—about 130 miles from the coast. Sustained hurricane force winds were reported along the immediate coast from east of Galveston to the Corpus Christi area.

Sustained winds (fastest mile) were reported at 145 m.p.h. at Matagorda and Port Lavaca; 135 m.p.h., estimated, at Aransas Pass and 110 m.p.h. at Victoria. Gust speeds, all estimated, near the center reached 160 m.p.h. at Matagorda, 150 m.p.h at Aransas Pass, Austwell, Edna, Port Aransas, and Victoria. In the Galveston area sustained winds reached 80 m.p.h., with gusts to 112; at Corpus Christi highest gusts were near 90 m.p.h.

The duration of high winds along the coast was exceptionally long due to the large size and the unusually slow forward movement of 6 to 9 m.p.h. Winds were above gale force on most of the Texas coast for periods ranging from 30 to 50 hours. . . .

In Louisiana sustained winds along the coast were generally less than 50 m.p.h., with gusts of 60, 58, and 47 m.p.h. at Cameron, Lake Charles, and Burrwood, respectively.

Torrential rains accompanied Carla in Texas. More than 16 inches of precipitation fell in the coastal area from Galveston to Bay City, east of the storm center. Bay City had a storm total of 17.10 inches. Amounts up to 13 inches fell as far as 130 miles inland over a very irregular pattern. . . . Rainfall decreased northward away from the coast with most of northeastern Texas, east of the storm center, receiving 4 inches or more. Most Gulf drainage streams east of the storm track reached or exceeded flood stage, and flooding and ponding was extensive in the flat coastal plain. The river stage at Wharton, on the lower Colorado, read 30.8 feet at 0700 c.s.t. on the 15th, exceeding the previous record of 30 feet at the peak of the 1957 flood. West of the center, storm totals were generally lighter, exceeding 4 inches only from the eastern Edwards Plateau southward to the coast between Corpus Christi and Brownsville.

Some of the heaviest storm rainfalls were 17.10 inches, Bay City; 16.23 inches, Galveston Airport; 15.6 inches, Freeport; 15.58 inches, Deer Park; 15.26 inches, Galveston City Office; 14.97 inches, Danevang; 13.25 inches, Liberty; 13.23 inches, Giddings.

Rainfall in Louisiana associated with Carla ranged up to 6 inches at several coastal stations. . . .

Eight tornadoes accompanied Carla in Texas. The most severe of these occurred at Galveston at 0315 c.s.t. on the 12th, cutting a path across the island between 19th and 25th Streets, leaving 8 dead, 55 injured, and heavily damaging about 200 buildings, of which about 60 to 75 were totally destroyed. A second tornado moved across Galveston at 0600 c.s.t., destroyed 6 houses, but caused no additional injuries.

At Channelview, near Houston, a tornado at 1750 c.s.t. on the 11th injured 22 persons and caused $200,000 property damage. Two persons were injured in the tornado at Latex, Panola County, and 3 were injured near Jacksonville, Cherokee County. Other tornadoes occurred at Fulbright, Red River County; Hardin, Liberty County; and near Bay City, Matagorda County, with no casualties and relatively minor property damage.

Ten tornadoes were reported in Louisiana, with 6 deaths and 50 injuries.

The Galveston District of the U. S. Army Corps of Engineers has prepared a very comprehensive report of the damages, flooding and the available information about the maximum water levels and the changes in water level with time at many points. . . . The hydrographs in the original report, when interpreted in the light of the available land elevation data, show that large areas of the barrier islands were completely covered with water. The higher high water marks on the inland side of the bays show that the surfaces of these bays were tilted upward toward the inland regions by the effects of the wind over the bays. The local variability of 2 to 3 feet within a mile or two . . . is characteristic of the coastal flooding produced by severe storms. This local variability is believed to be due to the transport of water by breaking waves. This phenomenon is very local in nature and any attempt to draw lines of equal water elevation to these values would be misleading. The high water marks . . . for Laguna Madre north of Brownsville are the result of wind pile-up within the lagoon, not the effect of the hurricane on the open Gulf. . . .

The effects of winds and water in the coastal area near the storm center were devastating. Port O'Connor was virtually destroyed; Palacios, Edna, and Port Lavaca suffered severe damage. Most significant and widespread damage was inflicted along the coastal area between Corpus Christi and Port Arthur, plus the inland counties of Jackson, Wharton, and Harris. Damage was characterized as severe in Calhoun, Matagorda, Brazoria, and Galveston Counties; as heavy in Nueces, Refugio, Chambers, Jefferson, Victoria, Jackson, Wharton, and Harris Counties. Moderate damage occurred in Aransas, San Patricio, Orange, Goliad, Fort Bend, DeWitt, Lavaca, and Colorado Counties. Much of the damage in most places was caused by high water, both from tidal flooding and rainfall, rather than by the high winds. Storm damage gradually decreased inland and was relatively minor 100 miles from the coast.

Overall property and agricultural damage has been estimated by the U. S. Army Corps of Engineers at over $400 million following an extensive survey of the Texas coastal area by teams of experienced storm and flood damage survey personnel. The largest monetary losses occurred at Galveston, Texas City, and Freeport, due to the size and complexity of these cities. . . .

In addition, damage sustained by governmental and relief agencies totaled $4,706,000, making an estimated grand loss of $408,290,000.

In the 16 counties most heavily affected, the Red Cross reported 1,915 homes, 568 farm buildings, and 415 other buildings destroyed; 7,398 homes, 1,382 farm buildings, and 1,219 other buildings with major damage; and 43,325 homes, 4,238 farm buildings, and 9,268 other buildings with minor damage.

Severe damage occurred to the extensive acreages of cotton and rice in the Coastal Bend counties. These crops, nearing harvest, were blown down and waterlogged; losses ranged to complete in some areas. Lesser damage was done to corn, pecans, citrus, and pastures. Livestock losses were heavy in some places where cattle could not be moved to higher ground.

Reports indicate 46 deaths associated with Carla's passage through the Nation: 34 in Texas, 6 in Louisiana in tornadoes, 5 in Kansas, and 1 in Missouri in flash floods. Timely and accurate hurricane warnings produced the largest mass evacuation ever recorded in the United States. An estimated 350,000 persons fled inland from the coastal sections of Texas and Louisiana. This evacuation from areas of danger was near 100 percent in small coastal towns unprotected by sea walls or levees; of the order of 75 to 90 percent in the larger towns; and between 20 and 25 percent in the cities such as Corpus Christi and Galveston. Evacuation was a major factor in the comparatively very low death toll, about one-half of which was due to tornadoes and inland flooding.

# 127. THE ASSASSINATION OF PRESIDENT JOHN F. KENNEDY IN DALLAS

## NOVEMBER 22, 1963

Report of the President's Commission on the Assassination of President Kennedy, USGPO, Washington, 1964, p. 1-4

The assassination of President Kennedy was one of those moments that marked the life of the state and the nation, and marked the life of virtually every American alive at that time. With an eye toward the 1964 presidential election, President Kennedy came to Texas in November 1963 to give several speeches and shore up his support in the state. At that time Dallas had something of a reputation for harboring virulent conservatives. Although it has been suggested that this climate of anger in Dallas created an environment that led to the assassination, the probable assassin, Lee Harvey Oswald, was not allied with Dallas's conservative forces. He had defected to the Soviet Union, but returned to the United States, although he remained sympathetic toward the United States' Cold War enemies. Ironically, it was a disaffected leftist who so seriously tarnished the image of conservative Dallas.

The assassination was an event with enormous symbolic power. The fact that it occurred in Texas reinforced the long-standing image of Texas as a violent, frontier culture. Although this shocking act did dovetail with the popular-culture image of Texas, the assassination may tell us more about Lee Harvey Oswald or about the nation's overall tendencies toward violence in the political arena than about Texas culture itself. Many see this event as symbolizing the loss of American innocence, and the beginning of wide-spread cynicism and disillusionment with American culture and institutions. Although this may be true for the so-called "baby boomers" born in the immediate post-World War II period, the generation which endured the Depression in the 1930s and World War II in the 1940s was far from innocent of the harsh realities of life and death. Others interpret the assassination as symbolic of the loss of civility in American life, the tendency to move political decision-making into the streets where a gun, a riot, or a demonstration (violent or non-violent) drives the political and social process.

The so-called *Warren Report*, a multi-volume set commissioned to investigate the assassination, was issued quickly to ease the national shock. Immediately, however, critics began suggesting that it was not thorough enough, or even that it was a cynical cover-up. A cottage industry of assassination buffs and conspiracy theorists subsequently churned out hundreds of books, articles, even a major Hollywood movie (*JFK*), many of which find conspiracies involving the Soviet Union, Cubans, the CIA, the FBI, the Mafia, and even Kennedy's vice-president, Texan Lyndon B. Johnson, who was sworn in as president that same day. There are entire bibliographies on assassination materials and studies, many of which question the *Report's* summary and conclusions. As in any criminal or historical investigation there are discrepancies and missing evidence, yet the lone assassin conclusion reached by the Warren Commission appears, at this thirty-year remove, to be the only conclusion backed by substantial, convincing evidence.

## SUMMARY AND CONCLUSIONS

The Assassination of John Fitzgerald Kennedy on November 22, 1963, was a cruel and shocking act of violence directed against a man, a family, a nation, and against all mankind. A young and vigorous leader whose years of public and private life stretched before him was the victim of the fourth Presidential assassination in the history of a country dedicated to the concepts of reasoned argument and peaceful political change. This Commission was created on November 29, 1963, in recognition of the right of people everywhere to full and truthful knowledge concerning these events. This report endeavors to fulfill that right and to appraise this tragedy by the light of reason and the standard of fairness. It has been prepared with a deep awareness of the Commission's responsibility to present to the American people an objective report of the facts relating to the assassination.

## NARRATIVE OF EVENTS

At 11:40 a.m., c.s.t., on Friday, November 22, 1963, President John F. Kennedy, Mrs. Kennedy, and their party arrived at Love Field, Dallas, Tex. Behind them was the first day of a Texas trip planned 5 months before by the President, Vice President Lyndon B. Johnson, and John B. Connally, Jr., Governor of Texas. After leaving the White House on Thursday morning, the President had flown initially to San Antonio where Vice President Lyndon B. Johnson joined the party and the President dedicated new research facilities at the U.S. Air Force School of Aerospace Medicine. Following a testimonial dinner in Houston for U.S. Representative Albert Thomas, the President flew to Fort Worth where he spent the night and spoke at a large breakfast gathering on Friday.

Planned for later that day were a motorcade through downtown Dallas, a luncheon speech at the Trade Mart, and a flight to Austin where the President would attend a reception and speak at a Democratic fund-raising dinner. From Austin he would proceed to the Texas ranch of the Vice President. Evident on this trip were the varied roles which an American President performs—Head of State, Chief Executive, party leader, and, in this instance, prospective candidate for re-election

The Dallas motorcade, it was hoped, would evoke a demonstration of the President's personal popularity in a city which he had lost in the 1960 election. Once it had been decided that the trip to Texas would span 2 days, those responsible for planning, primarily Governor Connally and Kenneth O'Donnell, a special assistant to the President, agreed that a motorcade through Dallas would be desirable. The Secret Service was told on November 8 that 45 minutes had been allotted to a motorcade procession from Love Field to the site of a luncheon planned by Dallas business and civic leaders in honor of the President. After considering the facilities and security problems of several buildings, the Trade

Mart was chosen as the luncheon site. Given this selection, and in accordance with the customary practice of affording the greatest number of people an opportunity to see the President, the motorcade route selected was a natural one. The route was approved by the local host committee and White House representatives on November 18 and publicized in the local papers starting on November 19. This advance publicity made it clear that the motorcade would leave Main Street and pass the intersection of Elm and Houston Streets as it proceeded to the Trade Mart by way of the Stemmons Freeway.

By midmorning of November 22, clearing skies in Dallas dispelled the threat of rain and the President greeted the crowds from his open limousine without the "bubbletop," which was at that time a plastic shield furnishing protection only against inclement weather. To the left of the President in the rear seat was Mrs. Kennedy. In the jump seats were Governor Connally, who was in front of the President, and Mrs. Connally at the Governor's left. Agent William R. Greer of the Secret Service was driving, and Agent Roy H. Kellerman was sitting to his right.

Directly behind the Presidential limousine was an open "follow-up" car with eight Secret Service agents, two in the front seat, two in the rear, and two on each running board. These agents, in accordance with normal Secret Service procedures, were instructed to scan the crowds, the roofs, and windows of buildings, overpasses, and crossings for signs of trouble. Behind the "follow-up" car was the Vice-Presidential car carrying the Vice President and Mrs. Johnson and Senator Ralph W. Yarborough. Next were a Vice-Presidential "follow-up" car and several cars and buses for additional dignitaries, press representatives, and others.

The motorcade left Love Field shortly after 11:50 a.m., and proceeded through residential neighborhoods, stopping twice at the President's request to greet well-wishers among the friendly crowds. Each time the President's car halted, Secret Service agents from the "follow-up" car moved forward to assume a protective stance near the President and Mrs. Kennedy. As the motorcade reached Main Street, a principal east-west artery in downtown Dallas, the welcome became tumultuous. At the extreme west end of Main Street the motorcade turned right on Houston Street and proceeded north for one block in order to make a left turn on Elm Street, the most direct and convenient approach to the Stemmons Freeway and the Trade Mart. As the President's car approached the intersection of Houston and Elm Streets, there loomed directly ahead on the intersection's northwest corner a seven-story, orange brick warehouse and office building, the Texas School Book Depository. Riding in the Vice President's car, Agent Rufus W. Youngblood of the Secret Service noticed that the clock atop the building indicated 12:30 p.m., the scheduled arrival time at the Trade Mart.

The President's car which had been going north made a sharp turn toward the southwest onto Elm Street. At a speed of about 11 miles per hour, it started down the gradual descent toward a railroad overpass under which the motorcade would

proceed before reaching the Stemmons Freeway. The front of the Texas School Book Depository was now on the President's right, and he waved to the crowd assembled there as he passed the building. Dealey Plaza—an open, landscaped area marking the western end of downtown Dallas—stretched out to the President's left. A Secret Service agent riding in the motorcade radioed the Trade Mart that the President would arrive in 5 minutes.

Seconds later shots resounded in rapid succession. The President's hands moved to his neck. He appeared to stiffen momentarily and lurch slightly forward in his seat. A bullet had entered the base of the back of his neck slightly to the right of the spine. It traveled downward and exited from the front of the neck, causing a nick in the lower portion of the knot in the President's necktie. Before the shooting started, Governor Connally had been facing toward the crowd on the right. He started to turn toward the left and suddenly felt a blow on his back. The Governor had been hit by a bullet which entered at the extreme right side of his back at a point below his right armpit. The bullet traveled through his chest in a downward and forward direction, exited below his right nipple, passed through his right wrist which had been in his lap, and then caused a wound to his left thigh. The force of the bullet's impact appeared to spin the Governor to his right, and Mrs. Connally pulled him down into her lap. Another bullet then struck President Kennedy in the rear portion of his head, causing a massive and fatal wound. The President fell to the left into Mrs. Kennedy's lap.

Secret Service Agent Clinton J. Hill, riding on the left running board of the "follow-up" car, heard a noise which sounded like a firecracker and saw the President suddenly lean forward and to the left. Hill jumped off the car and raced toward the President's limousine. In the front seat of the Vice-Presidential car, Agent Youngblood heard an explosion and noticed unusual movements in the crowd. He vaulted into the rear seat and sat on the Vice President in order to protect him. At the same time Agent Kellerman in the front seat of the Presidential limousine turned to observe the President. Seeing that the President was struck, Kellerman instructed the driver, "Let's get out of here; we are hit." He radioed ahead to the lead car, "Get us to the hospital immediately." Agent Greer immediately accelerated the Presidential car. As it gained speed, Agent Hill managed to pull himself onto the back of the car where Mrs. Kennedy had climbed. Hill pushed her back into the rear seat and shielded the stricken President and Mrs. Kennedy as the President's car proceeded at high speed to Parkland Memorial Hospital, 4 miles away.

At Parkland, the President was immediately treated by a team of physicians who had been alerted for the President's arrival by the Dallas Police Department as the result of a radio message from the motorcade after the shooting. The doctors noted irregular breathing movements and a possible heartbeat, although they could not detect a pulsebeat. They observed the extensive wound in the President's head and a small wound approximately one-fourth inch in diameter in the lower third portion of his neck. In an effort to facilitate breathing, the physicians performed a tracheotomy by enlarging the throat wound and inserting a tube. Totally absorbed in the immediate task of trying to preserve the President's life, the attending doctors never turned the President over for an examination of his back. At 1 p.m., after all heart activity ceased and the Last Rites were administered by a priest, President Kennedy was pronounced dead. Governor Connally underwent surgery and ultimately recovered from his serious wounds.

Upon learning of the President's death, Vice President Johnson left Parkland Hospital under close guard and proceeded to the Presidential plane at Love Field. Mrs. Kennedy, accompanying her husband's body, boarded the plane shortly thereafter. At 2:38 p.m., in the central compartment of the plane, Lyndon B. Johnson was sworn in as the 36th President of the United States by Federal District Court Judge Sarah T. Hughes. The plane left immediately for Washington, D.C., arriving at Andrews AFB, Md., at 5:58 p.m., e.s.t.

## 128. LYNDON BAINES JOHNSON, PRESIDENT OF THE UNITED STATES

### 1963-1969

When Vice President Lyndon Baines Johnson of Texas was sworn in as president of the United States on November 22, 1963, hours after the assassination of John F. Kennedy, Texas had what many would say was the only true Texas president. Although Dwight D. Eisenhower was born in Texas, he lived in the state only briefly, and New England-born George Bush was a naturalized Texan who moved here following his service in World War II. Unlike these two, LBJ was perceived as the quintessential Texas politician and the quintessential Texas president: bigger than life, rough-hewn and outrageous but shrewd and intelligent, egocentric but in touch with the common man.

Reelected by a landslide in 1964, LBJ served until 1969. His tenure as president came during a volatile period in American life when civil rights battles at home and military conflict abroad resulted in great public debate and conflict over the direction of the country. Many see his "Great Society" domestic social policies—the War on Poverty, Civil Rights legislation, Medicare—as his greatest political success, although detractors believe that he attempted too much and that his tendency to prescribe a new, expensive program to deal with every social problem was fatally flawed. The following excerpts from his speeches include his May 22, 1964, remarks at the University of Michigan where he first put forward the concept of the Great Society and his vision of what America could become. This is followed by remarks from his "American Promise" speech delivered to Congress on March 15, 1965. This memorable civil rights speech included comments about his youthful experience in 1928 as a teacher in a small Mexican-American school in Cotulla, Texas, and the impact of that experience on his understanding of poverty and prejudice. Excerpts from a speech given at that Cotulla schoolhouse in 1966 expand on his earlier comments about the importance of education, and reveal how his life in Texas informed his future and the future of the nation.

Johnson's central foreign policy initiative—aggressively pursuing the war in Vietnam—is widely seen as his political Waterloo. Although some now regard that long and controversial war as an important facet of the containment policy that eventually won the Cold War against communism, the war's length, televised brutality, and divisiveness caused great anguish in the nation and brought Johnson's presidency to an abrupt and unhappy end. In a speech from the White House on March 31, 1968, President Johnson spoke movingly of his hopes for peace, his concern about the great divisions within the country, and his decision not to seek another term as president.

### 1. THE GREAT SOCIETY

#### May 22, 1964

From "Remarks at the University of Michigan, May 22, 1964." *Public Papers of the Presidents of the United States, Lyndon B. Johnson, 1963-1964*, 2 vols. (Washington, 1965), 1: pp. 704-707.

I have come today from the turmoil of your Capital to the tranquility of your campus to speak about the future of your country.

The purpose of protecting the life of our Nation and preserving the liberty of our citizens is to pursue the happiness of our people. Our success in that pursuit is the test of our success as a Nation.

For a century we labored to settle and to subdue a continent. For half a century we called upon unbounded invention and untiring industry to create an order of plenty for all of our people.

The challenge of the next half century is whether we have the wisdom to use that wealth to enrich and elevate our national life, and to advance the quality of our American civilization.

Your imagination, your initiative, and your indignation will determine whether we build a society where progress is the servant of our needs, or a society where old values and new visions are buried under unbridled growth. For in your time we have the opportunity to move not only toward the rich society and the powerful society, but upward to the Great Society.

The Great Society rests on abundance and liberty for all. It demands an end to poverty and racial injustice, to which we are totally committed in our time. But that is just the beginning.

The Great Society is a place where every child can find knowledge to enrich his mind and to enlarge his talents. It is a place where leisure is a welcome chance to build and reflect, not a feared cause of boredom and restlessness. It is a place where the city of man serves not only the needs of the body and the demands of commerce but the desire for beauty and the hunger for community.

It is a place where man can renew contact with nature. It is a place which honors creation for its own sake and for what it adds to the understanding of the race. It is a place where men are more concerned with the quality of their goals than the quantity of their goods.

But most of all, the Great Society is not a safe harbor, a resting place, a final objective, a finished work. It is a challenge constantly renewed, beckoning us toward a destiny where the meaning of our lives matches the marvelous products of our labor.

So I want to talk to you today about three places where we begin to build the Great Society—in our cities, in our countryside, and in our classrooms. . . .

These are three of the central issues of the Great Society. While our Government has many programs directed at those issues, I do not pretend that we have the full answer to those problems.

But I do promise this: We are going to assemble the best thought and the broadest knowledge from all over the world to find those answers for America. I intend to establish working groups to prepare a series of White House conferences and meetings—on the cities, on natural beauty, on the quality of education, and on other emerging challenges. And from these meetings and from this inspiration and from these studies we will begin to set our course toward the Great Society.

The solution to these problems does not rest on a massive program in Washington, nor can it rely solely on the strained resources of local authority. They require us to create new concepts of cooperation, a creative federalism, between the National Capital and the leaders of local communities.

Woodrow Wilson once wrote: "Every man sent out from his university should be a man of his Nation as well as a man of his time."

Within your lifetime powerful forces, already loosed, will take us toward a way of life beyond the realm of our experience, almost beyond the bounds of our imagination.

For better or for worse, your generation has been appointed by history to deal with those problems and to lead America toward a new age. You have the chance never before afforded to any people in any age. You can help build a society where the demands of morality, and the needs of the spirit, can be realized in the life of the Nation.

So, will you join in the battle to give every citizen an escape from the crushing weight of poverty?

Will you join in the battle to make it possible for all nations to live in enduring peace—as neighbors and not as mortal enemies?

Will you join in the battle to build the Great Society, to prove that our material progress is only the foundation on which we will build a richer life of mind and spirit?

There are those timid souls who say this battle cannot be won; that we are condemned to a soulless wealth. I do not

agree. We have the power to shape the civilization that we want. But we need your will, your labor, your hearts, if we are to build that kind of society.

Those who came to this land sought to build more than just a new country. They sought a new world. So I have come here today to your campus to say that you can make their vision our reality. So let us from this moment begin our work so that in the future men will look back and say: It was then, after a long and weary way, that man turned the exploits of his genius to the full enrichment of his life.

## 2. THE AMERICAN PROMISE

### March 15, 1965

From "Special Message to the Congress on the Right to Vote," *Public Papers of the Presidents of the United States, Lyndon B. Johnson, 1965*, 2 vols. (Washington, 1966), 1: pp. 287-291.

I speak tonight for the dignity of man and the destiny of democracy.

I urge every member of both parties, Americans of all religions and of all colors, from every section of this country, to join me in that cause.

At times history and fate meet at a single time in a single place to shape a turning point in man's unending search for freedom. So it was at Lexington and Concord. So it was a century ago at Appomattox. So it was last week in Selma, Alabama.

There, long-suffering men and women peacefully protested the denial of their rights as Americans. Many were brutally assaulted. One good man, a man of God, was killed.

There is no cause for pride in what has happened in Selma. There is no cause for self-satisfaction in the long denial of equal rights to millions of Amercans. But there is cause for hope and for faith in our democracy in what is happening here tonight.

For the cries of pain and the hymns and protests of oppressed people have summoned into convocation all the majesty of this great government of the greatest nation on earth.

Our mission is at once the oldest and the most basic of this country: to right wrong, to do justice, to serve man.

In our time we have come to live with moments of great crisis. Our lives have been marked with debate about great issues; issues of war and peace, of prosperity and depression. But rarely in any time does an issue lay bare the secret heart of America itself. Rarely are we met with a challenge, not to our growth or abundance, or welfare or our security, but rather to the values and the purposes and the meaning of our beloved nation.

The issue of equal rights for American Negroes is such an issue. And should we defeat every enemy, should we double our wealth and conquer the stars, and still be unequal to this issue, then we will have failed as a people and as a nation.

For with a country as with a person, "What is a man

profited, if he shall gain the whole world, and lose his own soul?"

There is no Negro problem. There is no Southern problem. There is no Northern problem. There is only an American problem. And we are met here tonight as Americans to solve that problem.

This was the first nation in the history of the world to be founded with a purpose. The great phrases of that purpose still sound in every American heart, North and South: "All men are created equal"—"government by consent of the governed"—"give me liberty or give me death." Those are not just clever words. Those are not just empty theories. In their name Americans have fought and died for two centuries, and tonight around the world they stand there are guardians of our liberty, risking their lives.

Those words are a promise to every citizen that he shall share in the dignity of man. This dignity cannot be found in a man's possessions, his power or his position. It rests on his right to be treated as a man equal in opportunity to all others. It says that he shall share in freedom, choose his leaders, educate his children, and provide for his family according to his ability and his merits as a human being.

To apply any other test—to deny a man his hopes because of his color or race, his religion or the place of his birth—is not only to do injustice, it is to deny America and to dishonor the dead who gave their lives for American freedom.

Our fathers believed that if this noble view of the rights of man was to flourish, it must be rooted in democracy. The most basic right of all was the right to choose your own leaders. The history of this country, in large measure, is the history of the expansion of that right to all of our people.

Many of the issues of civil rights are very complex and most difficult. But about this there can and should be no argument. Every American citizen must have an equal right to vote. There is no reason which can excuse the denial of that right. There is no duty which weighs more heavily on us than the duty we have to ensure that right. . . .

The last time a President sent a civil rights bill to the Congress it contained a provision to protect voting rights in Federal elections. That civil rights bill was passed after eight long months of debate. And when that bill came to my desk from the Congress, the heart of the voting provision had been eliminated.

This time, on this issue, there must be no delay, no hesitation and no compromise with our purpose.

We cannot, we must not, refuse to protect the right of every American to vote in every election that he may desire to participate in. We ought not, we must not, wait another eight months before we get a bill. We have already waited a hundred years and more, and the time for waiting is gone.

I ask you to join me in working long hours, nights, and weekends if necessary, to pass this bill. And I don't make that request lightly. For from the window where I sit with the problems of our country I am aware that outside this chamber is the outraged conscience of a nation, the grave concern of many nations, and the harsh judgment of history on our acts.

But even if we pass this bill, the battle will not be over. What happened in Selma is part of a far larger movement which reaches into every section and state of America. It is the effort of American Negroes to secure for themselves the full blessings of American life.

Their cause must be our cause too. It is not just Negroes, but it is all of us, who must overcome the crippling legacy of bigotry and injustice.

And we shall overcome.

As a man whose roots go deeply into Southern soil I know how agonizing racial feelings are. I know how difficult it is to reshape the attitudes and the structure of our society. . . .

The bill that I am presenting to you will be known as a civil rights bill. But, in a larger sense, most of the program I am recommending is a civil rights program. Its object is to open the city of hope to all people of all races.

All Americans must have the right to vote. And we are going to give them that right.

All Americans must have the privileges of citizenship regardless of race. And they are going to have those privileges of citizenship regardless of race. . . .

My first job after college was as a teacher in Cotulla, Texas, in a small Mexican-American school. Few of them could speak English, and I couldn't speak much Spanish. My students were poor and they often came to class without breakfast, hungry. They knew even in their youth the pain of prejudice. They never seemed to know why people disliked them. But they knew it was so, because I saw it in their eyes. I often walked home late in the afternoon, after the classes were finished, wishing there was more that I could do. But all I knew was to teach them the little that I knew, hoping that it might help them against the hardships that lay ahead.

Somehow you never forget what poverty and hatred can do when you see its scars on the hopeful face of a young child.

I never thought then, in 1928, that I would be standing here in 1965. It never occurred to me in my fondest dreams that I might have the chance to help the sons and daughters of those students and to help people like them all over this country.

But now I do have that chance—I'll let you in on a secret—I mean to use it. And I hope that you will use it with me. . . .

Above the pyramid on the great seal of the United States it says—in Latin—"God has favored our undertaking."

God will not favor everything that we do. It is rather our duty to divine His will. But I cannot help believing that He truly understands and that He really favors the undertaking that we begin here tonight.

### 3. COTULLA, TEXAS

November 7, 1966

From "Remarks at the Welhausen Elementary School, Cotulla, Texas, November 7, 1966," *Public Papers of the Presidents of the United States, Lyndon B. Johnson, 1966*, 2 vols. (Washington, 1967), 2: pp. 1347-1350.

Mayor Cotulla, my friend Dan Garcia, all of my former students, boys and girls:

I have come back to Cotulla this afternoon not just because this school is part of my past, but because this school is a part of America's future.

Everything I want to work for, as your President, to achieve peace, to conquer poverty, to build a worthy civilization—all of these depend in a very large degree on what happens in this school and what happens in other schools throughout our land.

Thirty-eight years ago I came to Cotulla. I was still a student myself. I was working my way through the San Marcos Teachers College.

In those days, neither America nor her schools shared any abundance. We had only five teachers here in the Welhausen public school. We had no lunch facilities. We had no school buses. We had very little money for educating people of this community. We did not have money to buy our playground equipment, our volleyballs, our softball bat. I took my first month's salary and invested in those things for my children.

About the only thing we had an ample supply of was determination—determination to see it through.

I worked as a teacher for the fifth, sixth, and seventh grades.

I worked as a principal of five teachers.

I worked as a playground supervisor.

I coached the boys' baseball team.

I was a debate coach.

I was the song leader. You would not believe that, but I tried to be, anyway.

In my spare time sometimes I acted as assistant janitor.

In that year, I think I learned far more than I taught. And the greatest lesson was this one: Nothing—nothing at all—matters more than trained intelligence. It is the key not only to success in life, but it is the key to meaning in life.

And that is true for a nation, too.

Our greatest national resource probably is not even listed in your textbooks. Our greatest resource is the skill, the vision, and the wisdom of our people.

That is why we invest more in education than in any other enterprise in this country, except our national defense.

That is why last year your National Government pledged billions of new dollars to help improve your school and schools all over America.

In the last 3 years, we have inaugurated more than 40 new programs for health and education for our children in this country.

The Welhausen School looks very much the way it did when I was here. It has not changed a lot in 38 years. But things are happening here and in other schools throughout this land.

We have new reading programs. We have new child nutrition programs. We have new health programs. We have after-hours education centers—all made possible because of the interest your Government has in educating its children. . . .

But it would help little for your Nation to put education first if you don't put education first.

Often young Americans write to ask their President, "What can we do to help our country?"

Well, this is my answer: If you want to help your country, stay in school as long as you can. Work to the limit of your ability and your ambition to get all the education you can absorb—all the education you can take.

What you are doing now is the most important work that you can possibly do for your country. . . .

I am so happpy to be back where these memories are so strong.

Thirty-eight years have passed, but I still see the faces of the children who sat in my class. I still hear their eager voices speaking Spanish as I came in. I still see their excited eyes speaking friendship.

Right here I had my first lessions in poverty. I had my first lessons in the high price we pay for poverty and prejudice right here.

Thirty-eight years later our Nation is still paying that price.

Three out of every four Mexican-American children now in a Texas school will drop out before they get to the eighth grade.

One out of every three Mexican-Americans in Texas who are older than 14 have had less than 5 years of school.

How long can we pay that price?

In one school district alone, one out of every two children is of Mexican-American descent. But two out of every three graduating seniors this year will be Anglo.

How long can we pay that kind of a price?

In five of our Southwestern States, 19 percent of the total population was less than 8 years of school. Almost one-fifth of the population in five States has less than 8 years in school.

What is the percent of the Mexican-Americans with less than 8 years of school? How many Mexican-Americans have less than 8 years of school? Fifty-three percent. Over half of all the Mexican-American children have less than 8 years of school.

How long can we pay that price?

I will give you that answer this afternoon. I will give that answer to America this afternoon. I will say: We can afford to pay that price no longer. No longer can we afford second-class education for children who know that they have a right to be first-class citizens. . . .

Here in Cotulla, 38 years ago, under the leadership of Judge Welhausen, you provided this beautiful brick building, one of the most modern of its kind in its time. You provided the children with modern facilities—with free textbooks—with generally good teachers. You set the example and you gave the inspiration.

As I walked in today, I saw the faces of many who grew up in this area—many who grew up here who went on and went to college.

I rode in with one of my students whom I had paddled right here in this room—who now has two daughters in one of our senior schools.

To the people of Cotulla for the vision that you exercised many years ago in building this beautiful plant—almost 40 years ago—for the sacrifices that you made to provide good teachers, for the products that you have turned out as represented here on this platform today, we say: Thank you.

But we say to all the Nation that we have not yet done enough. The time for action is now.

## 4. PEACE

### March 31, 1968

From "The President's Address to the Nation Announcing Steps to Limit the War in Vietnam and Reporting His Decision Not to Seek Reelection, March 31, 1968," *Public Papers of the Presidents of The United States, Lyndon B. Johnson, 1968-1969*, 2 vols. (Washington, 1969), 1: pp. 469-476.

Good evening, my fellow Americans. Tonight I want to speak to you of peace in Vietnam and Southeast Asia. No other question so preoccupies our people. No other dream so absorbs the 250 million human beings who live in that part of the world. No other goal motivates American policy in Southeast Asia.

For years, representatives of our government and others have travelled the world—seeking to find a basis for peace talks.

Since last September, they have carried the offer that I made public at San Antonio.

That offer was this:

That the United States would stop its bombardment of North Vietnam when that would lead promptly to productive discussions—and that we would assume that North Vietnam would not take military advantage of our restraint.

Hanoi denounced this offer, both privately and publicly. Even while the search for peace was going on, North Vietnam rushed their preparations for a savage assault on the people, the government, and the allies of South Vietnam.

Their attack—during the Tet holidays—failed to achieve its principal objectives.

It did not collapse the elected government of South Vietnam or shatter its army—as the Communists had hoped.

It did not produce a "general uprising" among the people of the cities as they had predicted.

The Communists were unable to maintain control of any of the more than 30 cities that they attacked. And they took very heavy casualties.

But they did compel the South Vietnamese and their allies to move certain forces from the countryside, into the cities.

They caused widespread disruption and suffering. Their attacks, and the battles that followed, made refugees of half a million human beings.

The Communists may renew their attack any day.

They are, it appears, trying to make 1968 the year of decision in South Vietnam—the year that brings, if not final victory or defeat, at least a turning point in the struggle. . . .

Tonight, I renew the offer I made last August—to stop the bombardment of North Vietnam. We ask that talks begin promptly, that they be serious talks on the substances of peace. We assume that during those talks Hanoi will not take advantage of our restraint.

We are prepared to move immediately toward peace through negotiations.

So, tonight, in the hope that this action will lead to early talks, I am taking the first step to de-escalate the conflict. We are reducing—substantially reducing—the present level of hostilities. And we are doing so unilaterally, and at once.

Tonight, I have ordered our aircraft and our naval vessels to make no attacks on North Vietnam, except in the area north of the Demilitarized Zone where the continuing enemy build-up directly threatens allied forward positions and where the movements of their troops and supplies are clearly related to that threat. . . .

I cannot promise that the initiative that I have announced tonight will be completely successful in achieving peace any more than the 30 others that we have undertaken and agreed to in recent years.

But it is our fervent hope that North Vietnam, after years of fighting that has left the issue unresolved, will now cease its efforts to achieve a military victory and will join with us in moving toward the peace table.

And there may come a time when South Vietnamese—on both sides—are able to work out a way to settle their own differences by free political choice rather than by war.

As Hanoi considers its course, it should be in no doubt of our intentions. It must not miscalculate the pressures within our democracy in this election year.

We have no intention of widening this war.

But the United States will never accept a fake solution to this long and arduous struggle and call it peace. . . .

So tonight I reaffirm the pledge that we made at Manila—that we are prepared to withdraw our forces from South Vietnam as the other side withdraws its forces to the North, stops the infiltration, and the level of violence thus subsides.

Our goal of peace and self-determination in Vietnam is directly related to the future of all of Southeast Asia—where much has happened to inspire confidence during the past 10 years. We have done all that we knew how to do to contribute and to help build that confidence. . . .

I think every American can take a great deal of pride in the role that we have played in bringing this about in Southeast Asia. We can rightly judge—as responsible Southeast Asians themselves do—that the progress of the past three years would have been far less likely—if not completely impossible—if America's sons and others had not made their stand in Vietnam. . . .

But the heart of our involvement in South Vietnam—under three Presidents, three separate Administrations—has always been America's own security.

And the larger purpose of our involvement has always been to help the nations of Southeast Asia become independent and stand alone, self-sustaining as members of a great world community . . . at peace with themselves, and at peace with all others. . . .

Finally, my fellow Americans, let me say this:

Of those to whom much is given, much is asked. I cannot say and no man could say that no more will be asked of us.

Yet, I believe that now, no less than when the decade began, this generation of Americans is willing to "pay any price, bear any burden, meet any hardship, support any friend, oppose any foe, to assure the survival and the success of liberty."

Since those words were spoken by John F. Kennedy, the people of America have kept that compact with mankind's noblest cause.

And we shall continue to keep it.

Yet, I believe that we must always be mindful of this one thing, whatever the trials and the tests ahead. The ultimate strength of our country and our cause will lie not in powerful weapons or infinite resources or boundless wealth, but will lie in the unity of our people.

This, I believe very deeply.

Throughout my entire public career I have followed the personal philosophy that I am a free man, an American, a public servant, and a member of my party, in that order always and only.

For 37 years in the service of our Nation, first as a Congressman, as a Senator, and as Vice President, and now as your President, I have put the unity of the people first. I have put it ahead of any divisive partisanship.

And in these items as in times before, it is true that a house divided against itself by the spirit of faction, of party, of religion, of race, is a house that cannot stand.

There is division in the American house now. There is divisiveness among us all tonight. And holding the trust that is mine, as President of all the people, I cannot disregard the peril to the progress of the American people and the hope and the prospect of peace for all peoples.

So, I would ask all Americans, whatever their personal interests or concern, to guard against divisiveness and all its ugly consequences.

Fifty-two months and ten days ago, in a moment of tragedy and trauma, the duties of this office fell upon me. I asked then for your help and God's, that we might continue America on its course, binding up our wounds, healing our history, moving forward in new unity, to clear the American agenda and to keep the American commitment for all of our people.

United we have kept that commitment. United we have enlarged that commitment.

Through all time to come, I think America will be a stronger nation, a more just society, and a land of greater opportunity and fulfillment because of what we have all done together in these years of unparalleled achievement.

Our reward will come in the life of freedom, peace, and hope that our children will enjoy through ages ahead.

What we won when all of our people united just must not now be lost in suspicion, distrust, selfishness, and politics among any of our people.

Believing this as I do, I have concluded that I should not permit the Presidency to become involved in the partisan divisions that are developing in this political year.

With America's sons in the fields far away, with America's future under challenge right here at home, with our hopes and the world's hopes for peace in the balance every day, I do not believe that I should devote an hour or a day of my time to any personal partisan causes or to any duties other than the awesome duties of this office—the Presidency of your country.

Accordingly, I shall not seek, and I will not accept, the nomination of my party for another term as your President.

But let men everywhere know, however, that a strong, a confident, and a vigilant America stands ready tonight to seek an honorable peace—and stands ready tonight to defend an honored cause—whatever the price, whatever the burden, whatever the sacrifices that duty may require.

Thank you for listening.

Good night and God bless all of you.

# 129. VIOLENCE IN TEXAS: THE CHARLES J. WHITMAN SHOOTING

## AUGUST 1, 1966

From Press Conference, Report to the Governor, Medical Aspects, Charles J. Whitman
Catastrophe, September 8, 1966

In the public imagination, the history of Texas has been marked by extreme violence. The historical record indeed shows that the peopling and development of Texas has produced its share of violence, although this violence may not have been any more common or extreme than in other Southern and Western states or, for that matter, urban industrial states in the East or Midwest.

Before Europeans arrived in the New World, Native American tribes in what would someday be called Texas fought among themselves, sometimes displacing entire peoples, and in turn Spaniards, Mexicans, and Americans moved in and fought against Indians and each other. A violent revolution with pivotal, mythic battles at the Alamo and San Jacinto established an independent Texas, born in blood. Texas's soldiers in the Mexican War and the Civil War, and every war thereafter, have been celebrated for their skill and ferocity.

Feuds, lynchings, race riots, and atrocities on the part of citizens, vigilantes, and police alike have been a part of the Texas experience. World War II's great American soldier hero was Texan Audie Murphy, and Norman Mailer's quintessential fictional soldier for the same war was violent Texan Sam Croft in *The Naked and The Dead*.

Popular culture figures, from Davy Crockett going down swinging his rifle at the Alamo to Bonnie and Clyde racing across Texas a century later, have created powerful images of Texas as a land dominated by violence and populated exclusively by cowboys and Indians, Rangers and vaqueros, outlaws and lawmen, oil-field roughnecks and rodeo riders. In the last thirty years, the Texas experience has included the Kennedy assassination, Charles Whitman's deadly fusillade of bullets from the University of Texas tower, several notorious serial killers, mass murder in a restaurant in Killeen, and the shootout and deadly fire near Waco between the Branch Davidian religious cult and the Bureau of Alcohol, Tobacco, and Firearms and the FBI. All of these prominent events reinforced the perception of Texas as an especially violent culture whose frontier-born heritage has outlived its usefulness in what is now a predominantly urban state. This official report to the governor on the Whitman massacre on the University of Texas campus touches on the concern, fear, and fascination that Texans and Americans in general have with violence. Among the numerous recommendations in the report is one heard repeatedly for thirty years in many contexts: that the news media and entertainment industry must examine their frequent emphasis on violence.

Pursuant to the request of the Governor of the State of Texas and the Chairman of the Board of Regents of The University of Texas that a detailed investigation be made of all the available medical and related psychiatric facts concerning the late Charles J. Whitman, perpetrator of the catastrophe which occurred in Austin, Texas, on August 1, 1966, the objectives of study were outlined:

1. To determine the events and circumstances which surrounded the actions of Charles J. Whitman on August 1, 1966.

2. To explore the findings and make such additional examinations as might be indicated by the factual information which is available.

3. To prepare the material for its maximal utilization in evaluating the problem for our society. . . .

Charles Joseph Whitman was born on June 24, 1941, following an apparently full-term pregnancy and normal delivery. He had the usual childhood illnesses, none of which had any recorded sequelae. At the age of 16 he underwent an appendectomy, and three months later was hospitalized because of a motorbike accident.

During the first six years of his life, he and his family moved eight times. They settled in their present home in Lake Worth, Florida, in June, 1947. In September of that year, Charles entered the Catholic grade school. His brother Patrick was born in 1945, and his brother John Mike in 1947. In 1948, Charles began piano lessons, in which his father expected him to excel. Charles joined the Boy Scouts in 1952 at the age of 11. When he was 12, he had attained the rank of Eagle Scout, and received national recognition for being the youngest Scout to achieve that rating. At that same time he was considered to be quite good at the piano. Charles gradu-

ated from the eighth grade in June, 1955, and in September of that year he entered a Catholic high school. He was graduated from that same school in June, 1959, in the upper 25 per cent of his class.

Although he was reported as having been accepted for enrollment at the Georgia Institute of Technology after graduating from high school, Whitman enlisted in the Marine Corps at the age of 18. During the next 26 months of active duty, he underwent the normal physical examinations, which indicated no unusual findings.

In September, 1961, at the age of 20, Whitman was awarded a Naval Enlisted Science Education Program (NESEP) scholarship to The University of Texas in Austin. In the next 17 months (until February, 1963, when his scholarship was withdrawn for unacceptable academic performance) he underwent several complete routine physical examinations which showed no new data.

In February of 1962, Whitman began dating Kathryn Leissner of Needville, Texas, then a student at The University of Texas at Austin. They were married on August 17, 1962. During this period at The University of Texas before his marriage, Whitman had served as a dormitory counselor. At some time during the preceding year, (November, 1961), he was found guilty of illegal possession of a deer which he had "poached," and for which he was fined. In March of 1962, a check given for a gambling debt (he gambled often) was returned for insufficient funds.

Following withdrawal of his scholarship, Whitman returned to active duty with the Marine Corps in February, 1963. His wife "Kathy" was graduated from the University and stayed in Austin as a teacher. In April, 1963, he attempted unsuccessfully to re-enroll in the NESEP program.

During his second period of active duty in the Marine Corps, he again underwent the usual physical examinations. At one time he was hospitalized for four days following a jeep accident in which Whitman and another Marine went over an embankment. According to witnesses, Whitman, although groggy, lifted the jeep from his pinned companion, then collapsed and was unconscious for several hours. His medical records stated that the findings were unremarkable. His physical examination for release from the service in November, 1964, revealed nothing of note.

By July, 1963, Whitman had advanced to the rank of Lance Corporal in the Marine Corps. However, on February 7, 1964, his rank was reduced to that of Private as the result of a summary court martial convicting him to 90 days of hard labor because he had loaned money at usurious rates.

In January, 1965, Whitman returned to The University of Texas. During this period of study, he maintained a B average, with an A minus average for one semester. In January, 1965, Whitman became a Scout Master, a position which he filled for a year. From April to June, 1965, he served as a bank teller to earn extra money. On May 1, 1965, he was bonded as an insurance agent and as a real estate broker. He received two traffic tickets for speeding in 1966, one on February 24, and one on March 20.

In late February, 1966, his parents' marital problems reached a climax, and on March 2, Whitman drove to Florida and assisted his mother in moving to Austin and she left her husband. In Austin, Whitman made arrangements for a separate apartment for his mother.

It is known that Whitman visited the Tower at The University of Texas twice during the recent months of 1966, once on April 5 with a friend, and once on July 22 with relatives.

On March 29, 1966, he sought psychiatric help at the Student Health Center and after approximately an hour's session with the psychiatrist, was told to return in one week and whom to call if he needed help in the meantime. He did not return nor did he call.

Following the Tower Incident, close friends and associates were questioned regarding possible neurologic deficit. No evidence of disability in speech, gait, face, or hand movements, or state of consciousness was described by those interviewed.

It required nearly an hour and a half to positively identify the sniper as 25-year-old college junior, Charles Joseph Whitman. A check of his and his mother's apartments then revealed two additional murders. His wife of four years was found stabbed four times in the chest and his mother dead with a stab wound in the chest and a gunshot wound in the back of the head.

Whitman had begun about midnight by killing his wife and mother, according to notes found with the bodies. In the morning, after calmly purchasing guns and ammunition from three stores and preparing an elaborate trunk full of supplies, he had ascended the Tower to continue his murderous action which left 16 dead and 32 wounded. Whitman's own death brought the toll to 49.

Since Whitman's father signed a release granting permission for the study, the study of the autopsy findings and related consultations was undertaken by a group of nine specialists with the assistance of Dr. Coloman de Chenar who had performed the autopsy on the 25-year-old, white male, in Austin on August 2, 1966. . . .

The malignant tumor removed from the brain by Dr. de Chenar microscopically exhibited the features of a glioblastoma multiforme with a remarkable vascular component of the nature of a small congenital vascular malformation. It contained widespread areas of necrosis with palisading of cells characteristic of glioblastoma multiforme.

No evidence of other diseases or previous trauma was observed although the destruction of the brain by the gunshot wounds was so extensive that anatomic relationships could not be completely evaluated and the examination of all the major nerve tracts and nuclei of the brain was impossible.

Specialists at the Armed Forces Institute of Pathology in Washington, D.C., reviewed formalin-fixed and embalmed specimens of tissue from the brain, kidney, stomach, and liver for toxicological analysis. The report indicated:

Kidney, stomach and brain — no finding of basic drugs

Liver — no findings of barbituates

Kidney — no findings of neutral drugs

Consultation with the Office of Drug Surveillance, Bureau of Medicine, Food and Drug Administration also confirmed the negative findings.

The data obtained provide no evidence that this man had a clinical neurological abnormality, and there is no evidence from the pathological reports that its [ the tumor's ] presence interrupted pathways leading to detectable neurological signs.

However the committee of neurologists, neurosurgeons, and neurophysiologists interested in the clinical and physiological aspects of the nervous system recognizes that abnormal aggressive behavior may be a manifestation of organic brain disease.

While both physiological and clinical studies are pointing increasingly to certain deeper portions of the brain and the temporal lobe as the substrate for normal and abnormal behavioral patterns evolving emotion, the application of existing knowledge of organic brain function does not enable us to explain the actions of Whitman on August first. . . .

The review of behavioral data received in confidence led to the conclusions that:

1.  Charles J. Whitman was an intelligent, intense, and driven young man;

2.  Charles J. Whitman was living under conditions of increasing personal stress from which he felt he could not escape, and which he could not master. He experienced this stress essentially in increasing personal psychological isolation, and had done so for years;

3.  Charles J. Whitman experienced profound personal dissatisfactions. His inner image of himself seems to have been poorly formulated, resulting in a deep sense of unrest;

4.  Charles J. Whitman was prone to impulsive action and loss of control at times, not always adhering to the expectations of the groups to which he belonged;

5.  Charles J. Whitman had acquired skill with firearms from childhood and this had been supplemented through intensive training in military service;

6.  Charles J. Whitman, despite reasonable good grades, had not chosen academic pursuits for which he was best equipped, and he experienced much difficulty in the abstraction of ideas and organization of his studies. He took stimulating drugs to assist him in keeping academic deadlines, the net effect of which was further loss of efficiency and a decrease in clarity of thinking at these times. However, there was no evidence of acute or chronic drug toxicity on August 1, 1966;

7.  Charles J. Whitman was deeply concerned over the chronic marital discord and recent separation of his parents. He often had strong, variable, inconsistent feelings of hostility toward members of his family, particularly his father. Because of his emotional conflicts and at the suggestion of his wife and friends he consulted a psychiatrist on March 29, 1966; no diagnosis was made; he was requested to return for further evaluation, but did not do so;

8.  There is much evidence that Charles J. Whitman had developed strong loving ties to his wife though his behavior toward her was inconsistent;

9. There is evidence that Charles J. Whitman made good friends and was admired and respected by many;

10. Charles J. Whitman was known to express his concern about physical symptoms frequently; however, he is not known to have consulted a physician in the last four months of his life for physical complaints, including headaches;

11. It is the opinion of the task force that the relationship between the brain tumor and Charles J. Whitman's actions on the last day of his life cannot be established with clarity. However, the highly malignant brain tumor conceivably could have contributed to his inability to control his emotions and actions;

12. Without a recent psychiatric evaluation of Charles J. Whitman, the task force finds it impossible to make a formal psychiatric diagnosis.

The Governor's Committee composed of the Fact-Finding Committees and the invited consultants have made the following recommendations: . . . .

It is recommended that specific responsibility for following the progress of the injured survivors and assisting them in meeting their needs be assigned to an existing group or element of The University of Texas or of the State, or to a group commissioned for this purpose. . . .

It is desirable that The University of Texas have the best possible health program in the broadest meaning of the term for both students and faculty. . . .

It is recommended that consideration be given by The University of Texas to the formulation of a broad health program for both students and faculty of all divisions of the University. . . .

It is recommended that the planning for the Mental Health Program utilize all of the appropriate University resources, coordinated with the guidance of the Vice-Chancellor for Health Affairs. . . .

Closely allied to the above recommendations is the need for the development of an effective student counseling service.

It is recommended that The University of Texas develop a student counseling service of such depth and scope as to personalize the abilities and educational and life goals of, and provide counsel and aid to, each student in need at any time. This program should be coordinated with the Mental Health Program for most effective implementation. . . .

It is recommended that there be instituted a study of safety factors of the individual campuses of the University system with a view to anticipation of problems which may arise and the devising of plans for their ready solution. . . .

## Social Implications of the Tragedy

### 1. Medical Examiner System

The investigation of violent deaths should be conducted by a qualified Medical Examiner, preferably a qualified forensic pathologist. Present laws in Texas permit the establishment of an Office of the Medical Examiner at the county level subject to population requirements.

#### Recommendation

It is recommended that appropriate legislation be introduced to establish an Office of the Medical Examiner on a statewide basis.

### 2. Self-study by news media concerning dissemination of information on acts of violence

Acts of violence and tragedy are given prominence in all news media. Additionally, there is much discussion currently concerning the presentation of acts of brutality and violence in entertainment programs freely accessible to young as well as old.

#### Recommendation

It is recommended that the communications media review their own role and attitude in obtaining and disseminating information concerning acts of violence and conduct research, with appropriate educational agencies, to determine means to best serve the public welfare in regard to these matters.

### 3. Re-learning process for combat-trained military personnel

It is believed possible for military personnel who have been trained to kill to re-learn in such a way as to de-emphasize in their minds those hostile acts taught as laudatory in time of war.

#### Recommendation

It is recommended that appropriate consideration be given to programs for re-learning among combat-trained military personnel prior to their return to civilian life and that, if such programs are found to be effective, they be required by all military forces as a prerequisite for separation from the service.

### 4. Special Studies on abnormal behavior

This case is a dramatic indication of the urgent need for further understanding of brain function related to behavior, and particularly to violent and aggressive behavior. With sufficient knowledge in this area, logical approaches to correction of abnormal behavior can be pursued. . . .

### 5. Confidentiality of health records

The individual's free cooperation with his physician or psychiatrist in time of illness or distress is dependent upon his feeling secure from injury or embarrassment in making personal revelations in matters of health and emotion. . . .

The qualities of man are best tested in times of danger and stress. A heartening aspect of the catastrophe on August 1 was the heroic behavior of many individuals.

#### Recommendation

It is recommended that the appropriate officials take cognizance of this heroism in commending those peace officers, university officials, students, doctors, hospital personnel, and other citizens who rose so courageously to the occasion on that fateful day.

# 130.  THE FIRST MAN ON THE MOON TALKS TO HOUSTON

## JULY 20,1969

From Apollo 11 Technical Air-to-Ground Voice Transmission, National Aeronautics and Space Administration, Manned Spacecraft Center, Houston, Texas

The first word spoken by a human on the moon was the name of the largest city in Texas: "Houston, Tranquility Base here. The Eagle has landed." Spoken by American astronaut Neil Armstrong, these words were transmitted to the ground crew at the National Aeronautics and Space Administration's Manned Spacecraft Center in Houston and simultaneously broadcast around the world.

If the location of the nation's highly technical space center seemed incongruous in the midst of a state associated in the public mind with cattle drives across a bald prairie, it was actually not surprising at all. The vice president of the United States at the time NASA was looking for a site was Lyndon B. Johnson, a Texan, and the presence of many powerful Texas politicians in Washington over the years had resulted in the placement of numerous military bases in the state. Just as important was the fact that, contrary to its rural, dusty image, Texas had a long tradition of technological innovation. The oil industry, which blossomed in Texas in the first decades of the twentieth century, was highly technical. In recent decades, Texas has been the home of major medical centers, including Houston's Methodist Hospital which has been an international leader in heart transplants. Texas Instruments has been an international leader in the development and use of transistors and microchips, and Texas is a national center for the computer industry. It was also the site of the controversial super-conducting super collider---a recently cancelled project on the cutting edge of scientific knowledge. These transcripts, which capture Neil Armstrong's messages to Houston as he first lands on the moon and later steps out onto its surface, symbolize this significant aspect of contemporary Texas.

This is a transcription of the Technical Air-to-Ground Voice Transmission (GOSS NET 1) from the Apollo 11 mission.

Communicators in the text may be identified according to the following list.

Spacecraft:

| | | |
|---|---|---|
| CDR | Commander | Neil A. Armstrong |
| CMP | Command module pilot | Michael Collins |
| LMP | Lunar module pilot | Edwin E. Aldrin, Jr. |

Mission Control Center:

| | |
|---|---|
| CC | Capsule Commander (CAP COMM) |

A series of three dots (. . .) is used to designate those portions of the communications that could not be transcribed because of garbling. One dash (-) is used to indicate a speaker's pause or a self-interruption and subsequent completion of a thought. Two dashes (—) are used to indicate an interruption by another speaker or a point at which a recording was terminated abruptly. Three asterisks (***) denote clipping of words and phrases.

| | |
|---|---|
| LMP (EAGLE) | 350 feet, down at 4. |
| LMP (EAGLE) | 30,. . . one-half down. |
| LMP (EAGLE) | We're pegged on horizontal velocity. |
| LMP (EAGLE) | 300 feet, down 3 1/2, 47 forward |
| LMP (EAGLE) | . . . up. |
| LMP (EAGLE) | On 1 a minute, 1 1/2 down. |
| LMP (EAGLE) | 70. |
| LMP (EAGLE) | Watch your shadow out there. |
| LMP (EAGLE) | 50, down at 2 1/2, 19 forward. |
| LMP (EAGLE) | Altitude-velocity light. |
| LMP (EAGLE) | 3 1/2 down, 220 feet, 13 forward. |
| LMP (EAGLE) | 11 forward. Coming down nicely. |
| LMP (EAGLE) | 200 feet, 4 1/2 down. |
| LMP (EAGLE) | 5 1/2 down. |
| LMP (EAGLE) | 160, 6 - 6 1/2 down. |
| LMP (EAGLE) | 5 1/2 down, 9 forward. That's good. |
| LMP (EAGLE) | 120 feet. |
| LMP (EAGLE) | 100 feet, 3 1/2 down, 9 forward. Five percent. |
| LMP (EAGLE) | . . . |
| LMP (EAGLE) | Okay. 75 feet. There's looking good. Down a half, 6 forward |
| CC | 60 seconds. |
| LMP (EAGLE) | Lights on. . . . |
| LMP (EAGLE) | Down 2 1/2. Forward. Forward. Good |
| LMP (EAGLE) | 40 feet, down 2 1/2. Kicking up some dust. |

LMP (EAGLE)    30 feet, 2 1/2 down. Faint shadow.

LMP (EAGLE)    4 forward. 4 forward. Drifting to the right a little. Okay. Down a half.

CC    30 seconds.

CDR (EAGLE)    Forward drift?

LMP (EAGLE)    Yes.

LMP (EAGLE)    Okay.

LMP (EAGLE)    CONTACT LIGHT.

LMP (EAGLE)    Okay. ENGINE STOP.

LMP (EAGLE)    ACA - out of DETENT.

CDR    Out of DETENT.

LMP (EAGLE)    MODE CONTROL - both AUTO. DESCENT ENGINE COMMAND OVERRIDE - OFF. ENGINE ARM - OFF.

LMP (EAGLE)    413 is in.

CC    We copy you down, Eagle.

CDR (TRANQ)    Houston, Tranquility Base here.

CDR (TRANQ)    THE EAGLE HAS LANDED.

CC    Roger, Tranquility. We copy you on the ground. You got a bunch of guys about to turn blue. We're breathing again. Thanks a lot.

CDR (TRANQ)    Thank you.

CC    You're looking good here.

CDR (TRANQ)    Okay. We're going to be busy for a minute.

LMP (TRANQ)    MASTER ARM, ON. Take care of the . . . I'll get this . . .

LMP (TRANQ)    Very smooth touchdown. . . .

CDR (TRANQ)    Hey, Houston, that may have seemed like a very long final phase. The AUTO targeting was taking us right into a football-field size - football-field sized crater, with a large number of big boulders and rocks for about. . . one or two crater diameters around it, and it required a . . . in P66 and flying manually over the rock field to find a reasonable good area.

CC    Roger. We copy. It was beautiful from here, Tranquility. Over.

LMP (TRANQ)    We'll get to the details of what's around here, but it looks like a collection of just about every variety of shape, angularity, granularity, about every variety of rock you could find. The colors - Well, it varies pretty much depending on how your're looking relative to the zero-phase point. There doesn't appear to be too much of a general color at all. However, it looks as though some of the rocks and boulders, of which there are quite a few in the near area, it looks as though they're going to have some interesting colors to them. Over.

CC    Roger. Copy. Sounds good to us, Tranquility. We'll let you press on through the simulated countdown, and we'll talk to you later. Over.

CDR (TRANQ)    Roger.

LMP (TRANQ)    Okay. This one-sixth goes just like the airplane.

CC    Roger. Tranquility. Be advised there's lots of smiling faces in this room and all over the world. Over.

CDR (TRANQ)    Well, there are two of them up here.

CC    Roger. That was a beautiful job, you guys.

CMP (Columbia)    And don't forget one in the command module. . . .

CDR (TRANQ)    How am I doing?

LMP (TRANQ)    You're doing fine.

LMP (TRANQ)    Okay. Do you want those bags.

CDR (TRANQ)    Yes. Got it.

CDR (TRANQ)    Okay. Houston, I'm on the porch.

CC    Roger, Neil.

LMP (TRANQ)    Okay. Stand by, Neil.

CC    Columbia, Columbia, this is Houston. One minute and 30 seconds to LOS. All systems GO. Over.

CMP (Columbia)    Columbia. Thank you.

LMP (TRANQ)    Stay where you are a minute, Neil.

CDR (TRANQ)    Okay. Need a little slack?

CDR (TRANQ)    You need more slack, Buzz?

LMP (TRANQ)    No. Hold it just a minute.

CDR (TRANQ)    Okay.

LMP (TRANQ)    Okay. Everything's nice and straight in here.

CDR (TRANQ)    Okay. Can you pull the door open a little more?

LMP (TRANQ)    All right.

| | |
|---|---|
| CDR (TRANQ) | Okay. |
| LMP (TRANQ) | Did you get the MESA out? |
| CDR (TRANQ) | I'm going to pull it now. |
| CDR (TRANQ) | Houston, the MESA came down all right. |
| CC | This is Houston. Roger. We copy. And we're standing by for your TV. |
| CDR (TRANQ) | Houston, this is Neil. Radio check. |
| CC | Neil, this is Houston. Loud and clear. Break. Break. Buzz, this is Houston. Radio check, and verify TV circuit breaker in. |
| LMP (TRANQ) | Roger, TV circuit breaker's in, and read you five-square. |
| CC | Roger. We're getting a picture on the TV. |
| LMP (TRANQ) | You got a good picture, huh? |
| CC | There's a great deal of contrast in it, and currently it's upside-down on our monitor, but we can make out a fair amount of detail. |
| LMP (TRANQ) | Okay. Will you verify the position - the opening I ought to have on the camera? |
| CC | Stand by. |
| CC (TRANQ) | Okay. Neil, we can see you coming down the ladder now. |
| CDR (TRANQ) | Okay. I just checked getting back up to that first step, Buzz. It's - not even collapsed too far, but it's adequate to get back up. |
| CC | Roger. We copy. |
| CDR (TRANQ) | It takes a pretty good little jump. |
| CC | Buzz, this is Houston. F/2 - 1/160th second for shadow photography on the sequence camera. |
| LMP (TRANQ) | Okay. |
| CDR (TRANQ) | I'm at the foot of the ladder. The LM footpads are only depressed in the surface about 1 or 2 inches, although the surface appears to be very, very fine grained, as you get close to it. It's almost like a powder. Down there, it's very fine. |
| CDR (TRANQ) | I'm going to step off the LM now. |
| CDR (TRANQ) | THAT'S ONE SMALL STEP FOR MAN, ONE GIANT LEAP FOR MANKIND. |
| CDR (TRANQ) | And the - the surface is fine and powdery. I can - I can pick it up loosely with my toe. It does adhere in fine layers like powdered charcoal to the sole and sides of my boots. I only go in a small fraction of an inch, maybe an eighth of an inch, but I can see the footprints of my boots and the treads in the fine, sandy particles. |
| CC | Neil, this is Houston. We're copying. |
| CDR | There seems to be no difficulty in moving around as we suspected. It's even perhaps easier than the simulations at one-sixth g that we performed in the various simulations on the ground. It's actually no trouble to walk around. Okay. The descent engine did not leave a crater of any size. It has about 1 foot clearance on the ground. We're essentially on a very level place here. I can see some evidence of rays emanating from the descent engine, but a very insignificant amount. . . . |
| CDR | This is very interesting. It's a very soft surface, but here and there where I plug with the contingency sample collector, I run into a very hard surface, but it appears to be very cohesive material of the same sort. I'll try to get a rock in here. Just a couple. |
| LMP | That looks beautiful from here, Neil. |
| CDR | It has a stark beauty all its own. It's like much of the high desert of the United States. It's different but it's very pretty out here. Be advised that a lot of the rock samples out here, the hard rock samples, have what appear to be vesicles in the surface, Also, I am looking at one now that appears to have some sort of phenocryst. . . . |
| CC | This is Houston. Roger, Neil. |
| LMP | Okay. I have got the cameras on at one frame a second. |
| CDR | Okay. |
| LMP | And I've got the 80 percent, no flags. |
| CDR | Are you getting a TV picture now, Houston? |
| CC | Neil, yes we are getting a TV picture. |
| CC | Neil, this is Houston. We're getting a picture. You're not in it at the present time. We can see the bag on the LEC being moved by Buzz, though. Here you come into our field of view. . . . |
| LMP | Okay. Now I want to back up and partially close the hatch. |
| LMP | Making sure not to lock it on my way out. |
| CDR | (Laughter) A pretty good thought. |
| LMP | That's our home for the next couple of hours and we want to take good care of it. Okay. I'm on the top step and I can look down over the RCU, landing gear pads. It's a very simple mattter to hop down from one step to the next. |
| CDR | Yes. I found I could be very comfortable, and walking is also very comfortable. |
| CDR | You've got three more steps and then a long one. |
| LMP | Okay. I'm going to leave that one foot up there and both hands down to about the fourth rung up. |
| CDR | There you go. |
| LMP | Okay. Now I think I'll do the same *** |
| CDR | A little more. About another inch. |
| CDR | THERE YOU GOT IT. |

| | |
|---|---|
| CDR | That's a good step. About a 3-footer. |
| LMP | Beautiful view! |

| | |
|---|---|
| CDR | Isn't that something! Magnificent sight out here. |
| LMP | Magnificent desolation. |

## 131.  LA RAZA UNIDA PARTY

### 1970

From "Mexicanos Need to Control Their Own Destinies" by José Angel Gutiérrez,
originally published in *The Militant*, June 19, 1970.

Organized in Texas in 1970 by young Mexican American political activists, La Raza Unida (United Race or United People) political party won a major success in April 1970 when the party's candidates won school board elections in the South Texas community of Crystal City. La Raza Unida founder and chairman José Angel Gutiérrez was elected chairman of the school board, and other party members won seats in city council elections in other South Texas towns. Founded on the principle that a politically active party of proud Mexican Americans could bring about justice and social, economic, and political change, La Raza Unida spread across the state and nation. Its successes promised to be the beginning of a powerful, self-determined Mexican-American movement.

Despite strong showings on the part of Raza Unida candidates in statewide races, the party experienced growing pains, a leadership crisis, and serious dissension within its ranks by the mid-to-late 1970s. Eventually the party foundered and disappeared, but not before helping to politically energize Mexican Americans in South Texas and elsewhere. La Raza Unida helped foster the cultural pride and political change that led to the election of many new Mexican-American officeholders. The ideas and emotions that led to its initial significant victories are evident in this speech by José Angel Gutiérrez delivered on May 4, 1970, in San Antonio. It reflects the anger, idealism, and ethnic pride that were at the base of many political movements in the late 1960s and early 1970s, and that are still a factor in Texas and national politics into the present.

As you know, there is a new political party in Southwest Texas. It's called La Raza Unida Party. The history of this party is rather interesting.

For years the Chicano farmworker has made up the majority of the population in the South Texas counties. But he goes trucking across this country on his summer vacation (laughter), and so he's never there to vote. Yet this is precisely the time the primaries are held—in May. And he is already vacationing in his resort area by the time the runoffs are held in June. So, you see, we are in fact not even able to vote.

We have had other problems which we have known about for a long time. For instance, the fact that the mexicano can't cope with the culture of the monolingual creatures that abound in South Texas. You see, we're literate in Spanish, so we can't recognize the name of John Waltberger on the ballot, but we sure as hell recognize Juan Garcia. (Laughter)

Supposedly in this kind of democratic society the citizenry is encouraged to participate in political process—but not so in South Texas.

Someone asked me recently whether I thought any type of system other than the American political system could work in South Texas. I thought about it for a minute and suggested that the question be reworded because we ought to try the American system first. (Applause)

They accuse me and mexicanos in Cristal (Crystal City), in Cotulla and Carrizo Springs, of being unfair. One gringo lady put it very well. She was being interviewed around April 6, right after the school board elections and before the city council elections. The guy from *Newsweek* asked her to explain the strange phenomena that were occurring in these counties: a tremendous voter turnout and a tremendous amount of bloc voting. She said, "Well, this is just terrible! Horrible! A few days ago we elected a bunch of bum Mexicans to the city council." And the reporter said, "Well, they are 85 percent of this county." And she replied, "That's what I mean! They think they ought to run this place!"

By all these little things you can begin to understand how to define the word "gringo," which seems to be such a problem all the time. It's funny, because the mexicano knows what a gringo is. It's the gringos themselves that are worried about what the hell it is. (Laughter) Let me elaborate on it.

I'm not going to give you a one sentence thing on them; I feel they deserve as least two sentences. (Laughter) The basic idea in using the word "gringo" is that it means "foreigner." The gringos themselves say, "It's Greek to me." So the mexicanos says, "It's griego [Greek] to me." That is one explanation of its origins, according to Professor Americo Paredes of the University of Texas. Another is, of course, the traditional one about the United States troops coming into Mexico with "green coats." The mexicanos would say, with our own pronunciation, "Here come the green coats.'" And there are other explanations.

The word itself describes an attitude of supremacy, of xenophobia—that means you're afraid of strangers. I pick up a fancy word here and there. This attitude is also found in institutions, such as the Democratic Party. It's in policies like the one that says you can't speak Spanish in school because it's un-American. It's in the values of people who feel that unless Mexican music is played by the Tijuana Brass or the Baja Marimba Band it's no good. You can't eat *tacos de choriza* [sausage tacos] around the corner for 20 cents. You've got to go up there to La Fonda [fancy anglo-owned Mexican restaurant] and eat a $3.50 Mexican plate that gives you indigestion.

(Applause and laughter)

The formation of this party came about because of the critical need for the people to experience justice. It's just like being hungry. You've got to get food in there immediately, otherwise you get nauseous, you get headaches and pains in your stomach.

We were Chicanos who were starved for any kind of meaningful participation in decision making, policy making and leadership positions. For a long time we have not been satisfied with the type of leadership that has been picked for us. And this is what a political party does, particularly the ones we have here. I shouldn't use the plural because we only have one, and that's the gringo party. It doesn't matter what name it goes by. It can be Kelloggs, All-Bran or Shredded Wheat, but it's still the same crap.

Those parties, or party, have traditionally picked our leadership. They have transformed this leadership into a kind of broker, a real estate guy who deals in the number of votes or precincts he can deliver or the geographical areas he can control. And he is a tape recorder—he puts out what the party says.

A beautiful example of this is Ralph Yarborough [Democratic senator from Texas]. The only thing he does for Chicanos is hire one every six years. He's perfectly content with the bigoted sheriff and Captain Allee [Texas Rangers] and the guys that break the strikes in El Rio Grande City and with [Wayne] Connally [brother of former Texas governor John Connally] and all these other people. Well, he gets beaten, and he knows why. The Republicans, the Birchers, the Wallace-ites and all these people went over to support Bentsen in the primaries. Yet I just read in the paper this afternoon that he said, "As always, I will vote a straight Democratic ticket in November."

There is only one other kind of individual who does that kind of work and that's a prostitute. . . .

Four years ago, when the guy who is now running for commissioner in La Salle County in La Raza Unida Party ran in the Democratic primaries, it cost him one-third of his annual income! That's how much it costs a Chicano with a median income of $1,574 per family per year. With the third party it didn't cost him a cent.

On top of the excessive filing fees, they have set fixed dates for political activity, knowing that we have to migrate to make a living. We are simply not here for the May primaries. Did you know that in Cotulla, Erasmo Andrade [running in the Democratic primary for state senator in opposition to Wayne Connally] lost by over 300 votes because the migrants weren't there? In the Democratic primaries you're not going to cut it. In May there are only 16 more Chicano votes than gringo votes in La Salle County. But in November the margin is two and one-half to one in favor of Chicanos.

So you see that what's happening is not any big miracle. It's just common sense. The trouble is that everybody was always bothered and said, "We can't get out of the Democratic Party. Why bite the hand that feeds you?" Well, you bite it because it feeds you slop. (Laughter and applause)

Others say, "Well, why don't you switch over and join the Republican Party?" Well, let's not even touch on that one.

Why can't you begin to think very selfishly as a Chicano? I still haven't found a good argument from anyone as to why we should not have a Chicano party. Particularly when you are the majority. If you want to implement and see democracy in action—the will of the majority—you are not going to do it in the Democratic Party. You can only do it through a Chicano party. (Applause)

But you see there is another, more important, reason, and that is that mexicanos need to be in control of their destiny. They need to make their own decisions. We need to make the decisions that are going to affect our brothers and maybe our children. We have been complacent for too long.

Did you know that not one of our candidates in La Salle County had a job the whole time they were running, and that they still can't get jobs? The same thing happened in Dimmit County. In Uvalde this is one of the reasons there's a walkout. They refused to renew the teaching contract of Jose Garcia, who ran for county judge. That's a hell of a price to pay. But that's the kind of treatment that you've gotten.

You've got a median educational level among mexicanos in Zavala County of 2.3 grades. In La Salle it's just a little worse—about 1.5 grades.

The median family income in La Salle is $1,574 a year. In Zavala it's about $1,754. The ratio of doctors, the number of newspapers, the health, housing, hunger, malnutrition, illiteracy, poverty, lack of political representation—all these things put together spell one word: colonialism. You've got a handful of gringos controlling the lives of muchos mexicanos. And it's been that way for a long time.

Do you think things are going to get better by putting faith in the Democratic Party and Bentsen? Or that things are going to get better because you've got a few more Chicanos elected to office now within the traditional parties? Do you think that things are going to get better now that the U.S. Commission on Civil Rights has officially claimed that there is discrimination against mexicanos? They've finally found out it's for real—we're discriminated against! (Laughter) Do you think that things are going to get better simply because kids are walking out of schools—kids who can't vote, who in many cases can't convince the community to stand behind them?

Not, it's not going to get better. We are going to have to devise some pretty ingenious ways of eliminating these gringos. Yet they don't really have to be too ingenious. All you have to do is go out there and look around and have a little common sense.

It stands to reason that if there are two grocery stores in town and we are the ones who buy from them, then if we stop buying from them they are going to go down. If you talk about transferring the wealth, that's how you do it. . . .

In 1960 there were 26 Texas counties in which Chicanos were a majority, yet not one of those counties was in the control of Chicanos. If you want to stand there and take that you can. You can be perfectly content just like your father and your grandfather were, *con el sombrero en el mano* (with hat in hand).

That's why most of our traditional organizations will sit there and pass resolutions and mouth off at conventions, but they'll never take on the gringo. They'll never stand up to him and say, "Hey, man, things have got to change from now on. *Que pase lo que pase* [Let whatever happens happen]. We've had it long enough!"

This is what we've got to start doing. If you don't go third party, then you've got to go the independent route, because there is no other way you are going to get on the November ballot. And don't try to put in a write-in candidate. That never works. . . .

The recent elections here in April for school board and city council demonstrated something that many people knew was a fact. It was almost like predicting that the sun is going to come up in the morning; if you can count, you know what the results are going to be. But an interesting factor is going to enter in now. We won in an off year in the nonpartisan races, which means that we were able to elect a minority to these positions. So now the establishment has all summer long to figure out how to stop the mexicano. This is where we get back to the old tricks and lies of the gringo.

They tried the "outside agitator" bit on me but it didn't work because I was born in Crystal City. So they changed gears. Then they tried the "communist" one for a while—until they found out I was in the U.S. Army Reserves. (Laughter and applause) Then somewhere they dug up my "kill a gringo" thing of about a year ago when I said that I would kill a gringo in self-defense if I were attacked. . . .

Another lie is the white liberal approach. "I like Mexican food. Oh, I just love it!" And this is the kind of guy who's got the *molcajete* [Aztec mortar and pestle for cooking] sitting as an ash try in his living room. (Applause and laughter)

This kind of character is the one that cautions you, "Be careful. Don't be racist in reverse. It's bad enough that gringos don't like 'Meskins' and 'Meskins' don't like gringos. You have to talk things over. You have to turn the other cheek. You've got to be nice. You've got to be polite. You can't use foul language in public. You have to have a constructive program."

They ask us, "What are you going to do for the schools in Crystal City?" And when we answer, "Bring education," they don't know what the hell we're talking about.

You see, that's another thing about the liberal. They always love to make you feel bad. And oh, my God, we hate to hurt the feelings of a good anglo liberal, don't we? Well, hell, tell them the truth!

We've been hurting for a long time. They think we've got education, but we know different. How come we have 71 percent dropouts in Crystal City? It's miseducation. We ain't got teachers down there, we've got neanderthals.

These are the kinds of problems we are going to be faced with by the time November comes along. But a lot of people ain't going to buy it. The kids in the schools aren't going to stand for it. They see what this whole gringo thing has done

to their parents, what it's done to our community, what it's done to our organizations. And nothing is going to prevent them from getting what is due them.

There's no generation gap in Crystal City. To the old people who are experienced this is nothing new. The older people in Crystal City, who have experienced years and years of humiliation and blows to their dignity, know what's going on. There was a problem for a while with the 25- to 45-year-olds who were trying to be gringos. But that's no longer true. You see, those are the parents of these kids, and these kids got their parents straight very early in the game. (Applause). . . .

You know, civil rights are not just for those under 21. They're for everybody—for grandma, for daddy and mama, and *los chamaquitos* [children] and *primos* [cousins] and sisters, and so on. We've all got to work together. That means that all of us have to pitch in. And this is why in Crystal City you no longer hear "Viva La Raza" and "Chicano Power" and "La Raza Unida" all over the place. We don't talk about it anymore because it's a reality. You see, there *la familia mexicana esta organizada* [the Mexican family is organized]. Aztlan has begun in the southwest part of Texas. (Prolonged applause)

Our actions have made "La Raza Unida" more than just a slogan. Beginning with the walkout, we began organizing and moving in to counter-attack every time the gringo tried to put pressure on the mexicano. Boycott his store. Point the finger at him. Expose him for the animal that he is. Bring in the newspapers and photographers and the tape recorders. Let the world see it. . . .

So don't let anybody kid you. We are the consumers, we are the majority. We can stop anything and we can make anything in South Texas if we stick together and begin using common sense.

This third party is a very viable kind of alternative. It's a solution. For once you can sit in your own courthouse and you don't have to talk about community control because you are the community. And we are not talking about trying to run for Congress because you are sitting on the school board and then four years from now you're going to run for county judge. That's not the name of the game either.

We are talking about bringing some very basic elements into the lives of mexicanos—like education and like making urban renewal work for mexicanos instead of being the new way of stealing land. We got screwed once with the Treaty of Guadalupe-Hidalgo and now we're getting it under "Model Cities" and urban renewal. (Applause)

You can be as imaginative as you want and do almost anything you want once you run units of government. I'll give you an example. Everyone publicizes the fact that the Panthers are feeding kids all over the country. And everybody pours out money at cocktail parties and gets very concerned about little kids eating in the morning.

Well, the gringos in Cristal pulled out another one of their gimmicks and just a few days before the elections they decided to experiment with a pilot program of feeding kids in the morning. It was going to last for six weeks and feed 30 kids.

They were going to watch them. They were going to experiment, study, conduct a survey to see if they grew an inch. (Laughter)

Well, right now in Crystal City any kid who wants to eat can eat. Free breakfast in all the schools. You can do that, you see. You can also be very, very friendly to your opposition. You can rule them out of order when they get out of hand. You can slap them on the hand: "That's a no no!"

They can't hold an illegal meeting—like they tried yesterday with the school board while I was out of town. They tried to take advantage of the fact that I was out of town to hold a special meeting. But the law says you must give three days' notice. So the gringos failed in their attempt to hire a principal to their liking. We don't need to be experts in parliamentary procedure. All we have to do is follow the book and tell them, "No, no! You can't do that!" (Laughter and applause)

Let me be serious for a few minutes because I think we have laughed enough. Mario was talking about having a third party in Bexar County by 1972. Good luck, Mario. (Applause)

It doesn't matter if you don't agree with MAYO because this thing is no longer just MAYO. The response that we've had to this third party in all sections of our communities has been overwhelming. You saw the results. You can count votes just as I did.

The third party is not going to get smaller. It's going to be bigger.

You have three choices. First, you can be very active in this thing. For once we are not talking about being anti-Democratic or pro-Republican or pro-Democrat and anti-Republican. We are talking about being for La Raza, the majority of the people in South Texas. So there are a lot of things you can do and be very actively involved in.

If you don't choose that route, you can stay home and watch baseball and just come out and vote. But otherwise stay home. Don't get in the way.

The third thing you can do is lend your support, your general agreement. Often we are too critical of ourselves, and the gringo misunderstands that. He says, "You're disorganized, there's no unity among you." Hell, he can't understand an honest discussion when he hears one.

So, you've got these three roles that you can play. Or you can get very, very defensive and say, "This is wrong, this is un-American because you're bloc voting." But don't forget that the Democrats do it too. You can say that this is racism in reverse, but don't forget that we are the majority. And you can say that this is going to upset the whole situation in the state of Texas because we will never be able to elect a senator, because we're segregating ourselves and cutting ourselves apart and that this is not what we should be trying to do, that we should be trying to integrate, etc., etc. Well, before you go on your warpath or campaign, come down and tell that to my sheriff. Tell him how much you like him. Or, better yet, move on down the road a bit and tell it to Ranger Allee himself.

Build your constituency, build your community—that's how we will be electing three and possibly four congressmen in the very near future. There's going to be another congressman in Bexar County, and there's not room for all of them on the North side [anglo section of San Antonio]. (Laughter and applause)  So we have some very interesting developments coming up.

To the gringos in the audience, I have one final message to convey: Up yours, baby. You've had it, from now on. (Standing ovation)

# 132. THE SHARPSTOWN SCANDAL

## 1971

From "Sharpstown Scandal Judgement Set" by Ron Calhoun, Dallas *Times Herald*, August 20, 1978, p. 1

The 1971 Sharpstown scandal, a foreshadowing of the later national scandal known as Watergate, had much the same story line and much the same result: prominent elected officials betrayed their public trust by breaking the law, and a public scandal ensued, followed by an outcry for reform that evicted numerous incumbents from office and replaced them with supposedly nobler politicians.

Houston wheeler-dealer Frank W. Sharp, a developer and banker, attempted to influence state officials by cutting them in on a lucrative stock deal just at the time the state legislature was considering bills that would protect Sharp from federal regulators. On the eve of the very day in January 1971 on which Gov. Preston Smith and Lt. Gov. Ben Barnes were being inaugurated, the Securities and Exchange Commission filed suit against Sharp for stock manipula-

tions. The capital was abuzz with rumors and filled with grim-faced politicans, including Governor Smith and Speaker Gus Mutscher, who had traded heavily in Sharp's suspect stock.

When the house of cards came tumbling down during months of revelations in the press, many prominent Texas politicans fell with it. The voters had the chance to elect new politicians in 1972, and they did so with a vengeance. More than one-half of the incumbents were defeated or did not seek reelection. Rep. Gib Lewis, then a freshman legislator and later speaker of the Texas House, said of the scandal: "It cost many, many people many things. It cost Ben Barnes the governor's chair and Gus Mutscher his reputation. In fact, it changed the entire course of Texas political history." Along with court-ordered reapportionment and single-member districts, the

Sharpstown scandal was indeed one of the most important factors for political change in the 1960s and 1970s. A fresh breeze of reform blew open the often closed door of Texas politics. Republicans, women, minorities, and reform-minded newcomers would soon walk through that door into positions of influence that would change forever the face of Texas politics and Texas itself.

The final judgment in the Sharpstown scandal, which brought down some of the biggest names in Texas politics back in the early 1970s, has been rendered in Houston.

With the settlement of a five-year-old $13.5 million suit in the court of U.S. District Judge Carl O. Bue Jr., the case is officially closed.

In its wake lie the ruined political careers of a former governor, a former lieutenant governor touted as having presidential potential, a former Texas House speaker who was married to a former Miss America, two former attorneys general, a former state insurance board chairman, a former state Democratic chairman and several lesser figures.

It played a significant role in bringing about reforms in state government, including tightened campaign finance reporting and lobby control laws, financial disclosure by elected state officials and a state ethics code.

The story began quietly with the filing of a Securities and Exchange Commission suit in a Dallas federal court against Houston financier Frank W. Sharp and several of his business associates. The word spread quickly that "something big" was to be found in the numerous depositions filed with the case.

The headlines rocked the state the next day, on Jan. 21, 1971, when Preston Smith was inaugurated for his second term as governor.

Depositions filed with the case indicated that Smith, House Speaker Gus Mutscher, Mutscher aide Rush McGinty, Fort Worth Rep. Tommy Shannon and state Democratic chairman Elmer Baum had profited from sales of stock in one of the key firms named in the charges—National Bankers Life Insurance Co. (NBL) of Dallas.

It was alleged that Sharp, through former Atty. Gen. Waggoner Carr and former State Insurance Board chairman John Osorio, had enlisted the help of Smith, Mutscher, Shannon, Baum and Lt. Gov. Ben Barnes to pave the way for passage of two banking bills sought by Sharp.

Sharp, head of a financially troubled banking and real estate empire in Houston, subsequently testified that he wanted the bills to "get the Federal Deposit Insurance Corporation off my back." The FDIC had questioned various loans placed through his Sharpstown State Bank to finance stock purchases.

Court cases spawned by the SEC action were front-page news for the next four years. They reached all the way to Washington, D.C., and ultimately required testimony by several former Nixon administration figures who had themselves been accused of crimes by that time in the Watergate scandal.

Revelations of wheeling and dealing were so complex that many of the Sharpstown figures had trouble keeping things straight.

The political fallout, which was only a part of the overall scheme, can be capsuled thusly:

*In 1972, Smith and Barnes, tarred by the Sharpstown brush, were decisively defeated in the Democratic gubernatorial primary.

Smith, seeking a third term, ran a poor fourth. Barnes, the young protege of former Gov. John Connally who had been described as presidential material by none other than Lyndon Baines Johnson, ran third behind Frances "Sissy" Farenthold and Dolph Briscoe.

Briscoe subsequently beat Mrs. Farenthold in a runoff. Barnes' once-bright political career came to a screeching halt. Smith's attempt at a comeback in this year's gubernatorial race failed miserably.

*Mutscher, McGinty and Shannon, a key Mutscher lieutenant who carried the "Sharpstown bills" in a special session in 1969, were convicted on March 14, 1972, in an Abilene state court for conspiracy to accept bribes and were given five-year probated sentences.

Mutscher was forced to step down as speaker and he lost his legislative seat in the May 1972 primary. His marriage to former Miss America Donna Ausum ended in divorce. But he subsequently obtained a release from his probation and was elected county judge of Washington County, a post he holds today.

*Former Dallas Dist. Atty. and State Atty. Gen. Will Wilson was forced to resign as head of the criminal division of the U.S. Department of Justice after it was revealed that he had spent a highly profitable six years as Sharp's personal attorney, and had unwittingly paid for a device to "bug" a room at Sharp's bank used by bank examiners.

Wilson, who switched from the Democratic to the Republican party in 1966, steadfastly denied that he had aided Sharp in any questionable financial dealings, and claimed he had turned over the Justice Department's involvement in the Sharpstown prosecution to an assistant to avoid any conflict. His ambition to become Texas' first GOP governor since Reconstruction was shattered.

*Former Atty. Gen. Waggoner Carr, a U.S. Senate candidate in 1966 and candidate for governor in 1968, was left in deep debt and his law practice all but ruined by the Sharpstown affair.

Along with his law partner, Osorio, he was accused of illegally manipulating stock in several firms. Vowing to "fight for my life" and accusing the Nixon administration and the Republican party of instigating the charges for partisan reasons, he was placed along with Osorio and others under a permanent civil injunction by U.S. Dist. Judge Sarah T. Hughes. But he later beat criminal charges in a widely publicized jury trial in Judge Hughes' court.

*Osorio, the flamboyant, wise-cracking president of National Bankers Life, was convicted on three counts of conspiracy and embezzlement in a federal court in Amarillo.

Sharp himself became the focus of much criticism when it was announced that he was given immunity from further prosecution when he agreed to plead guilty to two minor banking law violations. He was fined $5,000 and given a three-year probated sentence. In return, he testified against his onetime friends.

The Sharpstown scandal had many ramifications and involved convoluted stock and business dealings. But it had two main phases.

The first involved Sharp and his dealings with the politicians. Sharp bought controlling interest in National Bankers Life from former Gov. Allan Shivers in 1968 for $7.5 million. In 1969 he started loaning large sums from his bank to Smith and his close friend Baum, and to Mutscher, McGinty and Shannon to buy NBL stock.

Sharp acted through a Dallas stock brokerage, the now-defunct Ling & Co., to drive up the price of the NBL stock, primarily by inducing the Jesuit Fathers of Houston Inc. to buy it at inflated prices. At one point he was selling the Jesuit Fathers the stock at $24 per share to produce profits for the politicians when it was selling for $5 on the open market.

Smith placed two of the banking bills Sharp wanted passed in his call for a second special legislative session in September of 1969. One of the bills would authorize non-profit corporations to insure state banks. The other would create a state deposit insurance corporation.

Both bills sailed through the House and Senate. In a deposition, Sharp claimed that Osorio told him that Barnes, as presiding officer of the Senate, had been instrumental in getting the bills through the Senate.

"Are you about to tell me I am indebted to Ben for his part in the passage of this bill?" Sharp claimed he asked Osorio.

Osorio, according to Sharp, replied, "Oh, no, no, no. I have already taken care of that. Ben is smarter than most of these other politicians. He wants cash."

That quote was widely reported in Texas newspapers and undoubtedly had much to do with Barnes' political demise. Osorio later denied he had given Barnes any money, but the damage was done.

Barnes vigorously denied he even knew Sharp, much less anything about his scheme. However, Barnes was tarred by another aspect of the case. It was revealed that he had borrowed $60,000 from a Dallas bank controlled by Osorio and Carr to buy stock in a firm called National Data Communications.

Smith and Baum also denied complicity, although they jointly profited by $125,000 in the sale of their NBL stock. Sharp obtained the profits by selling the stock to the hapless Jesuit Fathers.

Smith and Baum were spared criminal charges, possibly because Smith subsequently vetoed the two bills sought by Sharp, ironically, on the advice of Shivers.

The second major phase of the Sharpstown scandal centered on Carr's and Osorio's alleged manipulations of the stock of a Florida holding firm called the South Atlantic Co. and its subsidiary, RIC International. Carr was a vice president of South Atlantic and the "controlling person" in RIC International.

The two were accused of illegally taking money from the NBL pension fund to refinance their debts from the stock dealings.

In the final judgment rendered by Judge Bue, Sharp agreed to pay the Houston Educational Foundation Inc., formerly the Jesuit Fathers of Houston Inc., $900,000 plus interest.

Osorio agreed to pay the foundation $150,000, and Joe Novotny, former president of the Sharpstown State Bank, agreed to pay $100,000.

In all, the case involved 78 defendants.

# 133. *ROE v. WADE*: ABORTION LEGALIZED

## JANUARY 22, 1973

### From *Roe v. Wade*, 410 U.S. 113, 113-114, 93 S. Ct. 705, 35 L. Ed. 2d 147 (1973)

Numerous Texas legal cases, some of them argued before the United States Supreme Court, have had a significant impact within the state and beyond. Examples include *Nixon v. Herndon* (1927), which declared unconstitutional the 1923 "White Primary" Law that excluded African Americans from voting. *Ruiz v. Estelle* (1972), which found that confinement in the Texas prison system constituted cruel and unusual punishment, resulted in numerous changes in that system. In *Stanford v. Texas* (1965), Texan Maury Maverick Jr. set an important precedent when he successfully argued before the United States Supreme Court that a San Antonio book dealer's home had been illegally searched and his books and papers illegally seized under a vague warrant enforcing a Texas law which sought to control the dissemination of unpopular ideas.

Perhaps no Supreme Court decision in recent years has raised more profound constitutional issues, and touched on more legal, ethical, and cultural sore points, than *Roe v. Wade*. This highly controversial decision which legalized abortion under certain circumstances was based on a Texas case argued before the U.S. Supreme Court by Texas attorneys Sarah Weddington and Robert C. Flowers. Despite its Texas origins, this case has become a national lightning rod for moral, legal, and political issues. Just as important as the specific issue of abortion itself are the numerous social issues reflected in the partisan warfare over the case. Like many other legal cases in the past three decades, *Roe v. Wade* was a complex battleground between those holding traditional views of society and culture and those seeking social change and new cultural standards.

ROE et al. v. WADE, DISTRICT ATTORNEY OF
DALLAS COUNTY
APPEAL FROM THE UNITED STATES DISTRICT COURT FOR
THE NORTHERN DISTRICT OF TEXAS
No. 70-18. Argued December 13, 1971—Reargued
October 11, 1972—Decided January 22, 1973

A pregnant single woman (Roe) brought a class action challenging the constitutionality of the Texas criminal abortion laws, which proscribe procuring or attempting an abortion except on medical advice for the purpose of saving the mother's life. A licensed physician (Hallford), who had two state abortion prosecutions pending against him, was permitted to intervene. A childless married couple (The Does), the wife not being pregnant, separately attacked the laws, basing alleged injury on the future possibilities of contraceptive failure, pregnancy, unpreparedness for parenthood, and impairment of the wife's health. A three-judge District Court, which consolidated the actions, held that Roe and Hallford, and members of their classes, had standing to sue and presented justiciable controversies. Ruling that declaratory, though not injunctive, relief was warranted, the court declared the abortion statutes void as vague and overbroadly infringing those plaintiffs' Ninth and Fourteenth Amendment rights. The court ruled the Does' complaint not justiciable. Appellants directly appealed to this Court on the injunctive rulings, and appellee cross-appealed from the District Court's grant of declaratory relief to Roe and Hallford. *Held*:

1. While 28 U.S.C.§ 1253 authorizes no direct appeal to this Court from the grant or denial of declaratory relief alone, review is not foreclosed when the case is properly before the Court on appeal from specific denial of injunctive relief and the arguments as to both injunctive and declaratory relief are necessarily identical. P. 123.

2. Roe has standing to sue; the Does and Hallford do not. Pp. 123-129.

(a) Contrary to appellee's contention, the natural termination of Roe's pregnancy did not moot her suit. Litigation involving pregnancy, which is "capable of repetition, yet evading review," is an exception to the usual federal rule that an actual controversy must exist at review stages and not simply when the action is initiated. Pp. 124-125.

(b) The District Court correctly refused injunctive, but erred in granting declaratory, relief to Hallford, who alleged no federally protected right not assertable as a defense against the good-faith state prosecutions pending against him. *Samuels v. Mackell*, 401 U.S. 66. Pp. 125-127.

(c) The Does' complaint, based as it is on contingencies, any one or more of which may not occur, is too speculative to present an actual case or controversy. Pp. 127-129.

3. State criminal abortion laws, like those involved here,

that except from criminality only a life-saving procedure on the mother's behalf without regard to the stage of her pregnancy and other interests involved violate the Due Process Clause of the Fourteenth Amendment, which protects against state action the right to privacy, including a woman's qualified right to terminate her pregnancy. Though the State cannot override that right, it has legitimate interests in protecting both the pregnant woman's health and the potentiality of human life, each of which interests grows and reaches a "compelling" point at various stages of the woman's approach to term. Pp. 147-164.

(a) For the stage prior to approximately the end of the first trimester, the abortion decision and its effectuation must be left to the medical judgment of the pregnant woman's attending physician. Pp. 163, 164

(b) For the stage subsequent to approximately the end of the first trimester, the State, in promoting its interest in the health of the mother, may, if it chooses, regulate the abortion procedure in ways that are reasonably related to maternal health. Pp. 163, 164.

(c) For the stage subsequent to viability the State, in promoting its interest in the potentiality of human life, may, if it chooses, regulate, and even proscribe, abortion except where necessary, in appropriate medical judgment, for the preservation of the life or health of the mother. Pp. 163-164; 164-165.

4. The State may define the term "physician" to mean only a physician currently licensed by the State, and may proscribe any abortion by a person who is not a physician as so defined. P. 165.

5. It is unnecessary to decide the injunctive relief issue since the Texas authorities will doubtless fully recognize the Court's ruling that the Texas criminal abortion statutes are unconstitutional. P. 166.

314 F. Supp. 1217, affirmed in part and reversed in part.

BLACKMUN, J., delivered the opinion of the Court, in which BURGER,C.J., and DOUGLAS,BRENNAN, STEWART,MARSHALL, and POWELL,JJ., joined. BURGER, C.J., *post*, p. 207, DOUGLAS,J., post, P. 209, and STEWART,J., *post*, p. 167, filed concurring opinions. WHITE,J., filed a dissenting opinion, in which REHNQUISTJ., joined, *post*, p. 221. REHNQUISTJ. filed a dissenting opinion, *post*, p. 171

Sarah Weddington reargued the cause for appellants. With her on the briefs were Roy Lucas, Fred Bruner, Roy L. Merrill, Jr., and Norman Dorsen.

Robert C. Flowers, Assistant Attorney General of Texas, argued the cause for appellee on the reargument. Jay Floyd, Assistant Attorney General, argued the cause for appellee on the original argument. With them on the brief were Crawford C. Martin, Attorney General, Nola White, First Assistant Attorney General, Alfred Walker, Executive Assistant Attorney General, Henry Wade, and John B. Tolle.

## 134. THE BIG THICKET NATIONAL PRESERVE ESTABLISHED

### OCTOBER 11, 1974

It has been said that the history of Texas is the story of men doing things out of doors. Indeed, the activities of men on the land—cowboys, cotton farmers, lawmen, oil wildcatters, football players—have dominated the state's culture and history. Land in particular has been important to the state. It was one of the great lures that brought Spanish conquistadors and Anglo-American farmers and entrepreneurs to this distant frontier. In fact, when Texas joined the union in 1845, it was the only state in the American West which held onto its land rather than deeding it over to the federal goverment. As a result, Texas has much more land in private hands than other Western states where great percentages of land are owned by the federal goverment. And because of their love affair with the land, Texans have perhaps been more reluctant to cede control of it to the state and federal goverments. In the spirit of the national environmental movement, however, Texas has created a number of major national parks, sites, and monuments in recent decades.

The Big Thicket National Preserve, an 84,555-acre preserve formed of twelve units of land in seven East Texas counties, is an ecological crossroads of North America, featuring an incredible diversity of plant and animal life. When the legislation establishing the preserve was finally passed in 1974, it was the culmination of a nearly fifty-year struggle among loggers, farmers, local landowners, environmentalists, and some of Texas's most prominent politicans, including Ralph Yarborough, Lloyd Bentsen, and John Tower. The debate over the preservation of the Big Thicket was long and sometimes bitter, and it reflected the great national debates over the ownership, use, and stewardship of land.

### 1. BIG THICKET CONTROVERSY

From "The Main Battle of the Big Thicket is About Over" by Craig Hines, *Houston Chronicle*, September 29, 1974

Washington—Without a roll call vote, without much hoopla, a major chapter in Texas politics is expected to end Tuesday.

There will be a few words on the Senate floor, some pleasantries. Then the gavel will bang, and it will be over.

If things go as planned, that will be the scenario as Congress passes and sends to the White House a bill to create a Big Thicket National Preserve.

However, behind that tame little show—and a good-natured bill signing being urged on President Ford—are years of political wrangling so full of twists ands turns that one of the gnarled cypress tree in a thicket swamp looks smooth in comparison.

Discussions on putting parts of the Big Thicket under federal supervision date back to the 1920s. The National Park Service found a big park in the Thicket area just north of Beaumont, feasible in a 1938-39 study, but World War II intervened.

Interest warmed up about 10 years ago, and since then the controversy over the interesting variety of scarce plants and animals has sparked dozen of bills—as well as allegations and conspiracy theories.

One of the main figures in the fight has been former Sen.

Ralph W. Yarborough, D-Texas, who viewed his battle for a national park in the Big Thicket as a symbol of his fight with the state's conservative Democratic establishment.

Just as Yarborough's term was ending in 1970, as a sort of a going-away present, the Senate approved a bill which would establish a thicket national park of no more than 100,000 acres. The House did not have the time—or inclination—to act on the bill and it died.

During Yarborough's tenure, the thicket area was represented by conservative Rep. John Dowdy, D-Athens, who was generally opposed to creation of a national park. Before he retired in 1973—after being convicted of perjury in connection with a bribery deal—Dowdy did say he would support a 35,000-acre park made up of little pieces of the thicket. Conservationists turned up their noses.

In the process of his fight for a park of at least 100,000 acres, Yarborough made two converts—the current U.S. senators from Texas, Republican John G. Tower and Democrat Lloyd M. Bentsen.

Bentsen beat Yarborough in the 1970 Democratic primary and in the campaign found that Yarborough's Thicket position was favored by the ecologists who generally lived not in the Thicket but in vote-rich Houston and Dallas.

Tower came over to the 100,000-acre proposal when it looked in 1972 that he might have to face Yarborough in the general election. Yarborough, however, was defeated in a primary runoff.

Thicket prospects changed in the House in 1973 when Charles Wilson, D-Lufkin, succeeded Dowdy.

But it has not been altogether smooth sailing.

(Even before the current session, thicket proponents Reps. Bob Eckhardt, D-Houston, and Jack Brooks, D-Beaumont, tangled over differing proposals in 1972. Eckhardt criticized Brooks' 100,000-acre bill which would have left selection of the land to the government as "an invitation to a lumber interest hornswoggle.")

Wilson said he wanted a 75,000-acre park. He said that was generous because many of his constituents in the thicket area wanted no park at all.

On the other side in the House was another freshman, Rep. Alan W. Steelman, R-Dallas. He pressed on behalf of environmentalists for a 100,000-acre bill. He also had a seat on the House Interior Committee which handled the legislation.

Although Wilson says he likes Steelman personally, Wilson has been in Dallas campaigning for Steelman's Democratic opponent, old state Senate colleague Mike McKool.

Wilson has also joked—apparently—that next year he was going to introduce a bill to create a Little Thicket Park in Steelman's backyard in Dallas.

Without mentioning Steelman by name, Wilson said he would "certainly hold a resentment for those who showed no sensitivity to the people who live in my district and the problems it creates for me as their representative."

The plot thickens when the future political plans of Wilson and Steelman—two young, articulate politicians—are considered.

Wilson admittedly would like to move to the U.S. Senate, and he has his eye on Tower's seat which would be up in 1978. Steelman has similar ambitions, but they do not include a race against Tower.

With some pride, Wilson pointed out, "they messed around with thicket legislation for 12 years and passed it the first session I was here. It ain't the first session Tower has been here."

Wilson became so perturbed during negotiations on the 84,550-acre compromise bill that is headed for approval Tuesday that at one point he declared the only people interested in the project were "the radical ecologists and two Houston newspapers."

When some conservationists demanded inclusion of some Sandy Bog lands in the preserve, Wilson dismissed them as "fern fanciers and bog studiers."

But as the end of the hassle approaches, Wilson seems genuinely relieved that the thicket question seems headed for a settlement.

There is also relief among the major timber companies who have agreed since 1967 not to cut trees in the general areas that had been discussed for inclusion in the park.

Under the bill that seems headed for enactment, the Department of Interior has one year to map out a five-year acquisition plan.

There may be some controversy when the government starts trying to buy the land—there usually is in public projects like this. But the main battle of the Big Thicket is about over.

## 2. BIG THICKET LEGISLATION

From United States Code, 93rd Congress—Second Session, 1974, Public Law 93-439

An Act to authorize the establishment of the Big Thicket National Preserve in the State of Texas, and for other purposes.

Be it enacted by the Senate and House of Representatives of the United States of America in Congress assembled, That:

(a) In order to assure the preservation, conservation, and protection of the natural, scenic, and recreational values of a significant portion of the Big Thicket area in the State of Texas and to provide for the enhancement and public enjoyment thereof, the Big Thicket National Preserve is hereby established.

(b) The Big Thicket National Preserve (hereafter referred to as the "preserve") shall include the units generally depicted on the map entitled "Big Thicket National Preserve", dated November 1973 and numbered NBR BT 91,027 which shall be on file and available for public inspection in the offices of the National Park Service , Department of the Interior,

Washington, District of Columbia, and shall be filed with appropriate offices of Tyler, Hardin, Jasper, Polk, Liberty, Jefferson, and Orange Counties in the State of Texas. The Secretary of the Interior (hereafter referred to as the "Secretary") shall, as soon as practicable, but no later than six months after the date of enactment of this Act, publish a detailed description of the boundaries of the preserve in the Federal Register. In establishing such boundaries, the Secretary shall locate stream corridor unit boundaries referenced from the stream bank on each side thereof and he shall further make every reasonable effort to exclude from the units hereafter described any improved year-round residential properties which he determines, in his discretion, are not necessary for the protection of the values of the area or for its proper administration. . . .

Sec. 4. (a) The area within the boundaries depicted on the map referred to in section 1 shall be known as the Big Thicket National Preserve. Such lands shall be administered by the Secretary as a unit of the National Park System in a manner which will assure their natural and ecological integrity in perpetuity in accordance with the provisions of this Act and with the provisions of the Act of August 25, 1916 (39 Stat. 535; 16 U.S.C. 1-4), as amended and supplemented.

(b) In the interest of maintaining the ecological integrity of the preserve, the Secretary shall limit the construction of roads, vehicular campgrounds, employee housing, and other public use and administrative facilities and he shall promulgate and publish such rules and regulations in the Federal Register as he deems necessary and appropriate to limit and control the use of, and activities on, Federal lands and waters with respect to:

(1) motorized land and water vehicles;

(2) exploration for, and extraction of, oil, gas, and other minerals;

(3) new construction of any kind;

(4) grazing and agriculture; and

(5) such other uses as the Secretary determines must be limited or controlled in order to carry out the purposes of this Act.

(c) The Secretary shall permit hunting, fishing, and trapping on lands and waters under his jurisdiction within the preserve in accordance with the applicable laws of the United States and the State of Texas, except that he may designate zones where and periods when, no hunting, fishing, trapping, or entry may be permitted for reasons of public safety, administration, floral and faunal protection and management, or public use and enjoyment. Except in emergencies, any regulations prescribing such restrictions relating to hunting, fishing, or trapping shall be put into effect only after consultation with the appropriate State agency have jurisdiction over hunting, fishing, and trapping activities.

Sec. 5. Within five years from the date of enactment of this Act, the Secretary shall review the area within the preserve and shall report to the President, in accordance with section 3(c) and (d) of the Wilderness Act (78 Stat. 891; 16 U.S.C. 1132(c) and (d)), his recommendations as to the suitability or nonsuitability of any area within the preserve for preservation as wilderness, and any designation of any such areas as a wilderness shall be accomplished in accordance with said subsections of the Wilderness Act.

Sec. 6. There are authorized to be appropriated such sums as may be necessary to carry out the provisions of this Act, but not to exceed $63,812,000 for the acquisition of lands and interests in lands and not to exceed $7,000,000 for development.

Approved Oct. 11, 1974.

## 135.  A REPUBLICAN AND A WOMAN INAUGURATED AS GOVERNORS OF TEXAS

### JANUARY 16, 1979, and JANUARY 15, 1991

The traditionally Democratic, male-dominated political world of Texas was upended in 1978 and again in 1990 with the elections of Republican William Clements and Democrat Ann Richards to the governorship of Texas. The so-called Southern Strategy of Republican presidential candidate Richard Nixon in 1968 and 1972 drew significant numbers of converts from the ranks of the Democratic faithful in Texas and elsewhere. They believed that they had been abandoned by a radicalized Democratic Party beholden to various special interest groups. Voters in Texas crossed party voting lines and even, like former governor John Connally, changed party affiliation. In this atmosphere, Texas became a two-party state and in 1979 William Clements became the first Republican governor since Reconstruction.

The rise of women, and women's issues, into the political limelight was an important component of the women's movement of the 1960s and 1970s which, in turn, had important roots in the civil rights movement of the 1950s and 1960s. The increasingly important political roles played by African Americans, Mexican Americans, and women in Texas are reflected in the sheer numbers of minority officials elected statewide. Ann Richards is the only woman elected governor of Texas in her own right (Miriam "Ma" Ferguson rode the coattails of her husband, former governor Jim "Pa" Ferguson, into the statehouse in 1924 and 1932) and Richards has assumed a national prominence heretofore reserved for the likes of LBJ or Sam Rayburn. In 1993, Kay Bailey Hutchison, a Republican woman from Texas, was elected to the United States Senate, an event symbolizing this remarkable revolution in Texas life and politics.

### 1. William P. Clements Jr.: Inauguration Speech

### January 16, 1979

From *Journal of the Senate of the State of Texas* (January 16, 1979)

Lieutenant Governor Hobby, Mr. Speaker, members of the Sixty-Sixth Texas Legislature, distinguished officials and guests, my fellow Texans:

An inauguration traditionally marks the beginning of a new administration, and any beginning requires an awareness and an understanding of the past.

So, an inauguration is a time when we must pause to reflect on our past before embarking on the future.

An inauguration also is a time to offer thanks and I would like to begin by thanking our Divine Leader who is the fountainhead of our very existence.

The first Governor of the State of Texas, the Honorable J. Pinckney Henderson, said in his Inaugural Address of 1846:

"Who can look back upon our history, and not be fully and deeply impressed with the consideration that the arm of Deity has shielded our nation, and His justice and wisdom guided us in our path? It is therefore our duty, in deep humility, to make our acknowledgements for His many favors."

As your public servant, I want to thank you for the trust you have placed in me and for the opportunity you have given me to represent you.

This being the first time I have ever taken the oath of public office as an elected official, I take it with extreme seriousness and with a keen awareness of its meaning and obligations.

To take this oath is an honor because to be your Governor is to be the leader of the most exceptional state in the union, a state made great by its people.

This inauguration would be incomplete if we do not stop to publicly thank our outgoing elected leaders for their contributions to this state.

As a citizen, I want to thank Governor Dolph Briscoe for his six years of distinguished and unselfish service to this state.

He will be remembered as the Governor who successfully fought the creation of any new state taxes.

And, he will be remembered as the Governor who took the first steps toward returning the tax-generated surplus in our state treasury back to its rightful owners.

This is Governor Briscoe's legacy to Texas, and it's one he can be proud of and one this state will always appreciate.

As your Governor, I too, have goals for Texas and I am committed to making our state government accountable to the taxpayers.

I want to conduct government in a business-like manner, with elected officials and government leaders responsible to the taxpayers just as a board of directors and company officials are responsible to the stockholders.

You will hear voices during my administration expressing doubts about some of my proposals. But, I will persist, we will prevail.

I will persist because I believe that you, the people, have made clear your desire for better government and for less government.

I will persist with my plans to return to you, the taxpayers, one billion dollars of the state's surplus. I will persist with my plans to give you long-term, constitutional safeguards—including the right of initiative and referendum—to protect against excessive taxation and wasteful government spending.

I will persist with my plans to reduce the size of our state bureaucracy.

And, I will persist with my plans to improve the quality of our education system so that we can give our children the basic building blocks they need to develop meaningful careers.

I will persist with these and many other priorities because I believe you have clearly stated that we must persist, together.

I believe we will be successful because these are issues and concerns that cut across partisan lines. These are not just Republican issues or Democrat issues. These are Texas issues and the people of Texas are the ultimate beneficiaries.

I believe we will be successful because Texans have elected a unique leadership team to address these issues and concerns.

This inauguration, where a Republican governor takes office with a Democratic lieutenant governor, stands as living proof of the independent thinking of the people of this state.

I am uplifted and encouraged by that kind of spirit, and in that expression from the people of Texas, I see the clear message that I must be a governor who puts quality, excellence, achievement, and the best interests of this state, above partisan loyalties.

We have a healthy blend of leaders, who like myself, are assuming the responsibilities and challenges of elective office for the first time; and, we have leaders like Lieutenant Governor Bill Hobby and House Speaker Bill Clayton who have dedicated many years of their lives to public service.

This leadership team is one of enthusiasm and experience, but foremost, it is one of dedication and unity of purpose.

As public servants, we all were elected by the people of Texas and we must be responsive to the needs and concerns of the same electorate.

The challenge to government is to help people deal with their needs and concerns. I believe our founding fathers provided us with the framework for doing this.

I believe this framework is often overlooked and that we often forget the words upon which our state and our nation were founded.

These are not the words of demagogues for demagogues are quickly forgotten. History has proven the value and meaning of these words and they bear repeating.

For Texans, these words are found in the first three sections of Article One, the Bill of Rights, in the State Constitution.

The first section states: "Texas is a free and independent state, subject only to the Constitution of the United States, and the maintenance of our free institutions and the perpetuity of the union depends upon the preservation of the right of local self-government, unimpaired to all the states."

This Bill of Rights is saying that while we must work with other states and with the federal government for the betterment of the entire nation, we must be vigilant and protect our independence as a sovereign state,

For when the federal government weakens the power and independence of the states, the union itself is weakened.

In recent years, we have seen a disturbing trend toward the creation of a new branch of the federal government, the regulatory branch, a branch that doesn't include you and me among its constituency.

It is not elected by anyone and, in fact, is accountable to no one.

By an excessive and improper transfer of authority to these regulatory agencies, the congress and the president have further removed government from the reach of the people and further weakened the power of the states.

This must not be condoned by Texans. We must assert our rights and our spirit at every opportunity.

And, at the same time, we must take steps to ensure that our state government does not usurp the rights of individuals or of local governments within our boundaries.

The best government is that government which is closest to the people. The second section of the Bill of Rights in our state constitution speaks to that relationship between the people and their government.

It states, "All political power is inherent in the people and all free governments are founded on their authority, and instituted for their benefit, the faith of the people of Texas stands pledged to the preservation of a Republican form of government, and, subject to this limitation only. They have at all times the inalienable right to alter, reform or abolish their government in such manner as they may think expedient."

Those are potent words and they create a straightforward message. That message is this: Power in this state and in this nation rests not with political parties, not with governmental institutions, not with elected leaders, but with the people.

Like many other citizens, I have seen the governmental bureaucracy and some politicians trying to infringe on our rights as individuals.

We have seen the consequences of such infringement by government in other parts of the United States. When excessive intrusion by government into the lives of individuals is permitted, government becomes an economic master and the people become its slaves.

Texas, though, has had the benefit of more enlightened leaders through the years. We are still in the position of being able to control our state government, but warning signs are present and we must be aware of them.

Now is the time for us to set firm limits on our government. Now is the time for us to emphatically state that we want our government to serve us, not to dominate us.

In controlling government, in making it our servant, we must proceed without diminishing the rights of any citizen.

Section three of the Bill of Rights in our state constitution says: "All free men, when they form a social compact, have equal rights, and no man, or set of men, is entitled to exclusive separate emoluments, or privileges, but in consideration of public services."

That same section also says: "Equality under the law shall not be denied or abridged because of sex, race, color, creed, or national origin."

The greatest strength of Texas long has been the vitality and diversity of its people. They came to this land as Indians, as Spaniards, as Frenchmen, as Englishmen, as Germans, as blacks, as browns, as whites, as people from many different backgrounds. And, they are still coming.

Yet when they arrive, they  become Texans, people bound together by a common quest for a better life for themselves and for their children and grandchildren.

We must respect the rights of all Texans. Regardless of their cultural background. And, we must continually work to safeguard those rights. We must see that equal opportunity is a reality for all of our citizens.

People came here because this was the land of opportunity. It still is today.

Texas was a frontier then and it is today. It is a frontier in the sense of unparalleled economic opportunity. It is a place where people can realize their dreams and aspirations—and a place where free enterprise can flourish—without laboring under the yoke of a burdensome government.

It's not difficult to explain these vast opportunities, but it is becoming increasingly difficult to protect them and extend them to all Texans.

By being ever mindful of these three sections in the Bill of Rights—by stepping back to that firm foundation of government outlined in our state constitution—our steps forward in the future will be steadier and longer.

These three sections in our state constitution help form what will be a guiding philosophy of my administration.

Condensed to its most basic form, my philosophy is this: The proper function of government is not to guarantee prosperity for its citizens; rather, it is to guarantee them the opportunity to achieve prosperity.

Putting our government into its proper perspective is a job too large for me, or Lieutenant Governor Hobby, or Speaker Clayton, or the members of the legislature, or for any public official, without the direct involvement of the citizens of Texas.

You, too, have a responsibility to help achieve good government, and that responsibility goes beyond voting on election day.

When we as individuals, and as a state are silent—when we let others make decisions for us without stating our beliefs—we forfeit some of our freedom.

When we stand up and speak out, when we express our desires and concerns, then and only then, will we have effective government.

I am confident we can achieve that kind of effective government because the people of Texas are the state's most outstanding natural resource.

I am confident, too, that we can achieve the abundant potential with which our state has been endowed.

Now is the time for us to begin. I ask all of you to join with me, to put the best interests of Texas at the forefront of your thoughts.

We must be diligent, we must be bold, we must be energetic.

All of us, all Texans, must lock arms and work together. We must shape a new alliance of greatness, an alliance that will perpetuate and enhance the blessings our Almighty God has bestowed on our state.

### 2. Ann Richards: Inauguration Speech

#### January 15, 1991

From *Journal of the House of Representatives of the State of Texas* (January 15, 1991)

Welcome to the first day of the new Texas!

And welcome to the official representatives of 35 countries and the governors of the four Mexican border states who have joined us today.

I want to thank all of you for being with us. I hope we will see you often in the Capitol. We look forward to working cooperatively with your governments and to excellent relationships with your people.

Bienvenidos, mis amigos!

Eighteen months ago, I stood with many of you a few hundred yards from this platform and announced my candidacy for governor.

If you were there—in fact or in spirit—on that hot June day, if you gave your time and your energy to our campaign, if you held your ground and continued to believe when the odds seemed long and the outcome uncertain, my gratitude to you is profound.

Today is a day of celebration.

Today, we marched up Congress Avenue and said that we are reclaiming the Capitol for the people of Texas.

We say proudly that the people of Texas are back.

That statement will be given meaning by our actions during the next four years.

Today, the historians will record that a new administration, different from any in the past, began.

Twenty, fifty, one hundred years from now, school children will open their textbooks—or perhaps, switch on their video texts—and they will see a picture.

They will see us standing proudly on this bright winter noon. And looking through the eyes of a child will seem as distant and ancient as portraits of our ancestors seem to us.

Those children will read that on January 15, 1991, a woman named Ann W. Richards took the oath of office as the 45th Governor of Texas.

That much is certain.

Today, the headline has been written, but the pages that follow are blank.

Tomorrow, we begin filling in the pages, writing line by line the story that will be told long after the joy of this day is forgotten.

Like the Reverend Martin Luther King, Jr., who was born on this day, we have come this far on the strength of a dream.

Our challenge is to transform that dream into reality: to fill the pages of history with the story of Texans who came into office envisioning a new era of greatness, and breathed life into that vision.

Today, we have a vision of a Texas where opportunity knows no race or color or gender——a glimpse of the possibilities that can be when the barriers fall and the doors of government swing open.

Tomorrow, we must build that Texas.

Today, we have a vision of a Texas with clean air and land and water, a Texas where a strong economy lives in harmony with a safe environment.

Tomorrow, we must build that Texas.

Today, we have vision of a Texas where every child receives an education that allows them to claim the full promise of their lives.

Tomorrow, we must build that Texas.

Today, we have a vision of a Texas where the government treats every citizen with respect and dignity and honesty, where consumers are protected, where business is nurtured and valued, where good jobs are plentiful, where those in need find compassion and help, where every decision is measured against a high standard of ethics and true commitment to the public trust.

Tomorrow, we must build that Texas.

The people of Texas are back, and they are waiting and watching, anxious to see if their government can rise above personal interest, rancor and division, and get on with the business of building a Texas where the people come first.

Years ago, John Kennedy said that, "Life isn't fair."

Life is not fair, but government must be.

And if tomorrow, we begin with the understanding that government must stop telling people what they want, and start listening to the people and hearing what the people need, we will make government mean something good in people's lives.

Nothing is more fundamentally important to me than the understanding that this administration exists to serve the taxpayers.

Because service to the people is government's bottom line, we are creating a new position in the governor's office: a citizen's advocate who will cut red tape and bureaucratic stonewalling, who will report to me those agencies who fail to meet the test of the highest quality of service, efficiency, and financial management.

The oath I have taken today is mine, but the responsibility, the trust we have sought and been given, belongs to all of us.

And I hope that as we invoke the blessing of God on this adventure, we will all ask, in the words of the old gospel song, that the Lord lift us to higher ground, and that we will be wise enough and strong enough to do what we have set out to do.

Because when my time in office is finished, I want us to be able to look back together and say we——not he, not she, not me——but we came to this moment with a vision worthy of a great heritage, and we realized that vision in a way that was worthy of a great future.

And as we turn the corner on a new millennium, I want us to be able to look forward——to see a small child with a textbook, thumbing through the pages, coming upon a picture of a group of people standing on the Capitol steps looking out at that child across years and changes that we cannot even begin to imagine.

I want us to be able to read words beneath that picture that say that on this date in the year of our Lord nineteen hundred and ninety-one a new era began in Texas.

And I want us to know that what we started here will reach out across time to that child, and do us honor.

## 136.  LARRY MCMURTRY PUBLISHES NOVEL *LONESOME DOVE*

### 1985

From "Tall in the Saddle" by Nicholas Lemann in *The New York Times Book Review*, June 9, 1985, p. 7.

Texas's folk and popular arts——music, literature, movies, and more——have exerted a tremendous hold on the world's imagination for a very long time. Stories, songs, novels, and other artistic expressions by Texans about their home state, and by outsiders borrowing Texas for their own artistic (and commercial) purposes, have run the gamut from traditional cowboy ballads to the television hit *Dallas*. Regardless of the medium or the artistic point of view, Texas artists (or those who use Texas as a subject) often have, in one way or another, dealt with the enduring public stereotypes which have defined Texas for more than a century: colorful, outsized, violent, rebellious, humorous, mercenary, independent, folksy, and tough. The positive and negative images of Texas disseminated in popular culture have significance because they help determine how others perceive Texas and even how Texans perceive themselves.

Over the past three decades, few Texas artists have been more prolific, popular, and critically acclaimed than novelist Larry McMurtry, the son and grandson of cattlemen. His novels have covered a wide range of topics encompassing Texas's ranch life, small towns, and urban/suburban sprawl. The cultural change which marks the past thirty years of Texas life has been a dominant theme in McMurtry's work——the wrenching shifts involved in the passing of the old ranchers and cowboys, the coming of new values and new money, the rise of great cities and new kinds of Texans. In novels as different as *Horseman Pass By*, *The Last Picture Show*, and *Terms of Endearment*, each of which was made into an exceptional movie, McMurtry captured Texas as it was, as it is, and as it is becoming.

When commenting on the state of writing in his native Texas, McMurtry often chided his fellow writers for incessantly delving into the state's rich frontier and rural past instead of working with the urban present, and he himself began writing more and more of cities such as contemporary Houston. Ironically, however, as McMurtry's call went out to write of Texas's urban present, he was also researching the romantic past of Texas Rangers and cattle drives for what may turn out to be his greatest literary achievement—the novel *Lonesome Dove*. Irony of ironies, it not only looked to the past, but it was in many ways the closest thing he had ever done to a formulaic Western novel. Like all important art, however, it exploded and transcended the formulas which it drew upon. And it was as relevant to today's Texas, and as popular with today's audience, as anything he had written about the messy urban sprawl of Houston.

This positive and perceptive review of *Lonesome Dove* which appeared in the *New York Times Book Review* foreshadowed the novel's bestseller status and its capture of the Pulitzer Prize for fiction in 1986. Like McMurtry's earlier novels, *Lonesome Dove* was made into a critically acclaimed movie (this time a serialized television movie) that brought his work to an even wider audience and reinforced his stature as a writer who has powerfully evoked the history of Texas and the story of the human condition.

The practice of trail-driving herds of beef cattle over long distances from ranch to railhead flourished for just a moment after the Civil War and before the widespread use of barbed wire. It was the tiniest fraction of our national experience and did not directly involve more than a few thousand people. But maybe more than anything else—more than wars, more than slavery, more than urbanization or immigration—it has animated a part of our imagination out of which flows a vital branch of popular culture. Cowboyana in the form of dime fiction and stage shows flourished even before the short era of the trail drives ended. It nourished movies and television when they were young. Even today, it seems to be everywhere, in clothing, in advertising, in political rhetoric.

Unlike other themes that have obsessed us, though, the trail drive has not made the transition from low art to high art very well. The South has "Gone With the Wind" but also Faulkner; the cowboy has "Red River" and J. Frank Dobie. It seems mysterious that so rich a subject has not produced a great novel—perhaps it has become so stylized that there is no juice left in it.

Readers who held out hope have been getting sustenance for years from the rumors that Larry McMurtry was writing a big trail-driving novel. As much as anyone, he knows the subject: he comes from a large west Texas family that he has described as "cowboys first and last," and his essays show that he has done considerable digging around in obscure first-hand accounts of trail drives. Also, if the myth-making machine has expropriated the subject, well, Mr. McMurtry knows about that too. It is hard to think of an American novelist who has been so lucky in Hollywood for so long ("Hud," "The Last Picture Show," "Terms of Endearment") without becoming a part of it. By now a cowboy novel probably would have to show some underlying awareness of the movies. Mr. McMurtry seems ideally equipped for that.

At its beginning, "Lonesome Dove" seems to be an anti-western, the literary equivalent of movies like "Cat Ballou" and "McCabe and Mrs. Miller." The novel's title comes from the name of a Godforsaken one-saloon town on the dusty south Texas plain near the Rio Grande. Two former captains in the Texas Rangers have retired from the long wars against Indians and Mexicans to run the Hat Creek Cattle Company—when a customer wants horses or cattle, the former lawmen drop into Mexico at night and steal them. One of the captains, Augustus McCrae, is a lazy, hard-drinking, falsely erudite old coot; the other, W.F. Call, is strong and silent in circumstances that don't call for strength or silence. Surrounded by a motley crew of cowboys, Mexicans, old Rangers and flea-bitten animals, they have been living this funky life for nearly 15 years.

Then an old Ranger comrade of theirs rides into town, on the lam because he accidently killed a man in Arkansas. He suggests they drive a herd of cattle to the unsettled country in Montana, where he has been on his wanderings. In no hurry to stop the picaresque fun, Mr. McMurtry lets the idea of a cattle drive gradually take hold among his characters. Call steals some horses and a herd of cattle and lines up some cowhands; grumbling and wisecracking and pulling on his jug, McCrae ambles along; the old friend brings the town prostitute as his guest.

As they get underway, the novel's scope begins to become clear. Mr. McMurtry weaves a dense web of subplots involving secondary characters and out-of-the-way places, with the idea of using the form of a long, old-fashioned realistic novel to create an accurate picture of life on the American frontier, from Mexico to Canada, during the late 1870's. He gives us conversationless cowboys whose greatest fear is that they will have to speak to a woman, beastly buffalo hunters, murderous Indians, destitute Indians, prairie pioneers, river boat men, gamblers, scouts, cavalry officers, prostitutes, backwoodsmen; open plains and cow towns; the Nueces River and the Platte and the Yellowstone. Everything about the book feels true, being anti-mythic is a great aid to accuracy about the lonely, ignorant, violent West.

Mr. McMurtry plows right into the big themes. The lack of a good reason for Call and McCrae's epic trail drive— "Here you've brought these cattle all this way, with all this inconvenience to me and everybody else, and you don't have no reason in this world to be doing it," McCrae says to Call at one point—makes the drive seem oddly profound. It becomes a way of exploring whether what gives our lives meaning is the way we live (as Call and McCrae believe, though in different ways), or what we accomplish, or nothing at all. The trail drive and the turns of plot provide many loves and deaths by which to measure the degree of meaning in the frontier's codes and imperatives. Even Call and McCrae's ages—just at the far edge of middle are—are conducive to mellow, sad tallyings up.

The characters in "Lonesome Dove" seem always to be putting their horses into easy lopes that could be sustained all day, and this is the way Mr. McMurtry writes. His writing is almost always offhand and laconic, with barely any sustained passages intended to be beautiful or fervent. He always has time for another funny minor character to pirouette on stage, or for McCrae to produce a new bon mot. And he leisurely pursues familiar themes—two friends in love with the same woman ("Leaving Cheyenne"), a 17-year-old coming of age ("The Last Picture Show"), a formidable middle-aged woman surrounded by terrified men who love her ("Terms of Endearment"). During the last decade or so, the idea that eccentricity is the best way to deal with life has permeated Mr. McMurtry's work, and he makes an awfully good case for it again here. The question is whether it is possible to be eccentric and "major" in the same novel.

The scenes that best put the matter to rest are the most traditionally Western ones—the gunfights, stampedes, hangings and horse-stealings. Every one of these is thrilling and almost perfectly realized. In describing violence, Mr. McMurtry does not need to raise the stakes with labored prose—they are already high. When a young boy rides into a nest of poisonous snakes in a river and dies of the bites, or when McCrae single-handedly fights off a band of Indians on an open plain with only a dead horse for shelter, it is unforgettable.

Such moments give "Lonesome Dove" its power. They demonstrate what underlies all the banter, and they transform Call and McCrae from burnt-out cases into—there is no other word—heroes. They are absolutely courageous, tough, strong, cool, loyal, fabulously good fighters. They and their men live through incredible travails, and, once they get to Montana, it is a paradise, worth everything. When McCrae explains the journey to the woman he loves by saying "I'd like to see one more place that ain't settled before I get decrepit and have to take up the rocking chair," it is moving, not silly. Whether this response is justified by the grandeur of their mission to tame the frontier, or conditioned by popular culture, it is there and cannot be denied.

All of Mr. McMurtry's antimythic groundwork—his refusal to glorify the West—works to reinforce the strength of the traditionally mythic parts of "Lonesome Dove," by making it far more credible than the old familiar horse operas. These are real people, and they are still larger than life. The aspects of cowboying that we have found stirring for so long are, inevitably, the aspects that are stirring when given full-dress treatment by a first-rate novelist. Toward the end, through a complicated series of plot twists, Mr. McMurtry tries to show how pathetically inadequate the frontier ethos is when confronted with any facet of life but the frontier; but by that time the reader's emotional response is it does not matter—these men drove cattle to Montana!

The potential of the open range as material for fiction seems unavoidably tied to presenting it as fundamentally heroic and mythic, even though not to any real purpose. If there is a novel to be written about traildriving that will be lasting and deep without being about brave men—and about an endless, harsh, lovely country where life is short but rich—it is still to be written. For now, for the Great Cowboy Novel, "Lonesome Dove" will do.

## 137. THE OIL BOOM AND BUST AND THE SAVINGS & LOAN SCANDAL

### 1990

From "Lone Star Assault" by Seth Kantor in the Austin *American Statesman*, August 20, 1990

The Arab-Israeli War of 1973 led to an oil embargo of the United States by OPEC (the Organization of Petroleum-Exporting Countries) which abruptly changed the face of America. The great American economic and military colossus, which had dominated the world since the end of World War II, suddenly found itself tangled in long lines and paying new high prices at gasoline stations. The inflationary pressure created by the new costs associated with petroleum and its many byproducts had an enormous impact on the American economy and culture. A severe recession followed. The embargo made big American cars instant dinosaurs (which accelerated a serious trade deficit with Japan), helped turn the U.S. into a debtor nation, and gave a profound body blow to American self-confidence and to the assumption that each generation's opportunities were bigger and better than those which came before.

Texas felt all of these changes and upheavals, but as it was a leading oil-producing state, the new high price for petroleum also gave Texas a signficant economic boost in the late 1970s and early 1980s. The state's revenues climbed dramatically, and the overheated oil economy which dominated the state generated frenzies of business expansion and speculation in land and real estate. Texas's cities boomed. So many thousands of outsiders poured into the state in search of jobs and entrepreneurial opportunities that a bumper sticker of the day proclaimed, "Welcome to Texas. Now go home."

The boom times in Texas, fueled by the dizzying price of oil, coincided with deregulation in the banking and savings and loan industries. The S&Ls were now allowed to pay almost any amount of interest to attract deposits—which they did from around the state and country. In turn the S&Ls aggressively loaned out money, especially to real estate speculators who drove the cost of land and real estate sky high. In addition, some fraudulent S&L operators were siphoning off money for their own high-flying lifestyles and carelessly using money to their own advantage and to the detriment of their institutions.

Throughout its history, Texas had been a provincial colony of outside forces and economies, be they Spanish, Mexican, or American. It seemed, with the oil boom and its attendant growth and wealth, that Texas was finally controlling its own economic destiny. This decade-long success story that began in the mid-1970s started to unravel in the early to mid-1980s, however, when the high price of oil stalled and then fell, and Texas's economic house of cards, based in large part upon that high price, collapsed. The oil patch was suddenly deserted and recession set in. State income plummeted, the overpriced real estate market cratered, overbuilt office space went unfilled, jobs evaporated, and people and institution couldn't pay off their loans. The Texas banks and S&Ls found themselves holding countless bad loans based on the high price of oil. As they inevitably collapsed—more banks and S&L thrifts failed than at any time since the 1930s—they were bought up once again by the outsiders who had called the economic shots in Texas for so long. In 1992 the federal government set up the Resolution Trust Corporation, an agency created to close scores of failing S&Ls and take over management of billions of dollars' worth of overpriced land and real estate. Texas led the nation in the number of failed S&Ls, and the cost to taxpayers nationally was in the hundreds of billions.

The ripple effect of the economic collapse spread over the entire pool of oil which underlay the Texas economy. Texas's freedom from colonial economic status had lasted perhaps ten years. Since the mid-1980s, however, Texas has climbed back out of recession, and by the mid-1990s it was once again booming, although not on the basis of oil. Texas now has a much more diversified economy that resembles the national model rather than the oil/cotton/cattle triangle of the past. The oil boom and bust, and the related bank and savings and loan problems, were, in a sense, the last great hurrah of the freewheeling Texas wildcatter mentality and the beginning of a newer economy still driven by Texas daring and dreaming, but less dependent on the magic elixir of oil.

This newspaper report written during the height of the S&L crisis in 1990 focuses on that event in the wake of the collapsed oil boom. Of particular interest are the attitudes of non-Texans to the oil boom and bust: envy, resentment, gloating, and the outright dislike of Texans and Texas.

WASHINGTON—Texas under siege: As killer bees close in from the South, more treacherous enemies are preparing to bash the state from up North.

Professional Texas-bashing is certain to become a team sport for lawmakers from the Northeast and Midwest. When Congress returns from its recess after Labor Day, it will be forced to come to grips with federal spending cuts while bickering over who must pay for America's staggering savings and loan scandal.

Texans are bracing for severe budgetary assaults on the supercollider and military and space projects as a result of the No. 1 blame-it-on-Texas issue: the S&L bailout.

Centered to a large extent on 81 failed thrifts in the Lone Star State, the scandal has become a sore point in Congress as the nation's taxpayers are faced with underwriting at least $130 billion in S&L bailout costs, plus billions more in interest payments.

"In effect, Texas opened the vaults of the U.S. Mint, handed the keys to a bunch of crooks and reckless cowboys, and said, 'Come in, y'all,'" complains Sen. Frank Lautenberg, D-N.J.

Rep. David Wolpe, D-Mich., has introduced a bill that would punish Texas, forcing the state to pay a $2.1 billion penalty, because 72 percent of all state-chartered thrift failures have occurred in Texas.

Wolpe's get-Texas bill has 60 co-sponsors so far, including New York's senior Republican Rep. Frank Horton, a native Texan. [The bill did not pass.]

Horton points out that only 5 percent of the S&L failures took place in the Northeast and Midwest.

"Is it really fair to ask those who have caused 5 percent of the problem to pay for 47 percent of the solution, while those who have caused 72 percent of the problem pay for 6 percent of the solution?" he asks, referring to a study conducted by a Cleveland State University professor.

But Texas Reps. Jim Chapman, D-Sulphur Springs, and Tom DeLay, R-Sugar Land, say that they are sick and tired of Wolpe and Horton "twisting facts." And Texas is gearing up to fight back.

Next month, the Texas Finance Commission, a state government office that oversees the banking and consumer credit industries, will complete a study expected to arm Texas' 27 House members with "hard information to refute simplistic and incorrect charges being leveled against us," said Randy Erben, director of the Texas Office of State-Federal Relations.

"It's easy to demagogue the S&L thing," Erben said, "but difficult to explain away what happened in a quick sentence.

"For instance, Wolpe claims 98 percent of the investors in Texas state-chartered thrifts are Texans," Erben said. "The Finance Commission study may show that to be true. But the remaining 2 percent is where the real action was. It came from the high-rollers up North, who pumped huge investments into the S&Ls."

Rep. Henry Gonzalez, D-San Antonio, chairman of the House Banking Committee, agrees. "Costs of the (Texas) bailout could have been substantially lower, had it not been necessary to use funds to pay off depositors from other states—including the Midwest and Northeast."

Those depositors, Gonzalez says, took advantage of high interest rates offered by Texas savings and loans.

Edward Hill, associate professor of urban studies at Cleveland State University, unleashed savage anti-Texas feelings when he published a report this summer, showing that based on a total S&L bailout cost of $203 billion:

*Taxpayers in 37 states will shell out more than they receive in bailout benefits.

*Texas will be the nation's largest beneficiary, with a net gain of $4,775 per person. In contrast, in New Jersey, the bailout will cost $1,074 for every man, woman and child.

Hill's findings roused Lautenberg, New Jersey's usually temperate senator, to uncharacteristic rantings on the chamber's floor.

"This massive theft of New Jerseyans' pocketbooks was not some random bolt of lightning from God," thundered Lautenberg. "It was largely the result of conscious, calculated decisions made by Texas itself."

"Nonsense," said Rep. Mike Andrews, D-Houston. "The S&Ls are a national problem. Pitting one region against another is not the way our government works."

Gonzalez agrees. He points out that taxpayers in Texas contributed to the federal guarantees that helped Chrysler Corp. survive financial ruin in Wolpe's home state, and to the financial rebuilding of New York City in the state represented by Horton.

While the S&L scandal is the focal point of mouth-foaming distemper over Texas, a number of House and Senate members from Yankee states make it clear they have other grievances.

Some are bitter about the $8.6 billion superconducting supercollider, an atom smasher to be built by the federal government south of Dallas. Its projected costs have nearly doubled over the past two years.

New York Rep. Sherwood Boehlert, ranking Republican on the House Science Subcommittee, is rallying opposition to the collider, which would be the world's most expensive scientific instrument.

"This project is threatened by only two factors," he says. "They are the Energy Department's overly optimistic assessments of the SSC's costs and benefits, and a sober assessment of whether the nation's top science priority should be the building of a 54-mile tunnel in Texas."

Erben fears that budget negotiators may be forced next month to trim the $318 million that Congress has agreed to appropriate for the collider for the new fiscal year.

Or worse, Erben says, "Texas haters like Boehlert will seize on any SSC delay to try to kill the program."

If Boehlert is a Texas hater, he spent several years concealing it—until after Jim Wright of Fort Worth resigned under

fire last year as House speaker.

Wright and Boehlert were good congressional friends, despite political party differences. But after Wright resigned during an ethics scandal in June 1989, Boethlert began to launch his attacks against the supercollider, a project Wright had fought for.

Other Northeast and Midwest congressmen who bear no strong feelings against the collider say they still bitterly resent attitudes in Texas a decade ago, when oil was selling at $36 a barrel.

That pumped up the price of heating oil up North. New England residents, suffering hard economic times and a cold winter, complained about their spiraling utility bills.

But some Houston residents were driving up and down that booming city's freeways, gleefully displaying bumper stickers that declared: "Let the Bastards Freeze in the Dark."

In Hartford, Conn., and Providence, R.I., and Boston, they haven't forgotten. Neither has the *Chigaco Tribune*, which in a recent editorial proposed a new bumper sticker: "Let Texans Rot in Their Empty Skyscrapers."

## 138. *EDGEWOOD v. KIRBY*: THE FUNDING OF EDUCATION IN TEXAS

### JANUARY 22, 1991

### From 804 S. W. 2d 491

Public education in Texas has historically been a source of controversy. The public education system has had its successes, such as the creation of what historian Joe B. Frantz called two "near great" public universities—The University of Texas at Austin and Texas A&M University—but the system has also had its failures. In 1968, Demetrio Rodriguez of San Antonio's Edgewood school district filed a federal class action suit claiming that Texas's school finance system violated the U.S. Constitution because it was based largely on property wealth, which varies greatly from district to district, thereby insuring wide discrepancies between school systems and a lack of equality in educational opportunities between wealthy and poor districts. The funding system was ruled unconstitutional in 1971, but the U.S. Supreme Court overturned this decision in 1973, saying that school finance was a state constitutional issue.

In 1984 thirteen school districts filed a followup lawsuit, *Edgewood v. Kirby*, which claimed that the school finance system violated their residents' rights to an adequate education and to equal and uniform taxation. The central question was how the disparities between the systems in rich and poor school districts could be fairly reduced so that all school children would have equal opportunity for quality education and educational facilities.

In a unanimous 1989 decision known as Edgewood I, and in another unanimous decision in 1991 known as Edgewood II (which is reproduced here), the Texas Supreme Court declared the school finance system unconstitutional because it did not provide for an efficient way to address the great disparities between poor and rich districts' abilities to tax and spend on education. In 1994, the Texas legislature still struggled with this controversy: how to efficiently

provide quality education to all Texans regardless of their economic or social condition.

### OPINION

We have previously held in this case that the state public school finance system violates article VII, section 1 of the Texas Constitution. 777 S.W.2d 391 ("*Edgewood I*"). Now we decide whether this violation remains following enactment of Senate Bill 1 by the 71st Legislature. We hold that it does.

### I

This action commenced in May 1984 when numerous school districts and individuals sought a judicial declaration that the state public school finance system was unconstitutional. After trial on the merits in 1987, the district court found that the system violated the Texas Constitution in several respects and enjoined the State from funding it after September 1, 1989, unless the Legislature repaired the constitutional defects by that date. The court of appeals reversed the district court's judgment in December 1988. 761 S.W.2d 859. On October 2, 1989, this Court in *Edgewood I* reversed the judgment of the court of appeals and reinstated the injunction issued by the district court, but postponed its effect until May 1, 1990. On that date, state funding of public schools was to cease unless the Legislature conformed the system to the requirements of the Constitution. 777 S.W.2d 391.

The district court extended the May 1 deadline to allow the Legislature to complete its work on what became Senate Bill 1, which the Governor signed into law June 7, 1990. Once Senate Bill 1 became law, plaintiffs returned to the district court seeking both a declaration that the system remained unconstitutional and an order enforcing the injunction affirmed by this Court in *Edgewood I*. After a lengthy hearing, the district court found that despite the changes in Senate Bill 1, the school finance system remained unconstitutional. Nevertheless, the district court vacated our injunction and denied any other injunctive relief or enforcement of this Court's mandate. The district court stated in its judgment that it would not entertain requests for further relief until it became apparent that the Legislature would adopt a constitutional school funding system to be implemented beginning September 1, 1991.

Plaintiffs now seek relief from this judgment, arguing in substance that the district court exceeded its authority by vacating this Court's injunction and postponing consideration of further injunctive relief. Defendant state officials also complain by cross-appeal that the district court erred in finding that the school finance system continues to violate the Constitution after enactment of Senate Bill 1. Defendant-intervenor school districts challenge the Court's jurisdiction to consider any of these contentions. . . .

III

Senate Bill 1 does make certain improvements in public school finance. It attempts to realize the long-articulated objective of assuring school districts substantially similar educational revenue for similar levels of local tax effort by providing for a wide array of biennial studies to detect deviations from fiscal neutrality and inform senior policy makers when increased state funding is required. These policy makers then recommend to the Legislature the amount of funds that should be allocated for public education for the succeeding biennium. Thus, for the first time, the system contains a mandate for biennial adjustment, based upon information from a battery of studies, with the intention of preventing the opportunity gap between poor and rich districts from re-widening each time legislative action narrows it.

However, Senate Bill 1 leaves essentially intact the same funding system with the same deficiencies we reviewed in *Edgewood I*. Senate Bill 1 maintains the basic two-tiered education finance structure known as the Foundation School Program. The first tier is a basic allotment designed to enable all districts to provide a basic education to all pupils. Each district that taxes itself at or above a minimum level is guaranteed a certain base level of funding, composed of state and local revenue, per weighted student in average daily attendance. The second tier is the guaranteed yield or equalized enrichment tier, which is designed to equalize the ability

of school districts to raise revenue to supplement their basic allotment. At this tier, all districts receive a guaranteed revenue per weighted student for each cent of local tax effort above the tier one minimum level. The State funds the difference between the guaranteed revenue and the amount each cent of local tax effort generates. If a district is so wealthy that each cent of tax effort generates more than the guaranteed revenue per weighted student, it receives no tier two revenue from the State. To maximize their entitlement to state funding under tiers one and two, Senate Bill 1 contains incentives for most school districts to set their effective local tax rates at or above a state-designated minimum level.

The State asserts that as districts respond to these incentives and as it shifts more of its funds to lower wealth districts, Senate Bill 1 will achieve substantial equity among the districts that educate 95% of our students. The State maintains that excluding the districts with the wealthiest 5% of the students is reasonable and within the *Edgewood I* requirement of "substantially equal access to similar revenues per pupil at similar levels of tax effort." 777 S.W.2d at 397. It argues that the annual cost of equalizing all districts to the revenue levels attainable by the richest districts would be approximately four times the annual cost of operating the entire state government. Even if the incentives in the new law do not produce the anticipated results, the State contends that the newly mandated studies will lead to increased state funding, which will in turn produce equity. Plaintiffs complain of both the manner in which the State has attempted to achieve fiscal neutrality and the State's decision to exclude the wealthiest districts from the equalization formula. . . .

In analyzing the constitutionality of the system after Senate Bill 1, we begin with the following conclusion in *Edgewood I*, grounded on the Texas Constitution:

> The legislature's recent efforts have focused primarily on increasing the state's contributions. More money allocated under the present system would reduce some of the existing disparities between districts but would at best only postpone the reform that is necessary to make the system efficient. A Band-Aid will not suffice; the system itself must be changed.

777 S.W.2d at 397. Even if the approach of Senate Bill 1 produces a more equitable utilization of state educational dollars, it does not remedy the major causes of the wide opportunity gaps between rich and poor districts. It does not change the boundaries of any of the current 1052 school districts, the wealthiest of which continues to draw funds from a tax base roughly 450 times greater per weighted pupil than the poorest district. It does not change the basic funding allocation, with approximately half of all education funds coming from local property taxes rather than state revenue. And it makes no attempt to equalize access to funds among all districts. By limiting the funding formula to districts in which 95% of the students attend school, the Legislature

excluded 132 districts which educate approximately 170,000 students and harbor about 15% of the property wealth in the state. A third of our students attend school in the poorest districts which also have about 15% of the property wealth in the state. Consequently, after Senate Bill 1, the 170,000 students in the wealthiest districts are still supported by local revenues drawn from the same tax base as the 1,000,000 students in the poorest districts.

These factors compel the conclusion as a matter of law that the State has made an unconstitutionally inefficient use of its resources. The fundamental flaw of Senate Bill 1 lies not in any particular provisions but in its overall failure to restructure the system. Most property owners must bear a heavier tax burden to provide a less expensive education for students in their districts, while property owners in a few districts bear a much lighter burden to provide more funds for their students. Thus, Senate Bill I fails to provide "a direct and close correlation between a district's tax effort and the educational resources available to it." 777 S.W.2d at 397....

There are vast inefficiencies in the structure of the current system. With 1052 school districts, some having as few as two students, and with up to twenty districts within a single county, duplicative administrative costs are unavoidable. Consolidation of school districts is one available avenue toward greater efficiency in our school finance system....

Article VII of the Constitution accords the Legislature broad discretion to create school districts and define their taxing authority. The Constitution does not present a barrier to the general concept of tax base consolidation, and nothing in *Love* [*Love v. City of Dallas*] prevents creation of school districts along county or other lines for the purpose of collecting tax revenue and distributing it to other school districts within their boundaries. While consolidating tax bases may not alone assure substantially equal access to similar revenues, the district court erred in concluding that it is constitutionally prohibited.

We do not undertake lightly to strike down an act of the Legislature. We are mindful of the very serious practical and historical difficulties which attend the Legislature in devising an efficient system, and we recognize the efforts of the legislature and executive departments to achieve this goal. We do not prescribe the means which the Legislature must employ in fulfilling its duty. Nor do we suggest that an efficient funding system will, by itself, solve all of the many challenges facing public education in Texas today. Nevertheless, our duty is plain: we must measure the public school finance system by the standard of efficiency ordained by the people in our Constitution. The test for whether a system meets that standard is set forth in *Edgewood I*. 777 S.W.2d at 397-98. Under that standard, we therefore hold as a matter of law that the public school finance system continues to violate article VII, section 1 of the Constitution.

While we share the district court's desire to avoid disruption of the educational process, we must heed our duty to ensure Texas students the efficient education system guaranteed them by the Constitution. See Morton v. Gordon, Dallam 396, 397-98 (Tex. 1841). If the educational process is to be disrupted, it will be because the demands of the Constitution cannot be further postponed.

IV

The district court concluded that conditions have not changed since *Edgewood I* because the public school finance system has not been altered to comply with article VII, section 1 of the Texas Constitution. The district court clearly abused its discretion in refusing to enforce the mandate of this Court issued in *Edgewood I*.

We therefore direct the district court to vacate that portion of its judgment which vacates the injunction affirmed by this Court in *Edgewood I*. Because the deadlines set by that injunction have passed, we must modify those deadlines. However, the need for an efficient system remains as compelling today as it was when we last visited this issue, at which time we stated: "A remedy is long overdue. The legislature must take immediate action." 777 S.W.2d at 399. Balancing the need for immediate action against the realities of the legislative process, and desiring to avoid or minimize disruption of the educational process, we stay the effect of the injunction until April 1, 1991. The district court is directed not to extend this deadline or to modify this injunction.

We trust the district court will promptly comply, and we will withhold issuance of our writ unless it fails to do so.

## 139. THE TEXAS LOTTERY

### 1991

Changing cultural attitudes, and great influxes of outsiders in the last three decades, have resulted in legislation in Texas over recent years which challenged generations of traditional values. Although the concepts of individualism and individual rights have a permanent place in Texas law, culture, and mystique, the religious culture of the state, including the powerful Southern Baptist church, had long resisted alcohol, gambling, and other perceived vices. The creation of a Texas state lottery was highly controversial, and many religious and secular organizations opposed it. The group Texans Who Care, an anti-lottery coalition, compiled a fact sheet outling their opposition to the lottery. In spite of this stout resistance, however, the 72nd Texas State Legislature established a lottery in 1991.

In the past thirty years numerous changes—the abandoning of blue laws which kept stores closed on Sundays, legislation allowing liquor by the drink and pari-mutuel wagering—have combined to chip away at Texas's reputation as a solid, stolid culture. The rural

Bible Belt has loosened a few notches in recent years to become the Sunbelt, an urban landscape of growth and change. However, the continued activities of the "religious right" on issues such as the lottery and sex education suggest that the Bible Belt has not been completely loosened. The 1991 addition of Texas to the ranks of states holding lotteries reflected both difficult economic times and changing values, particularly the diminution of religious influence on Texas culture and American life.

## 1. OPPOSITION TO THE LOTTERY

From "Six Reasons Why The Lottery is a Bad Idea for Texas", Texas Alliance for Human Needs Fact Sheet, October, 1991.

1. The lottery is a regressive tax that hurts the poor.

Studies in Indiana, Michigan, California, Illinois, Florida, New Jersey, Iowa and Connecticut all showed that the lottery is substantially a regressive tax, that is, that it is effectively higher on poor people than on rich. Two-thirds of Detroit players earned less than $20,000 per year. Per-capita purchases were three times as much in the zip codes with the lowest income versus the highest in Chicago, twice in California, nine times in Iowa, etc.

2. Merchandising a lottery is not an appropriate function of government.

The lottery competes with retail and service goods. It also diverts revenue from local sales taxes to the state. The real winners are the purveyors of lottery equipment.

3. The lottery creates a new generation of gamblers, some of whom become compulsive gamblers.

A National Center for Pathological Gambling study of callers to gamblers assistance hotline showed that the lottery was the most preferred form of gambling for 22% of Maryland callers. Experts have testified that the lottery is a major factor in the increase of compulsive gambling in this country.

4. The lottery is a bad buy, sold through deceptive advertising.

Lotteries spend millions of dollars on advertising, particularly to target poor people who are generally misinformed about the limited chances to win. One study in Detroit showed that their lottery ran 50 ads on a classical radio station where demographics showed most listeners were highly-educated and did not often play, but 1700 ads on a urban radio station targeted toward a minority community. Advertisements are timed to be most intense when public assistance checks arrive.

5. Lotteries are destructive to good government and fiscal responsibility.

The projected revenue from a lottery in Texas is $462 million in its first full year, less than 2% of state revenues and only 1/20th of the amount projected by human services advocates to bring Texas services into the moderate range.

A major purpose of the lottery is to distract citizenry from the terrible plight of Texas' poor population and our failure to make building a caring infrastructure a high priority. This happens by promising significant revenues which would allay costly embarrassments like the federal court orders on

MHMR, public education, prisons, and TDHS.

6. Lotteries show evidence of increasing crime in the states where they exist.

Facts to start with . . .

-Thirty-three states have lotteries; the biggest is in California where 1991 lottery revenue is down 13% from previous years.

-Based on history in states with lotteries, a person has a much better chance of getting murdered on the way to a convenience store to buy a lottery ticket than to win the multi-million dollar prize.

-Of each $1 bet on a Texas lottery, probably 45% would be returned in prizes, 40% would go to the state's general fund and 15% would be eaten up in administrative costs.

-90% of lottery states also have a state income tax.

-Each man, woman, and child in Massachusetts averaged spending $265.68 in 1990 on the lottery.

-Some state lotteries authorize bingo and poker video games on video lottery terminals (VLT's) which are similar to casino video slot machines.

-The California lottery's advertising budget for 1987 was $39 million, making it one of the largest advertisers in the state.

-70% of Connecticut high school students say they have gambled; many confess they have bought a lottery ticket despite being under the legal age for purchasing one. . . .

## 2. THE LOTTERY ESTABLISHED

From House Bill No. 54, 72nd Legislature. First Called Session

Be it enacted by the Legislature of the State of Texas:

Section 1. The purpose of this Act is to establish and efficiently operate a lottery that is free of criminal influence and that is a self-supporting, revenue-producing division in the office of the comptroller of public accounts. The legislature recognizes that the operation of a lottery is a unique activity for state government and that the structures and procedures appropriate to the performance of other governmental functions are not necessarily appropriate to the operation of a state lottery. . . .

ARTICLE 2. ADMINISTRATION

Sect. 2.01. LOTTERY DIVISION. (a) A division to administer a state lottery is created in the office of the comptroller. The division is administered by the director.

(b) The comptroller shall appoint a person to serve as director and chief executive officer of the division subject to the comptroller's direction. . . .

Sec. 2.02. POWERS AND DUTIES OF COMPTROLLER, DIRECTOR, AND DIVISION. (a) The comptroller and director have broad authority and shall exercise strict control and close supervision over all lottery games conducted in this state to promote and ensure integrity, security, honesty, and fairness in the operation and administration of the lottery. . . .

Sec. 2.03 CERTAIN GAMES PROHIBITED. (a) The director or lottery operator may not establish or operate a lottery game or activity in which the winner is chosen on the basis of the outcome of a sports event.

(b) In this section, "sports event" means a football, basketball, or similar game, or a horse or dog race on which pari-mutuel wagering is allowed. . . .

Sec. 2.05. PREFERENCE FOR TEXAS BUSINESSES. (a) In all contracts for lottery equipment, supplies, services, and advertising, the division and each lottery operator shall give preference to equipment and supplies produced in this state or services or advertising offered by bidders from this state, the cost to the state and quality being equal. . . .

2.09. AUDIT. The director shall provide for a certified public accountant to conduct an independent audit for each fiscal year of all accounts and transactions of the lottery. . . . The certified public accountant shall present an audit report to the director, the comptroller, the governor, and the legislature not later than April 1 of the year following the fiscal year for which the audit was performed. . . .

2.13. DEMOGRAPHIC STUDIES. (a) The director shall, every two years, employ an independent firm experienced in demographic analysis to conduct a demographic study of lottery players. The study shall include the income, age, sex, education and frequency of participation of players. . . .

Sec. 2.14. CONFIDENTIAL INFORMATION. The following information is confidential and is exempt from disclosure under the open records law . . .

(1) security plans and procedures of the division or office of the comptroller designed to ensure the integrity and security of the operation of the lottery;

(2) information of a nature that is designed to ensure the integrity and security of the selection of winning tickets or numbers in the lottery, other than information describing the general procedures for selecting winning tickets or numbers; and

(3) the street address and telephone number of a prize winner, if the prize winner has not consented to the release of the information. . . .

ARTICLE 3. LICENSING; CRIMINAL HISTORY INVESTIGATIONS

Sec. 3.01. LICENSING OF SALES AGENTS. (a) The director shall attempt to license minority businesses as sales agents in at least 20 percent of the licenses issued. . . .

(b) The director may license as a sales agent each person the director believes will best serve the public convenience. The director may not issue a license to a person to engage in business exclusively as a sales agent. A license may not be transferred or assigned to any other person or location. . . .

ARTICLE 4. REGULATION OF GAMES AND ACTIVITIES; OFFENSES

Sec. 4.01. TICKETS. (a) The director shall prescribe the form of tickets. The toll-free "800" telephone number established by the Texas Commission on Alcohol and Drug Abuse...must be printed on each ticket. The overall estimated odds of winning a prize in a given game or activity must be printed on each ticket and prominently displayed in association with the sale of lottery products. . . .

(b) By purchasing a ticket in a particular lottery game or activity, a player agrees to abide by and be bound by the division's rules, including the rules applicable to the particular lottery game or activity involved. . . .

Sec. 4.02. CERTAIN SALES OF TICKETS PROHIBITED. (a) A person commits an offense if the person intentionally sells a ticket at a price the person knows is greater than that fixed by the division or by the lottery operator authorized to set that price. . . .

(b) Except as provided by this subsection, a person who is not a sales agent or an employee of a sales agent commits an offense if the person intentionally or knowingly sells a ticket. . . .

(d) A sales agent or an employee of a sales agent may not intentionally or knowingly sell or offer to sell a ticket to an individual that the person knows is younger than 18 years of age. . . .

(f) A person 18 years of age or older may purchase a ticket to give as a gift to another person, including an individual younger than 18 years of age. . . .

(g) A Sales agent or an employee of a sales agent commits an offense if the person intentionally or knowingly sells a ticket to another person by extending credit or lending money to the person to enable the person to purchase the ticket. . . .

(h) A person may not purchase a ticket: (1) with a food stamp coupon issued under the food stamp program administered under Chapter 33, Human Resources Code; (2) with a credit card or a debit card; (3) over the telephone; or (4) by mail-order sales.

(i) A person may not pay for a ticket with the proceeds of a check issued as payment under the Aid to Families with Dependent Children program administered under Chapter 31, Human Resources Code. . . .

ARTICLE 5. REVENUE AND PRIZES

. . . .Sec. 5.02. DISPOSITION OF REVENUES. (a) A special account in the general revenue fund to be known as the state lottery account is established. . . .

(b) Money in the state lottery account shall be used only for the following purposes and shall be distributed as follows:

(1) the payment of prizes to the holders of winning tickets; (2) the payment of costs incurred in the operation and administration of the lottery . . . (3) the transfer of amounts to the state lottery stabilization fund. . . .

(f) The state treasurer periodically shall file reports with the director providing information regarding the revenue credited to the state lottery account, the investments of the money in the account, and the distributions made from the account.

(g) For purposes of Article III, Section 49a, and Article VIII, Section 22, of the Texas Constitution: (1) funds received from the operation of a lottery are not revenue; and (2) expenses of operating the lottery and paying prizes are not expenses of state government. . . ..

Sec. 5.03. CERTIFICATION OF PRIZEWINNERS; PAYMENT OF PRIZES.

(a) The department of security shall supervise ticket validation and lottery drawings.

(b) If a lottery game or activity involves a drawing, the drawing must be open to the public. An independent certified public accountant must witness the drawing.

(c) An employee of the division and the independent certified public accountant witnessing the drawing shall inspect any equipment used in the drawing. The equipment must be inspected immediately before and after the drawing. The drawing and inspections must be recorded on video and audio tape.

(d) The director may authorize prizes to be paid by warrants to be drawn on the state lottery account. . . .

(e) Payment of a prize in an amount of $600 or more shall be made by the director.

(f) The director may authorize a sales agent to pay a prize in an amount less than $600 after performing procedures to validate the winning ticket as required by the director. . . .

(g) Except as otherwise provided by this subsection, the right of any person to a prize is not assignable. Payment of a prize may be made to the estate of a deceased prizewinner. . . .

(h) A specific prize as set forth by the prize structure of a specific lottery game or activity may not be paid more than once. . . .

(i) The director shall pay the cash equivalent of a prize other than prize money if more than one person is entitled to share the prize as provided by Subsection (h) of this section.

(j) The director shall deduct the amount of a delinquent tax or other money from the winnings of a person who has been fully determined to be:

(1) delinquent in the payment of a tax or other money collected by the comptroller, the state treasurer, or the Texas Alcoholic Beverage Commission; (2) delinquent in making child support payments administered or collected by the attorney general; (3) in default on a loan guaranteed under Chapter 57, Education Code.

(k) If a person's winnings exceed a delinquency under Subsection (j) of this section, the director shall pay the balance to the person. The director shall transfer the amount deducted to the appropriate agency. . . .

Sec. 5.05 UNCLAIMED PRIZES, REPORTS OF TICKETS SOLD AND PRIZES AWARDED.

(a) The division shall retain an unclaimed prize on a winning ticket for payment or delivery to the person entitled to the prize for 180 days after the date on which the winner was selected. . . .

(b) If a claim in not made for a prize other than prize money on or before the 180th day after the day on which the winner was selected, the prize shall revert to the division for use in subsequent games.

(c) A ticket holder forfeits any claim or entitlement to a prize after the expiration of the 180th day after the date on which the prizewinner was selected.

(d) For each lottery game, after the last date on which a prize may be claimed under Subsection (c) of this section, the director shall prepare a report that shows the total number of tickets sold and the number and amounts of prizes awarded in the game. The report must be available for public inspection. . . .

Sec. 5.07 EXEMPTION FROM TAXATION.

(a) A political subdivision of this state may not impose: (1) a tax on the sale of a ticket; (2) a tax on the payment of a prize under this Act; or (3) an ad valorem tax on tickets.

(b) The receipts from the sale, use, or other consumption of a ticket are exempt from taxation under Chapter 151, Tax Code.

# 140. BARBARA JORDAN'S KEYNOTE ADDRESS TO THE DEMOCRATIC NATIONAL CONVENTION

## JULY 13, 1992

### "Change: From What to What?"

In 1966 Houston sent Barbara Jordan to the Texas state Senate. A black woman walking the floor of the Texas statehouse as an elected official does not seem so remarkable today, but three decades ago it was ground-breaking. She was the first black woman senator in Texas history.

Born in 1936 into a strong black family in Houston's Fifth Ward, Barbara Jordan succeeded in spite of the obstacles placed in her path by a segregated society. After attending law school at Boston University, she returned to Texas, began a law practice, and eventually won the Senate seat in 1966. Jordan quickly established herself as a respected and savvy politician, and was elected to the United States Congress in 1972—one of the few black House members from the South since Reconstruction.

Although she was highly regarded by many Texans, the rest of the country knew little about Barbara Jordan until her national exposure in 1974 during the U.S. House of Representatives Judiciary Committee's Watergate hearings regarding the impeachment of President Nixon. Her thoughtful comments on the Constitution, her sonorous voice, and her appearance of calm dignity and absolute integrity in a period marked by deep cynicism about public officials elevated her to a rare position of trust and respect in the public eye. Although she retired to a life of teaching at the Lyndon Baines

Johnson School of Public Affairs, a program at the University of Texas at Austin named for her beloved mentor, Barbara Jordan has continued to play a role in Texas and national politics.

In 1976, in the wake of Watergate, Jordan presented the keynote address at the Democratic national convention. Hoping that lightning would strike twice—Democrat Jimmy Carter was elected to the White House that year—she was invited to address the Democratic convention again in 1992. That 1992 keynote address is reproduced here. Although some would argue with her politics, with her assessment of recent American history, and with her suggested solutions, her speech resoundingly addressed the subject of change and the controversial issues of the day from her perspective as a highly successful black woman who grew up in segregated Houston. References in this speech to her Texas past reveal the sources of her faith in activist government, a legacy shared with her friend and mentor Lyndon Johnson and with numerous prominent Texas Democrats before her.

At this time; at this place; at this event sixteen years ago—I presented a keynote address. I thank you for the return engagement and with modesty would remind you that we won the presidency in November, 1976. Why not 1992?

It is possible to win. It is possible but you must believe that we can and will do it. I will talk with you for the next few minutes about some of the changes which are necessary for victory. I have entitled my remarks—"Change: From What to What?"

Change has become the watchword of this year's electioneering. Candidates contend with each other, arguing, debating—which of them is the authentic agent of change. Such jostling acquires substance when we comprehend the public mind. There appears to be a general apprehension about the future which undermines our confidence in ourselves and each other. The American idea that tomorrow will be better than today has become de-stabilized by a stubborn, sluggish economy. Jobs lost have become permanent unemployment rather than cyclical unemployment. Public policy makers are held in low regard. Mistrust abounds. Given such an environment, is it not understandable that the prevailing issue of this political season is identifying the catalyst for change that is required. I see that catalyst as: the Democratic Party and its nominee for President.

We are not strangers to change. We calmed the national unrest in the wake of the Watergate abuses and we, The Democratic Party, can seize this moment. We know what needs to be done and how to do it. We have been the instrument of change in policies which impact education, human rights, civil rights, economic and social opportunity and the environment. These are policies firmly imbedded in the soul of our party. We will do nothing to erode our essence. However, some things need to change. The Democratic Party is alive and well. It will change in order to faithfully serve the present and the future, but it will not die.

Change: From What to What? We will change from a party with a reputation of tax and spend to one of investment and growth. A growth economy is a must. We can expand the economy and at the same time sustain and even improve our environment. When the economy is growing and we are treating our air, water and soil kindly, all of us prosper. We all benefit from economic expansion. I certainly do not mean the thinly disguised racism and elitism of some kind of trickle down economics. I mean an economy where a young black woman or man from the Fifth Ward in Houston or south-central Los Angeles, or a young person in the *colonias* of the lower Rio Grande valley, can attend public schools and learn the skills that will enable her or him to prosper. We must have an economy that does not force the migrant worker's child to miss school in order to earn less than the minimum wage just so the family can have one meal a day. That is the moral bankruptcy that trickle down economics is all about. We can change the direction of America's economic engine and become proud and competitive again. The American dream is not dead. True, it is gasping for breath but it is not dead. However, there is no time to waste because the American Dream is slipping away from too many. It is slipping away from too many black and brown mothers and their children; from the homeless of every color and sex; from the immigrants living in communities without water and sewer systems. The American Dream is slipping away from the workers whose jobs are no longer there because we are better at building war equipment that sits in warehouses than we are at building decent housing; from the workers on indefinite layoffs while their chief executive officers are making bonuses that are more than the worker will take home in 10 or 20 or 30 years.

We need to change the decaying inner cities into places where hope lives. We should answer Rodney King's haunting question, "can we all get along?" with a resounding "YES." We must profoundly change from the deleterious environment of the Eighties, characterized by greed, selfishness, mega-mergers and debt overhang to one characterized by devotion to the public interest and tolerance. And yes, love.

We are one, we Americans, and we reject any intruder who seeks to divide us by race or class. We honor cultural identity. However, separatism is not allowed. Separatism is not the American way. And we should not permit ideas like political correctness to become some fad that could reverse our hard-won achievements in civil rights and human rights. Xenophobia, has no place in the Democratic Party. We seek to unite people not divide them and we reject both white racism and black racism. This party will not tolerate bigotry under any guise. America's strength is rooted in its diversity. Our history bears witness to that statement. *E Pluribus Unum* was a good motto in the early days of our country and it is a good motto today. From the many, one. It still identifies us—because we are Americans.

We must frankly acknowledge our complicity in the creation of the unconscionable budget deficit and recognize that to seriously address it will put entitlements at risk. The idea of justice between generations mandates such sacrifice for growth—provided there is equity in sacrifice. Equity means all will sacrifice—equally. That includes the retiree living on a fixed income, the day laborer, the corporate executive, the college professor, the Member of Congress . . . all means all.

One overdue change already underway is the number of women challenging the councils of political power dominated by white-male policy makers. That horizon is limitless. What we see today is simply a dress rehearsal for the day and time we meet in convention to nominate . . . Madame President. This country can ill afford to continue to function using less than half of its human resources, brain power and kinetic energy. Our 19th century visitor from France, de Tocqueville, observed in his work *Democracy in America*, "If I were asked to what singular substance do I mainly attribute the prosperity and growing strength of the American people, I should reply: To the superiority of their women." The 20th century will not close without our presence being keenly felt.

We must leave this convention with a determination to convince the American people to trust us, the Democrats, to govern again. That is not an easy task, but it is a doable one.

Public apprehension and fears about the future have provided fertile ground for a chorus of cynics. Their refrain is that it makes no difference who is elected President. Advocates of that point of view perpetuate a fraud. It does make a difference who is President. A Democratic President would appoint a Supreme Court Justice who would protect liberty not burden it. A Democratic President would promote those policies and programs which help us help ourselves: such as . . . health care and job training.

Character has become an agenda item this political season. A well-reasoned examination of the question of character reveals more emotionalism than fact. James Madison warned us of the perils of acting out of passion rather than reason. When reason prevails, we prevail. As William Allen White, the late editor of the Emporia, Kansas *Gazette*, said, "Reason never failed man. Only fear and oppression have made the wrecks in the world." It is reason and not passion which should guide our decisions. The question persists: Who can best lead this country at this moment in our history?

I close by quoting from Franklin Roosevelt's first inaugural address to a people longing for change from the despair of the great depression. That was 1933, he said: "In every dark hour of our national life a leadership of frankness and vigor has met with that understanding and support of the people themselves which is essential to victory." Given the ingredients of today's national environment, maybe . . . just maybe, we Americans are poised for a second "Rendezvous with Destiny."

## 141. THE DALLAS COWBOYS: AMERICA'S TEAM

### 1994

From "Jones, Johnson Reach 'Mutual Decision' to Part" by Tim Cowlishaw in the Dallas *Morning News*, March 30, 1994

Sports have long had an important place in Texas culture. Some of the state's great athletes—Babe Didrickson, Nolan Ryan, George Foreman, and numerous others—have climbed the pinnacles of national acclaim, and have epitomized the competitive Texas spirit.

Football has had a special hold on the state's affections. It has been said that the best time and place to commit a robbery in Texas is on a Friday night in any town when the local high school football team has an away game. The fanatical devotion to football has been lampooned by Texas novelist Larry McMurtry and critiqued in exposés of ruthless high school coaches and programs. Texas billionaire and political gadfly Ross Perot has even attacked Texas's football culture by successfully promoting a "no pass/no play" rule as part of an educational reform act (House Bill 72) that he helped push through the Texas legislature in 1984. This act mandated that students who did not maintain a certain academic level could not take part in extracurricular activities, including sports. Many Texans agreed that winning at sports must take a backseat to winning at academics if Texas students are to compete nationally and internationally.

Nevertheless, Texans continued to take their sports very seriously. The Dallas Cowboys, with long-time coach Tom Landry and celebrated players such as Roger Staubach, Drew Pearson, Walt Garrison, Emmitt Smith, and Troy Aikman, were heroes of recent decades. Since the first edition of this book appeared in 1963, the Cowboys have been one of the dominant teams in professional sports. Because of their winning record over three decades, their colorful, talented players, and their cowboy moniker (and the celebrated Cowboy Cheerleaders), the Cowboys became known as "America's team" and sold nationwide a tremendous volume of memorabilia with their logo.

After several uncharacteristically lackluster years in the late 1980s, however, new owner Jerry Jones put the great Landry out to pasture and brought in new coach Jimmy Johnson. Many Texans were outraged that the beloved old coach was unceremoniously retired, but when the new owner, coach, and team turned around and won the Super Bowl in 1993 (and again in 1994), the Cowboys were once again America's team—heroes across the state and nation.

When a long-simmering feud between old friends Jones and Johnson led to Johnson's resignation only a few months after the 1994 Super Bowl victory, it was headline news in Texas—witness this front-page story from the Dallas *Morning News*—and across the nation. ABC television's award-winning late night news program, *Nightline with Ted Koppel*, spent an entire evening on the topic of Johnson's resignation and what it meant for the future of America's team.

IRVING—Jimmy Johnson wasn't sure of the proper word for what had happened—quit, resigned, fired, rode off into the sunset. All he and Jerry Jones really knew Tuesday was that it was over.

What Mr. Jones had described as "one of the greatest

stories in sports" reached a bizarre conclusion at the team's Valley Ranch headquarters after the coach and owner met for a little more than an hour Tuesday morning. After five years and consecutive Super Bowl titles the past two seasons, Mr. Johnson said it was a "mutual decision" that he no longer serve as coach.

Mr. Johnson and Mr. Jones each claimed last week's verbal battle in the media, which began with the owner's threats to fire Mr. Johnson, had nothing to do with Tuesday's separation. For more than 30 minutes, they sat side by side and assured the huge news media assemblage that they were parting as friends, had enjoyed their years together and that all was in the best interest for the future of the Cowboys' franchise.

"We've had hours of candid discussions the last two days," said Mr. Johnson, "and I can sincerely tell you that I fell better today about Jerry Jones as a friend than I have in our entire relationship. After our discussions, we mutually decided I would no longer be the head coach of the Dallas Cowboys."

Mr. Jones refused to discuss possible successors, although last week's mention of former Oklahoma coach Barry Switzer may be more realistic than first believed. With all the current Cowboys' assistants under contract for 1994, Mr. Jones needs to hire someone who won't be interested in bringing along his own staff. Mr. Switzer has been out of coaching since the 1988 season.

As for Mr. Johnson, the buyout of his contract was not detailed. Mr. Jones called it "a big-time thank you," but now Mr. Johnson is free and clear to pursue coaching jobs. Mr. Johnson had five years remaining on a contract with Mr. Jones that restricted him from pursuing other jobs.

Mr. Johnson said it's unlikely that he will coach anywhere in 1994 but said he expects to be coaching again after that.

"Personally, I think it was time to pull back some" said Mr. Johnson, who met Mr. Jones when they were teammates at Arkansas during the early 1960s. "I have always been 100 percent totally into it, but as Jerry was starting to see, I was starting to lose my focus."

Mr. Johnson told a friend recently that it was tough to come back from trips to Miami, where he coached the University of Miami Hurricanes for five seasons and won one national title. In the past, Mr. Johnson has taken only rare, brief vacations.

Mr. Johnson said he began to sense that he was losing his drive near the end of the 1993 season. It was not evident on the field, however, where the Cowboys won their last eight games and claimed their second straight Super Bowl title. No coach has ever won three in a row.

"Our relationship is one that is different from any in the NFL," said Mr. Jones. "We mutually agreed that if we didn't look out, we would take one of the greatest stories ever told in sports, take all those positives and turn it into something that we didn't think would be in the best interest of the Dallas Cowboys.

"This isn't something that has just been frivolously talked about. We have analyzed this from stem to stern."

Mr. Jones said he intends to periodically consult Mr. Johnson. "I've probably asked him for advice in three different areas in the last few hours," he said.

When tough questions were asked of Mr. Jones, Mr. Johnson almost always intervened on the owner's behalf. Just three days earlier, Mr. Johnson had said Mr. Jones was a man he could no longer respect or trust. He said winning a third Super Bowl had lost meaning as long as Mr. Jones was the owner. On Tuesday, he did nothing but credit Mr. Jones for his contributions to their mutual success.

"There's no way in the world we could have accomplished what we did without each other," Mr. Johnson said. "Some people might describe it as rocky, but something about our relationship worked."

Mr. Johnson didn't call it burnout but indicated that the pressure of the job was a factor in his decision.

"I don't think anybody in this room or anybody watching really understands until they've walked in our shoes what this is about," Mr. Johnson said. "You think there was pressure in the 1989 season when we lost all but one game? But there's just as much pressure to win a Super Bowl and to win another Super Bowl."

If there is a candidate on the current staff to lead the Cowboys, it is defensive coordinator Butch Davis. He said Tuesday that he would be interested in the job.

Mr. Johnson said only that he wants to see the best man get the job.

"I want the next head coach to be the best coach there is," he said. "I've got confidence Jerry will research and pick the best there is."

Mr. Johnson and Mr. Jones shook hands after Mr. Johnson's opening statement, in which he announced that he was leaving. After the news conference, they hugged. Between, they continually deflected all questioning of the timing of the change.

It reached a laughable stage when Mr. Johnson said at one point, "We're going through a little transition here." When the media interrupted him with its laughter, Mr. Johnson smiled and said, "Well, maybe it's a big transition."

Mr. Johnson has compiled a 31-7 record the past two seasons, tops in the NFL. His career record with the Cowboys was 44-36 in the regular season, despite that 1-15 start. Mr. Johnson's teams were 7-1 in the postseason, the second-best winning percentage in the NFL behind Vince Lombardi's 9-1.

Mr. Jones and Mr. Johnson each denied that Mr. Jones' efforts to exercise more control was a factor. "Really, 99 percent of every decision was made working together," Mr. Johnson said.

Said Mr. Jones: "Jimmy, did I ever try to call a play? The facts are that we never had a disagreement when it came to football."

Players, assistants and employees were understandably surprised at Tuesday's turn of events. Offensive coordinator Ernie Zampese has been on the payroll less than eight weeks after spending his entire life on the West Coast.

"I think we're all in a state of shock," Mr. Zampese said. "But I get paid to do a job, and I'll do it the best I can."

"Whoever comes in here is going to have his hands full," said center Mark Stepnoski. "You'd think these guys could have ironed something out. But this thing didn't happen overnight."

Quarterback Troy Aikman said he could begin to see that Mr. Johnson's interest was diminishing this off-season. "It's tough even for us as players to always keep that drive," he said. "The main thing for us now is to try to take care of the guys who are free agents."

To many, Mr. Jones now will be regarded as the man who fired Tom Landry and ran Mr. Johnson out of town. The owner's reaction: "Well, they will just have to keep pointing fingers at me. I think we have more Cowboys fans now than we had in 1989, and there was a lot of skepticism then. But I've always committed everything I've ever done to the Dallas Cowboys."

For five years, Mr. Johnson gave the same commitment. But his first two head coaching jobs, at Oklahoma State and Miami, also ended after five years. It will be the same here.

The Jimmy Johnson era of Cowboys' football is finished.

# Index

# INDEX